Advanced, Automated and Electric Vehicle Law

Advanced, Automated and Electric Vehicle Law

Alex Glassbrook
Barrister, Temple Garden Chambers
Honorary Senior Research Fellow in Road Transport Law, Department of
Civil and Environmental Engineering, Imperial College London

Bloomsbury Professional

LONDON · DUBLIN · EDINBURGH · NEW YORK · NEW DELHI · SYDNEY

BLOOMSBURY PROFESSIONAL

Bloomsbury Publishing Plc
50 Bedford Square, London, WC1B 3DP, UK
1385 Broadway, New York, NY 10018, USA
29 Earlsfort Terrace, Dublin 2, Ireland

BLOOMSBURY and the Diana logo are trademarks of Bloomsbury Publishing Plc

© Alex Glassbrook 2024

British Library Cataloguing-in-Publication Data

A catalogue record for this book is available from the British Library.

ISBN:	PB	978 1 52651 690 9
	ePDF	978 1 52651 692 3
	ePub	978 1 52651 691 6

Typeset by Evolution Design and Digital (Kent)
Printed and bound by CPI Group (UK) Ltd, Croydon, CR0 4YY

To find out more about our authors and books visit www.bloomsburyprofessional.com. Here you will find extracts, author information, details of forthcoming events and the option to sign up for our newsletters

Foreword

In a short story written in 1953 Isaac Asimov imagined a world of 2057 in which the only cars allowed on the road were fully autonomous and guided by a 'positronic' brain. In 2023 most of us have yet to encounter a vehicle without a human driver present but there can be no doubt that this will come. A future of the sort imagined by Asimov will soon be upon us.

The shift towards a transport infrastructure with high levels of automation or remote control is the inevitable consequence of increases in computational power and advances in automotive and communications technology. At the same time a new era of electrically powered vehicles has arrived; it marks a return to a path tentatively taken but then abandoned in the late nineteenth and early twentieth centuries with the additional feature that small, powerful motors and compact batteries have extended the categories of vehicle which can now be motorised. The practical and legal boundaries between large, powered vehicles and everything else on the roads are disappearing as electric micro-mobility vehicles become commonplace in our cities. The transition to a powered transport system which is multi-modal, largely electrified and includes self–driving vehicles will bring with it significant societal change and the promise of less pollution, reduced congestion and safer and more accessible travel.

The technical and infrastructure challenges that accompany this revolution are matched by the ethical and legal problems to which it has given rise. Questions of civil liability, insurance and regulation have begun to be addressed but the law is still evolving to deal with issues which range across the legal spectrum. The extent to which established principles and approaches can be mapped onto new problems is, as ever, a starting point but it is clear that significant adaptation and innovation will be required. Identifying the existing legal framework, drawn from disparate areas of civil, criminal and public law is often a difficult task. Anticipating how the law will and should develop is more difficult still and demands an overview of a fragmented legal landscape.

A comprehensive and informative guide to the law, set in its historical and technical context, by an author with a deep understanding of transformative technology could not be more timely. I can think of no better guide in this field than Alex Glassbrook, who combines the academic rigour of his teaching and research with the insight of the legal practitioner into how the law works in practice. The clarity with which the law is explained and analysed makes the text accessible to the lawyer, student and general reader alike. The commentary will be invaluable to those who want to know how the law is applied as well as those interested in its development.

I congratulate him on an authoritative and thoughtful book that I am sure will become an essential addition to the library of anyone practising in this area and high on the reading list of those interested in understanding more about the law as it relates to automated and electric vehicles.

Derek Sweeting
The Royal Courts of Justice
27 October 2023

Preface and Acknowledgments

A multidisciplinary approach is essential to good regulation. While this book was in its earliest stages I was invited by Professor Washington Ochieng, now Head of the Department of Civil and Environmental Engineering at Imperial College London, to work with the college's Centre for Transport Studies addressing legal and regulatory challenges of increasing levels of automation. This led to my appointment as Honorary Senior Research Fellow in Road Transport Law and to my teaching regulation at Imperial College under the director of postgraduate studies for transport, Dr Panagiotis Angeloudis. I can do no better than refer to the inaugural lecture in May 2023 of Professor Arnab Majumdar, Professor of Transport Risk and Safety at Imperial College, when Arnab emphasised the importance of transport users, engineers, social scientists, doctors, lawyers and others working together to tackle the numerous challenges of the field. As Arnab said, such multidisciplinary conversations relate to complex matters, are nuanced and need to be given every opportunity to happen. I am especially grateful to Washington, Arnab, Pan and to all at Imperial College for their commitment, their expertise and the great privilege of my appointment.

My heartfelt thanks to Mr Justice Sweeting for writing the Foreword and, longer ago, for his support as my Middle Temple sponsor barrister when I was a student at the City University then the Inns of Court School of Law. Our shared interest in technology has lasted.

At the bar, I owe a great debt of gratitude to all members of chambers, pupils and staff at Temple Garden Chambers, especially to the clerks who are led by Dean Norton, Nancy Rice and Keith Sharman and to our recently retired chambers' administrator, Gaye Spencer-King. Among barrister colleagues in chambers I mention in particular my fellow automated and electric vehicle law specialist Emma Northey, who set up and co-edits our AEV law blog, AEVlaw.com, to which numerous colleagues and guest writers have contributed. Those include my room-mate Paul Erdunast, who luckily shares my enthusiasm for the topic (sharing a room with me might otherwise have been a challenge).

In my case, thanking my family unusually involves a part-denial of reliance, as my wife Karen is a full-time judge. In all matters of law her judgement is so superior to mine that I would not dare to ask a technical question. The same is true of our children, Isaac and Theo, who both study computer science and who, from the iPhone onwards, have treated my excitement at technology with a weary indulgence. They are all infinitely supportive and wonderful.

To my parents, David and Juliet, all possible thanks – particularly for the twin interests of debating and cars, which seem to have led to where we are now. Thanks to my sister, Pippa, for wisdom from Cornwall.

My thanks to Jane Bradford, my editor, and to Andy Hill, Head of Legal Publishing, at Bloomsbury Professional. Both have been constantly enthusiastic friends and advisers. They understand my envy of their living in Yorkshire.

Finally, thanks to all my fellow parkrun volunteers, for giving me the perfect metaphor for writing a book and the wherewithal to finish.

Jurisdiction

This book deals with the law of England and Wales.

Date to which the law is described

The law in this first edition of *Advanced, Automated and Electric Vehicle Law* is up to date to 1 December 2023, to take account of the Automated Vehicles Bill 2023–24 (HL Bill 1) and the government's updating of its guidance on automated vehicle testing on 30 November 2023 (see Chapter 3, 'testing').

AAEV law is a fast-developing area, so the reader should take care to check current law.

External sources

Much material is available only or mainly online so external sources including links to websites are cited. I cannot guarantee the content of any websites, nor give any assurance relating to links to websites including hyperlinks in the online and e-book editions of this book.

ChatGPT is an important part of the recent history, so the reader will want to know whether I have used it to write this book. I have not. Any errors are mine and are human.

Alex Glassbrook
London
December 2023

Contents

Table of Cases

All references are to paragraph number

Table of Statutes

All references are to paragraph number

xxxi

Table of Statutory Instruments

All references are to paragraph number

Part I

Introduction

Chapter 1

Introduction to AAEV law

'Law, being a practical thing, must found itself on actual forces.'[1]

(Oliver Wendell Holmes, Jr., 1881)

1.01   In 1881, Oliver Wendell Holmes, Jr. was not yet Justice Holmes but a law lecturer[2]. The motor car would imminently be a mass-manufactured product. In 1884, Karl Benz would build the first motor car, a three-wheeled petrol-driven vehicle with an internal combustion engine[3]. The following decade saw numerous engineering refinements[4] and the car grew in popularity. In 1895 the automotive magazine launched in New York, *The Horseless Age*, wrote that:

> 'All over the country mechanics and inventors are wrestling with the problems of trackless traction. Much of their work is in an unfinished state; many of their theories lack demonstration; but enough has already been achieved to prove absolutely the practicability of the motor vehicle.'[5]

Lawyers also wrestled with the problems of motor cars. Judges in England and Wales were among those facing the challenges to legal thinking brought on by 'the coming of the Machine Age' in which 'technological advances and changing social conceptions had introduced into legal problems unforeseen facts and conflicts'[6]. Judges imagined future technologies:

> 'Suppose in the future locomotion by aerial vehicles becomes common; could a passenger in such a vehicle complain that the proprietor was guilty of a breach of duty or warranty towards him, if, a very high wind springing up, the aerial vehicle was carried against a building, without any fault of those in charge of it, whereby the passenger was injured?'[7]

---

1   *The Common Law* (1881), Lecture VI, 'possession'.
2   Holmes became a full professor at Harvard Law School and Associate Justice of the Supreme Judicial Court of Massachusetts in 1882, Chief Justice of that court in 1899 and Associate Justice of the US Supreme Court in 1902. See *Justice Oliver Wendell Holmes: A biography* by Silas Bent (AMS Press, New York, 1932) and *The Legacy of Oliver Wendell Holmes, Jr.* (ed Robert W Gordon, Stanford, 1992).
3   James J Flink, *The Automobile Age* (MIT press, 1990, 2001 edition), p 12; Robert Merkin and Maggie Hemsworth, *The Law of Motor Insurance* (2nd edition, 2015), 1-06.
4   See the Appendix to this book, History.
5   *Horseless Age* Vol. I, No. 1, New York, November 1895, 'Salutary'.
6   Bent, chapter 9, 'early writings: 'The Common Law'.
7   Vaughan Williams LJ, question to counsel in *Wing v London General Omnibus Company* [1909] 2 KB 652, 654 (CA).

1.02   Solutions which were both practical and coherent were occasionally hard to find. The debate in Britain as to regulation of road traffic generated as much heat as energy[8]. The law of compulsory third-party motor insurance – the method adopted to ensure payment of compensation to the growing number of road traffic accident victims – was especially active, producing two acts of Parliament within its first four years (the Road Traffic Acts 1930 and 1934): the first to enact third-party coverage, the second to defend it against the proliferation of exemption clauses seeking to avoid it[9]. The innovative method adopted to ensure payment of compensation for victims of uninsured drivers (the foundation of the Motor Insurers' Bureau in 1946) was the subject of withering judicial comment in 1968, when Lord Justice (later Lord) Diplock wrote that:

> '… instead of amending the legislation so as to impose upon the Motor Insurers' Bureau a statutory liability to the unsatisfied judgment creditor as had been done by the Road Traffic Act, 1934, in respect of the liability of insurers to satisfy judgments against defendants covered by a valid policy of insurance, the matter was dealt with by an agreement of June 17, 1946, between the Minister of Transport and the Motor Insurers' Bureau…. What reasons influenced the Government to adopt this oblique and extra-statutory way of imposing liability upon the bureau, despite the legal complications this involves, I do not know. But the courts must accept it as it is and try, so far as they are permitted by the rules, to make it work with justice to the bureau as well as to the persons for whose benefit the Minister made the contract.'[10]

Just as the innovations of the late 19th and early 20th centuries demanded that 'new wine could not be poured into old bottles' and required the law 'to find fresh containers'[11], so the technological revolutions in electronics and computing of the late twentieth and early twenty first centuries now require

> 'legal doctrine [to] adapt to processes governed without human agency, by artificial intelligence – that is, by autonomous computers generating their own solutions, free from any direct human control'[12].

1.03   In the era of smartphones, the 'internet of things' and ChatGPT, we are used to the notion of a disruptive technology. The motor car was (and remains) just such a technology; as revolutionary in its benefits (foremost, providing individual mobility across great distances) as in its harms (injuries in collisions, illness caused by pollution and environmental damage).

Today's innovations in cars are in computer software and hardware, in electric motors and batteries. Computer technologies are achieving both higher levels of advanced driver assistance through ADAS systems and the start of complete automation of driving. Increasing electrification of road vehicles reduces pollution but adds its own challenges – especially in the safety implications of adapting smaller vehicles to electric propulsion and the environmental effects of manufacturing sophisticated

---

8   See Chapter 6, 'insurance'.
9   As above: 'outline', 'inherent tension'.
10 *Gurtner v Circuit* [1968] 2 QB 587 at 598, 602, discussed in Chapter 6, 'insurance'.
11 Bent, chapter 9, 'early writings: 'The Common Law'.
12 Lord Sales JSC 'Algorithms, Artificial Intelligence and the Law' (the Sir Henry Brooke Lecture for BAILII, 12 November 2019).

and large vehicles for mainly individual use, including the challenges of recycling and of particulate pollution.

As Oliver Wendell Holmes reminds us, making effective laws is a practical matter. Part of the process is understanding the history of our current laws. As Holmes put it:

> 'History must be a part of the study, because without it we cannot know the precise scope of rules which it is our business to know… it is the first step toward an enlightened scepticism, that is, towards a deliberate reconsideration of the worth of those rules.'[13]

The scope of rules applicable to motor vehicles is wide; spanning civil, criminal and public law fields and topics from vehicle specification to the laws of equality. This book puts topics into their factual and legal contexts primarily by reference to their history, which each chapter summarises in an 'outline' section.

A detailed chronological history appears in the Appendix. The eras into which this chronology is divided and the choice of events are entirely my own, to serve the topics in this book. My chronology attempts to provide both the detailed and panoramic views. I hope that it puts the regulation into context. An important feature is that it shows the profound effect upon regulation of some events which were only in the loosest way connected to the technology – for example, the effect of post-second world war economic reconstruction upon international regulation of vehicles by standards[14].

---

13 'The Path of the Law' 10 Harvard Law Review (1897).
14 See Chapter 2, 'specifications'.

Chapter 2

The law of vehicle specifications

'Standards govern the design, operation, manufacture, and use of nearly everything that mankind produces... Standards generally go unnoticed. They are mostly quiet, unseen forces, such as specifications, regulations and protocols, which ensure that things work properly, interactively and responsibly. How standards come about is a mystery to most people should they even ponder the question.'

John H Gibbons, Director of the Office of Technology Assessment of the US Congress (1992)[1]

'Existing law reflects a division between rules governing vehicle design on the one hand and the behaviour of drivers on the other. This is true at both international level ... and at domestic level. Legislating for self-driving requires an integrated approach, bridging these two regulatory spheres: the automated driving system (ADS) constitutes equipment fitted in a vehicle, but it also determines the behaviour of the vehicle. To accommodate AVs [automated vehicles], we need a new vocabulary, new legal actors and new regulatory schemes'

The Law Commission of England and Wales and the Scottish Law Commission (2022)[2]

'... the comfort, capabilities, and convenience of the electromobile are so vastly greater, that, in a remarkably short space of time, it has become quite a familiar feature of our streets, many hundred being in regular use to-day. The distances travelled by these cars is extraordinary, it being no uncommon thing for them to average thirty miles daily. They are, moreover, very speedy, besides being thoroughly safe and trustworthy.'

The editor of *The Automotor Journal* (London, 1906)[3]

---

1   Foreword to *'Global Standards: Building Blocks for the Future'*, US Congress Office of Technology Assessment (March 1992). With thanks to Andrea Barrios Villareal, who quotes the second part in the Introduction to *International Standardization and the Agreement on Technical Barriers to Trade* (Cambridge, 2018).

2   Law Commissions' final report on automated vehicles, *Automated Vehicles: Joint Report*, Law Com No 404, Scot Law Com No 258 (January 2022), 2.2, 2.3.

3   *Motors and Motor Driving* (the Badminton library of sports and pastimes, ed. Alfred E. T. Watson, 4th edn, Longmans, Green and Co, 1906) at pp 278-279 (chapter XIII, 'electric cars'). That and *The Automotor Journal* accessed online via Google Books.

> **Chapter Contents**
>

A   Outline of the Law of Vehicle Specifications

Introduction

2.01   The laws of motor vehicle specifications flow from several sources. Domestic statutory regulation, industrial standards and international laws all contribute. There is a strong historical context.

Parts of the history are surprising. For example:

- We are (as the 1906 quotation above illustrates) not in the first but the second major era of electric road vehicles[4].

- The laws of vehicle specifications are more international than they are domestic.

- The mainly international nature of vehicle specification laws is explained in part by commerciality but also by events wholly independent of the motor industry. Arguably, the strongest influence upon modern automotive regulation was the economic reconstruction overseen by the United Nations after the Second World War. Internationally observed standards and regulations were important tools of that reconstruction[5].

Domestic construction and use regulations

2.02   Domestic statutory rules as to the construction and use[6] of vehicles appeared at an early stage in automotive history. Both the Locomotives Act 1865 (the 'Red Flag Act'[7]) and the Locomotives on Highways Act 1896 contained rules as to the construction of 'light locomotive' vehicles – the early motor cars.

---

4   See the 'Motors, 1901 to 1938' section of the 'History' Appendix to this book. For the history of the electric car see James J Flink, *The Automobile Age* (MIT Press, 1990, 2001 edition), Levi Tillemann, *The Great Race: The Global Quest for the Car of the Future* (Simon and Schuster, 2015) and Tom Standage, *A Brief History of Motion: From the Wheel to the Car to What Comes Next* (Bloomsbury, 2021).

5   See 'Standards', below.

6   Essentially meaning rules as to the specifications of vehicles and as to how they should be driven, loaded etc.

7   Locomotives Act 1865, s 3: 'one of [the three] such Persons [employed to drive or conduct the locomotive], while any Locomotive is in Motion, shall precede such Locomotive on Foot by not less than Sixty Yards, and shall carry a Red Flag constantly displayed, and shall warn the Riders and Drivers of Horses of the Approach of such Locomotives, and shall signal the Driver thereof when it shall be necessary to stop, and shall assist Horses, and Carriages drawn by Horses, passing the same'.

Those rules included construction and use requirements. For example, the 1865 Red Flag Act (which sought effectively to prohibit the use of motor cars on roads) prohibited the sounding of a whistle on a road locomotive 'for any purpose whatever'[8]. By contrast with that rule, the 1896 Act (whose policy was to enable motor car use) required every light locomotive to carry a bell 'capable of giving audible and sufficient warning of the approach or position of the carriages'[9].

In addition to requiring a bell, the 1896 Act also required the person in charge of a light locomotive 'During the period between one hour after sunset and one hour before sunrise' to 'carry attached thereto a lamp so constructed and placed as to exhibit a light in accordance with the regulations to be made by the Local Government Board'[10] and empowered the Local Government Board to 'make regulations with respect to the use of light locomotives on highways, and their construction, and the conditions under which they may be used'[11] (a model followed by the extensive regulation-making powers of the Automated Vehicles Bill 2023-24[12]).

During the nearly 130 years since the 1896 Act, the volume of construction and use regulations has increased, as technologies affecting vehicle construction (including electronic components[13]) have grown more sophisticated and devices affecting their use (recently including handheld mobile communications devices) have proliferated. Compared with the five articles of the Motor Cars (Use and Construction) Regulations 1904[14], the regulation governing the use of mobile telephones in road vehicles is the Road Vehicles (Construction and Use) Regulations 1986[15] (CUR 1986), reg 110.

The statutory requirements as to the construction and use of vehicles and equipment are now in Part II of the Road Traffic Act 1988 and CUR 1986 (as amended).

The Automated Vehicles Bill 2023-2024, set to become the Automated Vehicles Act 2024 (AVA 2024), provides the Secretary of State for Transport with an important – and arguably overdue – power to make regulations to amend or impose new type approval requirements, not only for automated vehicles but also for vehicles with advanced driver assistance systems – 'any other type of vehicle that: (i) includes equipment designed to allow its motion to be controlled other than by an individual in it, or to facilitate its being so controlled; or (ii) is designed to incorporate or interact with software', as of the AV Bill, cl 91(1) puts it.

---

8   As above (the whistle-sounding prohibition was the fourth of six rules in LA 1865, s 3; the Red Flag was the second).
9   Locomotives on Highways Act 1896, s 3.
10   LOHA 1896, s 2.
11   LOHA 1896, s 6(1).
12   AV Bill 2023-24 (HL Bill 1).
13   See the 'History' Appendix to this book, especially in relation to the miniaturisation of electronic devices, the development of semiconductors and the use of computers in cars.
14   Motor Cars (Use and Construction) Regulations 1904, reproduced in *Motors and Motor-driving* (1906), above, at pp 480-483 ('the motor laws as they exist'), accessed online via Google Books.
15   SI 1986/1078 (as amended). The Secretary of State for Transport's power to make such regulations is now under RTA 1988, s 41. RTA 1988 also enacts particular construction and use offences: for example, s 41D(b) makes it an offence to contravene or fail to comply with a construction and use requirement in relation to driving (or supervising driving) while using a hand-held mobile telephone or other hand-held interactive communication device, or causing or permitting the same.

Standards

2.03   As the Vehicle Certification Agency says:

> 'Many industrial sectors are subject to some form of approval or certification system but road vehicles are a special case, because of their importance to and impact upon society, and have been subject to specific technical standards almost from their first invention.'[16]

Industrial technical standards are historically distinct from statutory rules, in that industrial standards are motivated primarily by the commercial interests of manufacturers, whereas statutory rules tend to be motivated mainly by considerations of public safety.

In the early stages of automotive legislation in Great Britain, industrial standards relating to motor cars lagged in time behind statutory rules. However, standards were soon adopted as an effective commercial tool and proliferated. The rise of industrial standards is apparent in the history of manufacture of motor vehicles in the early twentieth century, and especially in the foundation of three organisations (BSI, SAE and ISO) which remain key both to road vehicle safety in general and to the safety of advanced, automated and electric vehicles in particular.

In 1901, the British Standards Institution (BSI) was founded, with the original title of the Engineering Standards Committee, by Sir John Wolfe-Barry, the designer of Tower Bridge. Wolfe-Barry believed that agreed technical standards for the manufacture of goods and services would speed up production and reduce costs. The BSI received its royal charter in 1929 and changed its title to BSI in 1931. The BSI 'kitemark' was registered in 1903[17].

In 1905, the Society of Automotive Engineers (SAE) was founded in the USA: 'a small but influential group of American automobile trade journalists and engineers who organised in 1905 to improve the state of automotive technology through the publication of articles'[18].

In 1908, the American manufacturer Cadillac became the first to demonstrate the interchangeability of its parts in the Cadillac Model B, winning the Dewar Trophy of the Royal Automobile Club (RAC) in the UK by reassembling three Cadillac cars from their mixed parts and driving them 500 miles, with perfect scores[19].

In 1910, the SAE produced the first common standard for automobile parts, adopting 224 standards by 1921. The SAE President Howard E Coffin said that the lack of intercompany standardisation was 'responsible for nine tenths of the production troubles and most of the needless expense in the manufacture of motorcars'[20].

---

16   Vehicle Certification Agency, *Type Approval for Automotive Systems and Components* (VCA004, revision 15), p 1, 'Introduction'.
17   See the 'Motors, 1901 to 1938' section of the 'History' Appendix to this book.
18   As above.
19   As above.
20   As above.

After the Second World War (1939-1945), industrial standards became a tool of economic reconstruction. The restoration of the motor car manufacturing industry worldwide was key to post-war economic recovery[21] and the efficiencies of standardised manufacturing processes had their part to play. In 1946, the International Organisation for Standardization (abbreviated worldwide to ISO) was founded, with a meeting of delegates from 25 countries at the Institute of Civil Engineers in London to discuss the future of international standardisation[22]. Standards became written into law as requirements of international trade agreements (including the General Agreement on Tariffs and Trade (GATT) of 1947, which underpins the World Trade Organisation, founded in 1995)[23].

In 1947, The United Nations Economic Commission for Europe (UNECE) was established as one of the UN's five regional commissions[24]. In 1958, UNECE produced its agreement to harmonise vehicle standards (the 1958 Agreement)[25]. 'Building a better world', in President Truman's description of the purpose of the 1945 UN Charter[26], included restoring and expanding the motor industry.

The aim of the 1958 agreement was to reduce technical barriers to international trade in vehicles and vehicle parts. The UK became a party in 1963. The World Forum for Harmonisation of Vehicle Regulations – also known as Working party 29 of UNECE (WP 29) – still sets regulations to standardise motor vehicles[27]. As at the date of writing, there are 167 regulations attached as addenda to the 1958 Agreement[28], and the number of regulations has increased steadily. The regulations under the 1958 Agreement include regulations as to steering (regulation 79), electric power trained vehicles (regulation 100), automated lane keeping systems (regulation 157) and event data recorders (160). UNECE is considering a new

---

21 See the 'Road Transport Law, 1939 to 1972' section of the 'History' Appendix to this book.
22 See the 'Motors, 1939 to 1972' section of the 'History' Appendix to this book. For a detailed account of the history and of the process of standardisation, see Nick Rich and F Tegwen Malik, *International Standards for Design and Manufacturing: Quality Management and International Best Practice* (Kogan Page, 2020).
23 See the 'Road Transport Law, 1939 to 1972' section of the 'History' Appendix to this book. For a detailed account of GATT and discussion of the status of standards in international law, see Andrea Barrios Villareal, *International Standardization and the Agreement on Technical Barriers to Trade* (Cambridge, 2018).
24 See above (UNECE, 1947).
25 Now titled 'Agreement concerning the Adoption of Harmonized Technical United Nations Regulations for Wheeled Vehicles, Equipment and Parts which can be Fitted and/or be Used on Wheeled Vehicles and the Conditions for Reciprocal Recognition of Approvals Granted on the Basis of these United Nations Regulations (Revision 3)'. See UNECE WP 29 website 'Text of the 1958 Agreement: https://unece.org/trans/main/wp29/wp29regs.
26 Speech of President Harry S Truman at the closing session of the United Nations Conference (26 June 1945), website of the American Presidency Project, University of California, Santa Barbara
27 Although UN regulatory approval of a vehicle as a whole is an ongoing project. As the 'introduction' to the UN WP 29 website (accessed 9 January 2023) puts it, 'provisions established under the 1958 Agreement include the reciprocal acceptance of approvals of vehicle systems, parts and equipment issued by other Contracting Parties (the reciprocal recognition of the entire vehicle is not yet possible under the 1958 Agreement, even if procedures for the whole vehicle type approval of vehicles have been established in EU Member States. In order to address this issue, WP.29 launched the International Whole Vehicle Type Approval (IWVTA) project in March 2010)'.
28 See UNECE website 'UN regulations: addenda to the 1958 Agreement'.

regulation relating to approval of Driver Control Assistance Systems (a type of ADAS)[29].

Evidential status of standards in courts in England and Wales

2.04   The mainly commercial purpose of industrial standards is reflected in the evidential weight which the law affords to them as evidence of safety. Law is concerned less with industrial efficiency than it is with liabilities and their corollary in individual rights, including consumer rights. So, absent an express rule[30] to the contrary, the courts do not presume that industrial standards fix an acceptable level of safety. Absent a rule to the contrary, industrial standards do not have the force of law[31].

This is apparent in a judgment relating to civil liability under the Consumer Protection Act 1987 for alleged defects in metal hip replacements, *Gee v DePuy International Limited (the DePuy Pinnacle Metal on Metal Hip Litigation)*[32], where Mrs Justice Andrews (as she then was) said as follows in relation to the evidential weight of standards (relevant in that case to the issue of whether or not a product was defective).

'...the existence of regulations or standards are material factors because they indicate that the product is of a nature that requires regulations or standards to be imposed on the producer, thereby generating a heightened expectation of safety in comparison to unregulated products ...'

'No-one has suggested that compliance with standards or regulations affords a defence or creates any *prima facie* presumption in favour of the producer. The weight to be ascribed to these factors will depend on the facts and circumstances of the individual case.'

'... the standards set by a regulatory regime cannot be used as a substitute for the statutory test of safety, even when the regulatory regime expressly addresses safety. The level of safety that the public is entitled to expect may be lower than a particular safety standard ... [or] it may be higher, for example if the product complied in all material respects with particular safety features required by the regulatory regime, but there was some additional feature that made it unsafe; or where the generic products complied with the regulatory regime but there was a faulty batch that would have failed the safety assessment ... The weight to be placed on such compliance is a matter of fact and degree in the individual case, and it may be of no relevance at all.'

---

29   ECE/TRANS/WP.29/GRVA/2023/20, 'Proposal for a new UN Regulation on uniform provisions concerning the approval of vehicles with regards to Driver Control Assistance Systems' (11 July 2023).

30   See, for example, RTA 1988, s 38(7), AV Bill 2023-2024, cl 93(7) and HSWA 1974, s 17(2), discussed below.

31   As, for example, Lord Denning said of the Highway Code: 'It contains many propositions of good sense which may be taken into account in considering whether reasonable care has been taken, but it would be a mistake to elevate them into propositions of law.' (*Qualcast (Wolverhampton) Ltd v Haynes* [1959] AC 743, 759 (HL)). The Highway Code was not evidence in the case; Lord Denning cited the Code as an example of evidence of good practice.

32   [2018] EWHC 1208 (QB).

'... in an appropriate case compliance with [mandatory] standards will have considerable weight, because they have been set at a level which the appropriate regulatory authority has determined is appropriate for safety purposes. However, the standards must have a relevance to the defect that is alleged; it would be no good establishing that a child's toy met all the safety standards in terms of toxicity, for example, if the complaint was that one of the components was a choking hazard.'[33]

(In *Gee v DePuy*, the court held that there was no defect in the metal hips. The relevance of standards was limited, due to the unquantifiable risk of some patients suffering the effects of metal debris:

'All the components of the Pinnacle system met all relevant UK and European safety standards. However, there were no specific safety standards addressing what would be regarded as an acceptable rate of failure within 10 years, or the incidence of failure for osteolysis or soft tissue damage. The achievement of regulatory approval, whilst a positive factor, is therefore of limited assistance in the overall evaluation of the entitled expectation of safety in this case.'[34])

So standards are (absent a different evidential rule) material but non-decisive factors, depending upon their application to the facts of a particular case.

However, a statute or regulation can give a particular effect to guidance contained in standards, guidance or a code of practice. The Road Traffic Act 1988, s 38(7) does this for the guidance to road-users in the Highway Code, by providing that:

'A failure on the part of a person to observe a provision of the Highway Code shall not of itself render that person liable to criminal proceedings of any kind but any such failure may in any proceedings (whether civil or criminal, and including proceedings for an offence under the Traffic Acts, the Public Passenger Vehicles Act 1981 or sections 18 to 23 of the Transport Act 1985) be relied upon by any party to the proceedings as tending to establish or negative any liability which is in question in those proceedings.'

The Automated Vehicles Bill 2023-2024, cl 93(7) allows regulations made as to the manner and form in which information as to traffic regulation measures is provided by traffic regulation authorities to assist automated or other electronic vehicle systems 'to be provided in accordance with a specified model, standard or set of specifications as it exists from time to time'.

Another example is the Health and Safety at Work Act 1974, s 17 which provides for the 'use of approved codes of practice in criminal proceedings'. In that part of HSWA 1974, a 'code of practice ... includes a standard, a specification and any other documentary form of practical guidance'[35]. Approval of codes of practice by the Health and Safety Executive is provided for in s 16. HSWA 1974, s 17(2) reads:

'Any provision of the code of practice which appears to the court to be relevant to the requirement or prohibition alleged to have been contravened shall be admissible in evidence in the proceedings; and if it is proved that

---

33 Extracts from [170-178] of the judgment, 'Legally Relevant Circumstances', 'Regulations and Standards'.
34 See above, 'Was the Product Defective?' [488-489].
35 HSWA 1974, s 53(1).

there was at any material time a failure to observe any provision of the code which appears to the court to be relevant to any matter which it is necessary for the prosecution to prove in order to establish a contravention of that requirement or prohibition, that matter shall be taken as proved unless the court is satisfied that the requirement or prohibition was in respect of that matter complied with otherwise than by way of observance of that provision of the code.'

In relation to civil liability for damage caused by an automated vehicle when driving itself, the Automated and Electric Vehicles Act 2018 maintains the orthodoxy of leaving the relevance and evidential effect of standards to the court. AEVA 2018 avoids reference to any industrial standard, including the most celebrated standard defining automated vehicles, the SAE's Levels of Driving Automation (J3016[36], which was first published on 16 January 2014 and was in its third revision when AEVA 2018 was enacted[37]). AEVA 2018 contains its own definition of 'automated vehicle', without reference to the SAE Levels of Driving Automation or to any other industrial standard[38].

However, while maintaining that orthodoxy of not replicating an industrial standard, the AV Bill 2023-24 would (if enacted in terms of AV Bill 2023-24 (HL Bill 1)) amend the definition of 'automated vehicle' both for its own purposes and in AEVA 2018[39]. The AV Bill 2023-24 would redefine 'automated vehicle' to:

'authorised automated vehicle' which 'means a vehicle authorised under section 3 of the Automated Vehicles Act 2024'[40]

That redefinition is discussed below.

United Nations Road Safety Instruments

2.05   The 1958 Agreement to harmonise vehicle standards is not the only UN legal instrument in relation to the safety of road traffic. Overall, there are five categories of UN legal instruments which cover road safety[41]:

- The 'vehicle regulations' agreements (the 1958, 1997 and 1998 agreements, of which the 1958 Agreement is for present purposes the most relevant[42])

- The Road Traffic Convention (1968, also known as 'the Vienna Convention'; the successor to the 1949 Convention of the same title, signed in Geneva)

---

36 In its fourth revision (30 April 2021) as at the time of writing: 'Taxonomy and Definition for Terms Related to Driving Automated Systems for On-Road Motor Vehicles' (SAE J3016). See summary of SAE J3016 at figure 1, below.
37 Third revision of the SAE levels of driving automation (15 June 2018). AEVA 2018 was enacted on 19 July 2018.
38 AEVA 2018, ss 1 and 8(1)(a).
39 AV Bill 2023-24, HL Bill 1, cl 45, Sch 2, para 5.
40 As above, Sch 2, para 5(6)(b)(i).
41 See UNECE website 'Introduction to United Nations Road Safety Conventions'.
42 The 1997 and 1998 agreements added to the 1958 agreement: the 1997 agreement by providing for periodic technical inspections, the 1998 agreement by allowing a mechanism whereby nations not party to the 1958 agreement (so not bound by the requirement of mutual recognition of another signatory nation's type approval) could contribute to global technical regulations for vehicles. See UNECE document 'Road map for accession to and implementation of the United Nations 1998 agreement' (May 2021).

- The Road Signs and Signals Convention (1968)

- The European Agreement for the International Carriage of Dangerous Goods by Road (1957), and

- In relation to professional driver fatigue, the European Agreement concerning the Work of Crews of Vehicles Engaged in International Road Transport (1970).

As the Law Commissions have noted, 'Existing law reflects a division between rules governing vehicle design on the one hand and the behaviour of drivers on the other. This is true at both [the] international … and domestic level'[43].

At the international level, the main UN instruments governing vehicle design and driver behaviour are, respectively, the 1958 Agreement on harmonising vehicle regulations and the 1968 Vienna Convention on Road Traffic. As for the 1958 Agreement (in the care of working party 29 or WP 29), UN regulation for road traffic safety is also in the care of a UNECE working party – working party 1, the Working Party on Road Traffic Safety (WP 1).

For the purposes of considering advanced, automated and electric vehicles, the first two categories of UN instrument relating to road safety – vehicle standards (the 1958 Agreement) and road traffic (the 1968 Convention) are the two most relevant categories.

In the AAEV field, these two are the closest siblings, bound by the increasing ability of the vehicle (or its systems) to assist in and to take over the activity of driving. As the Law Commissions wrote, 'Legislating for self-driving requires an integrated approach, bridging these two regulatory spheres'[44].

Type approval

2.06   As the Vehicle Certification Agency says, 'Put simply, type approval is the confirmation that production samples of a design will meet specified performance standards'[45].

Type approval for road vehicles arose at about the same time as the standardisation of parts and processes by manufacturers, to meet the need of each national government to regulate, within its borders, the safety of motor cars manufactured elsewhere.

In 1909, Great Britain was among the signatories to the Convention with respect to the international circulation of motor vehicles (the Paris Convention), which was agreed between nations 'with a view of facilitating, as far as possible, the international circulation of motor vehicles' [46].

---

43   Law Commissions' final report on automated vehicles, *Automated Vehicles: Joint Report*, Law Com No 404, Scot Law Com No 258 (January 2022), 2.2, 2.3.
44   Quotation at head of this chapter.
45   Vehicle Certification Agency, *Type Approval for Automotive Systems and Components* (VCA004, revision 15), p 2, 'What is Automotive Type Approval?'.
46   *Convention with respect to the international circulation of motor vehicles*, signed at Paris, 11 October 1909. A copy of the Convention, published in the American Journal of International Law in October 1910, is available on JSTOR, at https://archive.org/details/jstor-2212082.

The 1909 Paris convention (which was not as full as later agreements) covered both vehicle specifications and driver behaviour. In relation to specifications, article 1 set out conditions for examination, by a competent authority or authorised association, of the suitability for use on the highway of 'every motor car' but provided alternatively that the car 'must belong to a *type approved* in the same manner' [italics added].

Type approval therefore allows for examination and approval not of every individual vehicle (which, in relation to mass-manufactured vehicles, would be an onerous requirement of the examining authority) but approval of a *type* of vehicle by reference to examination of a sample. So RTA 1988, s 55(1) ('type approval certificates') provides that:

> '(1) Where the Secretary of State is satisfied on application made to him by the manufacturer of a vehicle of a class to which regulations under section 54 of this Act apply and after examination of the vehicle –
>
> (a) that the vehicle complies with the relevant type approval requirements, and
>
> (b) that adequate arrangements have been made to secure that other vehicles purporting to conform with that vehicle in the relevant aspects of design, construction, equipment and marking will so conform in all respects or with such variations as may be permitted,
>
> he may approve that vehicle as a type vehicle.'

Under RTA 1988, s 63(1) it is an offence to use on a road a vehicle to which type approval requirements apply without certificates of conformity complying with RTA 1988, ss 54–58.

In the UK, vehicle type approval is carried out by the Vehicle Certification Agency (VCA): 'VCA is the designated UK Type Approval Authority for automotive products and also a designated Technical Service for type approval testing in the United Nations (UN) scheme. VCA is also responsible for certification under UK type approval schemes.'[47]

Type approval is a long-established method. But its limitations have become clear in recent years, with the use by certain manufacturers of devices designed to cheat the approval test in the 'Dieselgate' cases, where 'defeat devices' in software were used by manufacturers to hide non-compliance with emissions standards[48]. The Court of Justice of the European Union (CJEU) has affirmed that type approval provided by the European Union can be withdrawn, and that the fact of type approval does not prove compliance with consumer protection law[49].

---

47 UK Government website (Vehicle Certification Agency), 'Vehicle Type Approval' (accessed 12 January 2023).

48 See *Crossley and others v Volkswagen Aktiengesellschaft and others (the VW NOx Emissions Group Litigation)* [2021] EWHC 3444 (the summary judgment decision, 20 December 2021) summary of background at paras 3-7, and [2020] EWHC 783 (the preliminary issues judgment, 6 April 2020, both QBD, Waksman J). The VW NOx Emissions Group Litigation settled on confidential terms in May 2022: see Volkswagen press release on its website, 25 May 2022.

49 *DS v Porsche Inter Auto GmbH & Co KG and another* (Case C-145/20) EU:C:2022:572; [2022] 4 WLR 91 [56]. See the domestic statutory position in RTA 1988 Part II, especially ss 56 and 61, and see the AV Bill 2023-24 (HL Bill 1), cll 8, 9 and Sch 1.

Relationship with international vehicle specifications law after Brexit

2.07 Type approval is a method applicable to international trade in road vehicles. Great Britain's extraction from its membership of the European Union removed it from membership of a trade bloc (the EU) which has both a single relationship with the main international body regulating vehicle specifications (UNECE, above) and its own internal system of EU vehicle type approval.

After Brexit, Great Britain has reinforced its existing relationship with the primary vehicle-regulating international body, the UN[50]. In relation to type approval of automated vehicles, the UK government's explanatory memorandum on amendment of the 1968 UN Convention on Road Traffic (12 October 2021) explained that:

> 'The deployment of AVs on UK roads will be subject to vehicle type approval and domestic rules on use. The UK has flexibility to define rules on use provided they are in compliance with international obligations.'[51]

Future domestic regulation and the Automated Vehicles Bill 2023-24

2.08 In May 2022, in the Queen's Speech, the government announced that it would publish a Transport Bill, to include regulation of automated vehicles and e-scooters[52]. In October 2022 (during the Truss administration), the then Secretary of State for Transport indicated that no full Transport Bill would proceed during that parliamentary session, although a smaller, 'Future of Transport' Bill might proceed[53]. In December 2022 (during the Sunak administration), her successor as Transport Secretary stated that no Transport Bill would proceed during the 2022-2023 parliamentary session[54].

In the King's Speech of 7 November 2023, a model closer to the smaller, 'Future of Transport' Bill approach was adopted.

As at the time of writing, the Automated Vehicles Bill 2023-24 has had its first reading in Parliament (with its announcement in the House of Lords as HL Bill 1 on 8 November 2023) and is expected to pass into law as the Automated Vehicles Act 2024. It complements and will amend some terms of definition in the already-

---

50 The post-Brexit reinforcement of the UK-UNECE relationship on road safety was not confined to vehicle specifications. According to the UK Government (Department for Transport) Explanatory Memorandum to the Motor Vehicles (International Circulation) (Amendment) (EU Exit) Order 2019, SI 2019 No. 563 p 2, 7.1, 'The UK originally signed the [UN] 1968 Convention [on Road Traffic] in November 1968, but only ratified it in 2018 because of the decision to leave the EU and the need to ensure the continued recognition of UK driving licences.'

51 Explanatory Memorandum on the Proposal of Amendment to Article 1 and new Article 34 BIS of the 1968 Convention on Road Traffic, Command Paper No: CP 540 (12 October 2021), 3.1.

52 Baroness Vere, House of Lords Hansard volume 822, columns 30 to 31 (11 May 2022).

53 Parliament Live TV, Transport Select Committee 19 October 2022 at 9:42 to 9:45, Sec of St for Transport the Rt Hon Anne-Marie Trevelyan MP.

54 Parliament Live TV, Transport Select Committee 7 December 2022 at 9:43, Sec of St for Transport the Rt Hon Mark Harper MP.

enacted motor insurance statute for automated vehicles, AEVA 2018, Part 1 (see Chapter 6, 'insurance').

The AV Bill 2023-24 would enact the scheme for the criminal and public law regulation of automated vehicles recommended to the government by the Law Commission of England and Wales and the Scottish Law Commission after their joint review of the law of automated vehicles (2018 to 2022). Those recommendations were largely accepted by the government in its response paper of August 2022, the 'Connected and Automated Mobility 2025' paper (CAM 2025)[55].

There are numerous regulation-making powers under the AV Bill 2023-24 (and a duty to consult representative organisations before regulating: cl 97(2)). The Bill sets a rigorous regulatory scheme affecting not only automated but advanced vehicle technologies, including statutory inspection of vehicles and criminal offences which can be committed by using non-permitted terms or language 'likely to confuse' as to autonomous capability.

The AV Bill 2023-24 presents an expansive regulatory scheme. It expands the lexicon for automated vehicles (after a period in exile[56], the word 'autonomous' returns). It introduces to automated vehicles the practice of official accident investigation practised in marine, rail, air and space transport. It expands the reach of safety regulation beyond roads (in the powers of statutory inspectors to investigate automated vehicle incidents under cl 62(3)) and has an armoury of criminal offences governing conduct including the unlicensed use of unauthorised automated vehicles (cl 53) and misleading marketing of non-automated systems as automated (cll 78-81).

The AV Bill 2023-24 also provides the Secretary of State with an important – and arguably overdue – power to make regulations to amend or impose new type approval requirements not only for automated vehicles but also for vehicles with advanced driver assistance systems – 'any other type of vehicle that: (i) includes equipment designed to allow its motion to be controlled other than by an individual in it, or to facilitate its being so controlled; or (ii) is designed to incorporate or interact with software', as cl 91(1) puts it.

The AV Bill 2023-24 does not extend to ADAS systems the rigorous, in-use safety regime policed by statutory inspectors which it applies to automated vehicles, but it nonetheless brings a new proactivity by central government (statutory inspectors must, notably, be civil servants: cl 60(2)(a)) to the authorisation and safety regulation of motor vehicle technologies.

The regulation of smaller electric vehicles such as e-scooters (whose legalisation was promised in the Queen's Speech in May 2022 then postponed) did not appear in any other Transport Bill in the King's Speech in November 2023. That is still awaited. But 2024 will see a flurry of regulations for both advanced and automated vehicles under what will become the Automated Vehicles Act 2024.

---

55 Government paper 'Connected & Automated Mobility 2025: Realising the benefits of self-driving vehicles in the UK' (August 2022).
56 The Centre for Connected and Autonomous Vehicles (CCAV) was founded as the government's specialist unit in 2015, but 'automated' was the word adopted for AEVA 2018.

B   The Law of Advanced Driver Assistance Systems (ADAS) Specifications

What are 'Advanced Driver Assistance Systems'?

2.09   'Advanced Driver Assistance System' ('ADAS') is a technical term, which BSI and the UK government's Centre for Connected and Autonomous Vehicles (CCAV) defines in its vocabulary[57] as an

> 'entity consisting of interdependent components that supports human drivers by performing a part of the dynamic driving task[58] … or providing safety relevant information. *NOTE Examples include adaptive cruise control*[59] *and automatic emergency braking.*'

The Department for Transport defines Advanced Driver Assistance Systems as 'Individual automation features such as adaptive cruise control or lane changing features which assist the driver' [60] falling within either level 1 or level 2 of the six levels of vehicle automation described by the SAE levels of driving automation, (J3016)[61].

As well as providing for the authorisation of automated systems, the AV Bill 2023-24, cl 91(1)(b) would (if enacted per HL Bill 1) for the first time provide a definition of driver assistance systems for the purpose of type approval. The AV Bill 2023-24, cl 91would provide a power to the Secretary of State by regulations to update type approval requirements, of a sort similar to the general power to prescribe TA requirements provided by RTA 1988, s 54, but specifically

> 'for the purpose of making the assimilated[62] type approval legislation more suitable for:
>
> …
>
> (b)   any other type of vehicle that –

---

57   Connected and automated vehicles – Vocabulary BSI Flex 1890 v4.0:2022-03 (the BSI CAV vocabulary).

58   The BSI CAV vocabulary defines Dynamic driving task (DDT) as the 'real-time operational and tactical functions required to operate a vehicle … safely in on-road traffic'.

59   The BSI CAV vocabulary defines adaptive cruise control (ACC) as follows: 'system that attempts to maintain the vehicle (2.1.87) at a driver-selected target speed and following distance, using sensors and automation to regulate vehicle speed. NOTE 1 The purpose is to keep a safe distance relative to other slower moving vehicles ahead before reverting to the set speed when the lane clears. NOTE 2 Some early adaptive cruise control systems, especially those vehicles with manual transmission, are not capable of bringing the vehicle to a complete stop and require the human driver to intervene to do so. Systems that are capable of controlling the vehicle to a stop have a variety of additional names such as "Stop & Go".'

60   'Acronym glossary' at page 45 of Department for Transport, 'Safe use of automated lane keeping system (ALKS): summary of responses and next steps – moving Britain ahead' (April 2021).

61   See figure 1.

62   'The assimilated type approval legislation' is defined by AV Bill 2023-24, cl 91(4) and consists mainly of EU regulations including Regulation 2018/858 of the European Parliament and of the Council of 30 May 2018 on the approval and market surveillance of motor vehicles and their trailers, and of systems, components and separate technical units intended for such vehicles (cl 91(4)(j)).

    (i)   includes equipment designed to allow its motion to be controlled other than by an individual in it, or to facilitate its being so controlled, or

    (ii)   is designed to incorporate or interact with software.'

Domestic Regulation of ADAS

2.10   As at the time of writing, unless a vehicle is listed as automated under AEVA 2018, s 1, it is not 'automated' for the purposes of the 2018 Act, and the liability and insurance provisions of AEVA 2018, Part 1 would not apply in the event of an accident causing damage.

Although the AV Bill 2023-24 (per HL Bill 1) would repeal the 'listing' process for automated vehicles under AEVA 2018, s 1 and replace it with the AVA 2024 process of authorisation[63], the effect would be the same: an accident causing injury or damage because of the use of an ADAS, non-automated system would not afford the injured claimant a direct claim against the insurer of the person using that vehicle under AEVA 2018, s 2.

It is at present unclear whether the Department of Transport will classify the Automated Lane Keeping System (ALKS) as an ADAS or as an 'automated' vehicle within AEVA 2018 s 1 or its succeeding authorisation mechanism under AVA 2024.

The UK government's intention, as expressed in April 2021, was that it intended to classify a vehicle equipped with ALKS as an automated vehicle under AEVA 2018, s 1, though it would make decisions 'on a case by case basis'[64]. However, that intention preceded the publication of the AV Bill 2023-24 (HL Bill 1). The government's view on the point had also altered: it had previously, before AEVA 2018 was enacted, indicated opposition to classifying an SAE Level 3 vehicle as 'automated'[65].

A key factor will be the approach of the AV Bill 2023-24 to the difficulty of classifying an SAE Level 3 vehicle in which both human and automated driving are possible – the 'mushy middle' (as the Law Commissions had described it). The AV Bill 2023-24, fashioned by the Law Commissions, proposes a solution. We should first understand the problem.

---

63   AV Bill 2023-24 (HL Bill 1), cl 45, Sch 2, para 5(2).

64   UK government (VCA) website, 'Automated Lane Keeping Systems (ALKS) and Listing of Self-Driving Vehicles' (29 July 2022): 'ALKS Listing Review. Vehicles which are approved to UNECE R157 and include the United Kingdom within their Operational Design Domain (ODD) should meet the threshold of self-driving and therefore be added to the Secretary of State's List. Decisions will be made on a case by case basis. VCA will carry out a thorough review of all approvals submitted which include ALKS, in order that the decision to list the vehicles based on them having a UNECE Regulation 157 approval can be confirmed as valid in each case.'

65   See 'Will Write' 'Letters from [Minister of State] John Hayes MP to Edward Leigh and Adrian Bailey MP, as referenced in letter dated 15/11/2017 regarding levels of automation' and 'Letter dated 13/03/2018 from Baroness Sugg regarding whether the Automated and Electric Vehicles Bill's provisions cover Level 3 vehicles', both at UK Parliament, Parliamentary Bills, 'Automated and Electric Vehicles Act 2018', 'Publications'.

Standards for ADAS

2.11   The most well-known categorisation of the levels of driving automation is in the SAE standard, 'Taxonomy and Definitions for Terms Related to Driving Automation Systems for On-Road Motor Vehicles' (J3016), more often known by its short title 'Levels of Driving Automation'. It is summarised by the well-known graphic at figure 1:

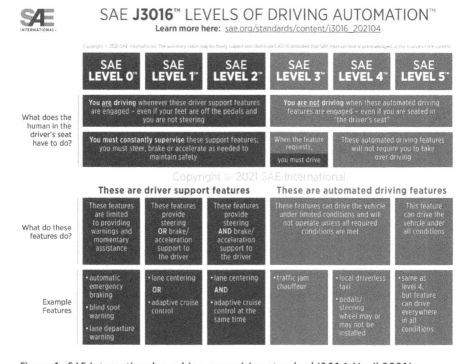

Figure 1: SAE International graphic summarising standard J3016 (April 2021)

SAE J3016 encompasses (within levels 0, 1 and 2) 'driver support systems' such as automatic emergency braking (AEB, at level 0), adaptive cruise control (ACC, at level 1) and lane centring and ACC simultaneously (at level 2).

In the SAE's summary of its levels of driving automation (figure 1), Levels 0, 1 and 2 are coloured blue (the darker background in the monochrome Figure 1 above) to denote the distinction in the SAE levels between 'driver support' features and (in its language) the 'automated' driving features at levels 3, 4 and 5, which are coloured green (the lighter background in the monochrome Figure 1 above).

The problem appears in the first of the three 'automated' levels: Level 3. SAE Level 3 does not denote entirely attention-free driving. As the SAE graphic (figure 1) shows, 'When the [Level 3] feature requests' the driver to take back control 'you [the driver] must drive'. So Level 3 requires at least residual attention on the part of the driver. In the SAE graphic, the question 'what does the human in the driver's seat have to do?' is written in both blue and green text (denoting both non-automated and automated driving). This led to elaborate systemising of the human driver's responsibilities when using a Level 3 system, including the responsibility to react in a timely way to a request by the vehicle to resume human control: a 'transition demand'. As the Law Commissions have noted, SAE Level 3 'has been described as the 'mushy middle' of driving automation'[66].

It has always been accepted in the UK (whether under AEVA 2018, s 1 or the AV Bill 2023-2024) that legalisation of systems equivalent to SAE Level 3 depends upon the national regulating authority's assessment of whether or not vehicles equipped with such a system are sufficiently safe to operate as 'automated' vehicles.

UN regulations for ADAS

UN regulation 157 on ALKS

2.12   The Automated Lane Keeping System (ALKS) is a system which steers and controls vehicle speed in lane for extended periods on motorways at speeds of 60 km/h (37 mph) or less.

In January 2021, the UN published its regulation for ALKS, regulation 157[67]. In June 2022, regulation 157 was amended, with effect from January 2023 in those contracting parties which decide to apply it, to allow operation of ALKS equipped vehicles at motorway speeds of up to 130 km per hour (80.78 mph)[68]. The UK government's position on the UN regulation 157 is that the 'ALKS Regulation sets out technical requirements for ALKS, but certain aspects of its use require further consideration at a national level, for example rules on safe use'[69]. As at the date of writing, no vehicle has been listed as automated under AEVA 2018, s 1 (the current legal instrument for classifying a vehicle as automated).

The UK government's intention in April 2021 was to classify a vehicle equipped with ALKS as an automated vehicle under AEVA 2018, s 1[70], 'on a case by case basis'[71]. But this intention should now be read in the light of AV Bill 2023-24 (HL Bill 1), which would repeal AEVA 2018, s 1 and replace it with a new system of authorisation. It should also be read with the prospect of a new UN rule affecting ADAS in mind.

Proposed new UN ADAS rule

2.13   UNECE Working Party 29 is, as at the time of writing, considering new regulation of Driver Control Assistance Systems (DCAS) in relation to UN Regulation

---

66 The Law Commissions 'Automated Vehicles: Summary of the Preliminary Consultation Paper' (November 2018), p 4, 2.9.
67 UN Regulation No. 157, Uniform provisions concerning the approval of vehicles with regard to Automated Lane Keeping Systems ('UN Regulation 157'), in force as an annex to the 1958 Agreement, 22 January 2021.
68 UNECE 'Proposal for the 01 series of amendments to UN Regulation No. 157 (Automated Lane Keeping Systems)' ECE/TRANS/WP.29/2022/59/Rev.1 (30 May 2022), Art 5.2.3.1 and 5.2.6; UNECE website 'UN Regulation extends automated driving up to 130 km/h in certain conditions' (22 June 2022).
69 UK government website 'Rules on the safe use of automated vehicles: summary of responses and government response' (updated 25 April 2022).
70 See UK government (VCA) website, 'Automated Lane Keeping Systems (ALKS) and Listing of Self-Driving Vehicles' (29 July 2022) (accessed 12 January 2023).
71 As above.

No 79 (regulation 79 relates to steering equipment) [72]. No final version of the DCAS regulation is yet available.

Existing (pre-Automated Vehicles Act 2024) domestic construction and use regulations applicable to ADAS

2.14 As described above, the AV Bill 2023-24, cl 91 indicates the likelihood of new domestic regulations for type approval of ADAS.

To date, emerging motor vehicle technologies have been regulated by incremental additions to the Construction and Use Regulations. This has produced a patchy regulatory picture for ADAS.

The rule on screens in vehicles provides an example. Originally intended to prevent the use of portable television sets in vehicles for entertainment during driving[73], CUR 1986, reg 109 ('Television sets') is now relevant to the use of flat screens, to view images from navigation software or from rear or side cameras. Before its amendment to apply to automated vehicles (see below), CUR reg 109 provided as follows:

'(1) No person shall drive, or cause or permit to be driven, a motor vehicle on a road, if the driver is in such a position as to be able to see, whether directly or by reflection, a television receiving apparatus or other cinematographic apparatus used to display anything other than information—

(a) about the state of the vehicle or its equipment;

(b) about the location of the vehicle and the road on which it is located;

(c) to assist the driver to see the road adjacent to the vehicle; or

(d) to assist the driver to reach his destination.

(2) In this regulation *'television receiving apparatus'* means any cathode ray tube carried on a vehicle and on which there can be displayed an image derived from a television broadcast, a recording or a camera or computer.'

See Chapter 4, 'driving', for discussion of other CUR 1986 requirements for ADAS and automated vehicles, in particular:

* For AVs, the amendment of CUR 1986, reg 109 from 1 July 2022, to include new rules for the use of screens in automated vehicles, during self-driving[74], and

* For all vehicles, the current regs 104 ('driver's control') and 110 (mobile telephones, as amended).

---

72 ECE/TRANS/WP.29/GRVA/2023/20, 'Proposal for a new UN Regulation on uniform provisions concerning the approval of vehicles with regards to Driver Control Assistance Systems' (11 July 2023).

73 See CUR 1986, SI 1986/1078 reg 109 and explanatory note para 2(xxvi), both as originally made, at https://www.legislation.gov.uk/uksi/1986/1078/note/made.

74 Road Vehicles (Construction and Use) (Automated Vehicles) Order 2022, SI 2022/470, in force from 1 July 2022 (art 1(1)).

The pace of domestic legislation for advanced and automated vehicles has been criticised, particularly by reference to the pace of European Union regulation[75]. One illustration of the outdatedness of current rules (as at the time of writing) is the persistence of the 'cathode ray tube' definition in CUR 1986, reg 109(2), above, which is obsolete in the era of LED flatscreens.

The AV Bill 2023-24, cl 91 appears to take a new approach, by providing a regulation-making power expressly for a 'type of vehicle that: (i) includes equipment designed to allow its motion to be controlled other than by an individual in it, or to facilitate its being so controlled; or (ii) is designed to incorporate or interact with software.'

Influence of European Union (EU) vehicle specifications law upon British AAEV regulation after Brexit

2.15   Since 2018, the EU has reformed its vehicle approval regulations, both as a reaction to technological developments to date and to 'future-proof' its regulatory regime for further advances in driver support and automation (higher levels of ADAS and automation).

The first reform was to counter a malign use of technology. In 2018, in the wake of the Dieselgate scandal, the EU passed regulation 2018/858, to allow greater powers of monitoring passenger and goods vehicles and their trailers[76] while in use in the market (the EU approval and market surveillance regulation)[77]. The use of software 'defeat devices' by certain manufacturers to cheat emissions testing was the reason for a more secure version of vehicle approval which would take greater account of software:

> 'The need for control and monitoring of technical services has increased because technical progress has increased the risk of technical services not possessing the necessary competence to test new technologies or devices that emerge within their scope of designation'[78]

> 'The approval authority and technical services shall have the access to the software and algorithms of the vehicle that they consider to be necessary for the purpose of carrying out their activities.'[79]

2.16   In November 2019, the EU executed a larger revision of its vehicle approval regulations with the Vehicle General Safety Regulation 2019 (EU VGSR 2019,

---

75 House of Commons European Scrutiny Committee, Twelfth Report of Session 2022-2023, chapter 1, 'EU regulations for 'self-driving' vehicles: potential implications for the UK' (17 January 2023)
76 Respectively categories M (passenger) and N (goods) vehicles and their trailers (category O). EU reg 2018/858, preamble [8].
77 Regulation (EU) 2018/858 of the European Parliament and of the Council of 30 May 2018 on the approval and market surveillance of motor vehicles and their trailers, and of systems, components and separate technical units intended for such vehicles, amending Regulations (EC) No 715/2007 and (EC) No 595/2009 and repealing Directive 2007/46/EC.
78 EU reg 2018/858, preamble [13].
79 EU reg 2018/858, art 25(4) ('Additional information to be provided with an application for EU type-approval').

sometimes referred to as the General Safety Regulation)[80]. EU VGSR 2019 was directed particularly at the safety of vehicle occupants and vulnerable road users, and looked towards higher levels of driver support and vehicle automation. It approached those possible advances in a notably commercial way:

'Detailed technical requirements and adequate test procedures, as well as provisions concerning uniform procedures and technical specifications, for type-approval of motor vehicles and their trailers, and of systems, components and separate technical units should be laid down in delegated acts and implementing acts sufficiently in advance before their date of application in order to allow enough time for manufacturers to adapt to the requirements of this Regulation and the delegated acts and implementing acts adopted pursuant to it. Some vehicles are produced in small quantities. Therefore, it is appropriate that requirements set out in this Regulation and the delegated acts and implementing acts adopted pursuant to it take into account such vehicles or classes of vehicles where such requirements are incompatible with the use or design of such vehicles, or where the additional burden imposed by them is disproportionate. Therefore, the application of this Regulation should be deferred'[81]

EU VGSR 2019 laid the ground for 'a range of mandatory advanced driver assistant[82] systems to improve road safety and … the legal framework for the approval of automated and fully driverless vehicles in the EU'[83].

The EU approval and market surveillance regulation (EU 2018/858) was amended on 20 June 2022 by the EU Commission Delegated Regulation 2022/2236[84]. The amendment took 'into account technological and regulatory developments by updating some of the references in [the] table [at Annex II, Part I to EU regulation 2018/858] setting out the requirements for vehicles, systems, components and separate technical units' and to refer to EU VGSR 2019[85]. But it was

---

80 Regulation (EU) 2019/2144 of the European Parliament and of the Council of 27 November 2019 on type-approval requirements for motor vehicles and their trailers, and, systems, components and separate technical units intended for such vehicles, as regards their general safety and the protection of vehicle occupants and vulnerable road users, amending Regulation (EU) 2018/858 of the European Parliament and of the Council and repealing Regulations (EC) No 78/2009, (EC) No 79/2009 and (EC) No 661/2009 of the European Parliament and of the Council and Commission Regulations (EC) No 631/2009, (EU) No 406/2010, (EU) No 672/2010, (EU) No 1003/2010, (EU) No 1005/2010, (EU) No 1008/2010, (EU) No 1009/2010, (EU) No 19/2011, (EU) No 109/2011, (EU) No 458/2011, (EU) No 65/2012, (EU) No 130/2012, (EU) No 347/2012, (EU) No 351/2012, (EU) No 1230/2012 and (EU) 2015/166.
81 EU VGSR 2019 preamble (35). See [10] for the reference to future-proofing EU regulation. EU VGSR 2019 was deferred to apply from 6 July 2022 (art 19).
82 As the Commission described them, i.e. ADAS.
83 European Commission press release 'New rules to improve road safety and enable driverless vehicles in the EU' (6 July 2022).
84 Commission Delegated Regulation (EU) 2022/2236 of 20 June 2022 amending Annexes I, II, IV and V to Regulation (EU) 2018/858 of the European Parliament and of the Council as regards the technical requirements for vehicles produced in unlimited series, vehicles produced in small series, fully automated vehicles produced in small series and special purpose vehicles, and as regards software update.
85 Above, preamble [2].

'also necessary to set out the requirements that should apply to the EU whole-vehicle type approval of fully automated vehicles produced in small series[86] to allow for a progressive but quick introduction of the technology in line with the application dates set out in Regulation (EU) 2019/2144. As a next stage, the Commission will continue the work to further develop and adopt by July 2024 the necessary requirements for the EU whole vehicle type approval of fully automated vehicles produced in unlimited series.'[87]

EU VGSR 2019 applied from 6 July 2022[88].

2.17   The rules for EU approval of automated driving systems of 'fully-automated' vehicles as provided by EU VGSR 2019 were brought into force for certain use cases in September 2022[89], by the EU Commission Implementing Regulation 2022/1426[90]. The particular use cases were:

'(a) Fully automated vehicles, including dual mode vehicles, designed and constructed for the carriage of passengers or carriage of goods on a predefined area.

(b) "Hub-to-hub": fully automated vehicles, including dual mode vehicles, designed and constructed for the carriage of passengers or carriage of goods on a predefined route with fixed start and end points of a journey/ trip.

(c) "Automated valet parking": dual mode vehicles with a fully automated driving mode for parking applications within predefined parking facilities. The system may use or not external infrastructure (e.g. localization markers, perception sensors, etc.) of the parking facility to perform the dynamic driving task.'[91]

Although the title to EU Regulation 2022/1426 refers to 'fully-automated vehicles', the geographical restrictions in parts (a) and (b) of article 1 (above) and the reference in the preamble to EU Regulation 2022/2236 to requirements for fully automated vehicles being adopted by July 2024[92] tend to show that the regulation applies to automated driving systems equivalent to SAE Level 4, and not yet to SAE Level 5.

The automated lane keeping system, ALKS (considered by most to be equivalent to SAE Level 3) was not included in this EU regulation. EU approval 'of the automated driving systems of automated vehicles should not be covered by this regulation as it is intended to cover them with a reference to UN Regulation 157 on automated

---

86   See discussion in the 'automated vehicles' section, below.

87   Above, [3].

88   EU VGSR 2019 art 19.

89   EU Regulation 2022/1426 (below), art 4 ('Entry into force'): 'This Regulation shall enter into force on the twentieth day following that of its publication in the Official Journal of the European Union'. The date shown by the OJEU for the regulation is 26.8.2022.

90   Commission Implementing Regulation (EU) 2022/1426 of 5 August 2022 laying down rules for the application of Regulation (EU) 2019/2144 of the European Parliament and of the Council as regards uniform procedures and technical specifications for the type-approval of the automated driving system (ADS) of fully automated vehicles

91   EU Reg 2022/1426, art 1.

92   EU Reg 2022/2236, preamble [3], quoted above.

lane keeping systems in Annex I to Regulation (EU) 2019/2144 listing the UN regulations that shall apply on a compulsory basis in the EU'[93].

2.18   The effects of those EU regulations in relation to ADAS are that, from 6 July 2022, all new vehicles that are placed onto the market or registered or entered into service in the European Union must be equipped with certain ADAS systems[94]. Those systems include Advanced Emergency Braking (AEB) and Intelligent Speed Assistance (ISA, which signals to the driver that the applicable speed limit is exceeded).

The EU regulation is not mandatory as it allows for systems to be overridden and allows the speed limit to be exceeded by the driver[95] (so, insofar as the ISA system is concerned, it is not a full 'speed limiter' as the media has sometimes described it).

Post-Brexit, EU law remains relevant to domestic regulation of both advanced and automated vehicle technologies, mainly because any British vehicle system not complying with EU regulations could not be deployed or sold into the EU, but also because the system of regulation through common vehicle standards is – in both the practical and legal senses – rooted in international agreements[96].

The UK government's position on the relevance of EU vehicle specifications law in September 2022 was as follows:

'Whilst there is currently no equivalent regulation for the rest of the UK [outside Northern Ireland], the Department for Transport is in the process of producing a safety assurance and legal framework for self-driving vehicles (i.e. fully automated vehicles) in Great Britain. The approach taken by the European Commission when developing the implementing Regulation is the same as the planned GB equivalent, which will take into consideration guidelines being developed at an international level by the Working Party on Automated and Connected Vehicle (GRVA[97]) under the United Nations Economic Commission for Europe (UNECE) (of which the UK is a contributor). Therefore, the general concepts and a considerable number of requirements are likely to be similar or compatible. Any technical divergence is likely to result from areas which GRVA have not addressed, or if there are provisions required to account for nuances for deployment in Great Britain.'[98]

---

93   Above, preamble [1].
94   EU Regulation 2019/2144 of the European Parliament and of the Council of 27 November 2019.
95   Article 6(2) of EU Regulation 2019/2144.
96   See the discussion above.
97   Groupe de travail des véhicules automatisés/autonomes et connectés (GRVA), the specialist group within UNECE working party 29.
98   UK government (Department for Transport), 'Explanatory Memorandum for European Union Legislation within the scope of the UK/EU Withdrawal Agreement and Northern Ireland Protocol: Commission implementing Regulation (EU) 2022/1426 of 5.8.2022 laying down rules for the application of Regulation (EU) 2019/2144 of the European Parliament and of the Council as regards uniform procedures and technical specifications for the type-approval of the automated driving system (ADS) of fully automated vehicles[;] Annexes to the Commission Implementing Regulation laying down rules for the application of Regulation (EU) 2019/2144 of the European Parliament and of the Council as regards uniform procedures and technical specifications for the type-approval of the automated driving system (ADS) of fully automated vehicles' (29 September 2022) [12].

A committee of the House of Commons had understood this to mean that:

> '... the Department [for Transport] has indicated its planned legislation for Great Britain will largely mirror what the EU has done in terms of AV technical safety.'[99]

The AV Bill 2023-24 reiterates the important and lasting effect of international regulation upon domestic British regulation of new vehicle technologies. In particular:

- consistently with the revision to articles 1 and 34 of the UN Vienna Convention on Road Traffic 1968 (below), the AV Bill 2023-24 adopts official vehicle authorisation by reference to objective criteria[100] as the definitional factor as to whether or not a vehicle is 'automated' in law (the broader ministerial discretion of AEVA 2018, s 1 'listing' is abandoned[101]);

- the AV Bill 2023-24, cl 91 cites assimilated EU type approval legislation (including EU Regulation 2018, SI 2018/858) as among the legal foundations from which British law may be adapted.

C The Law of Automated Vehicle Specifications

Definition of 'automated' vehicle under AEVA 2018

2.19   The current legal definition of 'automated vehicle' is in AEVA 2018, s 1 ('Listing of automated vehicles by the Secretary of State') of which provides that:

> '(1) The Secretary of State must prepare, and keep up to date, a list of all motor vehicles that—
>
> (a) are in the Secretary of State's opinion designed or adapted to be capable, in at least some circumstances or situations, of safely driving themselves, and
>
> (b) may lawfully be used when driving themselves, in at least some circumstances or situations, on roads or other public places in Great Britain.
>
> (2) The list may identify vehicles—
>
> (a) by type,
>
> (b) by reference to information recorded in a registration document issued under regulations made under section 22 of the Vehicle Excise and Registration Act 1994, or
>
> (c) in some other way.
>
> (3) The Secretary of State must publish the list when it is first prepared and each time it is revised.

---

99 House of Commons European Scrutiny Committee, Twelfth Report of Session 2022-2023, chapter 1, 'EU regulations for 'self-driving' vehicles: potential implications for the UK' (17 January 2023), p 3.

100 See AV Bill 2023-24, cll 3-5.

101 By the prospective repeal of AEVA 2018, s 1 by AV Bill 2023-24, cl 45, Sch 2, para 5(2).

(4) In this Part 'automated vehicle' means a vehicle listed under this section.'

AEVA 2018, s 8 ('interpretation') provides that:

'(1) For the purposes of this Part—

(a) a vehicle is 'driving itself' if it is operating in a mode in which it is not being controlled, and does not need to be monitored, by an individual;

…

(2) In this Part 'automated vehicle' has the meaning given by section 1(4)'

However, this definition is set to change, with the repeal of AEVA 2018, s 1 and the amendment of s 8, if the AV Bill 2023-24 is enacted as the AVA 2024.

SAE Standard J3016 Levels 3 to 5 for AVs

2.20   See figure 1, above, for a summary of the SAE's six levels of driving automation (levels 0 to 5 inclusive).

As noted in the 'Outline' section above, standards do not have the force of law. The Law Commissions note that SAE J3016 'is the most widely used description of driving automation' but also that it 'is described as 'descriptive and informative, rather than normative' and is 'technical rather than legal'[102]. AEVA 2018 does not refer to the SAE Levels.

SAE J3016 was produced by SAE and ISO. It proposes three levels of automated driving:

- SAE Level 3 (conditional driving automation);

- SAE Level 4 (high driving automation); and

- SAE Level 5 (full driving automation).

For reasons already discussed, Level 3 is problematic. The first problem is that the driver must remain ready to take back control; the second is that Level 3 combines that requirement of driver readiness with the apparent permission to the driver to distract themselves.

The text of J3016 contains a fuller account of the roles of the human user and the driving automation system, by level of driving automation, in a table of that title[103]. The table describes in some detail the respective roles of driver and automated system, including at SAE Level 3. The content of the text of J3016 cannot be reproduced without permission so the reader is directed to that text[104]. In particular, at Level 3 J3016 requires the driver to remain vigilant, not only to matters external to the vehicle but also to the occurrence of faults in the vehicle and its systems.

---

102 Law Commissions' third AV law consultation paper (December 2020), p 39.
103 J3016 (April 2021) table 2, p 28.
104 Via https://www.sae.org/blog/sae-j3016-update (SAE blog 3 May 2021).

As noted above, AEVA 2018 does not refer to the SAE Levels. As discussed in the 'driving' chapter of this book[105], the proposed revision to the Highway Code for automated vehicles (made in anticipation of the government's intended listing of ALKS as an automated system), appears closer to the requirements of UN regulation 157 on ALKS (which contains detailed practical requirements of an ALKS system, including the suspension of entertainment during a transition demand to the user[106]) than to the guidance in SAE J3016. Nevertheless, on the law as it now stands in AEVA 2018, the tension between driver readiness and driver distraction remains.

SAE Level 3 and the question of classification under AEVA 2018, s 1

2.21   As the law stands at the time of writing, the classification of a vehicle as 'automated' is determined by its presence on the list of automated vehicles which the Secretary of State for Transport is required to prepare by AEVA 2018, s 1.

The current law is that the Secretary of State for Transport certifies motor vehicles as automated, having determined that such vehicles are, in the Secretary of State's opinion: '(a) ... designed or adapted to be capable, in at least some circumstances or situations, of safely driving themselves; and (b) may lawfully be used when driving themselves, in at least some circumstances or situations, on roads or other public places in Great Britain': AEVA 2018, s 1(1).

However, in August 2022 the government agreed with the Law Commissions' recommendation that this 'listing' process should be replaced, and that the authorisation of a vehicle as 'automated' should occur within a new, more detailed vehicle approval process to be set out in a forthcoming Transport Bill:

> 'it is now right that the authorisation decision replaces 'listing' ..., which is more limited in scope. Any vehicles that have already been listed by the time the new framework is commenced will have time to convert to authorisation prior to the regime coming into force.'[107]

The 'Transport Bill' appeared as the Automated Vehicles Bill 2023-24 (HL Bill 1), published on 8 November 2023. The AV Bill 2023-24 provides clarity on the method by which a vehicle would be classified officially as 'automated'. Before the AV Bill, the government's approach to the method of classifying a vehicle as automated had not always been consistent. The parliamentary materials on the Bill which became AEVA 2018 appear to show that in November 2017 the government considered the SAE levels relevant to listing under AEVA, particularly SAE Level 3 in which a human driver is required to remain sufficiently alert to retake control of a self-driving car. Government 'will write' letters on the issue of SAE level classification

---

105 Chapter 4, section: 'Revision of the Highway Code guidance to drivers in relation to automated vehicles'.

106 UN regulation 157, 'Uniform provisions concerning the approval of vehicles with regard to Automated Lane Keeping Systems' (4 March 2021) Art 6.1.4.

107 UK Government paper 'Connected and Automated Mobility 2025' (CAM 2025, 19 August 2022) page 126, Annex D.

seemed then to indicate a view that an SAE Level 3 vehicle would *not* be within the AEV Bill's definition of 'automated vehicle'[108].

However, after enactment of AEVA 2018, the government described its intention to list as an automated vehicle under the 2018 Act any vehicle equipped with the Automated Lane Keeping System (ALKS)[109], despite ALKS requiring driver vigilance within SAE Level 3[110]. Listing an ALKS-equipped vehicle under AEVA 2018, s 1 would result in the direct liability of insurer or permitted uninsured owner of that vehicle under AEVA 2018, s 2, in the event of an accident caused by the vehicle when driving itself on a road or other public place in Great Britain, as well as the application of the insurance rules which AEVA 2018 adds to the RTA 1988, Part VI motor insurance scheme[111].

So the SAE standard J3016 highlighted a persistent question, as to how the statutory definition of 'automated vehicle' under AEVA 2018 corresponded to the practical reality of automated driving systems – and especially as to which systems should lead to the statutory classification of a vehicle as 'automated'[112].

As at the time of writing, no automated vehicle (whether an ALKS-equipped vehicle or otherwise) has yet been listed as such under AEVA 2018, s 1. Depending upon the pace of enactment of the AV Bill 2023-2024 as AVA 2024, it is possible that no automated vehicle will be listed as such under AEVA 2018, s 1 and that such authorisation will happen under the more detailed provisions of AVA 2024 (described below) and its regulations which are yet to be published.

UN regulation of AVs

2.22   As set out above, the UN published its regulation for ALKS, regulation 157, in January 2021. Whether in Great Britain an ALKS-equipped vehicle would be an automated vehicle is a matter of law which has yet to be settled by listing under AEVA 2018, s 1 (the current legal instrument for such classification) or authorisation under AVA 2024 (if and when enacted in the terms of HL Bill 1).

Also in January 2021 (and taking effect on 14 July 2022[113]), the UN amended articles 1 and 34 of the Vienna Convention on Road Traffic 1968 to read as follows, in anticipation of self-driving systems:

---

108 See 'Will Write' 'Letter from John Hayes MP to Edward Leigh and Adrian Bailey MP, as referenced in letter dated 15/11/2017 regarding levels of automation' and 'Letter dated 13/03/2018 from Baroness Sugg regarding whether the Automated and Electric Vehicles Bill's provisions cover Level 3 vehicles', both at UK Parliament, Parliamentary Bills, 'Automated and Electric Vehicles Act 2018', 'Publications'.

109 Department for Transport, 'Safe use of automated lane keeping system (ALKS): summary of responses and next steps – moving Britain ahead' (April 2021) p 41.

110 See as evidence of this the subsequent terms of UN Regulation no 157 (under the 1958 Agreement) 'to establish uniform provisions concerning the approval of vehicles with regard to Automated Lane Keeping Systems (ALKS)', which requires that 'The activated system shall recognise all situations in which it needs to transition control back to the driver' and then to 'generate a transition demand to the driver' (Art 5.4.1). As the SAE graphic (figure 1 above) describes SAE Level 3, 'When the feature requests, you must drive'.

111 See Chapter 6, 'insurance'.

112 Under AEVA 2018, ss 1 and 8(1)(a). See Chapter 6, 'Insurance', 'Insurance law for automated vehicles', 'Controversy as to the Listing of ALKS vehicles as 'automated', ie. 'capable … of safely driving themselves', under AEVA 2018'.

113 Communication of Secretary-General of the UN, 21 January 2022, at https://treaties.un.org/doc/Publication/CN/2022/CN.26.2022-Eng.pdf

'*Amendment of Article 1:*

Two new definitions 'ab' and 'ac' are added, to read:

ARTICLE 1

Definitions

(ab) 'Automated driving system' refers to a vehicle system that uses both hardware and software to exercise dynamic control of a vehicle on a sustained basis.

(ac) 'Dynamic control' refers to carrying out all the real-time operational and tactical functions required to move the vehicle. This includes controlling the vehicle's lateral and longitudinal motion, monitoring the road, responding to events in the road traffic, and planning and signalling for manoeuvres.

Insertion of new Article 34 bis:

A new article 'Article 34 bis' is added, to read:

ARTICLE 34 bis

Automated driving

The requirement that every moving vehicle or combination of vehicles shall have a driver is deemed to be satisfied while the vehicle is using an automated driving system which complies with:

(a) domestic technical regulations, and any applicable international legal instrument, concerning wheeled vehicles, equipment and parts which can be fitted and/or be used on wheeled vehicles, and

(b) domestic legislation governing operation.

The effect of this Article is limited to the territory of the Contracting Party where the relevant domestic technical regulations and legislation governing operation apply.'[114]

That amendment was described by the UK government as 'the first binding international law relating to automated vehicles'[115]. The UK government described its position in relation to the amendment as follows:

---

114 UK Government website (Foreign, Commonwealth and Development Office) (12 October 2021), 'Proposal of Amendment to Article 1 and new Article 34 BIS of the 1968 Convention on Road Traffic, Presented to Parliament by the Secretary of State for Foreign, Commonwealth and Development Affairs by Command of Her Majesty October 2021, Miscellaneous series No.5 (2021), Command Paper 540

115 Explanatory Memorandum on the Proposal of Amendment to Article 1 and new Article 34 BIS of the 1968 Convention on Road Traffic, Command Paper No: CP 540 (12 October 2021), 3.1.

'For the UK the amendment to the 1968 Convention is merely clarificatory, setting out a route whereby countries can regulate automated driving to continue to adhere to the requirement, (common to both [the 1949 and 1968 UN Road Traffic] Conventions), that every vehicle shall have a driver in a way which suits their own domestic law and traffic rules. As the UK is already regulating automated driving in accordance with the principles set out in the amendment to the 1968 Convention, its wording is no more than a restatement for the UK of what we are doing already.'[116]

The Automated Vehicles Bill 2023-24 (HL Bill 1)

2.23   The AV Bill 2023-24 (here discussed in its first published version introduced to Parliament on 8 November 2023 as HL Bill 1[117]) takes an approach to classification of 'automated' vehicles which is closer to the January 2021 amendments to the UN Vienna Convention on Road Traffic 1968 arts 1 and 34 (above) than to AEVA 2018, s 1. In other words, the AV Bill 2023-24 makes compliance with technical regulations the main consideration and replaces the AEVA 2018, s 1 Secretary of State's 'list' of automated vehicles with a more detailed process of technical authorisation. That authorisation, envisaged as part of a type approval process, underpins the Secretary of State's legal power to authorise a road vehicle for use as an automated vehicle under what is expected to become AVA 2024, s 3 (now AV Bill 2023-24, cl 3).

There are seven Parts to the AV Bill 2023-24 (HL Bill 1) –

1   Regulatory scheme for automated vehicles (cll 1-45);

2   Criminal liability for vehicle use (cll 46-56);

3   Policing and investigation (cll 57-59);

4   Marketing restrictions (cll 78-81);

5   Permits for automated passenger services (cll 82-90);

6   Adaptation of existing regimes (cll 91-93);

7   General provision (cll 94-100).

– as well as six Schedules:

Sch 1   Enforcement action under Part 1: procedure

       Part 1   Unilateral variation, suspension or withdrawal of authorisation;

       Part 2   Civil sanctions

Sch 2   Amendments related to Part 1 (the regulatory scheme)

Sch 3   Amendments related to cll 53 and 54 (offences of use of vehicle without driver or licensed oversight, and dangerous use etc)

Sch 4   Amendments related to cl 66(3) (offence of failing to comply with the direction of a statutory inspector under cl 65)

---

116 As above.
117 See the progress of the AV Bill 2023-24 (HL Bill 1) at https://bills.parliament.uk/bills/3506.

Sch 5 Enforcement of marketing restrictions

Sch 6 Civil sanctions for infringing passenger permit scheme.

This chapter (vehicle specifications) is concerned with the AV Bill 2023-24, Part 1 – the regulatory scheme for automated vehicles – and those sections in other parts which affect Part 1. So this chapter deals with Parts:

1 Regulatory scheme for automated vehicles (cll 1-45);

6 Adaptation of existing regimes (cll 91-93);

7 General provision (cll 94-100).

– and, in the Schedules:

Sch 1 Enforcement action under Part 1: procedure

       Part 1 Unilateral variation, suspension or withdrawal of authorisation

Sch 2 Amendments related to Part 1 (the regulatory scheme)

The AV Bill 2023-24, Part 1 regulatory scheme for automated vehicles

2.24 Under AV Bill 2023-24 (HL Bill 1), cl 3, the Secretary of State has a power to authorise a road vehicle for use as an automated vehicle, if:

'(a) in the opinion of the Secretary of State, the vehicle satisfies the self-driving test by reference to intended travel on a road (in at least some circumstances), and

(b) any applicable initial authorisation requirements are met (see section 5).'[118]

(That cl 3 authorisation is central also to AEVA 2018, Part 1, as prospectively amended by AV Bill 2023-24, cl 45, Sch 2, para 5 to substitute 'authorised automated vehicle' for 'automated vehicle' in AEVA 2018 (see the AV Bill 2023-24 (HL Bill 1), cl 45, Sch 2, para 5 amendments to AEVA 2018, Part 1 in Chapter 6, 'insurance'). The AV Bill 2023-24, cl 94 ('general definitions') provides that '"authorised automated vehicle" means a vehicle authorised under section 3' of AVA 2024.)

The 'self-driving test' is defined in AV Bill 2023-24, cl 1, 'basic concepts':

'...

(2) A vehicle "satisfies the self-driving test" if –

(a) it is designed or adapted with the intention that a feature of the vehicle will allow it to travel autonomously, and

(b) it is capable of doing so, by means of that feature, safely and legally.

(3) Whether a vehicle satisfies the test is to be assessed by reference to the location and circumstances of that intended travel (and may differ in respect of different locations and circumstances).

---

118 AV Bill 2023-24 (HL Bill 1), cl 3(1).

(4) A "feature" of a vehicle is a combination of mechanical or electronic operations that equipment of the vehicle performs.

(5) A vehicle travels "autonomously" if –

(a) it is being controlled not by an individual but by equipment of the vehicle, and

(b) neither the vehicle nor its surroundings are being monitored by an individual with a view to immediate intervention in the driving of the vehicle.

(6) References to "control" of a vehicle are to control of the motion of the vehicle.

(7) A vehicle that travels autonomously does so –

(a) "safely" if it travels to an acceptably safe standard, and

(b) "legally" if it travels with an acceptably low risk of committing a traffic infraction.

(8) In assessing whether a vehicle is capable of travelling autonomously and safely, the Secretary of State must have particular regard to the statement of safety principles.'

(The 'interpretation' provision for Part 1 of the AV Bill, cl 44, provides that:

'(2) For the purposes of this Part, a vehicle "commits a traffic infraction" if, while an authorised automation feature of the vehicle is engaged, the vehicle does anything that would, were an individual in control of it –

(a) amount to the commission of an offence by that individual, or

(b) cause a person to become liable to a penalty charge under an enactment relating to road traffic.

(3) For the purposes of subsection (2)(a), it is to be assumed that nothing can be proved about the mental state of the notional individual.')

The 'statement of safety principles' is governed by AV Bill 2023-24, cl 2(1) to (4) of which provide that:

'(1) The Secretary of State must prepare a statement of the principles that the Secretary of State proposes to apply in assessing, for the purposes of this Part, whether a vehicle is capable of travelling autonomously and safely.

(2) The principles must be framed with a view to securing that road safety in Great Britain will be better as a result of the use of authorised automated vehicles on roads than it would otherwise be.

(3) In preparing the statement, the Secretary of State must consult such representative organisations as the Secretary of State thinks fit.

(4) The prepared statement must be laid before Parliament...'

AV Bill 2023-24, cl 2(6) to (8) allow for the statement to take effect 'at the end of the period of 40 days beginning with the day on which it is laid, unless either House resolves before then that the statement should not take effect' and for the timescale in the events of statements being laid before different Houses of Parliament on different days and negative resolution(s). As at the time of writing, no statement of safety principles has yet been laid before Parliament. Under cl 2(9), 'The power in section 3 may not be exercised until a statement has effect under this section'.

The AV Bill 2023-24, cl 4 prescribes certain details which must be contained in an automated vehicle authorisation:

'(1) An automated vehicle authorisation must identify the feature or features by virtue of which (in the opinion of the Secretary of State) the vehicle satisfies the self-driving test.

(2) More than one feature may be identified if it appears to the Secretary of State that each can reasonably be characterised as amounting to a distinct capability of the vehicle.

(3) In relation to each feature identified in the authorisation, the authorisation must specify—

(a) whether the mode of operation of the feature is "user-in-charge" or "no-user-in-charge",

(b) how the feature is engaged and disengaged, and

(c) the locations and circumstances by reference to which (in the opinion of the Secretary of State) the vehicle satisfies the self-driving test by virtue of the feature.

(4) The locations specified or described in the authorisation may include places other than roads.

(5) If more than one feature is identified in an authorisation, the Secretary of State must discharge the duty in subsection (3)(b) in a way that will make it possible to ascertain which feature (if any) is engaged at any given moment.'

A 'no-user-in-charge journey' is defined by AV Bill 2023-24 (HL Bill 1), cl 12(2) and by the interpretation clause of Part 1, cl 44(1), as 'a journey by a vehicle with an authorised no-user-in-charge feature during which (at any point) – (a) that feature is engaged, or (b) there is no individual in the vehicle who is exercising control of it'[119]. The explanatory note to the AV Bill 2023-24 explains the difference between the two features as follows:

'Subsection (3)(a) clarifies that a 'mode of operation' is either as a 'user-in-charge' (UiC) feature or a 'no-user-in-charge' NUiC feature. A UiC feature is one that can drive itself for only part of a journey and therefore requires an individual to be a driver for the remainder of the journey, for example a motorway chauffeur system. A NUiC feature is one that can drive itself for an entire journey and does not require an individual to be capable of taking control, for example a self-driving airport shuttle bus.'

'The distinction between UiC and NUiC features set out in subsection (3)(a) will determine the safety requirements for each. For example, a UiC feature can issue transition demands to ensure safe transition of control

---

119 And see (in the criminal liability Part of the AV Bill 2023-24), cl 46, 'meaning of user-in-charge'.

from the vehicle to a driver (see clause 7). A NUiC feature will require a licensed operator (a no-user-in-charge operator NUiCO – see Chapter 2) to ensure the safe operation of the vehicle. For example, taking responsibility for insurance.'[120]

AV Bill 2023-24, cl 5 describes the two types of authorisation requirements which the Secretary of State may,

' .. by regulations impose and which must be met –

(a) for a vehicle to be authorised under section 3 ("initial authorisation requirements"), or

(b) as a condition of a vehicle remaining authorised ("ongoing authorisation requirements").

(2) Ongoing authorisation requirements may include a requirement for compliance with any conditions that the Secretary of State attaches to an individual authorisation ("authorisation conditions").

(3) Authorisation conditions may relate to anything to which authorisation requirements may relate.

(4) A duty in relation to the imposition of authorisation requirements may be met (in whole or in part) by means of an authorisation requirement of the sort described in subsection (2) in combination with authorisation conditions.'

(AV Bill 2023-24, cl 5(1)(b) is one of the measures in the Bill serving the ongoing monitoring of safety-in-use which was a central feature of the Law Commissions' recommendations.)

AV Bill 2023-24, cl 6 places ongoing responsibility for an authorised AV upon 'a person' who 'is designated as the "authorised self-driving entity" for the authorised vehicle at all times' and who must satisfy authorisation requirements which 'may include requirements that a person has to satisfy in order to be, or remain, an authorised self-driving entity' (cll 6(1) and (2)). Those requirements should, so far as reasonably practicable, meet the objectives of cl 6(4):

'(4) The objectives are –

(a) that an authorised self-driving entity should have general responsibility for ensuring that an authorised automated vehicle continues to satisfy the self-driving test by virtue of its authorised automation features, and

(b) that an authorised self-driving entity should be –

(i) of good repute,

(ii) of good financial standing, and

(iii) capable of competently discharging any authorisation requirements imposed on it for the purposes of paragraph (a).

(5) Authorisation requirements may include requirements as to the payment of fees by authorised self-driving entities for the grant or continuation of an automated vehicle authorisation.'

---

120 Explanatory note to AV Bill 2023-24 (HL Bill 1 – EN) paras 97, 98.

AV Bill 2023-24, cl 7 deals with authorisation requirements relating to transition demands – the topic which caused difficulty in SAE's taxonomy relating to Level 3 of vehicle automation (the Law Commissions' 'mushy middle' of automated driving) and on the first enacted version of AEVA 2018 where it defined an automated vehicle as one which 'does not need to be monitored, by an individual'[121]. As the insurance industry and others had observed, that phrase invited contrast with the reality of 'traffic jam chauffeur' systems such as the automated lane keeping system (ALKS). The AV Bill 2023-24 approaches the point differently to AEVA 2018 (which the Bill amends[122]), by subjecting the vehicle's 'transition' system to more precise authorisation requirements:

'(1) Subsection (3) applies if authorisation requirements in relation to a vehicle with an authorised user-in-charge feature require the vehicle to be able to issue a transition demand while that feature is engaged.

(2) A "transition demand" is a demand, communicated by equipment of a vehicle in which an authorised user-in-charge feature is engaged, that the user-in-charge assume control of the vehicle by the end of a period of time beginning with the communication of the demand (the "transition period").

(3) The Secretary of State must impose authorisation requirements designed to secure, so far as Secretary of State considers reasonably practicable, that –

(a) the transition demand will be capable of being perceived by anyone who might legally be a user-in-charge of the vehicle (having regard in particular to users-in-charge with disabilities),

(b) the transition period will be long enough for the user-in-charge to prepare to assume, and assume, control of the vehicle,

(c) the vehicle will continue to travel autonomously, safely and legally during the transition period,

(d) equipment of the vehicle will make a further communication at the end of the transition period to alert the user-in-charge to the ending of the period, and

(e) the vehicle will deal safely with a situation where the user-in-charge fails to assume control by the end of the transition period.'

AV Bill 2023-24, cll 8 and 9 provide powers to vary, suspend and withdraw authorisations. AV Bill 2023-24 , cll 10 and 11 provide for a public register of AV authorisations and regulations for the grant, variation etc of authorisations. Sch 1 Part 1 sets out the procedure in relation to the unilateral variation, suspension or withdrawal of authorisation, including appeals. Part 2 of the schedule deals with civil sanctions, which are described further in the public law part of this book.

---

121 AEVA 2018 s 8(1)(a), as at the time of writing. AV Bill 2023-24 (HL Bill 1), cl 45, Sch 2, para 5(2) would amend that definition in AEVA 2018, s 8(1)(a) as follows: 'an authorised automated vehicle is "driving itself" if it is travelling while an authorised automation feature of the vehicle is engaged'.
122 AV Bill 2023-24 (HL Bill 1), cl 45, Sch 2, para 5.

AV Bill 2023-24, Part 1, Chapter 2 (cll 12-13) deals with the 'licensing of operators for vehicle use without user-in-charge'. Cl 12 provides the Secretary of State with a power to establish a NUIC operator scheme. AV Bill 2023-24, cl 12(2) defines a NUIC journey as follows and the remainder of cll 12 and 13 provide for features of the NUIC operator regulations. Cl 12 reads in its entirety:

'(1) The Secretary of State may, by regulations ("operator licensing regulations"), make provision –

   (a) for the licensing of persons as no-user-in-charge operators;

   (b) imposing requirements on those persons in connection with no-user-in-charge journeys or the vehicles that undertake them;

   (c) for the keeping of a public register of those persons (and associated information).

(2) A "no-user-in-charge journey" is a journey by a vehicle with an authorised no-user-in-charge feature during which (at any point) –

   (a) that feature is engaged, or

   (b) there is no individual in the vehicle who is exercising control of it.

(3) For the purposes of this Part, a no-user-in-charge journey is "overseen" by a licensed no-user-in-charge operator if the operator is, in respect of the journey, subject to requirements imposed under subsection (1)(b).

(4) If the Secretary of State makes operator licensing regulations, the Secretary of State must do so in a way that is designed to secure, so far as the Secretary of State considers reasonably practicable, that the following objectives are met.

(5) The objectives are –

   (a) that a licensed no-user-in-charge operator should have general responsibility for the detection of, and response to, problems arising during a no-user-in-charge journey overseen by the operator, and

   (b) that a licensed no-user-in-charge operator should be –

      (i) of good repute,

      (ii) of good financial standing, and

      (iii) capable of competently discharging any requirements imposed on it for the purposes of paragraph (a).'

Regulated bodies are subject to measures set out in Part 1, Chapter 3 ('provision of information by regulated bodies'), Chapter 4 ('power to investigate premises used by regulated bodies') and Chapter 5 ('civil sanctions against regulated bodies'). Those provisions are described in the 'criminal law' and 'public law' parts of this book.

The Secretary of State is required to put in place arrangements to monitor the safe performance of automated vehicles while they are in use. These arrangements are set out in Part 1, chapter 6 ('other regulatory powers and duties') and comprise the duties in:

- cl 38 ('the general monitoring duty') whereby the Secretary of State 'must put in place arrangements that the Secretary of State considers effective and proportionate for monitoring and assessing the general performance of authorised automated vehicles on roads and other public places in Great Britain' including 'monitoring and assessing the extent to which that performance is consistent with the statement of safety principles', upon which the Secretary of State must publish an annual report starting from the first effective date of an AV authorisation, setting out the Secretary of State's conclusions;

- cl 39 (the 'duty with respect to incidents with potential regulatory consequences') requiring similar provision for arrangements for reporting into, enquiring into the causes of and considering enforcement powers in relation to incidents ('relevant incidents') that occur on a road or other public place, involve an authorised automated vehicle, and reveal grounds for enquiring into whether any of the enforcement powers has become exercisable as a result of the incident; and

- cl 40 (the 'power to require reports from police and local authorities') which empowers the Secretary of State by regulations to require authorities defined by cl 40(3) (including a chief officer for police, county council and Transport for London, for example) to report to the Secretary of State relevant incidents about which that authority has obtained information in the performance of its functions.

Supplementary provisions (in Part 1, Chapter 7, cll 41-44) provide for administrative matters relating to the regulatory powers including the service of notices and fees, protection of information obtained (cl 42) as well as the interpretation section for the AV Bill 2023-24, Part 1(cl 44).

Guided Transport Modes

2.25   A further avenue of regulation relating to the development of infrastructure for automated driving systems in passenger and goods transport was opened in 2022, with the amendment (after consultation[123]) of the Transport and Works (Guided Transport Modes) Order 1992[124] to allow orders for the construction and operation of non-physical guidance systems, guided by sensors, in passenger and goods transport. This amendment took effect on 26 December 2022 and allows the Secretary of State for Transport to 'make an order relating to, or to matters ancillary to, the construction or operation' of a guided transport system including one using sensors rather than physical guidance 'so far as it is in England and Wales'[125]. See Chapters 5 (passenger services and public transport) and 14 (delivery claims).

---

123 See UK government (Department for Transport) website, 'Outcome of consultation: allowing non-physical guided transport modes to be authorised by a Transport and Works Act order' (29 July 2022).

124 SI 1992/3231, as amended by the Transport and Works (Guided Transport Modes) (Amendment) Order 2022, SI 2022/1380.

125 TWA 1992, s 1(1)(d), as now permitted under s 1(2) by SI 1992/3231 as amended by SI 2022/1380.

D The Law of Electric Vehicle Specifications

What is an 'electric' vehicle?

2.26   The history of motor vehicles includes, from the late 19th century, electric vehicles (see the quotation at the head of this chapter). Factors including the striking of oil in the United States in 1901[126] and their greater geographical range contributed to the dominance of vehicles powered by the internal combustion engine, but the ICE's victory had not been certain[127].

A characteristic of the development of both types of engine – ICE and electric – was the innovation of users. The British case which established that an electrically propelled vehicle was in law a motor vehicle arose from the installation of an electric motor on a bathchair, about which the court said:

> 'Though I doubt very much whether it was in the mind of the Legislature that a vehicle of this kind would come into existence, I am forced to the conclusion on the language of the Act that this is a motor car within the Act'[128]

The precursor of the e-scooter was the Autoped, popular in the early twentieth century and used by the U.S. Postal Service, among others[129]. Although the historical record is unclear, the Autoped might with the addition of a seat have morphed into the moped, which is how the UK government now classifies e-scooters[130].

So the history of motor vehicles is of innovation. E-scooters and the current trend for 'micromobility' vehicles are not new.

A vehicle is a 'motor' vehicle even if powered by electricity (so an electric car and an e-scooter are both motor vehicles), although some electric vehicles which would otherwise fit the definition are exempted (such as e-bikes). See Chapters 4 ('driving') and 6 ('insurance') for discussion of those classifications and the consequences, particularly in relation to insurance.

Domestic and international regulation of EVs

2.27   The regulation of EVs is mainly domestic (with the exception of specific UN regulations such as UN reg 100 on electric power trained vehicles). As described above, in its modern form it goes back to 1917, to *Elieson v Parker*.

Future domestic regulation of EVs and the Transport Bill

2.28   The pressing issue in relation to EVs is whether the widespread public use of e-scooters, beyond trial areas, is to be legalised. The government's stated

---

126 See the 'Motors, 1901 to 1938' section of the 'History' Appendix to this book.
127 See Flink and Tillemann, above.
128 Lord Reading CJ in *Elieson v Parker* (1917) 81 JP 265.
129 Jackie Mansky, 'The motorised scooter boom that hit a century before dockless scooters', The Smithsonian Magazine (18 April 2019)
130 UK Parliament website 'Questions, Statements, Written Answers: Question 20 June 2020 by Jim Shannon MP for DfT on e-scooters, answer 23 June 2020 by Trudy Harrison MP.

intention (in May 2022) was that it would legalise such vehicles by the creation of a new category of vehicles, although the insurance implications of such legalisation (including the suggestion of less than full indemnity in relation to compensation, which seems to assume a tariff rather than judge-assessed compensation scheme) have yet to be proposed in detail. See Chapters 4 ('driving'), 6 ('insurance') and 16 ('smaller electric vehicle claims') for discussion of those points.

In contrast to the AV Bill 2023-24 (HL Bill 1), the Transport Bill announced to include legislation for e-scooters announced in the Queen's Speech in May 2022 then postponed by the government in December 2022[131] did not appear in the King's Speech on 7 November 2023. Mandated trials of e-scooters are due to run until 31 May 2024[132]. The future regulation of e-scooters remains unclear.

---

131 Parliament Live TV, Transport Select Committee 7 December 2022 at 9:43, Sec of St for Transport the Rt Hon Mark Harper MP.
132 DfT answer 6 July 2022 to parliamentary question by Gill Furniss MP 1 July 2022, UIN 28907

Chapter 3

The law of testing prototypes

'Automation poses challenges for the testing process. One consultee expressed the view that the current testing system is based on the concerns of the 1970s and often involves 'throwing metal at walls'. The process of testing artificial intelligence requires a new expertise.'[1]

The Law Commissions (2018)

A Outline of the laws of testing prototype vehicles

3.01   In this chapter:

- The word 'prototype' is used to indicate that the testing under discussion is of new technologies, rather than the periodic testing of vehicles for roadworthiness including roadside inspection;

- The government guidance on automated vehicle testing described is the post-Automated Vehicles Bill 2023-24 (HL Bill 1) updated version of 30 November 2023[2]. However, the law on AV testing remains in a state of flux, with regulations under the powers in the AV Bill 2023-24 yet to be made and with further updating of official guidance on testing a possibility.

---

1   'Automated Vehicles: a joint preliminary consultation paper', Law Commission of England and Wales Consultation Paper No 240, Scottish Law Commission Discussion Paper No 166, 8 November 2018 (cited below as 'Law Commissions' first AV law consultation paper (November 2018)') page 62, paragraph 4.45.
2   UK government (gov.uk) guidance 'Trialling automated vehicle technologies in public' (updated 30 November 2023).

Construction and use requirements for road vehicles under RTA 1988, ss 41 and 42

3.02 RTA 1988, s 41 and the Road Vehicles (Construction and Use) Regulations[3] ('CUR 1986'), set requirements for the construction of road vehicles and for the ways in which they are used. Those include the 'driver's control' requirement in CUR 1986, reg 104:

> 'No person shall drive or cause or permit any other person to drive, a motor vehicle on a road if he is in such a position that he cannot have proper control of the vehicle or have a full view of the road and traffic ahead'

– and the CUR 1986, reg 110 prohibition (subject to exceptions for a 'genuine emergency', remote-parking and contactless payments) of driving a motor vehicle on a road when using a 'hand-held mobile telephone' or a 'hand-held device ... other than a two-way radio, which is capable of transmitting and receiving data, whether or not those capabilities are enabled'.

Breaches of the RTA 1988, s 41 and CUR 1986 requirements are criminal offences under ss 41A to 42, including s 41D in relation to control and to use of a mobile telephone (relating to CUR 1986, regs 104 and 110) which provides that:

> 'A person who contravenes or fails to comply with a construction and use requirement–
>
> (a) as to not driving a motor vehicle in a position which does not give proper control or a full view of the road and traffic ahead, or not causing or permitting the driving of a motor vehicle by another person in such a position, or
>
> (b) as to not driving or supervising the driving of a motor vehicle while using a hand-held mobile telephone or other hand-held interactive communication device, or not causing or permitting the driving of a motor vehicle by another person using such a telephone or other device,
>
> is guilty of an offence.'

RTA 1988, s 40A makes it a further offence to use a vehicle in a dangerous condition:

> 'A person is guilty of an offence if he uses, or causes or permits another to use, a motor vehicle or trailer on a road when—
>
> (a) the condition of the motor vehicle or trailer, or of its accessories or equipment, or
>
> (b) the purpose for which it is used, or
>
> (c) the number of passengers carried by it, or the manner in which they are carried, or
>
> (d) the weight, position or distribution of its load, or the manner in which it is secured,

---

3 SI 1986/1078 (as amended)

is such that the use of the motor vehicle or trailer involves a danger of injury to any person.'

and CUR 1986, reg 100 ('maintenance and use of vehicle so as not to be a danger, etc') echoes those requirements.

The Automated Vehicles Bill 2023-24 (HL Bill 1) would, if enacted, add stringent conditions relevant to testing, relating to the provision of information and the use of 'no user-in-charge' technologies, reinforced by powers of investigation, criminal offences and civil sanctions. It features one provision permitting testing, in automated passenger services. See the discussion below.

Testing prototype road vehicles under RTA 1988, s 44

3.03   RTA 1988 allows for the testing of prototype vehicles. RTA 1988, s 44 (particularly s 44(1)(a) and (c)) provides as follows:

'44.— Authorisation of use on roads of special vehicles not complying with regulations under section 41.

(1) The Secretary of State may by order authorise, subject to such restrictions and conditions as may be specified by or under the order, the use on roads—

    (a) of special motor vehicles or trailers, or special types of motor vehicles or trailers, which are constructed either for special purposes or for tests or trials,

    (b) of vehicles or trailers, or types of vehicles or trailers, constructed for use outside the United Kingdom,

    (c) of new or improved types of motor vehicles or trailers, whether wheeled or wheelless, or of motor vehicles or trailers equipped with new or improved equipment or types of equipment, and

    (d) of vehicles or trailers carrying loads of exceptional dimensions,

and sections 40A to 42 of this Act shall not apply in relation to the use of such vehicles, trailers, or types in accordance with the order.

(2) The Secretary of State may by order make provision for securing that, subject to such restrictions and conditions as may be specified by or under the order, regulations under section 41 of this Act shall have effect in their application to such vehicles, trailers and types of vehicles and trailers as are mentioned in subsection (1) above subject to such modifications or exceptions as may be specified in the order.

(3) The powers conferred by this section on the Secretary of State to make orders shall be exercisable by statutory instrument except in the case of orders applying only to specified vehicles or to vehicles of specified persons, but in that excepted case (as in others) the order may be varied or revoked by subsequent order of the Secretary of State.

(4) The function of the Secretary of State under subsection (1) in the case of orders applying only to—

    (a) specified vehicles, or

(b) vehicles of specified persons,

may be delegated to a strategic highways company.

(5) A delegation under subsection (4) may specify—

(a) the extent to which the function is delegated;

(b) any conditions to which the delegation is subject.'

Special Types General Orders

3.04   The statutory instrument referred to in RTA 1998, s 44(3) is the Road Vehicles (Authorisation of Special Types) (General) Order 2003 ('RV(AST)(G) O 2003')[4]. Under art 9(1):

'A vehicle that falls within a recognised category of special vehicles is authorised to be used on roads by virtue of this Order if (but only if) it complies with the authorisation requirements applicable to vehicles in that category'.

So, as per the government's guidance as to complex connected and autonomous vehicle trials [italics added][5]:

A 'Special Type General Order (STGO) ... allows a vehicle that meets the criteria to be exempt from certain C&U regulations. There is no application process. The order lists the construction and use regulations that continue to apply. There are conditions, such as that the vehicle must be for sole use in trials and tests.'

'For vehicles and use-cases that fall within the scope of STGO [*this appears to refer to the statutory instrument, RV(AST)(G)O 2003*], there is no application process to make use of the provisions afforded by STGO.'

'However, it should be noted that some provisions of STGO require 'authorisation' (for example, in the case that a vehicle that exceeds a certain mass or dimensions, STGO requires police notification). Refer to STGO for further details.'[6]

Each test of a prototype turns on its own facts

3.05   Whether or not an intended vehicle trial qualifies for an STGO under RV(AST)(G)O 2003 depends upon the specifications of the particular vehicle and

---

4 RV(AST)(G)O 2003, SI 2003/1998, as amended. I suggest the acronym 'RV(AST)(G)O 2003' (pronounced 'ReVASTGO') to distinguish between the statutory instrument and a 'special types general order' for which a vehicle can qualify under the SI. If the SI is abbreviated to 'STGO 2003' or to 'the 2003 Order', then the SI and an STGO (both 'orders') are easily confused – as in the government guidance quoted below, where 'STGO' is used for both.

5 UK government (gov.uk) guidance 'Trialling automated vehicle technologies in public' (updated 30 November 2023).

6 RV(AST)(G)O 2003 Parts 2, 3 and 4. As the guidance says, police notification is required in certain cases where the vehicle's mass or dimensions (including projection of a load) exceed prescribed limits. See RTA 1988 s 44(1)(d) (authorisation of use on roads of '... vehicles or trailers carrying loads of exceptional dimensions').

the facts of its intended use on the roads. So, the testing organisation or person considering their qualification for an STGO under RV(AST)(GO) 2003 should first consider the detail of their proposed test carefully against the requirements set out in RV(AST)(GO) 2003, in light of current guidance from the Department for Transport and its agencies.

The Law Commission's advice to government on remote driving (discussed below) is also relevant and is referred to in the updated government guidance of 30 November 2023.

In addition to satisfying RTA 1988, s 44, compliance with other laws is also required for any test, as carrying out a test will have legal implications broader than satisfying RV(AST)(G)O 2003 or, failing that, succeeding in obtaining a Vehicle Special Order (see below). Other potential liabilities may arise from the conduct of the test (in private law to those affected by the test, including employees; in public law in terms of potential criminal liabilities and compliance with local regulations). Compulsory motor insurance will be a pre-requisite of any test taking place on a road or other public place.[7] As the UK government's guidance to trialling organisations states,

> 'It is the responsibility of those carrying out trials to ensure that their trials comply with all relevant legal requirements. Deploying a service may require appropriate licensing.'[8]

Further updated guidance on testing is likely to be among the information published as the AV Bill 2023-24 (HL Bill 1) passes into law. A feature of the AV Bill 2023-24 (HL Bill 1), even absent such guidance, is that it does permit 'trials' of automated passenger services within the permit process as described in the Bill (see cl 82(2)(b), below).

Overview of criteria for an STGO under RV(AST)(G)O 2003

3.06   As the law stands at the time of writing[9], obtaining an STGO – if the proposed test of the prototype satisfies the requirements of RV(AST)(G)O 2003 – is essentially a self-certifying exercise for a testing organisation, albeit an exercise which cannot practically succeed without the cooperation and scrutiny of others (including the compulsory motor insurer, where the vehicle is a motor vehicle whose use requires such insurance[10]).

However, that ability to 'self-certify' in an automated vehicle test should now be treated with some caution in light of the Law Commission's advice to government on remote driving (February 2023) which tended towards a Vehicle Special Order

---

7   RTA 1988, s 143.
8   UK government (gov.uk) guidance 'Trialling automated vehicle technologies in public' (updated 30 November 2023): 'Code of Practice: automated vehicle trialling' 'legal requirements'.
9   Please note in particular (a) the recommendation in the Law Commission of England and Wales 'Remote Driving: Advice to Government', February 2023 that a Vehicle Special Order (VSO) should become the government's preferred order for testing where remote driving is used (although the 30 November 2023 updated guidance still otherwise holds STGOs open for automated vehicle testing) and (b) the AV Bill 2023-24 (HL Bill 1, introduced 8 November 2023).
10 So not, for example, an exempted vehicle such as an e-bike (see RTA 1989, s 189).

as the preferred type of authorisation where remote driving plays a part in a test. That advice is referred to in the current (30 November 2023) version of the government guidance on automated vehicle testing. VSOs, that guidance and the Law Commission's advice are discussed below.

As a general overview, the parts of RV(AST)(G)O 2003 likely to be of relevance to a test of a new advanced, automated or electric vehicle (or such a vehicle with new equipment) are as follows.

RV(AST)(G)O 2003, art 8 ('Application of this order') provides that:

'(1) This Order applies only to motor vehicles or trailers–

   (a) that do not comply in all respects with the standard construction and use requirements; and

   (b) that fall within a recognised category of special vehicles.

(2) In this Order 'recognised category of special vehicles' means a description of vehicles that is stated by a provision of this Order to be a recognised category of special vehicles.

(3) In paragraph (1), 'standard construction and use requirements', in relation to a motor vehicle or trailer, means the requirements of such of the regulations made under section 41 of the Road Traffic Act 1988 as would, apart from this Order, apply to that motor vehicle or trailer.'

RV(AST)(G)O 2003, art 9 provides for 'authorisation of particular vehicles falling within recognised category of special vehicles', as follows:

'(1) A vehicle that falls within a recognised category of special vehicles is authorised to be used on roads by virtue of this Order if (but only if) it complies with the authorisation requirements applicable to vehicles in that category.

(2) In this Order 'authorisation requirements', in relation to a recognised category of special vehicles–

   (a) means all the requirements specified in this Order as being applicable to vehicles in that category; and

   (b) includes such of the requirements of regulations made under section 41 of the Road Traffic Act 1988 as are specified in this Order as being applicable to vehicles in that category (subject to any modifications or exceptions so specified).

(3) Where any provision of this Order specifies any of the regulations mentioned in paragraph (2)(b) as being applicable to any recognised category of special vehicles, that provision is not to be construed as applying any requirement of those regulations to a vehicle in that category if that requirement may reasonably be regarded, in all the circumstances, as not relevant to the vehicle in question (for example, if the requirement relates to trailers and the vehicle in question is not a trailer).'

Within Part 4 of the order, in RV(AST)(G)O 2003, arts 36–40, is provision for 'vehicles for tests, trials or non-UK use etc'. RV(AST)(G)O 2003, art 36(1) includes the following categories of special vehicles:

'(c) any new or improved type of motor vehicle or trailer which is constructed for tests or trials;

(d) any motor vehicle or trailer which is equipped with new or improved equipment;

(e) any motor vehicle or trailer which is equipped with new or improved types of equipment.'

RV(AST)(G)O 2003, art 37 provides that:

'The authorisation requirements applicable to vehicles falling within any of the recognised categories of special vehicles mentioned in article 36(1) are–

(a) the requirements specified in articles 38 to 40; and

(b) the requirements specified in Schedule 11.'

RV(AST)(G)O 2003, art 38 states requirements as to length, Art 39 as to width and Art 40 as to weight.

RV(AST)(G)O 2003, Sch 11 ('Vehicles for tests, trials or non-UK use etc) has the following requirements:

In Sch 11, para 2:

'A relevant vehicle may only be used on roads for–

(a) testing;

(b) demonstration;

(c) delivery on sale;

(d) proceeding to, or returning from, a manufacturer or repairer for construction, repair or overhaul.'

RV(AST)(G)O 2003, Sch 11, para 3(2) disapplies para 2 in circumstances where a person A (approved by the Secretary of State) 'has lent the vehicle to B on terms that include a requirement for B to supply A with information or opinions derived from his use of it, and for B to return the vehicle to A on demand; and (b) that the vehicle is being used by B in accordance with those terms'. Sch 11 para 3(1) allows para 2 to be disapplied in that situation, or where a vehicle registered only in A's name is being used 'by A for the sole purpose of making an evaluation of it' and the person A 'has been approved by the Secretary of State for the purposes of this Schedule'.

RV(AST)(G)O 2003, Sch 11, para 4 provides that:

'A relevant vehicle must not be used in such a way as to cause a danger of injury to any person by reason of–

(a) the condition of the vehicle, its accessories or equipment;

(b) the purpose for which it is used;

(c) the number of passengers carried by it;

(d) the manner in which such passengers are carried;

(e) the weight, position or distribution of any load carried on the vehicle; or

(f) the manner in which any such load is secured.'

RV(AST)(G)O 2003, Sch 11, para 5 provides that:

'(1) A relevant vehicle that is used on roads must not carry any load or transport goods or burden.

(2) But that is subject to paragraphs 6 and 7.'

RV(AST)(G)O 2003, Sch 11, para.6 provides that:

'A relevant vehicle may carry–

(a) its own necessary gear and equipment; and

(b) any apparatus or ballast necessary for the purpose of carrying out a test or trial of the vehicle.'

RV(AST)(G)O 2003, Sch 11, para 7 provides that the vehicle may carry a load if it complies with the applicable maximum weight regulations.

RV(AST)(G)O 2003, Sch 11, paras 8, 9, 10 and Tables 16 and 17 set out how various requirements of the CUR 1986 (including requirements for braking systems and lighting) are to apply to special vehicles. From 31 May 2023, CUR 1986, reg 110 (mobile telephones) applies[11]. For reasons of space those paragraphs and tables are not reproduced here and the reader is referred to the text of RV(AST)(G)O 2003 (as amended).

Vehicle Special Orders

3.07   Where a trial vehicle does not qualify for an STGO, the trialling organisation may apply for an alternative order, a 'vehicle special order' ('VSO').

This arises under RTA 1988, s 41(3) which (with the writer's note in italics) provides that:

'(3) The powers conferred by this section on the Secretary of State to make orders shall be exercisable by statutory instrument [*currently RV(AST)(G) O 2003*] except in the case of orders applying only to specified vehicles or to vehicles of specified persons, but in that excepted case (as in others) the order may be varied or revoked by subsequent order of the Secretary of State.'

A VSO is the 'excepted case' for an order 'applying only to specified vehicles or to vehicles of specified persons'.

---

11 Road Vehicles (Authorisation of Special Types) (General) (Amendment) Order 2023, SI 2023/524, art 5.

The UK government's guidance on applying for a VSO appears online[12]. The first two paragraphs of that guidance introduce a VSO as follows:

'By exception, if the vehicle cannot comply with the required construction regulations for use in trials and testing, even after investing time and effort, then the Department for Transport (DfT) may still allow the vehicle to be used on the road. This is also true if the required use of the vehicle falls outside the restrictions of STGO.'

'In these cases, the trialling organisation must make a reasoned case for exemption from the regulations that they cannot comply with and apply to the Vehicle Certification Agency (VCA) to be considered for a VSO under section 44 of the Road Traffic Act 1988, on the basis that the vehicle is either for 'tests and trials', a 'new or improved type', or that it is 'special'.

As discussed below and cited in the 30 November 2023 version of that guidance, the Law Commission has advised government that the VSO should be the preferred means of allowing vehicle tests involving remote driving[13].

Compulsory insurance of prototype motor vehicles

3.08   RTA 1988, s 143(1) and (2) provide as follows:

'(1) Subject to the provisions of this Part of this Act—

(a) a person must not use a motor vehicle on a road or other public place unless there is in force in relation to the use of the vehicle by that person such a policy of insurance as complies with the requirements of this Part of this Act, and

(b) a person must not cause or permit any other person to use a motor vehicle on a road or other public place unless there is in force in relation to the use of the vehicle by that other person such a policy of insurance as complies with the requirements of this Part of this Act.

(2) If a person acts in contravention of subsection (1) above he is guilty of an offence.'

So, unless (as in the case of an invalid carriage, e-bicycle or other vehicle excepted from the insurance requirement[14]) the vehicle is not a 'motor vehicle', a prototype vehicle under testing on a road or other public place[15] must be insured by a policy compliant with RTA 1988 Part VI.[16]

---

12 UK government (gov.uk) guidance 'Trialling automated vehicle technologies in public' (updated 30 November 2023), 'Code of practice: vehicle authorisations and exemptions for more complex CAV trials'.
13 Law Commission of England and Wales 'Remote Driving: Advice to Government', February 2023.
14 RTA 1988, ss 143(4), 189.
15 For discussion of 'road or other public place', see Appendix 2 to the Law Commissions' third AV law consultation paper (December 2020), chapter 1 of *Wilkinson's Road Traffic Offences* (30th edn) and footnote 9 in chapter 6 (Insurance) of this book.
16 And see UK government (gov.uk) guidance 'Trialling automated vehicle technologies in public' (updated 30 November 2023).

B Laws of testing prototype advanced driver assistance systems (ADAS)

Same laws apply for testing ADAS prototypes as apply to conventional vehicles

3.09   The laws described above also apply to vehicles with advanced driver assistance systems.

Standards

3.10   Particular standards relevant to testing may apply to particular systems, including ADAS, depending upon the issues and other relevant evidence in a case.

For example (and this is not an exhaustive list):

- a subproject of the integrated project PReVENT, a European automotive industry activity, co-funded by the European Commission produced a 'Code of Practice for the Design and Evaluation of ADAS' in 2009[17].

- The Centre for Connected and Autonomous Vehicles Code of Practice for the trialling of automated vehicles (described below) suggests that the Code might be applied more widely, including to ADAS:

    'This Code has not been developed with a view to the testing and development of driver assistance systems (such as adaptive cruise control) or to trials and pilots carried out on private test tracks or other areas not accessible by the public. Those undertaking such trials are nonetheless encouraged to consider whether the guidelines may be relevant.'[18]

Of stronger legal effect than standards alone[19], the AV Bill 2023-24, cl 91(1)(b) might result in type approval regulations specific to ADAS (see below).

Law Commission's recommended reforms of testing regulations for advanced vehicles

3.11   As discussed below in relation to testing prototype automated vehicles, in February 2023 the Law Commission of England and Wales published its advice to government on Remote Driving, after its consultation on the topic. It noted that

'Remote driving has potential advantages, both to support and test automated driving, and to pioneer new forms of transport. It is therefore desirable for

---

17 'Code of Practice for the Design and Evaluation of ADAS', Information Society Technologies, PReVENT Preventive and Active Safety Applications Integrated Project Contract Number FP6-507075, version 5.0 (August 2009)
18 UK government (gov.uk) guidance 'Trialling automated vehicle technologies in public' (updated 30 November 2023).
19 See chapter 2, 'vehicle specifications'.

trials to take place, provided that this can be done without unacceptable risks to safety. This requires robust regulation.'[20]

But it noted concerns as to both the safety of remote driving in testing and the lack of clarity in current regulations and guidance as to its use.

Its advice to government was that, in the short term, VSOs should be the means of obtaining permission for the use of beyond line-of-sight remote driving in testing and, in the longer term, it envisaged a requirement for licensed operators.[21]

'VSOs would be available both where remote drivers are used in trials of automated vehicles, and where they are used independently of automated driving. Each use case would need to be assessed on its merits.'[22]

Provision for regulations for type approval of driver assistance systems in the Automated Vehicles Bill 2023-24 (HL Bill 1)

3.12   Testing of prototypes is not expressly described in the Automated Vehicles Bill 2023-24 (HL Bill 1). However it does include provisions relevant to prototype testing. See the discussion in relation to automated vehicles, below.

Of relevance to testing prototype ADAS, cl 91(1)(b) would provide a power to make regulations to amend or impose new type approval requirements not only for automated vehicles but also for vehicles with driver assistance systems:

'The Secretary of State may exercise the power in subsection (2) if the Secretary of State considers it appropriate to do so for the purpose of making the assimilated type approval legislation more suitable for—

(a) vehicles that are designed to travel autonomously, or

(b) any other type of vehicle that

(i)   includes equipment designed to allow its motion to be controlled other than by an individual in it, or to facilitate its being so controlled, or

I(ii) s designed to incorporate or interact with software.'

C Laws of testing prototype automated vehicles

UK Government Code of Practice for Trialling Automated Vehicles

3.13   The Centre for Connected and Autonomous Vehicles (a joint unit of the Department for Transport and the Department for Business, Energy and Industrial Strategy) produced a Code of Practice for Trialling Automated Vehicles in 2015. The Code was updated in February 2019 and in January 2022, latterly including the guidance on vehicle authorisations and exemptions for more complex CAV trials

---

20 Law Commission of England and Wales 'Remote Driving: Advice to Government', February 2023, p 20, 2.65.
21 Ibid, p 20, 2.66.
22 Ibid, p 51, 5-14-5.15.

described above in relation to STGOs and VSOs[23]. It was most recently updated on 30 November 2023, after publication of the AV Bill 2023-24 (HL Bill 1).

BSI pre-standards for AV trials

3.14   The British Standards Institution has to date published several standards including publicly acknowledged specifications (PAS – an early version of a full standard) and a 'flex' (guidance and advisory) paper in relation to trials of automated vehicles, including:

- PAS 1881:2020 'Assuring the safety of automated vehicle trials and testing'
- PAS 1882:2021 'Data collection and management for automated vehicle trials for the purpose of incident investigation – Specification'
- PAS 1884:2021 'Safety operators in automated vehicle testing and trialling – Guide'
- BSI Flex 1886 v1.0 2023-08 'System aspects for remote operation of vehicles – Guide'[24]

CUR 1986, regs 104 and 107 in tests of prototype automated vehicles with an off-board driver

3.15   CUR 1986, regs 104 and 107 are among the construction and use regulations which apply to prototype vehicles under RV(AST)(G)O 2003[25] (from 31 May 2023 CUR 1986, reg 110 on mobile telephones also applies[26]). Regulations 104 and 107 are not the only regulations relevant to trials of prototype automated vehicles and automated driving systems, but they raise the issue of permissibility of an off-board driver or safety operator who is outside the prototype automated vehicle during the test.

CUR 1986, reg 104 ('driver's control') provides that

> 'No person shall drive or cause or permit any other person to drive, a motor vehicle on a road if he is in such a position that he cannot have proper control of the vehicle or have a full view of the road and traffic ahead.'

CUR 1986, reg 107 ('leaving motor vehicles unattended') provides as follows:

> '(1) Save as provided in paragraph (2), no person shall leave, or cause or permit to be left, on a road a motor vehicle which is not attended by a person licensed to drive it unless the engine is stopped and any parking brake with which the vehicle is required to be equipped is effectively set.

---

23 Both documents at UK government webpage: 'Guidance: Trialling automated vehicle technologies in public – How to organise safe trials for automated vehicle technologies on public roads and in public places', updated 28 January 2022
24 All at BSI webpage 'CAV Resources – Standards, guidelines, research and viewpoints'.
25 RV(AST)(G)O 2003 Sched 11, Tables 16 and 17
26 Road Vehicles (Authorisation of Special Types) (General) (Amendment) Order 2023, SI 2023/524, art 5.

(2) The requirement specified in paragraph (1) as to the stopping of the engine shall not apply in respect of a vehicle—

(a) being used for Scottish Fire and Rescue Service or, in England or Wales, fire and rescue authority or police purposes; or

(aa) being used for ambulance purposes or for the purpose of providing a response to an emergency at the request of an NHS ambulance service;

(b) in such a position and condition as not to be likely to endanger any person or property and engaged in an operation which requires its engine to be used to—

(i) drive machinery forming part of, or mounted on, the vehicle and used for purposes other than driving the vehicle; or

(ii) maintain the electrical power of the batteries of the vehicle at a level required for driving that machinery or apparatus.

(3) In this regulation 'parking brake' means a brake fitted to a vehicle in accordance with requirement 16 or 18 in Schedule 3.'

In case law, 'attended by' has been defined as 'either in [the vehicle] or in close attendance on it ... the word 'close' is not there but it is clearly implicit'[27].

Consistent with that definition, the UK government's guidance is that testing with an off-board driver *is* possible, provided that the driver is still able to observe the environment around the vehicle and control it.

'As stated in the [*CCAV trialling*] Code of Practice, it is possible under UK law to operate a vehicle whose driver is not in the vehicle.'

'Where this is done, all relevant legislation must still be complied with, including the driver's ability to observe the driving environment around the vehicle, to have adequate control of the vehicle and responsibility for certain passengers (for example, seatbelt wearing). Refer in particular to regulations 104 and 107 of the Construction and Use Regulations 1986.'

'The trialling organisation must make a thorough analysis of the compliance of any vehicle operated in this way and, where necessary, an organisation may need to present a thorough safety case as part of an application for a VSO [Vehicle Special Order].'[28]

This is also consistent with CUR 1986, reg 30 (which is applicable to tests under RV(AST)(G)O 2003, Sch 11, Table 16), which requires that 'Every motor vehicle shall be so designed and constructed that the driver thereof while controlling the vehicle can at all times have a full view of the road and traffic ahead of the motor vehicle ...' – and see the alternative to that requirement under reg 30(2) ('Instead of complying with the requirement of paragraph (1) a vehicle may comply with

---

27 *Bulman v Godbold* [1981] RTR 242, 244 to 245 (Donaldson LJ). And see *Wilkinsons' Road Traffic Offences* (30th edn), 8-54.

28 UK government (gov.uk) guidance 'Trialling automated vehicle technologies in public' (updated 30 November 2023), 'vehicle authorisations and exemptions for more complex CAV trials', 'considerations for trialling vehicles with an off-board driver'.

Community Directive 77/649, 81/643, 88/366, 90/630 or, in the case of an agricultural motor vehicle, 79/1073').

The Law Commissions were of a similar view in their first consultation paper on AV law, in November 2018:

'Regulation 107 … does not necessarily require a licensed person within the vehicle. A vehicle may still be 'attended' by a person who is near the vehicle or in a remote control centre. However, Regulation 107 would appear to be incompatible with some forms of highly automated vehicles, such as where the vehicle is empty and not remotely controlled.'[29]

– as was the Law Commission of England and Wales in its June 2022 issue paper on remote driving:

'[CUR 1986] regulation 107 would appear to be compatible with remote driving. The courts have held that the driver does not need to be in the vehicle if they are in a position to observe it. This suggests that a vehicle may still be 'attended' by a person who is near the vehicle or in a remote-control centre. However, the issue is not beyond all doubt. If in practice a remote driver could not see the vehicle or was not in a position to prevent interference with it, the courts might consider the regulation to have been breached.'[30]

The government's 30 November 2023 update to its automated vehicle trialling guidance reiterates in several places that 'it is possible under UK law to operate a vehicle whose driver is not in the vehicle'. It adds (for example) that:

'Safety drivers and operators, at all levels of automated vehicle technologies, must be able to take control of the vehicle at all times and are required to have a full view of the road ahead. Trialling organisations should consider the use of more than one safety driver or operator ready and willing to take control of the vehicle to provide as a high level of safety as possible.'

'…The safety driver or operator may be outside of the vehicle, as long as they have the necessary capability to be able to resume control of the vehicle.'

'For remote-controlled tests, safety drivers or safety operators should understand any risks associated with remote access. This includes handling any communication or control latency and mitigating and responding to any network problems.'

'The transition system should be easily and clearly understood by the safety driver or safety operator…'[31]

---

29 Law Commissions' first AV law paper (November 2018), p 127, 7.8
30 Law Commission of England and Wales 'Remote Driving Issues Paper' 24 June 2022, p 19, 3.27
31 UK government (gov.uk) guidance 'Trialling automated vehicle technologies in public' (updated 30 November 2023), 'code of practice; automated vehicle trialling'.

Law Commission's recommended reforms of testing regulations for automated vehicles

3.16   In its February 2023 paper 'Remote Driving: Advice to Government', published after the consultation launched by the June 2022 issue paper (above), the Law Commission pointed out the importance of remote driving to testing of automated vehicles:

'Some AVs are designed without a driving seat or have no on-board controls. For such vehicles, an in-vehicle safety driver may not be an option. A remote safety driver might be the only way to bring the vehicle through testing to deployment.'[32]

Respondents to the Law Commission's June 2022 paper had expressed concerns both as to the potential risks of testing using beyond line-of-sight remote driving and as to ambiguity in current regulations and guidance as to the application of CUR 1986 regs such as 104 and 107 in automated vehicle testing. The Law Commission concluded that

'There is no clear answer to the question of whether remote driving is sufficiently safe to be permitted on the roads. Although remote driving gives rise to many serious safety concerns, it may be safe enough in some limited circumstances, provided sufficient care is taken over each aspect of the operation.'[33]

The Law Commission's advice to government was that a new approach should be adopted to testing, namely that a VSO must be obtained in order to use beyond line-of-sight remote driving without an in-vehicle safety driver:

'We start by proposing a new construction and use regulation to prohibit beyond line-of-sight remote driving without an in-vehicle safety driver. The regulation would apply unless the organisation obtains a Vehicle Special Order."

"In our opinion, the Road Vehicles (Construction and Use) Regulations 1986 should be amended to include a new prohibition. Beyond line-of-sight remote driving should only be allowed with an in-vehicle safety driver or (in the absence of a safety driver) when authorised by a VSO. Anyone acting in contravention of this rule would commit the offence of breaching construction and use regulations, under section 42 of the Road Traffic Act 1988.'[34]

An application for such a VSO should be supported by a rigorous safety case:

'Those wishing to use remote driving without a safety driver would need to submit a safety case and any other relevant information to the [Vehicle Certification Agency]. The VCA should then, as a minimum, check the safety

---

32 Law Commission of England and Wales 'Remote Driving: Advice to Government', February 2023, p 2, 1.7, and p 7-8, 2.2-2.8.
33 Ibid, p 20, 2.64.
34 Ibid, p 49, 5.3 and 5.5.

case against the checklist outlined in Chapter 2[35] and the provisions of the Government's Code of Practice on automated vehicle trialling.

'VSOs could be issued subject to specific requirements covering (for example): areas of operation; how vehicles must be constructed; inspections; and maintenance. Any breach of these conditions may result in a VSO being revoked.

'VSOs would be available both where remote drivers are used in trials of automated vehicles, and where they are used independently of automated driving. Each use case would need to be assessed on its merits.'[36]

In the longer term, the Law Commission advised that

'once an opportunity arises, a statutory licensing scheme should be introduced for entities that undertake beyond line-of-sight remote driving operations, whether alongside automated driving or not. Once these statutory schemes have been introduced, we think that construction and use regulations should be amended to clarify that neither regulation 104 nor regulation 107 apply to licensed remote driving operations.'[37]

'Following the reforms, the Government's Code of Practice on automated vehicle trialling should communicate how to apply for a VSO.'[38]

Testing prototype automated vehicles in the Automated Vehicles Bill 2023-24 (HL Bill 1)

3.17 The AV Bill 2023-24 (HL Bill 1) does not deal distinctly with testing of prototype vehicles, other than in its definition of 'automated passenger services' to include 'a trial with the aim of developing vehicles that are so designed or adapted' (cl 82(2)(b), see below). However, its regulatory scheme is broad and includes measures which emerge from the Law Commissions' joint recommendations on AV law and from the Law Commission of England and Wales' advice to government on remote driving, the latter of which dealt particularly with the use of remote driving in automated vehicle testing[39]. In particular, following the recommendations of the Law Commission:

- Part 1 Chapter 2 'Licensing of operators for vehicle use without user-in-charge' (cll 12-13) allows for the establishment of a statutory licensing scheme. In that scheme:

    'A "no-user-in-charge journey" is a journey by a vehicle with an authorised no-user-in-charge feature during which (at any point)—

    (a)   that feature is engaged, or

    (b)   there is no individual in the vehicle who is exercising control of it.'[40]

---

35 Ibid, p 21, 'Conclusion 1', 2.70.
36 Ibid, p 51, 5-14-5.15.
37 Ibid, p 52, 5.22.
38 Ibid, p 54, 'Conclusion 5', 5.30.
39 Law Commission of England and Wales' Remote Driving: advice to government, February 2023
40 AV Bill 2023-24 (HL Bill 1) cl 12(2).

- Part 1 Chapter 3 ('provision of information by regulated bodies) specifies that automated vehicle authorisation requirements 'may include requirements as to the collection and sharing of information by an authorised self-driving entity' (cl 14(1)), may require an authorised self-driving entity to 'nominate an individual to be responsible for information that is, or has to be, provided by the person to the Secretary to the State for the purposes of this Part', empowers the Secretary of State to serve notices requiring information or interview (cll 16-19) and creates offences of non-compliance (cl 20), providing false or withholding information relating to vehicle safety (sl 24) and an aggravated offence where death or serious injury occurs (cl 25). Also of note are the liability of the nominated individual for information to which the offence relates (cl 26) and the criminal liability of a consenting or conniving senior manager (cl 27). Chapter 3 of Part 1 provides powers to investigate premises used by regulated bodies including warrant powers (cll 28-32);

- Clause 53 proposes offences relating to 'road vehicles used without human control', the first of which would become RTA 1988, s 34B:

    '34B Using vehicle without driver or licensed oversight

    (1)   A person commits an offence if—

        (a)   the person uses, or causes or permits another person to use, a road vehicle on a road or other public place,

        (b)   at any time while the vehicle is so used –

            (i)   the vehicle is mechanically propelled, and

            (ii)   there is no individual who is exercising, or in position to exercise, control of the vehicle, and

        (c)   subsection (2) does not apply.

    (2)   This subsection applies if—

        (a)   an authorised no-user-in-charge feature is engaged at all times when subsection (1)(b) is satisfied, and

        (b)   the journey undertaken by the vehicle is overseen by a licensed no-user-in-charge operator.

    (3)   It is a defence for a person accused of an offence under this section to prove that, at the time of the acts said to constitute the offence, the person did not know, and could not reasonably have been expected to know, that—

        (a)   the facts were, or would be, as described in subsection (1)(b), or

        (b)   the facts were not, or would not be, as described in subsection (2).

    (4)   Subsection (1) does not apply to the use of a vehicle on a public place other than a road if the vehicle is designed primarily for a purpose other than –

        (a)   the carriage of persons, or

        (b)   the carriage of goods on roads.

    (5)   Section 44 of the Automated Vehicles Act 2024 applies for the interpretation of this section as it applies for the interpretation of Part 1 of that Act.

> (6) In this section, "road vehicle" means a mechanically propelled vehicle intended or adapted for use on roads.'

The explanatory note to the AV Bill says of cl 53 that:

> 'The purpose is to ensure that there is a human or corporate entity responsible for the operation of the vehicle at all times...'

> 'These new offences prevent use of NUiC technology unless it has been authorised and is overseen by a licensed operator. It also prevents use of an authorised user-in-charge feature where the user-in-charge has moved out of a position to be able to exercise control of the vehicle, for example by moving to an alternative seat.'

> 'In the case of vehicles without authorised self-driving technologies and appropriate oversight, a human driver is still required. That driver remains responsible for exercising proper control of the vehicle and any feature could only be used as driver assistance technology.'[41]

The effect of AV Bill 2023-24, cl 53 (the new RTA 1988, s 34B offence) upon pre-authorisation AV prototype testing on a road or other public place is not described expressly in the draft s 34B offence at cl 53, nor in the explanatory note to HL Bill 1.

However, cl 53 allows for a safety driver to be outside the vehicle within the proposed RTA 1988, s 34B(1)(b)(ii): '...there is no individual who is exercising, or in position to exercise, control of the vehicle' (italics added). Albeit not explicitly in relation to that proposed offence, the government's 30 November 2023 update to its AV testing guidance elaborates upon that requirement. For example:

> 'Safety drivers and operators, at all levels of automated vehicle technologies, must be able to take control of the vehicle at all times and are required to have a full view of the road ahead. Trialling organisations should consider the use of more than one safety driver or operator ready and willing to take control of the vehicle to provide as a high level of safety as possible.'

> '...The safety driver or operator may be outside of the vehicle, as long as they have the necessary capability to be able to resume control of the vehicle.'

> 'For remote-controlled tests, safety drivers or safety operators should understand any risks associated with remote access. This includes handling any communication or control latency and mitigating and responding to any network problems.'

> 'The transition system should be easily and clearly understood by the safety driver or safety operator...'[42]

---

41 Explanatory note to AV Bill 2023-24 (HL Bill 1 – EN) paras 235, 237-238.
42 UK government (gov.uk) guidance 'Trialling automated vehicle technologies in public' (updated 30 November 2023), 'code of practice; automated vehicle trialling'.

Definition of 'automated passenger service' in AV Bill 2023-24 (HL Bill 1) permits 'a trial with the aim of developing vehicles…'

3.18   The AV Bill 2023-24 (HL Bill 1), cl 82(2) (in cl 82, 'power to grant permits') provides that:

> 'An "automated passenger service" is a service that consists of the carrying of passengers in a road vehicle that—
>
> (a) is designed or adapted to travel autonomously, or
>
> (b) is being used for a trial with the aim of developing vehicles that are so designed or adapted.'

'Trial' is not further defined by the AV Bill 2023-24 (HL Bill 1). The explanatory notes to the AV Bill 2023-24 (HL Bill 1) state (at para 336) that:

> 'Subsection (2) defines an automated passenger service as a service carrying passengers in road vehicles which is designed or adapted to travel autonomously or is being used as part of a trial which is aimed at developing the autonomous design or adaptation of a vehicle. This enables not only vehicles which have already satisfied the self-driving test, under Part 1 (Regulatory scheme for automated vehicles), to be granted a permit, but also enables the grant of a permit to vehicles operated under a trial with a safety driver. Technology is still developing and therefore trialling of new technologies and vehicles with the aim of developing new automated passenger services that meet the self-driving test is likely to be needed for some time. This definition allows for regulatory flexibility for these vehicles as they are in development.'[43]

Clause 82 reflects the Law Commission's observation in February 2023 (in its advice to government on remote driving) that current law allows the Secretary of State for Transport to dispense with conditions for fitness for a public passenger vehicle adapted to carry more than eight passengers but lacking type approval 'where it is expedient to do so for the purpose of making tests or trials of a vehicle or its equipment' (Public Passenger Vehicles Act 1981, s 11)[44]. The AV Bill 2023-24 (HL Bill 1) would disapply PPVA 1981 for permitted automated passenger services (cl 83(2)(c)), but the 'trial' provision of AV Bill 2023-24 (HL Bill 1) is influenced by that Act.

D Laws of testing prototype electric vehicles

Use of VSOs for e-scooter rental trials

3.19   VSOs have been granted for trial rental schemes for e-scooters[45]. It might be that VSOs (rather than STGOs) were thought appropriate in part due to issues

---

43 As above, para 336.
44 Law Commission of England and Wales' Remote Driving: advice to government, February 2023 p 44, 4.30-31. See chapter 5 of this book, 'passenger services and public transport', section on 'The Law Commissions' consultations relevant to AAEV passenger services and public transport'.
45 Department for Transport, 'Guidance: E-scooter trials: guidance for local authorities and rental operators' (updated 22 February 2022), 'Annex: Minimum technical requirements for e-scooters', accessed 20 October 2022.

relating to the stability of e-scooters. The published VSO specification relates in part to stability.

The use of VSOs for e-scooter trials was a model for the Law Commission's February 2023 advice that VSOs be used as the means for authorising the use of remote, beyond line-of-sight driving in testing more broadly:

> 'VSOs provide considerable flexibility. Recently VSOs have been used extensively to enable the trialling of electric scooters in the UK. VSOs enabling the trials exempted scooters from certain construction and use regulations whilst also setting specific requirements to ensure safety.'[46]

3.20   The King's Speech in November 2023 did not include the wider Transport Bill which had been announced (in the Queen's Speech in May 2022) as a measure to legislate for smaller electric vehicles including e-scooters. At the time of writing that legislation remains postponed.

---

46 Law Commission of England and Wales 'Remote Driving: Advice to Government', February 2023, p 50, 5.11.

Chapter 4

The law of driving

'It is not possible to produce a set of rules purporting to describe what a man should do in every conceivable set of circumstances. One might for instance have a rule that one is to stop when one sees a red traffic light, and to go if one sees a green one, but what if by some fault both appear together? One may perhaps decide that it is safest to stop. But some further difficulty may well arise from this decision later. To attempt to provide rules of conduct to cover every eventuality, even those arising from traffic lights, appears to be impossible. With all this I agree.'

Alan Turing (Computing Machinery and Intelligence, 1950)[1]

Chapter Contents

A Outline of the Law of Driving

The meaning of 'driver'

4.01   'Driver' is defined in the Road Traffic Act 1988, s 192(1) (the general interpretation section) as follows:

' *"driver"*, where a separate person acts as a steersman of a motor vehicle, includes (except for the purposes of section 1 of this Act [causing death by dangerous driving]) that person as well as any other person engaged in the driving of the vehicle, and *"drive"* is to be interpreted accordingly'

The interpretation section of the Road Traffic Regulation Act 1974, s 142(1), contains a similar definition:

---

1   The Alan Turing Internet Scrapbook (maintained by biographer Andrew Hodges).

' *"driver"*, where a separate person acts as steersman of a motor vehicle, includes that person as well as any other person engaged in the driving of the vehicle, and "drive" and "driving" shall be construed accordingly'

The term 'steersman' originates in the early days of motor vehicles on the road. A steersman was the second of two people required to drive a steam locomotive[2]. The driver was (as the Law Commission has noted):

'responsible for getting steam up, applying the brakes and generally looking after the firing and mechanical side of the engine. When the engine goes downhill the driver... has to see that his fire is properly damped down, that he has not got too much steam up, and that his brakes are properly on'[3]

– whereas (as the title implied) the steersman's job was to steer the vehicle. The steersman was nevertheless released from some of the duties of the driver. For example, under the Road Traffic (Driving Licences) Act 1936, s 1:

'a person who is not the holder of a licence to drive a motor vehicle issued under Part I of that Act [the Road Traffic Act 1930] may act as steersman of a motor vehicle (being a vehicle on which a speed limit of five miles per hour or less is imposed by or under section ten of that Act) under the orders of another person engaged in the driving of the vehicle who is licensed in that behalf ...'

The Road Traffic Act 1988 retains the possibility of a 'steersman'. Thus, as the Law Commission explains:

'... the current position under the Road Traffic Act 1988 is that both the person who brakes/accelerates (longitudinal control) and the person who steers (lateral control) are drivers. The person with longitudinal control has full responsibility for all aspects of driving, while the person with lateral control is responsible for everything except for the most serious crime – causing death by dangerous driving.'[4]

The current equivalent of the 'steersman' is the attendant to an exceedingly long load, who is permitted to use a remote controlled steering device to assist the driver.[5]

More than one driver

4.02   So a notable feature of the established statutory definition of 'driver' is that it allows for the possibility of a vehicle being driven by more than one person.

---

2   See the 'History' appendix to this book for the part played by road steam locomotives in the largely prohibitive Locomotives Act 1865 (the 'red flag' Act) and, after the development of the internal combustion engine and production of lighter cars, the liberalisation of road vehicle law by the permissive Locomotives on Highways Act 1896.
3   Sir George Fox, House of Commons debates 8 May 1936, volume 311 columns 2070 to 2071, quoted by the Law Commission of England and Wales in its Remote Driving Issues Paper, 24 June 2022 at Annex 1, page 82, 1.2.
4   The Law Commission of England and Wales, Remote Driving Issues Paper, 24 June 2022 at Annex 1, page 82, 1.3.
5   Road Vehicles (Authorisation of Special Types) General Order 2003, SI 2003/1998, Sch 6, para 2.

This is true for cars. For example, in *Tyler v Whatmore*[6] the defendant front-seat passenger of a car asked her friend (a Mr Payne), in the driving seat, to let her steer. The friend in the driving seat had 'had a fair amount to drink'[7]. In leaning across the driver to hold the steering wheel with both hands, the front-seat passenger substantially obstructed the driver's view of the road. He had let go of the wheel. He could not have reached the handbrake because the defendant was sitting across it. The car crashed off the road at a bend. Both Payne and the defendant were charged – the defendant with contravening the Construction and Use Regulations[8] by being in such a position that she could not have proper control of the vehicle while actually driving it. The Justices convicted her on the basis that:

'although the defendant did not control the propulsion of the vehicle, nevertheless she as steersman and [her friend in the driver's seat] in the operation of the gears and foot controls were together engaged in driving the vehicle in pursuance of a common agreed arrangement between them.'[9]

The defendant appealed on the ground that she was not (in the language of the 1973 regulation) 'actually driving'. The High Court rejected the defendant's argument and dismissed the appeal:

'If one asks oneself who was the driver of this car on the assumption that there could only be one driver, it is difficult to say who was the driver. The man Payne who was in the driving seat was able to control the propulsion, but he was perhaps unable to control the footbrake. He certainly could not control the handbrake because the defendant was sitting over the top of it. On the other hand, he was not in a position to control the steering. The defendant, on the other hand, was controlling the steering and she was in a position to control the braking.'

'In my view this was a question of fact. It was a question of fact on which the justices reasonably came to the conclusion that the defendant was driving, and they had also come to the conclusion that the man Payne had been a driver at a separate hearing. I think, for my part, that both those convictions were right and that this appeal accordingly should be dismissed.'[10]

So dual driving is a legal approach adopted for the practicalities of steam technology, retained for cars and of potential application to imminent technologies such as remotely-driven and automated vehicles.

But that still begs the question: 'what does 'driving' mean?'

The meaning of 'driving'

4.03 'Driving' is defined by criminal case law[11] in relation to driving offences.

---

6 [1976] RTR 83.
7 [1976] RTR 83, 86.
8 Motor Vehicles (Construction and Use) Regulations 1973, SI 1973/24, reg 111, now Road Vehicles (Construction and Use) Regulations 1986, SI 1986/1078, reg 104. The phrase 'actually driving' in the 1973 regulation became 'No person shall drive …' in the 1986 regulations.
9 [1976] RTR 83, 85.
10 [1976] RTR 83, 87.
11 As Lord Goddard CJ noted in *Wallace v Major* [1946] KB 473, 477 (quoted in *R v MacDonagh*, discussed below, at 451h), the criminal context affects interpretation: 'After all, we have to remember that this is a penal Act and we are bound to construe it strictly and ought not to stretch the language in any way'.

Criminal case law draws a distinction between 'moving traffic offences'[12] and other driving offences such as RTA 1988, s 170 which imposes upon a driver a 'duty to stop, report accident and give information or documents'. In a s 170 case, the question is not whether which person or people was in control of the vehicle at the time of the accident; instead, 'For the purposes of that section the 'driver' is the person who takes out the vehicle, and he remains the driver until he finishes his journey'[13]. So, while it applies to a driver, the courts have described the offence under the RTA 1988, s 170(4) as 'not a driving offence as such'[14].

In relation to 'moving traffic offences', the position is different.

The approach differs between the law of England and Wales and the law of Scotland. This book is concerned with the law of England and Wales[15].

The test of the word 'driving' in the law of England and Wales derives from the judgment of the Court of Appeal in *R v MacDonagh*[16]. The defendant pushed his car, with both of his feet on the ground outside the car and one hand on the steering wheel to control its steering. The assumption on which the appeal proceeded was the defendant's evidence that the engine was not running. The question was whether he was 'driving' the car. If so, he would have been committing the offence of driving while disqualified, as he was so disqualified and was moving the car in order to comply with a police officer's request that he prevent it obstructing the road. The Court of Appeal held that he was not 'driving' so had not committed the offence.

The High Court of Justiciary in Scotland had previously dealt with essentially the same question, reaching the other answer (that the appellant so moving the car was 'driving') in the case of *Ames v MacLeod*[17]. An indication of how clearly the court regarded its answer was that counsel for the respondent was not called upon[18]. Notably relying upon English authorities, the High Court of Justiciary held that:

> 'The issue as to whether the appellant was driving within the meaning of the section depends, in my view, upon whether he was in a substantial sense controlling the movement and direction of the car. It is not essential for the purpose of establishing that he was driving it that the engine was running at the time, and it is in my view not essential to constitute driving that the appellant should be sitting in the driving seat... [T]he extent of the appellant's powers of intervention with the movement and direction of this

---

12 *Cawthorn v Director of Public Prosecutions* [2000] RTR 45 (QB).
13 Lord Goddard CJ in *Jones v Prothero* [1952] 1 ALL ER 434, applied in *Cawthorn v DPP* (above).
14 *Cawthorn v DPP* (above) at 50g to 51a (Mr Justice Forbes).
15 See *Wilkinson's Road Traffic Offences* (30th edition) at 1-93 ('Driving') for a discussion of the approach in Scottish law.
16 [1974] 1 QB 448 (CA).
17 *Ames v MacLeod* 1969 JC 1. The offence in *Ames* (driving with excessive alcohol) was different to that in *MacDonagh* (driving while disqualified). The numbers of people involved in the incidents and precise motions of the cars also varied. But the common legal question (whether 'driving') and relevant facts of the two cases are – as Wilkinson's puts it at 1-93 – 'virtually indistinguishable'.
18 *Ames v MacLeod* (above) at 2.

vehicle was sufficient to establish that within the meaning of the section he was driving ...'[19]

'... the appellant was driving the car ... since he was controlling it in movement, although he was not in the driving seat and the engine of the car was not running. That conclusion seems to me to be sound in law.'[20]

The Court of Appeal took a different view in *MacDonagh*. The Court of Appeal did so by adding a filter to the test set out in *Ames*:

'Although the word 'drive' must be given a wide meaning, the courts must be alert to see that the net is not thrown so widely that it includes activities which cannot be said to be driving a motor vehicle in any ordinary use of that word in the English language. Unless this is done, absurdity may result by requiring the obtaining of a driving licence and third-party insurance in circumstances which cannot have been contemplated by Parliament.'[21]

The Court of Appeal quoted Lord Parker CJ in the 1965 case of *R v Roberts*:

'on the authorities, a man cannot be said to be a driver unless he is in the driving seat or in control of the steering wheel and also has something to do with the propulsion ... There are no cases, so far as this court knows, where a man has been held to be guilty of ... driving ... if, although he has something to do with the movement and the propulsion, he is not driving in any ordinary sense of the word.'[22]

The test in English and Welsh law is therefore that set out in *MacDonagh*, and can be said to comprise two elements:

1. Whether the alleged driver 'was in a substantial sense controlling the movement and direction of the car'[23]; and

2. The additional filter (which in effect contradicted *Ames*) that:

'It is still necessary to consider whether the activity in question can fall within the ordinary meaning of the word 'driving'. Giving the words their ordinary meaning there must be a distinction between driving a car and pushing it. The dividing line will not always be easy to draw, and the distinction will often turn on the extent and degree to which the defendant was relying on the use of the driver's controls.'[24]

The leading work on road traffic offences interprets *Ames* and *MacDonagh* as adding an overarching element of the test in the context of criminal cases, that:

---

19   Lord Justice General (Clyde) at 3.
20   Lord Guthrie at 3 and 4.
21   Lord Widgery CJ at 451f.
22   *R v Roberts* [1965] 1 QB 85, 88, applied by Lord Widgery CJ in *R v MacDonagh* at 452d-e.
23   *Ames v MacLeod*, Lord Justice General (Clyde) at 3. Part 1 of the test in English and Welsh law follows from *R v MacDonagh* at 452g: 'We respectfully agree that a person cannot be driving unless he satisfies the test adopted by the Court of Session, and we recognise the importance that this legislation should be given the same meaning in England as in Scotland'. The Court of Appeal then applied a different approach, by adding its own second part to the test.
24   *R v MacDonagh* at 452h.

'the primary consideration as to whether a person is 'driving' is essentially a question of fact, dependent on the degree and extent to which the person has control of the direction and movement of the vehicle' [25]

In a civil claim, that would not add a further element to the test of 'driving'. Every road traffic accident claim is determined on its own facts: 'The root of this liability is negligence, and what is negligence depends on the facts with which you have to deal'[26].

But even in a civil liability context the fact-sensitivity of judicial interpretations of 'driving' deserves emphasis, because it tells us something about the way in which the issue of 'driving' has been decided by the courts over time.

Judgments on 'driving' affected by contemporary technology and driver behaviour

4.04   As the leading work on road traffic offences puts it, 'There are a number of cases on whether a person can be said to be 'driving'. Some are not easy to reconcile.'[27] The prime example of this is the disagreement of the Scottish and the English and Welsh authorities in *Ames* and *MacDonagh*.[28]

There are disparities. However, a possible explanation appears in the caselaw, namely judicial awareness of driving technology and driving behaviours at the time that a particular case is decided. In *MacDonagh*, this is shown by the Court of Appeal's resistance to pushing a vehicle being described as 'driving':

'... we do not think that any ordinary meaning of the word 'drive' could extend to a man who is not in the motor car, who has both feet on the road, and who is making no use of the controls apart from an occasional adjustment of the steering wheel.'[29]

That was written in 1974, when the possibility of a driver remotely parking their car using an App on a smartphone was unforeseen. Both the Construction and Use Regulations and the Highway Code now permit use of a mobile telephone or other device to perform a remote controlled parking function[30].

The Court of Appeal implicitly acknowledged the role of changing technology and behaviour in its judgment in *MacDonagh*:

'The dividing line will not always be easy to draw, and the distinction will often turn on the extent and degree to which the defendant was relying on the use of the driver's controls'[31]

---

25 *Wilkinson's Road Traffic Offences* (30th edition), 1-93.
26 Lord Dunedin in *Fardon v Harcourt-Rivington* (1932) 146 LT 391, quoted by Lord Justice May in *Foskett v Mistry* [1984] RTR 1, 4c.
27 *Wilkinson's Road Traffic Offences* (30th edition), 1-92.
28 See the discussion in *Wilkinson's* for other examples.
29 *R v MacDonagh* at 453c.
30 Road Vehicles (Construction and Use) Regulations 1986, SI 1986/1078 (as amended), regulation 110(5A)(a); Highway Code Rule 149.
31 *R v MacDonagh* at 452h.

A further example of the courts taking into account the features of contemporary technology appears in *MacDonagh*. The court doubted whether merely pushing smaller vehicles 'which must from their nature be manhandled from time to time' and which then required no driving licence could fairly be made subject to moving traffic offences.[32] That is a point which might affect judgments differently in the age of e-scooters and micro-mobility vehicles.

Judicial notice of vehicle technology in use at the time of a decision therefore forms part of the factual background of a case in which 'driving' is in issue – as does judicial awareness of changes in driving trends, including types of recklessness.

In 2003, in *Director for Public Prosecutions v Alderton,*[33] the question before the High Court was whether use of the accelerator, clutch and steering wheel, with a vehicle in gear and its handbrake on, to produce wheel spinning – whereby the vehicle did not move forwards or backwards – was 'driving', despite the emphasis in the legal test on control of 'movement'.[34]

Mr Justice Harrison applied a 2000 Scottish case described by the High Court of Justiciary as 'unusual', in which a driver had been prosecuted for driving while disqualified on the basis of the slight forward lurch of the car when he switched off its engine. The lurch was said to result from the need to take the vehicle out of gear and depress the brake pedal in order to compensate for a defect in the handbrake. In that Scottish case, Lord Sutherland interpreted the facts as follows:

'The fact that there was movement at the end of the proceedings is a clear indication in our view that the appellant must have been driving because there would have been no movement but for the intervention on his part by disengaging the gear and using the footbrake.'[35]

This (in Lord Sutherland's view) affected the legal test, and particularly the interpretation of 'movement':

'The correct test is to look at what the appellant was doing and not necessarily the result. For example, if the car had in fact rolled forward and hit another car perhaps a foot or two in front of it there can be no question but that the appellant would have been driving the car. The things that he was doing would have been exactly the same as he was doing in the present case. This shows that the question of movement of the car is not essential if the driver's activities have got beyond the stage of mere preparation for driving but have got to the stage when there is active intervention on his part to prevent movement and direction of the vehicle.'[36]

That interpretation of movement to include its prevention fitted the needs of the first case on wheel spinning, as Mr Justice Harrison held:

'… it is important to remember that each case must depend on its own facts. This is, I am told, the first case of its kind (i.e. wheel spinning) that has come

---

32   *R v MacDonagh* at 453b.
33   [2003] EWHC 2917 (Admin); [2004] RTR 23.
34   The *Ames* test as applied in *MacDonagh* (above).
35   *Hoy v McFadyen* 2000 SLT 1060, quoted at paragraph 15 of *DPP v Alderton*.
36   As above.

before the court. In dealing with the first test in *MacDonagh*, namely the degree of control over the movement and direction of the vehicle, I consider that the defendant was controlling the movement and direction of the vehicle by preventing it going forwards by virtue of the handbrake being on.'[37]

So the legal meaning of 'driving' has shifted over time, as judicial perceptions of vehicle technology and driver behaviours have altered. Whether 'driving' can be given an 'ordinary meaning'[38] as driving becomes automated, remote and more technically defined remains to be seen. The two-part test in *R v MacDonagh* might be due for a change.

Presumption that person in driving seat of moving car is the 'driver'

4.05   In 1958, the High Court held in the case of *Hill v Baxter* that:

'In any ordinary case, when once it has been proved that the accused was in the driving seat of a moving car, there is, prima facie, an obvious and irresistible inference that he was driving it. No dispute or doubt will arise on that point unless and until there is evidence tending to show that by some extraordinary mischance he was rendered unconscious or otherwise incapacitated from controlling the car.'[39]

Hill v Baxter was a criminal case, whereas in civil liability automatism is *not* the only defence open to a driver. In *Mansfield v Weetabix Ltd* a lorry driver lost consciousness and crashed the lorry into the Claimant's shop, causing damage. The lorry driver had no reason to suspect that he had 'very rare' malignant insulinoma and that he might lose consciousness at the wheel.

The claim against the lorry driver's employer failed. 'There is no reason in principle why a driver should not escape liability where the disabling event is not sudden, but gradual, provided that the driver is unaware of it.' The claim might have succeeded if the driver had 'continued to drive when he was unfit to do so and when he should have been aware of his unfitness'[40].

The *Mansfield v Weetabix* case limits to criminal cases the *Hill v Baxter* presumption that, absent automatism, the person in the driver's seat has control of the vehicle.

Riding

4.06   'Driving' means controlling the movement and direction of the vehicle so includes riding a two-wheeled motor vehicle such as a motorcycle, provided that the ordinary meaning of the word 'driving' is also met in any particular case[41].

---

37   *DPP v Alderton*, paragraphs 22 and 23.
38   *R v MacDonagh* at 452h.
39   *Hill v Baxter* [1958] 1 QB 277, 286 per Pearson J.
40   [1998] 1 WLR 1263 at 1266-7 per Leggatt LJ.
41   *McKoen v Ellis* [1987] RTR 26 (QB).

The driver's standard of care

4.07   The standard of care which a non-police driver is required to satisfy to avoid liability has remained constant since the early 1970s. Whether a driver is a learner or an experienced driver, the standard of care is the same – they:

'must drive in as good a manner as a driver of skill, experience and care, who is sound in wind and limb[42], who makes no errors of judgment, has good eyesight and hearing, and is free from any infirmity'[43]

(The phrase 'free from any infirmity' 'does not refer to cases in which a driver is unaware that he is subject to a disability'. Liability might arise if a defendant driver 'continued to drive when he was unfit to do so and when he should have been aware of his unfitness'[44].)

It is a demanding standard. In particular:

'The court "has consistently imposed upon the drivers of cars a high burden to reflect the fact that the car is potentially a dangerous weapon"'[45]

The demanding nature of the common law standard does not, however, result in strict liability[46]. In particular:

There is no 'golden rule' of driving that a driver should never drive at a speed at which they cannot stop in time, if a sudden and unexpected danger arises (in that case, a pedestrian stepping out from a concealed position behind a van, as the defendant driver was almost level with that position): 'It would be an unattainable counsel of perfection to hold that the defendant should have driven at such a speed and in such a way that she should have avoided this accident'[47].

A driver placed in a position of peril and emergency must not be judged by too critical a standard when they act on the spur of the moment to avoid an accident[48].

In criminal law, the standard of care has been altered in relation to police drivers, to invoke their training as a characteristic of lawful driving. Since 26 October 2022[49], the standard of care has been altered by statute (the Police, Crime, Sentencing

---

42   An equestrian metaphor, meaning able to breathe and move freely.
43   *Nettleship v Weston* [1971] 2 QB 691, 699g, Lord Denning MR.
44   *Mansfield v Weetabix Ltd* [1998] 1 WLR 1263 at 1266 to 1267, Leggatt LJ.
45   *Lunt v Khelifa* [2002] EWCA Civ 801 (20), as quoted by Hale LJ in *Eagle v Chambers* [2003] EWCA Civ 1107; [2004] RTR 9, [16].
46   In 1971 Lord Denning MR appeared to suggest a trend towards strict liability for third party road traffic accident injuries in *Nettleship v Weston* (above) at 699h to 700b: 'The high standard thus imposed by the judges is, I believe, largely the result of the policy of the Road Traffic Acts. Parliament requires every driver to be insured against third party risks.... Thus we are, in this branch of the law, moving away from the concept: "No liability without fault," We are beginning to apply the test: "On whom should the risk fall?".'
47   *Sam v Atkins* [2005] EWCA Civ 1452; [2006] RTR 14, 171, at 175, 176 [18], [23].
48   *Ng Chun Pui v Lee Chuen Tat* [1988] RTR 298, 302d (Privy Council).
49   Police, Crime, Sentencing and Courts Act 2022 (Commencement No.3) Regulations 2022, SI 2022/1075, reg 3(a) and (b); non-retrospectivity provisions at PCSCA 2022 s 5(5) and 6(5).

and Courts Act 2022) in relation to the criminal offences of careless driving[50] and dangerous driving[51] where the driver is a police driver (a 'designated person' driving in one of several prescribed police roles), is driving for police purposes and has undertaken prescribed training[52].

In relation to careless driving:

> 'The designated person is to be regarded as driving without due care and attention if (and only if) the way the person drives falls below what would be expected of a competent and careful constable who has undertaken the same prescribed training.'[53]

In relation to dangerous driving, the 'designated person' is to be regarded as driving dangerously:

> '... if (and, subject to subsection (2) below, only if) –
>
> (a) the way the person drives falls far below what would be expected of a competent and careful constable who has undertaken the same prescribed training, and
>
> (b) it would be obvious to such a competent and careful constable that driving in that way would be dangerous.
>
> ...
>
> (2) A person is also to be regarded as driving dangerously for the purposes of sections 1, 1A and 2 above if it would be obvious to a competent and careful driver that driving the vehicle in its current state would be dangerous.'[54]

The regulations providing for training are the Road Traffic Act (Police Driving: Prescribed Training) Regulations 2023[55].

Omissions by driver treated as part of activity of driving

4.08   The usual rule is that, save for in special circumstances, there is no justification for "the imposition of liability upon someone who simply does nothing: who neither creates the risk nor undertakes to do anything to avert it"[56].

If applied to individual omissions by the driver of a vehicle, however, that rule would allow a defence which might ignore a broader lack of care. Failures to apply a brake or to keep a proper lookout might be described as omissions. The

---

50   RTA 1988, s 3ZA, as added by PCSCA 2022, s 6.
51   RTA 1988, s 2A, as added by PCSCA 2022, s 5.
52   PCSCA 2022, ss 5(3) and 6(3).
53   RTA 1988, s 3ZA(2B), as added by PCSCA 2022, s 6(3).
54   RTA 1988, s 2A(1B), as added by PCSCA 2022, s 5(3).
55   SI 2023/185 (in force from 20 March 2023: reg 1(1)).
56   See *Gorringe v Calderdale Metropolitan Borough Council* [2004] UKHL 15; [2004] 1 WLR 1057, Lord Hoffmann [17]. See Chapter 13, 'highway claims' for discussion of the rule as it applies to public authorities.

courts have therefore treated such omissions while driving as part of the activity of driving[57].

The Highway Code

4.09   The Highway Code is the statutory code 'comprising directions for the guidance of persons using roads'.[58] The Road Traffic Act 1988 provides that:

> 'A failure on the part of a person to observe a provision of the Highway Code shall not of itself render that person liable to criminal proceedings of any kind but any such failure may in any proceedings (whether civil or criminal, …) be relied upon by any party to the proceedings as tending to establish or negative any liability which is in question in those proceedings.'[59]

The evidential effect of a breach of the Highway Code is that 'any breach of the Highway Code is relevant but not determinative'.[60] As Lord Denning wrote in 1959:

> 'It contains many propositions of good sense which may be taken into account in considering whether reasonable care has been taken, but it would be a mistake to elevate them into propositions of law.'[61]

The Highway Code is frequently updated. The Secretary of State for Transport 'may from time to time revise the Highway Code by revoking, varying, amending or adding to the provisions of the Code in such manner as he thinks fit'[62].

Any proposed alterations to the Highway Code that are not 'merely consequential on the passing, amendment or repeal of any statutory provision' must be laid before both Houses of Parliament and the proposed alterations must not be made to the Code 'until after the end of a period of forty days beginning with the day on which the alterations were so laid'[63].

This is not a mere formality. There is a statutory duty on the Secretary of State to 'consult with such representative organisations as he thinks fit' before 'revising the Highway Code by making any alterations in its provisions which are required by subsection (3) above to be laid before Parliament'[64].

---

57   See *Kelly v Metropolitan Railway Company* [1895] 1 QB 944 (CA); *Stovin v Wise, Norfolk County Council (Third Party)* [1996] AC 923 (HL), Lord Nicholls at 930 A-B and Lord Hoffmann at 945 D-E; *Valentine v Transport for London* [2010] EWCA Civ 1358; [2011] RTR 24, Hughes LJ (as he then was) [32]; *Mitchell v Glasgow City Council* [2009] 1 AC 874, Baroness Hale, 904 [76].

58   RTA 1988, s 38(8).

59   RTA 1988, s 38(7)

60   See for example *Wakeling v McDonagh & MIB* [2007] EWHC 1201 (QB), His Honour Judge MacKie QC [24].

61   *Qualcast (Wolverhampton) Ltd v Haynes* [1959] AC 743, 759 (HL). The Highway Code was not evidence in the case; Lord Denning cited the Code as an example of evidence of good practice.

62   RTA 1988, s 38(2).

63   RTA 1988, s 38(3).

64   RTA 1988, s 38(5).

A resolution by either House of Parliament that the proposed alterations be not made prevents the Secretary of State making the proposed revision, '(but without prejudice to the laying before Parliament of further proposals for alteration in accordance with that subsection)'.[65]

The current judicial approach to driver negligence

4.10   Judges are aware of the relative calm and slow pace of the court room, as compared to the reality of fast-developing events in a road traffic accident. Lord Justice Laws warned of the:

> 'danger in cases of negligence that the court may evaluate the standard of care owed by the defendant by reference to fine considerations elicited in the leisure of the court room, perhaps with the liberal use of hindsight'.[66]

Current and future approaches to expert evidence

4.11   For similar reasons, the courts have tended to adopt a cautious attitude when balancing the weight given to expert accident reconstruction evidence against 'the primary factual evidence which is of the greatest importance in a case of this kind'. Mr Justice Coulson put the point this way, in 2009:

> 'The expert evidence comprises a useful way in which that factual evidence, and the inferences to be drawn from it, can be tested. It is, however, very important to ensure that the expert evidence is not elevated into a fixed framework or formula, against which the defendant's actions are then to be rigidly judged with a mathematical precision.'[67]

While the courts will avoid rigidity, advanced driver assistance systems and automated vehicles might alter that balance. For example, issues as to when the transition from driving to self-driving occurred, so as to give rise to a claim against the insurer under the Automated and Electric Vehicles Act 2018, s 2, as well as questions of contributory negligence (s 3) and claims by liable insurer/owner against other responsible parties (s 5), are likely to require expert comment in order to be adjudicated.

More primary data is available in road traffic accident cases than in the early 2000s, especially from on-vehicle cameras. Vehicles with the Automated Lane Keeping System will be equipped with a Data Storage System for Automated Driving (DSSAD)[68].

Again, the factual setting will change the legal approach. In particular, the judicial fact-finding approach when balancing accident data against other sources of evidence is likely to alter, as expert evidence is likely more often to be required to interpret data from devices incorporated within vehicles. Cases involving ADAS

---

65   RTA 1988, s 38(4).
66   *Ahanonu v South East London and Kent Bus Company Ltd* [2008] EWCA Civ 274 [23].
67   *Stewart v Glaze* [2009] EWHC 704 [10].
68   See Article 8 of UN Regulation 157 (the Automated Lane Keeping System regulation)

systems on the cusp of full automation and early automated vehicles might lead to a greater need for expert opinion as to the likely reasons for a collision[69].

Remote driving

4.12   The law permits the use of remote driving in several contexts:

1   'Pedestrian-controlled road maintenance vehicles that are not constructed or used to carry a driver or passenger' which 'are a recognised category of special vehicles', under the Road Vehicles (Authorisation of Special Types) General Order 2003[70], art 50 and RTA 1988, s 44 ('Authorisation of use on roads of special vehicles not complying with [construction, weight, equipment and use] regulations under section 41'). Under RV(AST)GO 2003, art 50(5):

> '"*Road maintenance vehicle*" means a motor vehicle that is specially constructed or adapted for the purposes of carrying out one or more of the following operations–
>
> (a) gritting roads;
>
> (b) laying road markings;
>
> (c) clearing frost, snow or ice from roads; or
>
> (d) any other work of maintaining roads.'

2   The attendant accompanying the driver of an exceedingly long vehicle under RV(AST)GO 2003 may use a 'remote controlled steering device to assist the driver' (Sch 6, para 2).

3   Under RV(AST)GO 2003,[71] art 53, there is a wide exemption, by certification by the Secretary of State, for "operational military vehicles …where compliance with any regulations made under section 41 of the Road Traffic Act 1988 by any such vehicle would directly compromise the vehicle's operational capability". This appears capable of applying to remotely-controlled vehicles.

4   Remote parking, as provided by the Road Vehicles (Construction and Use) Regulations 1986, reg 110(5A), to which from 11 June 2018 was added[72] the following exception to the prohibition in reg 110(1) and (4) ('No person shall drive a motor vehicle on a road if he is using: (a) a hand-held mobile telephone; or (b) a hand-held device … other than a two-way radio, which performs an interactive communication function by transmitting and receiving data'):

> '(5A) A person does not contravene a provision of this regulation if, at the time of the alleged contravention—

---

69   See the test for admissibility of expert evidence at Civil Procedure Rules 1998, Part 35.1: 'Expert evidence shall be restricted to that which is reasonably required to resolve the proceedings' and the classic exposition of the need for expert evidence in road traffic accident claims (just prior to the Civil Procedure Rules 1998) in *Liddell v Middleton* [1996] PIQR P36 (CA).

70   SI 2003/1998. See Chapter 3, 'Testing'.

71   Made under RTA 1988, s 44 ('Authorisation of use on roads of special vehicles not complying with regulations under section 41').

72   Road Vehicles (Construction and Use) (Amendment) Regulations 2018, SI 2018/592, reg 1 and 2(2).

(a) that person is using the mobile telephone or other device only to perform a remote controlled parking function of the motor vehicle; and

(b) that mobile telephone or other device only enables the motor vehicle to move where the following conditions are satisfied—

   (i) there is continuous activation of the remote control application of the telephone or device by the driver;

   (ii) the signal between the motor vehicle and the telephone or the motor vehicle and the device, as appropriate, is maintained; and

   (iii) the distance between the motor vehicle and the telephone or the motor vehicle and the device, as appropriate, is not more than 6 metres.'

On 24 June 2022, at the request of the Department for Transport's International Vehicle Standards division and Centre for Connected and Autonomous Vehicles (CCAV, a joint unit of DfT and the Department for Business, Energy and Industrial Strategy (BEIS)) the Law Commission of England and Wales launched its consultation on:

'the law surrounding remote driving, where a person outside a vehicle uses wireless connectivity to control a vehicle on a public road.'[73]

Remote driving, as the Law Commission noted:

'has proved to be particularly useful in dangerous or unpleasant environments, such as mines. It is increasingly being used in other off-road environments, such as farms, ports and warehouses. Until now, its use on public roads has been limited to low speed and short range, for abnormal loads and remote control parking. However, its use is set to expand, for two main reasons. The first is that remote driving can be used as an adjunct to automated driving, both in trials and in the longer term. The second reason is the increasing interest in delivering rental vehicles by remotely driving them to the customer's door. Cheaper car rental services, delivered to the hirer's door, could reduce dependency on private car ownership, bringing many social benefits. However, at present, car delivery is expensive because the delivery driver must return to base. Placing the delivery driver in a remote control centre has the potential to remove the cost of a return journey. Trials are currently taking place to deliver conventional vehicles by remote driving.'[74]

After its June 2022 consultation, the Law Commission published 'Remote Driving: Advice to Government', in February 2023[75]. It approached the definition of 'driver' in the context of remote driving as follows.

'A driver is an individual who performs one or more of the following tasks: steering; braking, releasing a brake, or accelerating; or monitoring the vehicle or driving environment with a view to immediate and safety-critical intervention in the way the vehicle drives.'[76]

---

73   Remote Driving Issues Paper, 24 June 2022, page i.
74   Remote Driving: Advice to Government (the Law Commission, February 2023), p 7, 2.2-4.
75   Ibid.
76   Ibid, p 3, 1,13.

The Law Commission distinguished the particular roles of a 'within line-of-sight' and 'beyond line of sight' remote driver, where:

'A "beyond line-of-sight" remote driver is a driver who is outside the vehicle or its trailer; and who relies on external aids (other than corrective spectacles) to see some or all safety-critical elements of the driving environment.'[77]

B Laws of Driving Vehicles with Advanced Driver Assistance Systems (ADAS)

Overview of ADAS

4.13 'Advanced Driver Assistance System' ('ADAS') is a technical term, which the British Standards Institute and the UK government's Centre for Connected and Autonomous Vehicles define in their vocabulary[78] as an:

'entity consisting of interdependent components that supports human drivers by performing a part of the dynamic driving task[79] ... or providing safety relevant information. *NOTE Examples include adaptive cruise control*[80] *and automatic emergency braking.*'

The Department for Transport defines Advanced Driver Assistance Systems as 'Individual automation features such as adaptive cruise control or lane changing features which assist the driver' [81] falling within either level 1 or level 2 of the six levels of vehicle automation described by the American Society of Automotive Engineers (the SAE levels[82]).

ADAS is described in the Highway Code, which uses the term 'driver assistance systems'[83].

As well as providing for the authorisation of automated systems, the AV Bill 2023-24, cl 91(1)(b) would (if enacted per HL Bill 1) for the first time provide a definition of driver assistance systems for the purpose of type approval. The AV Bill 2023-24 (HL Bill 1), cl 91 would provide a power to the Secretary of State by regulations

---

77 Ibid.
78 Connected and automated vehicles – Vocabulary, BSI Flex 1890 v4.0:2022-03.
79 The BSI CAV vocabulary defines Dynamic driving task (DDT) as the 'real-time operational and tactical functions required to operate a vehicle ... safely in on-road traffic'.
80 The BSI CAV vocabulary defines adaptive cruise control (ACC) as follows: 'system that attempts to maintain the vehicle (2.1.87) at a driver-selected target speed and following distance, using sensors and automation to regulate vehicle speed. NOTE 1 The purpose is to keep a safe distance relative to other slower moving vehicles ahead before reverting to the set speed when the lane clears. NOTE 2 Some early adaptive cruise control systems, especially those vehicles with manual transmission, are not capable of bringing the vehicle to a complete stop and require the human driver to intervene to do so. Systems that are capable of controlling the vehicle to a stop have a variety of additional names such as 'Stop & Go'.'
81 'Acronym glossary' at page 45 of Safe Use of Automated Lane Keeping System (ALKS) Summary of Responses and Next Steps, Moving Britain Ahead (Centre for Connected and Autonomous Vehicles, Department for Transport, April 2021).
82 The SAE levels are often cited in discussions of automated driving. See diagram 'the SAE taxonomy' at page 12 of Law Commissions' final report on automated vehicles, *Automated Vehicles: Joint Report*, Law Com No 404, Scot Law Com No 258 (January 2022).
83 The Highway Code (Department for Transport, 2022) at rules 150 and 160.

to update type approval requirements, of a sort similar to the general power to prescribe TA requirements provided by RTA 1988, s 54, but specifically

'for the purpose of making the assimilated[84] type approval legislation more suitable for –

(a) vehicles that are designed to travel autonomously, or

(b) any other type of vehicle that –

  (i) includes equipment designed to allow its motion to be controlled other than by an individual in it, or to facilitate its being so controlled, or

  (ii) is designed to incorporate or interact with software.'

The Highway Code on ADAS

4.14   The Highway Code in its current version provides as follows in relation to ADAS systems:

'You **MUST** exercise proper control of your vehicle at all times. You **MUST NOT** use a hand-held mobile phone, or similar device, capable of interactive communication (such as a tablet) for any purpose when driving or when supervising a learner driver. This ban covers all use of a hand-held interactive communication device and it applies even when the interactive communication capability is turned off or unavailable. You **MUST NOT** pick up the phone or similar device while driving to dial a number and then put it in the cradle for the duration of the conversation. You **MUST NOT** pick up and use your hand-held phone or similar device while stationary in traffic.

There is an exception to call 999 or 112 in a genuine emergency when it is unsafe or impractical to stop. There is also an exception if you are using a hand-held mobile phone or similar device to make a contactless payment at a contactless payment terminal. Your vehicle **MUST** be stationary, and the goods or services **MUST** be received at the same time as, or after, the contactless payment.

Never use a hand-held microphone when driving. Using hands-free equipment is also likely to distract your attention from the road. It is far safer not to use any telephone or similar device while you are driving or riding – find a safe place to stop first or use the voicemail facility and listen to messages later.

You may park your vehicle using a handheld remote control app or device. The app or device **MUST** be legal, and you should not put other people in danger when you use it.'

(Rule 149)

---

84 'The assimilated type approval legislation' is defined by the AV Bill 2023-24 (HL Bill 1), cl 91(4) and consists mainly of EU regulations including Regulation 2018/858 of the European Parliament and of the Council of 30 May 2018 on the approval and market surveillance of motor vehicles and their trailers, and of systems, components and separate technical units intended for such vehicles (cl 91(4)(j)).

'There is a danger of driver distraction being caused by in-vehicle systems such as satellite navigation systems, congestion warning systems, PCs, multi-media, etc. You **MUST** exercise proper control of your vehicle at all times. Do not rely on driver assistance systems such as motorway assist, lane departure warnings, or remote control parking. They are available to assist but you should not reduce your concentration levels. Do not be distracted by maps or screen-based information (such as navigation or vehicle management systems) while driving or riding. If necessary find a safe place to stop.

As the driver, you are still responsible for the vehicle if you use a driver assistance system (like motorway assist). This is also the case if you use a hand-held remote control parking app or device. You **MUST** have full control over these systems at all times.'

(Rule 150)

'**Once moving** you should:

…

drive or ride with both hands on the wheel or handlebars where possible. This will help you to remain in full control of the vehicle at all times. You may use driver assistance systems while you are driving. Make sure you use any system according to the manufacturer's instructions.'

(Rule 160)

ADAS and Mobile Devices

4.15   The Highway Code cites in support of rules 149 and 150 the RTA 1988, ss 2 and 3 and the Road Vehicles (Construction and Use) Regulations 1986 ('CUR 1986'), regs 104 and 110[85]. These rules all focus upon 'driver's control':

Offence of dangerous driving (RTA 1988, s 2)

Offences of careless and inconsiderate driving (RTA 1988, s 3)

'Driver's Control' 'No person shall drive or cause or permit any other person to drive, a motor vehicle on a road if he is in such a position that he cannot have proper control of the vehicle or have a full view of the road and traffic ahead.' (CUR 1986, reg 104 and RTA 1988, s 41D[86])

---

85   SI 1986/1078 (as amended).

86   RTA 1988, s 41D (offences of 'Breach of requirements as to control of vehicle, mobile telephones etc'). Reform of the control rules for automated driving is underway at national level (by the Transport Bill, unpublished at the time of writing but described by the government in May 2022 in terms echoing the Law Commissions' recommendations for future AV regulation) and internationally (by the Amendment to Article 1 and new Article 34 BIS of the 1968 UN Convention on Road Traffic) 'by 'deeming' the 1968 Convention's requirement that every moving vehicle shall have a driver, to be satisfied provided it is using an automated driving system that complies with domestic and international technical regulations, and domestic legislation governing operation' (UK government's explanatory memorandum on the proposal, Command Paper CP No 540, at 2.1). See Chapter 2 of this book, 'specifications'.

'Mobile telephones' 'No person shall drive a motor vehicle on a road if he is using–

(a) a hand-held mobile telephone; or

(b) a hand-held device of a kind specified in paragraph (4)…

(4) A device referred to in paragraphs (1)(b), (2)(b) and (3)(b) is a device, other than a two-way radio, which is capable of transmitting and receiving data[87], whether or not those capabilities are enabled.'

There are exceptions in CUR 1986, reg 110(5), (5A), (5B) for using a mobile telephone in a 'genuine emergency', for remote controlled parking functions (see above) and for contactless payments (CUR 1986, reg 110 and RTA 1988, s 41D).

ADAS systems which might soon be required by law

4.16   From 6 July 2022, all new vehicles that are placed onto the market or registered or entered into service in the European Union must be equipped with certain ADAS systems[88]. Those systems include Advanced Emergency Braking (AEB) and Intelligent Speed Assistance (ISA, which signal to the driver that the applicable speed limit is exceeded).

The EU regulation is not mandatory as it allows for systems to be overridden and allows the speed limit to be exceeded by the driver[89] (so, insofar as the ISA system is concerned, it is not a full 'speed limiter' as the media has sometimes described it).

It seems likely but has yet to be officially confirmed that the British government will adopt a similar rule – both to achieve parity for British drivers and manufacturers but also because such systems are common to many current new vehicles.

Remote driving systems

4.17   As the Law Commission has noted, the main current use of in line-of-sight remote driving in a driver assistance system is remote-controlled parking. It is also used to steer very long loads, which 'often require a separate steersperson to operate the back wheels' and where for 'particularly difficult bends or bridges, the steersperson may use remote control, either from the side of the road or from an accompanying vehicle'[90].

For those 'in line-of sight' remote driving systems, the Law Commission's view is that 'existing driving laws' such as the Road Vehicles (Authorisation of Special

---

87   Including transmissions within the vehicle, eg. via Bluetooth: *Bendt v Crown Prosecution Service* [2022] EWHC 502 (Admin).

88   EU Regulation 2019/2144 of the European Parliament and of the Council of 27 November 2019.

89   Article 6(2) of EU Regulation 2019/2144.

90   Remote Driving: Advice to Government (the Law Commission, February 2023) p 11, 2.24. See RV(AST)GO 2003, Sch 6 para 2, above.

Types) (General) Order 2003[91] for abnormal loads 'are generally sufficient'[92]. In relation to proposed laws at the international level, the Law Commission noted the 'very cautious approach' of UNECE in relation to the approval regulation for remote control parking, including the low range and low speeds for permitted use, the requirement for automatic obstacle detection and braking[93].

For 'beyond line-of-sight' systems, however, the Law Commission identified particular safety concerns including the possibility of delay in transmission of information to the remote driver from the vehicle, or entire breakdown of that connectivity[94].

In the short term, especially in relation to testing of prototype vehicles using a beyond line-of-sight driver, the Law Commission's view was that 'all those who use remote beyond line-of-sight driving should be required to demonstrate that their system is safe and obtain a VSO [Vehicle Special Order]' (see Chapter 3, 'Testing'). In the longer term, the Law Commission advised the government by new primary legislation to introduce 'a licensing scheme to promote safety and shift responsibility to the organisation behind remote driving'.

How future ADAS might affect the standard of care: a lesson from cruise control?

4.18   British case law on civil liability has not yet treated the use of any advanced driver assistance system as altering the driver's standard of care in law.

There is, however, some case law in relation to a long-established and familiar driver assistance system: cruise control.

Cruise control was invented in the 1950s, came into widespread use initially in the USA after the fuel shortage crises of the early 1970s and has been a feature of conventional vehicles since (both in internal combustion engine-propelled and, more recently, electric vehicles)[95].

No test has been articulated by the courts of England and Wales as to what constitutes negligent driving when using cruise control.

Some clues as to a test are, however, provided by reported criminal cases relating to sentencing.

In *R v Brian France*[96], an appeal against sentence for six counts of causing death by dangerous driving, by a lorry driver who had collided with stationary vehicles, there was evidence both that cruise control had been engaged at just over the maximum permitted speed (by police examination of the tachograph and cruise control) and (on the basis of eye-witness evidence and the presence of documents in the cab) that the appellant had been reading documents while driving and appeared tired.

---

91   SI 2003/1998. See Chapter 3, 'Testing'.
92   Remote Driving: Advice to Government (the Law Commission, February 2023) p 34, 3.61.
93   Ibid, p 34, 3.65 and p 35, 3.67.
94   Ibid, p 34, 3.62.
95   See the 'History' appendix to this book for a fuller account of cruise control.
96   [2002] EWCA Crim 1419; [2003] 1 Cr App R (S) 25

The Court of Appeal Criminal Division set out the reasoning of the sentencing judge as to the use of cruise control as follows (italics added):

'He [the judge] said that over a protracted distance and time the appellant had displayed an indifference to exercising the degree of control which any driver should exert over his vehicle and a consequent criminal disregard to the safety of others. He had been in negligible control of his vehicle because of a combination of factors exclusively within his control. It was not an offence to set the cruise control to the maximum possible speed, but to do so called for *a corresponding degree of vigilance in the steering and braking of the vehicle.*'[97]

The Court of Appeal said of the degree of the appellant's responsibility that:

'Continuing to drive while fighting off sleep is one thing. A driver may be optimistic (with or without justification) that his fight will be successful. Reading documents while driving on cruise control is another matter. It is a *deliberate, not simply a negligent, removal of one's attention from driving.*'[98]

That is a point directed at sentencing, not at the underlying question of criminal liability. But the phrase 'deliberate removal of one's attention from driving' provides an indication of where fault in the use of cruise control might arise, in an ADAS case[99].

In *R v Gareth Jones*[100], another appeal against sentence:

'The appellant was convicted of causing death by careless driving. The appellant was driving his car on a dual carriageway. The car was set on cruise control with the speed set at 70mph. The appellant came up behind a 16-year-old boy who was riding a moped in the same direction as the appellant. The appellant drove into the back of the boy's moped, knocking him from the moped. The boy subsequently died from his injuries.'[101]

The evidence was that the road was straight, long and that the appellant had good visibility of the moped for at least 16 seconds prior to the impact. There was no logical reason why the appellant failed to see the moped.

As in the *R v France* case, the appellant's vehicle had at all times been travelling at 'considerable (albeit legal) speed'[102]. The car was nevertheless under his control, and:

'Taking the otherwise unexplained failure to see the moped over a lengthy period, together with the appellant's unconvincing reaction when asked about the question of sleep[103], the judge was entitled to conclude that lack

---

97   At 113 (para.18).
98   At 119 (para 47). The writer has corrected a spelling error in the report ('optomistic').
99   The position in relation to liability for control of an automated vehicle while it is driving itself is different: see section C of this chapter, below.
100 [2012] EWCA Crim 972; [2013] 1 Cr App R (S) 20.
101 From the headnote to [2013] 1 Cr App R (S) 20.
102 *R v Gareth Jones* (above) at 112 (para 18).
103 This appears to be a reference to the appellant's 'behaviour in seeking wrongly to blame the victim … in a variety of ways for the collision' (112, para.17).

of adequate sleep or rest provided the explanation for what had happened. This being so, it is an aggravating feature of this offence.'[104]

'The bald fact is that the only reasonable conclusion is that the appellant, for a prolonged period at considerable (albeit legal) speed, was not paying attention to what he was doing.'[105]

In *R v Michael Spencer*[106], the appellant lorry driver appealed against sentence after pleading guilty to dangerous driving. He had driven his lorry into a vehicle broken down in the nearside lane of a motorway, which CCTV evidence showed to be displaying hazard lights. The hard shoulder of the motorway was closed due to roadworks. Another lorry had flashed its headlights at the appellant in an attempt to make him aware of the obstruction in the road and moved behind the appellant's lorry, allowing him space to make the evasive manoeuvre. However the appellant had driven his lorry into the stationary vehicle, fatally injuring the driver, Mr Raguckas.

The evidence of the appellant was that he had been driving with cruise control engaged at 50 mph, and this was accepted by the sentencing judge:

'I have come to the firm conclusion that your driving by the use of a cruise control at 50 mph through roadworks when you were fatigued created itself a substantial risk of danger.'[107]

The use of cruise control was argued by the appellant not to be a factor that ought to raise the seriousness of the offence for sentencing purposes:

'He [counsel for the appellant] argues that it would be wrong [to] mark the fact that the appellant was driving on cruise control as a determinative factor since, given the nature of the roadworks and the importance of the tachograph and other considerations, that it was natural for a lorry driver in those circumstances to engage the same. That point made, he nevertheless acknowledges it must be seen in the context of an appellant who was quite clearly tired, driving an HGV, at risk of falling asleep and who had failed to acknowledge and act upon what should be regarded as warnings by a following vehicle.'[108]

The Court of Appeal's judgment does not mention the cruise control point further but it is clear that the argument was rejected as the court came:

'... to the clear conclusion that the judge was entitled to and appropriately weighted a number of features elevate a significant risk of danger into one of substantial risk. That is that this appellant was driving: at a speed which was inappropriate for prevailing conditions, namely at a time when he knew that the hard shoulder was out of use; when he was knowingly deprived of adequate sleep and rest, including from the day before, continued to drive; and, by failing to have regard to a vulnerable road user, namely Mr Raguckas,

---

104 112 to 113 (para.19).
105 112 (para.18).
106 [2016] EWCA Crim 1882.
107 Paras 10 and 14.
108 Para.15.

in his stationary car. We are not persuaded that Mr Raguckas' failure to exit the vehicle should play any part in the sentencing exercise.'[109]

So the caselaw does not clearly define a test for driver's negligence in the use of cruise control.

However, the criminal appeal cases support the position taken in the Highway Code that a driver 'must exercise proper control of your vehicle at all times' and must 'not rely on driver assistance systems'[110]. Setting cruise control to or within the speed limit will not absolve the driver from liability based upon inattention.

Although it is not derived from a case considering the bounds of liability (civil or criminal), the phrase 'deliberate removal of one's attention from driving' provides an indication of where fault might arise in the use of cruise control and, by extension, in the use of an Advanced Driver Assistance System[111].

Furthermore, setting cruise control to 'the maximum possible speed ... called for a corresponding degree of vigilance in the steering and braking of the vehicle'[112].

So it is possible that, as the construction and use of ADAS in vehicles becomes more common, the courts will rule as to how this affects the driver's standard of care. A possible outcome is that the already-demanding standard of care is not altered but is particularised by requiring 'a corresponding degree of vigilance' when using ADAS.

C Laws of Driving Automated Vehicles

The meanings of 'driving' and 'driving itself'/'self-driving' in automated vehicle cases

4.19   As discussed above, the law might develop a different meaning for 'driving' (and, for example, the courts of England and Wales might reform the *MacDonagh* test) in light of experience of more ADAS vehicles and of automated vehicles on the roads.

AEVA 2018, before amendment by the AV Bill 2023-24: 'driving itself'

4.20   The law in relation to automated vehicles, as it stands at the time of writing, is in the Automated and Electric Vehicles Act 2018. AEVA 2018 adds to the phrase to produce a new legal description: 'driving itself'.

An accident occurring when an automated vehicle is 'driving itself' is the essential element of the insurer or permitted uninsured owner's civil liability under AEVA 2018, s 2. The phrase is defined by AEVA 2018, s 8(1)(a):

---

109 Para.17.
110 Highway Code, Rule 150.
111 The position in relation to liability for control of an automated vehicle while it is driving itself is different: see section C of this chapter, below.
112 *R. v France* (above) at 113 (para.18).

'a vehicle is 'driving itself' if it is operating in a mode in which it is not being controlled, and does not need to be monitored, by an individual'

The first part of the *MacDonagh* test for 'driving', derived from *Ames*, is whether the alleged driver 'was in a substantial sense controlling the movement and direction of the car'[113]. So, as the Law Commissions noted,

'The concept of 'control' in the AEV Act covers functions influencing and indicating the vehicle's motion. However, the crucial issue is what it means for an individual not to 'need to monitor' a vehicle.'[114]

The meanings of 'monitor' and 'need to monitor' are not provided by AEVA 2018. The Law Commissions noted, from the most widely-used taxonomy of automated vehicle specifications, SAE J3016[115], that an automated driving system (ADS)[116] 'must monitor the environment and the way that the ADS performs the [Dynamic Driving Task] DDT', which 'consists not only of steering, braking and signalling. It also involves monitoring the driving environment and responding to objects and events'[117].

The Law Commissions noted that the 'great majority of consultees' to its consultation on automated vehicle law:

'agreed that only systems which are safe without the need for human monitoring should be described as 'self-driving' under our authorisation scheme... Furthermore, manufacturers need to know what to aim for if society is to unlock the productivity benefits that can be gained from allowing users to do other things. The law must ensure there is a clear commercial advantage to producing a vehicle that is safe without human monitoring.'[118]

On that basis, the Law Commissions recommended to government:

'that an ADS feature should only be regarded as self-driving if a human is not required to monitor the driving environment, the vehicle or the way that it drives... a user may be required to respond to a clear and timely transition demand. However, the user must not be relied on to respond to events in the absence of a transition demand.'[119]

The Law Commissions considered whether there should be exceptions to that high requirement for an ADS, such as a sudden blowing-out of a tyre or giving way to an emergency vehicle. In contrast to the approach in some other jurisdictions, the

---

113 *Ames v MacLeod,* Lord Justice General (Clyde) at 3; *R v MacDonagh* at 452g (both discussed above).
114 Law Commissions' final AV law report, 'Automated Vehicles: Joint Report', Law Com No 404, Scots Law Com No 258, 25 January 2022 at page 37, 3.12.
115 SAE levels of driving automation (J3016), revised May 2021.
116 Although the abbreviations are similar, an ADS (automated driving system) is distinct from an ADAS (advanced driver assistance system): the former denotes a self-driving vehicle, the latter assistance to a human driver.
117 Law Commissions' final AV law report, 'Automated Vehicles: Joint Report', Law Com No 404, Scots Law Com No 258, 25 January 2022 at pages 37 to 38, 3.13 and 3.15.
118 As above, page 38, 3.17.
119 As above, 3.18.

Law Commissions were clear that this high standard of operating for an ADS should not be diluted:

'In Consultation Paper 3 we expressed 'grave reservations' about all these examples...'

'There is a danger that the list of external circumstances may be based on things the ADS cannot do rather than on things which the user can reasonably respond to when not monitoring the driving environment. Requirements to respond to external circumstances could be used to blame human users for failures within the ADS.'

'In our view, to be classified as self-driving, an ADS feature must meet the criteria prescribed as part of the safety authorisation process. It must be found to be safe enough even if the human user does not intervene in response to any event except a clear and timely transition demand. This does not mean that the ADS feature must be able to deal with absolutely everything. Some events, such as a meteor strike or a plane landing on the motorway, are so unlikely that they do not need to be considered.'

'However, in the early stages of automated driving, there may be many relatively common events which the ADS cannot handle, from floods to emergency vehicles. In these cases, the ADS will need to recognise that it is outside its [operational design domain[120]] ODD and issue a transition demand. An ADS feature should not be considered as self-driving if it relies on a disengaged user-in-charge to notice such events in the absence of a transition demand.'[121]

AEVA 2018 does not provide the regulatory requirements for an ADS capable of monitoring the environment to that extent. The Law Commissions recommended a new Act, a recommendation accepted by the government and announced as the Transport Bill in the Queen's Speech on 10 May 2022[122]. The requirements for approval of an ADS were to become part of the vehicle type approval process[123].

In its August 2022 paper accepting the Law Commissions' recommendations (CAM 2025), the government announced that vehicles would be authorised to self-drive upon certain criteria, to be set out in published National Safety Principles (page 45). Those criteria will 'build on existing work' carried out in relation to the Automated Lane Keeping System (ALKS) which has included the following, 5-part 'monitoring test' (pages 37, 120):

'A vehicle must:

- Comply with relevant road traffic rules

---

120 'Operational design domain (ODD): A term used in the SAE Taxonomy to describe the domain within which an automated driving system can drive itself. It may be limited by geography, time, type of road, weather or by some other criteria.' Glossary to the Law Commissions' final AV law report, 'Automated Vehicles: Joint Report', Law Com No 404, Scots Law Com No 258, 25 January 2022.
121 As above, pages 46 and 47, 3.54 to 3.58.
122 See the government's paper dated 19 August 2022, 'Connected and Automated Mobility 2025' paper (CAM 2025).
123 See Chapter 2 of this book for the law of automated vehicle specifications.

- Avoid collisions which a competent and careful driver could avoid

- Treat other road users with reasonable consideration

- Avoid putting itself in a position where it would be the cause of a collision

- Recognise when it is operating outside of its operational design domain'[124]

On 8 November 2023, the AV Bill 2023-24 was published after its first reading in Parliament as HL Bill 1. It was not a wider 'Transport Bill' and the 'national safety principles' described in CAM 2025 had also been renamed. But the principles of the Bill are essentially those of CAM 2025.

AV Bill 2023-24 (HL Bill 1): satisfying 'the self-driving test'

4.21   Under AV Bill 2023-24 (HL Bill 1), cl 3, the Secretary of State has a power to authorise a road vehicle for use as an automated vehicle, if:

'(a) in the opinion of the Secretary of State, the vehicle satisfies the self-driving test by reference to intended travel on a road (in at least some circumstances), and

(b) any applicable initial authorisation requirements are met (see section 5).'[125]

(That cl 3 authorisation is central also to AEVA 2018, Part 1, as prospectively amended by AV Bill 2023-24, cl 45, Sch 2, para 5 to substitute 'authorised automated vehicle' for 'automated vehicle' in AEVA 2018 (see Text of AV Bill 2023-24 (HL Bill 1) cl 45, Sch 2, para 5 amendments to AEVA 2018 Part 1 in Chapter 6, 'insurance'). AV Bill 2023-24, cl 94 ('general definitions') provides that '"authorised automated vehicle" means a vehicle authorised under section 3' of AVA 2024.)

The 'self-driving test' is defined in the AV Bill 2023-24 (HL Bill 1), cl 1, 'basic concepts':

'...

(2) A vehicle "satisfies the self-driving test" if –

(a) it is designed or adapted with the intention that a feature of the vehicle will allow it to travel autonomously, and

(b) it is capable of doing so, by means of that feature, safely and legally.

(3) Whether a vehicle satisfies the test is to be assessed by reference to the location and circumstances of that intended travel (and may differ in respect of different locations and circumstances).

(4) A "feature" of a vehicle is a combination of mechanical or electronic operations that equipment of the vehicle performs.

(5) A vehicle travels "autonomously" if –

(a) it is being controlled not by an individual but by equipment of the vehicle, and

---

124 'Connected and Automated Mobility 2025' paper (CAM 2025) pages 37 and 120.
125 AV Bill 2023-24 (HL Bill 1), cl 3(1).

(b) neither the vehicle nor its surroundings are being monitored by an individual with a view to immediate intervention in the driving of the vehicle.

(6) References to "control" of a vehicle are to control of the motion of the vehicle.

(7) A vehicle that travels autonomously does so –

(a) "safely" if it travels to an acceptably safe standard, and

(b) "legally" if it travels with an acceptably low risk of committing a traffic infraction.

(8) In assessing whether a vehicle is capable of travelling autonomously and safely, the Secretary of State must have particular regard to the statement of safety principles.'

(The 'interpretation' provision for Part 1 of the AV Bill 2023-24 (HL Bill 1), cl 44, provides that:

'(2) For the purposes of this Part, a vehicle "commits a traffic infraction" if, while an authorised automation feature of the vehicle is engaged, the vehicle does anything that would, were an individual in control of it –

(a) amount to the commission of an offence by that individual, or

(b) cause a person to become liable to a penalty charge under an enactment relating to road traffic.

(3) For the purposes of subsection (2)(a), it is to be assumed that nothing can be proved about the mental state of the notional individual.')

The 'statement of safety principles' is governed by the AV Bill 2023–24 (HL Bill 1)cl 2, (1) to (4) of which provide that

'(1) The Secretary of State must prepare a statement of the principles that the Secretary of State proposes to apply in assessing, for the purposes of this Part, whether a vehicle is capable of travelling autonomously and safely.

(2) The principles must be framed with a view to securing that road safety in Great Britain will be better as a result of the use of authorised automated vehicles on roads than it would otherwise be.

(3) In preparing the statement, the Secretary of State must consult such representative organisations as the Secretary of State thinks fit.

(4) The prepared statement must be laid before Parliament...'

The AV Bill 2023-24 (HL Bill 1), cl 2(6) to (8) allow for the statement to take effect 'at the end of the period of 40 days beginning with the day on which it is laid, unless either House resolves before then that the statement should not take effect' and for the timescale in the events of statements being laid before different Houses of Parliament on different days and negative resolution(s). As at the time of writing, no statement of safety principles has yet been laid before Parliament. Under cl 2(9), 'The power in section 3 may not be exercised until a statement has effect under this section'.

Although, as at the time of writing, the statement of safety principles to which the Secretary of State must have regard (cl 1(8)) when applying the 'safe travel' element of the self-driving test (cll 1(7)(a), 2(b), 1(8)) have yet to be published, it is clear from the language of the clauses above that the standard of driving required of an automated vehicle under the AV Bill 2023-24 (HL Bill 1) would not be an absolute standard. In particular:

- Clause 1(7)(a) defines autonomous travel as happening 'safely' if the AV 'travels to an acceptably safe standard' (and 'legally' in cl 1(7)(b) is similarly qualified).

- The statement of safety principles is not required to stipulate a higher standard, eg. that no automated vehicle will cause injury. Clause 2(2) instead requires the safety principles to be 'framed with a view to securing that road safety in Great Britain will be better as a result of the use of authorised automated vehicles on roads than it would otherwise be'.

Not imposing an absolute standard of care upon an automated vehicle would be consistent with the common law principles discussed in the 'outline' section above.

In what terms the statement of safety principles will describe an automated vehicle's standard of care is unknown, pending sight of the document. However, the Law Commissions' recommendation, accepted by government in its CAM 2025 paper, was that

'self-driving vehicles should be held to the same standard of behaviour as that expected of human drivers; competent and careful. This standard is higher than that of the average human driver – which includes, for example, drivers who are fatigued, distracted or under the influence of drink or drugs.'[126]

That is the standard applied to a human in some criminal offences proposed in the AV Bill:

- 'the standard that could reasonably be expected of a careful and competent driver' is the standard which a human driver (the 'user-in-charge' during operation of the automated system: cl 46) of a UIC automated vehicle must reach to have the immunity from criminal liability for an offence which 'results from something done by the vehicle while the individual was its user-in-charge' (cl 47(3)); and

- 'it would have been obvious to a competent and careful user of the vehicle, at the moment when the authorised user-in-charge feature in question was engaged, that the current state of the vehicle would make it dangerous to use it in the way in which it is being used' is the mental element of the offence of using an automated vehicle in a dangerous state (cl 54(1), the proposed new offence at RTA 1988, s 3C(1)(c)).

The context of discussing the standard of care applicable to a vehicle is important: the AV Bill provisions above go to an automated vehicle's authorisation by the Secretary of State for use on a road. The standard of care applicable to civil liability might attach to a vehicle's driving for the purpose of assessing its negligence as compared to that of a claimant, for the purpose of assessing contributory negligence

---

126 'Connected and Automated Mobility 2025' paper (CAM 2025) UK government, 19 August 2022, page 35.

in an AEVA 2018 claim pursuant to AEVA 2018, s 3(1) ('whatever reduction ... would apply ... against a person...'[127]).

The transition of control of an automated vehicle between vehicle and human

4.22   Engineering and law meet in the question of how to fix in time the moment at which human control of a vehicle ceases, and automated control begins (and vice versa). The United Nations, the Law Commissions and the writers of engineering standards have grappled with the problem.

As to the passing of control from human to vehicle, AEVA 2018, s 3(2) provides for the potential extinction of a civil claim:

> "The insurer or owner of an [authorised[128]] automated vehicle is not liable under section 2 to the person in charge of the vehicle where the accident that it caused was wholly due to the person's negligence in allowing the vehicle to begin driving itself when it was not appropriate to do so.'

The passing back of control from car to human has taken more consideration, due to the danger of loss of human concentration and the need for warning signals – a 'transition demand' – from the vehicle to the human, to the effect that the machine has reached the limit of its capability and must yield control to the human. The Law Commissions have recommended, in summary: (a) that a rigorous authorisation scheme (see Chapter 2) ensures that this is a rare occurrence and that transition demands are reliable and safe; and (b) that the human user of an automated vehicle accordingly has immunity, up to the end of the 'transition period' during which the human driver can resume control, from liabilities arising from automated driving. Fixing the moment at which the transition period and the human immunities from liability end is therefore a key issue.

Fixing the moment of an occurrence is, however, notoriously difficult. As a forensic matter, even in a conventional road traffic collision case the moment at which driving goes wrong can be obscured by gaps in evidence, or by the clash of many evidential pieces. In civil cases, the balance of probabilities can assist, but with the birth of an alternative and to a claimant likely preferred legal basis of claim – AEVA 2018, s 2, with its stricter liability structure – the civil liability consequences of forensic doubt become greater.

Added to this is the resistance in English and Welsh legal culture to founding liability upon an omission. In driving cases to date, the courts have avoided the difficulty pragmatically by declaring all omissions (to brake etc) to be within the activity of driving. But can that be said of a failure to resume control, when the human user in charge is not driving (and not required to do so) when the vehicle asks them to resume control?

---

127 See the discussion of contributory negligence and an automated vehicle's standard of care, below.
128 Proposed amendment by AV Bill 2023-24 (HL Bill 1), cl 45, Sch 2, para 5(3)(b).

The AV Bill 2023-24 (HL Bill 1) codifies the transition of control, starting at cl 46 with the definition of a 'user-in-charge' of a vehicle, a role different from 'driver', taken on:

> '... if—
>
> (a) the vehicle is an authorised automated vehicle with an authorised user-in-charge feature,
>
> (b) that feature is engaged, and
>
> (c) the individual is in, and in position to exercise control of, the vehicle, but is not controlling it.'

The user-in-charge has immunity in criminal law under the AV Bill

> '... if the act that would constitute the offence—
>
> (a) results from something done by the vehicle while the individual was its user-in-charge, and
>
> (b) does not also result from the individual's conduct after ceasing to be the user-in-charge falling below the standard that could reasonably be expected of a careful and competent driver in the circumstances.' (cl 47(3))

The explanatory notes to the AV Bill 2023-24 (HL Bill 1) state that:

> 'Where a vehicle has been authorised for use as self-driving, it has been deemed capable of safely and lawfully driving itself without the need for human monitoring of the road environment with a view to safety critical intervention. If the vehicle was authorised for use with a user in charge (who must be within the vehicle and in a position to control it, hold a valid driving license and remain in a fit state to drive), it is appropriate to ensure that the user in charge is not held responsible for the behaviour of the vehicle when it is driving itself – particularly as there are many strict liability offences relating to how the vehicle behaves on the road.'[129]

There are exceptions to the immunity in cl 48, summarised by the explanatory notes:

> Under cl 48(1), ' ... the user-in-charge immunity ceases to apply when the period for responding to a valid transition demand issued by the vehicle expires', although under cl 48(2) 'the driver will not be liable if the vehicle does not behave in accordance with agreed authorisation requirements regarding how it will handle situations where the user-in-charge does not take control within the transition period. The subsection clarifies that the cessation of the immunity following a transition demand does not apply if the act causing the offence is committed by the vehicle behaving unpredictably and in breach of agreed authorisation requirements.'
>
> Under cl 48(3), 'the immunity does not apply in relation to parking offences or offences arising from the position where the vehicle is stopped or left

---

129 Explanatory note to AV Bill 2023-24 (HL Bill 1 – EN) para 221.

stationary where the user in charge has voluntarily left the vehicle. This clarifies that it is the user-in-charge's responsibility upon leaving the vehicle to ensure that it is parked or stopped lawfully.'

Under cl 48(4), 'the immunity does not apply in relation to offences arising from the vehicle's entering or remaining on a particular road or other area without a required toll or charge being paid. This clarifies that the user-in-charge will need to verify whether the route followed incurs any toll or charges.'

Under cl 48(5) and (6) the immunity 'does not apply to an offence that has arisen when the vehicle is driving itself outside of an authorised location or circumstance due to deliberate interference with vehicle equipment by the user-in-charge, or another person where the user-in-charge knows of the interference. This is to prevent tampering with vehicle equipment to enable use of the self-driving technology in inappropriate and potentially unsafe circumstances.'[130]

In civil liability law, the statutory claim under AEVA 2018, s 2, as proposed to be amended by the AV Bill 2023-24 (HL Bill 1), cl 45, Sch 2, para 5, will require judges to examine the terms of authorisation of the automated feature in the cases before them to determine disputes on transition of control. AEVA 2018 s 8(1), as proposed to be amended by the AV Bill 2023-24, would read (with the amendments shown):

'(1   For the purposes of this Part [AEVA 2018, Part 1] –

(a)   an authorised automated vehicle is "driving itself" if it is travelling while an authorised automation feature of the vehicle is engaged;

...

(1A) Section 44(5) of the Automated Vehicles Act 2024 (authorisation to determine when feature "engaged" or "disengaged") applies for the purposes of subsection (1)(a) as it applies for the purposes of Part 1 of that Act.'

The AV Bill 2023-24 (HL Bill 1), cl 44(5) provides that:

'Any question arising under this Part [AV Bill 2023-24 Part 1] as to whether an authorised automation feature is "engaged" or "disengaged" is to be determined in accordance with what is specified or described under section 4(3)(b).'

And cl 4(3)(b) provides that:

'In relation to each feature identified in the authorisation, the authorisation must specify—

...

(b)   how the feature is engaged and disengaged'

The application of those principles will be left to the courts to determine. The scheme poses questions for the judge: was the user-in-charge feature of the vehicle

---

130   As above, paras 223-227.

engaged, according to the requirements of its authorisation by the Secretary of State? There are several situations defined in the Bill as to when the immunity will and will not apply: did any of those situations apply to the case before the court?

The presumption that the person in the driver's seat is the driver, in an automated vehicle case

4.23   This relates to the 'obvious and irresistible inference' that the person in the driving seat is driving (*Hill v Baxter*[131]).

The AV Bill 2023-24 (HL Bill 1), cll 46 and 49 deal, in the context of criminal liability for vehicle use (the scope of Part 2 of the Bill) with the presumptive driver of a 'user-in-charge' automated vehicle:

Cause 46 defines 'user-in-charge':

'46 Meaning of "user-in-charge"

An individual is the "user-in-charge" of a vehicle if –

(a) the vehicle is an authorised automated vehicle with an authorised user-in-charge feature,

(b) that feature is engaged, and

(c) the individual is in, and in position to exercise control of, the vehicle, but is not controlling it.'

Clause 49 deems the user-in-charge of a vehicle to be liable as the 'driver' of that vehicle for the purpose of any enactment, and provides for that to be the case even if the UIC moves within the vehicle, absent a change in control:

'49 User-in-charge otherwise liable as driver

(1) The user-in-charge of a vehicle is to be taken for the purposes of any enactment to be the driver of, and driving, the vehicle.

(2) Subsection (1) –

(a) does mean that (subject to section 47[132]) an enactment applies to the user-in-charge as it would apply to a driver who acted in the same way as the user-in-charge in fact acts, but

(b) does not mean that any particular behaviour of the vehicle is to be treated as brought about by the user-in-charge when it is not in fact so brought about.

(3) If an individual is for a time the user-in-charge of a vehicle but moves so as no longer to be in position to control the vehicle, this section continues to apply to the individual as it applies to a user-in-charge until –

---

131 *Hill v Baxter* [1958] 1 QB 277 (discussed above).
132 Clause 47 'introduces an immunity from offences arising from how a vehicle drives itself for the user-in-charge, or where the vehicle hands back control to the driver in a situation where careful and competent driving could not have avoided an offence being committed …': explanatory note to AV Bill 2023-24 (HL Bill 1 – EN) para 220.

(a) another individual becomes the user-in-charge of the vehicle or takes control of it, or

(b) the authorised user-in-charge feature is disengaged.'

More than one driver, in an automated vehicle case

4.24   In an automated vehicle case, the provisions of AEVA 2018 and of the AV Bill 2023-24 (see above) point to singularity of driving at any one moment: the vehicle is either being driven by the human driver or the vehicle is driving itself.

That does not necessarily mean that an AV could only ever have one driver, as it is conceivable (for example in a misadventure type of case: see *Tyler v Whatmore*, above) that more than one human might have control of the vehicle at the relevant moment.

Remote driving used in tests of prototype automated vehicles

4.25   Where remote driving is used for testing prototype vehicles, the law is currently as set out in the Road Vehicles (Authorisation of Special Types) (General) Order 2003 and government guidance, as discussed in Chapter 3, 'testing'.

Regulating use of built-in screen in an automated vehicle

4.26   In accordance with the position that the driver of an automated vehicle may watch non-driving related material on an in-built screen while the vehicle is driving itself, the Road Vehicles (Construction and Use) Regulations 1986, reg 109(1) has already been amended to permit a driver 'to see … information … of any sort…' displayed on a built-in screen in an automated vehicle driving itself within the meaning of the AEVA 2018, s 8(1)(a) and providing that the vehicle is not requesting the driver to take back control[133].

Contributory negligence and the automated vehicle's standard of care

4.27   In August 2022, the British government accepted the recommendation of the Law Commission of England and Wales and the Scottish Law Commission that the conduct of a self-driving vehicle should be held to the same standard of civil and criminal liability as would apply in law to a human driver:

'self-driving vehicles should be held to the same standard of behaviour as that expected of human drivers; competent and careful. This standard is higher than that of the average human driver – which includes, for example, drivers who are fatigued, distracted or under the influence of drink or drugs.'[134]

---

133 Article 3 of the Road Vehicles (Construction and Use) (Automated Vehicles) Order 2022, SI 2022/470 (in force from 1 July 2022).

134 'Connected and Automated Mobility 2025' paper (CAM 2025) UK government, 19 August 2022, page 35.

The issue of the *vehicle's* standard of care is not merely theoretical. It is a matter relevant to pre-deployment approval of an automated driving system as safe for use[135]. It also arises under the contributory negligence provision of AEVA 2018.

AEVA 2018, s 3(1) addresses the assessment of comparative fault in an AEVA 2018 civil claim for damages where the injured party has to any extent caused the accident or the damage resulting from it.

The exercise of assessing contributory negligence involves considering 'the claimant's share of the responsibility for the damage' to reach a reduction in the claimant's recoverable damages 'to such extent as the court thinks just and equitable'[136]. 'This involves a consideration, not only of the causative potency of a particular factor, but also of its blameworthiness.'[137]

Considering the share of the claimant's responsibility is a comparative exercise, which involves considering the responsibility of other actor(s). In an AEVA 2018 claim, one of the actors is the automated vehicle.

AEVA 2018, s 3(1) provides that:

'(1) Where—

(a) an insurer or vehicle owner is liable under section 2 to a person ('the injured party') in respect of an accident, and

(b) the accident, or the damage resulting from it, was to any extent caused by the injured party,

the amount of the liability is subject to whatever reduction under the Law Reform (Contributory Negligence) Act 1945 would apply to a claim in respect of the accident brought by the injured party against a person other than the insurer or vehicle owner.'

The language of AEVA 2018, s 3(1)(b) is not easy to interpret, but it appears to describe a fictional comparator, whose behaviour stands in place of the behaviour of the automated vehicle.

For the purpose of assessing contributory negligence, AEVA 2018, s 6(3) creates (by the phrase 'as if') the legal fiction[138] that 'the behaviour of the automated vehicle were the fault of the person made liable for the damage by section 2 of this Act', presumably with the intention of making the insurer or permitted uninsured owner vicariously liable for the vehicle's fault. The phrase 'a person other than the insurer or vehicle owner' in AEVA 2018, s 3(1) might be intended to emphasise that this is a legal fiction (AEVA 2018, s 6(3)) and that the comparator is not the insurer or owner but a notional human driver standing in place of the automated vehicle.

---

135 See Chapter 2 'the law of AAEV specifications'.

136 Law Reform (Contributory Negligence) Act 1945, s 1(1).

137 *Davies v Swan Motor Company (Swansea) Ltd* [1949] 2 KB 291, 326, Denning LJ (as he then was).

138 AEVA 2018, s 6(3) [with AV Bill 2023-24 (HL Bill 1), cl 45, Sch 2, para 5 addition in square brackets] reads: 'For the purposes of section 3(1), the Law Reform (Contributory Negligence) Act 1945 and section 5 of the Fatal Accidents Act 1976 (contributory negligence) have effect as if the behaviour of the [authorised] automated vehicle were the fault of the person made liable for the damage by section 2 of this Act.'

The Law Commissions fairly criticised the clarity of the language of AEVA 2018, s 3 in their first consultation paper:

'The provisions require the reader to imagine two counter-factual situations: first, that the claim is brought against someone other than the insurer, and secondly that the insurer is at fault because of the behaviour of the automated vehicle. The combined effect of these provisions can be quite difficult to follow.'[139]

An interpretation of the sections might be that, in effect, ss 3(1) and 6(3) together:

- treat the automated vehicle as if it was a human driver, for the purpose of assessing contributory negligence (ie. comparative fault) under the 1945 Act and

- make the insurer or owner vicariously liable for whatever part of the fault is thereby attributed to the automated vehicle.

This interpretation would be consistent with the government's acceptance of the Law Commissions recommendation that automated vehicles be subject to the same standard of care as a human driver[140].

D Laws of Driving and Riding Electric Vehicles

E-scooters

4.28   An e-scooter is a 'motor vehicle' within RTA 1988, s 185[141]. In particular, the government classifies it as a moped[142]. Consequently, riding (which amounts to driving, provided that the ordinary meaning of the word 'driving' is also met in any particular case[143]) an e-scooter is subject to the requirements and penalties provided by RTA 1988 (including those relating to third party compulsory motor insurance[144] and requiring a driving licence[145]).

As at the time of writing, e-scooters may be used lawfully on public roads without full compliance with licensing, insurance and other requirements only in identified trial areas[146].

---

139 *Automated Vehicles: a joint preliminary consultation paper*, Law Commission Consultation Paper 240, Scottish Law Commission Discussion Paper 166, November 2018, at page 107, 6.36; repeated in the Law Commissions' final AV law report, 'Automated Vehicles: Joint Report', Law Com No 404, Scots Law Com No 258, 25 January 2022 at page 243, 13.15.

140 'Connected and Automated Mobility 2025' paper (CAM 2025) page 35, and see discussion of AV Bill 2023-24 and the standard of care above.

141 *DPP v King* [2008] EWHC 447 (Admin).

142 In an answer to a parliamentary question on 23 June 2022, the Department for Transport particularised an e-scooter as a moped: 'As motor vehicles having fewer than 4 wheels and weighing less than 410 kg unladen, e-scooters are classed as motorcycles as defined in Section 185 of the Road Traffic Act 1988 and, because of their low speed, within the subclass of moped'.

143 *McKoen v Ellis* [1987] RTR 26 (QB).

144 See the Insurance chapter of this book.

145 RTA 1988, s 87, 'drivers of motor vehicles to have driving licences'; Gov.uk: e-scooter trials guidance for users – registration-plates and vehicle excise duty, updated 31 March 2022

146 Electric Scooter Trials and Traffic Signs (Coronavirus) Regulations and General Directions 2020, SI 2020/663.

The purpose of temporarily loosening the law for public use of e-scooters in trial areas was to assess the suitability of e-scooters for permanent use on roads, and the appropriate regulations[147]. The details of future regulation – including the form of future liability insurance for e-scooters – have yet to be revealed in a Transport Bill such as that announced in the Queen's Speech on 10 May 2022 but then postponed[148]. No broader Transport Bill than the AV Bill 2023-24 appeared in the King's Speech in November 2023.

As the law stands, the use on public roads of all e-scooters (being 'motor vehicles') must be insured. But trial e-scooters are liberated from some other requirements: privately-owned e-scooters must be licensed and registered, whereas trial e-scooters are not subject to registration or licensing requirements[149].

The government announced in May 2022 that it intended to legalise the use of e-scooters on roads and other public places. This was elaborated in parliamentary debate following the 2022 Queen's Speech:

'…it is our intention that the Bill will create a low-speed, zero-emission vehicle category that is independent from the cycle and motor vehicle categories. New powers would allow the Government to decide the vehicles that fall into this new category in future and how they should be regulated to make sure that they are safe to use. We hope that e-scooters will be the first of these vehicles.'[150]

However, the timescale for bringing the proposed scheme into force was extended. E-scooter trials were due to end on 30 November 2022[151] but in an answer to a parliamentary question on 6 July 2022 the Department for Transport stated its preference for an 18-month extension of the trials:

'The Government has decided to allow current e-scooter trials, which are live in 30 areas across England, to be extended. The existing trials will continue to run until 30 November and participating local authorities will then have the option to end their local trial or extend it to 31 May 2024. Extensions will be restricted to existing trial areas only and will allow us to gather further evidence where gaps are identified, building on the findings of the current

---

147 Explanatory note to SI 2020/663.
148 See debate on day after the Queen's Speech, Baroness Vere, House of Lords Hansard Volume 822, columns 30 to 31, 11 May 2022. As noted above, the Transport Bill will no longer proceed during the 2022–23 parliamentary session (Secretary of State for Transport to House of Commons Transport Select Committee, 7 December 2022).
149 An electric vehicle is exempt from excise duty but must have a nil licence (unless it is an invalid carriage or a vehicle used by a disabled person). Upon a nil licence being granted it must be registered by the Secretary of State (VERA 1994, s 21). See Vehicle Excise and Registration Act 1994 (VERA 1994) and Road Vehicle (Registration and Licensing) Regulations 2002, as amended. The exception for electric scooters only applies to 'an electric scooter being used in a trial'. See Road Vehicle (Registration and Licensing) Regulations 2002, reg 4(2A)as amended by Electric Scooter Trials and Traffic Signs (Coronavirus) Regulations and General Directions 2020, reg 2(3); Gov.uk: e-scooter trials guidance for users – registration-plates and vehicle excise duty, updated 31 March 2022.
150 Baroness Vere, House of Lords Hansard Volume 822, columns 30 to 31, 11 May 2022.
151 Gov.uk: e-scooter trials: guidance for local authorities and rental operators, updated 22 February 2022.

evaluation. We hope that all areas will want to continue, but there is no compulsion.'[152]

E-bikes

4.29   E-bikes (or 'electrically assisted pedal cycles', as RTA 1988 labels them) are excluded from the definition 'motor vehicle' by RTA 1988, s 189(1)(c) and the Electrically Assisted Pedal Cycles Regulations 1983[153], reg 3 of which provides that

'The class of electrically assisted pedal cycles prescribed for the purposes of … section 189 of the Road Traffic Act 1988 consists of pedal cycles with two or more wheels which comply with the requirements specified in Regulation 4 below.'

Regulation 4 of the EAPC Regulations includes requirements

'that the vehicle shall: – …

(b) be fitted with pedals by means of which it is capable of being propelled; and

(c) be fitted with no motor other than an electric motor which –

(i)   has a maximum continuous rated power which does not exceed 250 watts;

(ii) cannot propel the vehicle when it is travelling at more than 15.5 miles per hour.'

The exception for EAPCs from the insurance requirement of RTA 1988, Part VI cannot be obtained by cosmetic means. The requirement of pedals 'by means of which [the EAPC] is capable of being propelled' is tested by an objective standard.

In *Winter v DPP*[154], exemption from the third party compulsory insurance requirement had been attempted by the installation of largely ineffective pedals to an electric tricycle. Michael Supperstone QC, sitting as a Deputy High Court Judge[155], interpreted:

'the words 'fitted with pedals by means of which it is capable of being propelled' as meaning that the vehicle is 'reasonably capable of being propelled' by the pedals'

While this means that an EAPC which falls objectively within its regulatory definition will not be subject to the same requirements applicable to a 'motor vehicle' under RTA 1988 (including but not limited to third party compulsory motor insurance relating to its use on public roads), that is not to say that the rider of an EAPC will be immune from all criminal and civil liabilities, whether under the 1988 Act or otherwise.

---

152 DfT answer 6 July 2022 to parliamentary question by Gill Furniss MP 1 July 2022, UIN 28907.
153 'The EAPC Regulations', SI 1983/1168, as amended by the Electrically Assisted Pedal Cycles (Amendment) Regulations 2015, SI 2015/24.
154 *Winter v DPP* [2002] EWHC 1524 (Admin).
155 Later Mr Justice Supperstone.

Riding amounts to driving, provided that the ordinary meaning of the word 'driving' is also met in any particular case[156] and an EAPC is a 'mechanically propelled vehicle'[157]. So, for example, an EAPC rider is subject to the offence of driving or being in charge of a mechanically propelled vehicle when under the influence of drink or drugs under RTA 1988, s 4.

Powered wheelchairs and mobility scooters

4.30   The 'motor vehicle' definition in RTA 1988, s 185 is:

''*motor vehicle*' means, subject to section 20 of the Chronically Sick and Disabled Persons Act 1970 (which makes special provision about invalid carriages, within the meaning of that Act), a mechanically propelled vehicle intended or adapted for use on roads'[158]

The Chronically Sick and Disabled Persons Act 1970, s 20 provides as follows:

'20 Use of invalid carriages on highways

(1) In the case of a vehicle which is an invalid carriage complying with the prescribed requirements and which is being used in accordance with the prescribed conditions—

  (a) no statutory provision prohibiting or restricting the use of footways shall prohibit or restrict the use of that vehicle on a footway;

  (b) if the vehicle is mechanically propelled, it shall be treated for the purposes of the Road Traffic Regulation Act 1984 and the Road Traffic Act 1988, except section 22A of that Act (causing danger to road users by interfering with motor vehicles etc), and the Road Traffic Offenders Act 1988 as not being a motor vehicle and sections 1 to 4 [certain driving offences], 21 [prohibition of use on cycle tracks], 34 [prohibition of driving elsewhere than roads], 163 [power of police to stop vehicles], 170 [duty of driver to stop, report accident and give information or documents] and 181[general provisions as to accident inquiries by Secretary of State] of the Road Traffic Act 1988 shall not apply to it; and

  (c) whether or not the vehicle is mechanically propelled, it shall be exempted from the requirements of the section 83 of the Road Traffic Act 1988 [offences to do with reflectors and tail lamps].

(2) In this section—

    …

    '*invalid carriage*' means a vehicle, whether mechanically propelled or not, constructed or adapted for use for the carriage of one person, being a person suffering from some physical defect or disability;'

RTA 1988, s 185 also defines 'invalid carriage':

---

156 *McKoen v Ellis* [1987] RTR 26 (QB).
157 *Elieson v Parker* (1917) 81 JP 265 (electrically powered vehicle is 'mechanically propelled').
158 RTA 1988, s 185(1).

''*invalid carriage*' means a mechanically propelled vehicle the weight of which unladen does not exceed 254 kilograms and which is specially designed and constructed, and not merely adapted, for the use of a person suffering from some physical defect or disability and is used solely by such a person'[159]

The Highway Code provides guidance on the use of powered wheelchairs and mobility scooters at rules 36 to 46. Rule 36 describes the classes of wheelchairs and mobility scooters:

'There is one class of manual wheelchair (called a Class 1 invalid carriage) and two classes of powered wheelchairs and powered mobility scooters. Manual wheelchairs and Class 2 vehicles are those with an upper speed limit of 4 mph (6 km/h) and are designed to be used on pavements. Class 3 vehicles are those with an upper speed limit of 8 mph (12 km/h) and are equipped to be used on the road as well as the pavement.'

Rule 37 provides that:

'When you are on the road you should obey the guidance and rules for other vehicles; when on the pavement you should follow the guidance and rules for pedestrians.'

Rules 38 to 40 provide guidance on use of powered wheelchairs and use of mobility scooters on pavements and rules 41 to 46 on roads.

---

159 As above.

Chapter 5

The law of passenger services and public transport

'In contrast to mass transit, in Chicago and in all American cities the private passenger car was massively subsidised by publicly funded street improvements to accommodate automobile traffic ... Providing the automobile an infrastructure of vastly improved city streets was not cost-effective in comparison with what it would have cost to provide excellent urban mass transit.' [1]

(James J. Flink, describing urban planning in US cities
from the early twentieth century)

'... our commercial men must be brought to see that there are great personal and public values in civic improvement, and they must learn from cities like Chicago, where commercial opinion is one of the chief factors in this class of reform, that there is an important work for them to do'[2]

(William Haywood, The Development of Birmingham: an Essay, 1918)

'Mass transit must remain fundamental to an efficient transport system.'[3]

(The UK government's fourth strategic principle for transport, 2019)

---

1 Flink, *The Automobile Age* (MIT Press, first paperback edition 1990, sixth printing 2001), pp.363 and 364.
2 Haywood, *The Development of Birmingham: an Essay* (Kynoch Ltd, Birmingham, 1918), p.101. See a digitised version of a copy held by the library of the University of California Los Angeles at https://openlibrary.org/works/OL210907W/The_ development_of_ Birmingham. The book (which went to a print run of 250) includes illustrations of Haywood's plans for the re-development of Birmingham and an introduction by Neville Chamberlain (later Prime Minister). William Haywood was an architect, the first secretary of the Birmingham Civic Society and special lecturer on town planning at the University of Birmingham, a post which he held for 25 years. See the Birmingham Civic Society's commemoration of William Haywood on its website.
3 Department for Transport, 'Future of Mobility: Urban Strategy – moving Britain ahead', March 2019, p 39; repeated in Department for Transport, 'Bus Back Better: National Bus Strategy for England', March 2021, p 51.

Chapter Contents

A Outline of the Laws of Passenger Services and Public Transport

Historical influences on laws of passenger services and public transport

5.01 The laws affecting passenger services and public transport have been formed by technological developments (from the internal combustion engine to electronics), by political and commercial decisions and by worldwide events including two world wars and a recent pandemic.

As the Law Commissions have noted, the result is a jagged regulatory landscape:

'current regulation is highly fragmented, with separate systems for taxis, private hire vehicles and public service vehicles… At one time, the distinctions reflected genuine market differences between a taxi, 'minicab' and bus. However, as the Government comments, 'traditional modal divisions, for instance between buses and taxis, are blurring'. These distinctions may disappear altogether in an automated environment.'[4]

The summary of responses to the government's Future of Transport Regulatory Review in 2020 described

'a dominant view from stakeholders that the regulatory framework for taxis, PHV [private hire vehicles] and buses is outdated. A siloed approach was no longer seen as appropriate, with a wide call for a consensus of standards across different types of passenger transport. Stakeholders were critical of historic regulatory distinctions based on the size of the vehicle rather than the purpose of service. The need for more flexibility was a key theme, both in the licensing framework and in the way that vehicles are used.'[5]

---

4   Automated Vehicles: Consultation Paper 2 on Passenger Services and Public Transport – a joint consultation paper (Law Commission of England and Wales Consultation Paper No 245, Scottish Law Commission Discussion Paper No 169, 16 October 2019) (the second of the Law Commissions' papers on automated vehicle law, so cited below as 'Law Commissions' second AV law consultation paper (October 2019)'), p.39, 3.9.
5   Summary of responses to the Future of Transport Regulatory Review (October 2020), pp 49 and 50.

While that view favoured wholesale reform, the courts were required to deal with the laws of passenger services as they stood. In 2022 the Court of Appeal confirmed that the concept of 'plying for hire', which has applied to the regulation of taxis since the 18th century, remains effective when applied to smartphone booking Apps[6].

But automated vehicle law is set to take the reforming route: the Automated Vehicles Bill 2023-24 (HL Bill 1), Part 5 ('permits for automated passenger services'), cl 83 provides for the 'Disapplication of taxi, private hire vehicle and bus legislation'.

Current overarching definition of 'public service vehicle' in law

5.02   The current, overarching definition of 'public service vehicle' involves three main characteristics: the number of passengers which the vehicle is designed to carry, whether the vehicle is used for carrying passengers 'for hire or reward' and the payment of separate fares by each passenger.

The definition is the Public Passenger Vehicles Act 1981 (PPVA 1981), s 1. The core of the definition of public service vehicle is as follows:

'(1) Subject to the provisions of this section, in this Act 'public service vehicle' means a motor vehicle (other than a tramcar) which –

(a) being a vehicle adapted to carry more than eight passengers, is used for carrying passengers for hire or reward[7]; or

(b) being a vehicle not so adapted, is used for carrying passengers for hire or reward at separate fares[8] in the course of a business of carrying passengers.'

Falling within the statutory definition of a public service vehicle (PSV) carries duties. For example, under PPVA 1981, s 12, a 'public service vehicle shall not be used on a road for carrying passengers for hire or reward except under a PSV operator's licence granted in accordance with the following provisions' of Part II of the Act.

However, the PPVA 1981, s 1 definition and the regulatory processes under the Act are subject to numerous qualifications and exceptions, which for reasons of space and relevance are not explored in detail in this book[9]. The modifications are part of the regulation's evolution, as the s 1 definition required some qualification to remain practically useful to passengers. As the leading work on road traffic offences observes,

---

6   *R (United Trade Action Group Ltd) v Transport for London* ('the *UTAG* case') [2022] EWCA Civ 1026; [2022] RTR 32.

7   The 'business test' of 'for hire and reward' is 'has there been a systematic carrying of passengers for reward which goes beyond the bounds of mere social kindness?': *Albert v Motor Insurers' Bureau* [1972] AC 301 (HL), 319c (Lord Donovan).

8   See *Wilkinson's Road Traffic Offences* (30th edition), Ch 13 for a detailed discussion. Wilkinson's notes (at 13-38) that the cases cited there in relation to the phrase 'separate fares' 'were decided on the old law and the 1960 Act [RTA 1960] (now repealed). What is now [PPVA 1981] s.1(5) … makes more stringent provision as to the payment of separate fares. The cases should be read in the light of it.'

9   See *Wilkinson's Road Traffic Offences* (30th edition), Ch 13 for a detailed discussion of the definition of public service vehicle, and chapters 3 and 8 of the Law Commissions' second AV law consultation paper (October 2019).

'There has been an increasing tendency to relax the laws relating to public service vehicles and in particular for small and socially beneficial operations.'[10]

So, for example, the Transport Act 1985 (TA 1985), s 10 allows for local schemes whereby taxis licensed in that area 'may be hired for use for the carriage of passengers for hire or reward at separate fares without thereby' becoming a public service vehicle. And TA 1985, s 11 allows a licensed taxi or licensed hire car to be used for the carriage of passengers for hire or reward at separate fares without thereby becoming a public service vehicle, where:

'(a) all the passengers carried on the occasion in question booked their journeys in advance; and

(b) each of them consented, when booking his journey, to sharing the use of the vehicle on that occasion with others on the basis that a separate fare would be payable by each passenger for his own journey on that occasion.'

The process of adaptation of existing law to new passenger technologies continues. The courts have fixed the position of booking Apps within the relatively ancient landscape of taxi regulation[11]. As the Law Commission has observed, the 'hire or reward' element might be capable of regulatory adaptation to technology[12].

The governments of the United Kingdom and of Wales have both indicated support for regulatory reform to support better, more flexible access to public road transport, especially considering emerging technologies[13]. The Law Commissions suggested that, in the longer term, legislators might 'start afresh, and remove the current distinctions between taxis, private hire and PSVs [public service vehicles]'[14]. In relation to 'permits for automated passenger services' the AV Bill 2023-24 (HL Bill 1), cl 83 follows that suggestion.

A brief history of bus regulation

5.03

'[T]he existing system of bus regulation in Great Britain… is complex, with both regulated and deregulated elements. There are minor differences between England, Wales and Scotland, and major differences between London and the rest of the country. These complexities are best understood in their historical context.'[15]

(The Law Commissions, 2019)

---

10   *Wilkinson's Road Traffic Offences* (30th edition), 13-167.
11   The *UTAG* case (above).
12   Law Commissions' second AV law consultation paper (October 2019) p 60, 4.12 to 4.13.
13   See for example the bus policy documents of the UK and Welsh governments cited in the footnotes to the 'history of bus regulation' section below.
14   Law Commissions, 'Automated Vehicles: joint report', Law Com No 404, Scot Law Com No 258 (25 January 2022), referred to below as 'Law Commissions' joint report at end of AV law consultation (January 2022)', pp 206 to 207, 10.64 to 10.66. See discussion of the Law Commissions' recommendations, below.
15   Law Commissions' second AV law consultation paper (October 2019), p.159, 8.3.

A whistle-stop history of bus regulation[16] in England and Wales shows the reasons for its complexity:

- concern as to the safety of motor vehicles, leading to the establishment by the Road Traffic Act 1930 of 'a licensing system for passenger carrying motor vehicles, controlled by regional Traffic Commissioners'[17];

- the rising popularity of the privately-owned car and a corresponding fall in the use of buses;

- increasing reliance by bus operators upon public subsidies, leading to public ownership of most bus companies in the UK by 1968[18];

- deregulation of bus services outside London, by the Conservative government of the 1980s, in the Transport Acts of 1980 (deregulation of express coach services) and 1985 (deregulation of local bus services). Deregulation stripped the traffic commissioners of their powers and required operators merely to register their intention to set up a service;

- after 1980s deregulation, 'bus wars'– including intimidation and the obstruction of services – which ensued between competing bus operators;

- the adoption of a different approach to privatisation – and regulation – of bus services in London, by the London Regional Transport Act 1984[19], which had required competitive tendering

  'on the basis of all the costs required to operate and maintain the specified service whilst London Transport retained the fares revenue. Routes were awarded to the operator who could run the best service at the most cost effective price.'[20]

  Bus services in London were privatised as 13 companies:

  'The result is a bus franchise system in London which continues to this day. Details of routes, fares and service levels are specified by a public body and the right to run services is contracted out to private companies on a tendered basis... Since franchising, bus passenger numbers have increased in London despite a decline elsewhere.'[21]

- the failure of the 1980s policy of deregulation to reverse the decline in bus services outside London[22], which resulted in a subsequent return of some powers to public authorities. In particular, (in a passage quoted by the House of Commons Library in 2022),

  'The Centre for Cities, in 2019, argued that [outside London] deregulation 'broke the link between cities and their bus services''

---

16 See 'Bus Regulation: a short history' in chapter 8 of the Law Commissions' second AV law consultation paper (October 2019) at pp.160 to 165.
17 Law Commissions' second AV law consultation paper (October 2019), p 160, 8.6.
18 Law Commissions' second AV law consultation paper (October 2019), p 160, 8.7.
19 Repealed by Greater London Authority Act 1999, Pt IV, Ch V of which regulates bus services in Greater London.
20 Transport for London website, quoted in the Law Commissions' second AV law consultation paper (October 2019) at p 161, 8.13.
21 Law Commissions' second AV law consultation paper (October 2019) p 161, 8.17
22 See House of Commons Library Research Briefing 'The National Bus Strategy: Bus policy in England outside London', CBP9464, 17 May 2022, pp 23 to 24.

by, in the words of the Centre for Cities, changing

> 'the focus from providing a citywide network to focusing only on running a profitable service. Largely unregulated private monopolies took charge of critical urban infrastructure, and made fully-integrated public transport harder to provide.'[23]

In England outside London, the response to the failure of deregulation included the expansion (via the Bus Services Act 2017) of the powers of directly elected mayors and local transport authorities in relation to bus services, through new forms of partnership working and franchising[24];

- the introduction of a 'flexible service' for bus services in England (outside London) and Wales in February 2004, defined as a service:

  '(i) which serves one or more local communities or neighbourhoods within a specific geographical area,

  (ii) which, while it may have fixed sections of route, is in the entirety of its operation so flexible that it is not practicable to identify in advance all the roads to be traversed at any given time,

  (iii) which is provided primarily for the purpose of carrying passengers who have booked in advance of the journey and whose collective requirements determine the route of each journey notwithstanding that other persons may also be travelling[25],

  (iv) all the seats of which are available for use by members of the general public, and

  (v) which is provided in consideration of the payment of individual passenger fares which are not subject to variation according to the number of passengers carried on the journey'[26]

- devolution of legislative competence to Senedd Cymru (the Welsh Parliament) in matters including transport, though *not* in relation to public service vehicle

---

23   Centre for Cities, 'Delivering Change: Improving urban bus services', November 2019, p 2 (quoted in House of Commons Library Research Briefing 'The National Bus Strategy: Bus policy in England outside London', CBP9464, 17 May 2022, p 25).

24   Although the House of Commons Library Research Briefing 'The National Bus Strategy: Bus policy in England outside London', CBP9464, 17 May 2022 reports that 'Prior to the National Bus Strategy, the uptake of powers within the Bus Services Act 2017 had been limited' (p 25).

25   The Department for Transport's 'Future of Transport Regulatory Review: Call for Evidence – Moving Britain Ahead' (March 2020) noted that 'Experience with taxi and PHV apps in recent years has indicated that the concept of pre-booking transport does not necessarily need to mean booking well in advance. PHVs can be pre-booked through an operator's App seconds before a car in that area arrives to pick up a customer' (p.34) and asked 'how could the carriage of more ad-hoc bus passengers be encouraged without impacting negatively on the service received by passengers who have booked in advance?' (p 35, question 3.5). The Summary of responses to the FoTTR review (October 2020) (pp 35 to 37) did not answer the point, revealing among respondents both aversion to and support for ad hoc passengers using a smartphone App to alter the route of a bus at short notice.

26   Public Service Vehicles (Registration of Local Services) (Amendment) (England and Wales) Regulations 2004, SI 2004/10, reg 3 (amending the Public Service Vehicles (Registration of Local Services) Regulations 1986, SI 1986/1671). For commentary on flexible bus services see chapter 3, p.30 of the Department for Transport's 'Future of Transport Regulatory Review: Call for Evidence – Moving Britain Ahead' (March 2020).

operator licensing which is a specifically reserved matter[27] (reflecting European Union law, as the Law Commissions have noted[28]);

• urgent environmental concerns as to the energy inefficiency and environmental damage resulting from private car use. In January 2019, the UK government's 'Future of Mobility' paper advocated a greater role for government:

> 'Behavioural shifts that change demand are unlikely to be significant if driven solely by soft options [such as changing perceptions of the merits of different methods of transport] … Soft options clearly have an impact, but to effect significant change, they need to be combined with harder options such as investments in services or infrastructure.'[29] 'Investment' included 'government and industry' investment into electrification and automation[30].

• the worldwide coronavirus pandemic in 2020, when social distancing measures, including remote working, diminished the use of public transport;

and, post-pandemic:

• the UK government's review of national bus strategy for England outside London (March 2021)[31]. This strategy has at its main aim the return of bus use outside London to pre-pandemic levels and beyond to achieve a 'substantial modal shift away from the car'. Proposed measures to encourage such use include an increase in the number of bus services, contactless payments, 'integrated ticketing across bus operators and different modes' and buses which are environmentally friendlier and more accessible.[32]

• the Welsh government's legislative proposals for the operating model for buses in Wales (March 2022)[33]. The three main legislative proposals are 'requiring the franchising of bus services across Wales', 'allowing local authorities to create new municipal bus companies' and 'relaxing restrictions on existing municipal bus companies to put them on the same footing as new ones'[34]. 'We will also need to continue work on demand-responsive travel options, such

---

27 Government of Wales Act 2006 (as amended), ss A2(1) (recognition of Welsh law), 108A(2) (c) (Acts of the Senedd – legislative competence) and Sch 7A, Pt 2 (specifically reserved matters) Head E (Transport), E1 (Road Transport), para 113: 'Public service vehicle operator licensing'. Construction and use regulation (para 104), road traffic offences (para 105) and vehicle insurance and vehicle registration (para 115) are among the other road transport matters specifically reserved to Westminster. Generally reserved matters under GWA 2006, Sch 7A, Pt 1 include courts, judges and civil and criminal proceedings (para's 8(1)(a) to (c)).
28 Law Commissions' second AV law consultation paper (October 2019) p 48, 3.47.
29 Government Office for Science, 'A time of unprecedented change in the transport system: the Future of Mobility', January 2019, p 84.
30 As above, p.85.
31 See House of Commons Library Research Briefing 'The National Bus Strategy: Bus policy in England outside London', CBP9464, 17 May 2022.
32 Department for Transport, 'Bus Back Better: National Bus Strategy for England', March 2021, House of Commons Library Research Briefing 'The National Bus Strategy: Bus policy in England outside London', CBP9464, 17 May 2022, chapter 4.
33 See Welsh Government consultation paper, 'One network, one timetable, one ticket: planning buses as a public service for Wales', 31 March 2022.
34 Welsh Government consultation paper, 'One network, one timetable, one ticket: planning buses as a public service for Wales', 31 March 2022, 'Outline legislative proposals'.

as the Fflecsi[35] service being piloted by Transport for Wales, to offer reliable, sustainable, affordable travel options in places and times when scheduled bus services are not available.'[36]. 'We are also proposing to give the Welsh Ministers powers to make regulations and guidance in relation to franchising, setting out key objectives we consider are necessary to successful franchising and to support the long-term growth of bus services and the bus industry...'[37].

A brief history of taxi and private hire vehicle (PHV) regulation

5.04   Taxi and private hire vehicle regulation has evolved piecemeal[38] over centuries, with many regional differences.

The history of taxi and PHV regulation includes:

- The 'two-tier' system[39], founded on the distinction 'between taxis, which can be hailed in the street or hired at ranks' (with the taxis 'plying for hire') 'and private hire services which must be pre-booked'[40].

- A long-established phrase for the central activity of taxis, 'plying for hire', meaning in 'essence ... that the vehicle in question should be on view, that the owner or driver should expressly or impliedly invite the public to use it, and that the member of the public should be able to use that vehicle if he wanted to'[41]. In 2022, in *R (United Trade Action Group Ltd) v Transport for London*[42] ('the *UTAG* case'), Bean LJ summarised the history of the phrase:

    'The legal term for a black cab is a hackney carriage: in 1715 the term used was hackney coaches. Section 3 of an Act with the short title of the Hackney Coaches Etc Act 1715 provided that no person 'shall presume to stand, ply, or drive for hire with any coach whatsoever' within the cities of London and Westminster or their suburbs, except such persons who were licensed by Commissioners appointed under an earlier statute. After some intervening statutes which I need not set out, the Metropolitan Public

---

35 A Transport for Wales App allowing flexible booking for buses: 'fflecsi buses can pick you up and drop you off in a service area and not just at a bus stop. You must book your ride via the App or phone, then a bus picks you up at your request, changing its route so that all passengers can get to where they need to go.' https://www.fflecsi.wales

36 Welsh Government consultation paper, 'One network, one timetable, one ticket: planning buses as a public service for Wales', 31 March 2022, 'What are the aims and objectives?'

37 Welsh Government consultation paper, 'One network, one timetable, one ticket: planning buses as a public service for Wales', 31 March 2022, 'additional requirements, regulations and guidance'.

38 'Taxi and Private Hire Services', Law Com No 347, May 2014, p.2, 1.4.

39 The description of the traditional taxi/private hire vehicle relationship as the 'two-tier system' is not to be confused with the 'Tier 1 and Tier 2 duties' which the Law Commissions propose be applied to operators of no user-in-charge (NUIC) automated vehicles: 'Tier 1 duties (such as supervision, insurance, maintenance and reporting accidents) would apply to all vehicles, including those that are privately owned. Tier 2 duties would depend on the use case, with separate duties for Highly Automated Road Passenger Services (HARPS) and freight services.': Law Commissions' Analysis of Responses to AV consultation paper 3 (26 January 2022), p.129, l.4.

40 Law Commission's summary of its paper on Taxis and Private Hire Services, May 2014, pp.2 to 3, 1.8.

41 *Cogley v Sherwood* [1959] 2 QB 311, 325-326 (Lord Parker CJ).

42 [2022] EWCA Civ 1026; [2022] RTR 32.

Carriage Act 1869 prohibited plying for hire in London except by licensed drivers of licensed hackney carriages.'[43]

The Law Commissions noted on occasions up to the end of January 2022 (in both the taxi and automated vehicle consultations) that, while the phrase 'plying for hire' is plentiful in the caselaw, it is not defined by 'particularly strong authority since the question has to be decided on the merits of each case'[44]. However, with the Court of Appeal's judgment in the *UTAG* case, there is now authority on the phrase in the context of smartphone App bookings (see section B of this chapter, below, for discussion of the *UTAG* case).

- The emergence of minicabs (private hire vehicles) in the 1970s, with consequent regulation first applying to Plymouth (the Plymouth City Council Act 1975), then England (excluding London) and Wales in 1976 (the Local Government (Miscellaneous Provisions) Act 1976). The Private Hire Vehicles (London) Act 1998 was not brought into force until 2004[45].

- The review of taxi and private hire vehicle law by the Law Commission of England and Wales's consultation of 2011 to 2014 (see below).

- The first Uber journey in London, in June 2012[46].

- The Law Commission of England and Wales and the Scottish Law Commission's joint consultation on the law of automated vehicles (November 2018 to January 2022), which considered the possibility of driverless, highly automated road passenger vehicles (HARPS) and their regulation[47].

- From 31 May 2022, the Taxis and Private Hire Vehicles (Safeguarding and Road Safety) Act 2022 was enacted to require a licensing authority to record on a database, for the purposes of the safeguarding of passengers and road safety, concerns as to drivers' conduct and to act on such concerns (and to do likewise in relation to concerns of which it becomes aware, relating to a driver licensed in another area).

- From 28 June 2022, the Taxis and Private Hire Vehicles (Disabled Persons) Act 2022 amended the 'sections of the Equality Act 2010 relating to the carriage of disabled people by taxi and PHV, to address inconsistencies in the current provision and expand the protections currently afforded to wheelchair and assistance dog users to all disabled people, regardless of the vehicle they travel in.' [48]

Car Rentals

5.05   As the Law Commissions noted in 2019:

---

43   At para 4 of the judgment.
44   Law Commissions' second AV law consultation paper (October 2019), p.40, footnote 162.
45   Private Hire Vehicles (London) Act 1998 (Commencement No. 3) Order 2004, SI 2004/241, art.2.
46   https://www.uber.com/en-GB/newsroom/5-years-moving-london/, accessed 12 October 2022.
47   See the Law Commissions' second AV law consultation paper (October 2019) (the HARPS paper). Some the proposals in the second AV paper were modified by the third and final papers (see discussion of the Law Commissions' consultations, below).
48   Explanatory note to the Bill, para 2.

'Although taxis, private hire and PSVs [public service vehicles] are all heavily regulated, there is no equivalent provision for car rental, where a vehicle is hired to a person without the services of a driver. In this market, general consumer protections apply ... However, there are no specific legal requirements for setting up a rental company beyond the normal legal requirements when setting up any other type of business.'[49]

In their HARPS paper, (October 2019), the Law Commissions did not consider this unregulated position for car rentals (as distinct from long-term leases of vehicles) appropriate for highly automated road passenger services:

'We do not think that this relatively relaxed legal position would be appropriate where vehicles travel empty or with passengers only. In these circumstances, the primary legal actor – the driver – is absent. Instead, the operator must assume primary responsibilities. We therefore see the operator licensing provisions as applying to HARPS which look like a development of car rental services as well as those which might previously have been thought of as buses, taxis or minicabs.'[50]

The Law Commissions' consultations relevant to AAEV passenger services and public transport

5.06   Three completed consultations by the Law Commissions are relevant:

- the first in relation to taxis and private hire vehicles (carried out by the Law Commission of England and Wales, from 2011 to 2014),

- the second (by both the Law Commission of England and Wales and the Scottish Law Commission, from 2018 to 2022) in relation to automated vehicles, and

- the third (by the Law Commission of England and Wales), in relation to remote driving[51]. After that consultation, the Law Commission published its advice to government on remote driving in February 2023[52].

The 2011 to 2014 consultation came during a period of innovation in taxi services, including (in June 2012) the entry of Uber into the UK market. Although in 2014 the Law Commission recommended the retention of the two-tier system, it also identified a lack of consistency in standards applied to taxis and private hire services by various local authorities ('There are over 300 different sets of standards across England and Wales'[53]) and 'an outdated legislative framework' which 'has become too extensive in some respects, imposing unnecessary burdens on business'[54]. The Law Commission made recommendations including the introduction both of national standards for all taxis and private hire vehicles, set by the Secretary of State, with the power for local licensing authorities to set additional standards for taxi services only, and the introduction of mandatory disability awareness training for all taxi and private hire drivers.

---

49   Law Commissions' second AV law consultation paper (October 2019) p.53, 3.68.
50   Law Commissions' second AV law consultation paper (October 2019) p.54, 3.71.
51   Law Commission of England and Wales' Remote Driving issues paper, 24 June 2022
52   Law Commission of England and Wales' Remote Driving: advice to government, February 2023.
53   'Taxi and Private Hire Services', Law Com No 347, May 2014, pp.78 to 79, 5.6.
54   'Taxi and Private Hire Services', Law Com No 347, May 2014, p.2, 1.4.

In 2014 the Law Commission also considered the effect of smartphone technology on bookings. However, having balanced arguments in favour of retention or abolition of the two-tier system, the Law Commission then recommended its retention, chiefly based on the choice of service and relative cost that it considered the two-tier system provided to the public. In particular:

> 'Whilst we recognise that technology is making enforcement of the distinction between plying for hire and pre-booking more difficult, it does not make the distinction meaningless. The legal definitions should be flexible enough to accommodate technological bookings, such as those made through smartphone applications.'[55]

However, by 2019 the Law Commission (now, together with the Scottish Law Commission, considering automated vehicles) had formed a different view. In 2019 the Law Commissions published their consultation paper on highly automated road passenger services (HARPS), a term coined by the Law Commissions 'to convey the idea of a new service which uses highly automated vehicles to supply road journeys to passengers without a human driver or user-in-charge'[56]. The Law Commissions implied that App technology had advanced further since the conclusion of the 2014 review of taxi and PHV law and opined that in future the 'hailing/booking' distinction supporting the two-tier system should not apply to HARPS:

> '... the widespread use of booking apps has placed the two-tier system under strain. Apps can make the booking process so quick and effortless that the user's experience may seem little different from hailing. Furthermore, some taxis, particularly in rural areas, may do little rank and hail work. The public often lack understanding of the difference between a taxi and private hire vehicle, which can undermine the usefulness of regulating them differently. As already mentioned, the legal dividing line between plying for hire and pre-booking is far from clear... Our current view is that there is no need to replicate the two-tier system for HARPS.'[57]

The Law Commissions' AV law consultation also noted the weight of the regulatory burden on local authorities, if the method of localising taxi and PHV regulations were to continue into a HARPS era: in addition to those tasks, 'We think that many existing licensing authorities would lack the resources to deal with the new regulatory demands of HARPS'[58]. The instantaneous nature of bookings could also evade local regulations: quoting a leading textbook on taxi law, the Law Commissions noted the:

> 'significant increase in vehicles licensed by other authorities being regularly used in areas where they are not actually licensed' which 'can make

---

55 'Taxi and Private Hire Services', Law Com No 347, May 2014 at p.16, 2.28.
56 The Law Commissions, 'Automated Vehicles: Summary of the Analysis of Responses to Consultation Paper 2 on Passenger Services and Public Transport', p.3, 2.1.
57 Law Commissions' second AV law consultation paper (October 2019) pp.42 to 43, 3.16 to 3.23. See also p.55, 3.76 to 3.78, which note current difficult areas for the PSV definition (including 'care services and childminders; and rental car (or other) services where a lift might be provided to a customer as an ancillary service') and the observation again that 'The distinctions between taxis, private hire vehicles and private hire services are likely to blur further in the face of app-based technologies and automation'.
58 Law Commissions' second AV law consultation paper (October 2019) p.44, 3.26.

enforcement difficult, and undermine attempts by local authorities to improve local standards of vehicles, drivers and operators.'[59]

The Law Commissions in 2019 noted the inflexibility of the current PSV rules to current needs, including 'care services and childminders; and rental car (or other) services where a lift might be provided to a customer as an ancillary service' [60] and their likely discouragement to ride-sharing[61].

The Law Commissions therefore proposed a single system of regulation for HARPS operators, with national standards:

'... we provisionally propose a single regulatory structure, which avoids arbitrary distinctions based on number of passengers or fare structures. We fear that such distinctions could warp decision making. They would be incompatible with the Government's seventh principle for the future of mobility, namely that the regulatory structure should stimulate innovation and give the best deal to consumers ... The main reason for licensing HARPS operators is to ensure that HARPS are operated safely, especially for issues related to updating, maintenance, insurance, cyber-security and remote supervision. We think all these issues should be subject to minimum national standards, irrespective of where the HARPS is based...[62]

'The operator licensing scheme would be *in addition* to the safety assurance scheme proposed in Consultation Paper 1, which focussed on the design of the automated driving system (ADS).'[63]

'We provisionally propose to define a HARPS operator as any business which carries passengers for hire or reward using highly automated vehicles on a road without a human driver or user-in-charge in the vehicle (or in line of sight of the vehicle).'[64]

The coronavirus outbreak was declared a pandemic by the World Health Organisation on 11 March 2020, during the Law Commissions' AV consultation[65]. The Law Commissions' first AV paper after the start of the pandemic (its analysis of responses to the HARPS report, in May 2020) acknowledged some likely effects on HARPS:

'Many consultees expressed strong concerns about ride-sharing in the absence of a human driver and how it would affect vulnerable people. Since February 2020, these concerns have been amplified by the need to practise and enforce social distancing. There are many issues about how to safeguard

---

59 Law Commissions' second AV law consultation paper (October 2019), p.45, 3.32, quoting J Button, *Button on Taxis: Licensing Law and Practice* (4th edition, 2017), pp.xi to xii.
60 Law Commissions' second AV law consultation paper (October 2019) p.55, 3.76 to 3.78.
61 Law Commissions' second AV law consultation paper (October 2019) p.56, 3.80.
62 Law Commissions' second AV law consultation paper (October 2019) p.56, 3.81 to 3.82.
63 The Law Commissions, 'Automated Vehicles: Summary of the Analysis of Responses to Consultation Paper 2 on Passenger Services and Public Transport', p.3, 2.3.
64 Law Commissions' second AV law consultation paper (October 2019) p.59, 4.7.
65 https://www.who.int/director-general/speeches/detail/who-director-general-s-opening-remarks-at-the-media-briefing-on-covid-19---11-march-2020

passengers in small shared automated vehicles which the industry has yet to overcome.'[66]

In their third AV law consultation paper[67] (December 2020), the Law Commissions rethought and streamlined their recommendation on regulation of HARPS, so that the proposed licensing of HARPS operators would not apply only to passenger vehicles but would apply to *all* automated vehicles with no user-in-charge (so would apply to all NUIC vehicles, 'irrespective of whether they are used for private or business purposes, and whether or not they carry passengers'). This was in response to concerns that safeguards in relation to the use of fully-automated, NUIC vehicles should not be restricted to passenger vehicles.[68] One consequence of this proposal (which now appears in the AV Bill 2023-24[69]) would be that:

'A private individual may still own a NUIC vehicle, but they must contract with a licensed operator for supervision and maintenance services. Maintenance for these purposes would include installing software and maintaining cybersecurity. The proposal would be backed by criminal sanctions. It would be a crime to use a self-driving vehicle on a road or public place without a user-in-charge unless it was either operated by a licensed operator or covered by a contract with a licensed operator.'[70]

In their final automated law paper, in January 2022, the Law Commissions wrote that:

'there is much that is not known about how passenger services will operate in the absence of a driver. The immediate need is to collect more evidence and gain more experience, particularly on issues such as accessibility and safeguarding. We therefore recommend a procedure to issue 'interim passenger permits' before designing a permanent regulatory scheme [for AV passenger services without a user-in-charge]'[71]

As to whether a new regulatory approach should be applied across the passenger and public transport sector, or confined to NUICs, the Law Commissions proposed two options:

'There are two main approaches to redesigning passenger regulation in the longer term. The first is the approach we took in Consultation Paper 2, which is to start afresh, and remove the current distinctions between taxis, private hire and PSVs. We provisionally proposed a new form of service, HARPS, with a new single scheme of national operator licensing. Responses to Consultation Paper 2 highlighted a lack of consensus on how this could work, both in

---

66   The Law Commissions, 'Automated Vehicles: Summary of the Analysis of Responses to Consultation Paper 2 on Passenger Services and Public Transport', p.6, 2.22.
67   The Law Commissions, 'Automated Vehicles: Consultation Paper 3 – A regulatory framework for automated vehicles', Law Com CP No 253, Scots Law Com DP No 171 (18 December 2020), referred to below as 'Law Commissions' third AV law consultation paper (December 2020)'.
68   Law Commissions' third AV law consultation paper (December 2020), pp.226 to 227, 13.73 to 13.80.
69   AV Bill 2023-24 (HL Bill 1), cll 12-13 and 53.
70   Law Commissions' third AV law consultation paper (December 2020), p.227, 13.79 and 13.80.
71   Law Commissions' joint report at end of AV consultation (January 2022), p.193, 10.4.

terms of local governance arrangements and the relationship with existing licensed modes to ensure fair competition.'

'The second approach is to amend existing taxi, private hire and PSV legislation (where necessary) so as to bring NUIC services unequivocally within the existing schemes. During this review, several stakeholders have told us that operators of NUIC vehicles would work with mixed fleets including conventional vehicles. In addition, the same vehicle might be used with no user-in-charge for some trips but not others. One advantage of bringing NUIC services within the existing model is that companies could run NUIC, user-in-charge and conventional services under the same type of licence.'

'Experience gathered from interim passenger permits could contribute the necessary evidence base to help decide which long-term option is preferable. Alternatively, amendment of existing taxi, private hire and PSV legislation to bring in NUIC services could be seen as an intermediate option.'[72]

The Law Commission of England and Wales' consultation on remote driving (June 2022 to February 2023) dealt with the immediate issue of testing prototype vehicles using remote driving, and particularly using a 'beyond line-of-sight' remote driver as a safety driver outside the vehicle. The Law Commission advised government that such testing should currently be permitted if within a Vehicle Special Order[73] or (in the longer term) a licensing system yet to be introduced by new primary legislation. In relation to the testing of public passenger vehicles, the Law Commission noted that current law allowed the Secretary of State for Transport to dispense with conditions for fitness for a PPV adapted to carry more than eight passengers but lacking type approval 'where it is expedient to do so for the purpose of making tests or trials of a vehicle or its equipment' (PPVA 1981, s 11)[74]. However, like regulations 104 and 107 of the Road Vehicles (Construction and Use) Regulations 1986[75], that was not a law drafted with remote driving in mind[76], and is subject to the Law Commission's conclusions in its advice to government that 'in the short term ... those who use remote 'beyond line-of-sight' driving should be required to demonstrate that their system is safe and obtain a VSO' and in 'the longer term ... all organisations who conduct remote driving should obtain a licence' under 'a licensing scheme to promote safety and shift responsibility to the organisation behind remote driving' which 'will require new primary legislation'[77]. The Law Commissions also noted a potential hazard of allowing commercial activity to take place during a trial, particularly in relation to the carriage of passengers, namely that 'it is possible that unscrupulous operators will try and avoid regulation by claiming they are trialling'[78] – a possibility which is illustrated by attempted evasion of the

---

72 Law Commissions' joint report at end of AV consultation (January 2022), pp.206 to 207, 10.64 to 10.66.

73 See Chapter 3, 'Testing'.

74 Law Commission of England and Wales' Remote Driving: advice to government, February 2023 p 44, 4.30-31. And see p 42, 4.18, in relation to CUR 1986 reg 107 (prohibition against leaving a vehicle unattended) and the RTA 1988 s 42 offence in relation to a passenger vehicle.

75 SI 1986/1078.

76 Law Commission of England and Wales' Remote Driving: advice to government, February 2023, p 42, 4.20.

77 Ibid, p 47, 4.48.

78 Ibid, p 54-55, 5.34.

compulsory insurance requirement in the case of some electric vehicles[79]. The Law Commission took 'a cautious approach to trials which provide a commercial service carrying passengers'[80] but concluded that 'VSOs should permit the commercial carriage of goods and delivery of vehicles on a case-by-case basis'[81].

Government responses to the Law Commissions' recommendations on automated vehicle passenger services and public transport

5.07   The UK government has repeatedly aligned itself with the Law Commissions' recommended approaches to regulation of automated vehicles. In its national bus strategy document in March 2021, it agreed with the Law Commissions' observations as to the outdatedness of passenger services and public transport law in light of imminent technologies, and stated that:

> 'We will review how legislation that separately covers buses, taxis, private hire vehicles and light rail may be brought together to reflect the blurring boundaries between these forms of travel, within the Future of Transport Regulatory Review. This will give service providers a clear, long-term, regulatory framework, which will allow new forms of service to be provided to passengers by removing obstacles to innovation and allowing greater flexibility.'[82]

In its CAM 2025 report in August 2022, the government accepted the substance of the Law Commissions' recommendations in its final paper for automated passenger-only services. It did not support the Law Commissions' 'interim permit' proposal. As to accessibility:

> 'Whilst we fully support the need for a new accessibility advisory panel to sign off permits, we do not believe it need be statutory for the moment. Instead, we commit to establishing an identical panel in time for commencement of the permitting regime, though this panel will not be established through legislation.'

> 'The Secretary of State for Transport will need to pay due regard to accessibility when issuing a permit. We also expect that this panel would help design a national minimum standard for the accessibility of self-driving passenger service vehicles over time as learning improves.'[83]

The Welsh government welcomed the Law Commission of England and Wales's automated vehicle law proposals in its report on the Welsh Ministers' implementation of Law Commission proposals covering the period 15 February 2021 to 14 February

---

79 See *Winter v DPP* [2002] EWHC 1524 (cosmetic pedals not reasonably capable of propelling electric tricycle, which was therefore a motor vehicle) discussed in Chapter 4, 'Driving'.

80 Law Commission of England and Wales' Remote Driving: advice to government, February 2023, p 55, 5.38.

81 Ibid, p 55-56, 5.38 to 5.41 (conclusion 6).

82 Department for Transport, 'Bus Back Better: National Bus Strategy for England', March 2021, p.51.

83 UK government paper 'Connected & Automated Mobility 2025: Realising the benefits of self-driving vehicles in the UK' ('CAM 2025') (August 2022), Annex D, p.125.

2022. The report also recorded the Welsh government's 'further progress in taking forward Law Commission proposals in relation to taxi and private hire services'.[84]

The Automated Vehicles Bill 2023-24 (HL Bill 1) and passenger services and public transport

5.08 The AV Bill 2023-24 (HL Bill 1) reflects both the government's overwhelming acceptance of the Law Commissions' recommendations on AV law and the Law Commission of England and Wales' advice to government on remote driving. See in particular the following clauses of the Bill:

- a scheme of licensing of operators for vehicle use without a user-in-charge (Part 1, Chapter 2, cll 12-13);
- a new offence of use of a vehicle without a driver or licensed oversight (Part 2, Chapter 2, cl 53);
- a power to grant permits for the provision of automated passenger services (Part 5, cl 82); and
- the disapplication of taxi, private hire vehicle and bus legislation 'while a permit holder is providing an automated passenger service in an area in which, and in a vehicle in which, services may be provided under the permit' (Part 5, cl 83).

The provisions are set out in detail in the 'automated vehicles' section below.

E-bike and e-scooter rentals

5.09 The rental market is not limited to electric cars, and now includes rental schemes both for e-bikes and e-scooters (the latter currently only in permitted trial areas). While those rental schemes provide vehicles designed for single-occupancy, they play a particular part in the rental market for electric vehicles and in the promotion of zero-emission public transport.

These rental schemes are considered below in section D, below: 'Laws of Passenger Services and Public Transport involving Electric Vehicles'. E-scooter and e-bike claims are considered in chapter 16, 'smaller electric vehicle claims'.

Tramcars

5.10 A 'tramcar'[85] is treated differently from other public service vehicles and is excluded from the definition of 'public service vehicle' under the Public Passenger Vehicles Act 1981, s 1.

---

84 Welsh Government 'Report on the Implementation of Law Commission proposals 2021-2022'

85 PPVA 1981 s.82 defines 'tramcar' as including 'any carriage used on a road by virtue of an order made under the Light Railways Act 1896'. The 1896 Act (which allowed the Light Railway Commission and local councils etc to co-operate in the development of light railways) was repealed, except insofar as it applies in Scotland, by the Transport and Works Act 1992.

A tramcar is exempted from some requirements applicable to other road vehicles, including in particular the requirements of Parts II, III and IV of the Road Vehicles (Construction and Use) Regulations 1986[86] ('CUR'), which include regulations of significance for advanced and automated vehicle technologies and trialling (such as the requirement for driver control under CUR 104 and the regulations in relation to the use of screens and mobile telephone use under CUR 109 and 110).

Case law on 'lee-way' in bus driver liability

5.11   A strand of the case law on the duties of bus and tram drivers to passengers suffering injury is (as a leading textbook has described it) the 'lee-way' that 'the courts have tended to afford … to drivers of public service vehicles who are forced to brake or swerve suddenly in response to extraneous events'[87].

In *Wooller v London Transport Board* (judgment handed down in 1968 but not reported until 1976)[88] the Claimant was standing in a bus, ready to get off at a stop, when the bus driver braked suddenly from about 25 mph because a pedestrian had suddenly walked in front of the bus. The Claimant fell and was injured. The judge at first instance found the lorry driver to have driven negligently on the basis that he was driving too close to the lorry in front of the bus and too fast for the circumstances (namely the approach to both a pedestrian crossing and a bus stop where passengers would alight), but also reduced the Claimant's damages by a third for his failure not to hold onto a handrail or bar in the bus to steady himself.

The Court of Appeal allowed the appeal of the bus company, noting that there had been no collision with the lorry and that no other passengers had fallen. Edmund Davies LJ rejected submissions for the Claimant which concluded that 'public service vehicle drivers must take particular care to travel so far behind a leading vehicle when a pedestrian crossing is being approached so that, even if that vehicle should brake suddenly, the bus can be pulled up behind it without having to brake suddenly'. Edmund Davies LJ considered this 'a counsel of perfection' which ignored both:

> 'modern traffic conditions and the likelihood of other vehicles nipping in if a substantial gap is allowed to develop, and so increasing traffic dangers. Above all, they ignore the fact that pure accidents do occur; and unfortunately this was such an accident.'[89]

The rejection of a 'counsel of perfection' in driving was repeated by the Court of Appeal again in the *Sam v Atkins*[90] case (which did not involve a public service vehicle but a defendant driving in her private capacity) in 2005[91].

---

86   Road Vehicle (Construction and Use) Regulations 1986, SI 1986/1078, reg.4(4) (as amended by reg.13 of the Tramcars and Trolley Vehicles (Modification of Enactments) Regulations, SI 1992/1217, to exclude tramcars from the regulations in Parts II, III and IV of CUR 1986).

87   'Emergency braking' at p.262, 23.4 of the *APIL Guide to RTA Liability* (3rd edn, 2018), chapter 23, *Public Service Vehicle Liability* by Kate Lamont.

88   [1976] RTR 206 (CA).

89   At 207-8.

90   [2005] EWCA Civ 1452; [2006] RTR 14, discussed in 'Driver's standard of care' in the 'Laws of driving AAEVs' chapter.

91   And see *Ahanonu v South East London & Kent Bus Company Ltd* [2008] EWCA Civ 274 and *Zanatta v Metroline Travel Ltd* [2023] EWCA Civ 224, discussed in Chapter 11, 'passenger claims'.

Whether the operators of HARPS vehicles would be allowed 'lee-way' in relation to injuries to passengers remains to be seen. AEVA 2018 provides for direct liability of the insurer (or permitted uninsured owner) of an automated vehicle where 'an accident is caused by an [authorised] automated vehicle when driving itself on a road or other public place in Great Britain' and a person 'suffers damage as a result of the accident'[92], and 'a reference to an accident caused by an [authorised] automated vehicle includes a reference to an accident that is partly caused by an [authorised] automated vehicle'[93]. So even partial causation of an accident by an automated vehicle driving itself would trigger the direct liability under AEVA 2018, s 2. As noted in chapter 4, 'driving', the standard of care for driving by the vehicle itself as described in the AV Bill 2023-24 (HL Bill 1) is not an absolute standard, which reflects the common law.

Mobility as a Service (MaaS)

5.12   Future developments in passenger road transport might include Mobility as a Service ('MaaS'), which has been described as:

> 'a digital platform which provides information on a wide range of transport options, often in real time. This platform is accessed via a smartphone app, so that the user has a straight-forward way to plan and pay for their transport, even if a journey involves more than one mode of transport... A key concept is that a user would only pay once for the entire trip, rather than paying separately for each leg of the journey. It is also possible to create subscription models so that it becomes unnecessary to pay separately for each trip. A goal of the MaaS movement is to create a unified transport market, so that users can travel freely and have a simple and consistent user experience. However, making MaaS a reality is difficult, as it requires operators to share information and cooperate over fare structures to an unprecedented degree.' [94]

The UK government published its code of practice for MaaS in August 2023[95].

B Laws of Advanced Passenger Services and Public Transport

'Plying for hire' and smartphone PHV booking Apps

5.13   Whether the use of a smartphone booking App amounts to 'plying for hire' has been considered in two cases: by the Divisional Court in *Reading BC v Ali*[96] and by the Court of Appeal in *R (United Trade Action Group Ltd) v Transport for London*[97] (the *UTAG* case).

---

92   AEVA 2018, s 2(1) and (2), with prospective amendments per AV Bill 2023-24 (HL Bill 1), Sch 2, para 5(3)(a) in square brackets.
93   AEVA 2018, s 8(3)(b), with prospective amendments per AV Bill 2023-24 (HL Bill 1), Sch 2, para 5(3)(e) in square brackets.
94   Law Commissions' second AV law consultation paper (October 2019) p.178, 8.101 and 102.
95   Department for Transport 'Guidance. Mobility as a Service: code of practice' (30 August 2023).
96   [2019] 1 WLR 2635
97   [2022] EWCA Civ 1026; [2022] RTR 32

In both cases, the courts found that inviting bookings on a smartphone App did not amount to 'plying for hire' within the test in the leading case of *Cogley v Sherwood* ('the vehicle in question should be on view, that the owner or driver should expressly or impliedly invite the public to use it, and that the member of the public should be able to use that vehicle if he wanted to'[98]). The Court of Appeal in *UTAG* labelled the relevant elements of the *Cogley* test as: (1) exhibition of the vehicle; and (2) soliciting business from prospective customers[99].

In *Reading Borough Council v Ali*, the Divisional Court considered a case stated by the Chief Magistrate on questions going to 'plying for hire' in relation to a booking App (the Uber app) used in Reading. The Divisional Court held that there was no 'exhibition' because:

'depiction of the vehicle on the App does not involve any exhibition of that kind, but is for the assistance of the Uber customer using the App, who can see that there are vehicles in the vicinity of the type he or she wishes to hire. I agree ... that the App is simply the use of modern technology to effect a similar transaction to those which have been carried out by PHV operators over the telephone for many years. If I ring a minicab firm and ask for a car to come to my house within five minutes and the operator says 'I've got five cars round the corner from you. One of them will be with you in five minutes,' there is nothing in that transaction which amounts to plying for hire. As a matter of principle, I do not consider that the position should be different because the use of internet technology avoids the need for the phone call.'[100]

And there was no 'soliciting' because the driver:

'only proceeded to the pick-up point after the customer had confirmed the booking and the respondent as driver had accepted the job. Whenever any contract was concluded, I have little doubt that this was not plying for hire, because on the facts found in this case, the customer could not use the respondent's car without making a prior booking through the App... [The driver] was waiting in his vehicle until a customer confirmed a booking on the Uber App and he accepted that booking. There was no question of his soliciting custom during the period of waiting. His vehicle did not advertise itself as available for hire nor did he do anything which would have suggested to the public that he was available for hire. Indeed, as the Chief Magistrate found, if a member of the public had approached the vehicle and sought a ride, the respondent would have refused to take such a passenger off the street without a prior booking through the Uber App.'[101]

In the *UTAG* case, the Court of Appeal considered whether a PHV in London booked using a different App (the FREE NOW App) was 'plying for hire' and required to comply with regulations governing London black cabs. Agreeing with the Divisional Court in *Reading BC v Ali*, the Court of Appeal (Lord Justice Bean) held that:

'Lord Parker's conclusion [in *Cogley v Sherwood*] that 'there is no decided case where a hackney carriage was held to be plying for hire where it was not

---

98   [1959] 2 QB 311, 325-326 (Lord Parker CJ).
99   *UTAG*, para's 20, 23 (Bean LJ).
100 *Reading BC v Ali* at para 34 (Flaux LJ)
101 *Reading BC v Ali*, para 38.

exhibited so as to be visible to would-be customers' is in my view correct. The two-stage test of exhibition of the vehicle and solicitation of passengers is clear and intelligible and has stood the test of time. If it is still necessary for *Cogley v Sherwood* to be approved in this court, I would approve it.'

'I agree with the Divisional Court in *Reading BC v Ali* that plying for hire requires a vehicle to be not just exhibited or on view but, while exhibited, to be soliciting custom in the sense of inviting members of the public to hire it without a prior contract. I do not consider that drivers of PHVs using the FREE NOW app can be said to be plying for hire. Neither the 'exhibition' nor the 'solicitation' element of the test is satisfied.'

'As to the element of exhibiting the vehicle, I do not consider that the depiction of the vehicle and others as rectangular blobs on the passenger's smartphone screen amounts to exhibiting. The passenger is not being given any details that would identify a vehicle and no means of finding it or contacting it directly. The individual vehicles depicted on the screen are neither 'visible' nor 'on view' in any real sense. I agree with Mr Matthias that the case would be the same if, instead of being shown a map of the area with a number of blobs representing cars, the customer was simply told by an on-screen message 'there are five cars currently available within five minutes of where you are waiting'. But that would not be exhibition either. Like Flaux LJ in the *Reading* case, I accept that the case is no different from that of the traditional minicab firm which takes phone calls from prospective customers and where the operator tells them 'we have five cars within five minutes of you'. All that the FREE NOW app does is to speed up that process.'[102]

Lord Justice Singh summarised the technological developments and the survival of the 'plying for hire' test throughout:

'... it was always possible, even in 1869, for a person to hire a private vehicle (to use modern terminology) which would not be plying for hire. At that time, there were carriages with horses and drivers available for hire from a 'jobmaster'. There were stables where such carriages and horses were kept. But the essential difference between such a hire and plying for hire by a hackney carriage was that a pre-booking had to be made. The coming of the motor car did not change this conceptual distinction, as the facts of *Cogley* themselves illustrate. The facts of *Cogley* also illustrate the point that it has for a long time been possible to go to an office (there a desk at the airport terminal) and make a booking physically for the hire of a vehicle. The subsequent widespread availability of telephones in the 20th century made it unnecessary to make a booking physically. Towards the end of the 20th century the mobile phone meant that a person could make a telephone booking even from the street. In the 21st century the advent of the smartphone has meant that, instead of having to make a telephone call, a person can use an app and almost instantaneously book a private hire vehicle.'

'Crucially, however, although these technological developments have reduced the amount of time needed to book a hire vehicle, they have not, in

---

102 *UTAG*, Para's 44 to 46 (Bean LJ)

my opinion, obliterated the conceptual distinction between the need for such a booking and plying for hire, where there is no need for a prior booking. As Salmon J said in *Cogley*, a member of the public can simply step into the vehicle and the driver will be expected to take them to their destination. If, in the circumstances of the present case, a member of the public stepped into a vehicle, the driver would not simply drive them to their destination. They would point out that they had not been booked on the relevant app and would (no doubt politely) ask the member of the public to leave their vehicle. In the circumstances of this case, therefore, I agree with Bean LJ that there was no plying for hire.'[103]

C Laws of Passenger Services and Public Transport involving Automated Vehicles

'Traditionally, road passenger services have been divided into taxis, private hire vehicles, public service vehicles and rental cars, with separate regulatory systems applying to each. At one stage, these separate categories corresponded to clearly recognised market divisions: people understood the difference between a taxi, minicab, bus, coach or car hire. However, ... these divisions are becoming blurred and may disappear altogether in an automated world.'

(*The Law Commissions*[104])

The Automated Vehicles Bill 2023-24 (HL Bill 1) and passenger services and public transport

5.14   The AV Bill 2023-24 (HL Bill 1) follows the recommendations of the Law Commissions which the government overwhelmingly accepted in August 2022 (see above). The AV Bill deals with passenger services in the following parts:

- 'Licensing of operators for vehicle use without user-in-charge' (Part 1 'Regulatory scheme for automated vehicles', Chapter 2, cll 12-13);

- Offence of use of a vehicle without a driver or licensed oversight (Part 2 'Criminal liability for vehicle use', Chapter 2, cl 53);

- 'Permits for automated passenger services' (Part 5, cll 82-90); and

- 'Civil sanctions for infringing passenger permit scheme' (cl 84, Sch 6).

'Licensing of operators for vehicle use without user-in-charge' (Part 1 'Regulatory scheme for automated vehicles', Chapter 2, cll 12-13)

5.15   The AV Bill 2023-24 (HL Bill 1), cl 12 provides as follows:

---

103 *UTAG*, para's 53 and 54
104 Law Commissions' second AV law consultation paper (October 2019) at p.4, 1.21.

'12 Power to establish operator licensing scheme

(1) The Secretary of State may, by regulations ("operator licensing regulations"), make provision—

    (a) for the licensing of persons as no-user-in-charge operators;

    (b) imposing requirements on those persons in connection with no-user-in-charge journeys or the vehicles that undertake them;

    (c) for the keeping of a public register of those persons (and associated information).

(2) A "no-user-in-charge journey" is a journey by a vehicle with an authorised no-user-in-charge feature during which (at any point)—

    (a) that feature is engaged, or

    (b) there is no individual in the vehicle who is exercising control of it.

(3) For the purposes of this Part, a no-user-in-charge journey is "overseen" by a licensed no-user-in-charge operator if the operator is, in respect of the journey, subject to requirements imposed under subsection (1)(b).

(4) If the Secretary of State makes operator licensing regulations, the Secretary of State must do so in a way that is designed to secure, so far as the Secretary of State considers reasonably practicable, that the following objectives are met.

(5) The objectives are—

    (a) that a licensed no-user-in-charge operator should have general responsibility for the detection of, and response to, problems arising during a no-user-in-charge journey overseen by the operator, and

    (b) that a licensed no-user-in-charge operator should be—

        (i)   of good repute,

        (ii)   of good financial standing, and

        (iii) capable of competently discharging any requirements imposed on it for the purposes of paragraph (a).'

(The definition of 'user-in-charge' in the AV Bill 2023-24 (HL Bill 1) is in the 'criminal liability' part at cl 46:

'An individual is the "user-in-charge" of a vehicle if—

(a) the vehicle is an authorised automated vehicle with an authorised user-in-charge feature,

(b) that feature is engaged, and

(c) the individual is in, and in position to exercise control of, the vehicle, but is not controlling it.')

Clause 13 provides makes further provision about operator licensing regulations, which 'may, in particular, make provision for and about the grant, retention, variation, renewal, expiry, suspension or withdrawal of licences' (cl 13(2)). Clause 13(4) provides that the 'regulations may impose on a licensed no-user-in-charge operator a requirement to comply with any conditions that are attached to an individual licence'.

Clause 13(3)(e) – despite the jettisoning of taxi, PHV and bus legislation by cl 83 – preserves a role in automated vehicle regulation for the traffic commissioners (see 'a brief history of bus regulation', above) by allowing regulations to confer functions on them in relation to NUIC operator licensing. The explanatory note to the AV Bill 2023-24 (HL Bill 1) states that

'Traffic Commissioners currently have responsibility for the licensing and regulation of those who operate conventional heavy goods vehicles, buses and coaches, and the registration of local bus services. They are appointed by the Secretary of State and operate at arm's length from the Department for Transport as independent regulators. The provision in this clause is intended to give the Secretary of State the flexibility to align the regulation of licensed operators of authorised automated vehicles with that of conventional vehicles in the future, should this be considered appropriate. Additionally, paragraph 8 of Schedule 1 [Enforcement action under Part 1: procedure] enables the Secretary of State to transfer the power to impose civil sanctions to the Traffic Commissioners.'[105]

Offence of use of a vehicle without a driver or licensed oversight (Part 2 'Criminal liability for vehicle use', Chapter 2, cl 53)

5.16 This offence is described in Chapter 3, in relation to 'testing'.

'Permits for automated passenger services' (Part 5, cll 82-90)

5.17 AV Bill 2023-24 (HL Bill 1), cl 82 provides as follows:

'82 Power to grant permits

(1) The appropriate national authority may grant a person a permit for the provision by the person of automated passenger services.

(2) An "automated passenger service" is a service that consists of the carrying of passengers in a road vehicle that—

  (a) is designed or adapted to travel autonomously, or

  (b) is being used for a trial with the aim of developing vehicles that are so designed or adapted.

(3) A permit may be granted for either or both of the following purposes—

  (a) securing the application of section 83 (disapplication of taxi, private hire vehicle and bus legislation);

  (b) satisfying a requirement imposed by regulations under section 12 (licensing of no-user-in-charge operators) in relation to the holding of a permit.

---

105 Explanatory note to AV Bill 2023-24 (HL Bill 1 – EN) para 126.

(4) A permit must specify—

    (a) the areas in which services may be provided under the permit,

    (b) the vehicles (or descriptions of vehicle) in which services may be provided under the permit,

    (c) the period for which the permit is valid, and

    (d) any conditions subject to which the permit is granted ("permit conditions").

(5) Permit conditions may take the form of—

    (a) further limitations on the services that may be provided under the permit, or

    (b) obligations that the permit holder has to fulfil as a condition of holding the permit.

(6) In subsection (2)(a), "travel autonomously" has the same meaning as in Part 1 (see section 1(5)[106]).'

Clause 83 provides for the disapplication of taxi, private hire vehicle and bus legislation (including that 'the vehicle is not to be treated for any purpose as being, or as being used or operated as ... a hackney carriage within the meaning of the Town Police Clauses Act 1847 or the Metropolitan Public Carriage Act 1869'[107]) 'while a permit holder is providing an automated passenger service in an area in which, and in a vehicle in which, services may be provided under the permit' (cl 83(1)).

Clause 84 provides for civil sanctions for infringing the passenger permit scheme.

Clause 85 deals with the situation where 'an automated passenger service resembles a taxi or private hire vehicle'. In that situation, cl 85:

'provides that the appropriate national authority may only grant a permit with the consent of each licensing authority in whose area the automated passenger service may be provided under the proposed permit. As the responsibility for granting taxi and private hire vehicle licenses currently sits with licensing authorities, obtaining the authorities' consent prior to granting a permit may ensure consideration is given to local issues relating to limits imposed on the number of taxis and private hire vehicles, and vehicle standards set by licensing authorities. Licensing authorities may also consider other factors as part of the consent process, for example local authority traffic calming measures and ensuring services are adequately overseen by the permit holder...'[108]

Clause 86 makes similar provision for the consent of each relevant franchising body in the case of automated passenger services resembling buses.

---

106 AV Bill 2023-24 (HL Bill 1), cl 1(5): 'A vehicle travels "autonomously" if (a) it is being controlled not by an individual but by equipment of the vehicle, and (b) neither the vehicle nor its surroundings are being monitored by an individual with a view to immediate intervention in the driving of the vehicle.'
107 AV Bill 2023-24 (HL Bill 1), cl 83(2)(a); cf the *UTAG* case, above.
108 Explanatory note to AV Bill 2023-24 (HL Bill 1) para 342 (both quoted passages).

Clause 87(1) requires the appropriate national authority, before granting a permit, to 'consult any traffic authorities and emergency services that it considers are likely to be substantially affected if the permit is granted'.

Clause 87(3) requires such authority, in deciding whether to grant a permit, to 'have regard to whether, and to what extent, the granting of the permit is likely to lead to an improvement in the understanding of how automated passenger services should best be designed for, and provided to, older or disabled passengers'.

Clause 87(4) provides that:

'Where the appropriate national authority grants a permit, it must include a permit condition (of the sort described in section 82(5)(b)) requiring the permit holder to publish reports about the automated passenger services which it provides, and in particular about the steps which it takes—

(a) to meet the needs of older or disabled passengers, and

(b) to safeguard passengers more generally.'

Clause 88, 'collection, sharing and protection of information', is described in chapter 26, 'public laws of data and privacy'.

Clause 89, 'procedural and administrative matters' (varying, renewal, suspension or withdrawal of automated passenger service permits), is described in chapter 31, 'public laws of vehicle safety'.

Clause 90 is the interpretation section, which includes the definition of 'appropriate national authority':

'(4) Subject to subsection (5), the "appropriate national authority" is—

(a) the Secretary of State, in relation to a permit for the provision of a service in England;

(b) the Scottish Ministers, in relation to a permit for the provision of a service in Scotland;

(c) the Welsh Ministers, in relation to a permit for the provision of a service in Wales.

(5) In relation to a permit for the provision of a service in a public service vehicle, the "appropriate national authority" is the Secretary of State.

...

(7) In relation to the exercise of power by a traffic commissioner further to regulations under section 89(7), references in this Part to the appropriate national authority are to be read as including a traffic commissioner.'

'Civil sanctions for infringing passenger permit scheme' (cl 84, Sch 6)

5.18   These sanctions are described in Chapter 31, 'public laws of vehicle safety'.

Guided transport systems

5.19   A self-driving passenger vehicle system has been in operation in the UK since 2011, though not on the open road[109].

The Heathrow pods (also known as the Personal Rapid Transit or PRT) system runs between a car park and Terminal 5 of Heathrow airport. The system:

> 'consists of a fleet of 18 low energy, battery powered, driverless vehicles capable of carrying around four passengers and their luggage, which travel along a dedicated guideway.'[110]

A PRT system is described by the organisation UK Tram as regulated by the Railways and Other Guided Transport Systems (Safety) Regulations 2006 ('ROGS 2006')[111], which define 'guided transport' as

> 'a system of transport, used wholly or mainly for the carriage of passengers, employing vehicles which for some or all of the time when they are in operation are guided by means of—
>
> (a) rails, beams, slots, guides or other apparatus, structures or devices which are fixed and not part of the vehicle; or
>
> (b) a guidance system which is automatic'.[112]

ROGS 2006 'impose prohibitions and requirements in relation to safety on railways and other guided transport systems' including, under Part 2, a safety management system and, under Part 3, 'general duties on transport operators subject to the duties in Part 2 to carry out risk assessment, co-operate with each other and certain other persons and to prepare an annual safety report to the Office of Rail Regulation'[113].

PRT is among the systems under consideration by the government for future mass transit. The CAM 2025 paper of 19 August 2022 included this passage:

> 'CAM could also offer a new mass transit option, integrated into our existing and planned transport system, as an alternative to traditional modes such as rail and bus. Operating on fully segregated 'track' infrastructure (no access for vehicles, pedestrians, or cyclists), self-driving vehicles could provide a public transport service that is safe, zero-emission, demand responsive and flexible, and cost effective. Unlike for public road use, which requires planned changes to legislation, self-driving vehicle services on fully segregated routes could potentially be regulated under existing arrangements for guided transport or guided bus systems.'[114]

---

109 Heathrow Airport YouTube channel 'How To: Use the T5 Pod Parking', accessed 16 October 2022
110 Heathrow media centre article 'Heathrow's Personal Rapid Transport ('PRT') system is on track as guideway construction phase is completed', accessed 16 October 2022.
111 SI 2006/599. See UK Tram 'Advice Note for Promoters Considering Personal Rapid Transit (PRT)', Version 1: July 2012, page 15, accessed 16 October 2022.
112 ROGS 2006, reg 2 ('Interpretation and application')
113 ROGS 2006, explanatory note.
114 CAM 2025, p.91, 4.3.2, 'Mass transit systems'.

The process of regulation for such services has started. In July 2022 the government consulted upon its intention to expand the scope of orders that can be made by the Secretary of State for Transport under the Transport and Works Act 1992 and secondary legislation, so that 'modes of guided transport' might be expanded from physical means of guidance such as cables or tracks, to non-physical guidance such as that provided by sensors.[115]

This was brought into law on 26 December 2022, with the amendment of the Transport and Works (Guided Transport Modes) Order 1992[116] to allow for the use of non-physical guidance systems, guided by sensors, in passenger and goods transport.

From 26 December 2022, the Transport and Works (Guided Transport Modes) (Amendment) Order 2022[117] added to the prescribed modes in relation to which the Secretary of State for Transport may under the Transport and Works Act 1992 'make an order relating to, or to matters ancillary to, the construction or operation of a transport system of any of the following kinds, so far as it is in England and Wales'[118] the following further modes[119] of guided transport:

'(g) road-based with sensor guidance;

(h) road-based with side guidance;

(i) track-based with sensor guidance;

(j) track-based with side guidance.'[120]

Where:

"road-based with sensor guidance" means a mode in which the vehicles—

(a) are capable of operating on a road; and

(b) are guided wholly or mainly by means of sensors on the vehicles which, by reference to the vehicles' external environment or to the receipt of electromagnetic information, provide data which is used to guide the vehicles;

"road-based with side guidance" means a mode in which the vehicles—

(a) are capable of operating on a road; and

(b) are guided wholly or mainly by means of wheels bearing outwards against fixed apparatus;

"track-based with sensor guidance" means a mode in which the vehicles—

(a) are supported by means of a track or other structure not being a road; and

---

115 Gov.uk, 'Consultation outcome – allowing new forms of guided transport to be authorised by a Transport and Works Act Order', updated 29 July 2022
116 SI 1992/3231.
117 SI 2022/1380.
118 TWA 1992, s 1(1)(d).
119 'Mode' means a mode of guided transport which employs vehicles used for the carriage of passengers or goods": The Transport and Works (Guided Transport Modes) Order 1992, SI 1992/3231 (as amended by SI 2022/1380), Art 3(2).
120 The Transport and Works (Guided Transport Modes) Order 1992, SI 1992/3231 (as amended by SI 2022/1380), Art 2.

(b) are guided wholly or mainly by means of sensors which, by reference to the vehicles' external environment or to the receipt of electromagnetic information, provide data which is used to guide the vehicles; and

"track-based with side guidance" means a mode in which the vehicles—

(a) are supported by means of a track or other structure not being a road; and

(b) are guided wholly or mainly by means of wheels bearing outwards against fixed apparatus.' And:

'In this Order –

"electromagnetic information" means information that is conveyed by some kind of radiation including radio waves, microwaves, infrared, visible light, ultraviolet, x-rays and gamma rays;

"goods" has the same meaning as in Part 1 (the provision of railway services) of the Railways Act 1993;[121]

"mode" means a mode of guided transport which employs vehicles used for the carriage of passengers or goods;

"road" has the same meaning as in the Road Traffic Regulation Act 1984.[122]'

Personal security of passengers using automated vehicles without a human supervisor in the vehicle

5.20   A no user-in-charge (NUIC) vehicle would be one in which only passengers are physically present. So concern as to security of passengers informs the debate as to the overall form of regulation of highly automated passenger services.

The history of deregulation of bus services (which at one stage involved 'bus wars' including criminal behaviour) and the absence of regulation at the outset of private hire both provide lessons as to the personal importance of effective regulation.

The Law Commissions made the point in their final report on AV law:

'Without some changes to the existing law, passenger services may either be banned or entirely unregulated. Where there is no 'driver' it could be argued that the service does not require licensing at all. That argument is strongest in respect of private hire services across Great Britain; and taxi services in Scotland. There is a risk that a determined operator might exploit legal gaps to run an entirely unlicensed service. Automated passenger services could emerge as unregulated competitors to private hire, as happened when private

---

121 RA 1993, s 83(1): '"*goods*" includes mail, parcels, animals, plants and any other creature, substance or thing capable of being transported, but does not include passengers".
122 RTRA 1984, s 142(1)(a): '"*road*" ... in England and Wales, means any length of highway or of any other road to which the public has access, and includes bridges over which a road passes'.

hire emerged as competition to taxis before the introduction of private hire regulation.'[123]

Regulations will also need to provide, in some detail, for safety of the passenger in an unattended vehicle. Regulation already provides in part for security of the passenger:

'Various legal provisions in existing law assume the presence of human staff on board and are calculated to ensure that disabled passengers can communicate with transport staff. For example, in a regulated PSV, a communication device must be fitted in various places, including adjacent to the wheelchair space and within reach of the priority seat and adjacent to at least every third row of seats. There are also requirements that ensure adequate communication with the driver of a PSV.'[124]

The Law Commissions note both the aspirations and the limits of technology:

'Artificial intelligence that can provide information and support is already widely available and increasingly sophisticated. Until public acceptance and technology develop to allow a human-machine interface to be as effective as ordinary human interaction, the option to speak to another person, rather than a machine, is likely to remain important, especially to disabled and older people.'[125]

– and the limitations of CCTV coverage, if there are even *insufficient* staff present on public transport:

'The Government report on the experiences of disabled rail passengers[126] noted that it was suggested in focus groups that good behaviour could be encouraged by the following four measures. First, preventing alcohol consumption on trains. Second, putting up posters 'nudging' other passengers to be considerate. Third, allowing passengers to activate CCTV, and for the activated camera to indicate that it was working. The CCTV feature was considered to act as a deterrent, although staff intervention when required was seen as critical to the success of the CCTV solution. Fourth, for there to be more staff on trains and at stations. It will be necessary to consider how such recommendations may apply to HARPS.'[127]

Whether and how, as a matter of fact, passenger security could be achieved in a no user-in-charge (NUIC) public vehicle are unanswered questions. In relation to oversight (not supervision in person) of such vehicles, the Law Commission in 2019 opined that:

---

123 Law Commissions' joint report at end of AV consultation (January 2022), p.194, 10.8.
124 Law Commissions' second AV law consultation paper (October 2019) at p.120, 6.84. For example, see the requirement for communication device to be fitted 'adjacent to a wheelchair space and in a position readily useable by any person who is using the wheelchair space': Public Service Vehicles Accessibility Regulations 2000, SI 2000/1970, Sch 1 para 9(1)(a).
125 Law Commissions' second AV law consultation paper (October 2019) at p.120, 6.87.
126 Department for Transport, 'Research on experiences of disabled rail passengers' (July 2019) at pp.37 38, 9.20 to 9.22.
127 Law Commissions' second AV law consultation paper (October 2019) at p.123, 6.99.

'In our view [CCTV] operators should be under a general duty to take reasonable steps to safeguard passengers from assault or abuse. Guidance on how this should be done will need to be developed in the light of experience.'[128]

Both vehicle design and the operating practices of passenger services operators will affect passenger safety. The provisions of the AV Bill 2023-24 (HL Bill 1) provide both that:

'The Secretary of State must prepare a statement of the principles that the Secretary of State proposes to apply in assessing, for the purposes of this Part, whether a vehicle is capable of travelling autonomously and safely' (cl 2(1))

and that:

'Where the appropriate national authority grants a[n automated passenger services] permit, it must include a permit condition (of the sort described in section 82(5)(b)) requiring the permit holder to publish reports about the automated passenger services which it provides, and in particular about the steps which it takes—

(a) to meet the needs of older or disabled passengers, and

(b) to safeguard passengers more generally' (cl 87(4)).

Whether those provisions are adequate will be a matter for Parliament. The disapplication of taxi, PHV and bus legislation by cl 83 leaves both a blank slate and the task of enacting an effective scheme for the safety of AV passengers.

Civil liability for assault by a third party in an unattended automated vehicle

5.21   Whether an assault on a passenger in a HARPS vehicle by another passenger, in the absence of a human supervisor provided by the operator, could lead to civil liability against the HARPS operator would be a matter of law applied to the facts of the case. The main obstacle to such a claim would be that the law does *not* recognise 'a general principle that, whenever the harmful conduct of another is reasonably foreseeable, it is our duty to take precautions against it' because 'the common law does not impose liability for what are called pure omissions'[129].

There are 'strictly limited'[130] exceptions to that position, where an affirmative duty may arise, for example: 'This may occur where the defender negligently causes or permits to be created a source of danger, and it is reasonably foreseeable that third parties may interfere with it and, sparking off the danger, thereby cause damage to persons in the position of the pursuer'[131]. The law does not decide this point without regard to habits and risks arising from contemporary technology – for example, in a claim arising from a fire:

---

128 Law Commissions' second AV law consultation paper (October 2019) at p.80, 4.123.
129 *Smith v Littlewoods Ltd* [1987] 1 AC 241 (HL), 270 to 271 (Lord Goff, in the first phrase quoting Hart and Honoré, *Causation in the Law* (2nd Edn, 1985)).
130 271h.
131 272 to 273.

'... it is not to be forgotten that, in ordinary households in this country, there are nowadays many things which might be described as possible sources of fire if interfered with by third parties, ranging from matches and firelighters to electric irons and gas cookers and even oil-fired central heating systems. These are commonplaces of modern life; and it would be quite wrong if householders were to be held liable in negligence for acting in a socially acceptable manner.'[132]

So the possibility of civil liability attaching to a HARPS operator for assault against a claimant passenger on an unattended HARPS vehicle by a third party passenger might arise for consideration by a court, strictly exceptionally, in the context of an allegation that the operator had negligently caused or permitted its unattended vehicle to be a source of danger. But the court's judgment would be fact-sensitive (including consideration of all measures taken by the operator, in relation to applicable law and safety standards).

The novelty of HARPS technology should not of itself point to liability, as the law recognises contemporary technology within its relevant assessment of what is 'socially acceptable' conduct by a defendant.

However, a driverless passenger vehicle would, especially in the early stages of public deployment, still be an unfamiliar technology to many. Safety issues in relation to HARPS should be always approached with care by operators, but especially in the early period of the technology and before it is a 'commonplace of modern life'.

D Laws of Passenger Services and Public Transport involving Electric Vehicles

5.22   (This section outlines regulation of e-scooter and e-bike rental schemes. E-bikes and e-scooters are discussed further in Chapter 16, 'smaller electric vehicle claims'.)

E-bike rental schemes

5.23   Bicycles and e-bicycles (the latter defined in law as 'electrically assisted pedal cycles' or EAPCs) are subject to regulations governing their safe construction.

Bicycles are subject to the Pedal Bicycles (Safety) Regulations 2010, which apply to non-mechanical bicycles, 'propelled solely by the muscular energy of a person on that vehicle by means of pedals ... not ... constructed or adapted for propulsion by mechanical power'[133]. An electric vehicle is propelled by mechanical power[134]. So bicycles are outside the scope of this book, though they play their part in the regulation of bicycle and e-bicycle rental schemes which have been adopted in many areas.

---

132 274B to C (Lord Goff).
133 SI 2010/198, reg.2.
134 *Elieson v Parker* (1917) 81 JP 265.

EAPCs are subject to the Electrically Assisted Pedal Cycles Regulations 1983 (EAPCR 1983)[135]. RTA 1988, s 189 treats an EAPC as defined by EAPCR 1983 as not being a 'motor vehicle' for the purposes of the Road Traffic Acts, so (for example) releasing the user of such a vehicle from the requirement to have compulsory insurance under RTA 1988, s 143. To be within EAPCR 1983, an EAPC must meet the following criteria:

- It must be a pedal cycle with two or more wheels (EAPCR 1983, reg 3);
- It must be fitted with pedals by means of which it is capable of being propelled[136] (EAPCR 1983, reg 4(b));
- It must be fitted with no motor other than an electric motor (EAPCR 1983, reg 4(c));
- Its electric motor must have a maximum continuous rated power (as defined by EAPCR 1983, reg 5) which does not exceed 250 watts (EAPCR 1983, reg 4(c)(i)), and
- Its electric motor cannot propel the vehicle when it is travelling at more than 15.5 miles per hour (EAPCR 1983, reg 4(c)(ii)).

Operators of e-bike rental schemes are subject to all applicable laws including tort laws (such as negligence and nuisance), contract and statutory law such as the Highways Act 1980 (s 149 of which allows for 'removal of things so deposited on the highway to be a nuisance', which is relevant to dockless bicycles[137]). However, as in the case of car rentals (above), bicycle and EAPC rental schemes are less regulated in terms of specific laws than public service vehicles and passenger transport.

The regulatory space is instead occupied by standards and codes of practice (such as Transport for London's 'Dockless bike share code of practice for operators in London' (September 2018)).

Trial e-scooter rental schemes

5.24 An 'electric scooter' is now defined (in relation to registration and licensing) by the Road Vehicle (Registration and Licensing) Regulations 2002, reg 33(1) ('nil licences')[138] as follows:

> ' "electric scooter" means a vehicle which—
>
> (a) is fitted with an electric motor with a maximum continuous power rating not exceeding 500 watts;
>
> (b) is not fitted with pedals that are capable of propelling the vehicle;
>
> (c) has two wheels, one front and one rear, aligned along the direction of travel;

---

135 SI 1983/1168.
136 See *Winter v DPP* (above and Chapter 4, 'Driving').
137 See page 8, part 7 of the TfL 'Dockless bike share code of practice for operators in London' (September 2018).
138 SI 2002/2742, as amended by the Electric Scooter Trials and Traffic Signs (Coronavirus) Regulations and General Directions 2020, reg 2(3).

(d) is designed to carry no more than one person;

(e) has a maximum weight, excluding the driver, not exceeding 55 kgs;

(f) has a maximum design speed not exceeding 15.5 miles per hour;

(g) has a means of directional control through the use of handlebars which are mechanically linked to the steered wheel;

(h) has a means of controlling the speed through hand controls; and

(i) has a power control that defaults to the "off" position;'

Trials of rental e-scooters are continuing to allow the government to assess how e-scooters should be regulated if their use is legalised on all public roads. The government has announced its intention eventually to legalise e-scooter use on public roads.

Trials of e-scooters are expressly regulated, by the Electric Scooter Trials and Traffic Signs (Coronavirus) Regulations and General Directions 2020 ('EST... Order 2020')[139]. The purpose of those regulations is 'to enable a trial of electric scooters to assess their suitability for use on roads'[140]. The UK government has published guidance to operators of trial e-scooter rental schemes[141].

The 2020 order liberates trial e-scooters from several of the requirements that would otherwise attach to their use, resulting from their legal status as 'motor vehicles'[142], such as registration[143]. But the requirement for insurance for use on a road or other public place remains[144] (which government guidance to users states will be provided by the rental scheme operator[145]) and a full or provisional driving licence permitting use of the scooter is still required[146].

As to vehicle specifications, the government has made Vehicle Special Orders (VSOs)[147] to allow e-scooters to be used as trial vehicles on public roads. The government has published online a summary of the specifications which have been met by rental operators under those VSOs for trial e-scooters (which are described as 'minimum technical requirements')[148].

Possible future reclassification of e-scooters

5.25 But an e-scooter might not be classified as a 'motor vehicle' in future. The government's proposal for future legalisation of all e-scooter use aims to change

---

139 SI 2020/663.
140 Explanatory note to SI 2020/663.
141 Department for Transport, 'Guidance: E-scooter trials: guidance for local authorities and rental operators' (updated 22 February 2022).
142 *DPP v King* [2008] EWHC 447 (Admin).
143 EST... Regulations 2020, reg 2.
144 RTA 1988, s 143.
145 UK government 'Guidance: E-scooter trials: guidance for users' 'Insurance' (updated 31 March 2022)
146 EST ... Regulations 2020, reg 4.
147 See chapter 3 of this book (the laws of testing AAEVs) for Vehicle Special Orders.
148 Department for Transport, 'Guidance: E-scooter trials: guidance for local authorities and rental operators' (updated 22 February 2022), 'Annex: Minimum technical requirements for e-scooters', accessed 12 October 2022.

the definition. Baroness Vere, speaking for the government, told the House of Lords on 11 May 2022 that:

> '...it is our intention that the [Transport] Bill will create a low-speed, zero-emission vehicle category that is independent from the cycle and motor vehicle categories. New powers would allow the Government to decide the vehicles that fall into this new category in future and how they should be regulated to make sure that they are safe to use. We hope that e-scooters will be the first of these vehicles.'[149]

That was a significant statement, as it indicated that the government had accepted the recommendation of the House of Commons Transport Select Committee (TSC) in October 2020, on relinquishing the requirement for compulsory insurance for e-scooters, that:

> 'In our view, an e-scooter is more akin to a bike or an e-bike, rather than a moped, and we share concerns that too many requirements on users or operators may be burdensome and discourage take-up.'[150]

In October 2022 the then Secretary of State for Transport (during the Truss administration) told the House of Commons Transport Committee that, contrary to the announcement to Parliament in the Queen's Speech, the Bill would not proceed during the 2022 to 2023 session, although it was not made clear whether e-scooter legislation would proceed in a smaller bill during that session[151]. In December 2022, the current Secretary of State for Transport told the same committee that the Transport Bill would not proceed during the 2022 to 2023 session[152].

Although the AV Bill 2023-24 (HL Bill 1) was announced in the King's Speech of 7 November 2023 and published the following day, no Transport Bill for smaller electric vehicles such as e-scooters has yet appeared.

Pedicabs in London

5.26   The Pedicabs (London) Bill 2023-24 (HL Bill 2) would, if enacted, empower Transport for London to regulate previously unregulated pedicabs by means of licensing, enforcement powers and criminal offences. The definition of pedicab includes a power-assisted pedal cycle (cll 1(2) and 7(1)).

The legal background is set out in the explanatory notes to the Bill (paras 5 to 7):

> 'There is no extant legislation which would allow the regulation of pedicabs in London. This is because the legislation which enables TfL to regulate taxis within London does not apply to pedicabs. Conflicting judicial decisions

---

149 Baroness Vere, House of Lords Hansard Volume 822, columns 30 to 31, 11 May 2022.
150 'E-scooters: pavement nuisance or transport innovation?', report of the Transport Select Committee of the House of Commons, 2 October 2020, Chapter 4, 'Accessibility of E-Scooters', 'Insurance'.
151 Parliament Live TV, Transport Select Committee 19 October 2022 at 9:42 to 9:45, Sec of St for Transport the Rt Hon Anne-Marie Trevelyan MP.
152 Parliament Live TV, Transport Select Committee 7 December 2022 at 9:43, Sec of St for Transport the Rt Hon Mark Harper MP.

mean that pedicabs can only be regulated outside London, where different legislation applies.

Outside London, in England and Wales, pedicabs are treated as taxis for the purposes of the Town Police Clauses Act 1847 and Part II of the Local Government (Miscellaneous Provisions) Act 1976. Accordingly, pedicabs may be regulated as taxis under the provisions of the 1847 and 1976 Acts.

By contrast, within London, pedicabs are not treated as taxis for the purpose of the Metropolitan Public Carriage Act 1869, which is the equivalent legislation in London. Pedicabs are instead considered stage carriages in London pursuant to section 4 of the Metropolitan Public Carriage Act. The legislation governing stage carriages is no longer in force; there are therefore no licensing provisions, so pedicabs are unregulated in London.'

Chapter 6

The law of motor insurance

'In the case of personal injuries, the great majority of claims are brought against defendants who are insured against liability. This means that the bill for damages awards is largely met by the premium paying population rather than by the wrongdoer. It follows that the tort system, at least in the personal injury context, is overwhelmingly financed by the public.'

Winfield and Jolowicz on Tort (2020)[1]

Contents at a glance:

A Outline of the law of insurance of advanced, automated and electric vehicles 6.01
B Insurance law for Advanced Driver Assistance Systems (ADAS) 6.10
C Insurance law for automated vehicles 6.15
D Insurance law for electric vehicles 6.33

A Outline of the law of insurance for advanced, automated and electric vehicles[2]

6.01   Insurance of the use[3] of motor vehicles equipped with advanced driver assistance system (ADAS) and of automated and electric vehicles exists within a

---

1   *Winfield and Jolowicz on Tort,* (20th edn by James Goudkamp and Donal Nolan, Sweet & Maxwell, 2020) at 1-028.
2   This is a summary aimed at putting AAEV insurance law into context, not at discussing all the numerous points of motor insurance law. For the whole topic, see in particular *The Development of Traffic Liability,* ed. Wolfgang Ernst (Cambridge, 2010), Chapter 1 of *The Law of Motor Insurance* by Robert Merkin and Maggie Hemsworth (2nd edn, Sweet and Maxwell, 2015), chapter 21 of *Birds' Modern Insurance Law* (11th edn, Sweet and Maxwell, 2019) *The Law of Compulsory Motor Insurance* by Özlem Gürses (Lloyd's Insurance Law Library, Routledge, 2020) and chapter 29 of *MacGillivray on Insurance Law* (15th edn, by John Birds, Ben Lynch QC and Simon Paul, Sweet and Maxwell, 2022). Other works on motor insurance (eg. Elliott and Street, *Law and Society: Road Accidents,* Penguin, 1968) are cited below, but those mentioned above are more current. The Law Commission of England and Wales and the Law Commission of Scotland publish all documents of the automated vehicle law consultation (2018 to 2022) at www.lawcom.gov.uk/project/automated-vehicles/.
3   '... what has to be covered by insurance is the use of a vehicle not the person using the vehicle': *Lees v MIB* Lloyds List Reports 1952 Vol.2 p. 210, Lord Goddard at 213, quoted

long-established but complicated scheme of road traffic accident compensation in Britain. That scheme rests upon insurance.

This section outlines AAEV insurance law in its context, within the British scheme for road traffic accident compensation.

The compensation gap

6.02   In the early 1900s, the use of motor vehicles on roads was increasing. So were accidents[4].

Some argued for strict liability for injury and damage caused by the users of motor vehicles to innocent victims of road traffic accidents. British courts resisted the call for strict liability but held that the law of negligence applied to the driver[5].

Anyone injured by another person's use of a car could seek redress through the civil courts, by securing a judgment for damages against the user.

However, motor insurance was then voluntary. So that left a gap. A claimant might succeed in getting a court judgment against the user of a vehicle but be unable to secure payment of their damages, if the user lacked funds and insurance.

Compulsory insurance against liability to third parties

6.03   In 1929, a system of compulsory third-party insurance for the use of motor vehicles on British roads was recommended as the means of ensuring payment of compensation to the victims of road traffic accidents[6].

That system was enacted in 1930. It was made a criminal offence to use (or cause or permit to be used) a motor vehicle on a road without a policy of insurance against the risks of injury and damage to third parties[7]. The policy was required to insure 'such person, persons or classes of persons as may be specified in the policy in respect of any liability which may be incurred by him or them in respect of the death of or bodily injury to any person caused by or arising out of the use of the vehicle on a road'[8].

---

  by Popplewell J in *R v Secretary of State for Transport ex parte National Insurance Guarantee Corporation Plc*, QBD 8 May 1996, 1996 WL 1090145. See section 143(1) of the Road Traffic Act 1988: 'A person must not use a motor vehicle' nor 'cause or permit any other person to use' such vehicle 'on a road or other public place unless there is in force in relation to the use of the vehicle by that person', or 'that other person', 'such a policy of insurance as complies with the requirements of this Part of this Act'.

4   The scale of road casualties was new and shocking. Winfield wrote in the first edition of his tort law textbook in 1937 that 'where the railway slew its scores, the motor vehicle killed its hundreds'. P Winfield, *A Text-Book of the Law of Tort* (Sweet and Maxwell, 1937) 209, quoted by Paul Mitchell in *A History of Tort Law 1900-1950* (Cambridge, 2015), page 208.

5   See, for example, *Wing v London General Omnibus Co* [1909] 2 KB 652 (CA).

6   Report of the Royal Commission on Transport, *The Control of Traffic on Roads,* Cmd 3365 (1929).

7   Road Traffic Act 1930, Part II ('Provision against third-party risks arising out of the use of motor vehicles'), section 35. Committing the section 35 offence was subsequently held to be actionable in damages as a breach of statutory duty, in *Monk v Warbey* [1935] 1 KB 75.

8   Road Traffic Act 1930, s 36, equivalent to the current RTA 1988, s 145.

Requiring a third-party insurance policy to use a motor vehicle on a road or other public place[9] remains a pillar of British motor insurance law today[10]. But the British system of compensating the victims of road traffic accidents has developed around that requirement in complex ways.

Inherent tension

6.04   The British system of road traffic accident compensation is complex because it is insurance-based.

Insurance is a matter of contract between two parties (the first party insured and the second party insurer). But any system for compensation for the public at large necessarily goes beyond that two-party relationship, to the rights of injured third parties. The rights of third parties to the insurance contract are uncertain, unless they are set out in law or agreed.

Added to the legal complexity are problems of cost for insurers: third-party insurance is 'in general … much more expensive and less efficient to operate than first party insurance'[11].

The chief source of legal complexity in compulsory motor insurance has been the terms on which it is given. The contractual terms of insurance are agreed between the insurance company and the insured but not by the third-party beneficiary of the insurance. Given the costs of providing third-party liability insurance, it is in the interests of the insurer to seek to limit its application, by terms written into the insurance policy.

That is what happened after the introduction of compulsory motor insurance in the Road Traffic Act 1930:

> 'Insurance was left in the hands of companies and underwriters who could impose what terms and conditions they chose. Nor was there any standard form of policy, and any company who could fulfill the not very onerous financial requirements that were necessary for acceptance as an approved insurer could hedge round the policies with so many warranties and conditions that no one advising an injured person could say with any certainty whether, if damages were recovered against the driver of the car, there was a prospect of recovering against the insurers.'[12]

---

9   ''Road' in relation to England and Wales, means any highway and any other road to which the public has access, and includes bridges over which a road passes': RTA 1988, s 192(1). For definitions, see *Harrison v Hill* [1932] JC 13 and subsequent cases, reviewed in September 2021 in *Brown v Fisk* [2021] EWHC 2769 (QB, Master Dagnall), [2022] 2 PIQR P4. The Supreme Court confirmed in *Pilling v UK Insurance* [2019] UKSC 16 [40, 41] that the requirement for insurance in the RTA 1988 could not be read down in a national court in a case between private persons to accommodate the wider definition of location in the CJEU judgment in *Vnuk v Zavarovalnica Triglav dd* (Case C-162/13) [2016] RTR 10. From 28 June 2022 the Motor Vehicles (Compulsory Insurance) Act 2022 removes the effect of *Vnuk* from British law.
10   Now in the Road Traffic Act 1988, Part VI ('Third-party liabilities'), s 143.
11   *Birds' Modern Insurance Law*, 1-04.
12   *Zurich General Accident and Liability Insurance Co Ltd v Morrison* [1942] 2 KB 53, Goddard LJ at 61, 62.

That commercial behaviour led to the Road Traffic Act 1934, which imposed a new duty upon motor insurers to satisfy a judgment obtained by a third party and limited the extent to which they could rely upon contractual terms to avoid payment to an injured third party.

The need for a second Road Traffic Act within four years of the first emphasises the practical role of regulation in British motor insurance law. Since its introduction, the legislature and the courts have guarded a tense border between the commercial nature and the public purpose of the British compulsory motor insurance scheme[13].

Unorthodox methods

6.05   Another example of that tension between public and commercial interests is the method of compensating the victims of uninsured drivers.

This was the result of negotiation between government and the motor insurance industry[14]. In 1946, an agreement was reached between government and motor insurers in which the latter took the form of the Motor Insurers' Bureau, a company incorporated for the purpose of securing payment of compensation for the victims of uninsured drivers. But this agreement was not put on a statutory basis[15]. Later complemented by an agreement in relation to victims of untraced drivers (1969), the government's agreement with the MIB was essentially commercial.

The need to compensate the many victims of road traffic accidents led to such unorthodox solutions. Alongside the 1930 statutory compulsory insurance scheme, the MIB extra-statutory agreement model (1946) became the other supporting pillar of the system of British road traffic accident compensation. That is still the position.

---

13   See, for example, Merkin and Hemsworth's summary of the debate after the 1937 Cassel committee's recommendations for reform of the motor insurance system, 'Waged through the pages of the Modern Law Review', including: 'Hughes ... argued that the proposals led to an imbalance against the rights of the insurers against the victim ... Finlay ... argued that the use of a motor vehicle was a privilege, for which an insurance premium was a justifiable charge, and that society had reached a state whereby common law rules alone were no longer satisfactory ... Lord Chorley ... noted that Parliament had created a new market for insurers, and as a result motor premiums had risen only slightly to cover the enhanced risks, so that the balance had been properly drawn ... Lord Chorley was accused of 'political and sociological speculation''. Merkin and Hemsworth, Chapter 1, 1-18, footnote 112.

14   'The UK motor insurance industry, anxious to avoid legislation requiring them to participate in [the 1937 Cassel committee]'s proposed guarantee fund, decided to accept a non-statutory scheme for the compensation of uninsured drivers... It has been suggested that the threat of nationalisation, one of the defining themes of the post-war Labour government, was instrumental in producing this agreement: Williams, (1973) 59 ABA Journal 73.' Merkin and Hemsworth Chapter 1, 1-20 and footnote 116.

15   Although the MIB agreements are not statutory, there is a structural link between the MIB and the statutory system of compulsory third party motor insurance, in that an 'authorised insurer' issuing a policy of insurance complying with the RTA 1988, Part VI is defined as 'an insurer who is a member of the Motor Insurers Bureau (a company limited by guarantee and incorporated under the Companies Act 1929 on 14th June 1946)' (RTA 1988, ss 95(2) and 145(5)).

Pragmatism leads to complexity

6.06   But the pragmatism of the system has produced layers of complexity.

The combination of statutory insurance under successive Road Traffic Acts and extra-statutory agreements between government and the MIB has been described as providing 'safety nets'[16] for road traffic accident victims.

But the courts have noted the difficulties.

On the statutory side of the system, the interpretation of policy terms in accordance with the layered rules of the Road Traffic Acts has led to much litigation[17].

On the non-statutory side, the position of the MIB has also generated complexity. Lord Justice (later Lord) Diplock wrote in 1968 (while adjudicating whether or not the MIB could be added as a party to a claim) that:

> '… instead of amending the legislation so as to impose upon the Motor Insurers' Bureau a statutory liability to the unsatisfied judgment creditor as had been done by the Road Traffic Act, 1934, in respect of the liability of insurers to satisfy judgments against defendants covered by a valid policy of insurance, the matter was dealt with by an agreement of June 17, 1946, between the Minister of Transport and the Motor Insurers' Bureau…. What reasons influenced the Government to adopt this oblique and extra-statutory way of imposing liability upon the bureau, despite the legal complications this involves, I do not know. But the courts must accept it as it is and try, so far as they are permitted by the rules, to make it work with justice to the bureau as well as to the persons for whose benefit the Minister made the contract.' [18]

Further complexity resulted from the adjustment of the safety nets over time. Listing the main developments in British motor insurance law from 1930 reveals no cogent pattern but many adjustments to the equipment of compensation. See **6.08**.

Those adjustments to the motor insurance system can be viewed as reactions to the behaviours of various actors. For example:

- vehicle users bought, drove and loaned more vehicles, and used them in their work,

---

16   The Motor Insurers' Bureau describes itself as providing 'a safety net for the innocent victim of an uninsured driver'. See its Articles of Association (first object, at article 2(1)(a)) and *MIB Notes for Guidance. MIB Uninsured Agreement (2015)*.

17   See, for example, the Court of Appeal's conclusion in 2013 that, although RTA 1988, s 145(3) provided that, in order to comply with the requirements of Part VI, a policy of motor insurance had to insure a driver in respect of liability for deliberate damage to property, it did not follow that such liability was to be treated as being covered by the terms of a policy, for the purposes of RTA 1988, s 151(2)(a), if the actual policy excluded such liability: *Bristol Alliance v Williams* [2013] QB 806. This judgment has been criticised (see Gürses at 7.96 to 7.103 and 8.50 to 8.56) but it reflects the point that the 1934 Act left gaps in the third-party liability provisions of the Road Traffic Acts, within which arguments of non-cover to third parties could develop.

18   Diplock LJ, as he then was, in *Gurtner v Circuit* [1968] 2 QB 587 at 598, 602. Matthew Channon has argued for the MIB to be placed on a statutory footing: *The Nature of the Motor Insurers' Bureau and Its Agreements: Time for a Radical New Approach?* European Journal of Comparative Law and Governance 7 (2020) 168-200.

- manufacturers introduced new technologies,
- victims of road traffic accidents sought compensation for injuries and other losses,
- litigation generated legal costs and novel heads of claim[19],
- insurers reacted to liability risks and to the costs of litigation, and
- government sought to balance public interests of effective compensation and of insurance costs.

Given the variety of behaviours and actors affecting it, and the mixture of statutory and extra-statutory materials used in its construction, the British system for road traffic accident compensation was vulnerable to complications.

The place of the Automated and Electric Vehicles Act 2018, Part 1 within the statutory motor insurance scheme

6.07   The Automated and Electric Vehicles Act 2018 (AEVA 2018), Part 1 can be seen as one of the adjustments to the British compensation system. It is a reaction to an especially radical technology: the vehicle which drives itself.

But AEVA 2018 also reacts to other behaviours. It reacts to the escalation of legal costs, which informs its adoption of a direct right of action by the victim against the insurer (or owner permitted to be uninsured) as a means of avoiding the burden for the accident victim of difficult and expensive litigation invoking product liability laws in the first instance (AEVA 2018, s 2).

AEVA 2018 passes that burden of expense to the liable insurer or permitted uninsured owner who (in the second instance) may seek contribution or indemnity under AEVA 2018, 5. That appears to be a measure aimed at managing costs – primarily for the victim but also for the insurer/owner. As Matthew Channon has pointed out, the 'single insurer model' on which AEVA 2018, Part 1 is premised was suggested by the motor insurance industry[20].

AEVA 2018 has yet to be put into practice so its mechanisms are untested (and might be amended by the Automated Vehicles Act 2024 – now the Automated Vehicles Bill 2023-24 (HL Bill 1), before it comes into practical effect with the authorisation of the first automated vehicle). AEVA 2018 is, in essence, a means of transferring the risk of litigation from victim to insurer. And victim includes not only the traditional third party but the 'insured person'[21].

---

19   Credit hire charges (charges by accident management companies for the provision of replacement vehicles during repair periods) provide an example of novel damages claims of significance to the motor insurance industry. Litigation first as to the recoverability and secondly as to the measure of such charges has been ongoing since the 1990s. See *Ellis on Credit Hire* (Aidan Ellis, 6th edn, Law Brief Publishing, 2019) and Gürses, chapter 9.

20   Matthew Channon, Lucy McCormick and Kyriaki Noussia, *The Law and Autonomous Vehicles* (Informa Law/Routledge, 2019) chapter 3, 3.24.

21   AEVA 2018. s 2(1)(c): 'Where – ... (c) an insured person or any other person suffers damage as a result of the accident, the insurer is liable for that damage'. RTA 1988, s 145(3A) (as amended by section 20 and schedule 1 AEVA 2018) accordingly requires 'the insurer's obligations to an insured person under section 2(1) of the [AEVA] 2018 (liability of insurers etc where accident caused by automated vehicle) to be obligations under the policy'.

So AEVA 2018 is a creature of the compulsory insurance scheme of 1930, even though it has expanded the bounds of that scheme significantly (eg in its provision for compulsory first party insurance and for insurance of employees).

List of the main developments in British motor insurance law[22]

6.08

Year	Development	British Law
1930	Third parties given a right against insurers on the bankruptcy etc of the insured	Third Parties (Rights Against Insurers) Act 1930, s 1
1930	Enactment of offence of using (or causing or permitting to be used) a motor vehicle on a road without compulsory third-party motor insurance	RTA 1930, s 35[23]
1934	Court of Appeal provides remedy to victims of some uninsured drivers by holding that a breach of the compulsory insurance requirement in the 1930 Act is a breach of statutory duty actionable in damages against the owner of a car who had allowed an uninsured person to drive it.	*Monk v Warbey*[24]
1934	Further Road Traffic Act to regulate excessive use of exemptions and conditions precedent by motor insurers in attempts to avoid coverage. Enactment of legal duty of insurers to satisfy judgments against persons insured in respect of third-party risks.	RTA 1934, ss 12 and 10
1937	Cassel Committee report on compulsory insurance[25] recommends, among other matters, establishment of central fund to compensate victims of uninsured drivers and prohibition of all but a small list of permitted exclusions to third party cover.	–

---

22 This is a table of the main developments which, in the writer's opinion, affect a view of AAEV insurance. Other statutes (eg relating to contribution and contributory negligence) arose in part from motor accident liabilities, to which motor insurance law is tied, but for the sake of focus those are discussed in other chapters.

23 See *Monk v Warbey* [1935] 1 KB 75, 80 (Greer LJ) for a summary of the two Acts of 1930: '… it had become apparent that people who were injured by the negligent driving of motor cars were in a parlous situation if the negligent person was unable to pay damages. Accordingly two statutes were passed, …'

24 [1935] 1 KB 75. Though reported in 1935, the facts of *Monk v Warbey* preceded the 1934 Act.

25 *Report of the Committee on Compulsory Insurance*, Cmnd 5528.

1946	Motor Insurers' Bureau (MIB) established as company limited by guarantee. First agreement between MIB and Ministry of Transport for MIB to compensate the victims of uninsured drivers (UDA).	–
1969	First MIB untraced drivers agreement (UtDA)	–
1972	European Communities Act 1972[26]. EU First Motor Insurance Directive[27]. British law already complies with compulsory motor insurance requirement.	European Communities Act 1972
1972	Cover for liability to passengers made compulsory (repealing exclusion originally in RTA 1930, s 36(1)(b)(ii)).	Motor Vehicles (Passenger Insurance) Act 1971, s 1[28]
1975	Statement issued by motor insurers that 'the receipt of contributions as part of a car-sharing arrangement for social or similar purposes in respect of passenger carriage in a private car would not be regarded as carriage for hire or reward, or the use of the vehicle for hiring'[29] subject to provisos as to the number of passengers and the absence of business or profit.	–
1987	EU Second Motor Insurance Directive[30] implemented into British law. Matters including property damage and liability incurred by a person not authorised or licensed to use the vehicle included in compulsory motor insurance	Motor Vehicles (Compulsory Insurance) Regulations 1987[31]
1988	RTA 1988 consolidates road traffic law	RTA 1988, Part VI
1990	EU Third Motor Insurance Directive[32] extends compulsory insurance to all passengers (not just family members) and requires coverage for a single premium across the EU.	
2000	Geographical scope of compulsory cover expanded from 'on a road' to 'on a road or other public place'	Motor Vehicles (Compulsory Insurance) Regulations 2000[33]

---

26 For brevity, the European Communities/European Economic Communities/European Union are labelled 'EU'.

27 First Motor Insurance Directive, Council Directive 72/166/EC.

28 For the history of this compulsory cover see *R v Secretary of State for Transport ex parte National Insurance Guarantee Corporation Plc*, QBD 8 May 1996 (Popplewell J), 1996 WL 1090145.

29 MacGillivray at 29-078 and 29-016. The precursor to RTA 1988, s 150.

30 Second Motor Insurance Directive, Council Directive 84/5/EEC.

31 SI 1987/2171.

32 Third Motor Insurance Directive, Council Directive 90/232/EEC. See *Merkin & Hemsworth* 1-36 to 1-38.

33 SI 2000/726.

2002	EU Fourth Motor Insurance Directive[34]. Draft provision for direct action against insurers does not make it into final draft of the Fourth Directive but is anticipated in Britain[35].	European Communities (Rights against Insurers) Regulations 2002[36]
2005	EU Fifth Motor Insurance Directive[37]. Allows member states to derogate from compulsory insurance obligation in cases of vehicles in particular cases, including public vehicles, if compensation is otherwise available.	RTA 1988, s 144 ('exceptions from requirement of third-party insurance or security')[38]
2006	Requirement to insure a vehicle extended from users to registered keepers	Road Safety Act 2006, s 22 (adding to RTA 1988, ss 144A–144D)
2009	EU Consolidated Motor Insurance Directive[39] consolidates previous directives	
2010	Third Parties (Rights against Insurers) 2010 updates the 1930 law, eg. removing requirement for third party first to establish insured's liability in separate proceedings by allowing single direct action against insurer[40]	Third Parties (Rights against Insurers) Act 2010[41]
2012	Consumer Insurance (Disclosure and Representations) Act 2012 'replaces the duty to volunteer information with a duty on consumers to take reasonable care to answer the insurer's questions fully and accurately'[42]	Consumer Insurance (Disclosure and Representations) Act 2012
2015	Insurance Act 2015. Further reforms laws originally 'designed to protect a fledgling insurance industry' but 'now out of line with best practice'[43] including insurer's right to avoid liability for breach of warranty, even if breached term would not have increased risk of loss.	Insurance Act 2015
2018	AEVA 2018 enacted	AEVA 2018

---

34 Fourth Motor Insurance Directive, Council Directive 200/26/EC
35 The direct action was subsequently introduced in the Fifth Directive and written retrospectively into the Third Directive. It had by then been brought into force in the UK by the EC (RAI) regulations 2002. See Merkin and Hemsworth 1-54.
36 SI 2002/3061.
37 Fifth Motor Insurance Directive, Council Directive 2005/14/EC.
38 This was already the case in British law, before the Fifth Motor Insurance Directive.
39 Consolidated Motor Insurance Directive, 2009/103/EC.
40 TP (RAI) Act 2010, s 1(3).
41 Not brought entirely into force until 1 August 2016: Third Parties (Rights against Insurers) Act 2010 (Commencement) Order, SI 2016/550, article 2.
42 'Consumer Insurance Law: Pre-Contract Disclosure and Misrepresentation' Law Com No 319, Scot Law Com No 219 (December 2009), page 38, 4.3.
43 Explanatory Notes to Insurance Bill [HL], Session 2014-15.

2018	European Union (Withdrawal) Act 2018 repeals European Communities Act 1972 and provides for retention of saved EU law at end of implementation period.	European Union (Withdrawal) Act 2018
2021	AEVA 2018, Part 1 brought into force (21 April), though without section 1 list of automated vehicles to which the Act will apply.	Automated and Electric Vehicles Act 2018 (Commencement No.1) Regulations 2021[44]
2022	Motor Vehicles (Compulsory Insurance) Act 2022 adds section 156A ('retained EU law relating to compulsory insurance') to the Road Traffic Act 1988, to remove from the law of Great Britain the retained effect of the *Vnuk* judgment of the Court of Justice of the EU[45] which had expanded the definition of 'public place' in EU law. MV(CI)A 2022 in force from 28 June 2022[46].	Motor Vehicles (Compulsory Insurance) Act 2022 (adding RTA 1988, s 156A(8))
2022	Amendment of regulation 109(1) of the Road Vehicles (Construction and Use) Regulations 1986, to permit a driver 'to see … information … of any sort…' displayed on a built-in screen in an automated vehicle, and providing that the vehicle is not requesting the driver to take back control: The Road Vehicles (Construction and Use) (Automated Vehicles) Order 2022[47]. In force from 1 July 2022.	The Road Vehicles (Construction and Use) (Automated Vehicles) Order 2022
2023	8 November: First reading of Automated Vehicles Bill 2023-24 (HL Bill 1), cl 45, Sch 2, para 5 of which would amend AEVA 2018 (see below)	

Summary of British motor insurance law for AAEVS

6.09   To summarise, the main features of current British motor insurance law are that:

---

44   SI 2021/396.
45   *Vnuk v Zavarovalnica Triglav dd* (Case C-162/13) [2016] RTR 10 (CJEU). The Supreme Court had already noted *Vnuk*'s lack of application before 'a national court, hearing a dispute between private persons', in *Pilling v UK Insurance* [2019] UKSC 16 [40, 41], following Ouseley J in *R (Roadpeace Ltd) v Secretary of State for Transport* [2017] EWHC 2725 (Admin), [2018] 1 WLR 1293 and Soole J in *Lewis v Tindale* [2018] EWHC 2376 (QB), [2019] 1 WLR 1785. The 2022 Act seems to be aimed at removing the effect of *Vnuk* against the MIB.
46   Motor Vehicles (Compulsory Insurance) Act 2022, s 2(1).
47   SI 2022/470.

- The payment of compensation for victims of road traffic accidents is provided through insurance. Insurance against liabilities to third parties using a motor vehicle on a road or public place in Great Britain has been compulsory at law since 1930[48], and driving without insurance is a criminal offence[49];

- After the introduction of compulsory third party liability insurance in 1930, insurers' attempts to exclude liabilities to third parties by means of exclusion terms in their policies proliferated, so further legislation was enacted in 1934[50] preventing certain insurance policy exclusions taking effect against third parties[51] and requiring an insurer (subject to procedural requirements including notice of the proceedings in which judgment was obtained) to satisfy an unpaid judgment made against its insured[52]. The same legislation also allowed an insurer making a payment to a third party on the basis of a policy term ineffective against the third party under the Act[53], or a payment exceeding that which it would have been required to pay under the policy terms[54], to recover its payment from its insured or from another liable person. This tool of recovery for the insurer was later described by the Court of Appeal as 'the other side' of the compulsory insurance bargain[55].

---

48 Road Traffic Act 1930, Part II 'Provision against third-party risks arising out of the use of motor vehicles', comprising ss 35 to 44, including: s 35 'Users of motor vehicles to be insured against third party risks' (equivalent to RTA 1988, s 143); s 36 'Requirements in respect of policies (equivalent to RTA 1988, s 145); section 38 'Certain conditions to policies or securities to be of no effect' ('Any condition in a policy or security issued or given for the purposes of this Part of this Act, providing that no liability shall arise under the policy or security or that any liability so arising shall cease, in the event of some specified thing being done or omitted to be done after the happening of the event giving rise to a claim under the policy or security, shall be of no effect' though not voiding provision requiring repayment of third party liability by insured to insurer – equivalent to RTA 1988, s 148(5), (6)).
49 RTA 1930, s 35(2) (equivalent to RTA 1988, s 143(2)).
50 Road Traffic Act 1934, Part II 'Amendments as to provision against third-party risks', ss 10 to 17 including: s 10 'duty of insurers to satisfy judgments against persons insured in respect of third-party risks', including s 10(4) 'If the amount which an insurer becomes liable under this section to pay in respect of a liability of a person insured by a policy exceeds the amount for which he would, apart from the provisions of this section, be liable under the policy in respect of that liability, he shall be entitled to recover the excess from that person' (equivalent to RTA 1988, s 151); s 12 'Avoidance of restriction on scope of policies covering third party risks' (the list of matters purporting to restrict cover which shall have no effect against third party risks, starting with '(a) the age or physical or mental condition of persons driving the vehicle …' and providing that 'any sum paid by an insurer in or towards the discharge of any liability of any person which is covered by the policy by virtue only of this section shall be recoverable by the insurer from that person' – equivalent to RTA 1988, s 148(1)–(4)); s 16 'Payments and insurance in respect of emergency treatment of injuries arising from the use of motor vehicles on roads' (equivalent to RTA 1988, s 158).
51 RTA 1934, s 12 later RTA 1988, s 148(1)–(4) (see footnote above).
52 RTA 1934, s 10, later RTA 1988, s 151.
53 RTA 1934, s 12, later RTA 1988, s 148(4).
54 RTA 1934, s 10(4), see later RTA 1988, s 151(8).
55 'Section 151(8) [RTA 1988] is, of course, a national rule; there is nothing equivalent in the [EU motor insurance] Directives. What does it do? It grants to a compulsory motor insurer who has had to satisfy a judgment pursuant to section 151(5) of the 1988 Act the right to recoup his payment from either the uninsured person who created the liability or an insured person who caused or permitted the use of the vehicle which gave rise to the liability. So, in a sense, the section is the other side of a bargain. It is the benefit that the compulsory motor insurer obtains in return for having to pay out in circumstances where it might otherwise have been able to avoid or cancel the policy.' *Wilkinson v Fitzgerald* [2012] EWCA Civ 1166, [2013] 1 WLR 1776 Aikens LJ at 1818 [61].

- Compensation to the victims of uninsured and untraced drivers is provided by agreement between the British government and the Motor Insurers' Bureau, a company established for the purpose in 1946. Diplock LJ described the legal position of the MIB in *Gurtner v Circuit*, in 1968:

  'The legal position of the Motor Insurers' Bureau … is unique … The bureau's legal obligation differs from the statutory obligation of an ordinary insurer under section 207 of the Road Traffic Act, 1960[56], owed to a judgment creditor in a running-down action to satisfy the judgment obtained against the assured, in that the insurer's legal obligation is directly enforceable by the plaintiff in the running-down action, whereas the bureau's legal obligation is not enforceable by the plaintiff himself but is enforceable for his benefit by the Minister, who is *not* a party to the action.'[57]

- As Lord Sumption said in 2018, 'The statutory regime' of compulsory motor insurance 'has become more elaborate and more comprehensive since 1934, but the basic framework has not changed'[58]. Waves of legal reform have affected motor insurance law, especially Britain's membership of the European Communities (later the European Union) from 1973 to 2020. The EU motor insurance directives have been highly influential in the formation of British motor insurance law. An example of the effect of Brexit was the Motor Vehicles (Compulsory Insurance) Act 2022, enacted to remove from British motor insurance law the effects of the Court of Justice of the European Union's broad interpretation of the phrase 'public place', in *Vnuk*[59], thus limiting the scope of compensation payable by the MIB[60]. The Queen's Speech on 10 May 2022 included the announcement of a bill 'to 'remove the special status' of retained EU law, which is currently conferred by the EU (Withdrawal) Act 2018 (as amended)'[61]. That Bill became the Retained EU Law (Revocation and Reform) Act 2023, gaining royal assent on 29 June 2023, but after:

  'At Lords Report Stage, the Government [had] announced a major change in approach. Instead of generically sunsetting [EU originating] legislation, there would be a "list". A Schedule in the Bill would identify all of the legislative instruments the Government considered no longer to be needed, and these would then expire at the end of 2023. The rest of [retained EU law] REUL would remain in place, but be susceptible to repeal under new delegated powers through to June 2026.'[62]

- AEVA 2018 was enacted on 19 July 2018 and brought into force on 21 April 2021[63]. AEVA 2018, s 2 introduced into British motor insurance law a direct, statutory right of action against a motor insurer (or owner permitted to be

---

56 Now provided by RTA 1988, s 151.
57 *Gurtner v Circuit* [1968] 2 QB 587, 602.
58 *Cameron v Liverpool Victoria Insurance (MIB intervening)* [2019] UKSC 6, [2019] 1 WLR 1471.
59 *Vnuk v Zavarovalnica Triglav dd* (Case C-162/13) [2016] RTR 10 (CJEU).
60 Before the MV(CI)A 2022, the Supreme Court had already confirmed that *Vnuk* did not apply before 'a national court, hearing a dispute between private persons': *Pilling v UK Insurance* [2019] UKSC 16 [40, 41].
61 House of Commons library paper 9521, 'Queen's Speech 2022', 8 April 2022, page 22. The bill was the Retained EU Law (Revocation and Reform) Bill 2022-23 (HC Bill 156).
62 House of Commons Library Research Briefing by Graeme Cowie 'Retained EU Law (Revocation and Reform) Act 2023' (CBP 09841, 28 July 2023), p 7.
63 Automated and Electric Vehicles Act 2018 (Commencement No.1) Regulations 2021, SI 2021/396.

uninsured) by a victim of an accident 'caused by an automated vehicle when driving itself on a road or other public place in Great Britain', balanced by a right of contribution for the insurer/permitted uninsured owner under s 5. AEVA 2018 made consequential amendments to the compulsory insurance scheme of the Road Traffic Act 1988, Part VI.

- As at the time of writing, the list of automated vehicles to which AEVA 2018 applies (AEVA 2018, s 1) has yet to be published. The Department of Transport indicated[64] in April 2021 that it intended to list vehicles equipped with the Automated Lane Keeping System (ALKS) as 'automated vehicles' under AEVA 2018, s 1 and the first revision of a Construction and Use Regulation has been made to accommodate use of automated vehicles, to take effect on 1 July 2022[65]. The Automated Vehicles Bill 2023-24 (HL Bill 1) will, if enacted as the Automated Vehicles Act 2024, repeal AEVA 2018, s 1 and replace the s1 'list' as the means of classifying vehicles as 'automated', instead providing that classification will form part of the new, post-Brexit 'GB type approval' system of approving road vehicles for use on UK roads. See the text of AV Bill 2023-24 amendments to AEVA 2018, below.

- As at the time of writing, the position of the Motor Insurers' Bureau in relation to automated vehicles is that 'At present, there are no Agreements in place between the MIB and the Secretary of State for Transport to deal with' claims by victims of uninsured automated vehicles. However, the same MIB document (its response to the Law Commissions' third consultation paper) engages in detail with the Law Commissions' recommendations for automated vehicle regulation insofar as they affect insurance (including discussion of data storage requirements and the effect of failure to update software in the context of claims under the MIB scheme) and states that the MIB 'would welcome a debate around these issues' [66].

B Insurance law for Advanced Driver Assistance Systems (ADAS)

Overview of ADAS

6.10 'Advanced Driver Assistance System' ('ADAS') is a technical term, which the British Standards Institution and the UK government's Centre for Connected and Autonomous Vehicles define in their vocabulary as an

'entity consisting of interdependent components that supports human drivers by performing a part of the dynamic driving task[67] ... or providing

---

64 Department for Transport, 'Safe use of automated lane keeping system (ALKS): summary of responses and next steps – moving Britain ahead' (April 2021)
65 Amendment of regulation 109(1) of the Road Vehicles (Construction and Use) Regulations 1986, to permit a driver 'to see ... information ... of any sort...' displayed on a built-in screen in an automated vehicle, and providing that the vehicle is not requesting the driver to take back control: The Road Vehicles (Construction and Use) (Automated Vehicles) Order 2022, SI 2022/470.
66 MIB's response to Law Commissions' third paper on AV law, March 2021 at page 6, response to question 53.
67 Dynamic driving task: the 'real-time operational and tactical functions required to operate a vehicle ... safely in on-road traffic'. Connected and automated vehicles – Vocabulary (BSI Flex 1890 v4.0:2022-03, March 2022)

safety relevant information. *NOTE Examples include adaptive cruise control and automatic emergency braking.'*[68]

The Department for Transport defines Advanced Driver Assistance Systems as 'Individual automation features such as adaptive cruise control or lane changing features which assist the driver'[69] falling within either level 1 or level 2 of the six levels of vehicle automation described by the American Society of Automotive Engineers (the SAE levels[70]).

The AV Bill 2023-24 (HL Bill 1) provides a regulation-making power for the type approval of vehicles fitting the description of ADAS, at cl 9(1)(b):

> 'any other type of vehicle [than one designed to travel autonomously] that –
>
> (i)   includes equipment designed to allow its motion to be controlled other than by an individual in it, or to facilitate its being so controlled, or
>
> (ii) is designed to incorporate or interact with software.'

If enacted (within the Automated Vehicles Act 2024), that provision would provide a statutory definition of ADAS.

ADAS are described in the Highway Code, which uses the term 'driver assistance systems'[71].

The Highway Code is guidance provided as a matter of statutory duty[72] by the Secretary of State for Transport. The Highway Code is not itself law but can be evidential of fault[73]. It is emphatic in relation to the driver's responsibility while using driver assistance systems:

> 'You MUST exercise proper control of your vehicle at all times … As the driver, you are still responsible for the vehicle if you use a driver assistance system (like motorway assist). This is also the case if you use a hand-held remote control parking app or device. You MUST have full control over these systems at all times.'[74]

The Highway Code cites, in support of rule 150, RTA 1988, ss 2 and 3 and the Road Vehicles (Construction and Use) Regulations 1986 ('CUR 1986'), regs 104 and 110[75]. Those rules all focus upon 'driver's control':

---

68 Connected and automated vehicles – Vocabulary (BSI Flex 1890 v4.0:2022-03, March 2022)

69 'Acronym glossary' at page 45 of Department for Transport, 'Safe use of automated lane keeping system (ALKS): summary of responses and next steps – moving Britain ahead' (April 2021).

70 The SAE levels are often cited in discussions of automated driving. See diagram 'the SAE taxonomy' at page 12 of Law Commissions' final report on automated vehicles, *Automated Vehicles: Joint Report*, Law Com No 404, Scot Law Com No 258 (January 2022). See chapter 2 (vehicle specifications) for discussion of the SAE levels of automation.

71 The Highway Code (Department for Transport, 2022) at rules 150 and 160.

72 RTA 1988, s 38. See especially the definition of the Code in s 38(8) as 'the code comprising directions for the guidance of persons using roads issued under Road Traffic Act 1930, s 45as from time to time revised under this section or under any previous enactment.'

73 RTA 1988, s 38(7).

74 The Highway Code (DfT, 2022) rule 150.

75 SI 1986/1078.

Offence of dangerous driving (RTA 1988, s 2)

Offences of careless and inconsiderate driving (RTA 1988, s 3)

'Driver's Control' 'No person shall drive or cause or permit any other person to drive, a motor vehicle on a road if he is in such a position that he cannot have proper control of the vehicle or have a full view of the road and traffic ahead.' (CUR 1986, reg 104 and RTA 1988, s 41D[76])

'Mobile telephones' 'No person shall drive a motor vehicle on a road if he is using–

(a) a hand-held mobile telephone; or

(b) a hand-held device of a kind specified in paragraph (4)...

(4) A device referred to in paragraphs (1)(b), (2)(b) and (3)(b) is a device, other than a two-way radio, which is capable of transmitting and receiving data[77], whether or not those capabilities are enabled.'

There are exceptions in parts (5), (5A) and (5B) of reg 110 for using a mobile telephone in a 'genuine emergency', for remote controlled parking functions and contactless payments) (CUR 1986, reg 110 and RTA 1988, s 41D).

No special statutory insurance scheme for ADAS-only vehicles

6.11 As at the time of writing there is no special statutory insurance scheme (whether actual or proposed by government) for vehicles equipped with driver assistance systems/ADAS which are not also autonomous.

Motor vehicles with driver assistance/ADAS systems which do not reach autonomy are regulated as 'motor vehicles' within RTA 1988, are subject to the construction and use requirements set out by RTA 1988, Part II (including those set out above) and are within the existing statutory insurance regime of RTA 1988, Part VI. If the AV Bill 2023-24 is enacted, the classification of a vehicle as 'an authorised automated vehicle' (in the amended phrase applied to the insurance provisions of AEVA 2018, Part 1 by the AV Bill, cl 45, Sch 2, para 5) will allow the provisions of AEVA 2018, Part 1, as amended, to apply (including the direct claim under AEVA 2018, s 2).

---

76 RTA 1988, 41D (offences of 'Breach of requirements as to control of vehicle, mobile telephones etc'). Reform of the control rules for automated driving is underway at national level (by the Transport Bill, unpublished at the time of writing but described by the government in May 2022 in terms echoing the Law Commissions' recommendations for future AV regulation) and internationally (by the Amendment to Article 1 and new Article 34 BIS of the 1968 UN Convention on Road Traffic) 'by 'deeming' the 1968 Convention's requirement that every moving vehicle shall have a driver, to be satisfied provided it is using an automated driving system that complies with domestic and international technical regulations, and domestic legislation governing operation' (UK government's explanatory memorandum on the proposal, Command Paper CP No 540, at 2.1). See the 'Law of AAEV Specifications' chapter of this book.

77 Including transmissions within the vehicle: *Bendt v Crown Prosecution Service* [2022] EWHC 502 (Admin).

Vehicles with driver assistance/ADAS systems are given no special definition in the RTA 1988[78] (unlike automated vehicles[79] or electric bicycles[80], for example) and are not (like those especially defined vehicles) given a distinct regulatory position in relation to insurance.

Vehicles equipped only with ADAS systems are therefore subject to the motor insurance scheme as it stands under Part VI of the Road Traffic Act 1988. Amendments to that scheme for 'automated' vehicles do not apply to an ADAS vehicle (unless and until such a vehicle is classified as an 'automated vehicle' under AEVA 2018 or (when enacted) AV 2024, denoting that its systems go beyond driver support and into self-driving).

The insurance scheme for vehicles with both ADAS and 'automated' capabilities

6.12   Insurance law for automated vehicles is discussed in the following part of this chapter. Which part of the motor vehicle insurance scheme (the pre or post-AEVA 2018 part) will apply in relation to vehicles equipped with both systems (ie vehicles equipped with driver assistance systems which are also capable of self-driving and classified as 'automated' under AEVA 2018, or (when enacted) AV 2024) has not yet been adjudicated by a court.

The policy intention behind AEVA 2018 is to provide a 'single insurer model' in which a policy of insurance provides both for non-automated and automated vehicle use. The language of AEVA 2018, s 2 is consistent with that intention: the direct liability of the insurer under s 2 applies only when 'an accident is caused by an [authorised[81]] automated vehicle *when driving itself* on a road or other public place in Great Britain'[82] (italics added).

So the language of the statute indicates that a vehicle listed as automated under AEVA 2018 section 1 will not generate AEVA 2018, s 2 rights and the insurance consequences under that Act, unless the accident occurs *when it is driving itself*.

If at the time of the accident an automated vehicle is not 'driving itself' but is under human control, with or without assistance from driver assistance/ADAS systems, then the accident victim's remedy will be outside AEVA 2018, often[83] in negligence. In such a case, the pre-AEVA insurance regime under RTA 1988, Part VI and (in

---

78   See the interpretation sections: RTA 1988, ss 161, 185-196.

79   See the definitions of automated vehicle in RTA 1988 and AEVA 2018, in both cases subject to amendment to 'authorised automated vehicle' should the AV Bill 2023-24 (HL Bill 1) be enacted as the Automated Vehicles Act 2024: see cl 45 and Sch 2, paras 4 and 5.

80   '[A]n electrically assisted pedal cycle of such a class as may be prescribed by regulations so made, is to be treated as not being a motor vehicle': RTA 1988, s 189(1)(c). So EAPCs within the regulations are not 'motor vehicles' required to be insured by RTA 1988, s 143. See 'Insurance Law for Electric Vehicles', below.

81   Prospective amendment of AEVA 2018 by AV Bill 2023-24 (HL Bill 1) cl 45, Sch 2, para 5(3) (a).

82   AEVA 2018, s 2(1)(a).

83   Negligence has been the usual legal basis of claim (see above) and will be so if there is no relationship between the victim and the injurious use of the vehicle other than the 'neighbour' relationship in negligence. Other relationships (contractual, employment, consumer etc) may provide other legal bases of claim: see chapters in Part 2 of this book, 'civil law'.

relation to uninsured and untraced drivers) the MIB agreements will apply to the recovery of compensation.

Must a vehicle with both ADAS and Automated capabilities be insured as an 'automated vehicle'?

6.13   The question of the legality of driving a vehicle with automated capabilities without AEVA 2018-compliant insurance is different to the question of whether or not the direct action arises under AEVA 2018, s 2 in relation to an accident.

As a matter of fact, the need for insurance precedes liability. As a matter of law, an automated vehicle is one listed by the Secretary of State under AEVA 2018, s 1. A vehicle not so listed (or authorised, per the AV Bill 2023-24) is not 'automated' within the meaning of AEVA 2018, and so AEVA 2018 liability does not arise if an unlisted/unauthorised vehicle causes an accident resulting in damage.

A driver who gave up control of a *non*-automated vehicle, behaving as if it was 'automated' when in fact it had only driver assistance systems, would be liable in negligence (not under AEVA 2018) to victims of an ensuing accident. In relation to compulsory insurance, that driver would be within the pre-AEVA 2018 regime of RTA 1988.

A vehicle that *is* listed/authorised as 'automated' within AEVA 2018 is capable of generating AEVA 2018 liability in the event of an accident when it is driving itself, so is required to be insured against such liability.

The point has not been adjudicated in court, but the government's view is that AEVA 2018-compliant compulsory insurance is required for an AEVA 2018, listed/authorised vehicle, whether or not the automated capability has been activated or even if it has been disabled:

> '… respondents [to the government's call for evidence] expressed concerns about a situation where a vehicle is registered as an Automated Vehicle but the registered keeper has decided not to use the self-driving function or has had it disabled.'

> 'If a vehicle is listed as an 'Automated Vehicle' then it must be insured as an Automated Vehicle, even if the registered keeper has no intention to use it as one.'

> 'The registered keeper is responsible for ensuring they have a valid insurance policy whether the vehicle is automated or not.'[84]

From the insurance perspective, that is a logical position. The insurance risk of AEVA 2018 liability for an AEVA 2018 listed/authorised automated vehicle exists at the outset of the insurance, even if the user's intention then is not to use that capability. The risk arises from the status in law of the vehicle as a type ('automated')

---

84   Department for Transport, 'Safe use of automated lane keeping system (ALKS): summary of responses and next steps – moving Britain ahead' (April 2021) chapter 4 ('The Listing Methodology for Automated Vehicles') pages 42 and 43. That guidance preceded the AV Bill 2023-24 (HL Bill 1) so spoke only of 'listing'.

capable of a particular activity ('driving itself') which gives rise to particular legal consequence material to the risk (the insurer's statutory liability under AEVA 2018, s 2(1)).

Driving without the correct compulsory insurance is a criminal offence under RTA 1988, s 143(2) (of using a vehicle without a policy of insurance compliant with RTA 1988, Part VI).

No special MIB scheme for vehicles only equipped with ADAS

6.14   As at the time of writing, ADAS-only equipped vehicles have no special insurance status within RTA 1988, Part VI nor in relation to the MIB agreements. ADAS-only equipped vehicles remain under the control of the human driver. The MIB agreements appear to apply to the use of ADAS-only equipped motor vehicles just as they do to other vehicles.

C Insurance law for automated vehicles

Reform of the statutory motor insurance system for automated vehicles (by AEVA 2018, Part 1)

6.15   The statutory law of insurance of automated vehicles is set out in AEVA 2018, Part 1. It reforms British motor insurance law in readiness for automated vehicles.

It does this in two ways:

- it provides new statutory remedies both for victims (by the direct action under AEVA 2018, s 2) and for liable insurers and permitted uninsured owners (by the right of contribution under AEVA 2018, s 5), and

- it consequentially amends other statutes (chiefly the insurance provisions of the RTA 1988, Part VI).

The insurance reforms of AEVA 2018 are set out below.

AEVA 2018 in detail

The arrangement of AEVA 2018 as a whole

6.16   AEVA 2018 describes itself as 'An Act to make provision about automated vehicles and electric vehicles'. It is an Act in three parts:

Part 1: 'Automated vehicles: liability of insurers, etc'

Part 2: 'Electric vehicles: charging'

Part 3: 'Miscellaneous and general'

AEVA 2018, Part 1 is of particular interest to litigants and insurers, as it creates:

- a new, direct statutory claim against the insurer or owner of an automated vehicle, for the victim of an accident caused at least partly by an automated vehicle when driving itself (s 2), and

- a new statutory claim for a liable insurer or owner against any other person responsible for the accident (s 5).

Summary of the provisions of AEVA 2018, Part 1, before amendment by the Automated Vehicles Act 2024

6.17   There are eight sections in AEVA 2018, Part 1. By section number, each provides (in summary) for:

1 **Listing of automated vehicles by the Secretary of State**. The mandatory duty of the Secretary of State for Transport to prepare, publish and keep up to date a list of all motor vehicles which are, are in the Secretary of State's opinion, designed or adapted to be capable, in at least some circumstances or situations, of safely driving themselves, and which may lawfully be used when driving themselves, in at least some circumstances or situations, on roads or other places in Great Britain. Defines 'automated vehicle' in AEVA 2018, Part 1 as meaning 'a vehicle listed under this section' (AEVA 2018, s 1(4)).

2 **Liability of insurers etc where accident caused by automated vehicle**. The key section of AEVA 2018, Part 1, providing that, where an accident is caused by an automated vehicle when driving itself on a road or other public place in Great Britain, the vehicle is insured at the time of the accident, and an insured person or any other person suffers damage as a result of the accident, the insurer is liable for that damage (or, where a public body or the Crown is permitted to use the vehicle without insurance, that owner is so liable). AEVA 2018, s 6(4) (below) provides that liability under AEVA 2018, s 2 is treated as liability in tort or, in Scotland, delict for the purposes of any enactment conferring jurisdiction on a court with respect to any matter.

3 **Contributory negligence etc**. Preserves the reduction of damages for which the insurer or permitted uninsured owner is liable, by reference to any contributory fault of the injured party. Sets the standard by which the fault of the automated system will be assessed, in the balancing of contributory faults, as that which 'would apply to a claim in respect of the accident brought by the injured party against a person other than the insurer or vehicle owner'. AEVA 2018, s 3(2) provides for an extinction of the s 2 liability of the insurer or permitted uninsured owner of an automated vehicle to the person in charge of the vehicle 'where the accident that it caused was wholly due to the person's negligence in allowing the vehicle to begin driving itself when it was not appropriate to do so'.

4 **Accident resulting from unauthorised software alterations or failure to update software**. Allows the insurer to avoid or limit its liability under AEVA 2018, s 2 by excluding or limiting cover in the policy for damage suffered by an insured person arising from an accident occurring as a direct result of prohibited software alterations made by the insured person, or a failure to install safety-critical software updates that the insured person knows, or ought reasonably to know, are safety-critical. AEVA 2018, s 2(6) provides that 'Except

as provided by AEVA 2018, s 4, liability under this section [section 2] may not be limited or excluded by a term of an insurance policy or in any other way'[85].

5   **Right of insurer etc to claim against person responsible for accident**. Allows the insurer or permitted uninsured owner to seek contribution to its liability to the injured party, where the amount of that liability (including any liability not imposed by AEVA 2018, s 2) is settled, from any other person liable to the injured party in respect of the accident.

6   **Application of enactments**. Provides for the application of other Acts. Notable points include:

–   for the purposes of various Acts, the behaviour of the automated vehicle is deemed to be the fault of the person liable under AEVA 2018, s 2 (s 6(1)–(3));

–   the tortious nature of AEVA 2018, s 2 remedy for jurisdictional purposes (s 6(4));

–   the exclusion (at AEVA 2018, s 6(5)) of the Civil Liability (Contribution) Act 1978, if the insurer or permitted uninsured owner seeks the right to claim against another liable person under AEVA 2018, s 5.

7   **Report by the Secretary of State on operation of this Part**. Requires the Secretary of State to lay before Parliament, not later than two years after the first publication of the list of automated vehicles under AEVA 2018, s 1, a report assessing the impact and effectiveness of AEVA 2018, Part 1 and the extent to which that Part's provisions ensure that appropriate insurance or other arrangements are made in respect of vehicles that are capable of safely driving themselves.

8   **Interpretation**. The interpretation section in relation to Part 1. AEVA 2018, s 8 defines 'automated vehicle' as having the meaning given by AEVA 2018, s 1(4) (which reads 'In this Part 'automated vehicle' means a vehicle listed under this section', ie. the section 1 list of safe and lawful automated vehicles prepared by the Secretary of State).

But s 8(1)(a) adds a further element to the definition within s 1, by elaborating upon the meaning of the phrase 'driving itself'. Section 8(1)(a) provides that 'For the purposes of this Part – a vehicle is 'driving itself' if it is operating in a mode in which it is not being controlled, and does not need to be monitored, by an individual'.

That further element – 'and does not need to be monitored' – spurred debate as to whether or not vehicles with the Automated Lane Keeping System (ALKS) ought to be listed under AEVA 2018, s 1 as the Secretary of State for Transport had indicated in April 2021 that he expected to do (see the discussion of ALKS in Chapter 2, 'vehicle specifications').

AEVA 2018, s 8(1)(b) defines 'insured' in a way that makes clear the connection between Part 1 of the 2018 Act and RTA 1988, Part VI ('Third-Party Liabilities'):

'(1) For the purposes of this Part– ...

---

85   AEVA 2018, s 2(6) might avoid the uncertainty as to the scope of permitted exceptions from statutory insurance coverage under the 2018 Act which has arisen under the RTA 1988. See for example *Bristol Alliance v Williams* [2013] QB 806.

(b) a vehicle is 'insured' if there is in force in relation to the use of the vehicle on a road or other public place in Great Britain a policy of insurance that satisfies the conditions in section 145 of the Road Traffic Act 1988.'

AEVA 2018, s 8(3) provides that a reference to an accident includes a reference to two or more causally related accidents, and that a reference to an accident caused by an automated vehicle includes a reference to an accident that is partly caused by an automated vehicle.

Limitation periods for actions under AEVA 2018 are set by Part 3 ('Miscellaneous and General'), s 20(1), and in the Schedule to the Act (by amendment of the Limitation Act 1980, setting limitation periods for the s 2 action against an insurer of three years and for the 'claim against other responsible person' action under AEVA 2018, s 5 of two years).

Under AEVA 2018, Part 3, the Secretary of State has a power by regulations to 'make provision that is consequential on any provision made by this Act' (s 20(2): 'minor and consequential amendments) and to bring the Act into force (s 21(2): 'Commencement'). The power to make regulations to commence the Act is exercisable by statutory instrument and may appoint different days for different purposes or different areas (s 21(4)(a)).

A statutory instrument containing regulations under AEVA 2018, s 20 ('Minor and consequential amendments'), any of which amend, repeal or revoke primary legislation (which includes legislation of devolved assemblies: (s 20(7)) may not be made unless a draft of the instrument has been laid before Parliament and approved by a resolution of each House (s 20(5)). A statutory instrument containing regulations under AEVA 2018, s 20 'none of which amends primary legislation is subject to annulment in pursuance of a resolution of either House of Parliament' (s 20(6)).

The Schedule to AEVA 2018 also made clear that it would not be open to the owner of an automated vehicle, as an alternative to insuring the AV, to make a deposit of a sum with the Accountant General of the Senior Courts (see paragraphs 17 and 18 of the Schedule). However, this provision of AEVA 2018 has since been subsumed by other legislation, which removes the option of security from the RTA 1988 motor insurance scheme generally[86].

Policy Background to AEVA 2018, Part 1

6.18   Upon its enactment in July 2018, AEVA 2018, Part 1 extended third-party compulsory motor insurance, for a driverless future. As the House of Commons library briefing paper on the Act put it, in August 2018:

'The application of 'intelligence' to cars is gathering pace and there is a strong push by manufacturers to develop automated vehicles which will drive themselves. Currently, insurance law is driver-centric: all (human)

---

86   The Motor Vehicles (Compulsory Insurance) (Miscellaneous Amendments) Regulations 2019, SI 2019/1047, Sch 1, paras 6 and 7, in force from 1 November 2019 (regulation 1).

drivers have to have insurance in order to provide compensation for third parties for personal injury or property damage due to a driving related incident. The Government's view is that such principles need to be extended to cover automated vehicles when the car is the driver and the 'driver' is sometimes a passenger. The intention behind the legislation is to emphasise that if there is an insurance 'event' (accident) the compensation route for the individual remains within the motor insurance settlement framework, rather than through a product liability framework against a manufacturer'[87].

AEVA 2018, s 2 direct action against insurer (or owner permitted to use vehicle without insurance)

6.19   The central feature of AEVA 2018 is the provision for a direct action against the insurer of an automated vehicle under s 2(1), which reads:

'2 Liability of insurers etc where accident caused by automated vehicle

(1) Where –

    (a) an accident is caused by an automated vehicle when driving itself on a road or other public place in Great Britain,

    (b) the vehicle is insured at the time of the accident, and

    (c) an insured person or any other person suffers damage as a result of the accident,

the insurer is liable for that damage.'

AEVA 2018, s 2(2) provides for the direct liability of an owner, in the place of an insurer, where the owner is a public body or the Crown permitted to use the vehicle without insurance[88] (in this book, the s 2(2) owner is referred to as the 'permitted uninsured owner', though that is the writer's paraphrase rather than statutory language).

The policy behind that direct liability was the avoidance of complex product liability claims in road traffic cases involving automated vehicles (AVs), whose arrival was thought to be 'gathering pace'. As the House of Commons library paper put it:

'The key policy point in this section is that following a claims 'event' the process follows the insurance route – as now – rather than becoming a 'consumer-manufacturer' product liability action, which is inevitably longer and more costly.'[89]

---

87   House of Commons library briefing paper CBP 8118, 'Automated and Electric Vehicles Act 2018' (15 August 2018), page 3.
88   AEVA 2018, s 2(2).
89   House of Commons library briefing paper CBP 8118, 'Automated and Electric Vehicles Act 2018' (15 August 2018), page 10.

Overview of the statutory reform: AEVA 2018 fits within but adjusts RTA 1988

6.20 AEVA 2018 has been designed to fit within the established system of British motor insurance law. We can see the points at which the two Acts coincide (as the law stands at the time of writing[90]):

- AEVA 2018, s 1 defines an automated vehicle as a 'motor vehicle' listed as an automated vehicle by the Secretary of State for Transport. RTA 1988, s 161 (the interpretation section for RTA 1988, Part VI) adopts the AEVA 2018, s 1 definition of automated vehicle[91].

- RTA 1988, s 143 requires 'users of motor vehicles to be insured' (the title and relevant effect of the section).

- AEVA 2018, s 8(1)(b) provides that 'a vehicle is "insured" if there is in force in relation to the use of the vehicle on a road or other public place in Great Britain a policy of insurance that satisfies the conditions in section 145 of the Road Traffic Act 1988'.

- Further to AEVA 2018, s 8(1)(b), RTA 1988, s 145(3A) (added by AEVA 2018[92]) implies – by the word '*also*' ('the policy must also provide for the insurer's obligations to an insured person under section 2(1) of the Automated and Electric Vehicles Act 2018…') – that an insurance policy in relation to an automated vehicle is subject to *all* of the requirements of RTA 1988, s 145 ('Requirements in respect of policies of insurance')[93]. But this point is made explicit by AEVA 2018, s 8(1)(b) (above).

On a broader view, AEVA 2018 uses many of the tools of the statutory insurance scheme developed since 1930 and follows the patterns of that scheme (eg. providing for compulsory insurance cover, allowing certain exemptions to compulsory cover and for the insurer's rights to recover expenditure). The government's statements to Parliament reflect that the provisions of the AEV Bill were:

> '… intended to mirror the existing conventional vehicle compulsory third-party insurance framework, found in the Road Traffic Act 1988, for automated vehicles. … the aim of the Bill is to provide consistency with conventional vehicles in the 1988 Act.'[94]

The practical need for 'consistency with conventional vehicles' arose not just from the desire for legal consistency but from the envisaged use of automated vehicles

---

90 For the revisions proposed by the AV Bill 2023-24, please see text of prospective revisions to AEVA 2018, Part 1 by the AV Bill 2023-24 (HL Bill 1), cl 45, Sch 2, para 5, below.

91 The 'listing' section of AEVA 2018, s 1, and the RTA 1988, 2 161 definition adopting AEVA 2018, s 1, will be repealed if the AV Bill 2023-24 is enacted as the Automated Vehicles Act 2024 (see chapter 2, 'vehicle specifications'). However, the AV Bill amendments to AEVA 2018 Part 1 and the Road Traffic Act 1988, Part VI (at cl 45, Sch 2, paras 4 and 5 of the AV Bill) replace 'listed' with 'authorised', to accord with Part 1 of the AV Bill (the new regulatory framework for automated vehicles). AEVA 2018, Part 1, so amended, would therefore remain within the RTA 1988, Part VI system of compulsory motor insurance.

92 AEVA 2018 section 20(1) and paragraph 19(2) of the Schedule, adding RTA 1988, s 145(3A).

93 See point 3 'scope of compulsory insurance for AVs expanded to first party' discussed below.

94 Baroness Sugg, House of Lords Hansard volume 791 column 201 (9 May 2018).

alongside non-automated vehicles on British roads. Both parts of the insurance system (for the use of non-automated and automated vehicles) must work together.

An established feature of the Road Traffic Act insurance regime is the criminalisation of using a vehicle on a road or other public place without insurance which complies with RTA 1988, Part VI. In the case of an automated vehicle listed as such under AEVA 2018, s 1, that requirement for AEVA 2018-compliant insurance[95] and the criminal offence of omission[96] are said to apply, whether or not the user intends to use the automated driving features and even if those features have been disabled[97].

So AEVA 2018 applies many existing insurance requirements under the Road Traffic Acts to the use of automated vehicles. However, at the core of AEVA 2018 was the fundamental switch from human control of a motor vehicle to the vehicle driving itself. Before AEVA 2018, the underlying assumption of all the Road Traffic Acts – and of British motor insurance – was human control of the vehicle while in use. The identification of a human driver as the object of legal proceedings[98] was key.

Automated vehicles, 'designed or adapted to be capable, in at least some circumstances or situations, of safely driving themselves'[99] alter that assumption of human control.

So, while fitting within the RTA 1988 scheme, automated vehicles are subject to their own particular rules within the scheme. To accommodate insurance needs arising from automated vehicle accidents, AEVA 2018 modifies several aspects of the third-party liability scheme in the RTA 1988, Part VI.

Key Adjustments made by AEVA 2018 to the RTA 1988 statutory insurance scheme

1 New statutory cause of action for Automated Vehicle (AV) accidents

6.21 AEVA 2018 creates a new statutory cause of action, under AEVA 2018, s 2. An accident caused at least in part[100] by an automated vehicle while driving itself gives rise to the victim's cause of action against the insurer (s 2(1)) or permitted uninsured owner (s 2(2)) of the automated vehicle.

---

95 Via AEVA 2018, s 8(1)(b) and RTA 1988, s 145(3A), as amended by AEVA 2018 (s 20(1)).
96 RTA 1988, s 143(2).
97 See the UK government's view in Department for Transport, 'Safe use of automated lane keeping system (ALKS): summary of responses and next steps – moving Britain ahead' (April 2021), discussed in 'Insurance Law for ADAS', above.
98 See *Cameron v Liverpool Victoria Insurance (MIB intervening)* [2019] UKSC 6, [2019] 1 WLR 1471. Although the judgment post-dated the enactment of AEVA 2018 (July 2018), it preceded its coming into force (April 2021) and was premised entirely upon pre-automated vehicles. The need for certainty of service of legal proceedings upon an identified Defendant driver was central to the judgment. Lord Sumption's assertion that 'It is a fundamental feature of the statutory scheme of compulsory insurance in the United Kingdom that it confers on the victim of a road accident no direct right against an insurer in respect of the underlying liability of the driver' [5] refers to human driving. It should now be read in light of AEVA 2018, s 2.
99 AEVA 2018, s 1(1).
100 AEVA 2018, s 8(3)(b).

AEVA 2018, s 2(1)–(4) provide (before any amendment by the AV Bill 2023-24) as follows:

'*2 Liability of insurers etc where accident caused by automated vehicle*

(1) Where –

    (a) an accident is caused by an automated vehicle when driving itself on a road or other public place in Great Britain,

    (b) the vehicle is insured at the time of the accident, and

    (c) an insured person or any other person suffers damage as a result of the accident,

the insurer is liable for that damage.

(2) Where –

    (a) an accident is caused by an automated vehicle when driving itself on a road or other public place in Great Britain,

    (b) the vehicle is not insured at the time of the accident,

    (c) section 143 of the Road Traffic Act 1988 (users of motor vehicles to be insured or secured against third-party risks) does not apply to the vehicle at that time –

        (i) because of section 144(2) of that Act (exemption for public bodies etc), or

        (ii) because the vehicle is in the public service of the Crown, and

    (d) a person suffers damage as a result of the accident,

the owner of the vehicle is liable for that damage.

(3) In this Part 'damage' means death or personal injury, and any damage to property other than –

    (a) the automated vehicle,

    (b) goods carried for hire or reward in or on that vehicle or in or on any trailer (whether or not coupled) drawn by it, or

    (c) property in the custody, or under the control, of—

        (i) the insured person (where subsection (1) applies), or

        (ii) the person in charge of the automated vehicle at the time of the accident (where subsection (2) applies).

(4) In respect of damage to property caused by, or arising out of, any one accident involving an automated vehicle, the amount of the liability under this section of the insurer or owner of the vehicle is limited to the amount for the time being specified in section 145(4)(b) of the Road Traffic Act 1988 (limit on compulsory insurance for property damage).'

In AEVA 2018, s 2(1), the statutory claim extends to the insured person[101]. This links with point 3, below ('scope of compulsory insurance for AVs expanded to first party').

---

101 AEVA 2018, s 2(1)(c).

In AEVA 2018, s 2(3), 'damage' is defined in a limited way – eg. excluding damage to the automated vehicle itself[102].

AEVA 2018, s 2(4) caps compulsory property damage cover at the limit for the time being applicable under the) RTA 1988, s 145(4)(b) (as at the time of writing, not more than £1.2 million[103]).

The further subsections of AEVA 2018, s 2 provide for:

- the application of contributory negligence (as defined in s 3) to a s 2 claim, which includes the possibility of extinguishing any such liability 'where the accident that [the vehicle driving itself] caused was wholly due to the person [in charge]'s negligence in allowing the vehicle to begin driving itself when it was not appropriate to do so'[104] (s 2(5)),

- the statutory permission to insurers to exclude or limit their liability for an automated vehicle accident resulting from unauthorised software alterations or failure to update safety-critical software, but not otherwise (s 2(6)), and

- The saving that the 'imposition by this section of liability on the insurer or vehicle owner does not affect any other person's liability in respect of the accident', so allowing for the insurer or owner's statutory right under s 5 to claim contribution to its liability for an automated vehicle accident under s 2(1) or (2), discussed below (s 2(7)).

2 New statutory right for insurer etc to claim against any other person liable

6.22 AEVA 2018 also creates a new statutory claim for the insurer or permitted uninsured owner liable to a victim under s 2 to claim, under s 5, against any other person liable to the injured party in respect of the accident.

This is independent of the right to recover contribution under the Civil Liability (Contribution) Act 1978, which AEVA 2018, s 6(5) provides is *not* a right available to an insurer or owner liable under AEVA 2018.

AEVA 2018, s 5(1)–(4) provide as follows:

'*5 Right of insurer etc to claim against person responsible for accident*

(1) Where –

(a) section 2 imposes on an insurer, or the owner of a vehicle, liability to a person who has suffered damage as a result of an accident ('the injured party'), and

(b) the amount of the insurer's or vehicle owner's liability to the injured party in respect of the accident (including any liability not imposed by section 2) is settled,

---

102 AEVA 2018, s 2(3)(a). This takes the expensive item of repairs to a damaged AV outside compulsory insurance and into optional comprehensive insurance.
103 Motor Vehicles (Compulsory Insurance) Regulations 2016, SI 2016/1193, reg 2(2) (since 31 December 2016).
104 AEVA 2018, s 3(2).

any other person liable to the injured party in respect of the accident is under the same liability to the insurer or vehicle owner.

(2) For the purposes of this section, the amount of the insurer's or vehicle owner's liability is settled when it is established –

    (a) by a judgment or decree,

    (b) by an award in arbitral proceedings or by an arbitration, or

    (c) by an enforceable agreement.

(3) If the amount recovered under this section by the insurer or vehicle owner exceeds the amount which that person has agreed or been ordered to pay to the injured party (ignoring so much of either amount as represents interest), the insurer or vehicle owner is liable to the injured party for the difference.

(4) Nothing in this section allows the insurer or vehicle owner and the injured party, between them, to recover from any person more than the amount of that person's liability to the injured party.'

Subsection 5(5) provides for the limitation period applicable to a section 5 AEVA 2018 claim:

'(5) For the purposes of—

    (a) section 10A of the Limitation Act 1980 (special time limit for actions by insurers etc in respect of automated vehicles),

    …

the right of action that an insurer or vehicle owner has by virtue of this section accrues at the time of the settlement referred to in subsection (1)(b).'

Limitation Periods for AEVA 2018, s 5 claim

6.23   The Limitation Act 1980, s 10A provides as follows:

'*10A Special time limit for actions by insurers etc in respect of automated vehicles*

(1) Where by virtue of section 5 of the Automated and Electric Vehicles Act 2018 an insurer or vehicle owner becomes entitled to bring an action against any person, the action shall not be brought after the expiration of two years from the date on which the right of action accrued (under subsection (5) of that section).

(2) An action referred to in subsection (1) shall be one to which sections 32, 33A and 35 of this Act apply, but otherwise Parts 2 and 3 of this Act (except sections 37 and 38) shall not apply for the purposes of this section.'

The position on limitation periods for a s 5 claim is therefore as follows:

- The insurer/permitted uninsured owner's section 5 right accrues at the time that the amount of its liability to the injured party is settled[105] and

- The limitation period expires two years from that date,[106] but:

---

105 AEVA 2018, s 5(1), (2), (5),
106 Limitation Act 1980, s 10A(1).

- In cases of fraud, concealment or mistake, 'the period of limitation shall not begin to run until the plaintiff has discovered the fraud, concealment or mistake (as the case may be) or could with reasonable diligence have discovered it',[107]

- In mediation of cross-border disputes where mediation began before 11pm on 31 December 2020[108] and the limitation period was then current but expired during the mediation, the limitation period may be extended under the Limitation Act 1980, s 33A (although the lack of legal force of AEVA 2018 as at 31 December 2020 means that this section is likely to have no effect), and. and:

- The Limitation Act 1980, s 35 applies the Civil Procedure Rules 1998, r 17.4 to new claims to be brought in pending actions,

- The Limitation Act applies to the Crown and the Duchy of Cornwall[109] and

- The Interpretation section of the Limitation Act 1980 applies[110].

It has been noted that the limitation period of two years from settlement might lead to injustice in insurers' and permitted uninsured owners' AEVA 2018, s 5 claims that are based upon the other party's liability under the Consumer Protection Act 1987, as the 1987 Act applies a ten-year long-stop period after which the CPA 1987 right of action is extinguished[111]. This pre-automated and ADAS vehicle law might have an unintended effect upon product liability cases relating to those vehicles, whose software is likely to be continuously updated over their lifetime[112].

3 Scope of compulsory insurance for AV accidents expanded to first party

6.24 Where an automated vehicle is insured at the time that it causes damage, AEVA 2018, s 2(1) extends cover for 'damage' to 'an insured person' in the alternative to 'any other person' (s 2(1)(c)[113]):

'*2 Liability of insurers etc where accident caused by automated vehicle*

(1) Where –

(a) an accident is caused by an automated vehicle when driving itself on a road or other public place in Great Britain,

(b) the vehicle is insured at the time of the accident, and

---

107 Limitation Act 1980, s 32(1).
108 Cross Border Mediation (EU Directive) (EU Exit) Regulations, SI 2019/469, reg 4, Sch 1, para 7 repeal Limitation Act 1980, s 33A from 11pm on 31 December 2020 ('IP completion day': European Union (Withdrawal Agreement) Act 2020, s 39(1)), save for mediations begun before IP completion day (reg 5).
109 Limitation Act 1980, ss 10A(2), 37.
110 Limitation Act 1980, ss 10A(2), 38.
111 Limitation Act 1980, s 11A(3), inserted by Consumer Protection Act 1987, s 6(6), Sch 1, para 1. See Chapter 10, 'vehicle defect claims'.
112 As above, and see Daniel West, *The Role of Product Liability Law in Civil Claims arising from Autonomous Vehicles*, www.AEVlaw.com, 19 May 2022.
113 And see the consequential amendments made by AEVA 2018 to RTA 1988, s 145 (addition of s 145(3A): '... the policy must also provide for the insurer's obligations to an insured person under section 2(1)') and to the Limitation Act 1980 (addition of s 11B including s 11B(2): 3-year limitation period applies also to 'an action by an insured person under a contract of insurance in respect of the insurer's obligations under' AEVA 2018, ss 2(1)), 20(1), Sch, paras 11 and 19(2).

(c) an insured person or any other person suffers damage as a result of the accident,

the insurer is liable for that damage.'

'Damage' is defined by AEVA 2018, s 2(3) as follows. It is subject to limits – including the exclusion of damage to the automated vehicle itself:

'(3) In this Part 'damage' means death or personal injury, and any damage to property other than –

(a) the automated vehicle,

(b) goods carried for hire or reward in or on that vehicle or in or on any trailer (whether or not coupled) drawn by it, or

(c) property in the custody, or under the control, of—

(i) the insured person (where subsection (1) applies), or

(ii) the person in charge of the automated vehicle at the time of the accident (where subsection (2)[114] applies).'

The addition (in effect) of first party insurance to the RTA 1988 scheme, insofar as it applies to automated vehicles, is confirmed by the consequential amendment (by AEVA 2018, s 20(1) and RTA 1988, Part VI, Sch, para 19(2) by addition of a new sub-section (3A)) to RTA 1988, s 145 ('Requirements in respect of policies of insurance'). The new RTA 1988, s 145(3A) reads as follows:

'(3A) In the case of an automated vehicle, the policy must also provide for the insurer's obligations to an insured person under section 2(1) of the Automated and Electric Vehicles Act 2018 (liability of insurers etc where accident caused by automated vehicle) to be obligations under the policy.

In this subsection 'insured person' means a person who is covered under the policy for using the vehicle on a road or public place in Great Britain.'

This is a distinct feature of AEVA 2018. Other than in relation to automated vehicle claims where it is amended by AEVA 2018 to add a 145(3A), RTA 1988 does not require insurance against liability to the driver[115].

The expansion of compulsory liability insurance to the user of the vehicle again reflects the major factual change brought about by automated vehicles: that the user ceases to be the liable controller of the vehicle 'when driving itself'[116] and becomes a passenger.

---

114 Section 2(2) imposes the direct liability upon an owner which is a public body or the Crown, permitted by statute to use a vehicle on a road or other public place without compulsory insurance.

115 See *R v Secretary of State for Transport ex parte National Insurance Guarantee Corporation Plc*, QBD 8 May 1996 (Popplewell J), 1996 WL 1090145. MacGillivray notes: 'However, it does include the owner of the vehicle, who is treated as a third party for these purposes when struck by his own car being driven by a thief – *Delgado Mendes v Credit Agricola Seguros – Companhia de Seguros de Ramos Reais SA* (C-503/16) EU:C:2017:681; [2018] Lloyd's Rep I.R. 16.' MacGillivray (15th edn, 2022) at 29-006, footnote 58.

116 The time requirement of the direct liability under AEVA 2018, s 2(1)(a), (2)(a).

4 Scope of compulsory motor insurance for AV accidents expanded to employees

6.25   'Where the vehicle in question is an automated vehicle', AEVA 2018 disapplies[117] RTA 1988, s 145(4)(a).

RTA 1988, s 145(4)(a) does not require a policy of insurance 'to cover liability in respect of the death, arising out of and in the course of his employment, of a person in the employment of a person insured by the policy or of bodily injury sustained by such a person arising out of and in the course of his employment'.

RTA 1988, s 145(4)(a) was originally enacted in the Road Traffic Act 1930[118], to release motor insurers from the obligation to insure for matters already covered by employer's liability insurance (later made compulsory pursuant to the Employers' Liability (Compulsory Insurance) Act 1969).

To comply with the requirement for cover of all passengers other than the driver under the European Union's Third Motor Insurance Directive[119], this permitted statutory exclusion was subsequently limited in its application by RTA 1988, s 145(4A) introduced in 1992[120], which provided that, in the case of a person 'carried in or upon a vehicle, or entering or getting on to, or alighting from, a vehicle', the exclusion under s 145(4)(a) would not apply 'unless cover in respect of the liability referred to in that paragraph is in fact provided pursuant to a requirement of the Employers' Liability (Compulsory Insurance) Act 1969'.

AEVA 2018 disallows the original permitted exemption for third party employee cover. This appears to recognise both the possible commercial use of automated vehicles carrying employees as passengers, and the complexity which resulted from the original exemption of employers' liability cover from third party insurance under the Road Traffic Acts.

5. Permitted policy exclusions or limitations to insurer's AEVA liability restricted to unauthorised software alterations or failure to update software

6.26   One of the generators of litigation and cost in the Road Traffic Acts has been the complexity of the regulation of terms of exclusion and limitation of third-party compulsory insurance by policy terms.

As discussed in the 'Outline' section (above), within a few years of the first Road Traffic Act a second Act became necessary in 1934 because the insurers' response to compulsory insurance was to proliferate the use of conditions to exclude it.

Another response to this tactic was available. However, the Cassel Committee in 1937:

---

117 End of RTA 1988, s 145, added by AEVA 2018, s 20, Sch 1, para 19(3).
118 RTA 1930, s 36(1)(b)(i).
119 Council Directive 90/232/EC
120 RTA 1988, s 145(4A) added from 31 December 1992 by Motor Vehicles (Compulsory Insurance) Regulations 1992, SI 1992/3036, reg 3(2). See commentary in Gürses at 4.17 to 4.30.

'rejected ... the notion that all conditions should be void ... on the basis of the impact of such a measure upon competition between insurers and upon premium levels. Cassel's approach was by way of compromise: to prohibit conditions generally but to allow only a limited number.'[121]

The disadvantage of that approach, however, was to increase the internal complexity of the compensation system. Permitted exceptions within the system seemed to clash – in confusing detail – with its central purpose of assuring payment of compensation for damage caused by the use of vehicles in public places[122].

AEVA 2018 does not do away with that paradigm. In common with the existing statutory scheme (now under RTA 1988), AEVA 2018 provides its own permitted exclusion or limitation. The first part of that (subject to its own qualifications in the remainder of s 4) is in AEVA 2018, s 4(1):

'4 Accident resulting from unauthorised software alterations or failure to update software

(1)   An insurance policy in respect of an automated vehicle may exclude or limit the insurer's liability under section 2(1) for damage suffered by an insured person arising from an accident occurring as a direct result of—

(a)   software alterations made by the insured person, or with the insured person's knowledge, that are prohibited under the policy, or

(b)   a failure to install safety-critical software updates that the insured person knows, or ought reasonably to know, are safety-critical.

...'

However, AEVA 2018 also contains this provision in relation to the s 2 claim, at s 2(6):

'2 Liability of insurers etc where accident caused by automated vehicle

...

(6)   Except as provided by section 4, liability under this section may not be limited or excluded by a term of an insurance policy or in any other way.'

That is an important limitation upon the scope of exclusion arguments in AEVA 2018 claims.

However, while limiting the effect of exclusion clauses, AEVA 2018, ss 4 and 2(6) potentially fuel arguments as to exclusions of AEVA liability. As in the period between the 1930 and 1934 Road Traffic Acts, there is the likelihood of exclusion arguments being run (especially given the potency of the direct action under AEVA 2018, s 2). The mechanics of updating software (which usually requires an effective WiFi connection and time for downloading and installation of software to take place) mean that cars might be driven without a safety-critical software update being installed. AEVA 2018, s 4 allows that point to be taken by the insurer. The scope of s 4 appears likely to generate disputes.

---

121 Merkin and Hemsworth, 1-18.
122 See for example *Bristol Alliance v Williams* [2013] QB 806.

Text of prospective revisions to AEVA 2018, Part 1 by the AV Bill 2023-24 (HL Bill 1), cl 45, Sch 2, para 5

6.27   The AV Bill 2023-24 (HL Bill 1), cl 45, Sch 2, para 5, amends AEVA 2018 Part 1. The text of the amendments to AEVA 2018, Part 1 (with deleted text removed and added text underlined) is as follows:

'1 Listing of automated vehicles by the Secretary of State

[Section deleted]

'2 Liability of insurers etc where accident caused by authorised automated vehicle

(1) Where –

  (a) an accident is caused by an authorised automated vehicle when driving itself on a road or other public place in Great Britain,

  (b) the vehicle is being used by an insured person[123] at the time of the accident, and

  (c) an insured person or any other person suffers damage as a result of the accident,

  the insurer is liable for that damage.

(2) Where –

  (a) an accident is caused by an authorised automated vehicle when driving itself on a road or other public place in Great Britain,

  (b) the vehicle is not being used by an insured person at the time of the accident,

  (c) section 143 of the Road Traffic Act 1988 (users of motor vehicles to be insured or secured against third-party risks) does not apply to the vehicle at that time—

    (i)   because of section 144(2) of that Act (exemption for public bodies etc), or

    (ii)   because the vehicle is in the public service of the Crown, and

  (d) a person suffers damage as a result of the accident,

  the owner of the vehicle is liable for that damage.

(3) In this Part *"damage"* means death or personal injury, and any damage to property other than –

  (a) the authorised automated vehicle,

  (b) goods carried for hire or reward in or on that vehicle or in or on any trailer (whether or not coupled) drawn by it, or

---

123 Amending the phrase 'the vehicle is insured'. The AV Bill 2023-24, cl 45, Sch 2, para 5 amendments to AEVA 2018, s 2(1)(b) onwards to focus upon the insured person (rather than the vehicle) are not explained in the Explanatory Note to the AV Bill 2023-24 (HL Bill 1 – EN) but might be in response to *Cameron v Liverpool Victoria Insurance (MIB intervening)* [2019] UKSC 6, [2019] 1 WLR 1471 (above).

(c) property in the custody, or under the control, of –

   (i)   the insured person (where subsection (1) applies), or

   (ii) the person in charge of the <u>authorised</u> automated vehicle at the time of the accident (where subsection (2) applies).

(4) In respect of damage to property caused by, or arising out of, any one accident involving an <u>authorised</u> automated vehicle, the amount of the liability under this section of the insurer or owner of the vehicle is limited to the amount for the time being specified in section 145(4)(b) of the Road Traffic Act 1988 (limit on compulsory insurance for property damage).

(5) This section has effect subject to section 3.

(6) Except as provided by section 4, liability under this section may not be limited or excluded by a term of an insurance policy or in any other way.

(7) The imposition by this section of liability on the insurer or vehicle owner does not affect any other person's liability in respect of the accident.

3 Contributory negligence etc

(1) Where—

   (a) an insurer or vehicle owner is liable under section 2 to a person ("the injured party") in respect of an accident, and

   (b) the accident, or the damage resulting from it, was to any extent caused by the injured party,

   the amount of the liability is subject to whatever reduction under the Law Reform (Contributory Negligence) Act 1945 would apply to a claim in respect of the accident brought by the injured party against a person other than the insurer or vehicle owner.

(2) The insurer or owner of an <u>authorised</u> automated vehicle is not liable under section 2 to the person in charge of the vehicle where the accident that it caused was wholly due to the person's negligence in allowing the vehicle to begin driving itself when it was not appropriate to do so.

4 Accident resulting from unauthorised software alterations or failure to update software

(1) An insurance policy in respect of an <u>authorised</u> automated vehicle may exclude or limit the insurer's liability under section 2(1) for damage suffered by an insured person arising from an accident occurring as a direct result of—

   (a) software alterations made by the insured person, or with the insured person's knowledge, that are prohibited under the policy, or

   (b) a failure to install safety-critical software updates that the insured person knows, or ought reasonably to know, are safety-critical.

(2) But as regards liability for damage suffered by an insured person who is not the holder of the policy, subsection (1)(a) applies only in relation to software alterations which, at the time of the accident, the person knows are prohibited under the policy.

(3) Subsection (4) applies where an amount is paid by an insurer under section 2(1) in respect of damage suffered, as a result of an accident, by someone who is not insured under the policy in question.

(4) If the accident occurred as a direct result of—

   (a) software alterations made by an insured person, or with an insured person's knowledge, that were prohibited under the policy, or

   (b) a failure to install safety-critical software updates that an insured person knew, or ought reasonably to have known, were safety-critical,

   the amount paid by the insurer is recoverable from that person to the extent provided for by the policy.

(5) But as regards recovery from an insured person who is not the holder of the policy, subsection (4)(a) applies only in relation to software alterations which, at the time of the accident, the person knew were prohibited under the policy.

(6) For the purposes of this section—

   (a) "*software alterations*" and "*software updates*", in relation to an authorised automated vehicle, mean (respectively) alterations and updates to the vehicle's software;

   (b) software updates are "safety-critical" if it would be unsafe to use the vehicle in question without the updates being installed.'

(AEVA 2018, **s 5, 'Right of insurer etc to claim against person responsible for accident'** is not amended by the AV Bill 2023-24 (HL Bill 1).)

'6 Application of enactments

(1) Any damage for which a person is liable under section 2 is treated as if it had been caused –

   (a) for the purposes of the Fatal Accidents Act 1976, by that person's wrongful act, neglect or default;

   (b) for the purposes of sections 3 to 6 of the Damages (Scotland) Act 2011 (asp 7) (rights of relatives of a deceased), by that person's act or omission;

   (c) for the purposes of Part 2 of the Administration of Justice Act 1982 (damages for personal injuries, etc Scotland), by an act or omission giving rise to liability in that person to pay damages.

(2) Section 1 of the Congenital Disabilities (Civil Liability) Act 1976 ("the 1976 Act") has effect for the purposes of section 2 of this Act—

   (a) as if a person were answerable to a child in respect of an accident caused by an authorised automated vehicle when driving itself if the person—

      (i) is or has been liable under section 2 in respect of any effect of the accident on a parent of the child, or

      (ii) would be so liable if the accident caused a parent of the child to suffer damage;

(b) as if the provisions of this Part relating to liability under section 2 applied in relation to liability by virtue of paragraph (a) above under section 1 of the 1976 Act;

(c) as if subsection (6) of section 1 of the 1976 Act (exclusion of liability) were omitted.

(3) For the purposes of section 3(1), the Law Reform (Contributory Negligence) Act 1945 and section 5 of the Fatal Accidents Act 1976 (contributory negligence) have effect as if the behaviour of the <u>authorised</u> automated vehicle were the fault of the person made liable for the damage by section 2 of this Act.

(4) Liability under section 2 is treated as liability in tort or, in Scotland, delict for the purposes of any enactment conferring jurisdiction on a court with respect to any matter.

(5) An insurer or vehicle owner who has a right of action against a person by virtue of section 5 does not have a right to recover contribution from that person under the Civil Liability (Contribution) Act 1978 or under section 3 of the Law Reform (Miscellaneous Provisions) (Scotland) Act 1940.

7 Report by Secretary of State on operation of this Part

(1) The Secretary of State must prepare a report assessing—

[subsection deleted];

(b) the extent to which the provisions of this Part ensure that appropriate insurance or other arrangements are made in respect of <u>authorised</u> <u>automated vehicles</u>.

(2) The report must be laid before Parliament no later than two years after the first <u>authorisation is granted under section 3 of the Automated Vehicles</u> <u>Act 2024</u>.

8 Interpretation

(1) For the purposes of this Part—

(a) an <u>authorised automated</u> vehicle is "driving itself" if it is <u>travelling while</u> <u>an authorised automation feature of the vehicle is engaged</u>[124];

(b) <u>a person is an "insured person", in relation to a vehicle</u>[125], if there is in force in relation to <u>that person's</u> use of the vehicle on a road or other public place in Great Britain a policy of insurance that satisfies the conditions in section 145 of the Road Traffic Act 1988.

(1A) <u>Section 44(5) of the Automated Vehicles Act 2024 (authorisation to</u> <u>determine when feature "engaged" or "disengaged") applies for the</u> <u>purposes of subsection (1)(a) as it applies for the purposes of Part 1 of</u> <u>that Act</u>.

---

124 Replacing the phrase 'operating in a mode in which it is not being controlled, and does not need to be monitored, by an individual'.

125 Replacing the phrase 'a vehicle is "insured"'.

(2) In this Part –

"*authorised automated vehicle*" <u>means a vehicle authorised under section 3 of the Automated Vehicles Act 2024;</u>

"<u>*authorised automation feature*</u>" <u>has the same meaning as in Part 1 of the Automated Vehicles Act 2024 (see section 44(1) of that Act);</u>

"*damage*" has the meaning given by section 2(3);

[Deletion][126]

"*insurer*", in relation to an insured <u>person,</u> means the insurer under that policy;

"*road*" has the same meaning as in the Road Traffic Act 1988 (see section 192(1) of that Act).

(3) In this Part—

(a) a reference to an accident includes a reference to two or more causally related accidents;

(b) a reference to an accident caused by an <u>authorised</u> automated vehicle includes a reference to an accident that is partly caused by an <u>authorised</u> automated vehicle.'

The AV Bill 2023-24 approach to liability in relation to the transition between human and self-driving in a user-in-charge (UIC) automated vehicle

6.28 As the law stands at the time of writing, AEVA 2018, Part 1 activates, in the practical sense of the s 2 remedy, where:

'an accident is caused by an automated vehicle when driving itself on a road or other public place in Great Britain'[127]

and a person (including the insured person, if there is insurance) suffers damage as a result of the accident[128].

Because AEVA 2018, s 2 remedies activate where there is an accident caused by an automated vehicle 'when driving itself', the time of the occurrence of the accident is likely to be of particular importance if the accident occurs when an automated vehicle is in the transition between human driving and self-driving modes or *vice versa*.

As it stands at the time of writing, AEVA 2018 does not provide any guidance as to when the time of the accident should be fixed in this period.

After the enactment of AEVA 2018, both the Department for Transport and the Law Commissions recommended that human control should not be found by a court to

---

126 Deletion of phrase '"insured person", in relation to an insured vehicle, means any person whose use of the vehicle is covered by the policy in question'.

127 AEVA 2018, s 2(1)(a), (2)(a).

128 AEVA 2018, 2(1)(c), (2)(d).

have resumed, generating civil or criminal liabilities for the driver, unless the driver has in fact taken control back from the automated system, or a transition period (the duration of transition from automated to human control) has ended:

'It is important to note that we [the Department for Transport] consider the vehicle to no longer be driving itself if the driver resumes manual control at any time or a transition demand times out (because a driver has not responded to the prompt). Therefore, the driver resumes their driving task responsibilities once either of these events occur, not once the system disengages itself after bringing the vehicle to a stop. If the driver has not resumed control and the vehicle has not made a transition demand, then the vehicle is still considered to be driving itself.'[129]

'We [the Law Commissions] continue to believe that a user-in-charge should be granted an immunity for dynamic driving offences that arise out of the dynamic driving task… [A]n individual in the driving seat acquires user-in-charge status (and therefore has the immunity) while a relevant ADS [a fully-Automated Driving System] feature is engaged. The ADS is engaged when it is switched on. It ceases to be engaged when an individual takes control of the vehicle or the transition period ends.'[130]

The AV Bill 2023-24 (HL Bill 1), cl 45,Sch 2, para 5(6) would amend AEVA 2018, s 8(1)(a) as follows and add a new s 8(1A):

'8(1) For the purposes of this Part—

    (a) an authorised automated vehicle is "driving itself" if it is travelling while an authorised automation feature of the vehicle is engaged;

    …

(1A) Section 44(5) of the Automated Vehicles Act 2024 (authorisation to determine when feature "engaged" or "disengaged") applies for the purposes of subsection (1)(a) as it applies for the purposes of Part 1 of that Act.'

AV Bill 2023-24 (HL Bill 1), cl 44(5) (AVA 2024, s 44(5), assuming its enactment) provides that:

'Any question arising under this Part as to whether an authorised automation feature is "engaged" or "disengaged" is to be determined in accordance with what is specified or described under section 4(3)(b).'

And cl 4(3)(b) reads:

'4 **Authorised automation features**

    …

---

129 Department for Transport, 'Safe use of automated lane keeping system (ALKS): summary of responses and next steps – moving Britain ahead' (April 2021), chapter 4 ('The Listing Methodology for Automated Vehicles') page 40.
130 The Law Commissions, 'Automated Vehicles: joint report', Law Com No 404, Scot Law Com No 258 (25 January 2022) page 148, 8.71.

(3) In relation to each feature identified in the authorisation, the authorisation must specify –

...

(b) how the feature is engaged and disengaged'

The explanatory note to AV Bill 2023-24 states that:

'Subsection [cl 4](3)(a) [of the AV Bill] clarifies that a 'mode of operation' is either as a 'user-in-charge' (UiC) feature or a 'no-user-in-charge' NUiC feature. A UiC feature is one that can drive itself for only part of a journey and therefore requires an individual to be a driver for the remainder of the journey, for example a motorway chauffeur system. A NUiC feature is one that can drive itself for an entire journey and does not require an individual to be capable of taking control, for example a self-driving airport shuttle bus.'

'The distinction between UiC and NUiC features set out in subsection (3) (a) will determine the safety requirements for each. For example, a UiC feature can issue transition demands to ensure safe transition of control from the vehicle to a driver (see clause 7). A NUiC feature will require a licensed operator (a no-user-in-charge operator NUiCO – see Chapter 2) to ensure the safe operation of the vehicle. For example, taking responsibility for insurance.'

'The description of the locations and circumstances under which a vehicle is authorised to drive itself will ensure that users of a vehicle understand where and when it can safely be used (subsection (4)) and will support the determination of responsibility for a vehicle's driving behaviour. The locations specified could include places that are not roads but are public places, for example car park areas that are not defined as roads, but in line with clause 3(1)(a) the feature must be intended for use on roads in at least some circumstances in order to limit the scope of authorisation powers. Subsection (5) requires that the description of how a feature is engaged and disengaged must ensure that, where more than one feature is authorised, it is possible to identify which feature, if any, is engaged at any given moment. Clause 44(5) sets out that any question on interpretation about whether a feature is engaged or disengaged will be determined by the authorisation description required by this clause.'[131]

AV Bill 2023-24 (HL Bill 1), cl 7 defines and deals with authorisation requirements relating to 'transition demands':

'(1) Subsection (3) applies if authorisation requirements in relation to a vehicle with an authorised user-in-charge feature require the vehicle to be able to issue a transition demand while that feature is engaged.

(2) A "transition demand" is a demand, communicated by equipment of a vehicle in which an authorised user-in-charge feature is engaged, that the user-in-charge assume control of the vehicle by the end of a period of time beginning with the communication of the demand (the "transition period").

---

131 Explanatory note to AV Bill 2023-24 (HL Bill 1 – EN) paras 97-99.

(3) The Secretary of State must impose authorisation requirements designed to secure, so far as Secretary of State considers reasonably practicable, that –

  (a) the transition demand will be capable of being perceived by anyone who might legally be a user-in-charge of the vehicle (having regard in particular to users-in-charge with disabilities),

  (b) the transition period will be long enough for the user-in-charge to prepare to assume, and assume, control of the vehicle,

  (c) the vehicle will continue to travel autonomously, safely and legally during the transition period,

  (d) equipment of the vehicle will make a further communication at the end of the transition period to alert the user-in-charge to the ending of the period, and

  (e) the vehicle will deal safely with a situation where the user-in-charge fails to assume control by the end of the transition period.'

Contributory negligence in AEVA 2018 claims

6.29   As in a negligence claim, the defendant to an AEVA 2018, s 2 claim has the defence of contributory negligence.

Unlike a negligence claim (in which an insurer may raise contributory negligence in the defendant's place), AEVA 2018 provides a statutory cause of action (under s 2). So contributory negligence is provided for by s 3 (as it stands at the time of writing, unamended by AVA 2024 so omitting 'authorised' automated vehicle):

'3 Contributory negligence etc

(1) Where –

  (a) an insurer or vehicle owner is liable under section 2 to a person ('the injured party') in respect of an accident, and

  (b) the accident, or the damage resulting from it, was to any extent caused by the injured party,

  the amount of the liability is subject to whatever reduction under the Law Reform (Contributory Negligence) Act 1945 would apply to a claim in respect of the accident brought by the injured party against a person other than the insurer or vehicle owner.

(2) The insurer or owner of an automated vehicle is not liable under section 2 to the person in charge of the vehicle where the accident that it caused was wholly due to the person's negligence in allowing the vehicle to begin driving itself when it was not appropriate to do so.'

AEVA 2018, s 3 applies the 1945 Act in relation to the amount of the reduction, as would happen in a negligence claim resulting from the driving of a non-automated vehicle.

The phrase at the end of s 3(1) identifies the comparator to whose conduct the court must compare the vehicle's driving, when assessing comparative fault between the human user (the driver) and the automated vehicle ('a person other than the insurer or vehicle owner').

The Law Commission[132] and others have challenged the clarity of the language of s 3(1), but it might be that it provides for a notional human comparator in place of the car, to avoid difficult comparisons between human and machine reasoning when assessing comparative fault. AEVA 2018, s 6(3) provides (also in its pre-AVA 2024 form, so omitting 'authorised' automated vehicle) that:

> 'For the purposes of section 3(1), the Law Reform (Contributory Negligence) Act 1945 and section 5 of the Fatal Accidents Act 1976 (contributory negligence) have effect as if the behaviour of the automated vehicle were the fault of the person made liable for the damage by section 2 of this Act.'

The Law Reform (Contributory Negligence) Act 1945 abolished the rule that contribution by the fault of the claimant to the damage of which they complained operated as a complete defence. The 1945 Act provided instead that 'the damages recoverable in respect thereof shall be reduced to such extent as the court thinks just and equitable having regard to the claimant's share in the responsibility for the damage'[133]. The Fatal Accidents Act 1976, s 5 applies the same principle to a fatal accident claim where 'any person dies partly as the result of his own fault and partly of the fault of any other person or persons'.

The exercise under the Law Reform (Contributory Negligence) Act, s 1(1) is essentially comparative, requiring comparison between the faults of two or more persons, one of whom is the claimant. The language of AEVA, s 3(1) might be intended to introduce a fictional human comparator to play the role of the automated vehicle in that exercise.

6.30   AEVA 2018, s 3(2) provides for a particular situation in which the user's fault will extinguish a s 2 claim: 'where the accident that [the automated vehicle] caused was wholly due to the person [in charge]'s negligence in allowing the vehicle to begin driving itself when it was not appropriate to do so.'

Section 3(2) raises a factual situation for determination by the court: whether 'it was not appropriate to allow the vehicle to begin driving itself' at the moment that the user activated the system.

Reform of the extra-statutory MIB agreements for automated vehicles

6.31   As at the time of writing, the position of the Motor Insurers' Bureau in relation to automated vehicles is that 'there are no agreements in place between the MIB and the Secretary of State for Transport to deal with' claims by victims of uninsured automated vehicles.

---

132 See the Law Commissions, 'Automated Vehicles: a joint preliminary consultation paper', Law Commission Consultation Paper 240, Scottish Law Commission Discussion Paper 166 (8 November 2018) and 'Automated Vehicles: Analysis of Responses to the Preliminary Consultation Paper' (19 June 2019) chapter 6, pages 86 to 88
133 Law Reform (Contributory Negligence) Act 1945, s1(1).

However, the same MIB document (its response to the Law Commissions' third consultation paper) engages in detail with the Law Commissions' recommendations for automated vehicle regulation insofar as they affect insurance (including discussion of data storage requirements and the effect of failure to update software in the context of claims under the MIB scheme) and states that the MIB 'would welcome a debate around these issues' [134].

There is force in the view that revision of the non-statutory part of the insurance scheme is required in light of AEVA 2018. In particular:

- Both the current Uninsured Drivers Agreement (2015, amended in 2017) and Untraced Drivers Agreement (2017) preceded AEVA 2018 (which was enacted in July 2018 and was brought into force in relation to insurance in April 2021[135]).

- AEVA 2018 alters the statutory motor insurance scheme, with which the extra-statutory MIB agreements ride in tandem. But the liability under AEVA 2018, s 2 for which an insurer would compensate is of a different type to the conventional liability in negligence of the human driver. Özlem Gürses has written that:

    'It is likely that the MIB will adjust their levies [on its authorised motor insurer members] for the reason of insuring the vehicle under two different regimes. The MIB Articles of Association and the relevant MIB Agreements will need to be amended to reflect such an expansion of the MIB's liability.'[136]

- Given the reforming effects of AEVA 2018, the language of the current agreements might require review generally.

However, the prospect of the MIB and government failing to agree to accommodate automated vehicles within the MIB scheme seems unlikely. In particular:

- The MIB has invited 'a debate' on how automated vehicles might be brought within the MIB scheme.

- Neither the MIB nor the government has (so far as is known) exercised their right to terminate either agreement on the 12 months permitted notice[137], and more than 12 months has elapsed both since AEVA 2018 was enacted (July 2018) and since it was brought into force (April 2021[138]).

- Since AEVA 2018 amends RTA 1988, Part VI[139], it is possible that automated vehicles as defined by AEVA 2018 already fall within the MIB's objects as defined in its Articles of Association. The primary object of the MIB is

    'To provide a safety net for innocent victims of identified and uninsured drivers to satisfy, or provide for the satisfaction of, claims, judgements, awards or settlements in respect of any liability required to be covered by contracts of insurance or security under Part VI of the Road Traffic Act 1988 or by any other statute, statutory instrument, rule, regulation, order,

---

134 MIB's response to Law Commissions' third paper on AV law, March 2021 at page 6, response to question 53.
135 Automated and Electric Vehicles Act 2018 (Commencement No.1) Regulations 2021, SI 2021/396.
136 Gürses, 13.25.
137 Clause 2(3) of both the Uninsured Drivers Agreement and Untraced Drivers Agreement.
138 SI 2021/396, above.
139 See discussion of AEVA 2018, above.

directive or similar measure introduced by any competent authority or at common law or by custom'[140]

and that includes amendments:

'A reference to a particular directive, regulation, rule, statute, statutory provision or subordinate legislation is a reference to it as it is in force from time to time, taking account of any amendment or re-enactment and includes any directive, regulation, rule, statute, statutory provision or subordinate legislation which it amends or re-enacts and subordinate legislation for the time being in force made under it.'[141]

- Whether or not an untraced driver was using an AEVA 2018, s 1-listed or AVA 2024-authorised automated vehicle might not be capable of detection, so the Untraced Drivers Agreement might (levies aside) be unaffected[142].

However, none of these points are yet agreed between the MIB and government. Clarity is required. As Özlem Gürses notes, 'Practical difficulties will reveal themselves after automated vehicles appear on the road'[143].

Summary: the first 'automated vehicles' in British motor insurance law, and beyond

6.32   In summary:

- The insurance scheme for automated vehicles is provided by AEVA 2018, which amends the RTA 1988, Part VI.

- The insurance scheme will be put into practical effect – either with the first listing by the Secretary of State of an 'automated vehicle' (or several such models of vehicle) under AEVA 2018, s 1 or as the result of authorisation of such a vehicle under the AV Bill 2023-24 (expected to become the Automated Vehicles Act 2024).

- The insurance scheme as modified for automated vehicles follows the 'single insurer' model proposed by the insurance industry, whereby AEVA 2018 cover supplements the existing RTA 1988 insurance scheme and comes into compensatory effect 'where an accident is caused by an [authorised[144]] automated vehicle when driving itself on a road or other public place in Great Britain'[145].

- There are as yet no published agreements between the Motor Insurers' Bureau and the government in relation to the compensation of victims of accidents caused by uninsured or untraced automated vehicles.

---

140 MIB Articles of Association, Article 2(1)(a) ('Objects').
141 MIB Articles of Association, Article 1(5) ('Interpretation').
142 Gürses (13.27) makes this point, although (depending upon the AEVA 2018, s 1 list, unpublished at the time of writing) it is possible that a vehicle in an 'untraced driver' incident might exceptionally be identifiable as a marque typically listed as automated under AEVA 2018.
143 Gürses, 13.26.
144 Addition to AEVA 2018, s 2 proposed by AV Bill 2023-24 (HL Bill 1), cl 45, Sch 2, para 5(3) (a).
145 AEVA 2018, s 2(1)(a).

D Insurance law for electric vehicles

The insurance provisions of AEVA 2018, Part 1 do not apply to non-automated electric vehicles

6.33 Despite its title, AEVA 2018 does not apply any special insurance scheme to electric vehicles.

In particular, there is nothing in AEVA 2018 as to insurance of 'micro-mobility' electric vehicles such as e-scooters.

Provisions as to which electric vehicles do and do not require compulsory insurance for use on roads or other public places appear elsewhere.

Electric 'motor vehicles' whose use requires compulsory insurance

6.34 RTA 1988, s 143 (the requirement for liability insurance) applies to use of 'a motor vehicle' on a road or other public place.[146]

Definition of 'motor vehicle' in RTA 1988, s 185

6.35 RTA 1988, s 185 provides the definition of 'motor vehicle' (as well as more particular definitions of some types of motor vehicle). The 'motor vehicle' definition in s 185 is:

'*'motor vehicle'* means, subject to section 20 of the Chronically Sick and Disabled Persons Act 1970 (which makes special provision about invalid carriages, within the meaning of that Act), a mechanically propelled vehicle intended or adapted for use on roads'[147]

And RTA 1988, s 185 also defines 'invalid carriage':

'*'invalid carriage'* means a mechanically propelled vehicle the weight of which unladen does not exceed 254 kilograms and which is specially designed and constructed, and not merely adapted, for the use of a person suffering from some physical defect or disability and is used solely by such a person'[148]

A 'motor cycle' and a 'motor car' are among the particular types of motor vehicle defined by RTA 1988, s 185[149].

As to whether an electric vehicle is 'intended or adapted for use on roads':

'The test is whether a reasonable person would say that one of [the vehicle's] uses would be use on the roads. That person must consider whether some general use on the roads must be contemplated and not merely isolated use or use by a man losing his senses. The design and capabilities of the

---

146 RTA 1988, s 143(1).
147 RTA 1988, s 185(1).
148 RTA 1988, s 185(1).
149 See RTA 1988, s 185(1).

[vehicle] and the possibilities it offers will be considered and considered in the context of an assessment of peoples' wish to get quickly through traffic and the pressure of time upon many people.'[150]

Factors *not* determinative of whether the vehicle is 'intended or adapted for use on roads' include whether a reasonable person would use the vehicle on the road, the vehicle's non-compliance with safety standards, explicit advice by the manufacturer not to use the vehicle on the roads and (on the other side of the argument) that there is no other surface than a road on which the vehicle could be used[151].

Novelty of vehicle irrelevant to its statutory definition as a 'motor vehicle'

6.36   The novelty of a vehicle is irrelevant to the issue of its definition as a motor vehicle, which is a matter of statutory construction. This has been the case since 1917:

'Though I doubt very much whether it was in the mind of the Legislature that a vehicle of this kind would come into existence, I am forced to the conclusion on the language of the Act that this is a motor car within the Act'[152]

In particular, it is a misdirection in law to describe an innovative vehicle as a 'toy'[153] if it fits the statutory definition. The 'toy' submission was made repeatedly until the Divisional Court confirmed in 2008 that it is a misdirection in law[154].

An electric vehicle is 'mechanically propelled'

6.37   An electric vehicle is 'mechanically propelled actuated by electricity'[155] so will fall within the definition of 'motor vehicle' unless otherwise excluded.

Statutory definition of 'electric vehicle'

6.38   An oddity on the face of AEVA 2018 is that it does not define the phrase 'electric vehicle'. The definitions section of AEVA 2018, Part 2 ('Electric Vehicles: Charging') only defines 'vehicle':

' "vehicle" means a vehicle that is intended or adapted for use on roads.'[156]

That was a deliberate legislative decision. Despite the title of the Act, AEVA 2018, Part 2 legislates beyond electric vehicles and includes provision for hydrogen-

---

150 *DPP v Saddington* [2001] RTR 15 (QBD) [19].
151 *DPP v Saddington* [9], [17], [19], [20].
152 Lord Reading CJ in *Elieson v Parker* (1917) 81 JP 265.
153 *DPP v King* [2008] EWHC 447 (Admin). See judgment of the Divisional Court at [13].
154 *Elieson v Parker* (1917), *DPP v Saddington* (2001), *DPP v King* (2008).
155 *Elieson v Parker* (1917), above: an electrically propelled bath chair. Today, the vehicle in *Elieson* would have been within the 'invalid carriage' exemption.
156 AEVA 2018, s 9.

fuelled vehicles. Parliamentary debate on what became AEVA 2018, s 9 included this passage:

> '… this part of the Bill is focused on charging or refuelling infrastructure for vehicles. Such infrastructure is defined by reference to its capacity to recharge either battery or hydrogen-propelled vehicles. We think that the Bill includes the relevant definitions necessary in relation to refuelling points. In addition, there is a definition of 'electric vehicle' in legislation already, as the definition contained in the Alternative Fuels Infrastructure Regulations made last year mirrors the definition proposed by the noble Baroness, Lady Worthington. Given that the definitions in the Bill already work as intended, we do not think there is a need to duplicate the definition of 'electric vehicle' within the Bill.'[157]

The definition of 'electric vehicle' appears in those 2017 regulations:

> ' *"electric vehicle"* means a motor vehicle equipped with a powertrain containing at least one non-peripheral electric machine as energy convertor with an electric rechargeable energy storage system, which can be recharged externally;'[158]

As an electric vehicle is 'mechanically propelled'[159], such a vehicle should already fall within the RTA 1988, s 185 definition, though it is possible that the definition in the 2017 regulations might also be relevant in future cases.

RTA 1988, s 189 – certain vehicles not to be treated as motor vehicles

6.39   RTA 1988, s 189 provides that certain vehicles are *not* to be treated as motor vehicles for the purpose of the Road Traffic Acts:

> '189 – *Certain vehicles not to be treated as motor vehicles.*
>
> (1) For the purposes of the Road Traffic Acts—
>
> > (a) a mechanically propelled vehicle being an implement for cutting grass which is controlled by a pedestrian and is not capable of being used or adapted for any other purpose,
> >
> > (b) any other mechanically propelled vehicle controlled by a pedestrian which may be specified by regulations made by the Secretary of State for the purposes of this section and section 140 of the Road Traffic Regulation Act 1984, and
> >
> > (c) an electrically assisted pedal cycle of such a class as may be prescribed by regulations so made,
> >
> > is to be treated as not being a motor vehicle.'
>
> (2) In subsection (1) above 'controlled by a pedestrian' means that the vehicle either –

---

157 Baroness Sugg, <u>House of Lords Hansard, volume 791, column 790 (17 May 2018)</u>.
158 Alternative Fuels Infrastructure Regulations 2017, SI 2017/897, reg 2, 'interpretation'.
159 Section 185 RTA 1988 and *Elieson v Parker* (1917), above.

(a) is constructed or adapted for use only under such control, or

(b) is constructed or adapted for use either under such control or under the control of a person carried on it, but is not for the time being in use under, or proceeding under, the control of a person carried on it.'

E-scooters

Whether an e-scooter is a motor vehicle for compulsory insurance purposes

6.40   An e-scooter is a 'motor vehicle' within RTA 1988, s 185[160]. So its use on a road or other public place is required to be insured under RTA 1988, Part VI[161]. As the government guidance on 'powered transporters' (which include e-scooters) puts it,

'It is illegal to use a powered transporter on a public road without complying with a number of legal requirements, which potential users will find very difficult'[162].

The government has relaxed some of the requirements for personal use of e-scooters in identified trial areas[163], including providing that insurance will be provided by commercial operators of trials[164].

The purpose of allowing trials of e-scooters was assess the long-term suitability of e-scooters for use on roads[165].

E-scooter trials were due to end on 30 November 2022[166] but in an answer to a parliamentary question on 6 July 2022 the Department for Transport stated its preference for an 18-month extension of the trials:

'The Government has decided to allow current e-scooter trials, which are live in 30 areas across England, to be extended. The existing trials will continue to run until 30 November and participating local authorities will then have the option to end their local trial or extend it to 31 May 2024. Extensions will be restricted to existing trial areas only and will allow us to gather further evidence where gaps are identified, building on the findings of the current evaluation. We hope that all areas will want to continue, but there is no compulsion.'[167]

---

160 *DPP v King* (above).
161 RTA 1988, s 143.
162 Gov.uk 'Guidance: Powered Transporters' (updated 13 July 2020).
163 Electric Scooter Trials and Traffic Signs (Coronavirus) Regulations and General Directions 2020, SI 2020/663.
164 UK government 'Guidance: E-scooter trials: guidance for users' (published 13 July 2020, updated 25 October 2022)
165 Explanatory note to SI 2020/663.
166 UK government 'Guidance: E-scooter trials: guidance for local authorities and rental operators' (updated 22 February 2022)
167 DfT answer 6 July 2022 to parliamentary question by Gill Furniss MP 1 July 2022, UIN 28907

The future of the insurance requirement for e-scooters?

6.41   The government announced in May 2022 that it intended to legalise the use of e-scooters on roads and other public places. This was elaborated in parliamentary debate following the Queen's Speech:

> '...it is our intention that the Bill will create a low-speed, zero-emission vehicle category that is independent from the cycle and motor vehicle categories. New powers would allow the Government to decide the vehicles that fall into this new category in future and how they should be regulated to make sure that they are safe to use. We hope that e-scooters will be the first of these vehicles.'[168]

The future form of insurance law for e-scooters is unknown. A possibility is that the duty to insure e-scooter use under RTA 1988, s 143 will pass to the individual user upon legalisation of private use beyond the trials. A possible alternative (perhaps indicated by the intended creation of a new category of vehicles 'that is independent from the cycle and motor vehicle categories') is that s 143 is repealed in relation to e-scooters. The Motor Insurers' Bureau has indicated the possibility of a 'lighter touch' insurance approach, in which the compulsory motor insurance requirement still applies to the use of e-scooters on roads but is subject to financial limits to compensation[169]. And some respondents to the government's 'Future of Transport Regulatory Review' in 2020

> 'suggested that different types of insurance could be available, rather than motor insurance which applies to mopeds. This included options such as add-ons to home insurance, a standalone personal liability product, or some form of taxation. It was also suggested insurance should also be required for EAPCs, or that requirements could be linked to the speed, weight or power of the vehicle.'[170]

In contrast to the AV Bill 2023-24 (HL Bill 1), the Transport Bill announced to include legislation for e-scooters in the Queen's Speech in May 2022 then postponed by the government in December 2022[171] did not appear in the King's Speech on 7 November 2023.

The Motor Insurers' Bureau and future regulation of e-scooters

6.42   On 9 August 2020, the MIB made this statement on the use of e-scooters:

---

168 Baroness Vere, House of Lords Hansard volume 822, columns 30 to 31 (11 May 2022).
169 The Motor Insurers' Bureau supported insurance for e-scooters, saying that they will 'inevitably give rise to additional accidents'. It said this should be a lighter-touch approach than car insurance requirements and that the amount of cover, and the cost, should reflect the lower risk presented by e-scooters: House of Commons Transport Select Committee 'E-scooters: pavement nuisance or transport innovation' (2 October 2020), para.54. And see Bolt Burdon Kemp solicitors, 'The Future of E-scooter Regulation: a stakeholder discussion', 6 July 2022
170 Department for Transport 'Future of Transport Regulatory Review: summary of responses' (October 2020), pages 26, 27.
171 Parliament Live TV, Transport Select Committee 7 December 2022 at 9:43, Sec of St for Transport the Rt Hon Mark Harper MP.

'The MIB (Motor Insurers' Bureau) supports the Department for Transport's trials and indeed the potential legalisation of e-scooters for use on the road, but we stand with 80% of the British public in calling for compulsory insurance of these motorised vehicles.'

'We welcome the fact that operators during the trials will be required to have Motor Third Party Liability (MTPL) insurance. However, it's important to remember that e-scooters (and other e-mobility devices) not used as part of the trials remain illegal for use on roads and in other public places.'

'As it stands there has been no announcement on insurance requirements should e-scooters become legal. The government's failure to implement relevant EU law since 2014[172] has left the MIB bearing the costs for compensating victims who are hit by e-scooters. These claims are effectively funded by premium paying motorists and result – completely unfairly – in increased motor insurance premiums for all decent road users. This situation continues after the transition period ends, as this EU law requirement remains in UK law until the government legislates to remove it. So far, they have not committed to doing so.'[173]

The MIB believes there are potentially catastrophic consequences for legalising e-scooters beyond these trials without the requirement for some form of compulsory insurance. There is a high risk of accidents – presenting a dangerous threat to the safety and security of pedestrians, children and other innocent road users. This increases the likelihood of victims enduring life-threatening and life changing consequences with no hope of compensation for the victims. This also poses a major risk to e-scooter users without insurance, who could be forced to pay out thousands of pounds in liability if they have an accident.'[174]

The May 2022 indication from government as to future regulation of e-scooters was that:

'the [Transport] Bill will create a low-speed, zero-emission vehicle category that is independent from the cycle and motor vehicle categories. New powers would allow the Government to decide the vehicles that fall into this new category in future and how they should be regulated to make sure that they are safe to use. We hope that e-scooters will be the first of these vehicles.'[175]

But whether or not e-scooters would remain subject to the RTA 1988, Part VI requirement of compulsory insurance for use on roads or other public places was not stated. The Transport Bill announced in May 2022 has not been published and did not appear in the King's Speech in November 2023.

---

172 This appears to refer to the judgment of the CJEU in *Vnuk v Zavarovalnica Triglav dd* (Case C-162/13) [2016] RTR 10, which gave a broad application to 'use' of a vehicle, which was found by UK courts not to apply in disputes between private individuals (see *Pilling v UK Insurance* [2019] UKSC 16 [40, 41]) but could be deployed against the MIB. From 28 June 2022 the Motor Vehicles (Compulsory Insurance) Act 2022 aims to remove the effect of *Vnuk* from British law.
173 See MV(CI)A 2022, footnote above.
174 'MIB statement on the use of e-scooters, Mail on Sunday, 9 August 2020' (MIB website, accessed 31 October 2022)
175 Baroness Vere, House of Lords Hansard volume 822, columns 30 to 31 (11 May 2022).

Electrically Assisted Pedal Cycles (EAPCs)

Whether an EAPC is a motor vehicle

6.43   RTA 1988, s 189(1)(c) provides that:

'For the purposes of the Road Traffic Acts – … an electrically assisted pedal cycle of such a class as may be prescribed by regulations so made, is to be treated as not being a motor vehicle.'[176]

The regulations are the Electrically Assisted Pedal Cycles Regulations 1983 (the EPAC Regulations)[177], reg 3 of which provides that

'The class of electrically assisted pedal cycles prescribed for the purposes of … section 189 of the Road Traffic Act 1988 consists of pedal cycles with two or more wheels which comply with the requirements specified in Regulation 4 below.'

The EAPC Regulations, reg 4 specifies those requirements as

'that the vehicle shall: – …

(b)   be fitted with pedals by means of which it is capable of being propelled; and

(c)   be fitted with no motor other than an electric motor which –

(i)   has a maximum continuous rated power which does not exceed 250 watts;

(ii)   cannot propel the vehicle when it is travelling at more than 15.5 miles per hour.'

The exception for EAPCs from the insurance requirement of RTA 1988, Part VI cannot be obtained by cosmetic means. The requirement of pedals 'by means of which [the EAPC] is capable of being propelled' is (as in the case of intention or adaptation for use on roads) tested by an objective standard. In *Winter v DPP*[178], exemption from the insurance requirement had been attempted by the installation of largely ineffective pedals to an electric tricycle. Michael Supperstone KC, sitting as a Deputy High Court Judge[179], interpreted:

'the words 'fitted with pedals by means of which it is capable of being propelled' as meaning that the vehicle is 'reasonably capable of being propelled' by the pedals'

Because:

'the policy behind s.143 of the Road Traffic Act 1988, namely to safeguard road users and pedestrians from uninsured injury from a mechanically powered vehicle, by providing for compulsory insurance'

---

176 RTA 1988, s 189(1)(c).
177 'The EAPC Regulations', SI 1983/1168, as amended by the Electrically Assisted Pedal Cycles (Amendment) Regulations 2015, SI 2015/24.
178 *Winter v DPP* [2002] EWHC 1524 (Admin).
179 Later Mr Justice Supperstone.

requires that:

> 'a purposive construction should be adopted to reg.4(b) to give effect to the intention of Parliament, which must be to require the pedals on an electrically assisted pedal cycle to be capable of propelling the vehicle in a safe manner in its normal day-to-day use.'

So the installation of pedals not 'reasonably' capable of propelling the vehicle 'in a safe manner in its normal day-to-day use' failed to avoid (via the EAPC exemption) the 'motor vehicle' classification and the consequent requirement for third party insurance.

So, an electrically assisted pedal cycle within the RTA 1988, s 189(1)(c) and the EAPC regulations on that objective test will not require insurance.

An Electric Vehicle 'use' issue: does the use of charging cables on a road or other public place fall within RTA 1988 compulsory insurance?

6.44   Under RTA 1988, s 145 an insurance policy must insure a person in respect of:

> 'any liability which may be incurred by him or them in respect of the death of or bodily injury to any person or damage to property caused by, or arising out of, the use of the vehicle on a road or other public place in Great Britain'[180]

The concept of 'use' is broad. 'Use' is not restricted to 'driving', and 'or arising out of, the use…' expands the possibilities of liability.

In particular, it includes liabilities arising from refuelling a vehicle. In *Dunthorne v Bentley*[181], the defendant ran across the road from her car, which she had stopped as she had run out of petrol. She ran across the road towards a colleague. The claimant was unable to stop his car before a collision with the defendant, which resulted in the defendant's death and serious injury to the claimant. The claimant sued the defendant's estate for his injury caused by her negligence.

By a majority (Pill LJ dissenting), the Court of Appeal held that the accident arose out of the defendant's use of her car. The majority (Rose LJ, Hutchison LJ agreeing) held in particular that:

- 'at the time Mrs Bentley crossed the road she was using the car even though not at that moment driving it, for a person uses a vehicle on a road if he has the use of it on a road'

- 'the phrase 'arising out of' contemplates a more remote consequence than is embraced by 'caused by'.'

- 'the matter … must be determined by the facts of the particular case.'

---

180 RTA 1988, 145(3)(a) ('Requirements in respect of policies of insurance').
181 *Dunthorne v Bentley* [1996] RTR 428.

- 'the reason why she was crossing was one of the factors which had to be considered when determining whether the accident was caused by or arose out of the use of her car.'

- 'it by no means follows that intention and motive are irrelevant to what can be said to have arisen out of the use of the vehicle. Indeed, this is demonstrated by [counsel for the defendant insurer] Mr O'Brien's acceptance that a driver of a parked car walking to the boot to get a can of petrol would be engaged in an activity arising out of the use of the car.'

- 'In each case how the act of crossing the road is to be categorised and, in particular, whether it can be said to arise out of some other activity is to be judged objectively according to all the circumstances of the particular case including the reason why the pedestrian was there. To exclude consideration of the pedestrian's purpose would be an unwarranted disregard of common sense and to close one's eyes to potentially important information as to the origins of the act of crossing the road.'

- 'The judge expressed his conclusion in this way: '(1) Mrs Bentley's running across the road was a negligent act which caused the plaintiff's injuries (as well as her own tragic death); (2) that act was closely and causally connected with her use of the car; and therefore (3) the plaintiff's injuries arose out of Mrs Bentley's use of the car, within the meaning of section 145(3) of the Act of 1988.' With that conclusion, I agree.'

- 'Once it is accepted, as it is by Mr O'Brien, that 'arising out of' is a wider concept than 'caused by,' the question for the judge was essentially one of fact rather than law. This accident was caused by Mrs Bentley's negligence when seeking help to continue the journey in her car. It arose from her use of the car because she would not have been crossing the road had her car not run out of petrol and because she was seeking help to continue her journey.'

Hutchison LJ added to the majority view that:

'It is easy to envisage facts which, on the one hand, plainly do and, on the other hand, plainly do not arise out of the use of the vehicle. The question for the judge, as is so often the case, was on which side of the line the present case fell. I would accept that this is a case close to that line and I agree with the observations of Pill LJ in that regard. However I am satisfied that, on the facts before him, the judge was entitled to reach the conclusion he did and I, too, would dismiss this appeal.'

Pill LJ agreed that it was open to the trial judge to infer that the defendant had crossed the road in order to seek help refuelling her car.

Pill LJ also agreed that:

'Had she, for example, been walking to the rear of the vehicle to fetch an emergency petrol can in the boot in order to fill the tank I would have had no difficulty' in 'deciding whether the conduct of Mrs Bentley is properly categorised as arising from her use of the motor car.'

Pill LJ's dissent was confined to the degree of elasticity of the phrase 'arising out of, the use':

'Walking across the road to seek assistance from a passing friend some time after having properly parked her vehicle gives me more difficulty… [quoting Australian authority] 'Arising out of' excludes cases of bodily injury in which the use of the vehicle is a merely causal concomitant, not considered to be, in a relevant causal sense, a contributing factor.' Applying that test, I could not regard it as a general principle that an act performed by someone seeking assistance of some kind because his vehicle has broken down is necessarily conduct which arises out of the use of the vehicle.'

In *Pilling v UK Insurance*, the Supreme Court approved *Dunthorne v Bentley*, rejecting a submission that it had been wrongly decided. It was 'close to the line', as Lord Hodge put it, 'but it is not apparent to me that the outcome of that borderline case was wrong, having regard to the close connection in time, place and circumstance between the use of the car on the road and the accident.'[182] Summarising the effect of the RTA 1988, s 145(3), Lord Hodge said that:

'The relevant use occurs where a person uses or has the use of a vehicle on a road or public place, including where he or she parks an immobilised vehicle in such a place (as the English case law requires), and the relevant damage has to have arisen out of that use.'[183]

How 'arising out of the use' would be applied to a case in which a pedestrian claimant trips over an unsafely arranged cable of an electric vehicle charging in a public place, unattended by the defendant owner or user of the EV, is as yet untested. Each case will turn upon its facts.

But the connection between refuelling and use is made by *Dunthorne*, and the similarity between refuelling and charging is clear. An EV cable tripping claim might be within RTA 1988 compulsory insurance.

---

182 *Pilling v UK Insurance* [2019] UKSC 16 [44].
183 *Pilling v UK Insurance* [45].

Chapter 7

Themes of AAEV Law

'Creating environmental and public health laws [*in the nineteenth century*] did not simply involve the granting of more powers to civil servants or agencies, but often involved the very refashioning of administrative structures and laws.'

Professor Elizabeth Fisher (2019)[1]

Chapter Contents

A   Some Themes of AAEV Law 7.01
B   Some Themes of Advanced Driver Assistance Systems (ADAS) Law 7.06
C   Some Themes of Automated Vehicle Law 7.09
D   Some Themes of Electric Vehicle Law 7.12

A   Some themes of AAEV Law

AAEV law's place within the tradition of regulating technology

7.01   Professor Fisher describes (in the broad setting of environmental law) the Victorian approach to regulation and its lasting influence:

'This history is complicated but it is important to appreciate that many of the features of contemporary environmental law can be traced to this time. These features include reliance on central-local government interrelationships, the negotiated nature of enforcement, and the creation of offences as a means of regulation.... [*Gavin*] Drewry notes one particular development [*in Victorian government*] – the heavy reliance on general public acts as a means of social reform... General Acts of Parliament still play a central role in UK environmental law and ... are the starting point for nearly all regulatory frameworks... We will also see, however, the significance of delegated legislation within these frameworks ...'[2]

---

1   Elizabeth Fisher, Bettina Lange and Eloise Scotford *Environmental Law: Text, Cases and Materials* (Oxford University Press, 2nd edn, 2019), chapter 10, 'Environmental law in the legal culture of the United Kingdom', p 298.
2   As above.

The same pattern is true of legislation for automated and electric vehicles – the subjects of AEVA 2018 and the Automated Vehicles Bill 2023-24 (HL Bill 1). ADAS systems have been regulated incrementally by delegated legislation, a tradition that would continue under the AV Bill. The insurance reforms of AEVA 2018 and adaptation of type approval requirements for new technology under regulations proposed by the AV Bill 2023-24 (HL Bill 1), cl 91(1) sit within a regulatory framework for motor vehicles built by the Road Traffic Acts – a superstructure which is close to a century old[3].

Some central themes of AAEV law emerge from the discussion in this book and are discussed here. As in the discussion of legal problems (Chapter 8), this is not an exhaustive list, and readers are likely to see other themes.

Internationalism

7.02   Professors Fisher, Lange and Scotford's observations that environmental law 'is a legally, scientifically, and socio-politically complex subject'[4], 'a pluralistic subject in scholarly terms'[5], rooted in national culture and drawing upon laws of numerous types and ages is apt to AAEV law. The lasting influence of EU law is obvious, but (as described in Chapter 2) there is a larger and longer-established international influence, from the UNECE legal instruments upon which national vehicle specification law is largely based. Those instruments sprung from the earlier agreements and industrial standards which had allowed international trade in motor vehicles to grow.

Much law springs from international roots and vehicle law is no exception. The discussion of regulation of automated vehicle specifications remains international, through UNECE. National autonomy as to traffic rules is a well-established exception to that.

Laws under pressure

7.03   Technology exerts pressure upon some laws to change. Consumer protection law – a system with international roots and (in the case of the Consumer Protection Act 1987) of EU design – feels that pressure (see Chapter 10 and below). It was designed at the birth of consumer electronics and did not have the worldwide web in its imagination; the inflexibility of its rules to over the air updating software shows its limits. Among the recommendations of the Law Commissions on AV law in January 2022 was a wholesale reconsideration of product liability law to take account of emerging technologies.

---

3   If we take the Road Traffic Act 1930 – with its central features of compulsory insurance and the Highway Code – as the starting point of the current road traffic regulatory scheme. See Chapters 2, 'specifications', and 6, 'insurance'.
4   Elizabeth Fisher, Bettina Lange and Eloise Scotford *Environmental Law: Text, Cases and Materials* (Oxford University Press, 2nd edn, 2019), p 2. See Chapter 30.
5   Above, chapter 10, 'Environmental law in the legal culture of the United Kingdom', p 293.

Variety of available laws

7.04   Some laws require replacement; others adaptation. The Consumer Rights Act 2015 does not offer a universal solution to the unactionable nature of downloaded software, but its provisions as to digital content allow a practical solution for consumers in many contract cases (see Chapter 10).

Other laws might attract new attention. The law of nuisance, a potential warrior against motor vehicles in the 1900s, was demoted in favour of negligence (see Chapter 4). The birth of AEVA 2018, s 2 has drawn attention back to stricter torts, and nuisance might have a role to play in a time of dockless, electric rental vehicles.

AI Bias: training datasets must be tested

7.05   In *R (Bridges) v Chief Constable of South Wales Police*[6] (the automated facial recognition case), the Court of Appeal held that the defendant police force's failure to satisfy itself that the AFR system did not have an unacceptable bias on grounds of race or sex was a breach of the public sector equality duty under EA 2010, s 149, even though there was no evidence that the system had any such bias. The lack of consideration of the dataset used to train the system was sufficient to show the breach[7].

B Some Themes of Advanced Driver Assistance Systems (ADAS) Law

ADAS have been regulated incrementally, by secondary legislation

7.06   ADAS have been regulated incrementally, for example by the addition of exemptions to the prohibition against use of a hand-held mobile device under CUR 1986, reg 110, so as to allow remote parking and contactless payments. See Chapter 2.

As at the time of writing, driver assistance and ADAS are not terms of British law. Unlike 'automated vehicle' (which is defined both in AEVA 2018 and in RTA 1988), as at the time of writing they have no statutory definition in British law.

However, the AV Bill 2023-24 (HL Bill 1) will, if it becomes law, change that: cl 91(1) would enable type approval requirements to be updated not only for automated vehicles but also for:

'(b) any other type of vehicle that—

    (i)   includes equipment designed to allow its motion to be controlled other than by an individual in it, or to facilitate its being so controlled, or

    (ii) is designed to incorporate or interact with software.'

---

6 [2020] EWCA Civ 1058; [2020] 1 WLR 5037.
7 *Bridges*, 5078D-E [193], 5079E-F [199].

The difficult fit of product liability law

7.07   As discussed in Chapter 10, consumer protection law was designed in a pre-worldwide web era, and important features of its design (for example, the 10-year longstop) depended upon the nature of products available then, whose character has since changed: the computerisation of cars being a case in point.

The current version of consumer protection law is complex and fragmented: the Consumer Rights Act 2015 provides remedies in relation to downloaded software which British law still fails to recognise in a broader commercial setting. The EU law giving legal character to downloaded software has been added only since the UK's exit.

The persistent software problem

7.08   The AV Bill 2023-24 appears to have clarified the actionability of downloaded software in an AEVA 2018, Part 1 claim, by its inclusion of software within the definitions for authorisation of an AV and its amendments to AEVA 2018. Whether it does the same for ADAS is debatable. But, beyond the remedies available in consumer to business contracts under the Consumer Rights Act 2015, the general actionability of defective downloaded software in non-automated vehicles, including ADAS, remains unclear. See Chapter 10.

C Some Themes of Automated Vehicle Law

The significance of standards

7.09   Many standards classify automated vehicles, attempting in particular to delineate the border between human and automated driving (especially the 'mushy middle' of SAE level 3, as the Law Commissions have described it). As discussed in Chapter 2, the origins of automotive standards are not easy to discern, but their influence upon the regulation of vehicle construction and use is clear.

AEVA 2018 does not adopt any particular standard. The relevance of standards to civil liability has been discussed mainly in consumer protection law (see Chapter 10). The evidential role of standards in automated vehicle cases is not yet clear, but they might be of relevance in primary civil liability cases under AEVA 2018, s 2 where there is an issue as to driver negligence in handover (s 3(2)) and in secondary claims by a liable insurer etc (s 5).

Standards might be overtaken by the statutory statement of safety principles proposed by the AV Bill 2023-24 (HL Bill 1), cl 2, and by the detail of the many regulations which the Automated Vehicles Act 2024 would empower. But the AV Bill might give standards a greater role. Some amendments presented on 1 December 2023, after the second reading of HL Bill 1 in the House of Lords, suggest possible express references to British Standards within the text of the Bill. Whether that course is adopted in the AVA 2024 remains to be seen.

Stricter liability

7.10   Increasingly sophisticated ADAS systems and automated vehicles (when they come) signal a shift from driving as an activity to the use of vehicle as equipment. In terms of liability, that is a shift from negligence, on the basis of driver responsibility, to stricter liabilities on economic actors such as insurers and manufacturers and developers etc, as in AEVA 2018, ss 2 and 5.

This might return the law to the question faced by the courts in the 1900s, as motor vehicles spread, as to whether strict liability or negligence was the appropriate response. Negligence was then preferred. Might a different answer have been given then? What is the appropriate answer now?

Primary liability shifting

7.11   AEVA 2018, Part 1 has at its core a pragmatic device: the shifting of the burden of proving product liability from the injured claimant to the defendant's motor insurer or (where so permitted by RTA 1988) to the defendant where it is permitted to use a vehicle on roads or other public places without RTA 1988 insurance, ie. the permitted uninsured defendant.

This is practical law-making. The burden of proving a case is not removed but shifted to another person: the insurer or permitted uninsured defendant. Like the reform of the laws of contribution in the 1930s (see Chapter 9) or the Government's agreements with the Motor Insurer's Bureau (see Chapter 6), it is a pragmatic response to the civil legal consequences of mass use of road vehicles.

D   Some Themes of Electric Vehicle Law

Smaller electric vehicles have long been innovators

7.12   Smaller electric vehicles have long been innovators. The definition of 'mechanically propelled vehicle' was held in 2017 to include a bath chair adapted to be propelled by an electric motor. The e-scooter is the successor to the 'Autoped' of the early twentieth century, the motorised scooter which was adapted to an electric motor. See Chapter 4.

The existing compulsory insurance regime persists (for now)

7.13   Electric vehicles precede the introduction of compulsory motor insurance (from RTA 1930) but exist within it. Some electric vehicles are exempted (eg. electrically assisted pedal cycles if within the exemption under RTA 1988, s 189).

Some reform of the place of smaller electric vehicles within the compulsory motor insurance system is likely. But it has not yet appeared, despite the promise of a Transport Bill since May 2022.

Different treatments for e-bikes and e-scooters

7.14   The law's different treatments of e-bikes (not a motor vehicle, RTA 1988, s 189) and e-scooters (a motor vehicle within RTA 1988) has been softened in the short term by the device of e-scooter trials but cannot be postponed indefinitely.

Trials of e-scooters were extended into 2024. The Transport Bill 2022-23 was postponed from that Parliamentary session.

Both are popular vehicles for hire. Dockless rentals make parked e-bikes a common sight in many urban areas. The extension of 'motor vehicle' status to e-bikes would be consequential, especially in relation to compulsory motor insurance. Whether the compulsory motor insurance requirement would remain for e-scooters in a post-trial regulatory scheme is unknown, although the insurance industry and House of Commons Transport Select Committee have mentioned a 'light' insurance approach.

The regulatory scene for smaller electric vehicles is likely to alter, even if the outcome is unpredictable. No Transport Bill dealing with smaller electric vehicles appeared in the King's Speech of November 2023. In contrast to the vehicles, the pace of regulation has slowed.

Chapter 8

Problems of AAEV law

'No one really doubts that the common law is a body of law which develops in process of time in response to the developments of the society in which it rules. Its movement may not be perceptible at any distinct point of time, nor can we always say how it gets from one point to another; but I do not think that, for all that, we need abandon the conviction of Galileo that somehow, by some means, there is a movement that takes place.'

(Lord Radcliffe, 1956)[1]

'Strict liability applies to the industrial steam locomotive, but fault to the motor-car designed for personal use. Global consistency has never been a feature of the common law process, nor social reform.'

(Dr Jonathan Morgan, 2010)[2]

Chapter Contents

A **An introduction to AAEV legal problems 8.01**
B **Some Advanced Driver Assistance Systems (ADAS)**
   legal problems 8.02
C **Some Automated Vehicle legal problems 8.05**
D **Some Electric Vehicle legal problems 8.07**

A An introduction to AAEV legal problems

8.01   This chapter considers a selection of problems – for ADAS vehicles, AVs and EVs – which can be identified from the discussions elsewhere in this book. This is not a list of every issue raised in this book (see chapters for discussion of particular topics) but a selection of points. Readers might perceive other problems of equal or greater urgency. Problems are likely to emerge as technologies are deployed.

---

1 *Lister v Romford Ice and Cold Storage Co Ltd* [1957] AC 555 (HL), 591-2 (dissenting).
2 'Technological change and the development of liability for fault in England and Wales', chapter 2 of *The development of liability in relation to technological change* (ed. Miquel Martín-Casals, Cambridge, 2010, paperback edition 2014), p 48.

B Some Advanced Driver Assistance Systems (ADAS) legal problems

The lack of distinct regulation to date for ADAS systems, either in primary legislation or in judicial decisions

8.02 As discussed in Chapter 4, 'driving', the courts have rarely been asked to consider the effect of ADAS systems, and (perhaps for that reason) the standard of care applicable to driving has not altered substantially since 1971, despite the growth in assistive systems since then.

There is the possibility of over-reliance upon a common law system to regulate emerging technologies – a function which it is not designed to achieve. A common law system determines motor vehicle liability issues mainly in private law cases, where the common law is still characterised (as John P S McLaren described its workings in the 19th century) by:

'its basically reactive quality, [*and*] the capricious nature of its operation, which depended so much on individual initiative and staying power, and its lack of general enforcement mechanisms and supervisory powers.'[3]

The Law Commissions' recommendations for a pre-deployment and in-use safety monitoring system for automated vehicles recognised the point and were accepted by government, in its 'CAM 2025' paper of August 2022. However, unlike AVs, ADAS systems are already in widespread use, and April 2023 saw the approval for use on some British motorways of a new 'hands-free' driving system, whose use is (as at the time of writing) not covered by guidance in the Highway Code.

Perhaps for those reasons, the Automated Vehicles Bill 2023-24 (HL Bill 1) not only sets out the authorisation and safety monitoring schemes for automated vehicles, with allied criminal offences and public law powers, but proposes for the first time the adaptation of existing type approval legislation to both types of driving technology, advanced and automated:

'for the purpose of making the assimilated type approval legislation more suitable for—

(a) vehicles that are designed to travel autonomously, or

(b) any other type of vehicle that—

(i) includes equipment designed to allow its motion to be controlled other than by an individual in it, or to facilitate its being so controlled, or

(ii) is designed to incorporate or interact with software.' (cl 91(1))

At the time of writing, no drafts have been published of the many regulations to be made under the AV Bill 2023-24, when enacted as the Automated Vehicles Act 2024.

---

3 'Nuisance law and the Industrial Revolution: some lessons from social history' (1983) 3 OJLS 155, 220-221, quoted by Professor Fisher in *Environmental Law: Text, Cases and Materials* (above), chapter 10, p 297.

How should official guidance be provided to persons using roads?

8.03   The requirement that the Secretary of State prepare a Highway Code 'comprising such directions as appear to him to be proper for the guidance of persons using roads and may from time to time revise the code by revoking, varying, amending or adding to the provisions thereof in such manner as he thinks fit' originated in the Road Traffic Act 1930. It remains the means of providing such guidance (RTA 1988, s 38).

The first Highway Code (1931) ran to 21 pages (with additional advertisements, for petrol, insurance and both the AA and RAC) and started with the excellent advice for motoring and otherwise: 'Always be careful and considerate towards others'.

In its 2022 paper edition the Highway Code ran to 166 pages, excluding advertisements but including a 10-page index. It undergoes frequent amendment online. Nevertheless, it features no advice specific to hands-free driving (cf rule 160, which appears to prohibit it), a driver assistive system which was approved by the government for use on extensive stretches of British motorways in April 2023[4].

Apart from its content, the question arises as to whether a written Highway Code, designed as a paper document, is still fit for purpose.

Should an assisted driving system change the driver's standard of care?

8.04   As discussed in Chapter 4, no British case has yet considered the effect of an advanced driver assistance system upon the driver's standard of care. The closest decisions arise in sentencing, in cases where cruise control has played a part in events, but those cases do not address the point.

Driver assistance systems have been absorbed into the regulatory framework incrementally, through amendments to secondary legislation (the Construction and Use Regulations – the amendments to reg 110 to allow use of handheld devices for remote parking and contactless payments being a prominent example). But the ripples have not yet spread into the broader regulatory system. That is not an effective regulatory approach as ADAS systems become more sophisticated – and more radically challenge the tenets of current regulation, as they invite drivers to cede control of functions such as steering. AV Bill 2023-24 (HL Bill 1), cl 91 ('power to update type approval requirements', above) recognises the point.

Might a reformed driver's standard of care for ADAS heighten the duty, to require particular vigilance? Or would that be contrary to the ADAS function? Should reform arguably reduce the burden on the driver? Would others' liabilities flow into the point, with stricter liabilities for system developers and manufacturers? How might consumer protection law catch up?

---

4   Rt Hon Jesse Norman MP, Minister of State, Department for Transport, in oral evidence to Transport Committee of House of Commons (oral evidence: self-driving vehicles, HC 519, 17 May 2023) at Q271.

C Some Automated Vehicle legal problems

Fixing transition of control

8.05   Engineering and law meet in the question of how to fix in time the moment at which human control of a vehicle ceases, and automated control begins, and vice versa. The United Nations, the Law Commissions and the writers of engineering standards have grappled with the problem. The drafters of the AV Bill 2023-24 have joined the fray, with cll 46 to 49 (in Part 2 'criminal liability for vehicle use' Chapter 1 'legal position of user-in-charge'). The scheme is brought into the civil statutory claim for automated vehicle accidents by the revision to the definition section of AEVA 2018, Part 1, s 8(1) by the AV Bill 2023-24 (HL Bill 1), cl 45, Sch 2, para 5(6)(a). See Chapter 4.

The scheme of the AV Bill 2023-24 poses questions for the judge: was the user-in-charge feature of the vehicle engaged, according to the requirements of its authorisation by the Secretary of State? There are several situations defined in the Bill as to when the immunity will and will not apply: did any of those situations apply to the case before the court?

The scheme will be left to the courts to apply. The experience of statutory exemptions in the related context of compulsory motor insurance (see chapter 6) indicates the likelihood of dispute and the possibility of counter-intuitive results.

Adjudicating a machine's reasoning

8.06   AEVA 2018, s 2 avoids the task of proving a machine's unreasonableness. But the problem lingers, in the comparisons of fault essential both to contributory negligence and to the contribution of others.

Road traffic law required new liability schemes allowing comparative fault, and legal scholars and the legislature provided those schemes in the reforming Acts of the 1930s and 1940s. The 'internet of things' will require its own legal methods. The shape of some of those innovations has started to emerge: the commercial case of *B2C2 v Quoine*[5] shaped the law of mistake elegantly to the reasoning of AI currency trading gone awry, even while behaving entirely within its programming. But we are still (as the court acknowledged in that case) dependent upon legal reasoning based upon personification[6]. How essential is personification to liability and justice?

D Some Electric Vehicle legal problems

Incomplete regulation of smaller electric vehicles such as e-scooters

8.07   The lack of a regulatory scheme for vehicles in widespread use but which fall outside the existing scheme (notably privately-owned but publicly used

---

5   [2019] SGHC(I) 03 (Singapore International Commercial Court).
6   As to non-personality of an AI as inventor, see *Thaler v Comptroller General of Patents* [2021] EWCA Civ 1374; [2022] Bus LR 375; appeal heard by the Supreme Court in March 2023, judgment still pending at the time of writing.

e-scooters and other smaller electric vehicles such as u-wheels) is not just a problem of legal theory: the law serves the practical purpose of telling people what they can and cannot do, and there must be a position one way or the other (a point reiterated by the Court of Appeal in 2020, in *Bridges*[7], the AFR case).

Vehicles are either lawful for use or not[8]. But continued public misunderstanding of the lawful conditions for the use of smaller electric vehicles is understandable: smaller electric vehicles are available for purchase; those legal conditions are numerous and locked (from a non-lawyer's perspective) in the many drawers of the cabinet of road traffic law, a container almost a century old; and the government has yet to provide laws for many smaller electric vehicles actually in use. Regulation for privately-owned e-scooters remains stalled, the Transport Bill announced in May 2022 not having appeared in the most recent Monarch's Speech to Parliament in November 2023.

Court procedural rules for e-disclosure

8.08   The current Civil Procedural Rules (CPR 1998, as amended) arguably do not reflect the ubiquity and usefulness of electronic evidence. AAEV cases are likely to accentuate the problem, unless the scope of rules for e-disclosure is reconsidered. This point applies to all AAEV claims. See Chapter 9.

---

7   *Regina (Bridges) v Chief Constable of South Wales Police (Information Commissioner and others intervening)* [2020] EWCA Civ 1058; [2020] 1 WLR 5037.
8   See *Rex v Tudor Manolache* [2023] EWCA Crim 1116 (offences committed by rider of electric unicycle).

Part II

Civil law

Chapter 9

Road traffic accident claims

'… the process of determining and apportioning liability in the event of an incident will remain the same as now, with the courts ultimately making judgments based on the facts. That will include taking account of evidence as to whether the human driver or the automated vehicle system was in control at the time of the accident, and related issues.'

'I recognise that this is a new area, but our courts have a long history of making complex judgments in the determination and apportionment of liability, including following the introduction of new and emerging technologies. For this reason, we believe they are best placed to make judgments in that area, but of course, it is an incredibly complex one.'

(UK government 2018[1])

Contents at a glance:
A Outline of the laws of RTA claims 9.01
B Laws of RTA claims involving Advanced Driver
 Assistance Systems (ADAS) 9.15
C Laws of RTA claims involving Automated Vehicles 9.21
D Laws of RTA claims involving Electric Vehicles 9.31

A Outline of the laws of RTA claims

Legal bases of liability in RTA claims

9.01   Currently, the typical legal basis of liability in a road traffic accident claim is the tort of negligence, based on the negligent driving or riding of the defendant. In essence, the allegation in most cases is of carelessness in the control of a moving vehicle.

(In the writer's experience, RTA injury claims typically involve two central allegations of carelessness while driving or riding: moving too fast and too close to other vehicles. Inattention is often a factor.)

---

1   Baroness Sugg, speaking for the government on the Automated and Electric Vehicles Bill, House of Lords Hansard volume 791, column 202 (9 May 2018).

Other legal bases of liability than negligence could apply to a road traffic accident claim. The possibility of the tort of nuisance being the usual legal basis of liability arose in the early years of accident claims involving motor vehicles but was rejected (though not forever excluded) in favour of negligence[2]. Nuisance remains a possibility in a case of obstruction of the highway[3] or (in the judgment of the Court of Appeal in 1909):

> 'If a man places on the streets vehicles so wholly unmanageable as necessarily to be a continuing danger to other vehicles, either at all times or under special conditions of weather, I have no doubt that he does it at his peril, and that he is responsible for injuries arising therefrom, even though there has been no negligence in the management of his vehicle.'[4]

The possibility of a 'wholly unmanageable' vehicle being placed on the roads is much reduced (but not excluded) by the many requirements for the construction and use of vehicles created by statute, reinforced by criminal offences[5].

Where human driving is concerned, civil liability demands a high standard of the driver but liability is not strict: it is not 'a counsel of perfection'[6].

However, in automated (self-driving) vehicle claims the statutory liability of the insurer or permitted uninsured owner under AEVA 2018, s 2 will soon apply (when the first automated vehicles are listed as such by the Secretary of State for Transport, or authorised under the Automated Vehicles Act 2024[7]). So a regime resembling (and perhaps amounting to[8]) strict liability will apply in relation to civil liability for damage caused by a self-driving vehicle.

Liability under AEVA 2018, s 2 will allow the liable insurer or permitted uninsured owner a statutory claim 'against any other person liable to the injured party in respect of the accident' under AEVA 2018, s 5.

Currently, the tort of negligence is the most likely legal basis of liability where there is a road traffic accident claim involving conventional and ADAS-equipped

---

2   See *Wing v London General Omnibus Company* [1909] 2 KB 652 (CA).
3   See *East Hertfordshire District Council v Isabel Hospice Trading Ltd*, Jack Beatson QC sitting as a Deputy High Court Judge (as he then was), 29 August 2000, QB (unreported).
4   *Wing v London General Omnibus Company*, Fletcher Moulton LJ at 665. There are parallels in criminal law, in the offences under RTA 1988, s 40A ('using vehicle in dangerous condition etc'), s 42 ('breach of other construction and use requirements') and the Road Vehicles (Construction and Use) Regulations 1986, 1986/1078, reg 100 ('maintenance and use of vehicle so as not to be a danger, etc').
5   See RTA 1988, Part II, and the Road Vehicles (Construction and Use) Regulations 1986, SI 1986/1078.
6   *Sam v Atkins* [2005] EWCA Civ 1452; [2006] RTR 14. See discussion of the driver's standard of care in Chapter 4.
7   As at the time of writing, before Parliament as the Automated Vehicles Bill 2023-24 (HL Bill 1).
8   AEVA 2018, s 2 has been described as imposing strict liability (see eg. 'Law Commission, Remote Driving, A response by the Association of Personal Injury Lawyers, August 2022' p 2), but it is not yet established that this is the case. No 'automated vehicle' having been listed under AEVA 2018, s 1 as at the time of writing, no AEVA 2018 claim has yet arisen and the elements of an AEVA 2018, s 2 claim have yet to be considered by the courts. See discussion of RTA claims involving automated vehicles, below. See also James Goudkamp's article *Rethinking fault liability and strict liability in the law of torts* LQR 2023, 139 (April) 269-289.

vehicles. However, that is not to exclude other legal bases of liability, depending upon the facts of the case. The reader is referred to the other chapters in this part (about vehicle defects, employer's liability, highway claims etc) for discussion of other potential legal bases of liability.

Apportioning liability in RTA claims

Principles of apportionment

9.02   The court can be asked to apportion liability between actors in an RTA claim. This can happen in various ways. It could be an apportionment between:

(a) the claimant on the one hand and the defendant(s) on the other, where the claimant has contributed by their own fault to their injury. The law allows for reduction of the claimant's damages for contributory negligence under the **Law Reform (Contributory Negligence) Act 1945**.

and/or between

(b) a plurality of defendants liable to the claimant in respect of 'the same damage'[9], where those defendants *either* act 'by concerted actions towards a common end … in furtherance of a common design'[10], so that there is 'a concurrence in the act or acts causing damage'[11] (joint tortfeasors), *or* (as is typical in a claim by an injured passenger in one vehicle against the drivers of several vehicles) where they are 'separate actors whose concurrent acts caused'[12] the same damage to the claimant, ie. 'a coincidence of separate acts which by their conjoined effect cause damage'[13] (several tortfeasors). In both cases there is concurrence (happening at the same time), whether the acts are co-ordinated (joint) or coincidental (several). The tool for apportioning between joint or several tortfeasors their contributions to the 'same damage' suffered by a claimant (apportionment of the contributions of concurrent tortfeasors) is provided by the **Civil Liability (Contribution) Act 1978**.

or

(c) where there is a question before the court as to the distinct parts of different injury and damage caused by several defendant tortfeasors (non-concurrent tortfeasors), the court may assess the damages that each non-concurrent tortfeasor is liable to pay the claimant by reference to **other principles of law**, eg. the laws of causation, as it did in the case of *Rahman v Arearose Ltd and another*[14], discussed below. This has also been described as 'apportionment'.

(a)   Contributory negligence

9.03   The Law Reform (Contributory Negligence) Act 1945, s 1 provides for 'apportionment in case of contributory negligence'. LR(CN)A 1945, sub-s 1(1) and (2) provide as follows.

---

9   Civil Liability (Contribution) Act 1978, s 1.
10   *The Koursk* [1924] P. 140 (CA), 151 (Bankes LJ).
11   *The Koursk*, 160 (Sargant LJ).
12   *Drinkwater v Kimber* [1952] 2 QB 281 (CA), 292 (Morris LJ).
13   *The Koursk*, 160 (Sargant LJ).
14   Rahman v Arearose Ltd and another [2001] QB 351 (CA).

'1(1) Where any person suffers damage[15] as the result partly of his own fault[16] and partly of the fault of any other person or persons, a claim in respect of that damage shall not be defeated by reason of the fault of the person suffering the damage, but the damages recoverable in respect thereof shall be reduced to such extent as the court thinks just and equitable having regard to the claimant's share in the responsibility for the damage:

Provided that—

(a) this subsection shall not operate to defeat any defence arising under a contract;

(b) where any contract or enactment providing for the limitation of liability is applicable to the claim, the amount of damages recoverable by the claimant by virtue of this subsection shall not exceed the maximum limit so applicable.

(2) Where damages are recoverable by any person by virtue of the foregoing subsection subject to such reduction as is therein mentioned, the court shall find and record the total damages which would have been recoverable if the claimant had not been at fault.'

(b) Concurrent wrongs allowing for contribution under CL(C)A 1978 – joint or several wrongdoers causing 'the same damage'

9.04   The key characteristic allowing contribution under the 1978 Act is the 'concurrent' nature of the joint or several tortfeasors' wrongs. 'Tortfeasors are concurrent when their wrongful acts or omissions cause a single indivisible injury', so that 'the characteristic of such torts is the logical impossibility of apportioning the damage among the different tortfeasors'[17].

CL(C)A 1978, s 1(1) ('entitlement to contribution') provides that:

'Subject to the following provisions of this section, any person liable in respect of any damage suffered by another person may recover contribution from any other person liable in respect of the same damage (whether jointly with him or otherwise).'

Where (under s 6(1)):

'A person is liable in respect of any damage for the purposes of this Act if the person who suffered it (or anyone representing his estate or dependants) is entitled to recover compensation from him in respect of that damage (whatever the legal basis of his liability, whether tort, breach of contract, breach of trust or otherwise).'

---

15   ' "Damage" includes loss of life and personal injury': LR(CN)A 1945, s 4.
16   ' "Fault" means negligence, breach of statutory duty or other act or omission which gives rise to a liability in tort or would, apart from this Act, give rise to the defence of contributory negligence.': LR(CN)A 1945, s 4.
17   *Rahman v Arearose* (above), 361-362 [16-17] (Laws LJ).

The precursor to the 1978 Act – the Law Reform (Married Women and Tortfeasors) Act 1935 – abolished the previous rule that judgment[18] against one concurrent tortfeasor prevented any further claim against another concurrent tortfeasor, even if judgment against the first tortfeasor went unsatisfied. The abolition of the pre-1935 rule is now in CL(C)A 1978, s 3:

'Judgment recovered against any person liable in respect of any debt or damage shall not be a bar to an action, or to the continuance of an action, against any other person who is (apart from any such bar) jointly liable with him in respect of the same debt or damage.'

The 'same damage' created by concurrent wrongs being logically indivisible, the CL(C)A 1978 allows the court the means to 'attempt some rough division'[19]. Without the statutory abolition of the pre-1935 rule, a claimant would be unable to 'prove that either tortfeasor singly caused the damage, or caused any particular part or portion of the damage. Accordingly his claim would fall to be dismissed, for want of proof of causation. But that would be the plainest injustice; hence the rule'[20].

'However, the rule was a potential source of another injustice. A defendant against whom judgment had been given, under the rule, for the whole of the claimant's damages had at common law no legal basis of liability against his fellow concurrent tortfeasor to recover any part of what he had to pay under the judgment; so that the second tortfeasor, if for whatever reason he was not sued by the claimant, might escape scot free. Hence the 1978 Act and its predecessor the Law Reform (Married Women and Tortfeasors) Act 1935. It provides a right of contribution between concurrent tortfeasors. The expression 'same damage' in section 1(1) therefore means (and means only) the kind of single indivisible injury as arises at common law in a case of concurrent torts.' [21]

A contribution claim can be determined between concurrently liable drivers of two motor vehicles who are already joined as defendants to an existing road traffic accident claim, without the need for separate contribution proceedings[22].

---

18   The position in relation to *compromises* is different: 'Parliament has since intervened to abolish that rule in relation to judgments, in what is now s.3 of the Civil Liability (Contribution) Act 1978, replacing a similar provision in the Law Reform (Married Women and Tortfeasors) Act 1935. But the common law rule remains in full force and effect in relation to compromises ...': *Gladman Commercial Properties v Fisher Hargreaves Proctor and others* [2013] EWCA Civ 1466, [2014] PNLR 11 [22]. See discussion of the 'juridical relic' of compromise against one concurrent tortfeasor ending the claim, and the exceptions to that rule, in *Watts v Lord Aldington (Note)* [1999] L&TR 578, 598 (Simon Brown LJ, as he then was). See specialist works (eg. *Foskett on Compromise*).
19   *Rahman v Arearose* (above) at 361-362 (Laws LJ, quoting the 'rough division' phrase from the American textbook, *Prosser & Keeton on Torts*).
20   As above.
21   *Rahman v Arearose* (above) at 362 (Laws LJ). The increase in road traffic accidents, with the growth of the motor car industry, had influenced the 1935 reform: the Law Revision Committee (precursor of the Law Commission) had pointed out the frequency of concurrent torts as a result of claimants sustaining 'a single damage from the combined negligence of two motor car drivers'. See Professor Paul Mitchell, *A history of tort law 1900-1950* (Cambridge, 2015), Chapter 11.
22   *Croston v Vaughan* [1938] 1 KB 540 (CA).

(c) Apportionment otherwise than under CL(C)A 1978

9.05 Concurrent torts contrast with the position where a claimant suffers distinct torts each committed by a different defendant tortfeasor, each causing different damage. There, the claimant has distinct causes of action against each tortfeasor and may recover compensation from each tortfeasor only for the damage that they have each caused[23]. That would *not* be a claim against joint or several defendant tortfeasors for the 'same damage' (concurrent tortfeasors under CL(C)A 1978, s 1, so this situation would not allow contribution between defendants under the 1978 Act[24].

However, the courts have still occasionally used the phrase 'apportionment' to describe the process of attributing damage to different causes, in a non-concurrent tort case. An example is provided by *Rahman v Arearose*, where Laws LJ dealt with the attribution of ongoing psychiatric symptoms where 'on the evidence the respective torts committed by the defendants were the causes of distinct aspects of the claimant's overall psychiatric condition, and it is positively established that neither caused the whole psychiatric condition'[25].

In *Rahman v Arearose*, the court solved the problem of unavailability of CL(C)A 1978, s 1 apportionment (as it was not a concurrent torts case[26]) by treating this as an issue of causation[27] and by applying the principle that later negligence does not always extinguish the causative potency of an earlier tort[28]. While accepting that this was not such a case, Laws LJ quoted Lord Mustill's description of the method of apportionment for concurrent torts:

'What justice does demand, to my mind, is that the court should make the best estimate it can, in the light of the evidence, making the fullest allowances in favour of the plaintiffs for the uncertainties known to be involved in any apportionment.'[29]

Laws LJ added that:

'The fact-finding court's duty is to arrive at a just conclusion on the evidence as to the respective damage caused by each defendant, even if it can only do it on a broad-brush basis which then has to be translated into percentages.'[30]

In *Rahman v Arearose*, the Court of Appeal upheld the judge's apportionment of three quarters/one quarter of the ongoing psychological injury against the Second

---

23 Performance Cars Ltd v Abraham [1962] 1 QB 33 (CA).
24 *Rahman v Arearose* (above), 364 [23].
25 Above, 364c [22].
26 Above, 364d [23].
27 Above, 365f [26].
28 Above, 366g [29].
29 Above, 364c [22], quoting Lord Mustill (when he was Mustill J) in *Thompson v Smiths Shiprepairers (North Shields) Ltd* [1984] QB 405, 441. Later in the judgment Laws LJ quotes a lecture by Lord Hoffmann: 'the concept of concurrent tortfeasors are all no more and no less than tools or mechanisms which the law has developed to articulate in practice the extent of any liable defendant's responsibility for the loss and damage which the claimant has suffered.' 368 [33].
30 Rahman v Arearose, 364f [23].

Defendant, though not applying it to all heads of loss (the apportionment was limited to compensation for the psychological injury, and chronologically only the First Defendant could be liable for the first three years of past losses which flowed from the first tort alone). While this was described as an 'apportionment'[31] between the defendants of some of the ongoing injury compensation and loss (albeit an apportionment of the continuing losses that could not be divided forensically or chronologically), the Court of Appeal held that the judge had been wrong to consider the case as a concurrent torts case within the Civil Liability (Contribution) Act 1978[32].

The overriding principle in *Rahman v Arearose* was, in the Court of Appeal's view, 'that every tortfeasor should compensate the injured claimant in respect of that loss and damage for which he should justly be held responsible'[33]. So the use of the word 'apportionment' in this third category is an unusual application of the term, outside CL(C)A 1978 and using other legal principles – in *Rahman* the principles of causation and of personal injury compensation.

Prohibition against contribution action under CL(C)A 1978 in relation to different damage

9.06   In *Royal Brompton Hospital NHS Trust v Hammond and others*[34], the House of Lords held that the phrase 'the same damage' in CL(C)A 1978 is to be given its 'natural and ordinary meaning' and that 'no glosses, extensive or restricted, are warranted'. Lord Steyn observed that the phrase 'the same damage' referred to damage in the singular, not to 'damages', and that 'the closest synonym of damage is harm'[35]. The phrase was to be interpreted within the context of the 1978 Act, and its own particular scheme for concurrent wrongs:

> 'The legislative technique of limiting the contribution principle under the 1978 Act to the same damage was a considered policy decision. The context does not therefore justify an expansive interpretation of the words 'the same damage' so as to mean substantially or materially similar damage. Such solutions could have been adopted but considerations of unfairness to parties who did not in truth cause or contribute to the same damage would have militated against them. Moreover, the adoption of such solutions would have led to uncertainty in the application of the law. That is the context of section 1(1) and the phrase 'the same damage'. It must be interpreted and applied on a correct evaluation and comparison of claims alleged to qualify for contribution under section 1(1).'[36]

On such a comparison, the harms raised respectively against the employer and the architect in the *Royal Brompton* case were different, so did not allow for contribution proceedings under CL(C)A 1978:

---

31   Above, 368 [35].
32   Above, 368-369 [35-37].
33   Above, 367f [33].
34   [2002] UKHL 14; [2002] 1 WLR 1397.
35   Above at [27].
36   As above.

'The damage or harm for which the architect is liable is the change in the employer's contractual position vis-à-vis the contractor[37]. This claim is fundamentally different from the employer's claim against the contractor in respect of the delay in completion of the building.'[38]

In *Burdis v Livsey; Clark v Ardington Electrical Systems and others*[39], the Court of Appeal made rulings as to the recoverability of credit hire charges over an extended period of car repairs attributable to damage resulting from the defendant driver's negligence, and in doing so stated that contribution proceedings would be available to the insurers of the defendant driver against a dilatory repairer:

'The defendants' actions damaged the cars of Mrs Clark and Mr Dennard. They should pay the loss caused by their actions... The insurers of the defendants should seek a contribution from the repairers for any unjustified length of repair.'[40]

In the subsequent credit hire case *Mason v TNT UK Ltd & Groupama*[41], the county court subsequently appeared to disagree, in effect, with the Court of Appeal in *Burdis*, by ruling that contribution was not available to a defendant tortfeasor in an RTA claim in relation to credit hire charges said to have been increased by delay. However, this was not necessarily a disagreement between courts, as the defendant in the *Mason* case framed its argument in a particular way: seeking contribution not from the repairer but 'from the claimant's insurer, the third party, because of its failure to provide her with a courtesy car pursuant to her contract of insurance and because it failed to ensure that the repairs which it organised were completed within a reasonable time'[42].

Applying *Royal Brompton*, His Honour Judge Charles Harris QC drew the distinction between those harms – the damage to the claimant's vehicle (measured by diminution in its value and consequential losses including hire of a replacement vehicle) and the damage said to flow from the alleged breach of contract by the claimant's insurer (whose contract excluded indemnity for loss of use[43]). In HHJ Harris's judgment, the two were not 'the same':

'The insurer has no responsibility at all for causing the diminution of the value of the claimant's car, nor for the need for a replacement vehicle while repairs are carried out. This was the loss or damage which the defendant caused.'[44]

So there was no commonality in the damage for which the defendant company (vicariously liable for the negligent driving which damaged the claimant's vehicle) and the claimant's insurer (only potentially liable for any breach of its insurance contract, which in fact excluded indemnity for the damage sought) were said both

---

37 The architect having granted extensions of time to the contractor, relieving the contractor of its contractual obligation to make payments to the claimant for delay.
38 [2002] UKHL 14 [32] (Lord Steyn).
39 [2002] EWCA Civ 510; [2003] QB 36 (CA).
40 Above, at [121].
41 Reading County Court (His Honour Judge Harris QC), 13 March 2009 (unreported).
42 Above at [6(d)] and [9].
43 Above [21(b)].
44 Above [23].

to be liable. On that basis, applying *Royal Brompton*, the county court in *Mason* held that there was no right of contribution against the claimant's insurers under the 1978 Act[45]. Whether or not the defendant would have succeeded in a CL(C)A 1978 contribution claim against the repairer, as envisaged by the Court of Appeal in *Burdis*, was not decided in *Mason*.

Conclusion on the legal principles of apportionment in RTA claims

9.07 So, in RTA claims, both the applicable legal rules of apportionment and the consequent factual apportionment of damages (as a whole and by item) will be particular to the facts of each case.

One situation common to many RTA claims is that several drivers, in different vehicles, cause the same indivisible damage to a single claimant (a passenger in one of the vehicles, for example). That situation would allow contribution under CL(C)A 1978.

However, the facts of claims will not always fit that pattern. Advanced, automated and electric vehicles are likely to create new situations and claims might rest upon legal bases of liability other than negligence (for example, the contractual liability of operators of electric vehicle rental schemes).

In relation to damage resulting from an accident caused by an automated vehicle when driving itself, the Automated and Electric Vehicles Act 2018 reforms the law of contribution significantly, by creating its own mechanism whereby the insurer or owner liable under AEVA 2018, s 2 can claim 'against any other person liable to the injured party in respect of the accident' (s 5). This is a remedy unique to AEVA 2018 liability, as the 2018 Act excludes the right of contribution under the 1978 Act:

> 'An insurer or vehicle owner who has a right of action against a person by virtue of section 5 does not have a right to recover contribution from that person under the Civil Liability (Contribution) Act 1978 or under section 3 of the Law Reform (Miscellaneous Provisions) (Scotland) Act 1940.'[46]

How courts have apportioned in practice

9.08 Having explored the legal principles, how do the courts divide up the resulting responsibilities where the claimant has been negligent and/or there are multiple tortfeasors in road traffic accident claims? The following cases illustrate methods of reduction and apportionment of damages in RTA claims involving conventional vehicles (neither ADAS-equipped nor automated vehicles).

The principles and the calculations will be dictated by the facts of each case. But some patterns have emerged.

---

45   Above [18]-[29].
46   AEVA 2018, s 6(5). See the 'RTA claims involving AVs' section, below.

The Law Reform (Contributory Negligence) Act 1945, s 1 provides for 'apportionment in case of contributory negligence'. The LR(CN)A 1945, sub-ss 1(1) and (2) provide as follows.

'1(1) Where any person suffers damage[47] as the result partly of his own fault[48] and partly of the fault of any other person or persons, a claim in respect of that damage shall not be defeated by reason of the fault of the person suffering the damage, but the damages recoverable in respect thereof shall be reduced to such extent as the court thinks just and equitable having regard to the claimant's share in the responsibility for the damage:

Provided that—

(a) this subsection shall not operate to defeat any defence arising under a contract;

(b) where any contract or enactment providing for the limitation of liability is applicable to the claim, the amount of damages recoverable by the claimant by virtue of this subsection shall not exceed the maximum limit so applicable.

(2) Where damages are recoverable by any person by virtue of the foregoing subsection subject to such reduction as is therein mentioned, the court shall find and record the total damages which would have been recoverable if the claimant had not been at fault.'

Just as in relation to the negligence of a driver[49], contributory negligence is to be assessed by an essentially objective standard. This is not absolute: it 'is necessary to take into account at least some characteristics of the individual claimant: age is an obvious example'[50]. But the assessment is essentially objective. Failures by the particular claimant to take reasonable care for their own safety (e.g. the claimant's voluntary intoxication at the time of injury[51]) are not to be taken into account in the claimant's favour when assessing contributory negligence.

Contributory negligence is not limited to conduct that is at the time of injury unlawful. In *Froom v Butcher*, the Court of Appeal held that failure to wear a seatbelt was negligence contributing to injury even before it was required by law, on the basis that:

'Everyone knows, or ought to know, that when he goes out in a car he should fasten the seat belt. It is so well known that it goes without saying, not only for the driver, but also the passenger. If either the driver or the passenger fails to wear it and an accident happens—and the injuries would

---

47 ' "Damage" includes loss of life and personal injury': LR(CN)A 1945, s 4.
48 ' "Fault" means negligence, breach of statutory duty or other act or omission which gives rise to a liability in tort or would, apart from this Act, give rise to the defence of contributory negligence.': LR(CN)A 1945, s 4.
49 *Nettleship v Weston* [1971] 2 QB 691 (CA). See 'the driver's standard of care' in Chapter 4.
50 *Campbell v Advantage Insurance Co Ltd* [2021] EWCA Civ 1698; [2022] QB 354, 368e [49] (Underhill LJ).
51 *Campbell v Advantage Insurance Co Ltd*, above.

have been prevented or lessened if he had worn it—then his damages should be reduced.'[52]

The same approach has been applied by the High Court to a claimant's failure to wear a cycle helmet: 'It matters not that there is no legal compulsion for cyclists to wear helmets ...'[53].

In *Froom v Butcher*, the Court of Appeal suggested the following reductions for contributory negligence by failure to wear a seat belt:

- No reduction for contributory negligence if 'the failure made no difference' to the injury, and 'the damage would have been the same, even if a seat belt had been worn'.

- A reduction of 15% where the failure 'made a considerable difference': 'Some injuries to the head, for instance, would have been a good deal less severe if a seat belt had been worn, but there would still have been some injury to the head.'

- A reduction of 25% where the failure 'made all the difference' and 'the damage would have been prevented altogether if a seat belt had been worn'.[54]

The Court of Appeal has maintained that approach, seeing 'the undesirability of a prolonged or intensive enquiry in these cases':

'there is a powerful public interest in there being no such enquiry into fine degrees of contributory negligence, so that the vast majority of cases can be settled according to a well-understood formula and those few which entail trial do not mushroom out of control. *Froom v Butcher* so states, and is binding.'[55]

Not every contributory negligence assessment is made on the basis of guideline percentages, and there is a judicial 'discretion implicit in a test based on what is just and equitable'[56].

However, for the purpose of considering the effect of new vehicle technologies (particularly advanced driver assistance systems such as automated emergency braking, distance-keeping and collision avoidance systems), it is significant that the failure to use safety technologies such as bicycle helmets, not required by law but which 'everyone knows, or ought to know'[57] should be used, will reduce compensation for contributory negligence, and that assessment of contributory negligence for such an omission is usually by guideline percentages. ADAS systems (such as automated emergency braking and distance-keeping systems) might also reach that threshold of familiarity, and automated driving systems might follow. So similar reductions might in future apply for failure to use such systems protectively, in a way that contributes to injury.

---

52 *Froom v Butcher* [1976] 1 QB 286, 296e (Lord Denning MR).
53 *Smith v Finch* [2009] EWHC 53 (QB) [44] (Griffith Williams J).
54 Above, 296c-d.
55 *Stanton v Collinson* [2010] EWCA Civ 81 [2010] RTR 26, 284 at 294 [26] (Hughes LJ).
56 Clerk & Lindsell on Torts (23rd Edn), 3-100.
57 Froom v Butcher, above.

Similar principles apply to the assessment of contributions between tortfeasors.

As to assessment of the respective contributions of concurrent tortfeasors, CL(C) A 1978, s 2 ('assessment of contribution') provides in its entirety that:

'(1) Subject to subsection (3) below, in any proceedings for contribution under section 1 above the amount of the contribution recoverable from any person shall be such as may be found by the court to be just and equitable having regard to the extent of that person's responsibility for the damage in question.

(2) Subject to subsection (3) below, the court shall have power in any such proceedings to exempt any person from liability to make contribution, or to direct that the contribution to be recovered from any person shall amount to a complete indemnity.

(3) Where the amount of the damages which have or might have been awarded in respect of the damage in question in any action brought in England and Wales by or on behalf of the person who suffered it against the person from whom the contribution is sought was or would have been subject to—

(a) any limit imposed by or under any enactment or by any agreement made before the damage occurred;

(b) any reduction by virtue of section 1 of the Law Reform (Contributory Negligence) Act 1945 or section 5 of the Fatal Accidents Act 1976; or

(c) any corresponding limit or reduction under the law of a country outside England and Wales;

the person from whom the contribution is sought shall not by virtue of any contribution awarded under section 1 above be required to pay in respect of the damage a greater amount than the amount of those damages as so limited or reduced.'

In *Hughes v Williams & Williams*[58], the liable defendant driver sought contribution from the mother of the injured child claimant (the third party, also Williams but unrelated to the defendant), on the ground that the mother had contributed to the child claimant's injury by placing her on a booster seat which the mother knew from the instructions (which she had read) to be unsuitable due to the child's age and size. An alternative and safe child seat, with a five-point harness, had also been in the car at the time of the injury. The trial judge allowed the contribution claim and applied as a measure of the third party's contribution the reduction of 25% from *Froom v Butcher* applicable to a contributory negligence case. The Court of Appeal dismissed the third party's appeal, holding that the judge had been right to apply the *Froom v Butcher* approach to a 1978 Act contribution case[59].

As to apportionment of ongoing lifelong symptoms between distinct torts which cause different damage (non-concurrent torts), but where there are also some overlapping aspects of damage, the court is especially likely to adopt a forensic analysis of the evidence in the case (likely by reference to the chronological

---

58   [2013] EWCA Civ 455; PIQR P17, 248.
59   Above at 259 [54] (Black LJ, as she then was).

sequence of the injuries), in order to reduce to a minimum that part of the loss which it must apportion on a 'rough division' percentage basis. The division of responsibility for the lifelong psychological symptoms in *Rahman v Arearose* offers an illustration. See the discussion above.

Conclusion on apportionment

9.09   It is not possible to say that RTA claims will always generate concurrent torts, subject to CL(C)A 1978. Non-concurrent torts are a possibility. The analysis must be specific to the case.

As discussed below, new vehicle technologies – advanced, automated and electric – emphasise the importance of the fact-specific approach to the legal basis of apportionment.

As ADAS systems (especially collision-avoidance systems such as automated emergency braking and distance-keeping) become more familiar, an omission to use such system(s) might become a ground for contributory negligence or contribution.

AEVA 2018 takes matters even further, removing the remedy of 'contribution' under CL(C)A 1978[60] and allowing a different statutory remedy: the 'Right of insurer etc to claim against person responsible for accident' under AEVA 2018, s 5.

Evidence in RTA claims

9.10   This is not an exhaustive discussion of all evidential issues that might arise in an RTA claim. Two points are prominent in relation to advanced, automated and electric vehicles: electronic disclosure (e-disclosure) and expert evidence.

Electronic evidence in RTA claims

9.11   Electronic evidence is now ubiquitous in RTA claims. A host of personal devices are used even in conventional vehicles which do not incorporate those devices by design. Mobile telephones, SatNav and dashboard cameras provide electronic evidence as to the time, location and (by images and footage) numerous other aspects of a road traffic accident. Recently manufactured vehicles often incorporate such devices (including cameras and other sensors serving ADAS). Camera images can often be downloaded by the driver to a thumb-drive. Metadata within electronic documents is a potentially rich seam of precise, relevant information, if processed with sufficient care.

However, electronic evidence is not always deployed to its full potential in RTA claims, even on the multi-track[61]. There are a number of reasons for this, but the key reasons are:

---

60   AEVA 2018, s 6(5).
61   To which (subject to the points made below in relation to personal injury claims) the e-disclosure practice direction would normally apply: CPR 1998 Practice Direction 31B 'Disclosure of electronic documents', para 3 ('purpose, scope and interpretation').

- a lack of familiarity with current electronic technology in motor vehicles on the part of lawyers and judges (particularly at the early investigation and case management stages),[62]

- an underappreciation of the potential of electronic evidence to resolve issues and effectively reduce the costs of RTA litigation, and

- outdated procedural rules as to disclosure in RTA claims.

The outdatedness of procedural rules is not blameworthy, given the rapidity of recent technological change in motor vehicles (especially the growth of ADAS technologies in both internal combustion engine (ICE) and electric vehicles). But it is evident.

The Civil Procedure Rules 1998 include detailed provision for e-disclosure in multi-track cases, especially in the e-disclosure practice direction – PD 31B – which applies to all claims allocated to, or likely to be allocated to the multi-track[63].

Electronic evidence-generating devices are now commonplace in RTA claims. But this is not reflected in the Civil Procedure Rules 1998. The standard disclosure list annexed to the Pre-Action Protocol for Personal Injury Claims (applicable to fast track claims) makes no mention of electronic documents for RTA claims, but does in relation to workplace claims[64]. The CPR 1998, r 31.5(2) removes from multi-track claims 'which include a claim for personal injuries' the requirements for pre-case management consideration of disclosure matters including e-disclosure, 'unless the court otherwise orders'[65].

The rationale for the exclusion of e-disclosure management from personal injury claims appears to equate e-disclosure with cases involving large quantities of documents, whereas 'Personal injury litigation does not usually require large scale disclosure' (Jackson LJ, *Review of Civil Litigation Costs*, May 2009)[66].

The exclusion of pre-CMC disclosure measures from personal injury cases was a sensible cost-saving measure in 2009. But it might now have an unintended contrary effect. Electronic evidence from vehicle cameras has a high forensic (and costs-saving) value, by its capacity to resolve liability issues. Image evidence from cameras is usually easily accessible (sometimes via a thumb drive installed by the driver) and should usually generate no need for bulk disclosure.

Furthermore, the May 2009 argument for excluding pre-case management e-disclosure from personal injury claims preceded the current era of consumer

---

62 On lawyers' knowledge of e-disclosure in general, see Gloster LJ's foreword to *Electronic Disclosure: Law and Practice*, Michael Wheater and Charles Raffin (Oxford, 2017).

63 CPR 1998, PD 31B 3.

64 Pre-Action Protocol for Personal Injury Claims, Annex C. For a claim where the defendant is a commercial vehicle, Annex C lists 'tachograph charts', apparently by reference to outdated paper charts. It does not disregard electronic documents entirely, but confusingly requires 'copies of all electronic communications/documentation relating to the accident' in relation to workplace but not RTA claims.

65 CPR 1998, r 31.5(2), which disapplies r 31.5(3) to (8) in cases 'which include a claim for personal injuries', introduced on 1 April 2013 (see below).

66 *Review of Civil Litigation Costs: Preliminary Report (May 2009)*, Volume 2, Chapter 41 'Disclosure generally', section 3 'do the rules operate effectively?', p 392. And see commentary in the *White Book 2022*, volume 1, 31.5.1.

electronics[67] (coming only 18 months after the release in the UK of the iPhone[68] and five years before the release of the first Tesla electric car to enjoy widespread commercial success in the UK[69]). The rule was settled by statutory instrument in 2013[70] (again, before the current era of ADAS-equipped and electric vehicles had started in the UK).

The case for early case management of e-disclosure is made eloquently by Michael Wheater and Charles Raffin, in their 2017 book *Electronic Disclosure: Law and Practice*[71]. Among the many considerations is the sensitivity of metadata (information associated with an image or other electronic file, such as information as to the time that a file was created):

> 'Metadata can be an exceedingly useful tool in analysing electronic documents … However, metadata is also very sensitive and can be altered inadvertently if a file is used, accessed or copied. According, ensuring that ESI [electronically stored information] is collected and handled properly is an important factor that must be considered on a case-by-case basis.'[72]

The presumptive exclusion by CPR 1998, r 31.5(2) of personal injury claims from pre-CMC consideration of e-disclosure is likely to generate more cost and delay than it saves in advanced, automated and some electric vehicle RTA claims, increasing the risk of late disclosure and of consequent disruption to legal issues, allocation to track and even trial listings.

It might be argued that the CPR 1998, r 31.5(2) rule against pre-CMC disclosure measures in a personal injury claim would *not* apply to a contribution claim under CL(C)A 1978 or an insurer/owner's claim under AEVA 2018, s 5, by analogy with the similar phrase used in the different context of the qualified one-way costs shifting (QoCS) rules under CPR 1998, rr 44.13–44.17 (*Wagenaar v Weekend Travel Ltd (Serradj, Third Party)*[73]). That would meet some practical considerations, as contribution or AEVA 2018, s 5 claims would be likely to go into matters of system design and require more extensive e-disclosure than the primary victim's claim.

But the possible avoidance of CPR 1998, r 31.5(2) in a contribution or AEVA 2018, s 5 claim would not solve the problem created by CPR 1998, r 31.5(2) in the present context. A personal injury claimant after a road traffic accident involving an advanced vehicle who lacks the direct action under AEVA 2018, s 2 (either through lack of insurance for the AV or because the vehicle was not automated but ADAS-equipped) would be especially dependent upon well-managed, pre-CMC e-disclosure, which the current CPR 1998, r 31.5(2) presumptively denies.

So it is respectfully suggested that the presumptive exclusion of early management of e-disclosure in personal injury claims by CPR 1998, r 31.5(2) should be reconsidered, and should not apply to RTA claims where evidence as to the issues includes electronically stored information.

---

67 Above.
68 BBC News website 'Apple iPhone debuts in UK stores' (10 November 2007).
69 Tesla website 'Right hand drive model S arrives in the UK' (9 June 2014).
70 Civil Procedure (Amendment) Rules 2013, SI 2013/262, r 11.
71 (Oxford, 2017).
72 Wheater and Raffin [1.23].
73 [2014] EWCA Civ 1105; [2015] 1 WLR 1968.

Early management of e-disclosure is only the first part of the exercise: presentation of electronic evidence in RTA claims in court is also still wanting, sometimes due to insufficient case management (a symptom of the CPR 1998, r 31.5(2)) or to inadequate co-ordination for the use of technology at trial. This is a time and cost-inflating omission. As Gloster LJ pointed out:

> 'The advantages of electronic presentation, both for the judge and for the efficient and cost-effective conduct of a trial, cannot in my view be overstated.'[74]

Expert evidence in RTA claims

9.12 As discussed in Chapter 4, part A ('current and future approaches to expert evidence'), the courts have tended to adopt a cautious attitude when balancing the weight given to expert accident reconstruction evidence against 'the primary factual evidence which is of the greatest importance in a case of this kind'[75].

Stuart Smith LJ's classic exposition of the boundaries of expert opinion as to accident reconstruction in an RTA claim, from *Liddell v Middleton* in 1996, is still followed by the courts:

> '... the function of the expert is to furnish the judge with the necessary scientific criteria and assistance based upon his special skill and experience not possessed by ordinary laymen to enable the judge to interpret the factual evidence of the marks on the road, the damage or whatever it may be. What he is not entitled to do is to say in effect 'I have considered the statements and/or evidence of the eye-witnesses in this case and I conclude from there evidence that the defendant was going at a certain speed, or that he could have seen the plaintiff at a certain point'. These are facts for the trial judge to find based on the evidence that he accepts and such inferences that he draws from the primary facts found. Still less is the expert entitled to say that in his opinion the defendant should have sounded his horn, seen the plaintiff before he did or taken avoiding action and that in taking some action or failing to take some other action, a party was guilty of negligence. These are matters for the court, on which the expert's opinion is wholly irrelevant and therefore inadmissible.... We do not have trial by expert in this country; we have trial by Judge. In my judgment, the expert witnesses contributed nothing to the trial in this case except expense. For the reasons that I have indicated, their evidence was largely if not wholly irrelevant and inadmissible. Counsel on each side at the trial succumbed to the temptation of cross-examining them on their opinions, thereby lengthening and complicating a simple case.... In road traffic accidents it is the exception rather than the rule that expert witnesses are required.'[76]

The *Liddell* approach might be strengthened by greater reliance upon electronic primary evidence in RTA claims. Early e-disclosure of images (for example) should allow many liability issues to be resolved, significantly earlier than previously. To

---

74 Gloster LJ, foreword to Wheater and Raffin (2017).
75 *Stewart v Glaze* [2009] EWHC 704 [10].
76 [1996] PIQR P36 (CA), quoted in (for example) *Stewart v Glaze* above [9].

assist this (as discussed above), the procedural rules of e-disclosure as they relate to RTA claims should be reinforced.

In automated vehicle RTA claims for contribution or under AEVA 2018, s 5, however, liability issues are likely to range beyond driving negligence and into the design and construction of a vehicle and its systems, with different legal bases for liability. In claims involving design issues (for example), e-disclosure is likely to extend into e-documents of complexity, requiring expertise 'to furnish the judge with the necessary scientific criteria and assistance based upon his special skill and experience not possessed by ordinary laymen to enable the judge to interpret the factual evidence'[77].

In ADAS and automated vehicle cases where there is an actual or potential liability issue, expert assistance will be required both to preserve electronically stored information from the vehicle(s) and to interpret the ESI to the court. The Electronic Discovery Reference Model (EDRM) provides guidance as to the nine stages of the EDRM, and Wheater and Raffin have presented ten core principles of effective e-disclosure, including that the process is auditable[78].

The importance and detail of e-disclosure are likely to alter the court's approach to the issue of reasonable necessity for expert opinion to resolve the proceedings[79] in RTA claims involving ADAS and automated vehicles, and perhaps also some types of electric vehicles (eg. if location of the vehicle is an issue in a e-scooter case, engaging metadata or GPS evidence), expert opinion is likely to be required to interpret electronic evidence.

Costs in RTA claims

9.13   The thrust of both the civil procedural and costs reforms of the last quarter of a century has been the reduction of the costs of civil litigation to a level that is both economic and proportionate to the issues put to the court for adjudication[80].

In the context of RTA claims, as the current edition of *Winfield v Jolowicz on Torts* notes[81], the system of compensation is financed by the motor insurance premium-paying public. Recent years have seen several regulatory measures to control the litigation costs of RTA claims. Prominent costs-limiting measures have included the following:

- *Qualified one-way costs shifting*[82] – particularly to avoid the need for after the event (ATE) insurance to be taken out by claimants in personal injury claims, which had allowed ATE premiums to be recoverable as costs.

---

77   *Liddell*, above.
78   Wheater and Raffin [1.82] and Part III, 'e-disclosure in practice'.
79   The test for permission for expert evidence under CPR 1998, r 35.1.
80   The writer's summary. See the Civil Procedure Rules 1998, especially r 1.1(1): 'These Rules are a procedural code with the overriding objective of enabling the court to deal with cases justly and at proportionate cost.'
81   See the quotation at the start of Chapter 6 (insurance).
82   CPR 1998, r 44, Part II.

- *Costs management orders (costs budgeting)*[83] as part of the early management of multi-track claims with a value of up to £10 million[84].

- *The Protocol for Low Value Personal Injury Claims in Road Traffic Accidents.* The many details of the RTA low value PI claims protocol are not explored in this book, and the reader is referred to other works[85]. The essence of the RTA low value PI claims protocol is a three-stage procedure 'carefully designed to whittle down the disputes between the parties as the case passes through the various stages'[86] and thereby to limit costs to fixed amounts. As the Court of Appeal acknowledges, the effect of the procedure, for those issues which cannot be resolved before the final third stage, is 'to deliver fairly rough justice. This is justified because the sums in issue are usually small, and it is not appropriate to hold a full blown trial'[87]. Stage 3 hearings are typically listed with court time of less than one hour.

- *Whiplash injury claim reforms.* In May 2021, the government and insurance industry established a free online service – the Official Injury Claim Service – to resolve low value whiplash injury claims (valued at less than £5,000), based upon a tariff of awards[88].

- From 1 October 2023, the extension of the application of fixed recoverable costs ('FRC') to most civil proceedings allocated to the fast track and to the newly created 'intermediate track' of less complex multi-track cases valued at under £100,000 which will be banded in four levels of complexity[89].

Civil Liability (Contribution) Act 1978, s 4

9.14   In addition to those relatively recent measures, there is another, more established rule of costs limitation which should be considered in any RTA case involving multiple tortfeasors which might involve a CL(C)A 1978 claim. Where a claimant considers their right to bring successive actions under CL(C)A 1978, s 3, they should bear in mind the statutory limitation of costs in s 4:

'If more than one action is brought in respect of any damage by or on behalf of the person by whom it was suffered against persons liable in respect of the damage (whether jointly or otherwise) the plaintiff shall not be entitled to costs in any of those actions, other than that in which judgment is first given, unless the court is of the opinion that there was reasonable ground for bringing the action.'

---

83   CPR 1998, r 3, Part II.
84   CPR 1998, r 3.12(1).
85   See for example para's 5 to 9 of the judgment of Jackson LJ in *Phillips v Willis* [2016] EWCA Civ 401; [2017] RTR 4; and the current edition of the *White Book*.
86   *Phillips v Willis* (above), para 33.
87   *Phillips v Willis* (above), para 9.
88   Government website 'Guidance: Whiplash Reform Programme: Information and FAQ' (26 April 2021, updated 7 March 2022).
89   Civil Procedure (Amendment No 2) Rules 2023, SI 2023/572; and see Ministry of Justice note 'Extending Fixed Recoverable Costs: a note on the new rules' (May 2023), including 'It is worth emphasising that judges will retain the discretion to allocate more complex cases valued at under £100,000 to the multi-track, so that complex cases will not be inappropriately captured by the extended FRC regime in any event' (para 9).

B Laws of RTA claims involving Advanced Driver Assistance Systems (ADAS)

Legal bases of liability in ADAS claims

9.15 Vehicles equipped with advanced driver assistance systems (ADAS), such as automated emergency braking, are already in use on roads.

Regulation of ADAS and of mobile devices is in a state of flux, as vehicle construction and use regulations adapt to technology. The law as to use of screens and handheld mobile devices has already changed, with revisions to the construction and use regulations (prohibiting use of handheld mobile devices, subject to limited exceptions[90] and, in anticipation of automated vehicles, allowing screen use for other purposes while the vehicle is driving itself[91]).

The law has not yet changed in relation to the typical legal basis of civil liability in an ADAS case: the presumption of control by a human driver remains central[92]. So negligence remains the legal basis of liability for the primary victim.

The standard of care also remains essentially as set out in 1971, in *Nettleship v Weston*: to 'drive in as good a manner as a driver of skill, experience and care, who is sound in wind and limb, who makes no errors of judgment, has good eyesight and hearing, and is free from any infirmity'[93].

As discussed in Chapter 4, by analogy with sentencing comments in criminal cases involving cruise control, it is possible that the courts might particularise the civil standard of care applicable to ADAS if presented with a case or cases in which there is evidence of a 'deliberate removal of one's attention from driving'[94] (such as the use of ADAS as if it were in law an automated vehicle[95]). But this has yet to be adjudicated.

Other bases of legal liability than negligence might also apply, depending upon the facts of the case. Allegations of vehicle defect will engage a variety of legal bases of liability (see chapter 10, 'vehicle defect claims').

Apportioning liability in ADAS cases

Contributory Negligence in ADAS Cases

9.16 From 6 July 2022, all new vehicles that are placed onto the market or registered or entered into service in the European Union must be equipped with

---

90 Road Vehicles (Construction and Use) Regulations 1986, SI 1986/1078 (as amended), reg 110. See Chapter 4, 'driving', section B (ADAS).
91 CUR 1986, reg 109. See Chapter 4, 'driving', section C (AVs).
92 See Chapter 4, 'driving', section B (ADAS).
93 [1971] 2 QB 691, 699g, Lord Denning MR. See Chapter 4, 'driving'.
94 *R v Brian France* [2002] EWCA Crim 1419; [2003] 1 Cr. App. R. (S) 25. See Chapter 4, 'driving', section B (ADAS).
95 AEVA 2018, s 1: 'designed or adapted to be capable, in at least some circumstances or situations, of safely driving' itself, and lawful for such use on roads or other places in Great Britain.

certain ADAS systems[96]. Those systems include Advanced Emergency Braking (AEB) and Intelligent Speed Assistance (ISA, which signal to the driver that the applicable speed limit is exceeded).

The EU regulation is not mandatory as it allows for systems to be overridden and allows the speed limit to be exceeded by the driver[97] (so, insofar as the ISA system is concerned, it is not a full 'speed limiter' as the media has sometimes described it). So such systems will remain under the control of the human driver.

It seems likely but has yet to be officially confirmed that the British government will adopt a similar rule – both to achieve parity for British drivers and manufacturers but also because such systems are common to many current new vehicles. The AV Bill 2023-24 (HL Bill 1), cl 91 would enable the updating by regulations of type approval legislation for both automated and driver assistance systems.

So ADAS systems capable of improving safety are likely to become more common. By analogy with failure to use other familiar but not then mandatory safety technologies (seat belts[98] and bicycle helmets[99]), failure to use ADAS systems which reach such a level of familiarity is likely to become a ground for contributory negligence, even if such use is not required by law.

Contribution in ADAS cases

9.17   ADAS systems are not 'automated' unless they satisfy the conditions set out currently within AEVA 2018[100] or, when enacted, in the Automated Vehicles Act 2024, now the AV Bill 2023-24 (HL Bill 1) and AEVA 2018 amended by AVA 2024. The AV Bill does not remove the prohibition against CL(C)A 1978 contribution proceedings in AEVA 2018, s 6(5), so contribution proceedings would be available to a liable defendant in an ADAS, non-automated vehicle claim under CL(C)A 1978, if the requirements of the 1978 Act were satisfied (see section A above).

Electronic evidence in ADAS cases

9.18   Evidence in ADAS cases is highly likely to include electronic evidence and to engage the e-disclosure practice direction, PD 31B.

For the reasons given in section A, above, it is respectfully suggested that CPR 1998, r 31.5(2) should be amended to allow for early case management of e-disclosure in RTA claims including a claim for personal injuries.

---

96 EU Regulation 2019/2144 of the European Parliament and of the Council of 27 November 2019.
97 Article 6(2) of EU Regulation 2019/2144.
98 *Froom v Butcher*, above.
99 *Smith v Finch*, above.
100 AEVA 2018, s 1.

Expert evidence in ADAS cases

9.19   For the reasons given in section A above, expert evidence is likely to be required to interpret electronic evidence for the court in any significant ADAS case.

Costs in ADAS cases

9.20   The allocation of an ADAS claim to a track will depend largely upon the complexity of the factual and legal issues. At least in early ADAS claims (and taking into account the increasing sophistication of ADAS technology), it seems unlikely that contested liability ADAS cases will be allocated beneath the multi track, even in the proposed extended fast track (see above).

C Laws of RTA claims involving Automated Vehicles

Legal bases of liability in AV claims

Primary victim's statutory legal basis of liability under AEVA 2018, s 2

9.21   Automated vehicles – once self-driving on public roads – will bring the standard applicable to self-driving vehicles closer to a strict liability, by operation of AEVA 2018, s 2, which imposes the AEVA 2018 duty upon the insurer of an automated vehicle or upon the owner of such a vehicle who is permitted to use it on a road or other public place without insurance[101].

Liability under AEVA 2018, s 2 is treated as liability in tort[102].

Whether or not the courts describe AEVA 2018, s 2 as a 'strict' liability of the insurer or permitted uninsured owner remains to be seen. Some commentators have described the liability as strict[103], and the primary liability provision of AEVA 2018, s 2, does not (unlike the provision relating to contributory negligence, AEVA 2018, s 3, via s 6(3)) mention 'fault'. But the issue of strict liability under AEVA 2018, s 2 has also been described as unclear, because it involves assessing whether the 'driving' of the automated vehicle was at least a partial cause of the accident, so as to import questions of fault[104].

The AEVA 2018, s 2 liability is of the insurer or the owner of the AV where the latter is one of the public bodies or the Crown permitted to use the vehicle without insurance[105].

---

101 See Chapter 6 (insurance) for the detail of AEVA 2018.
102 AEVA 2018, s 6(4).
103 For example, the Association of Personal Injury Lawyers (APIL) wrote that the AEVA 2018 'introduced strict liability for autonomous vehicles' in its response to the Law Commission's consultation on remote driving ('Law Commission, Remote Driving, A response by the Association of Personal Injury Lawyers, August 2022' p 2).
104 AEVA 2018, ss 2(1), (2) and 8(3)(b) ('includes ... partly caused by'). The Law Commissions' first consultation paper on autonomous vehicles (November 2018) asked whether AEVA 2018 provides 'a no-fault liability?' (p 104, 6.20) and observed, among other points, that 'it is not possible to separate elements of causation from issues of fault completely' (p 109, 6.46). And see James Goudkamp's article *Rethinking fault liability and strict liability in the law of torts* LQR 2023, 139 (April) 269-289.
105 AEVA 2018, s 2(2)(c) and RTA 1988, s 144(2). See Chapter 6, insurance, for commentary on the AEVA 2018.

'Damage' is given a restricted meaning throughout AEVA 2018, Part 1, including death, personal injury and damage to some property, but excluding damage to the following property: (a) the automated vehicle (b) goods carried for hire or reward in or on that vehicle or in or on any trailer (whether or not coupled) drawn by it, or (c) property in the custody, or under the control, of the insured person or (where use of the vehicle by a public body or the Crown is permitted without insurance) in the custody, or under the control, of the person in charge of the automated vehicle at the time of the accident (AEVA 2018, s 2(3))[106]. Those exclusions echo exemptions for property damage in the policy of insurance upon which RTA 1988, s 145(4)(c-e) permits a motor insurer to rely against a third party. However, the exclusions in AEVA 2018 have a more direct effect – disallowing a direct claim against the insurer under AEVA 2018, s 2 in relation to those items. Unlike the general insurance scheme of RTA 1988, Part VI, AEVA 2018, Part 1 allows – particularly to automated vehicle RTA claims – both a direct statutory claim against the insurer and first-party compulsory cover[107].

Other legal bases of liability for primary victims of RTAs involving AVs

9.22   Where a road traffic accident is caused (at least in part) by an automated vehicle when driving itself, causing 'damage' as defined in AEVA 2018, Part 1, but the automated vehicle does not fall within AEVA 2018, s 2 because it is uninsured and is not permitted for use without insurance (s 2(2)), then the statutory legal basis of liability under AEVA 2018, s 2 would be unavailable to the claimant, and other legal bases of liability (likely including but not necessarily limited to negligence) would be required. The claimant would – subject to the MIB's position on automated vehicles which has not been finalised at the time of writing – look to the MIB (having complied with its procedures) in order to obtain compensation arising from the uninsured use of the AV.

As to the different situation of an untraced driver or user, it is conceivable that an AEVA 2018, s 2 claim could arise but that the giving of false particulars by the user of the vehicle could lead to a claim under the MIB's untraced drivers agreement (UtDA). As with the uninsured drivers agreement, the MIB has yet to state its position in relation to coverage for automated vehicles under the UtDA. The ways in which such AV use might arise factually are not yet clear in practice. So, in such a case, the solidity of AEVA 2018, s 2 legal basis of liability and the availability of other legal bases of liability (and defendants) would require careful consideration on the particular facts of the case.

Some items of damage fall outside the remedies provided by AEVA 2018, Part 1 (see above). So (for example) an action for damage to the automated vehicle itself[108] would have to be put on one or more alternative legal bases, depending upon the facts of the case.

---

106 AEVA 2018, s 2(3): 'In this Part …'.
107 AEVA 2018, s 2(1)(c): 'where … an insured person… suffers damage … the insurer is liable for that damage'. See Chapter 6, 'insurance'.
108 Excluded by AEVA 2018, s 2(3)(a).

Apportioning liability in AV claims

Contributory negligence of the primary victim entitled to claim against insurer or permitted uninsured owner of AV under AEVA 2018, s 2

9.23   AEVA 2018 makes its own provision for contributory negligence, importing principles from the LR(CN)A 1945 but also adding a particular instance of (in effect) entire statutory negligence by the person in charge of the vehicle (s 3(2) below, which operates by barring s 2 liability).

AEVA 2018, s 3 ('contributory negligence etc') provides that:

'3(1) Where—

(a) an insurer or vehicle owner is liable under section 2 to a person ('the injured party') in respect of an accident, and

(b) the accident, or the damage resulting from it, was to any extent caused by the injured party,

the amount of the liability is subject to whatever reduction under the Law Reform (Contributory Negligence) Act 1945 would apply to a claim in respect of the accident brought by the injured party against a person other than the insurer or vehicle owner.

(2) The insurer or owner of an [authorised[109]] automated vehicle is not liable under section 2 to the person in charge of the vehicle where the accident that it caused was wholly due to the person's negligence in allowing the vehicle to begin driving itself when it was not appropriate to do so.'

AEVA 2018, s 6(3) provides that:

'6(3) For the purposes of section 3(1), the Law Reform (Contributory Negligence) Act 1945 and section 5 of the Fatal Accidents Act 1976 (contributory negligence) have effect as if the behaviour of the [authorised[110]] automated vehicle were the fault of the person made liable for the damage by section 2 of this Act.'

The Law Commissions have noted the apparently clashing language of AEVA 2018, s 3(1) ('whatever reduction … would apply to a claim … brought by the injured party against a person *other than* the insurer or vehicle owner') and s 6(3) ('as if the behaviour of the automated vehicle were the fault of the *person made liable* for the damage by section 2', ie the insurer or vehicle owner).

The language does seem to clash, though that is due to the factual conflict which the AEVA 2018, tackles – between notions of human and machine liability – and its attempt to resolve those conflicts within long-established laws premised upon the former (such as the LR(CN)A 1945).

---

109 Amendment proposed by AV Bill 2023-24 (HL Bill 1), cl 45 Sch 2, para 5(3)(b).
110 As above, para 5(3)(d).

The conflict plays out in the language of AEVA 2018 and arguably resolves. The two subsections can be read as complementary. A possible interpretation is that:

- s 3(1) relates to assessment of the reduction for contributory negligence, so identifies the standard by which the vehicle is required to drive. The standard is that of a human driver (a 'person', as in LR(CN)A 1945, s 1).

- The 'person' cannot be the insurer or the owner, either of which is likely to be a company or organisation, itself incapable of driving. So a different, fictional person is required: 'a person other than the insurer or vehicle owner' (AEVA 2018, s 3(1)).

- The apportionment must attach to the parties to the AEVA 2018 claim. So the insurer or permitted uninsured owner liable under AEVA 2018, s 2 is made vicariously liable for the fault of the automated vehicle, for the purposes of the contributory negligence apportionment: 'For the purposes of section 3(1), the Law Reform (Contributory Negligence) Act 1945 and section 5 of the Fatal Accidents Act 1976 (contributory negligence) have effect as if the behaviour of the automated vehicle were the fault of the person made liable for the damage by section 2 of this Act' (AEVA 2018, s 6(3)).

Notably, AEVA 2018, s 2 does not mention 'fault' as an element of the insurer/owner's *primary* liability. The elements of AEVA 2018, s 2 liability are: causation (including partial causation – s 8(3)(b)) of the accident by an insured or permitted uninsured AV while driving itself on a road or other public place in Great Britain, causing the claimant to suffer AEVA-defined damage (sub-ss 2(1) and (2)).

'Fault' is, however, an element of the assessment of contributory negligence under LR(CN)A 1945, which scheme AEVA 2018 retains. For the comparative purpose of apportioning between the defendant's and the claimant's contributory fault, the element of human 'fault' is translated into machine terms by s 6(3), but solely 'For the purposes of section 3(1)' ('contributory negligence etc'). Fault is not expanded into s 2, so appears not to be among the matters which the primary claimant must prove in order to establish the insurer or permitted uninsured owner's liability under s 2.

Liable insurer or permitted uninsured owner's claim against any other person liable to the injured party in respect of the accident, under AEVA 2018, s 5

9.24   AEVA 2018, s 2 creates its own mechanism whereby an insurer or permitted uninsured owner of an automated vehicle liable under s 2 can claim 'against any other person liable to the injured party in respect of the accident' (s 5).

This is a remedy unique to AEVA 2018 liability, as the Act excludes the right of contribution under the 1978 Act:

'An insurer or vehicle owner who has a right of action against a person by virtue of section 5 does not have a right to recover contribution from that person under the Civil Liability (Contribution) Act 1978 or under section 3 of the Law Reform (Miscellaneous Provisions) (Scotland) Act 1940.'[111]

---

111 AEVA 2018, s 6(5).

Question as to whether the AEVA 2018, s 5 secondary claim extends only to AEVA 2018, s 2 liability or allows recovery of liabilities outside AEVA 2018

9.25   AEVA 2018, s 5(1) provides that:

'(1) Where—

(a) section 2 imposes on an insurer, or the owner of a vehicle, liability to a person who has suffered damage as a result of an accident ("the injured party"), and

(b) the amount of the insurer's or vehicle owner's liability to the injured party in respect of the accident (including any liability not imposed by section 2) is settled,

any other person liable to the injured party in respect of the accident is under the same liability to the insurer or vehicle owner.'

The parenthetical phrase in s 5(1)(b) '(including any liability not imposed by section 2)' might suggest that the AEVA 2018, s 5 claim can extend beyond AEVA 2018 liabilities, to all amounts paid by the s 2 liable insurer or owner even including those not within AEVA 2018, s 2 (such as damage to the automated vehicle itself, excluded from the AEVA 2018, s 2 claim by s 2(3)(a))). That might seem the more practical reading, as AEVA 2018, s 6(5) (above) excludes the CL(C)A 1978 right to contribution which might have allowed such extra-AEVA secondary claims.

However, the language of AEVA 2018 is not clear on the point. In particular, AEVA 2018, s 5(1) appears to define 'the same liability' so as to restrict the s 5 secondary claim to liability under AEVA 2018, s 2:

'Where section 2 imposes on the insurer, or owner of a vehicle, liability … any other person liable … is under the same liability'[112]

AEVA 2018, s 5 also contains provisions to prevent over-recovery by the liable insurer or owner in a secondary claim. AEVA 2018, s 5(4) provides that:

'Nothing in this section [5] allows the insurer or vehicle owner and the injured party, between them, to recover from any person more than the amount of that person's liability to the injured party'.

AEVA 2018, s 5(3) provides that:

'If the amount recovered under this section by the insurer or vehicle owner exceeds the amount which that person has agreed or been ordered to pay to the injured party (ignoring so much of either amount as represents interest), the insurer or vehicle owner is liable to the injured party for the difference.'

---

112 This anchoring of the AEVA 2018, s 5 remedy to AEVA 2018, s 2 contrasts with the breadth of the language in CL(C)A 1978, s 1(6): 'References in this section to a person's liability in respect of any damage are references to any such liability which has been or could be established in an action brought against him in England and Wales by or on behalf of the person who suffered the damage …'.

As noted above, a particular feature of AEVA 2018 in relation to the claim against any other person under s 5 is that it strips the insurer/owner of any right to make a claim for contribution under CL(C)A 1978. AEVA 2018, s 5 avoids the word 'contribution'. As already quoted, AEVA 2018, s 6(5) ('application of enactments') provides that:

> 'An insurer or vehicle owner who has a right of action against a person by virtue of section 5 does not have a right to recover contribution from that person under the Civil Liability (Contribution) Act 1978 or under section 3 of the Law Reform (Miscellaneous Provisions) (Scotland) Act 1940.'

On its face, that provision seems to be at odds with CL(C)A 1978, s 7 ('savings'), s 7(3) of which provides that:

> 'The right to recover contribution in accordance with [CL(C)A 1978] section 1 above supersedes any right, other than an express contractual right, to recover contribution (as distinct from indemnity) otherwise than under this Act in corresponding circumstances; but nothing in this Act shall affect—
>
> (a) any express or implied contractual or other right to indemnity; or
>
> (b) any express contractual provision regulating or excluding contribution;
>
> which would be enforceable apart from this Act (or render enforceable any agreement for indemnity or contribution which would not be enforceable apart from this Act).'

AEVA 2018 does not amend (which includes repeal or revoke) CL(C)A 1978, s 7[113]. Whether AEVA 2018, s 6(5) (removal of 1978 Act right in AEVA 2018 case) clashes with CL(C)A 1978, s 7(3) ('[CL(C)A 1978] section 1 above supersedes any right, other than an express contractual right, to recover contribution...') is not clear.

The effect of AEVA 2018 in relation to (for example) an insurer's right to seek contribution for property damage which might be subject to comprehensive insurance but is not within AEVA 2018, Part 1 (eg damage to the AV itself[114]) has not been settled by any judgment but it might be argued that it is unclear whether:

- AEVA 2018, s 6(5) only excludes a CL(C)A 1978 contribution claim for the purposes of damage for which the insurer/owner is held liable under AEVA 2018, s 2, while leaving a CL(C)A 1978 claim open for non-AEVA damages (such as a comprehensively but not compulsorily insured value of the automated vehicle);

  or whether

- AEVA 2018, s 6(5) deprives an insurer/owner of the right to seek contribution under CL(C)A 1978 to liability for *all* damage, including property damage which falls outside AEVA 2018, Part 1.

The point has not been adjudicated, but the second scenario (in which a liable party is deprived of a secondary claim for property damage paid under the non-compulsory part of a motor insurance policy) would be unwelcome to a liable s 2 defendant.

---

113 Cf AEVA 2018, s 20 and Schedule.
114 AEVA 2018, s 2(3)(a).

A possible reading of AEVA 2018 is that the s 5 claim by the insurer or permitted uninsured owner is a claim of its own kind (*sui generis*), confined to recovery of AEVA 2018, s 2 liability (or a part thereof), but going no further than that. That would accord with the interpretation of AEVA 2018, Part 1 as a modification for a subset of motor vehicles of an existing, larger insurance scheme[115], with the interpretation of AEVA 2018, s 5 set out above (as applying only to AEVA 2018, Part 1 'damage') and with the government's description of what became AEVA 2018, s 5, when the Automated and Electric Vehicles Bill was before the Public Bills Committee of the House of Commons:

> 'Clause 5 gives insurers the right of recovery against the person actually responsible for the incident to the same extent that the person is liable to the victim. The person actually responsible for the incident could be, for example, the manufacturer. This clause also defines when and how the amount of the person's liability is settled and when their right of action accrues. It sets out the arrangements and limits on the amounts they recover. This clause will therefore ensure that the insurers are able to recover from those responsible, to the extent that the victim will be able to do so. This will facilitate the effective functioning of clause 2, which imposes initial liability on the insurer or owner of the automated vehicle in respect of an accident.'[116]

If that ('recovery to the same extent as the victim') is correct, then the further question arises as to whether (providing the other requirements of the 1978 Act – including 'same damage' – are satisfied) the liable insurer/owner seeking contribution from another liable party in relation to comprehensively insured damage going beyond AEVA 2018 compulsory cover (such as the value of the damaged AV itself[117]) might be able to raise a contribution claim under CL(C)A 1978 against the other liable party for extra-AEVA 2018 damage.

That would involve challenging a wholesale exclusion of CL(C)A 1978 by AEVA 2018, s 6(5), by points which might include CL(C)A 1978, s 7.

Further, the insurer/owner might need to distinguish the underlying liability from AEVA 2018, in order to avoid the prohibition against a CL(C)A 1978 claim resulting from AEVA 2018, s 6(5). That might logically lead to a requirement on the insurer/owner to demonstrate an extra-AEVA 2018 liability[118] 'which has been or could be established in an action brought against him in England and Wales by or on behalf of the person who suffered the damage' (CL(C)A 1978, s 1(6), 'entitlement to contribution'). In the case of an insurer, that might (for example) lead to driver/user negligence.

So an insurer or permitted uninsured owner facing an AEVA 2018, s 2 claim should think ahead to its own potential remedies, and to the legal bases of liability that it might assert in a claim against another person responsible – both within AEVA 2018, s 5 and CL(C)A 1978.

---

115 See Chapter 6, insurance.
116 House of Commons Hansard, AEV Bill (Public Bills Committee, First Sitting), 14 November 2017, column 131, John Hayes MP (Minister for Transport Legislation and Maritime).
117 AEVA 2018, s 2(3)(a).
118 Or the factual basis of such a liability, where the insurer/owner has made a bona fide settlement or compromise: CL(C)A 1978, s 1(4).

No 'same damage' requirement in AEVA 2018, s 5?

9.26   In contrast to CL(C)A 1978, 'same damage' is not an express requirement of AEVA 2018, s 5.

The rationale of the *Royal Brompton* case is that CL(C)A 1978 is a statutory scheme to be interpreted within its own terms. Similar arguments of construction might be raised in relation to AEVA 2018, Part 1, for example:

- AEVA 2018, Part 1 (as noted in Chapter 6, 'insurance') sits within a larger, established scheme of compulsory motor insurance (now RTA 1988, Part VI). In common with the statutory scheme within which it sits, AEVA 2018 sets limits to compensation payable by the insurer.

- The AEVA 2018, s 5 claim against another responsible person is described, in the language of the section, expressly in terms of 'section 2'[119] AEVA 2018. The liability of the 'other person' against whom a s 5 claim might be brought is 'the same liability', meaning 'section 2' AEVA liability.

- AEVA 2018, s 2(3) prohibits recovery of compensation for certain property damage, including damage to the automated vehicle[120].

It might be argued that the AEVA 2018, s 5 claim should be construed as being restricted to the 'damage' permitted to be recovered by AEVA 2018, s 2(3).

On that interpretation, the AEVA 2018, s 5 claim would be a claim relating solely to AEVA 2018 'damage'.

Whether a liable AEVA 2018 s 2 defendant would then be able to raise a 1978 Act contribution claim for damage paid to the victim which falls outside damage recoverable under AEVA 2018, s 2 would then also fall to be decided by the court.

The point has not been adjudicated. The answer depends in part upon the scope of AEVA 2018 s 5 secondary claim and its relationship to CL(C)A 1978, discussed above.

Conclusion on contribution matters arising from automated vehicles

9.27   All these matters are uncertain: neither the interpretation of AEVA 2018, ss 5 and 6 nor their relationship to the right under CL(C)A 1978 have been adjudicated.

The thickets of contribution law – with its 'trap[s] for the unwary'[121] – have become thicker with the paradoxes of driving and driverless cars.

Evidence in AV claims

9.28   It seems inevitable that electronic evidence will be required in any contested AEVA claim, whether under s 2 (the primary victim's claim) or s 5 (the

---

119 AEVA 2018, s 2(1).
120 AEVA 2018, s 2(3)(a).
121 *Watts v Lord Aldington* (above) at 595 (Steyn LJ, as he then was).

insurer or permitted uninsured owner's claim against another responsible person). The Law Commissions' final report on AV law (January 2022) recommended that the authorisation authority for AVs 'should require data to be collected and stored to process insurance claims…', should impose 'a duty on those controlling AV data to disclose data to insurers, where the data is necessary to decide claims fairly and accurately' and that the in-use regulator of AVs 'should have a statutory power to issue a code of practice on AV data, to which all disclosing data must have regard'[122]. So e-disclosure, and the efficient early management of e-disclosure, will be essential in any contested AV claim.

A feature of the regulatory scheme for authorisation of automated vehicles proposed by the AV Bill 2023-24 is the importance of information relating to vehicle safety, which is reinforced by offences relating to the provision of false information (see the AV Bill 2023-24 (HL Bill 1), cll 24 and 25). The regulatory background therefore indicates the likelihood of substantial disclosure in a case where vehicle defect is an issue (which is more likely to be the case in an AEVA 2018, s 5, contractual, consumer protection or other claim than in a claim under AEVA 2018, s 2, which avoids the need for proof of defect).

E-disclosure in AV claims

9.29   For the reasons given in section A above, it is respectfully suggested that the CPR 1998, r 31.5(2) be amended to allow for early management of e-disclosure in RTA claims including claims for personal injuries.

As also discussed in section A, it is arguable by analogy with the *Wagenaar* case that the presumption against such early management in CPR 1998, r 31.5(2) might not apply to an AEVA 2018, s 5 claim by the insurer or permitted uninsured owner against another responsible person (a third party claim).

However, that would not remove the practical difficulty that the current presumption against early management of e-disclosure in personal injury cases (CPR 1998, r 31.5(2)) creates – especially for the primary claimant who might lack an AEVA 2018, s 2 direct claim (by reason of non-insurance of the vehicle, outside s 2), who would then be put to the task of proving negligence or another legal basis for a claim. That claimant would be heavily dependent upon well-managed e-disclosure.

Costs in AV claims

9.30   For the reasons set out above, it is suggested that contested AEVA 2018 claims are likely to be of significant complexity and should be allocated to the multi-track. At this time it is difficult to conceive of a contested AEVA 2018 claim – whether under s 2 or s 5 – which would not generate a significant e-disclosure task and forensic complexity, requiring expert opinion.

---

122 Recommendations 73 to 75.

D Laws of RTA claims involving Electric Vehicles

Legal bases of liability in EV claims

9.31   Electric cars are motor vehicles[123] so the usual legal basis of liability for driving is negligence. As with other motor vehicles, other legal bases of liability might apply, depending upon the facts.

Electric vehicles generate potential liabilities in nuisance or negligence if they obstruct the pavement or highway. This potentially arises in cases of charging cables left in unsafe positions, or in the case of dockless e-bikes left for retrieval[124].

Apportioning liability in EV claims

9.32   Liability will be apportioned in EV cases according to the principles described in section A above, depending upon the facts of the case.

A potential contributory negligence issue in e-scooter cases is the efficacy of using bicycle helmets without facial protection, especially at higher speeds[125]. So a contributory negligence issue might arise in an e-scooter case if a helmet found inappropriate for e-scooter use is used. The requirement for use of a helmet for a motorcycle (which is how the government classifies e-scooters[126]) is for a helmet complying with British Standard 6658:1985 or the EEA equivalent[127]. The helmet requirement has been removed for an e-scooter in a trial[128] but has not otherwise been removed, so privately owned e-scooters used in public require (among other matters including compulsory insurance) the use of a British Standard 6658:1985 or EEA equivalent helmet.

Evidence in EV claims

9.33   Electric vehicles (cars and others) equipped with electronic devices (whether recording, locating, speed limiting or other devices) are likely to require directions for e-disclosure, and early management of e-disclosure. The points made in section A above will apply. The extent of e-disclosure might not be extensive where ADAS or automated driving systems play no part in the accident.

The reasonable requirement for expert evidence to resolve the proceedings (CPR 1998, r 35.1) is likely to be determined by the *Liddell v Middelton* test: whether it 'furnish[es] the judge with the necessary scientific criteria and assistance based

---

123 *Elieson v Parker* (1917) 81 JP 265; RTA 1988, s 185.
124 See *East Hertfordshire District Council v Isabel Hospice Trading Ltd,* Jack Beatson QC sitting as a Deputy High Court Judge (as he then was) (QB), 29 August 2000 (unreported).
125 Sergeant Steve Wilson, head of cycle safety team (including e-scooters), Metropolitan Police Service, speaking at 'The Future of E-Scooter Regulation' (Bolt Burdon Kemp, 6 July 2022) (video at 35:50-36:45).
126 Answer by Trudy Harrison MP to parliamentary question by Jim Shannon MP, UN 21181, tabled on 20 June 2022, answered 23 June 2022.
127 Motor Cycle (Protective Helmets) Regulations 1998, SI 1998/1807, reg 4(1), 5(1).
128 MC(PH)R, 1998, reg 4(2A), added by the Electric Scooter Trials and Traffic Signs (Coronavirus) Regulations and General Directions 2020, SI 2020/663, reg 3(2)(b).

upon his special skill and experience not possessed by ordinary laymen to enable the judge to interpret the factual evidence'.

Costs in EV claims

9.34   Relatively low value EV claims not involving any liability issue related to ADAS or automated driving, involving some but not a large amount of electronic evidence, are likely to be capable of resolution on one of the less costly tracks.

EV claims involving more severe injuries and complex issues (of liability and/or value) are more likely to be allocated to the multi track.

In relation to e-scooters, at the time of writing there is the additional uncertainty as to whether they will remain subject to compulsory motor insurance under RTA 1988, Part VI or whether the government will, as per its announcement in the 2022 Queen's Speech:

> 'create a low-speed, zero-emission vehicle category that is independent from the cycle and motor vehicle categories. New powers would allow the Government to decide the vehicles that fall into this new category in future and how they should be regulated to make sure that they are safe to use. We hope that e-scooters will be the first of these vehicles.'[129]

Whether a lesser level of indemnity would be required of defendants' motor insurers even if compulsory cover were maintained, and the costs implications of a re-categorisation, are unknown.

---

129 Baroness Vere, House of Lords Hansard Volume 822, columns 30 to 31, 11 May 2022. See section D of Chapter 6, 'insurance'.

Chapter 10

Vehicle defect claims

'We hold, then, that the principle of *Thomas v. Winchester*[1] is not limited to poisons, explosives, and things of like nature, to things which in their normal operation are implements of destruction. If the nature of a thing is such that it is reasonably certain to place life and limb in peril when negligently made, it is then a thing of danger. Its nature gives warning of the consequences to be expected.'[2]

Cardozo J (1916)

'There is general agreement across business and consumer groups that the existing UK consumer law is unnecessarily complex. It is fragmented and, in places, unclear, for example where the law has not kept up with technological change or lacks precision or where it is couched in legalistic language.'[3]

Explanatory notes to the Consumer Rights Act 2015

'The report ['Product Liability in the European Union' (2003)] envisaged that a body of case law would develop that would give guidance with regard to the concept [of 'defect']. However, no such body of law has yet developed.'[4]

Hickinbottom J (2016)

Contents at a glance:

---

1   6 NY 397 (1852). A civil claim in relation to the mistaken sale of a bottle containing poison. 'The wrong done by the defendant was in putting the poison, mislabeled, into the hands of Aspinwall as an article of merchandise to be sold and afterwards used as the extract of dandelion, by some person then unknown.'. The duty was owed to the public, and therefore to persons outside the contract.
2   *MacPherson v Buick Motor Company* 217 NY 382, 111 NE 1050 (1916), a case cited by the majority in *Donoghue v Stevenson* [1932] AC 562 (HL) at 598-599 (Lord Atkin), 603 (Lord Thankerton) and 617-618 (Lord Macmillan).
3   CRA 2015 Explanatory Notes, para 5.
4   *Wilkes v DePuy International Ltd* [2016] EWHC 3096, [2018] QB 627, 643 [68] (Hickinbottom J, as he then was).

A Outline of the laws of vehicle defect claims

10.01 The laws potentially applicable to civil claims relating to defects in products (often described under the umbrella heading 'product liability') can be categorised as follows, in the historical sequence in which they emerged[5]:

1 Contract (including legislative development of the laws of implied terms from the Sale of Goods Act 1893 to the Consumer Rights Act 2015 (CRA 2015)).

2 Tort (particularly with the extension of duties in negligence, beyond privity of contract, by *Donoghue v Stevenson* in 1932, and by breaches of statutory duty, now including the statutory tort[6] under AEVA 2018, s 2).

3 European law as to product liability under the EU Product Liability Directive (EU PLD) 1985[7] as implemented in the UK by the Consumer Protection Act 1987 (CPA 1987). The EU PLD has been described as 'a strict liability special tort law framework' which 'neither require[s] a contractual relationship between the claimant and the defendant nor any kind of negligence or intent on the side of the defendant' [8]. It 'creates strict (risk-based) liability' which 'it imposes … on producers for any defectiveness of their products'[9]. However, it is a scheme which balances consumer protection and commercial interests[10], so it has its limitations by design (perhaps most controversially, the extinction of claims ten years from the time of supply of the product within the meaning of CPA 1987, s 4[11]).

Claims in relation to vehicle defects are 'closely connected to product compliance/conformity including product safety and type approval'[12]. Chapter 2 (vehicle specifications law, including the reforms proposed by the Automated Vehicles Bill 2023-24 (HL Bill 1)) should be read as background to this chapter.

The relevance of each category of liability in a vehicle defect claim will depend upon the circumstances of the case. When considering the law applicable to a defective advanced, automated or electric vehicle claim, a useful starting point is to consider the distinction between hardware (the vehicle and its components such

---

5 See *The Development of Product Liability* (ed. Simon Whittaker, Cambridge, 2010), chapters 1 and 2.

6 Defined as such by AEVA 2018, s 6(4).

7 EU Council Directive of 25 July 1985 on the approximation of the laws, regulations and administrative provisions of the Member States concerning liability for defective products (85/374/EEC) (OJ L 210, 7 August 1985, p 29), amended by Directive 1999/34/EC of the European Parliament and of the Council of 10 May 1999 (OJ L 141, 4 June 1999, p 20).

8 Dr Sebastian Polly, *EU Products Law: A Hogan Lovells Guide to Product Compliance, Product Conformity, Product Integrity, Product Liability and Product Safety for the Automotive Industry* (2nd edn, 2022), p 108.

9 *Liability for Damage Caused by Autonomous Vehicles*, Dr. E.F.D (Esther) Engelhard, R.W. (Roeland) de Bruin, LL.M. (Eleven International Publishing, Utrecht Centre for Accountability and Liability Law, 2018), p 11, 12.

10 '… the European Court recognised that the competence under which the Directive [the EU PLD] was enacted rested on the needs of the internal market, and the harmonisation of the law was intended as a means to the end of harmonising the costs of product liability to market operators.' Whittaker, chapter 1, p 25-26.

11 Limitation Act 1980, s 11A(3), inserted by CPA 1987, s 6(6) and Sch 1. See discussion of CPA 1987 below.

12 Polly, p 107.

as bodywork, tyres, sensors, chips etc) and software. For many AAEVs, software is as important as hardware.

Please note that this chapter does not provide an account of the entire field of 'product liability law', which includes the categories above. Each category includes numerous applicable laws (for example, contractual liability includes the possibility of misrepresentation). This chapter is not, for reasons of space, a review of the entire field. The reader should also refer to specialist works on product liability[13], as each case will raise different points of law depending upon its facts. AAEV law is a developing area, so is likely to raise unforeseen issues. However, it is possible to identify some of the issues to which AAEV claims might lead, including disputes as to the safety of novel technologies such as vehicles described as 'self-driving', the quality of software updates and the effect of public statements by vehicle manufacturers. This chapter focuses upon such points.

The role of software in vehicles will become increasingly important. The law currently provides only limited actionability of defects in downloaded software, for particular claimants via CRA 2015, although amendments proposed by the AV Bill 2023-24 (HL Bill 1) seem to ensure that a software defect would be within the scope of the direct claim under AEVA 2018, s 2 in relation to insured or permitted uninsured use of an automated vehicle which when driving itself causes an accident.

The persistent, circumstantial differences in the law's treatment of downloaded software is a matter of concern. It is a problem which spans the contractual and tortious bases of liability and which affects all three types of vehicle (advanced, automated and electric) with which we are concerned.

The general problem of the legal character of downloaded software

10.02   Defects in downloaded software are now open to action by a consumer against a trader in contract[14], via implied terms provided by CRA 2015. The pre-CRA 2015 position that downloaded software, being intangible[15], could not attract the protection of terms implied by sale of goods legislation has been supplemented in the case of business to consumer contracts by CRA 2015, by the creation of a new commodity identified in the Act as 'digital content'.

However, 'digital content' was a creation of its own type, which circumvented without disturbing the orthodox legal analysis that 'goods' must be tangible and that downloaded software is intangible, so cannot by itself be 'goods'[16]. That

---

13   See in particular Duncan Fairgrieve and Richard Goldberg, *Product Liability* (3rd edn, Oxford, 2020).
14   CRA 2015 s 1.
15   *St Albans City and District Council v International Computers Ltd* [1996] 4 ALL ER 481 (CA); in the Court of Appeal (before referral by the UK Supreme Court to the CJEU), *Computer Associates UK Ltd v Software Incubator Ltd* [2018] 2 All ER 398 (CA).
16   As Gloster LJ noted in the Court of Appeal's judgment in the *Computer Associates UK Ltd* case at para 62-68, the CRA 2015 adopted a *sui generis* [of its own type] solution for business to consumer contracts (going further than the EU Consumer Rights Directive) in which goods are still defined as 'tangible' but the consumer is given the benefit of statutory implied terms in relation to the quality etc of digital content, including digital content provided with goods. The Court of Appeal found that solution supportive of the survival of the 'tangibility' requirement for goods. The CJEU (below) disagreed.

definition of 'goods' reaches into the statutory product liability scheme, through the definition of 'product' in CPA 1987 as 'any goods or electricity ...'[17].

The approach of CRA 2015 was to work around instead of reforming the established definition of 'goods'. However, the established definition remained problematic. Even while upholding 'the well-established meaning of 'goods' being limited to tangible, moveable items'[18], the Court of Appeal in 2018 confessed to feeling 'somewhat uncomfortable with a conclusion that the tangible/intangible distinction leads to a construction of 'goods' that excludes the Software, which seems artificial in the modern age'[19].

The Court of Justice of the European Union subsequently took the reforming route. In September 2021 the CJEU, upon referral by the UK Supreme Court in *Computer Associates UK Ltd v Software Incubator Ltd*[20], tackled the issue of 'tangibility' of downloaded software by reforming EU law more broadly, holding in the context of a commercial agency but with general application to EU sale of goods law[21] that:

'the term 'goods', according to the Court [of Justice of the European Union]'s case-law, ... is to be understood as meaning products which can be valued in money and which are capable, as such, of forming the subject of commercial transactions'

'It follows that that term, as a result of its general definition, can cover computer software, such as the software at issue, since computer software has a commercial value and is capable of forming the subject of a commercial transaction'

'Furthermore, it must be stated that software can be classified as "goods" irrespective of whether it is supplied on a tangible medium or, as in the present case, by electronic download'

'... according to a commonly accepted definition, a "sale" is an agreement by which a person, in return for payment, transfers to another person his rights of ownership in an item of tangible or intangible property belonging to him ...'

'In the particular case of the sale of a copy of computer software, the Court has held that the downloading of a copy of a computer program and the conclusion of a user licence agreement for that copy form an indivisible whole. Downloading a copy of such a program is pointless if the copy cannot be used by its possessor. Those two operations must therefore be examined as a whole for the purposes of their legal classification ...'

'Accordingly, the Court has taken the view that the making available of a copy of computer software by means of a download and the conclusion of a

---

17   See CPA 1987 s 1(2) and (3).
18   Above, Gloster LJ at para 66(i).
19   Above, Gloster LJ at para 45.
20   *Computer Associates UK Ltd v Software Incubator Ltd* (Case C-410/19) EU:C:2020:1061EU:C:2021:742; [2022] 2 All ER (Comm) 139 (CJEU, Fourth Chamber). Software Incubator Ltd was by then the appellant in the UK Supreme Court.
21   Above, para 30 of the CJEU judgment: '... the concept of 'sale of goods' must be given an autonomous and uniform interpretation throughout the European Union ...'.

user licence agreement for that copy, intended to make the copy usable by the customer, permanently, and in return for payment of a fee designed to enable the copyright holder to obtain a remuneration corresponding to the economic value of the copy of the work of which it is the proprietor, involve the transfer of the right of ownership of that copy …'

'Consequently, in the light of the wording of art 1(2) of Directive 86/653[22], it must be held that the supply, in return for payment of a fee, of computer software to a customer by electronic means where that supply is accompanied by the grant of a perpetual licence to use that software can be covered by the concept of "sale of goods" within the meaning of that provision.'[23]

So: defects in downloaded software can be the subject of legal redress in British law – in contract, in business to consumer contracts via the implied terms extended to 'digital content' by CRA 2015, which nevertheless retains the 'tangible' element in its definition of 'goods'[24]. But other sales of goods remain governed by established laws, rooted in that same definition of 'goods' as 'tangible' and without a bespoke remedy for downloaded software (whether via a 'digital content' definition – as in CRA 2015 – or otherwise).

Whether the judgment of the CJEU in the *Computer Associates UK Ltd* case has a broader effect in British law is yet to be clarified. If it were so applied (whether by Parliament or by the courts), it would have potentially radical implications for British contract law, redefining downloaded software as 'goods' generally in sale of goods contracts (not only in business to consumer sales where CRA 2015 already applies, but in sales of goods between other parties, ie. bilateral commercial and bilateral consumer sales). If that were to be the case, how such a redefinition would knit with CRA 2015 providing the different legal approach of 'digital content' is unclear. A possibility (though this is speculation on the part of the writer) is that the CRA 2015 'digital content' commodity might be introduced to other pertinent statutes by amendment (much as the 'digital content' and 'mixed contract' concepts of CRA 2015 – discussed below – were placed onto the template of earlier statutes such as the Sale of Goods Act).

The UK Supreme Court will not give a judgment in the *Computer Associates UK Ltd* case, as Software Incubator Ltd's appeal to the Supreme Court was conceded by Computer Associates UK Ltd after the CJEU's judgment on the preliminary issues[25]. However, unless legislated it seems likely that the issue of the legal character of downloaded software will return to the Supreme Court in a future case, given the ubiquity of that type of software, the persistence of the 'tangible' element of 'goods' in British caselaw and statute and the precedent of the Supreme Court's reference to the CJEU – and its result – in the sunset of EU law[26].

---

22 The EU legal instrument which raised the issue in the *Computer Associates UK Ltd* case: Council Directive 86/653/EEC of 18 December 1986 on the coordination of the laws of the Member States relating to self-employed commercial agents, implemented in the UK by the Commercial Agents (Council Directive) Regulations 1993, SI 1993/3053.
23 CJEU judgment in the *Computer Associates UK Ltd* case (above), para 34-36 and 4-42.
24 See the discussion of CRA 2015 in the 'Contract' section below.
25 Information provided to the writer.
26 The UKSC referral was on 28 May 2019. See Advocate General Tanchev's opinion for the CJEU at para 22-23.

The effect of the CJEU judgment in *Computer Associates UK Ltd* in British law cannot be assumed, against the background of Brexit and its changes to the constitutional landscape. Because the appeal to the UK Supreme Court was conceded after the CJEU judgment, its effect will not be tested in the UK Supreme Court in the *Computer Associates UK Ltd* case[27]. But the probability of the point arising in another case seems high, given the ubiquity of downloaded software and the importance of its quality being a real contractual right generally.

But the solution is not clear. The CJEU approach is in contrast both to the previous EU law position and to the logic of the CRA 2015, where 'digital content' is an ingenious circumvention. Even if the CJEU approach were to be adopted by a British court in a future judgment, the legal basis of the actionability of defects in downloaded software would still need clarification, as CRA 2015 and its *sui generis*[28] approach to digital content in British consumer contract law would remain. The differences between the CRA 2015 and the CJEU *Computer Associates UK Ltd* approaches are:

- under a business to consumer agreement CRA 2015 applies 'special rules'[29] to allow terms to be implied for the quality etc of digital content, including software that is acquired with goods, while still defining 'goods' as 'tangible'[30]; but

- EU law now adopts the different solution of allowing downloaded software itself to be 'goods', irrespective of its tangibility[31].

So the law as to *how* defects in downloaded software are actionable (generally by a redefinition of 'goods' or only particularly by special rules such as those in CRA 2015), and *by whom* (eg. everyone to whom a duty is owed in tort or all purchasers of redefined 'goods' or only consumers in a business to consumer contracts under CRA 2015) remains 'fragmented'[32].

And the point spreads beyond contract law. If reformed (whether by Parliament or the courts), a legal understanding of downloaded software as a 'product'[33] might follow[34]. That is the EU's approach in its proposed updated Product Liability

---

27 Information provided to the writer.
28 'Of its own type'. See Gloster LJ in the *Computer Associates UK Ltd* case in the Court of Appeal (footnote 16, above).
29 See CRA 2015, s 33, CRA 2015 Explanatory Notes, para 39, and discussion below.
30 CRA 2015, s 8.
31 *Computer Associates UK Ltd v Software Incubator Ltd* (CJEU, Fourth Chamber), above. As Gloster LJ had noted in the Court of Appeal, the EU Consumer Rights Directive had not adopted that approach, expressly defining 'goods' as 'tangible' (EU CRD art 2(3), which became CRA 2015 s 2(8)).
32 See quotation from CRA 2015 Explanatory Notes, para 5, at the head of this chapter.
33 CPA 1987, s 1(2), 1(3) and 45(1): "'product' means any goods or electricity and (subject to subsection (3) below) includes a product which is comprised in another product, whether by virtue of being a component part or raw material or otherwise'; '(3) For the purposes of this Part a person who supplies any product in which products are comprised, whether by virtue of being component parts or raw materials or otherwise, shall not be treated by reason only of his supply of that product as supplying any of the products so comprised.'; '45(1) ... 'goods' includes substances, growing crops and things comprised in land by virtue of being attached to it and any ship, aircraft or vehicle'.
34 Apart from its retention of the orthodox 'tangibility' criterion of 'goods', CRA 2015 Part 1 describes the 'producer' of goods or digital content in a similar way to the defendants identified by CPA 1987 s 2(2): see CRA 2015 s 59.

Directive[35]. As Fairgrieve and Goldberg noted (in 2020, before the CJEU's judgment in *Computer Associates UK Ltd*):

> 'While a novel development of the Consumer Rights Act 2015 is the express inclusion of contracts for a trader to supply 'digital content' to a consumer[36], largely rendering previous discussion on whether computer software should be treated as goods obsolete, previous authority on whether software constitutes goods in the area of the sale of goods and analogous transactions and from the United States remains relevant in the context of the 1987 Act [CPA 1987]. The issue is of considerable general importance.'[37]

The actionability of defective downloaded software in a claim arising from an accident caused by an automated vehicle under AEVA 2018, s 2

10.03   The AV Bill 2023-24 (HL Bill 1) would, if enacted, potentially clarify the status of software in automated vehicles both for the purposes of the Automated Vehicles Act 2024 (as it would become, as the regulatory act for automated vehicles) and AEVA 2018, Part 1 (the insurance and liability act for AVs).

The AV Bill 2023-24 (HL Bill 1), cl 44(1) (the 'interpretation' section for the purposes of Part 1 of the Bill ('regulatory scheme for automated vehicles') provides that:

> '"equipment" of a vehicle includes software, and any electronic equipment outside the vehicle, that interacts with equipment in the vehicle.'

That definition carries into the AV Bill's proposed amendments of the criminal offences (under RTA 1988, ss 25 and 76 respectively) of tampering (cl 55) and fitting unsuitable parts (cl 56) under Part 2 of the Bill ('criminal liability for vehicle use').

That definition is also repeated at cl 81(1), for the purpose of the misinformation offences at cll 78-79, in Part 4 of the Bill ('marketing restrictions').

The AV Bill 2023-24 amends AEVA 2018 as set out in cl 45, Sch 2, para 5. Schedule 2, para 5(3) amends 'automated' vehicle in AEVA 2018, Part 1 to 'authorised automated vehicle'. AV Bill 2023-24 (HL Bill 1), cl 94 ('general definitions') defines 'authorised automated vehicle' as 'a vehicle authorised under section [cl] 3' of the Automated Vehicles Act 2024 (as the Bill would become if enacted).

The AV Bill 2023-24 also amends the interpretation section of RTA 1988, s 192, to incorporate into the RTA 1988 the Part 1 definitions section of the Automated Vehicles Act 2024, Part 1 (as cl 44 is expected to become), by this addition to RTA 1988 s 192(1), at AV Bill 2023-24 (HL Bill 1), cl 45, Sch 2, para 4(5):

> '(1ZA) Section 44 of the Automated Vehicles Act 2024 applies for the purposes of the provisions of this Act relating to authorised automated vehicles as it applies for the purposes of Part 1 of that Act.'

---

35 Proposal for a Directive of the European Parliament and of the Council on liability for defective products, COM(2022) 495 final 2022/0302 (COD) (28 September 2022).
36 See discussion below.
37 *Fairgrieve and Goldberg* (3rd edition, 2020), p 300, 9.98.

AEVA 2018 sits within the insurance scheme of RTA 1988 (see Chapter 6, 'insurance').

So the AV Bill appears to define an 'authorised automated vehicle', both for its purposes and (by its amendments to AEVA 2018) for the purposes of the liability and insurance provisions of AEVA 2018 as including 'software'. In relation to AEVA 2018, that would be consistent with the claim and insurance provisions of Part 1, even before amendment by the Bill, which envisage the possibility of downloaded software playing a part in the accident (hence, for example, the permitted exemptions to a claim and to insurance coverage under AEVA 2018, s 4, which relate to software alterations and inadequate updating).

Actionability of downloaded software in an ADAS system

10.04 Whether the AV Bill 2023-24 would also make defective downloaded software actionable in a non-automated, ADAS vehicle case (beyond the 'digital content' remedies of CRA 2015) is debatable.

Clause 44(1) (within AV Bill 2023-24 (HL Bill 1), Part 1, 'regulatory scheme for automated vehicles') does not restrict the definition of vehicle 'equipment', including software, to an 'authorised' vehicle.

Clause 91(1) (within Part 6, 'adaptation of existing regimes) allows for adaptation of type approval legislation governing

'(a) vehicles that are designed to travel autonomously, or

(b) any other type of vehicle that—

 (i) includes equipment designed to allow its motion to be controlled other than by an individual in it, or to facilitate its being so controlled, or

 (ii) is designed to incorporate or interact with software.'

But whether that mention of 'software' is sufficient to make defective downloaded software in an ADAS, non-automated vehicle actionable outside the remedies for 'digital content' in the Consumer Rights Act 2015 is not clear. Unlike AVs, there is no direct statutory claim against an insurer or permitted uninsured owner in relation to an accident caused entirely or in part by an ADAS system (cf AEVA 2018, s 2), so an ADAS claim would be based upon other laws. Future regulations under the Automated Vehicles Act 2024, if so enacted, might illuminate the point.

The three categories of legal bases of claim for defects in vehicles

(1) Contract

10.05 Professor Simon Whittaker describes how:

'the contractual aspect of product liability developed remarkably over the second half of the nineteenth century. The starting point remained (and has subsequently remained) the same (*caveat emptor*[38]) but the courts – and then, in 1893, the legislature – recognised a raft of important exceptions to this

---

38 'Buyer beware'.

principle by recourse to the increasingly widespread technique of implication of terms … In this way, the law of sale of goods became, and has remained, significant for what I have termed the "core concern" of product liability.'[39]

A useful summary of the history of British consumer protection law in contract before CRA 2015 and Brexit is provided by the explanatory notes to CRA 2015:

'The law that protects consumers when they enter into contracts has developed piecemeal over time. Initially it was the courts that recognised that a person buying goods has certain clear and justified, but sometimes unspoken, expectations. The courts developed a body of case law which gave buyers rights when these expectations were not met. This case law was then made into legislation that protected buyers when buying goods, originally in the Sale of Goods Act 1893, updated by the Sale of Goods Act 1979 ("SGA"). These rights were then extended by the introduction of the Supply of Goods and Services Act 1982 ("SGSA") to cover the situations when goods were provided other than by sale (for example when someone hires goods). The SGSA also covers (in relation to England, Wales and Northern Ireland) certain protections for the recipients of services supplied by traders. Legislation setting out rules on unfairness in contract terms was established domestically in the Unfair Contract Terms Act 1977 ("UCTA"). These pieces of legislation currently cover more than just consumer contracts but certain of their provisions offer extra protection to consumers (as opposed to other types of buyers).'

'The EU has also legislated to protect consumers and so the UK legislation has been amended to incorporate this European legislation; sometimes this has been implemented in domestic law without resolving inconsistencies or overlaps.'[40]

A claim in contract has advantages. As Fairgrieve and Goldberg note:

'contractual liability on breach of the implied terms is strict and not dependent on fault. Indeed, it is stricter even than the tort-based liability associated with the Consumer Protection Act 1987 in that it is not subject to a development risks defence. Hence a contractual claim for damages may be either a useful supplement to one made under the 1987 Act or an alternative to it where the Act is clearly or potentially inapplicable… for example, if the defendant is not a person who is potentially liable under the Act or if the damage is of a type or amount which falls outside its scope. Indeed, where the loss is purely financial or economic a claim in contract will usually be the sole potential source of liability since the general rule in English law is that such losses do not fall to be compensated by the law of tort.'[41]

This chapter focusses its examination of contract law as the basis of an AAEV defect claim upon CRA 2015, because of its codification of consumer contract law and its importance in relation to the legal treatment of software – especially of downloaded software. CRA 2015 is not the only avenue of contractual claim, and other statutes apply to claims between other parties (see, for example, the sale and supply of goods legislation in *Figure 1*, below). For those other claims the reader is referred to other

---

39 *Whittaker*, chapter 2 ('the development of product liability in England') p 61-62.
40 CRA 2015 Explanatory Notes, para 6 and 7.
41 *Fairgrieve and Goldberg*, p 151, 5.31. See other works (including Fairgrieve and Goldberg) for accounts of remedies in contract.

works. The following section is not an exhaustive account of points which might arise under CRA 2015 and the reader should refer to the full text of the Act in any event.

The importance of software to AAEVs is a significant development both in road vehicle design and in vehicle defect law, where defects considered in caselaw have mainly been mechanical[42]. The shift towards greater use of software alters the focus of vehicle defect law. That is the particular setting for our discussion of CRA 2015.

Consumer Rights Act 2015

10.06 CRA 2015 has a broader scope than digital content. It is in three parts, the first two of which (Part 1 'Consumer contracts for goods, digital content and services' and Part 2, 'Unfair terms') are concerned with contract[43]. In Parts 1 and 2, CRA 2015 'sets out a framework that consolidates in one place key consumer rights covering contracts for goods, services, digital content and the law relating to unfair terms in consumer contracts'[44].

As Fairgrieve and Goldberg have pointed out, CRA 2015 'operates as a consolidating measure which replaces much of the existing [statutory] law' on implied terms in business to consumer contracts, although 'the provisions which relate to other types of contracts (eg business to business contracts and consumer to consumer contracts) remain in the existing legislation'[45].

CRA 2015 both codified domestic law as to implied terms in business to consumer contracts and implemented EU laws, including some provisions of Directive 2011/83/EU of the European Parliament and of the Council on consumer rights (the 'EU CRD')[46]. As the explanatory note to CRA 2015 says:

---

42 By contrast, the 'Dieselgate' litigation, where the 'defeat devices' were in software, provides an example of the increasing importance of software to the functionality of motor vehicles. See *Crossley and others v Volkswagen Aktiengesellschaft and others (the VW NOx Emissions Group Litigation)* [2021] EWHC 3444 (the summary judgment decision, 20 December 2021) summary of background at paras 3-7, and [2020] EWHC 783 (the preliminary issues judgment, 6 April 2020, both QBD, Waksman J).

43 CRA 2015, Part 3, 'Miscellaneous and General', deals with matters including regulators' powers and competition law.

44 CRA 2015 Explanatory Notes, para 3.

45 *Fairgrieve and Goldberg* (3rd edn, 2020) p 70, 4.01.

46 CRA 2015 implemented Directive 99/44/EC of the European Parliament and of the Council on certain aspects of the sale of consumer goods and associated guarantees, Directive 93/13/EEC of the Council on unfair terms in consumer contracts and some provisions of Directive 2011/83/EU of the European Parliament and of the Council on consumer rights (the 'EU CRD'). It also implemented some provisions (in respect of enforcement) of Regulation (EC) No. 2006/2004 of the European Parliament and of the Council on cooperation between national authorities responsible for the enforcement of consumer protection laws, Regulation (EC) No. 765/2008 of the European Parliament and of the Council setting out the requirements for accreditation and market surveillance relating to the marketing of products, Directive 2001/95/EC of the European Parliament and of the Council on general product safety and Directive 98/27/EC of the European Parliament and of the Council on injunctions for the protection of consumers' interests. See CRA 2015 Explanatory Notes, para 9 and 10. The Consumer Contracts (Information, Cancellation and Additional Charges) Regulations, SI 2013/3134 had implemented provisions of the EU CRD from 13 June 2014; CRA 2015 also implemented EU CRD provisions, including that 'for all contracts where a trader supplies goods, services or digital content to a consumer, requires that a trader must provide certain information (for example on the main characteristics of the goods, services and digital content) before the consumer is bound by the contract' (CRA 2015 Explanatory Notes, para 11; CRA 2015, s 36).

'A consultation by the Department for Business Innovation and Skills ('BIS') in August 2012 sought views on implementing the [EU] CRD in particular highlighting those areas where the UK had some flexibility in the way it might be applied ... In developing proposals for the Consumer Rights Act 2015, the Government has taken into account the definitions and measures contained within the CRD and, as far as appropriate, has made the Act consistent with the CRD, with the intention of achieving overall a simple, coherent framework of consumer legislation.'[47]

A table showing the impact of CRA 2015 upon existing British legislation appears at para 24 of the explanatory notes to CRA 2015, which state that 'the provisions in the existing legislation listed below which cover trader to consumer contracts only will be repealed. The provisions which relate to other types of contract (for example contracts between businesses) will remain in the existing legislation'. The EN para 24 table is as follows:

Supply of Goods (Implied Terms) Act 1973	For business to consumer contracts the provisions of the Supply of Goods (Implied Terms) Act 1973 ('SGITA') will be replaced by CRA 2015. It will be amended so that it covers business to business contracts and consumer to consumer contracts only.
Sale of Goods Act 1979	For business to consumer contracts this will mainly be replaced by CRA 2015 but some provisions of SGA will still apply, for example, rules which are applicable to all contracts of sale of goods (as defined by that Act – essentially these are sales of goods for money), regarding matters such as when property in goods passes. The SGA will still apply to business to business contracts and to consumer to consumer contracts.
Supply of Goods and Services Act 1982	For business to consumer contracts, this Act's provisions will be replaced by CRA 2015. The SGSA will be amended so that it covers business to business contracts and consumer to consumer contracts only.
Sale and Supply of Goods Act 1994	This Act amended the SGA and the SGSA and as such will be superseded by provisions in CRA 2015 for business to consumer contracts.
Sale and Supply of Goods to Consumers Regulations 2002	These will be replaced by provisions in CRA 2015.
Unfair Contract Terms Act 1977	In respect of business to consumer contracts the Act's provisions will be replaced by CRA 2015. The UCTA will be amended so that it covers business to business and consumer to consumer contracts only.
Unfair Terms in Consumer Contracts Regulations 1999	These will be replaced by the CRA 2015.

---

47   CRA 2015 Explanatory Notes, para 12-13.

CRA 2015, Part 1, 'Consumer contracts for goods, digital content and services'

10.07 CRA 2015, Part 1 codifies a consumer's contractual rights in relation to goods, services and – in a distinctive way – in relation to digital content. It does not apply to all contracts; it does not apply to consumer-to-consumer contracts, for example. It applies 'where there is an agreement between a trader and a consumer for the trader to supply goods, digital content or services, if the agreement is a contract'[48] and 'it applies whether the contract is written or oral or implied from the parties' conduct, or more than one of these combined'[49].

The key definitions in CRA 2015, Part 1 are provided in s 2, including:

- ' "*Digital content*" is defined as 'data which are produced and supplied in digital form'[50].

- CRA 2015 retains the orthodox, pre-CJEU in *Computer Associates UK Ltd* definition of '*goods*' as 'any tangible moveable items'[51] including 'water, gas and electricity if and only if they are put up for supply in a limited volume or set quantity'[52].

- ' "*Trader*" means a person acting for purposes relating to that person's trade, business, craft or profession, whether acting personally or through another person acting in the trader's name or on the trader's behalf'[53] and ' "*Business*" includes the activities of any government department or local or public authority'.[54]

- ' "*Consumer*" means an individual acting for purposes that are wholly or mainly outside that individual's trade, business, craft or profession'[55], with exceptions for second hand goods sold at public auction and individuals who have the opportunity of attending the sale in person[56].

'Contracts for the hire of goods' are defined in CRA 2015, Part 1, Chapter 2 ('Goods' 'What goods contracts are covered?') by s 3(2)(b) and 6. CRA 2015, s 6 provides that:

'(1) A contract is for the hire of goods if under it the trader gives or agrees to give the consumer possession of the goods with the right to use them, subject to the terms of the contract, for a period determined in accordance with the contract.

(2) But a contract is not for the hire of goods if it is a hire-purchase agreement.'

(Hire-purchase agreements are defined in CRA 2015, Part 1, Chapter 2, s 7.)

---

48   CRA 2015, s 1(1).
49   CRA 2015, s 1(2).
50   CRA 2015, s 2(9).
51   It is established that a car is within the definition of 'goods'. See for example *Crowther v Shannon* [1975] 1 WLR 30 (CA) (second hand car unfit for purpose of use on roads under Sale of Goods Act 1893, s 14).
52   CRA 2015, s 2(8).
53   CRA 2015, s 2(2).
54   CRA 2015, s 2(7).
55   CRA 2015, s 2(3).
56   See CRA 2015, s 2(5) and (6).

As discussed in relation to the problem of the legal character of downloaded software, CRA 2015 treats digital content distinctly from contracts to supply goods (dealt with in CRA 2015, Part 1, Chapter 2), and it likewise distinguishes digital content (dealt with in Chapter 3) from services (dealt with in Chapter 4)[57]. However, CRA 2015, s 1 also provides for a 'mixed contract':

'(4) In each case the Chapter applies even if the contract also covers something covered by another Chapter (a mixed contract).

(5) Two or all three of those Chapters may apply to a mixed contract.

(6) For provisions about particular mixed contracts, see—

(a) section 15 (goods and installation);

(b) section 16 (goods and digital content).'[58]

The explanatory notes to CRA 2015 state that, in mixed contracts:

'the service element of the contract attracts service rights and remedies, the goods elements attract goods rights and remedies and the digital content elements attract the digital content rights and remedies. [Section 1] Subsection (3) therefore makes clear that, for such mixed contracts, it will be relevant to look at the rights and remedies for each element of the mixed contract. In most cases it will be relevant to look at the appropriate chapter of the Act (Chapter 2 for goods, 3 for digital content and 4 for services). Subsection (6) sets out that for particular mixed contracts (goods and installation services, and goods and digital content) it may also be relevant to look at sections 15 and 16.'[59]

(CRA 2015, s 16 will be relevant to AAEVs, as such vehicles are often supplied with their own software which then updates over WiFi or cellular networks; s 16 is discussed below, as are s 39 and s 40 in relation to software updates.)

Key statutory rights provided by implied terms under CRA 2015, Part 1

10.08 CRA 2015, Part 1 provides, in relation to goods contracts (Chapter 2) and digital content (Chapter 3) the following key statutory rights, by means of implied terms as to:

- Satisfactory quality (of goods at s 9 and digital content at s 34)

- Fitness for particular purpose (of goods at s 10 and digital content at s 35) and

- Conformity with description (of goods at s 11 and digital content at s 36)

CRA 2015, Part 1, Chapter 4 provides statutory rights for services, including that the service be performed with reasonable care and skill (s 49) and that the service shall be performed within a reasonable time (s 52).

---

57 CRA 2015, s 1(3).
58 CRA 2015, s 1(4)-(6).
59 CRA 2015 Explanatory Notes, para 32.

Terms seeking to exclude or restrict those implied terms are not binding on the consumer, as per ss 31, 47 and 57.

Application of CRA 2015 to 'digital content'

10.09   CRA 2015, s 33(1)–(3) provides as follows:

'*33 Contracts covered by this Chapter*

(1) This Chapter applies to a contract for a trader to supply digital content to a consumer, if it is supplied or to be supplied for a price paid by the consumer.

(2) This Chapter also applies to a contract for a trader to supply digital content to a consumer, if—

(a) it is supplied free with goods or services or other digital content for which the consumer pays a price, and

(b) it is not generally available to consumers unless they have paid a price for it or for goods or services or other digital content.

(3) The references in subsections (1) and (2) to the consumer paying a price include references to the consumer using, by way of payment, any facility for which money has been paid.'

The explanatory note to CRA 2015 says this of the definition of 'digital content' in CRA 2015, s 2(9):

'The definition of digital content in subsection (9) is the same as the definition in the [EU] CRD (data produced and supplied in digital form). Digital content may be supplied on a tangible medium (in which case special rules apply) for example a DVD or software, on a computer or not, for example an e-book or music download. The creation of a category of digital content in this Act does not affect the treatment of digital content in any other legislation.'[60]

As discussed in the 'Outline' section at the start of this chapter, British law and EU law have to date taken different approaches to the problem of identifying the legal character of downloaded software, since the CJEU judgment in the *Computer Associates UK Ltd* case (2021). But, putting the problem of the character of software aside, CRA 2015 already legislates for circumstances where digital content is supplied free with tangible goods and is not generally available otherwise to consumers[61] – a paradigm which appears to fit the supply to the consumer of an advanced, automated or electric vehicle with software, including downloaded software updates.

---

60   CRA 2015 Explanatory Notes, para 39.
61   CRA 2015, s 33(2)(a) ('contracts covered by this chapter'): 'This Chapter also applies to a contract for a trader to supply digital content to a consumer, if (a) it is supplied free with goods or services or other digital content for which the consumer pays a price, and; (b) it is not generally available to consumers unless they have paid a price for it or for goods or services or other digital content.'.

Implied terms for digital content in mixed contracts for goods and digital content, under CRA 2015, s 16

10.10 CRA 2015, s 1(4)–(6) (above) provides that several of the Chapters in Part 1 of the Act (the chapters for goods, digital content and services) can apply together to a 'mixed contract' and s 1(6)(b) refers to the particular 'mixed contract' provided for by s 16: a mixed contract for goods and digital content.

CRA 2015, s 16 reads as follows:

> '*16 Goods not conforming to contract if digital content does not conform*
>
> (1) Goods (whether or not they conform otherwise to a contract to supply goods) do not conform to it if—
>
>   (a) the goods are an item that includes digital content, and
>
>   (b) the digital content does not conform to the contract to supply that content (for which see section 42(1)).
>
> (2) See section 19 for the effect of goods not conforming to the contract.'

CRA 2015, s 42 provides the 'consumer's rights to enforce terms about digital content' and s 42(1) provides that, in ss 42 and 43 ('right to repair or replacement'), 'references to digital content conforming to a contract are references to the digital content conforming to the terms described in ss 34, 35 and 36', ie the implied terms for digital contents of satisfactory quality, fitness for a particular purpose and conformity with description (above).

CRA 2015, s 19 provides the 'consumer's rights to enforce terms about goods', including for breaches of s 16. The remedies sought will depend upon the facts in each case. For example, in relation to a breach of the implied term of conformity with description relating to digital content under s 16, s 19(3) provides that:

> '... the consumer's rights (and the provisions about them and when they are available) are—
>
> (a) the short-term right to reject (sections 20 and 22);
>
> (b) the right to repair or replacement (section 23); and
>
> (c) the right to a price reduction or the final right to reject (sections 20 and 24).'

– and, under s 19(9)–(11):

> '(9) This Chapter does not prevent the consumer seeking other remedies—
>
>   (a) for a breach of a term that this Chapter requires to be treated as included in the contract,
>
>   (b) on the grounds that, under section 15 or 16, goods do not conform to the contract, or
>
>   (c) for a breach of a requirement stated in the contract.
>
> (10) Those other remedies may be ones—

(a) in addition to a remedy referred to in subsections (3) to (6) (but not so as to recover twice for the same loss), or

(b) instead of such a remedy, or

(c) where no such remedy is provided for.

(11) Those other remedies include any of the following that is open to the consumer in the circumstances—

(a) claiming damages;

(b) seeking specific performance;

(c) seeking an order for specific implement;

(d) relying on the breach against a claim by the trader for the price;

(e) for breach of an express term, exercising a right to treat the contract as at an end.'

Responsibility for breaches of CRA 2015 implied term as to quality of downloaded software where there is a problem with the means of transmission of the software

10.11   CRA 2015, s 39 provides for 'supply by transmission and facilities for continued transmission'.

Section 39(2) provides that:

'For the purposes of this Chapter,' [ie. Part 1 Chapter 3, 'digital content', which includes the implied terms as to quality etc] the digital content is supplied—

(a) when the content reaches the device, or

(b) if earlier, when the content reaches another trader chosen by the consumer to supply, under a contract with the consumer, a service by which digital content reaches the device.'

The explanatory notes to CRA 2015, s 39 include these passages:

'When [digital content] is not supplied on a tangible medium, it will usually travel through one or more intermediaries before it reaches the consumer's device. Some of these intermediaries, for example an Internet Service Provider ('ISP'), have been chosen by and are within the contractual control of the consumer. Other intermediaries, however, will be within the contractual control of the trader, or under arrangements initiated by the trader. For example, a supplier of streamed movies (the trader) may contract with a content delivery network who will deliver the data from the trader's server to the ISPs who will then deliver the content to the consumer.'

'Subsection (2) provides that the trader (T) from whom the consumer purchased the digital content supplies the content at the point that it reaches either the consumer's device (for example, directly to a consumer's satellite dish) or an independent trader within the contractual control of the consumer (such as an ISP), whichever is sooner. T is responsible for ensuring that it meets all the relevant quality standards. A trader which is in the contractual control of the consumer and which only provides a service by which the digital content reaches the consumer is not providing digital content for the purposes of [CRA 2015 Part 1] Chapter 3 (see section 33(4)) but may be subject to the provision in Chapter 4 (Services)).'

'Where digital content fails to meet the quality standards because of a problem with the consumer's device or with the delivery service supplied by an independent trader with whom the consumer has contracted (e.g. ISP, mobile network provider, cable provider), T would not be liable for the failure to meet the quality standards as that trader (T) cannot be at fault in any way for the problem and has no way of rectifying it. If the problem is with the consumer's network access provider, then this service provider is liable under the services provision of the Act if, for example, the service is not provided with reasonable care and skill (see Chapter 4). However, where the digital content fails to meet the quality standards because of a problem for which T [the trader] or an intermediary in the contractual control of T (either directly or indirectly) is responsible, then T will be liable. This is similar to the rules on the passing of risk for goods ([CRA 2015] section 29) which provide that the trader carries the risk for the goods purchased until they come into the physical possession of the consumer, unless the delivery is arranged by the consumer in which case the consumer takes the risk for the delivery of the goods.'[62]

Trader's liability for software updates under CRA 2015, s 40

10.12 'Where under a contract a trader supplies digital content to a consumer subject to the right of the trader or a third party to modify the digital content' CRA 2015, s 40 ('quality, fitness and description of content supplied subject to modifications') applies the terms implied as to quality, fitness for a particular purpose and description (under CRA 2015, ss 34, 35 and 36) 'in relation to the digital content as modified as they apply in relation to the digital content as supplied under the contract' (s 40(1)).

Under s 40(2), modifications must comply with CRA 2015, s 36 ('digital content to be as described').

A claim made on the grounds under s 40(1) 'is to be treated as arising at the time when the digital content was supplied under the contract and not the time when it is modified' (s 40(3)).

The fact of a software update does not necessarily imply fault in the software before the update:

'It is for a consumer to prove that the digital content is faulty. Where a consumer has not identified a fault (and therefore not requested a repair or replacement), but a general update is sent in any case to the consumer, this does not necessarily mean that the quality rights were breached nor that the update constitutes a repair or replacement.'[63]

---

62   CRA 2015 Explanatory Notes, para 192-194.
63   CRA 2015 Explanatory Notes, para 198.

Remedy under CRA 2015 where digital content causes damage to a device or to other digital content

10.13   CRA 2015, s 46 provides remedies for the consumer where:

'(1) ...

> (a) a trader supplies digital content to a consumer under a contract,
>
> (b) the digital content causes damage to a device or to other digital content,
>
> (c) the device or digital content that is damaged belongs to the consumer, and
>
> (d) the damage is of a kind that would not have occurred if the trader had exercised reasonable care and skill.'

The remedies under s 46 are repair within a reasonable time and the costs of repair (s 46(3)) or compensation (s 46(2)). The consumer with a remedy may enforce it by civil proceedings (s 46(7)).

Public statements relevant to satisfactory quality under CRA 2015

10.14   The Sale of Goods Act 1979, s 14, the Supply of Goods and Services Act 1982, s 4 and the Consumer Rights Act 2015, ss 9 and 34 all provide for implied terms as to quality.

All three statutes provide that the quality of goods is satisfactory if they meet the standard that a reasonable person would regard as satisfactory, taking account of any description of the goods, the price (if relevant) and all other relevant circumstances (SGA 1979, s 14(2A); SGSA 1982, s 4(2A); CRA 2015, ss 9(2), 34(2)).

Significantly for advanced and automated vehicles – and particularly the manufacturer's description of the driving capabilities of some advanced and automated systems – all three statutes also provide that an implied term as to satisfactory quality does not apply where the relevant matter is specifically drawn to the consumer's attention before the contract is made, or where the buyer examines the goods or digital content before the contract is made and the examination ought to have revealed the unsatisfactory matter or where there is a contract for sale by sample (a 'trial version' in the case of digital content[64]) and the unsatisfactory matter would have been apparent on a reasonable examination of the sample (SGA 1979, s 14(2C); SGSA 1982, s 4(3); CRA 2015, ss 9(4) and 34(4)).

However, CRA 2015, s 9 ('goods to be of satisfactory quality') and 34 ('digital content to be of satisfactory quality') both have a longer list than the other statutes of considerations relevant to satisfactory quality. CRA 2015, ss 9(5)–(7) and 34(5)–(7) provide as follows:

---

64   CRA 2015, s 34(4)(c).

'(5) The relevant circumstances mentioned in subsection (2)(c)[65] include any public statement about the specific characteristics of the [goods/digital content] made by the trader, the producer or any representative of the trader or the producer.

(6) That includes, in particular, any public statement made in advertising or labelling.

(7) But a public statement is not a relevant circumstance for the purposes of subsection (2)(c) if the trader shows that—

(a) when the contract was made, the trader was not, and could not reasonably have been, aware of the statement,

(b) before the contract was made, the statement had been publicly withdrawn or, to the extent that it contained anything which was incorrect or misleading, it had been publicly corrected, or

(c) the consumer's decision to contract for the [goods/digital content] could not have been influenced by the statement.'

That expanded list of circumstances is relevant to the satisfactory quality of a novel technology in contracts subject to CRA 2015, where there has been a public statement relating to its capabilities. The scope of 'any public statement made in advertising' might – depending upon the facts of the case – include social media content. In general terms, the parties' knowledge of online content might need to be established in evidence in a case, as an assumption of such knowledge would generally be insufficient[66]. However, CRA 2015, ss 9(5)–(7) and 34(5)–(7) seem only to involve proof of 'any public statement' (not even one made 'in advertising or labelling' under (6)), after which it becomes the trader's burden to show any of the three points of rebuttal in (7).

In this regard, CRA 2015 legislates for implied terms as to digital content in a specific, though not exhaustive[67] way. The approach of the CRA 2015 echoes general principles of contractual interpretation, including the relevance of the matrix of fact and of the treatment of clauses inconsistent with the purpose of the contract as a whole[68]. In particular, the possibility of contradictory public statements by the trader about the specific characteristics of their goods and digital content is recognised, and dealt with in CRA 2015, ss 9 and 34 by the imposition of the burden of proving the irrelevance of any such public statement relied upon by the consumer upon the person who made that statement, ie upon the trader, the producer or their representative.

---

65 CRA 2015, ss 9(2)(c) and 34(2)(c): 'The quality of [goods/digital content] is satisfactory if [they/it] meets the standard that a reasonable person would consider satisfactory, taking account of … (c) all the other relevant circumstances (see subsection (5)).'

66 See *Lehman Bros International (Europe) (in administration) v Exotix Partners Llp* [2019] EWHC 2380 (Ch), Hildyard J at para 112-113, including at para 113: 'the court needs to be wary of assuming that the general availability of information is sufficient to make it 'reasonably available' in the requisite sense [for the purposes of constructing the words they used]: almost anything is available on the internet in the general sense.'

67 'include … in particular,': CRA 2015, ss 9(5)-(6), 34(5)-(6). Although the list of permitted rebuttals by the trader in ss 9(7) and 34(7) is limited to the three points capable of making a public statement irrelevant.

68 See larger works on contract law, eg *Chitty on Contracts* (34th edn, 2021), chapter 15, section 3, 'construction of terms'.

This is of likely application to any public statements by traders etc about the specific characteristics of their AAEVs, whether solely as goods or in relation to digital content provided under a mixed goods/digital contents contract.

(2)   Tort (other than CPA 1987)

Strict liability at common law for a 'wholly unmanageable' vehicle

10.15   As noted in Chapter 9 ('RTA claims'), nuisance remains a possible basis of claim for obstruction of the highway[69] or (in the judgment of the Court of Appeal in 1909):

> 'If a man places on the streets vehicles so wholly unmanageable as necessarily to be a continuing danger to other vehicles, either at all times or under special conditions of weather, I have no doubt that he does it at his peril, and that he is responsible for injuries arising therefrom, even though there has been no negligence in the management of his vehicle.'[70]

The possibility of a 'wholly unmanageable' vehicle being placed on the roads is much reduced (but not excluded) by the many requirements for the construction and use of vehicles created by statute, reinforced by criminal offences[71].

Duty in negligence in relation to defects in motor vehicles

10.16   It is established that there is a duty of care in negligence in relation to defects in motor vehicles:

> 'Beyond all question, the nature of an automobile gives warning of probable danger if its construction is defective.'[72]

Duty in negligence in relation to components

10.17   The duty extends to components. For AAEVs, components are as likely to be computer hardware and software as 'nuts and bolts' in conventional vehicles.

---

69   See *East Hertfordshire District Council v Isabel Hospice Trading Ltd*, Jack Beatson QC sitting as a Deputy High Court Judge (as he then was), 29 August 2000, QB (unreported).
70   *Wing v London General Omnibus Company*, Fletcher Moulton LJ at 665. There are parallels in criminal law, in the offences under RTA 1988, s 40A ('using vehicle in dangerous condition etc'), s 42 ('breach of other construction and use requirements') and the Road Vehicles (Construction and Use) Regulations 1986, 1986/1078, reg 100 ('maintenance and use of vehicle so as not to be a danger, etc'). Though see Chapter 13, 'highway claims', for discussion of the protean nature of the standard of duty in nuisance, which in the road traffic context is often related to the standard in negligence.
71   See RTA 1988, Part II, and the Road Vehicles (Construction and Use) Regulations 1986, SI 1986/1078. See also any type approval regulations made under the Automated Vehicles Act 2024 to adapt type approval legislation to automated and assistive technologies: AV Bill 2023-24 (HL Bill 1), cl 91.
72   Cardozo, J., in *MacPherson v Buick Motor Company* (1916), followed by the majority in *Donoghue v Stevenson* (1932, citations at the head of this chapter). For a fuller account of 'the producer's liability in negligence', including car producers, see Fairgrieve and Goldberg (3rd edn, 2020), chapter 14.

Citing American cases, Fairgrieve and Goldberg note that:

> 'there is no especial problem with such components as car tyres and brake units which have a single identifiable function. However, … the position is much more problematic with such multipurpose components as nuts and bolts or copper or plastic piping. The manufacturer of such components will frequently not know the specific use to which his product has been put and he will rarely be held accountable if it is used for an unsuitable purpose.'[73]

The problem of attribution of responsibility for a multi-purpose component is compounded by AAEV hardware (including sensors and chips) and software components.

The position in negligence is distinct from the strict liability position under CPA 1987, Part I (discussed below):

> '(2) In this Part, except in so far as the context otherwise requires—
>
> *'product'* means any goods or electricity and (subject to subsection (3) below) includes a product which is comprised in another product, whether by virtue of being a component part or raw material or otherwise; and
>
> …
>
> (3) For the purposes of this Part a person who supplies any product in which products are comprised, whether by virtue of being component parts or raw materials or otherwise, shall not be treated by reason only of his supply of that product as supplying any of the products so comprised.'[74]

Under CPA 1987, s 4(1)(f), the manufacturer of a defective component has a defence if they show:

> '(f) that the defect—
>
> (i) constituted a defect in a product ('the subsequent product') in which the product in question had been comprised; and
>
> (ii) was wholly attributable to the design of the subsequent product or to compliance by the producer of the product in question with instructions given by the producer of the subsequent product.'

However, the position in negligence is that there is no such specific defence, so 'the component manufacturer may be required to issue appropriate warnings'[75] or make other attempts to avoid misuse of its components.

Duty in negligence includes disrepair

10.18 The duty in negligence also extends to repair, if the evidence links the disrepair sufficiently closely to the defendant.

---

73 *Fairgrieve and Goldberg* (3rd edn, 2020) at 14.77.
74 CPA 1987 s 1 ('purpose and construction of Part I').
75 *Fairgrieve and Goldberg* (3rd edn, 2020), para 14.77.

In *Herschtal v Stewart and Ardern Ltd*[76], the claimant took delivery of a car reconditioned and supplied to the claimant's company by the defendant. A rear wheel detached while he was driving it the following day and caused him injury. Examination of the wheel and hub just after the accident showed that the nuts had not been properly tightened for some time and that the threads were stripped. The defendant argued that the claimant had the opportunity of intermediate inspection before the accident occurred, which (it argued) had the effect of ending the proximate relationship required by *Donoghue v Stevenson* for the duty of care in negligence to arise. In the judgment of Tucker J:

'I respectfully agree that the decision in *Donoghue v. Stevenson* is not intended to be limited only to manufacturers of goods but that it applies in a proper case to the repairer of an article, subject to the question which I have to decide as to the intermediate examination...'[77]

'... the mere existence of the opportunity for examination is not sufficient to break the chain or destroy the proximate relationship. I think that *Donoghue v. Stevenson* ought not to be so limited as to be confined only to the precise words used by Lord Atkin in the concluding part of his speech, which I have already pointed out were not necessary for the decision in that case. I think that one has to look at the whole basis of the judgment and apply it to the facts.'[78]

'In the present case, in my view, the defendants were the plaintiff's neighbour in law within the definition of Lord Atkin. I think that they were very immediate neighbours. They were supplying a dangerous article to a person with whom they were in actual contact. He was not some ultimate person or user who might have been envisaged. He was an actual man with whom they were dealing in the flesh. They were supplying his company through him with a dangerous vehicle, knowing that it was going to be used forthwith by him. In my view, there was a very close proximity or relationship existing between the plaintiff and the defendants, which imposed a duty on the defendants to take reasonable care to see that the article which they were delivering to the plaintiff, knowing that he was going immediately to put it on the road, was not in a condition whereby a wheel might rapidly fly off, causing possibly very severe and grave damage.'[79]

Employer's duty to provide safe work equipment

10.19 An employer's duty to employees includes the duty to provide safe equipment – see Chapter 12, 'employer's liability claims', and EL(DE)A 1969 (below).

---

76 [1940] 1 KB 155 (Tucker J).
77 Above, 167.
78 Above, 170.
79 Above, 171-172.

Duty to warn of danger

10.20 Where a potential danger in a product is known to the seller there is a duty on their part as sellers to take reasonable care to prevent injury to purchasers, by warning them of the possible danger, of which presumably they would be ignorant[80].

'The general existence of a duty to exercise reasonable care in warning that a product may have dangerous characteristics has long been recognised in English law.'[81]

'On any view, it is clear that there is a very substantial degree of overlap between the principles applicable to failure to warn cases in strict liability, negligence and, indeed, where the claim is based on contract.'[82]

In *Palmer v Palmer, MIB and PZ Products Ltd*[83], even though instructions had not been available to the users of the particular device (which had been provided second-hand), two warnings in instructions for a device which allowed the user to reduce the tension of a car seatbelt for reasons of comfort – that the user should be 'careful to avoid introducing excessive slack' and 'do not introduce excessive slack' – were found to be inadequate and part of the objective evidence both of a defect in the device within the meaning of CPA 1987 and of the manufacturer's negligence, by reason of their failure to specify 'excessive' slack. There was evidence (both in the material accident and generally) that users were able to use the device to loosen seatbelts beyond a safe level[84]. The device in question was first manufactured before the wearing of seatbelts became a legal requirement[85], although the instructions were revised on occasions thereafter[86]. The judge found that the device's 'very purpose is to introduce some slack'[87] and that the instructions (even if they had been available) were evidence of a failure by the manufacturer to notify the user how to set up the device safely[88].

Safety warnings and contradictory marketing in negligence

10.21 As Fairgrieve and Goldberg note, a 'statement which constitutes a mere puff has no legal effect … but the licence to puff is subject to limits' – especially where safety is concerned. 'Thus representations of safety have frequently been held to counteract the effect of an accompanying warning'[89].

An example of the conflict between safety warnings and contradictory marketing is provided by a Canadian negligence case, *Buchan v Ortho Pharmaceutical (Canada)*

---

80 *Clarke and Wife v Army and Navy Co-Operative Society, Ltd* [1902] 1 KB 155, 164 (Collins MR).
81 *Fairgrieve and Goldberg* (3rd edn, 2020), 14.79.
82 Above, 12.09.
83 [2006] EWHC 1284 (QB, HHJ McKenna).
84 Above at [53 – 54].
85 [37].
86 [25].
87 [51].
88 [53].
89 *Fairgrieve and Goldberg* (3rd edn, 2020), 3.02-3.03.

Ltd[90] (1971) which dealt with the duty to warn of danger and the counter-effect of prolonged marketing in favour of a product (a contraceptive pill). The core facts were as follows:

> 'The plaintiff, 23, suffered a stroke in September, 1971, which left her partially paralyzed, shortly after she started taking oral contraceptives manufactured and distributed by the defendant. The oral contraceptives had been prescribed for her by her doctor. Before the stroke, the plaintiff was a non-smoker and in excellent health. The evidence established that the stroke was caused by the oral contraceptives and that the defendant was aware of the risk of stroke. In an action for damages for personal injuries brought by the plaintiff against the defendant, the trial judge gave judgment for the plaintiff. The defendant appealed to the Ontario Court of Appeal.'[91]

The defendant's 'aggressive and professional' marketing (as the defendant described it) of the pill in Canada contrasted with less aggressive marketing of the product by the subsidiary of the same business in the United States. Neither arm of the company gave evidence at trial[92]. The evidence of the defendant's marketing and reliance upon it by the prescribing doctor deprived it of a causation argument that a better warning would not have changed the conduct of the prescribing doctor.

Buchan was a claim pursued in negligence. The principle as to the duty to warn was held to be as follows:

> 'It can now be taken as a legal truism that the duty of reasonable care which lies at the foundation of the law of negligence commonly comprehends a duty to warn of danger, the breach of which will, when it is the cause of injury, give rise to liability… Once a duty to warn is recognized, it is manifest that the warning must be adequate. It should be communicated clearly and understandably in a manner calculated to inform the user of the nature of the risk and the extent of the danger; it should be in terms commensurate with the gravity of the potential hazard, and it should not be neutralized or negated by collateral efforts on the part of the manufacturer. The nature and extent of any given warning will depend on what is reasonable having regard to all the facts and circumstances relevant to the product in question.'[93]

The evidence in *Buchan* included sales material produced by the manufacturer for its salesmen in Canada:

> 'This material was lengthy; it contained detailed 'sales presentations' in which suggested answers were given to questions likely to be asked by doctors. Salesmen were told throughout to stress that Ortho-Novum was a safe, well-proven and effective drug. For instance, in one bulletin, in answer to the question, 'What does Ortho have to say about the estrogen controversy in the British report?', the following appeared:
>
>> No new evidence has been introduced which would substantiate a relationship between estrogen and thrombophlebitis or cancer. All our

---

90   *Buchan v Ortho Pharmaceutical (Canada) Ltd* (54 O.R. (2d) 92, [1986] O.J. No. 2331.
91   Above, headnote.
92   Part V of the judgment.
93   Part III of the judgment.

medical data supports the fact that ORTHO- NOVUM 0.5 mg. is a safe, well-proven, 100% effective product, ideally suited to start your patient on.

In another bulletin in which reference was also made to the British study, the following appeared:

Many doctors will not be impressed with the findings of the British Committee. We are not attempting to convince anyone of its validity. When the doctor expresses no concern or no interest in the British Medical Journal report

SELL ORTHO-NOVUM* Tablets 0.5 mg.

Gentlemen: I cannot emphasize this strongly enough -- IN NO WAY should any strength of ORTHO-NOVUM be considered as 'dangerous'.

ORTHO-NOVUM 2 mg. is still the most widely used oral contraceptive and has been in continuous use in the market place for eight years. It should be remembered that ORTHO- NOVUM 0.5 mg contains exactly the same quantity of estrogen.

OUR SALES STRATEGY IS SOUND!

Make use of this advance information and sell ORTHO-NOVUM 1/ 50 aggressively and professionally.

The sales bulletins made no mention of stroke or other of the more serious thromboembolic complications, nor did they point to evidence of the increased morbidity and mortality in users of oral contraceptives. They appear designed to allay fears raised by the British study and, more generally, to exhort salesmen to pursue aggressive sales tactics emphasizing the safety of Ortho's products and de-emphasizing their potential hazards.

By way of contrast, it appears that at about the same time Ortho U.S. was instructing its sales representatives through sales bulletins of their responsibility to make full disclosure to doctors ...'[94]

On the evidence in the *Buchan* case, the effect of the manufacturer's marketing was to deprive it of an argument as to causation, namely that its marketing had no causative effect and that the doctor receiving the marketing would have prescribed the pills even without it. That submission was rejected on the evidence:

'The doctor's testimony concerning his knowledge of the pill's safety is extensively reproduced in the reasons below and need not be repeated. It is sufficient to observe that he considered these potent drugs to be 'totally' or 'perfectly' safe. In prescribing Ortho-Novum 1/50 for the plaintiff, it was his 'understanding at the time that birth control pills were totally safe and there was no problem that you ought to anticipate as per the various information sources that I had at the time'. The 'information sources' to which the doctor

---

94   Part V of judgment.

referred encompassed, in addition to the RX Bulletin and other medical journals, the material 'constantly' provided to him by Ortho, that is, its file cards, the CPS excerpt[95], its product sheets, its other literature, and, equally, if not more important, the representations made by Ortho's sales representatives about its products. As noted earlier, the doctor considered these representatives to be the best in the business and acknowledged relying in part on them and, no doubt in varying degrees, on the other material supplied by Ortho to substantiate his opinion that oral contraceptives were 'totally safe'. On the basis of that opinion, he confirmed in cross- examination that it was his view that 'there would be no need to unduly upset patients ... by discussing, going into detail with them'.'

'This, patently, is not a case in which the intervening doctor proceeded solely on independently acquired information. Ortho's failure to give physicians a warning commensurate with its actual knowledge of the dangers inherent in its products combined with the efforts of its sales representatives to minimize those dangers and counteract reports of adverse side-effects plainly influenced the doctor's opinion as to the drug's safety and the need to inform patients of the risks. It is, therefore, not unreasonable to conclude, as I infer the trial judge did, that the doctor's failure to disclose the risk of stroke (or, for that matter, any thromboembolic risk) to the plaintiff was contributed to by the inadequacy of Ortho's warnings, devoid as they were of any reference to stroke, and the promotional tactics of its pharmaceutical salesmen. In these circumstances, I cannot agree that there was no causal link between Ortho's breach of the duty to warn and the plaintiff's ingestion of the drug, and, it follows, the doctor's intervention cannot operate to exonerate Ortho from liability for its breach of duty.'[96]

The effect of marketing upon a tort claim relating to an AAEV is as yet untested in British law. Causation is fact-sensitive, and (as noted by Fairgrieve and Goldberg), 'an alleged failure to warn will be causally inoperative if the claimant accepts that he would not have heeded a warning if it had been given'[97]. Although they are not concerned with civil liability, the proposed 'marketing restrictions' of Part 4 of the AV Bill 2023-24 (HL Bill 1) will, if enacted as provisions of the Automated Vehicles Act 2024, form part of the regulatory background.

Direct sales of vehicles by some manufacturers (rather than via dealerships) might reduce the extent to which the intervention of an intermediary might affect causation in a pure negligence case (although *Buchan* illustrates a limitation to the use of intermediaries where they have a role advising the claimant). Questions are likely to arise as to the effect of positive marketing of AAEVs and their systems in

---

95   'The Compendium of Pharmaceuticals and Specialties ('CPS') is published annually by the Canadian Pharmaceutical Association Inc.; it contains a compilation of manufacturers' descriptions of their drugs on the market and serves as a vital source of information for prescribing physicians. Ortho's statement concerning its product in the 1971 CPS, headed 'Ortho-Novum Preparations', omits any mention of cerebral thrombosis or stroke when dealing with 'Adverse Effects'': Part V of judgment.

96   Part VIII of the judgment.

97   *Fairgrieve and Goldberg* (3rd edn, 2020), para 14-115, citing *Chubb Fire Ltd v Vicar of Spalding and others* [2010] EWCA Civ 981; [2010] 2 CLC 277: Vicar failed to prove that, if properly advised by Chubb on the advantages and disadvantages of using a particular type of fire extinguisher (which vandals used to damage his church), he would have acted differently: para 37 to 49.

relation to the duty to warn, including the extent of the effect of such marketing and as to how it would affect any apportionment of liability under CL(C)A 1978 or AEVA 2018, s 5 (see Chapter 9, 'RTA claims').

Continuing duty to warn

10.22 In *E Hobbs (Farms) Ltd v Baxenden Chemical Co Ltd*, Sir Michael Ogden QC sitting as a Deputy High Court Judge held (in an action for negligent misrepresentation and breach of warranty) that a misrepresentation based upon outdated safety information, that insulating foam was 'self-extinguishing', gave rise to a duty to warn which arose after the date of sale and which continued. The manufacturer's duty of care did not cease when the goods were sold and if it realised that an omission to warn past customers about potential injury might result in injury to them it must take reasonable steps to warn them, however lacking in negligence it was at the time the goods were sold.[98]

Fairgrieve and Goldberg also refer to American cases applying the same principle, including cases relating to automotive defects not detected by testing until after sale of the vehicle[99].

No need to warn of an obvious risk

10.23 The notorious example of the lack of need to warn of an obvious risk is the strict liability case of *B v MacDonalds Ltd*, where Field J adopted and summarised Burton J's analysis of the EU PLD 1985 in *A v NBA* including the proposition that 'products that are obviously dangerous (such as a knife) are not defective: the consumer has a free choice whether to expose himself to the risk, but that choice must be an informed choice'[100]. Field J found that:

> 'persons generally expect tea or coffee purchased to be consumed on the premises to be hot... They expect precautions to be taken to guard against this risk but not to the point that they are denied the basic utility of being able to buy hot drinks to be consumed on the premises from a cup with the lid off'[101].

What an 'obvious' risk will be will vary according to the facts of each case. Although a car is itself obviously dangerous if driven at excessive speed or carelessly, that does not release its manufacturer from its duty to its users[102]. Although the point has not been adjudicated, reports of the use of objects and devices to thwart driver attention sensors in ADAS and automated vehicles might raise arguments about 'obvious danger' and the scope of the vehicle manufacturer's duty to warn.[103]

---

98 [1992] 1 Lloyd's Rep 54
99 See *Fairgrieve and Goldberg* (3rd edition, 2020) at 14.120.
100 [2002] EWHC 490 (QB) [73].
101 Above [80].
102 See Cardozo J, in *MacPherson v Buick Motor Company* (1916), above.
103 In November 2022, the website Electrek reported that a manufacturer was building detection of such cheating devices into its system: Electrek article 'Tesla detects Autopilot cheating devices' (25 November 2022).

Causation: once fault proven, claimant not required to identify exact person in the chain who was responsible, or specify what he did wrong

10.24 The principle in *Grant v Australian Knitting Mills Ltd* that, once a fault has been proven:

> 'the appellant is not required to lay his finger on the exact person in all the chain who was responsible, or specify what he did wrong. Negligence is found as a matter of inference from the existence of the defect taken in connection with all the known circumstances'[104]

– has been applied both to negligence and product liability cases[105].

The principle has potential application to machine-learning software, whose 'reasoning' is opaque. This point is discussed in further detail in relation to CPA 1987, below.

Statutory torts other than CPA 1987

10.25 In addition to negligence, statutory torts other than CPA 1987 are available. This is not an exhaustive list. For the purposes of an AAEV claim, the potential statutory torts (other than CPA 1987, which is discussed below) include the following:

The statutory claim in tort under AEVA 2018, s 2 and liable insurer or owner's claim against any other person responsible for the accident under s 5

10.26 AEVA 2018, Part 1 provides a statutory tort[106], releasing the injured victim of a road accident caused by an automated vehicle when driving itself from the burden of mounting an expensive product liability claim against a manufacturer or developer of a complex AV system[107] and allowing instead a claim directly against the insurer or permitted uninsured owner of the AV.

In the AEVA 2018 scheme, other arguments (including as to the defectiveness of the AV or its components) are left to that better-resourced, primarily liable party to pursue in a secondary claim against any other person responsible for the accident (potentially including manufacturer, developer etc) under AEVA 2018, s 5.

See the 'outline' section above for discussion of amendments to AEVA 2018 proposed by the AV Bill 2023-24 (HL Bill 1) affecting the treatment of software.

---

104 [1936] AC 85, 101 (PC, Lord Wright).
105 *Carroll v Fearon, Bent and Dunlop Ltd* [1998] PIQR P6 P416, P421 (CA); and see *Wilkes v DePuy International Ltd* [2016] EWHC 3096, [2018] QB 627, 644-645 [73], discussed in 'CPA 1987', below.
106 AEVA 2018, ss 2 and 6(4).
107 House of Commons Library Briefing Paper 'Automated and Electric Vehicles Act 2018', CBP 8118 (15 August 2018), p 10.

See Chapters 6, 'insurance' and 9, 'RTA claims', for discussion of the AEVA 2018, ss 2 and 5 claims.

The statutory claim in tort under the Employer's Liability (Defective Equipment) Act 1969

10.27 See Chapter 12, 'employer's liability claims', for discussion of EL(DE) A 1969.

The common duty of care under Occupiers Liability Acts 1957 and 1984

10.28 The duties of care upon occupiers of premises 'to his visitors in respect of dangers due to the state of the premises or to things done or omitted to be done on them'[108] under OLA 1957 and 'to persons other than his visitors in respect of any risk of their suffering injury on the premises by reason of any danger due to the state of the premises or to things done or omitted to be done on them'[109] under OLA 1984 also apply to 'any moveable structure, including any vessel, vehicle or aircraft'.[110]

(3) Tort: product liability under CPA 1987

Outline of the scheme for product liability under CPA 1987: original design and current challenge

10.29 The UK product liability scheme stems from European Union law made during the UK's membership of the EU: CPA 1987, Part I 'was enacted for the purpose of making such provision as was necessary in order to comply with the product liability directive [EU PLD 1985[111]] and shall be construed accordingly'[112].

There had been statutes in relation to defective goods before 1987[113]. Under the Consumer Protection Act 1961 s 3(1), an obligation under regulations as to goods or parts for sale made by the Secretary of State under s 2 was made 'a duty which is owed by him to any other person who may be affected by the contravention of or non-compliance with the requirement in question, and a breach of that duty is actionable (subject to the defences and other incidents applying to actions for breach of statutory duty)'. But that was a narrower statutory duty than was required to allow fair redress for defective goods[114].

---

108 OLA 1957 s 1(1), s 2.
109 OLA 1984 s1(1)(a).
110 OLA 1957, s 1(3); OLA 1984, s 1(2) and (9).
111 CPA 1987, s 1(2): 'the Directive of the Council of the European Communities, dated 25th July 1985, (No. 85/374/EEC) on the approximation of the laws, regulations and administrative provisions of the member States concerning liability for defective products'.
112 CPA 1987, s 1(1) (as amended by the Product Safety and Metrology etc (Amendment etc) (EU Exit) Regulations 2019, SI 2019/696, reg 6 and sch 3, under the European Union (Withdrawal) Act 2018 s 8 ('dealing with deficiencies arising from withdrawal'). SI 2019/696 came into force on exit day (31 January 2020 at 11 pm: EU(W)A 2018 s 20(1)): SI 2019/696 reg 1.
113 See *Fairgrieve and Goldberg* (3rd edn, 2020) at p 895, footnote 12.
114 The Law Commission and the Scottish Law Commission 'Liability for Defective Products' (Law Com No 82, Scot Law Com No 45, June 1977), p 6 para 20.

As in negligence[115] American law was influential in relation to the design of the British product liability scheme[116] especially in relation to defects in automobiles[117]. In particular, the 1968 judgment of the Court of Appeals for the Eighth Circuit in *Larsen v General Motors Corporation* established that design features which gave rise to foreseeable risk of injury in the event of an accident were, even if not causative of the accident itself, themselves actionable[118].

The Law Commission of England and Wales and the Scottish Law Commission reported on liability for defective products in 1977, making their own detailed proposals for reform of existing national laws (with which it reported 'widespread dissatisfaction'[119]) and considering two European laws – the Council of Europe's 'Strasbourg Convention on Products Liability in regard to Personal Injury and Death' and the European Commission's 'Proposal for a Council Directive relating to the Approximation of the Laws, Regulations and Administrative Provisions of the Member States concerning Liability for Defective Products'[120]. The Law Commissions found broad consistency between their approach and that of the then European proposals, but noted inconsistencies which concerned them (for example, the apparent expansion of liability beyond commercial producers in the EEC Directive and the proposal to exclude cover for personal injury[121]).

As to the now-controversial 'cut-off' period of ten years which was to be enacted by CPA 1987[122] and whose effect upon software updates now causes concern, the Law Commissions were divided. The Scottish Law Commission accepted 'that there may be certain commercial advantages in releasing some producers from strict liability after a period such as ten years has elapsed from the date when the product was put into circulation', but 'if the introduction of strict liability can be justified, one of its principal justifications must be that liability should subsist for as long as the product can be regarded as defective ... It may be that insurance premiums in respect of such products may be higher if there is no cut-off period, but altogether to deprive an injured person of a right or a remedy in these circumstances seems too high a price to pay'[123]. It regarded ten years as an 'arbitrary' measure of the lifespan of a product, and likely to create difficulties in relation to components[124]. However, the Law Commission of England and Wales was unconcerned about the ten-year longstop which it felt was a fair reflection of the lifespan of a product,

---

115 See, quoted at the head of this chapter, Cardozo J in *MacPherson v Buick Motor Company* (1916), a case cited by the majority of the House of Lords (the predecessor to the UK Supreme Court) in *Donoghue v Stevenson*.

116 See Alistair Clark, 'The Conceptual Basis of Product Liability', The Modern Law Review, Volume 48, Issue 3 (May 1985), 325-339. Clark examined 'recent recommendations for a strict product liability scheme in this country ... in the light of the considerable experience of American product liability law' (p 325).

117 See Ralph Nader, *Unsafe at any Speed: the designed-in dangers of the American Automobile* (Grossman, New York, 1965).

118 391 F 2d 495 at 503 (8th Cir, 1968), quoted by Fairgrieve and Goldberg (3rd 3dn, 2020) at 14.71.

119 The Law Commission and the Scottish Law Commission 'Liability for Defective Products' (Law Com No 82, Scot Law Com No 45, June 1977), p 4 para 13.

120 Above, Appendices A and B.

121 See above, p 44-50.

122 Limitation Act 1980, s 11A(3), inserted by CPA 1987, s 6(6) and Sch 1.

123 The Law Commission and the Scottish Law Commission 'Liability for Defective Products' (Law Com No 82, Scot Law Com No 45, June 1977), p 47-48, para 154-155.

124 Above, p 48, para 157-158.

though its reasons (which imagined cars only as tangible products) emphasise, by contrast, the current difficulty which the longstop creates for software updates to vehicles throughout their lifetime:

> '… the cut-off period of 10 years is not likely to be of much relevance to perishable goods and as for durable goods, such as motor-cars and building materials, the Law Commission [of England and Wales] believe that a cut-off point is needed in fairness to the producers on whom the burden of strict liability must otherwise rest indefinitely.'[125]

CPA 1987 was (as s 1(1) makes clear) a creature of EU law. After Brexit, 'EU-derived domestic legislation, as it has effect in domestic law immediately before IP completion day [31 December 2020 at 11pm], continues to have effect in domestic law on and after IP completion day'[126], including CPA 1987 in an amended form[127]. It is a matter of speculation as to how far UK law will diverge from the EU product liability law in future, but further divergence is possible – not least in the future approach to the actionability across all bases of claim of defects in downloaded software (see the discussion above).

Although inapplicable in Great Britain after Brexit[128], in 2022 the EU proposed a revision to its PLD, in particular to provide 'liability rules that are adapted to the digital world, to ensure a high level of effective consumer protection and a level playing field with legal certainty for all businesses, while avoiding high costs and risks for small and medium-sized businesses (SMEs) and start-ups'[129]. Reforms within the revised EU PLD included the updating of several definitions: of 'product' to include software (art 4(1)), of circumstances relevant to defectiveness to include machine learning types of ability ('the effect on the product of any ability to continue to learn after deployment': art 6(1)(c)) and the possibility of the manufacturer retaining control over the product after the moment that it was placed on the market (art 6(1)(e) and see art 10(2) in relation to software updates)[130].

But the original EU PLD 1985, upon which CPA 1987 is still based, is outdated. Its design goes back as far as 1970, when the Council of Europe's committee of experts first met[131]. It was drafted in a pre-worldwide web and pre-WiFi world[132],

---

125 Above, p 47, para 151.
126 EU(W)A 2018, s 2 ('saving for EU-derived domestic legislation').
127 By SI 2019/696, above.
128 As the European Communities Act 1972 was repealed on exit day, 31 January 2020 at 11 pm (EU(W)A 2018 s 1, 20(1)), and the 2022 EU revised PLD was not operative immediately before IP completion day [31 December 2020 at 11pm: European Union (Withdrawal Agreement) Act 2020 s 39(1)]: EU(W)A 2018 s 3(1).
129 EU explanatory memorandum [1.1, 'context of the proposal'] to European Commission, Proposal for a Directive of the European Parliament and of the Council on liability for defective products, COM(2022) 495 final 2022/0302 (COD) (28 September 2022).
130 See Daniel West 'The Road Ahead: could UK insurers' claims against automated vehicle manufacturers benefit from a regime akin to the new EU Product Liability Directive?', AEVlaw.com (24 January 2023)
131 The Law Commission and the Scottish Law Commission 'Liability for Defective Products' (Law Com No 82, Scot Law Com No 45, June 1977), p 2 para 6.
132 Worldwide web (www) software was invented in 1989 and released in 1993; WiFi was coined as a term in 1999. See the 'computers, 1989 to 2004' section of the 'History' appendix to this book.

where an 'Internet of Things'[133] operating by intangible, downloaded software was not contemplated. Two eminent European legal writers concluded in 2018 (before the 2022 revision to the EU PLD) that:

'the current product liability regime has a rather limited role to play for autonomous vehicles as, generally speaking, it is limited to defects or risks that already existed prior to production and, more particularly, those that were scientifically known to or detectable for the producer, while also its scope of protection is limited (*e.g.* not all property damage is recoverable, the 500 Euro threshold, and, in some countries, monetary caps for compensation).'

…

'… the practical relevance of the PLD [for autonomous vehicles] will be limited: it will always, to some degree, 'compete' with the applicable national liability rules for motor vehicles, if these are risk based. In some countries, the latter rules are much more advantageous to traffic victims than product liability.'[134]

The product liability scheme (even in its revised 2022 form) retains the ten-year longstop limitation period on a claim, from the time of supply of the product within the meaning of CPA 1987, s 4[135]. Although this has been revised in EU PLD 2022, art 14 to include the trigger date of 'substantial modification … outside the original manufacturer's control' of a product already placed on the market under EU PLD 2022 art 7(4), even that revised EU right of action appears only to apply against the modifier of the product, who might lack the financial or insurance resources of the original manufacturer to be an attractive defendant to a claim. As noted above, the justification for *any* longstop on product liability had been opposed – presciently in relation to the current problem of software updates – by the Scottish Law Commission in 1977[136].

In May 2021 (so before the EU revised PLD of 2022), a House of Commons Library Briefing Paper, 'Brexit: UK consumer protection law' made this prediction as to UK divergence with EU consumer law policy:

'Retained EU law remains in force in the UK indefinitely, unless or until the Government decides to repeal or amend it. It is generally thought that amending UK consumer law will not be a priority for the Government in the short term. This is because the UK regime has already been overhauled, consolidating consumer rights and remedies in the CRA 2015. In addition, most of the EU-derived provisions of consumer law are long-standing, and generally accepted as establishing 'a fair balance' between the interests

---

133 'The Internet of Things describes a world in which everyday objects are connected to a network so that data can be shared … the introduction of Internet of Things technologies is likely to create new regulatory challenges in some areas of government policy. For example, the introduction of autonomous vehicles may significantly reduce road traffic incidents, but is unlikely to eliminate them completely.' Government Office for Science 'The Internet of Things: making the most of the Second Digital Revolution. A report by the UK Government Chief Scientific Adviser' (December 2014) p 6, 9.
134 Engelhard and de Bruin, p 78, 79.
135 Limitation Act 1980, s 11A(3), inserted by CPA 1987, s 6(6) and Sch 1.
136 The Law Commission and the Scottish Law Commission 'Liability for Defective Products' (Law Com No 82, Scot Law Com No 45, June 1977), p 47-49, para 154-160.

of consumers and traders. That said there is some impetus to modernise certain aspects of the UK's consumer regime, to address the needs of a digital society... Looking to the future it is likely that the UK's policy on consumer protection will diverge from the EU's position.'[137]

In November 2021, the government's Office for Product Safety & Standards (OPSS) published its response to evidence gathered during its UK Product Safety Review. On the issue of the 'effectiveness of the current framework for new products and technologies', OPSS recorded:

'a shared view across stakeholder groups that clarity was needed in some areas. This included whether the definition of 'product' includes software, the requirements for software updates, and where liability lies... Some respondents, particularly law firms, also highlighted that the increasing use of software and emerging technologies in consumer products could make them more complex and more challenging for consumers to understand and that this could make it difficult to determine who is responsible when something goes wrong. They flagged that the current product liability regime may not be adequate for more sophisticated products. For example, when a product's behaviour is driven by opaque data models and algorithms, or if it evolves or makes partially autonomous decisions based on learning (often described as 'Artificial Intelligence (AI)'). Law firms supported a liability regime that supports innovation but expressed some concern about whether the current regime would adequately enable consumers to make a claim if they were harmed by products that relied on more sophisticated technology. OPSS is continuing to work with relevant Government Departments and bodies to understand the impact of AI on product safety and liability.'[138]

– and in relation to 'duration of manufacturer liability':

'Some law firms, consumer groups and enforcement authorities stated that the 10-year limitation for consumers to seek redress should be extended as sometimes harms could appear many years later.'[139]

Among the Law Commissions' recommendations on automated vehicle law in January 2022 was a wholesale reconsideration of product liability law to take account of emerging technologies[140].

The provisions of CPA 1987, Part I

10.30   CPA 1987, s 1 ('purpose and construction of Part I' sets out key definitions, including 'product' ('any goods or electricity and (subject to subsection (3) below) includes a product which is comprised in another product, whether by virtue of being a component part or raw material or otherwise'), 'producer' (for present

---

137 House of Commons Library Briefing Paper 'Brexit: UK consumer protection law' by Lorraine Conway, Briefing Paper Number 9126 (21 May 2021), p 17-18, 22.
138 Government website 'Consultation Outcome. UK Product Safety Review: call for evidence' (25 November 2021) p 16.
139 Above, p 18.
140 Law Commission of England and Wales, Scottish Law Commission 'Automated Vehicles: joint report' (Law Com No 404, Scot Law Com No 258, January 2022), recommendation 71.

purposes 'the person who manufactured' a product, though see also s 1(2)(b) and (c)), and 'component parts' (as to the latter, 'a person who supplies any product in which products are comprised, whether by virtue of being component parts or raw materials or otherwise, shall not be treated by reason only of his supply of that product as supplying any of the products so comprised', s 1(3)).

CPA 1987, s 2 sets out the 'liability for defective products'. In its entirety, it provides as follows. As per s 2(6), it does not extinguish any liability arising outside CPA 1987, Part I, so leaves open the other legal bases of claim categorised above (contract and tort):

'(1) Subject to the following provisions of this Part, where any damage is caused wholly or partly by a defect in a product, every person to whom subsection (2) below applies shall be liable for the damage.

(2) This subsection applies to—

(a) the producer of the product;

(b) any person who, by putting his name on the product or using a trade mark or other distinguishing mark in relation to the product, has held himself out to be the producer of the product;

(c) any person who has imported the product into the United Kingdom in order, in the course of any business of his, to supply it to another.

(3) Subject as aforesaid, where any damage is caused wholly or partly by a defect in a product, any person who supplied the product (whether to the person who suffered the damage, to the producer of any product in which the product in question is comprised or to any other person) shall be liable for the damage if –

(a) the person who suffered the damage requests the supplier to identify one or more of the persons (whether still in existence or not) to whom subsection (2) above applies in relation to the product;

(b) that request is made within a reasonable period after the damage occurs and at a time when it is not reasonably practicable for the person making the request to identify all those persons; and

(c) the supplier fails, within a reasonable period after receiving the request, either to comply with the request or to identify the person who supplied the product to him.

[...]

(5) Where two or more persons are liable by virtue of this Part for the same damage, their liability shall be joint and several.

(6) This section shall be without prejudice to any liability arising otherwise than by virtue of this Part.'

(The Law Commissions' 'general approach to the imposition of strict liability in respect of defective products' in their 1977 report was 'that it should be channelled to the producer since he is the person best able to regulate the quality of the product'[141]. Fairgrieve and Goldberg note that CPA 1987, s 2(3) enhances this

---

141 The Law Commission and the Scottish Law Commission 'Liability for Defective Products' (Law Com No 82, Scot Law Com No 45, June 1977), p 29, para 98.

'channelling' process, 'by the provisional nature of the liability attaching to mere suppliers since they will often, but by no means invariably, have records which permit them to identify a primary producer'[142]; 'In many cases the most obvious choice will be the producer of the finished product since they will be readily identifiable and carry appropriate insurance cover'[143]; If that producer then has recourse against another, then it 'may then benefit from the standard provisions for obtaining contribution and recourse or indemnity contained in the Civil Liability Contribution Act 1978'[144].)

CPA 1987, s 3 defines 'defect':

'(1) Subject to the following provisions of this section, there is a defect in a product for the purposes of this Part if the safety of the product is not such as persons generally are entitled to expect; and for those purposes *'safety'*, in relation to a product, shall include safety with respect to products comprised in that product and safety in the context of risks of damage to property, as well as in the context of risks of death or personal injury.

(2) In determining for the purposes of subsection (1) above what persons generally are entitled to expect in relation to a product all the circumstances shall be taken into account, including—

(a) the manner in which, and purposes for which, the product has been marketed, its get-up, the use of any mark in relation to the product and any instructions for, or warnings with respect to, doing or refraining from doing anything with or in relation to the product;

(b) what might reasonably be expected to be done with or in relation to the product; and

(c) the time when the product was supplied by its producer to another;

and nothing in this section shall require a defect to be inferred from the fact alone that the safety of a product which is supplied after that time is greater than the safety of the product in question.'

(Alistair Clark wrote in 1985 that 'at the very core of a product liability regime' is 'the problem of defining defectiveness', which 'has exercised the minds of legal scholars perhaps more than any other aspect of product liability law'[145]. The difficulty of the issue is illustrated by the disagreement between the main High Court cases on the point – on the one hand *A v NBA* (2003) and on the other *Wilkes v DePuy* (2016), followed in *Gee v DePuy* (2018) – discussed below.)

CPA 1987, s 4 sets out defences:

'(1) In any civil proceedings by virtue of this Part against any person ('the person proceeded against') in respect of a defect in a product it shall be a defence for him to show –

---

142 *Fairgrieve and Goldberg* (3ʳᵈ edn, 2020), 8.03.
143 Above, 8.73.
144 Above, 8.73. And see Chapter 19 of this book, 'third party claims for contribution or indemnity'.
145 Clark, 'The Conceptual Basis of Product Liability', The Modern Law Review, Volume 48, Issue 3 (May 1985), 325-339.

    (a) that the defect is attributable to compliance with any requirement imposed by or under any enactment or with any retained EU obligation; or

    (b) that the person proceeded against did not at any time supply the product to another; or

    (c) that the following conditions are satisfied, that is to say—

        (i) that the only supply of the product to another by the person proceeded against was otherwise than in the course of a business of that person's; and

        (ii) that section 2(2) above does not apply to that person or applies to him by virtue only of things done otherwise than with a view to profit; or

    (d) that the defect did not exist in the product at the relevant time; or

    (e) that the state of scientific and technical knowledge at the relevant time was not such that a producer of products of the same description as the product in question might be expected to have discovered the defect if it had existed in his products while they were under his control; or

    (f) that the defect—

        (i) constituted a defect in a product ('the subsequent product') in which the product in question had been comprised; and

        (ii) was wholly attributable to the design of the subsequent product or to compliance by the producer of the product in question with instructions given by the producer of the subsequent product.

(2) In this section *'the relevant time'*, in relation to electricity, means the time at which it was generated, being a time before it was transmitted or distributed, and in relation to any other product, means—

    (a) if the person proceeded against is a person to whom subsection (2) of section 2 above applies in relation to the product, the time when he supplied the product to another;

    (b) if that subsection does not apply to that person in relation to the product, the time when the product was last supplied by a person to whom that subsection does apply in relation to the product.'

CPA 1987, s 5 provides for 'damage giving rise to liability' and, in particular, sets out the damage for which there is *not* liability under CPA 1987:

    '(1) Subject to the following provisions of this section, in this Part *'damage'* means death or personal injury or any loss of or damage to any property (including land).

    (2) A person shall not be liable under section 2 above in respect of any defect in a product for the loss of or any damage to the product itself or for the loss of or any damage to the whole or any part of any product which has been supplied with the product in question comprised in it.

    (3) A person shall not be liable under section 2 above for any loss of or damage to any property which, at the time it is lost or damaged, is not—

        (a) of a description of property ordinarily intended for private use, occupation or consumption; and

(b) intended by the person suffering the loss or damage mainly for his own private use, occupation or consumption.

(4) No damages shall be awarded to any person by virtue of this Part in respect of any loss of or damage to any property if the amount which would fall to be so awarded to that person, apart from this subsection and any liability for interest, does not exceed £275.

(5) In determining for the purposes of this Part who has suffered any loss of or damage to property and when any such loss or damage occurred, the loss or damage shall be regarded as having occurred at the earliest time at which a person with an interest in the property had knowledge of the material facts about the loss or damage.

(6) For the purposes of subsection (5) above the material facts about any loss of or damage to any property are such facts about the loss or damage as would lead a reasonable person with an interest in the property to consider the loss or damage sufficiently serious to justify his instituting proceedings for damages against a defendant who did not dispute liability and was able to satisfy a judgment.

(7) For the purposes of subsection (5) above a person's knowledge includes knowledge which he might reasonably have been expected to acquire—

(a) from facts observable or ascertainable by him; or

(b) from facts ascertainable by him with the help of appropriate expert advice which it is reasonable for him to seek;

but a person shall not be taken by virtue of this subsection to have knowledge of a fact ascertainable by him only with the help of expert advice unless he has failed to take all reasonable steps to obtain (and, where appropriate, to act on) that advice.

(8) Subsections (5) to (7) above shall not extend to Scotland.'

CPA 1987, s 6 ('application of certain enactments') includes provision for the application of the Law Reform (Contributory Negligence) Act 1945[146] and provides that liability under CPA 1987, Part I is to be treated as liability in tort[147].

CPA 1987 s 7 prohibits exclusion or limitation of the CPA 1987, Part I liability 'by any contract term, by any notice or by any other provision'.

CPA 1987, s 9 provides that CPA 1987, Part I applies to the Crown to the extent that it is made liable in tort or in reparation under the Crown Proceedings Act 1947, as that Act has effect from time to time.

Within Part V ('miscellaneous and supplemental'), CPA 1987, s 41(1) provides as follows:

'41. Civil proceedings.

(1) An obligation imposed by safety regulations shall be a duty owed to any person who may be affected by a contravention of the obligation and,

---

146 CPA 1987, s 6(4).
147 CPA 1987, s 6(7).

subject to any provision to the contrary in the regulations and to the defences and other incidents applying to actions for breach of statutory duty, a contravention of any such obligation shall be actionable accordingly.

(2) This Act shall not be construed as conferring any other right of action in civil proceedings, apart from the right conferred by virtue of Part I of this Act, in respect of any loss or damage suffered in consequence of a contravention of a safety provision.

(3) Subject to any provision to the contrary in the agreement itself, an agreement shall not be void or unenforceable by reason only of a contravention of a safety provision.

(4) Liability by virtue of subsection (1) above shall not be limited or excluded by any contract term, by any notice or (subject to the power contained in subsection (1) above to limit or exclude it in safety regulations) by any other provision.

(5) Nothing in subsection (1) above shall prejudice the operation of section 12 of the Nuclear Installations Act 1965 (rights to compensation for certain breaches of duties confined to rights under that Act).

(6) In this section *'damage'* includes personal injury and death.'

'Safety regulations' means regulations under CPA 1987, s 11[148], which empowers the Secretary of State to:

'(1) ... make such provision as he considers appropriate for the purpose of securing—

(a) that goods to which this section applies are safe;

(b) that goods to which this section applies which are unsafe, or would be unsafe in the hands of persons of a particular description, are not made available to persons generally or, as the case may be, to persons of that description; and

(c) that appropriate information is, and inappropriate information is not, provided in relation to goods to which this section applies.

(2) Without prejudice to the generality of subsection (1) above, safety regulations may contain provision—

(a) with respect to the composition or contents, design, construction, finish or packing of goods to which this section applies, with respect to standards for such goods and with respect to other matters relating to such goods;

(b) with respect to the giving, refusal, alteration or cancellation of approvals of such goods, of descriptions of such goods or of standards for such goods;

(c) with respect to the conditions that may be attached to any approval given under the regulations; ...'[149]

---

148 CPA 1987, s 45(1) ('interpretation').
149 CPA 1987, s 11(1) and (2)(a) to (c).

Regulations made under CPA 1987, s 11 relating to motor vehicles include the Motor Vehicle Tyres (Safety) Regulations 1994[150] and the Road Vehicles (Brake Linings Safety) Regulations 1999[151].

Also within Part V, CPA 1987, s 46 ('meaning of supply') includes the following provisions relating to the supply of vehicles in particular circumstances, disqualifying those circumstances from the protection of the Act:

'(8) Where any goods have at any time been supplied by being hired out or lent to any person, neither a continuation or renewal of the hire or loan (whether on the same or different terms) nor any transaction for the transfer after that time of any interest in the goods to the person to whom they were hired or lent shall be treated for the purposes of this Act as a further supply of the goods to that person.

(9) A ship, aircraft or motor vehicle shall not be treated for the purposes of this Act as supplied to any person by reason only that services consisting in the carriage of goods or passengers in that ship, aircraft or vehicle, or in its use for any other purpose, are provided to that person in pursuance of an agreement relating to the use of the ship, aircraft or vehicle for a particular period or for particular voyages, flights or journeys.'

CPA 1987 pre-dates the worldwide web software which enabled mass use of the internet[152]. As Engelhard and de Bruin have noted, it might not be the strongest of the potential legal bases of claim in an AAEV case:

'the current product liability regime has a rather limited role to play for autonomous vehicles as, generally speaking, it is limited to defects or risks that already existed prior to production and, more particularly, those that were scientifically known to or detectable for the producer, ...'[153]

However, such are the gaps in the available bases of claim for current technologies (especially the lack of civil remedy for downloaded software outside business to consumer contracts covered by CRA 2015) that the suitability of CPA 1987 to an AAEV claim should be considered.

How have the courts defined 'defect' in CPA 1987?

10.31   As the quotation from the judgment of Hickinbottom J in *Wilkes v Depuy International Ltd* (2016) at the head of this chapter shows, the expectation of a body of case law defining 'defect' across a range of circumstances has not been realised.

The three leading cases on the point relate to medical products (blood products and metal hip replacements). In those cases, there is a clear change of approach to the definition of 'defect', between the first case – *A and others v National Blood Authority and another* (2001, the judgment relating to 114 claims of Hepatitis C infection via

---

150 SI 1994/3117 (as amended).
151 SI 1999/2978 (as amended).
152 Worldwide web (www) software was developed in 1989 and released in 1993. See the 'computers, 1989 to 2004' section of the 'History' appendix to this book.
153 Engelhard and de Bruin, p 78.

blood transfusions)[154] – and the two metal hip replacement cases – *Wilkes v DePuy International Ltd* (2016, in which the claim under CPA 1987 was determined as a preliminary issue)[155] and *Gee v DePuy International Ltd* (the Pinnacle Metal on Metal Hips Group Litigation, 2018)[156].

The detail of those cases and of the definition will not be explored comprehensively here[157], so the points are summarised.

First, there were significant differences in the circumstances of the judgments themselves – *A v NBA* was the first exploration of the EU PLD 1985 in detail and considered the terms of the Directive in preference to those of the 1987 Act, as there were then EU law compliance questions as to the latter, whereas *Wilkes v DePuy* examined the terms of the CPA 1987, on the basis that it had not been suggested that there had been any material failure to implement the Directive[158]. *A v NBA* did not work mainly from industry standards and regulation as the particular risk (of Hepatitis C) had been unknown, whereas *Wilkes* (and subsequently *Gee*) worked from a full stock of standards and regulation of the hip replacements, and therefore of evidence of design which took those standards and rules into account. As Hickinbottom J noted of the law and academic writing surrounding 'defect', 'whilst some of the mountains in the distance are formidable, this claim does not require us to climb them all; and some of the foothills are relatively gentle'[159].

Secondly – and against that background – the detail of the *A v NBA* and *Wilkes* judgments differ. *A v NBA* is a highly detailed and lengthy judgment – largely because it deals with issues of purposive interpretation. *A v NBA* formed new legal concepts – in particular that of 'standard' and 'non-standard' products – either of which could (on the analysis in that case) be defective. It ranged widely, including brief consideration of how a 'new', 'imaginary', 'not a familiar or usual', 'pioneering' [160] product might be treated within that 'standard/non-standard' taxonomy.

Thirdly, *Wilkes* (and subsequently *Gee*, following *Wilkes*) explicitly disagrees with the *A v NBA* approach in several respects. In the opinion of the court in *Wilkes*:

'... all medicines carry risks as well as provide benefits to the patients. No medicine is 100% safe, and all medicines have side effects.'[161] '... safety is inherently and necessarily a relative concept... no medicinal product, if effective, can be absolutely safe.'[162]

The *A v NBA* approach whereby "The first step must be to identify the harmful characteristic which caused the injury' ... is self-evidently circular: proof of a causal connection between defect and damage cannot rationally,

---

154 [2001] All ER 289 (QB).
155 [2016] EWHC 3096, [2018] QB 627 (Hickinbottom J, as he then was).
156 [2018] EWHC 1208 (QB, Andrews J, as she then was).
157 See also eg. Fairgrieve and Goldberg (3rd edn, 2020) chapter 10.
158 *Wilkes v DePuy*, 640 [53].
159 642 [62].
160 *A v NBA* at 311 [31], 314 [33], 327 [50] and 340-341 [71]. Why the term 'scrid' was coined in submissions for such a novel product is not explained in the judgment.
161 *Wilkes v DePuy*, 631-632 [14], quoting Charles Gibson KC, Geraint Webb KC and James Purnell in *Powers & Barton, Clinical Negligence* (5th edn, 2015).
162 642 [65].

or even conceptually, be attempted without ascertainment of whether there is a defect, and, if so what that defect might be.'[163]

The element of the statutory tort that 'the safety of the product is not such as persons generally are entitled to expect' (CPA 1987 s 3(1)) is to be assessed objectively, as the phrase 'are entitled to' implies. 'In *A v NBA* the parties had agreed that the question raised by the definition of 'defect' under the Directive and Act concerned the 'legitimate expectation' of persons generally; a formulation to which Burton J assented … in considering whether a product suffered from a defect, the court must assess the appropriate level of safety, exercising its judgment, and taking into account the information and the circumstances before it, whether or not an actual or notional patient or patients, or indeed other members of the public, would in fact have considered each of those factors and all of that information.'[164]

'… whilst over time cases may indicate which characteristics may be relevant in particular sets of circumstances … any attempt at formal rigid categorisation of products for these purposes is in conflict with the inherent flexibility of the Directive, and is likely to be both difficult and unwise. The issue raised by the Act in terms of defect is necessarily one of open-textured judgment, untrammelled by any rigid rules outside the few that appear in the Act itself. … it would be wrong for domestic law to distort the balance of risk-bearing between producers and consumers of products set by the Directive… Like other such questions raised in the law, on the particular facts of a specific case, the assessment may be difficult in practice; but it is conceptually simple. In my view, the courts should guard against either over-complicating, or over-analysing, the exercise.'[165]

'… the practicability of producing a product of risk-benefit equivalence must therefore potentially be a relevant circumstance in the assessment of a product's safety… cost too must potentially be relevant.'[166]

Fourthly, the difference between *A v NBA* on the one hand and *Wilkes* and *Gee* on the other is also of outcome. *A v NBA* was a success for the claimants, on the basis of a strict liability based upon legitimate expectation; the claims in *Wilkes* and *Gee* were dismissed, on the basis of objective examination of whether or not the conditions of the strict liability were fulfilled. *Wilkes* acknowledges and is loyal to the policy behind EU PLD 1985, the source of CPA 1987: 'the Directive is not driven solely by those interests [of protection of the interests of consumers]: its aim is, rather, to 'solving the problem, peculiar to our age of increasing technicality, of a fair apportionment of the risks inherent in modern technological production…'[167]. As Fairgrieve and Goldberg note:

'The shift towards enhanced consumer protection through the legitimate expectations test in *A v National Blood Authority* was emphatically rejected

---

163 641 [58].
164 644 [71-72].
165 646 [79].
166 646-647 [82-83].
167 640 [54].

by Hickinbottom J in the landmark decision of *Wilkes v DePuy International Ltd.*'[168]

Fifthly, however, *Wilkes* also acknowledged points that might assist a CPA 1987 claimant:

'although a claimant must prove causation in the sense of showing a causal link between the defect and damage, and it may be helpful to one side or another to show the cause of the lack of safety that amounts to defect, a claimant is not required to prove the cause of that lack of safety or why the product failed: see, eg, *Ide v ATB Sales Ltd* [2009] RTR 8, paras 19-22, per Thomas LJ. The issue as to the degree of specificity with which the defect (ie lack of safety) has to be described and proved (which has been the subject of considerable academic debate, on the basis of such cases as *Richardson v LRC Products Ltd* [2000] PIQR P164 which, on one reading, suggest that considerable specificity might be required) is not in issue in this claim, and therefore I need say little about it; but one can imagine a pharmaceutical product that is highly beneficial to most patients but, in a minority, causes death or serious injury, for a reason unascertained and unascertainable, may nevertheless be held to lack the appropriate level of safety for the Act, and therefore be defective.'[169]

'In determining the level of safety which the public is entitled to expect in this sense, section 3 of the Act, directly reflecting article 6 of the Directive, requires 'all the circumstances' to be taken into account, 'including' three specific matters. 'All the circumstances' must mean 'all relevant circumstances': there can be no place for a requirement to consider the irrelevant, nor any basis for demanding less than all relevant circumstances be taken into account. The circumstances which are relevant in a particular case is itself a matter of law; but it is to be noted that neither the Directive nor the Act imposes any restriction on the considerations that may be taken into account. The three specific matters set out in section 3(2) are circumstances which must be considered ('shall be taken into account'); but they are clearly not intended to be an exhaustive list of relevant circumstances, nor are they such that any other circumstance, to be relevant, must be shown to be *eiusdem generis*[170]... 'the open-textured character of the prescribed safety standard provides the court with a very considerable degree of flexibility in relation to the matters to which it can properly have regard''[171]

So the current approach to finding a 'defect' proven in a CPA 1987 claim is a broad, objective approach, taking into account all the circumstances including the specified circumstances in s 3(2) (which include marketing, at 3(2)(a)) but without limiting other relevant circumstances, including guidance in standards and applicable regulations[172] and considerations such as risk and cost.

---

168 *Fairgrieve and Goldberg* (3rd end, 2020), 10.64.
169 *Wilkes v DePuy*, 644-645 [73].
170 'Of the same kind'.
171 *Wilkes v DePuy*, 645 [76-77, 78].
172 649-650 [97-98]. And see *Gee v DePuy* [170-178] ('Legally Relevant Circumstances', 'Regulations and Standards'), extracts from which are quoted in chapter 2, 'vehicle specifications'.

Observations in A v NBA on adjudicating 'defect' in cases involving new or pioneering technologies

10.32   Although *A v NBA* has lately not been followed by other judges of the High Court (as Hickinbottom J and Andrews J then were, when deciding *Wilkes* and *Gee*), an aspect of the judgment is that Burton J commented upon the evidence that might be relevant to the issue of 'defect' in a 'new', 'imaginary', 'not a familiar or usual' or 'pioneering' [173] product. That this was considered within the approaches to 'legitimate expectation' and to the 'standard/non-standard' taxonomy, which the High Court in *Wilkes* and *Gee* later rejected, does not necessarily deprive those comments of force.

The point arose first in *A v NBA* within the account of the common ground between the parties, including the following:

'... (iv) The question to be resolved is the safety or the degree or level of safety or safeness which persons generally are entitled to expect. The test is not that of an absolute level of safety, nor an absolute liability for any injury caused by the harmful characteristic. (v) In the assessment of that question the expectation is that of persons generally, or the public at large. (vi) The safety is not what is actually expected by the public at large, but what they are entitled to expect ... (vii) The court decides what the public is entitled to expect: Dr Harald Bartl in *Produkthaftung nach neuem EG-Recht* (1989) described the judge (as translated from the German) as 'an informed representative of the public at large' ... Such objectively assessed legitimate expectation may accord with actual expectation; but it may be more than the public actually expects, thus imposing a higher standard of safety, or it may be less than the public actually expects. Alternatively the public may have no actual expectation – eg in relation to a new product – the word coined in argument for such an imaginary product was a 'scrid'.'[174]

Burton J went on to describe the likely need for evidence in relation to an unfamiliar technology:

'Article 6[175] must then be considered against the background of this summary of the issues. In the establishment of the level of safety, art 6 provides that the court (on behalf of the public at large) takes into account all circumstances, including the following. (i) Presentation, ie the way in which the product is presented, eg warnings and price. As set out above, the expanded wording of s 3(2)(a) of the CPA is helpful. (ii) The use to which the product could reasonably be expected to be put, eg: (a) if the product is not a familiar or usual one, such as a scrid, it will be necessary to find out what its expected or foreseeable use is; ...'[176]

---

173   *A v NBA* at 311 [31], 314 [33], 327 [50] and 340-341 [71]. Why the term 'scrid' was coined in argument for such a novel product is not explained in the judgment.

174   311 [31].

175   EU PLD 1985 art 6 (from which CPA 1987 s 3 is derived): '1. A product is defective when it does not provide the safety which a person is entitled to expect, taking all circumstances into account, including: (a) the presentation of the product; (b) the use to which it could reasonably be expected that the product would be put; (c) the time when the product was put into circulation. 2. A product shall not be considered defective for the sole reason that a better product is subsequently put into circulation.'

176   *A v NBA*, 313-314 [33].

In particular, Burton J envisaged the possible need for expert evidence:

'If a standard product is unsafe, it is likely to be so as a result of alleged error in design, or at any rate as a result of an allegedly flawed system. The harmful characteristic must be identified, if necessary with the assistance of experts. The question of presentation/time/circumstances of supply/social acceptability etc will arise as above. The sole question will be safety for the foreseeable use. If there are any comparable products on the market, then it will obviously be relevant to compare the offending product with those other products, so as to identify, compare and contrast the relevant features. There will obviously need to be a full understanding of how the product works – particularly if it is a new product, such as a scrid, so as to assess its safety for such use.'[177]

There are many standards relating to automated vehicles but (as at the time of writing) few that could be regarded as comprehensive or final[178]. Regulation of automated vehicles is, as at the time of writing, a work in progress (including the AV Bill 2023–24 (HL Bill 1))[179]. The effect of the judgment of Andrews J in *Gee v DePuy* insofar as it relates to standards and regulation is that compliance is relevant but not necessarily conclusive, in particular because

'The level of safety that the public is entitled to expect may be lower than a particular safety standard … [or] it may be higher, for example if the product complied in all material respects with particular safety features required by the regulatory regime, but there was some additional feature that made it unsafe'[180]

Does CPA 1987, s 4(1)(d) allow a producer a defence in relation to defects in downloaded updates to software supplied with goods?

10.33 CPA 1987, s 4(1)(d) appears to afford the producer a defence in relation to such defects if:

- (as is now common practice) they are downloaded software updates, as the definition of 'product' as 'goods'[181] still requires tangibility (cf the CJEU judgment in *Computer Associates UK Ltd*) and, even but for that point:

- if (as is again commonplace) software updates are provided on occasions after supply of the product (the vehicle). The defence at CPA 1987, s 4(1)(d) seems to exclude any defect that did not exist at the time of supply of the product.

In retrospect, such a wide defence to producers seems artificial, but its availability seems to be a relic of the pre-worldwide web situation in which EU PLD 1985 and

---

177 340-341 [71].
178 The BSI standards for connected and autonomous vehicles are all (as at the time of writing) in PAS (publicly acknowledged specification) form. 'The PAS approach offers an effective means of quickly introducing standardization in such cases, and for testing the value or validity of a particular approach or methodology. It can also serve as the basis for subsequent development towards more formal standardization at UK, European or international level.' BSI 'Principles of PAS Standardization' (PAS 0:2012), p 4.
179 See other chapters, eg. Chapter 2, 'vehicle specifications'.
180 *Gee v DePuy* [170-178] ('Legally Relevant Circumstances', 'Regulations and Standards').
181 See CPA 1987 s 1 and 46.

CPA 1987 were designed and enacted[182]. There is no provision in CPA 1987 (eg. in s 46, 'meaning of supply') which offers a solution, such as the 'digital content' approach applied to business to consumer contracts by CRA 2015. How a court might approach such a legal anachronism in a CPA 1987 case is uncertain (see Gloster LJ's concern as to the artificial effect of the Court of Appeal's judgment in the *Computer Associates UK Ltd* case in 2018). But the exception is consistent with the limitation to EU PLD 1985 'to defects or risks that already existed prior to production'[183], as well as with the 'development risks/discoverability' and 'state of the art' defences discussed below. And see the discussion of the 'problem of the legal character of downloaded software', above.

Does the 'state of scientific knowledge' defence under CPA 1987, s 4(1)(e) apply to AAEV claims brought under CPA 1987?

10.34   Engelhard and de Bruin, writing about the EU PLD 1985, opine that 'the current product liability regime has a rather limited role to play for autonomous vehicles as, generally speaking, it is limited to defects or risks that already existed prior to production and, more particularly, those that were scientifically known to or detectable for the producer …'[184]

This raises the issue of the relevance of the 'state of scientific knowledge' defence under CPA 1987, s 4(1)(e) (otherwise known as the 'development risks' or 'discoverability' defence[185]) to AAEV claims.

Lucy McCormick's view is that the defence is 'highly relevant', pointing to a 2015 product recall which resulted from a hack by third parties of controls from outside a particular manufacturer's vehicle:

'Had such a hack been carried out maliciously and given rise to a collision, a manufacturer would need to try to show in its defence that it would not have been possible to envisage and counter the nature of the hacking at the time. For this reason, manufacturers would be well advised to keep detailed records of their state of knowledge during the development process.'[186]

Lucy McCormick also notes, however, the effect of the 'state of the art' defence implicit in the phrase at the end of CPA 1987, s 3, 'nothing in this section shall require a defect to be inferred from the fact alone that the safety of a product which is supplied after that time is greater than the safety of the product in question':

'This provides a certain degree of protection to older products where the next generation is safer. The 'development risks defence' seeks to protect defendants from liability for risks which could not have been foreseen at the time of supply, whereas the 'state of the art defence' ensures there is no liability simply because standards have improved since the product was first supplied.'[187]

---

182 See the 'computers, 1989 to 2004' section of the 'History' appendix to this book.
183 Engelhard and de Bruin p 78.
184 As above.
185 *A v NBA*, 325-326 [48].
186 Chapter 4, 'product liability' in Channon, McCormick and Noussia, *The Law and Autonomous Vehicles* (Routledge, 2019), p 42, 4.27.
187 Above, 4.28.

In relation to testing the 'foreseeability' of risks, however, Lucy McCormick points out a difficulty of proof in relation to machine-learning software, namely its opacity[188]. Professor Michael Wooldridge (head of computer science at Oxford University) has explained opacity as follows:

'The expertise that a neural network has captured is embedded in the numeric weights associated with the links between neurons, and, as yet, we have no way of getting at or interpreting this knowledge … [Some expert systems] were capable of a crude form of explanation – retracing the reasoning that was used to reach a conclusion or recommendation – but neural networks are not even capable of this crude form of explanation. There is a lot of work underway currently to try to deal with this issue. But, at present, we have no idea how to interpret the knowledge and representations that neural networks embody.'[189]

As John Zerilli and Adrian Weller put it, when considering the justice system's assumption that legality can be assessed by 'reasonableness' (the underlying assumption of the law of negligence):

'… deep neural networks have a rationality all of their own – they do not decide matters the way human reasoners do. Instead, they frequently exploit subtle correlations and regularities in data that evade human detection… In English law, if a public official were to decide a case on the basis of what appear to be egregiously spurious inferences, their decision would be quashed… But *just these sorts of correlations* are likely to proliferate with the steady march of machine learning in all areas of public and private decision-making.'[190]

This characteristic of software – to act unpredictably while acting within its programming – is known to the law. In the currency-trading case *B2C2 Ltd v Quoine Pte Ltd*, the Singapore International Commercial Court tackled the conceptual problem of attaching knowledge (for the purpose of applying the law of mistake) to such software. In order to apply the legal principles of mistake to the software, Simon Thorley IJ (later upheld by the Singapore Court of Appeals) attributed knowledge to its human programmer, and said this:

'Where the law is in a formative state it is, I think, appropriate for a court (of first instance at any rate) to develop the law only so far as necessitated by the facts of the case before it. With this in mind I do not intend to express any views on the precise legal relationship between computers and those who control or program them. The algorithmic programmes in the present case are deterministic, they do and only do what they have been programmed to do. They have no mind of their own. They operate when called upon to do so in the pre-ordained manner. They do not know why they are doing something or what the external events are that cause them to operate in the way that they do.'[191]

---

188 Above, 4.20.
189 Michael Wooldridge, *The Road to Conscious Machines: The Story of AI* (Pelican, 2020), chapter 5, p 188.
190 Chapter 2 ('The Technology') of *The Law of Artificial Intelligence*, ed. Matt Hervey and Matthew Lavy (Sweet & Maxwell, 2021) 2-037-2.038.
191 [2019] SGHC(I) 03, para 208.

From the claimant's perspective in a CPA 1987 claim, the solution to the foreseeability issue in a case involving such software is likely to lie in the threshold of proof required as to causation, both according to the principle in *Grant v Australian Knitting Mills Ltd*[192] and as described by Hickinbottom J in the *Wilkes* case:

'although a claimant must prove causation in the sense of showing a causal link between the defect and damage, and it may be helpful to one side or another to show the cause of the lack of safety that amounts to defect, a claimant is not required to prove the cause of that lack of safety or why the product failed: see, eg, *Ide v ATB Sales Ltd* [2009] RTR 8, paras 19-22, per Thomas LJ. The issue as to the degree of specificity with which the defect (ie lack of safety) has to be described and proved (which has been the subject of considerable academic debate, on the basis of such cases as *Richardson v LRC Products Ltd* [2000] PIQR P164 which, on one reading, suggest that considerable specificity might be required) is not in issue in this claim, and therefore I need say little about it; but one can imagine a pharmaceutical product that is highly beneficial to most patients but, in a minority, causes death or serious injury, for a reason unascertained and unascertainable, may nevertheless be held to lack the appropriate level of safety for the Act, and therefore be defective.'[193]

From the defendant's perspective, could the opacity of the workings of machine-learning software provide a blanket 'development risks/discoverability' defence in all CPA 1987 cases where that software is said to have been the cause of an accident? A blanket defence for a particular technology would not seem to have been the intention of the EU PLD 1985 (whose designers at one stage considered having no such defence at all[194]). Notwithstanding the comment in *Wilkes* (above), the High Court's judgment in *Richardson v LRC Products Ltd* (the split condom case) seems, while analysing the facts carefully, to have allowed a degree of generality in description of the defect, and to tend against applying the development risks defence where there is a known risk which cannot always be detected:

'The test provided by the statute is not what the defendants knew, but what they could have known if they consulted those who might be expected to know the state of research and all available literature sources. The provision is, to my mind, not apt to protect a defendant in the case of a defect of a known character, merely because there is no test which is apt to reveal its existence in every case.'[195]

Conclusion on CPA 1987

10.35 Innovation will overtake any scheme for strict product liability, but the EU PLD 1985 scheme which underpins CPA 1987 precedes the worldwide web, WiFI and common connected products – including vehicles – so is especially outdated. The law has provided more up-to-date remedies than CPA 1987 for products using digital content (CRA 2015) but those remedies are available only to a particular group of claimants in contract.

---

192 [1936] AC 85, 101 (PC, Lord Wright).
193 *Wilkes v DePuy*, 644-645 [73].
194 *A v NBA*, 329 [52].
195 [2000] PIQR P164, P172 (Ian Kennedy J).

Other claimants will seek the strict liability offered by the product liability scheme of CPA 1987; liable defendants will wish to raise it in support of their claims against others[196]. CPA 1987 requires attention. In terms of legal complexity, artificial intelligence is likely to take the courts back into the mountains[197] of CPA 1987 claims.

B Claims arising from defects in Advanced Driver Assistance System (ADAS) vehicles

10.36 The 'outline' section of this chapter (above) discusses several legal issues common to all AAEV vehicle defect claims. This and the following sections discuss further points of particular relevance to ADAS, automated and electric vehicles. None of these points have yet been adjudicated in relation to AAEVs.

Marketing and sale of ADAS systems in terms that suggest a higher level of automation

10.37 The phenomenon of 'market[ing] a vehicle as self-driving (or to use terminology that suggests self-driving) where that vehicle has not been authorised to drive itself'[198] is sufficiently concerning that the Law Commissions have recommended and the government have accepted and proposed in the AV Bill 2023-24 (HL Bill 1) that it should be a criminal offence (see the AV Bill 2023-24 (HL Bill 1), Part 4, cll 78-81). Such criminal liability was envisaged by the government, in its policy paper responding to the Law Commissions in 2022, as applying only to marketing to consumers: the government:

> 'would not wish these new offences to apply to interactions between businesses. A business that will not use the vehicle, but may be intending to seek authorisation in the future, is not at risk of using a vehicle unsafely'[199]

which is reflected in the definition of 'end-user' by cl 81 as:

> 'a person who uses the vehicle on a road or other public place other than for commercial purposes to do with the development, manufacture or supply of the vehicle'.

In terms of civil liability, such statements are now a circumstance relevant to the satisfactory quality of goods, digital content and goods provided with digital content, under CRA 2015, ss 9(5)–(7) and 34(5)–(7)[200]. So a consumer contracting with a business has significant protection in relation to such assertions; likewise a business cannot make such statements without expecting them to be taken account in an assessment of the quality of their goods, including their digital content.

---

196 In AAEV cases under AEVA 2018, s 5 and/or under the Civil Liability (Contribution) Act 1978.
197 See *Wilkes v DePuy*, 642 [62].
198 UK government paper 'Connected and Automated Mobility 2025: Realising the benefits of self-driving vehicles in the UK' (19 August 2022) ('CAM 2025') p 40.
199 CAM 2025, p 123.
200 See discussion above.

Fairgrieve and Goldberg opine of the 'any public statement …' factor that 'being no more than a relevant circumstance, it should not be construed narrowly'[201].

While CRA 2015 provides the most potent and up-to-date protection, warnings and instructions are also relevant in claims in negligence and under CPA 1987. Contradictory marketing (such as that in the Canadian *Buchan* case[202]) will again be relevant – explicitly so under CPA 1987, s 3(2)(a).

Actionability of downloaded software for ADAS vehicles

10.38 The position is as discussed in the 'Outline' section above – the CRA 2015 works around the orthodox definition of 'goods' as 'tangible' by introducing its own concept of 'digital content', which is subject to implied terms which also apply when digital content is provided in a 'mixed contract' with goods or services.

However, the CRA 2015 remedies apply only in contract and only for the benefit of consumers in business to consumer contracts as defined by the Act. Other claimants are left without remedy, until the actionability of downloaded software is clarified by the national courts, in the wake of the CJEU judgment in the *Computer Associates Ltd* case.

ADAS vehicles are not 'automated' until and unless they are classified as such by the procedure under AEVA 2018, s 1 (or its successor provision or regulation, if that classification is absorbed within the GB type approval process, as indicated by the government). Absent such classification, the remedies under AEVA 2018, Part 1 do not activate for ADAS vehicles, so the 'software updating' exceptions to an insured person's claim for failure to update software etc under AEVA 2018, s 4 would also not then apply.

(See also: the discussions above in relation to the AV Bill 2023-24 (HL Bill 1) and software in an ADAS claim and below in relation to AEVA 2018, s 4 and its relationship with the legal character of downloaded software problem in an automated vehicle accident claim under AEVA 2018.)

C Claims arising from defects in Automated Vehicles

(This section supplements the discussion in the sections above.)

Lack of clarity as to the legal character of software: how this might relate to exclusion of claims under AEVA 2018, s 4 (the software updating exclusion)

10.39 The legal tension resulting from the CJEU judgment in the *Computer Associates UK Ltd* case, accentuated by post-Brexit constitutional reform, is likely to increase if claims arising from downloaded software updates are pursued.

---

201 *Fairgrieve and Goldberg* (3rd edn, 2020), 4.77.
202 Discussed above.

This might happen especially in claims arising from accidents caused by automated vehicles when driving themselves, where the flawed software updating exceptions to AEVA 2018 compulsory insurance and s 2 liability under AEVA 2018, s 4 [203] might leave an insured person unable to claim under AEVA 2018, s 2 and so necessitate defect claims against others (eg. in relation to the adequacy of updating equipment including both hardware and software, whether in the vehicle or elsewhere).

In that situation the insured person excluded from an AEVA 2018, s 2 claim by s 4 might, if they are also the consumer of the automated vehicle itself, proceed against its manufacturer if they can show a breach of implied terms as to satisfactory quality etc provided by the Consumer Rights Act 2015 in relation to the vehicle and/or its digital content, including updating of that content. The dynamics of such a claim are untested but, in particular, the consumer would need to establish that the software updating problem was attributable to the manufacturer's breach of contract, and that it was not (for example) attributable to transmission problems with the consumer's own internet provider (see discussion of CRA 2015, s 39, above).

However, there will be such cases where the CRA 2015 is unavailable – for example if the insured person disqualified from an AEVA 2018 claim by s 4 of that Act is not a consumer within the meaning of the CRA 2015 because they are not 'acting for purposes that are wholly or mainly outside that individual's trade, business, craft or profession'[204]. In such a situation, the contractual and product liability remedies might be unavailable for downloaded software, if the orthodox 'tangibility' requirement for 'goods' were still effective.

Effect of the 'downloaded software' problem upon secondary claims by liable insurer/permitted uninsured owner against another person responsible for the accident under AEVA 2018, s 5

10.40 As well as providing simplicity for consumers and accident victims, the argument has been made that British legislators should adopt the EU approach to the actionability of defects in downloaded software (set out since the CJEU judgment in *Computer Associates UK Ltd* in the EU's revised product liability directive[205]) in the 'hope of simplifying future product liability claims against AV manufacturers'[206] by insurers exercising their right of secondary claim under AEVA 2018, s 5 in automated vehicle accident cases.

The present uncertainty for insurers etc as to whether or not defective downloaded software can be the subject of such an action works against the aim of EU PLD 1985 of allowing measurement of the commercial risks of innovation, to which insurance

---

203 See Chapter 6, 'insurance'.

204 CRA 2015, s 2(3) and see CRA 2015 Explanatory Notes, para 36.

205 European Commission, Proposal for a Directive of the European Parliament and of the Council of liability for defective products (28 September 2022) Art 4(1): "product' means all movables, even if integrated into another movable or into an immovable. 'Product' includes electricity, digital manufacturing files and software'.

206 Daniel West 'The Road Ahead: could UK insurers' claims against automated vehicle manufacturers benefit from a regime akin to the new EU Product Liability Directive?', AEVlaw.com (24 January 2023)

is essential. Insurers' ability to spread risk among all responsible parties (enshrined in AEVA 2018, s 5) is key to that aim.

If there were reform of the 'tangibility' requirement, it would be a matter for future and – in the light of the CJEU judgment in *Computer Associates UK Ltd* – extensive amending legislation, reaching into sale of goods, consumer and product law generally. If the CJEU approach were followed, that would include rewriting the CRA 2015's different approach. If, alternatively, the CRA 2015's 'digital content' approach were to be applied as the general solution, that would need to be imported into domestic sale of goods and product liability legislation.

No amendment to the language of AEVA 2018, s 5 is proposed by the AV Bill 2023-24 (HL Bill 1): see cl 45, Sch 2, para 5.

Is 'beta test' driving software susceptible to a claim?

10.41   'Beta testing' has been described as 'a type of user acceptance testing where the product team gives a nearly finished product to a group of target users to evaluate product performance in the real world'[207].

Liability for beta tests of driving software is untested in English and Welsh law. The most up-to-date statute relating to civil liability for software faults in contract – CRA 2015 – echoes sections of previous statutes providing that an implied term as to satisfactory quality does not apply where the relevant matter is specifically drawn to the consumer's attention before the contract is made, or where the buyer examines the goods or digital content before the contract is made and the examination ought to have revealed the unsatisfactory matter, or where there is a contract for sale by sample – a 'trial version' in the case of digital content under CRA 2015[208] – and the unsatisfactory matter would have been apparent on a reasonable examination of the sample[209].

So CRA 2015, s 34(4) reads as follows:

'(4) The term mentioned in subsection (1)[210] does not cover anything which makes the quality of the digital content unsatisfactory—

   (a) which is specifically drawn to the consumer's attention before the contract is made,

   (b) where the consumer examines the digital content before the contract is made, which that examination ought to reveal, or

   (c) where the consumer examines a trial version before the contract is made, which would have been apparent on a reasonable examination of the trial version.'

---

207 Article by Nick Babich on Adobe website 'Everything you need to know about Beta testing' (11 October 2019).
208 CRA 2015, s 34(4)(c).
209 SGA 1979, s 14(2C), SGSA 1982, s 4(3), CRA 2015, ss 9(4) and 34(4).
210 'Every contract to supply digital content is to be treated as including a term that the quality of the digital content is satisfactory.'

Whether that exclusion applies will depend upon the facts of a particular case. It operates within s 34 as a whole, so the provisions as to the effects of 'any public statement about the specific characteristics of the digital content made by the trader, the producer or any representative of the trader or the producer' (s 34(5)–(7), discussed above) may be among the circumstances relevant to the quality of the digital content.

D Claims arising from defects in Electric Vehicles

(This section supplements the discussion in the sections above.)

10.42 An electric vehicle is (unless exempted from such provisions) a motor vehicle subject to the requirements of the Road Traffic Act 1988 including (for example) insurance[211].

No reform of e-scooter law yet

10.43 As noted in Chapter 2, 'specifications', the conditions for approval and use of e-scooters were due to be regulated in the Transport Bill announced in the Queen's Speech in May 2022. That Transport Bill was postponed and did not appear in the King's Speech in November 2023.

Electricity as 'product' and 'goods'

10.44 Both CPA 1987 and CRA 2015 include 'electricity' in their definition of 'product' and 'goods' respectively:

' 'product' means any goods or electricity …' (CPA 1987, s 1(2)).

' 'Goods' means any tangible moveable items, but that includes water, gas and electricity if and only if they are put up for supply in a limited volume or set quantity.' (CRA 2015, s 2(8)).

---

211 See Chapters 2, 'specifications', 4, 'driving', and 6, 'insurance'.

Chapter 11

Passenger claims

"Suppose in the future locomotion by aerial vehicles becomes common; could a passenger in such a vehicle complain that the proprietor was guilty of a breach of duty or warranty towards him, if, a very high wind springing up, the aerial vehicle was carried against a building, without any fault of those in charge of it, whereby the passenger was injured?"

(Vaughan Williams LJ, question to counsel, 1909)[1]

Chapter Contents

A **Outline of the laws of passenger claims 11.01**
B **Passenger claims involving Advanced Driver Assistance Systems (ADAS) 11.13**
C **Passenger claims involving Automated Vehicles 11.16**
D **Passenger claims involving Electric Vehicles 11.18**

A Outline of the laws of passenger claims

11.01   For the regulatory history please see Chapter 5 'passenger services and public transport'.

Legal bases of a passenger's claim against a carrier

11.02   The legal basis or bases of claim available to a passenger will depend upon the facts of each case. For example:

- A passenger might have a contract with the carrier. In particular, the Consumer Rights Act 2015 provides implied terms to a consumer contracting with a trader, including that services will be performed with reasonable care and skill[2] and allowing for the actionability of 'digital content'[3].

---

1   *Wing v London General Omnibus Company* [1909] 2 KB 652, 654 (CA).
2   CRA 2015, s 49. See below in relation to the post-Brexit application of CRA 2015, Part 1 Chapter 4 to contracts for services for bus and coach services.
3   See Chapter 10, 'vehicle defect claims'.

- Duties in negligence are owed to the reasonably foreseeable claimant according to the neighbour principle[4] and in some circumstances more particularly (for example to an employee by their employer[5]).

- Certain statutes impose a duty of care. For example, the Occupier's Liability Act 1957 imposes "in place of the rules of the common law", upon "a person occupying or having control over … any … vehicle"[6] "a duty … to his visitors in respect of dangers due to the state of the [vehicle] or to things done or omitted to be done on"[7] the vehicle. The Employer's Liability (Defective Equipment) Act 1969 deems personal injury suffered in the course of employment, in consequence of a defect in equipment provided by the employer for the purposes of the employer's business, where the defect is attributable to the fault of a third party to be also attributable to negligence on the part of the employer[8]. AEVA 2018, s 2 will (when brought into practical effect either by the publication of the first list of automated vehicles under s 1 or by the authorisation process under the Automated Vehicles Act 2024, now the AV Bill 2023-24 (HL Bill 1)) provide the victim of an accident caused at least in part by an automated vehicle when driving itself on a road or other public place in Great Britain with a direct claim in tort against the insurer or permitted uninsured owner of the vehicle[9].

That is not an exhaustive list. The available legal bases of claim will depend upon the facts of each case.

Duty of carrier to passenger in relation to defects in vehicle

11.03   The duty of a carrier of passengers in relation to a defect in the vehicle is not absolute. There is not (as there is in relation to carriage of goods, via the law of bailment) a warranty that passengers will be carried safely from all defects, even from latent defects which could not reasonably have been discovered[10].

However, in *Henderson v Henry E Jenkins*[11], the House of Lords held by a majority that, to establish the defence of latent defect, a defendant must show that it took all reasonable care in the circumstances. The Court was not persuaded by the defendant lorry owners' submission that a visual inspection had been adequate to assure themselves of the safety of a pipe which was vulnerable to corrosion:

> "The defendants' answer was that they had followed a practice of relying solely on visual inspection of the pipes, and that this was a general and proper practice. The learned judge's finding was that 'it is plainly the custom in the ordinary course of things not to remove these fluid pipes.' This may be a

---

4   *Donoghue v Stevenson* [1932] AC 562 (HL).
5   See Chapter 12, 'employer's liability claims'.
6   OLA 1957, s 1(3)(a).
7   OLA 1957, s 1(1).
8   EL(DE)A 1969 s 1(1). See Chapter 12, 'employer's liability claims'.
9   See Chapter 6, 'insurance'.
10 *Readhead v Midland Railway* (1869) LR Vol IV QB 379. The reference to an absolute duty in bailment of goods should be read in light of the dwindling importance of the notion of the 'common carrier' of goods, in the face of standard terms of carriage excluding or limiting that categorisation; note also the effect of CRA 2015 in business to consumer contracts. See Chapter 14, 'delivery claims'.
11 [1970] AC 282 (HL).

general and proper practice for an ordinary case in which there are no special circumstances increasing the risk. But I think the defendants' answer should not have been accepted without evidence from the defendants sufficiently showing that this was an ordinary case without special circumstances increasing the risk."[12]

In particular:

"Mr. O'Brien, one of the defendants' expert witnesses, thought there was something unusual in this case because the brake pipes should not have become corroded, but corrosion had taken place by chemical action and the lorry must have been subjected to some unusual treatment from outside. The defendants might perhaps have been able to show by evidence that the lorry had not been used in any way, or involved in any incident, that would cause abnormal corrosion or require special inspection or treatment, or at any rate that they neither knew nor ought to have known of any such use or incident. But they did not call any such evidence. Their answer was incomplete. They did not displace the inference, arising from the physical facts of the case, that the accident must have been due to their default in respect of inspection or maintenance or both."[13]

In relation to manifest defects, the position is different. In *Rogers v Night Riders and Others*[14], two defendants who together operated a minicab firm and held themselves out to the general public as a car-hire firm undertaking to provide a vehicle to convey the claimant passenger to her destination could foresee that the claimant might be injured if the vehicle provided to her was defective, so owed the claimant a duty to take reasonable steps to ensure that a vehicle owned by a driver was properly maintained and reasonably fit for the purpose. An insecurely fastened rear door opened during the journey and then slammed shut again, trapping the claimant's left hand[15]. The trial judge found that the door lock had not been properly maintained and that there was negligence in the maintenance of the vehicle[16]. The duty to ensure proper maintenance could not be delegated by the defendants to a third party, such as the driver, whether an employee or independent contractor, so as to evade responsibility for breach of that duty. "It is possible to treat this case as one of contract and to say that the plaintiff and defendants entered into a contract whereby the defendants would provide a car for reward for a purpose and an implied term that the vehicle would be reasonably fit for that purpose. It is said that the vehicle would be reasonably fit for that purpose."[17]

As to the non-delegability of the duty, *Rogers v Night Riders* was not a case of vicarious liability nor of agency in contract but of a "duty owed directly by the

---

12 Above, 303 A-B (Lord Pearson).
13 303 F-H.
14 [1983] RTR 324 (CA, Eveleigh and Dunn LJJ).
15 326 D-F.
16 327 H.
17 328 L to 329 B (Eveleigh J). A contract for services was pleaded in the Amended Particulars of Claim (325 J, L). Dunn LJ, agreeing with and adding to the judgment of Eveleigh J, said that 'It matters not whether the duty is put in contract or in tort, either way it is a duty they could not delegate to a third person so as to evade responsibility if the car was not fit for that purpose' (331 G-H).

employer to the plaintiff … We are not concerned with the status of the driver, it is sufficient that he was a third person employed to perform the defendants' duty."[18]

Particularised statutory duties to passengers, including to children and consumers

11.04 Particular considerations may apply to a statutory duty of care. For example, the Occupier's Liability Act 1957, ss 1 and 2 'regulate the nature of the duty imposed by law in consequence of a person's occupation or control of premises and of any invitation or permission he gives (or is to be treated as giving) to another to enter or use the premises'[19], where 'premises' includes 'any moveable structure' including 'any vehicle'[20]. 'The extent of the occupier's ordinary duty' is defined by OLA 1957, s 2, and particularly by s 2(2) as 'a duty to take such care as in all the circumstances of the case is reasonable to see that the visitor will be reasonably safe in using the premises' including a vehicle 'for the purposes for which he is invited or permitted by the occupier to be there'. OLA 1957, s 2(3) provides that:

'(3) The circumstances relevant for the present purpose include the degree of care, and of want of care, which would ordinarily be looked for in such a visitor, so that (for example) in proper cases –

(a) an occupier must be prepared for children to be less careful than adults; and

(b) an occupier may expect that a person, in the exercise of his calling, will appreciate and guard against any special risks ordinarily incident to it, so far as the occupier leaves him free to do so.'

So, for example, an occupier of a vehicle carrying children 'must be prepared for children to be less careful than adults' when considering the safety of the children in the vehicle.

The Consumer Rights Act 2015 might also be relevant to a passenger claim. See Chapter 10, 'vehicle defect claims'.

Standard of care of driver of passenger vehicle

11.05 As in relation to driving generally, the common law standard of care required of the driver of a passenger vehicle is to exercise 'skill, experience and care', as if fully healthy and making no errors of judgement[21], mindful of the potential of a vehicle to do great harm[22]. Demanding though it is, the standard is not to be applied as if it were strict:

---

18   329 H and K
19   OLA 1957, s 1(2).
20   OLA 1957, s 1(3)(a).
21   *Nettleship v Weston* [1971] 2 QB 691, 699g, Lord Denning MR, though see *Mansfield v Weetabix Ltd* [1998] 1 WLR 1263 (CA) in relation to illness unknown to the driver (both discussed in Chapter 4, 'driving').
22   See eg. *Lunt v Khelifa* [2002] EWCA Civ 801 ('this court has consistently imposed on the drivers of cars a high burden to reflect the fact that a car is potentially a dangerous weapon' [20]), discussed in Chapter 4, 'driving'.

'[Seeking] to impose a counsel of perfection on a bus driver I think distorts the nature of the bus driver's duty which was of course no more nor less than a duty to take reasonable care. There is sometimes a danger in cases of negligence that the court may evaluate the standard of care owed by the defendant by reference to fine considerations elicited in the leisure of the court room, perhaps with the liberal use of hindsight. The obligation thus constructed can look more like a guarantee of the claimant's safety than a duty to take reasonable care.'[23]

In a 2023 case, the Court of Appeal endorsed both that approach and the following findings of the trial judge, in the claim of bus driver negligence before it, that

'Driving a vehicle and awareness of surroundings and people and vehicles cannot be categorised into all of these things being a threat (or hazard). It is a matter of awareness... The description of "keeping an eye on her" [*the pedestrian claimant on the pavement ahead and to the left of the moving bus*] is not to be taken, in my judgment as a fixed and unyielding view as opposed to keeping tabs on her position and movements as the situation develops... Any driver and in particular a driver of a large passenger vehicle has several things going on which includes constant checking of mirrors and spatial awareness of surrounds to the road boundaries and checking for the presence of other vehicles and pedestrians... I completely agree with the concept of anticipation and a driver having to anticipate problems as part of his/her responsibilities to other road users. However, the reality is that no motorist would proceed anywhere in reasonable time if the presence of every pedestrian on a pavement caused them to reduce their speed.'[24]

Attempted restriction or exclusion of a duty of care owed to a passenger

11.06 In principle, liability can be restricted. For example, the extent of the occupier's ordinary duty under OLA 1957 is defined by s 2(1) as being 'the same duty, the "common duty of care"' that the occupier owes 'to all his visitors, except in so far as he is free to and does extend, restrict, modify or exclude his duty to any visitor or visitors by agreement or otherwise'.

However, an attempt to exclude or limit liability to a passenger is itself subject to several limitations, including:

- The rule in the Unfair Contract Terms Act 1977 and (in relation to consumer contracts) the Consumer Rights Act 2015 that 'a person cannot by reference to any contract term or to a notice given to persons generally or to particular persons exclude or restrict his liability for death or personal injury resulting from negligence.'[25].

- 'In the case of other loss or damage, a person cannot so exclude or restrict his liability for negligence except in so far as the term or notice satisfies the requirement of reasonableness' (UCTA 1977, s 2(2)). Certain breaches of

23 *Ahanonu v South East London & Kent Bus Company Ltd* [2008] EWCA Civ 274, Laws LJ [23].
24 *Zanatta v Metroline Travel Ltd* [2023] EWCA Civ 224 [17, 42, 44].
25 UCTA 1977, s 2(1) and see CRA 2015, s 65(1).

standard contractual terms of business cannot be excluded or restricted 'except in so far as … the contract term satisfies the requirement of reasonableness' (UCTA 1977, s 3(2)). The Consumer Rights Act 2015 consolidates and extends the law as to implied and unfair terms in business to consumer contracts. It provides that an exclusion or restriction of certain terms implied, or rights and remedies provided by, the 2015 Act in relation to goods (see s 31), digital content (see s 47) and services contracts (see s 57) is not binding on the consumer. It provides that 'an unfair term of a consumer contract is not binding on the consumer'[26] and provides for the assessment of whether or not a term is unfair (s 62).

- A person's awareness of or agreement to a purported exclusion or limitation of liability in negligence 'is not of itself to be taken as indicating his voluntary acceptance of any risk' (UCTA 1977, s 2(3), CRA 2015, s 65(2)).

- There is a particular rule in relation to liability to passengers in a motor vehicle which is required to be insured for use on a road or other public place. Where that use is required to be insured by the Road Traffic Act 1988 s 143, in compliance with Part VI of that Act[27], the user's ability to raise a defence that a passenger consented to the risk of injury (*volenti non fit injuria*), or to 'restrict, modify or exclude his [the user's] duty to any visitor or visitors by agreement' (as per OLA 1957, s 2(1), for example) is itself restricted by RTA 1988, s 149, which provides as follows.

    '149. Avoidance of certain agreements as to liability towards passengers.

    (1) This section applies where a person uses a motor vehicle in circumstances such that under section 143 of this Act there is required to be in force in relation to his use of it such a policy of insurance as complies with the requirements of this Part of this Act.

    (2) If any other person is carried in or upon the vehicle while the user is so using it, any antecedent agreement or understanding between them (whether intended to be legally binding or not) shall be of no effect so far as it purports or might be held –

        (a) to negative or restrict any such liability of the user in respect of persons carried in or upon the vehicle as is required by section 145 of this Act to be covered by a policy of insurance, or

        (b) to impose any conditions with respect to the enforcement of any such liability of the user.

    (3) The fact that a person so carried has willingly accepted as his the risk of negligence on the part of the user shall not be treated as negativing any such liability of the user.

    (4) For the purposes of this section—

        (a) references to a person being carried in or upon a vehicle include references to a person entering or getting on to, or alighting from, the vehicle, and

        (b) the reference to an antecedent agreement is to one made at any time before the liability arose.'

---

26   CRA 2015, s 62(1).
27   See Chapter 6, 'insurance'.

RTA 1988, s 149 absorbs the principle first set out in the Road Traffic (Passenger Insurance) Act 1971, with effect from December 1972, that compulsory insurance is extended to passengers[28].

Consequently (as *Clerk and Lindsell on Torts* puts it),

'in no circumstances involving the use of a motor vehicle on a public road can it now be held that a passenger in or on the vehicle assumed any risk of injury arising out of his presence in or on the vehicle.'[29]

That includes driver inebriation cases[30].

However, the same conduct might give rise to defences other than consent, such as *ex turpi causa non oritur actio* (a claim does not arise from a base cause) and contributory negligence[31].

(While it does not affect a defence to liability, the effect of RTA 1988, s 148 upon compulsory insurance should also be noted: see below.)

RTA 1988, s 148: Avoidance of certain exceptions to compulsory insurance policies, by reference to number of persons that the vehicle carries and the time at which or the areas within which the vehicle is used

11.07   We have already discussed the ineffectiveness of 'any conditions with respect to the enforcement of any such liability of the user' arising from 'any antecedent agreement or understanding' between vehicle user and passenger 'to negative or restrict any such liability of the user in respect of persons carried in or upon the vehicle as is required by section 145 of this Act to be covered by a policy of insurance' under RTA 1988, s 149.

RTA 1988 prevents certain exceptions to compulsory motor insurance taking effect against third parties. RTA 1988, s 148(1) and (2)(c) and (e) are of particular relevance to electric vehicles which are insured under that Act, including e-scooters and especially e-scooters used in public trials. Those subsections provide as follows:

'*148. Avoidance of certain exceptions to policies*

(1)   Where a policy is issued for the purposes of this Part of this Act, so much of the policy as purports to restrict the insurance of the persons insured by

---

28   See Chapter 6, 'insurance', 'List of the main developments in British motor insurance law', *R v Secretary of State for Transport ex parte National Insurance Guarantee Corporation Plc*, QBD 8 May 1996 (Popplewell J), 1996 Westlaw document 1090145 and Merkin and Hemsworth, *The Law of Motor Insurance* (2nd edn, 2015) at 5-147 and 148.

29   *Clerk and Lindsell on Torts* (23rd edn, 3-125).

30   As above, and see the Fifth EU Motor Insurance Directive, 2005/14/EC, art 4 (now Consolidated Motor Insurance Directive, 2009/103/EC, art 13(3)): 'Member States shall take the necessary measures to ensure that any statutory provision or any contractual clause contained in an insurance policy which excludes a passenger from such cover on the basis that he knew or should have known that the driver of the vehicle was under the influence of alcohol or of any other intoxicating agent at the time of an accident, shall be deemed to be void in respect of the claims of such passenger'.

31   *Pitts v Hunt* [1991] 2 QB 24 (CA), 60 F to 61 A (Dillon LJ), 51 B (Balcombe LJ, agreeing). See discussion of *ex turpi causa* below.

the policy, by reference to any of the matters mentioned in subsection (2) below shall, as respects such liabilities as are required to be covered by a policy under section 145 of this Act, be of no effect.

(2) Those matters are—

...

(c) the number of persons that the vehicle carries,

...

(e) the time at which or the areas within which the vehicle is used'

In *R (Roadpeace Ltd) v Secretary of State for Transport*, Ouseley LJ summarised RTA 1988, s 148 and 149 as follows:

'Section 148 invalidates certain exceptions in a compulsory insurance policy in so far as they relate to the liabilities which have to be insured… Section 149 invalidates any restriction of liability to or acceptance of the risk of negligence on the part of a passenger.'[32]

Under s 148(4),

'Any sum paid by an insurer in or towards the discharge of any liability of any person which is covered by the policy by virtue only of subsection (1) above is recoverable by the insurer from that person'.

Duty of care of carrier in relation to passengers leaving the vehicle

11.08   As *Clerk & Lindsell on Torts* notes:

'There is much case law concerned with the standard of care of a [bus] conductor. Applied to modern conditions, it suggests that the person responsible for the transport should take reasonable care to warn his passengers of any dangers and prevent them from acting negligently.'[33]

For example, in *Prescott v Lancashire United Transport Co Ltd*[34], a bus driver was not at fault for stopping the bus, as the claimant and her husband ringing the bell had indicated that they would leave the bus when it stopped. However,

'When the bus did stop and when it stopped short of the stopping place, the conductor, in my judgment, ought either to have warned the passengers, or ought to have communicated with the driver in some way. It would be easily possible to inform the driver that passengers were getting off the bus. The conductor ought to have taken control. It is clear that he could have seen that the plaintiff's husband had got off the bus. There were others waiting to get off. That could have been seen by the conductor. The plaintiff was following her husband. The conductor ought to have given a warning, or

---

32   *R (Roadpeace Ltd) v Secretary of State for Transport* [2017] EWHC 2725, [2018] 1 WLR 1293 (Admin), 1300 E [12].
33   *Clerk and Lindsell on Torts* (23rd edn, 2020) at 7-222.
34   [1953] 1 WLR 232 (CA).

ought to have taken charge of the situation so as to ensure that either the plaintiff would be prevented from getting off the bus or that the bus should be prevented from going on while passengers were in the act of alighting.'[35]

The new regulatory background for automated passenger services under the Automated Vehicles Act 2024 (now the AV Bill 2023-2024 (HL Bill 1) is also likely to be relevant to the duty of care to passengers, especially in unattended vehicles. The AV Bill 2023-24 (HL Bill 1), cl 87 requires the national authority granting a permit to include a condition

'requiring the permit holder to publish reports about the automated passenger services which it provides, and in particular about the steps which it takes—

(a) to meet the needs of older or disabled passengers, and

(b) to safeguard passengers more generally.'

Carrier's responsibility for rowdy co-passengers and overcrowding

11.09   A carrier is not responsible for the action of a passenger causing injuries to other passengers unless it could reasonably have foreseen the danger[36]. A carrier must take reasonable steps to avoid overcrowding[37].

The defence of '*ex turpi causa non oritur actio*' (no claim arises from a base cause) against a passenger's claim

11.10   The principle *ex turpi causa non oritur actio* (no claim arises from a base cause) is often invoked, but its 'ritual incantation' is 'more likely to confuse than illuminate'[38]. In particular, the courts have moved away from a 'public conscience' test based upon the exercise of a discretion and towards principles which will better serve 'the practical operation of the law', while acknowledging that a practical approach 'will often produce disproportionately harsh consequences'[39].

---

35   Morris LJ at 234.
36   *East Indian Railway v Mukerjee* [1901] AC 396 (PC): explosion of fireworks in railway carriage where passengers smoked was not foreseeable by the railway company. 'The question then is reduced to this: whether there is any proof that the parcels carried by the two passengers exhibited such signs of their real nature as ought to have called the attention of the railway servants to them, and thus prevented such dangerous goods being carried. Their Lordships can find none.' (400-401); *Pounder v North Eastern Railway Company* [1892] 1 QB 385 (QBD): man whose job it was to evict pitmen assaulted by pitmen on defendant's train, defendant not liable: 'The railway company are bound to take reasonable care for the safety of their passengers. The controversy was as to how that reasonable care was to be measured, and I am clearly of opinion that it can only be ascertained by reference to the ordinary incidents of a railway journey, and by reference to what must be taken to have been in the contemplation of the parties when the contract of carriage was entered into' (Mathew J, 390).
37   *Metropolitan Railway Company v Jackson* (1877) 3 App Cas 193 at 209, 210 (HL).
38   *Pitts v Hunt* [1991] 2 QB 24, 49 F (Balcombe LJ).
39   *Les Laboratoires Servier v Apotex Inc* [2014] UKSC 55; [2015] AC 430, 442 [18].

In 2017, in *Patel v Mirza*, (a claim in tort and contract based upon a solicitor's breach of retainer) the Supreme Court applied what it subsequently described as 'the new policy-based approach'[40] to *ex turpi* whereby:

> 'one cannot judge whether allowing a claim which is in some way tainted by illegality would be contrary to the public interest, because it would be harmful to the integrity of the legal system, without (a) considering the underlying purpose of the prohibition which has been transgressed, (b) considering conversely any other relevant public policies which may be rendered ineffective or less effective by denial of the claim, and (c) keeping in mind the possibility of overkill unless the law is applied with a due sense of proportionality. We are, after all, in the area of public policy.'[41]

In 2014, Lord Sumption characterised *ex turpi* as follows:

> 'although described as a defence, it is in reality a rule of judicial abstention. It means that rather than regulating the consequences of an illegal act (for example by restoring the parties to the *status quo ante*, in the same way as on the rescission of a contract) the courts withhold judicial remedies, leaving the loss to lie where it falls... The *ex turpi causa* principle precludes the judge from performing his ordinary adjudicative function in a case where that would lend the authority of the state to the enforcement of an illegal transaction or to the determination of the legal consequences of an illegal act.'[42]

In the context of road traffic accident claims by passengers, the law of *ex turpi* had been clarified in 2015, before *Patel*, by the Court of Appeal in *McCracken v Smith*[43]. The claim was brought by M, the passenger on a stolen motorbike ridden negligently on a cycle path by his friend S. Both were 16 years old. They were committing several road traffic offences, including riding without insurance. The motorbike (a 'trials bike') was not designed for road use, nor to carry passengers. Neither M nor S were wearing helmets. They were riding with another trials bike, which was not involved in the accident but whose rider the judge found was known to S (and might, though it was immaterial, have been S's younger brother). The motorbike ridden by S crashed into a minibus driven by B, who drove into the path of the trials bike as it was proceeding along the path and was also found to have driven negligently. Both M and S were seriously injured. M claimed against his friend S, the rider of the motorbike, and the minibus driver B.

As far as M's claim against his friend S was concerned, the Court of Appeal held that *ex turpi* would have operated to bar the claim, if S had been the only negligent driver. Adopting the formulation of the principle by Elias LJ in *Joyce v O'Brien*[44], namely:

---

40   *Grondona v Stoffel & Co* [2020] UKSC 42; [2021] AC 540 [1].
41   *Patel v Mirza* [2016] UKSC 42; [2017] AC 467, 499-500 [101], Lord Toulson JSC.
42   *Les Laboratoires Servier* (above) at 445 [23].
43   *McCracken v Smith* [2015] EWCA Civ 380; [2015] PIQR P19.
44   *Joyce v O'Brien* [2013] EWCA Civ 546; [2014] 1 WLR 70.

'where the character of the joint criminal enterprise[45] is such that it is foreseeable that a party or parties may be subject to unusual or increased risks of harm as a consequence of the activities of the parties in pursuance of their criminal objectives, and the risk materialises, the injury can properly be said to be caused by the criminal act of the claimant even if it results from the negligent or intentional act of another party to the illegal enterprise'[46]

– the Court of Appeal in *McCracken* held that the trial judge had 'been wrong to reject the defence of *ex turpi causa* in relation to [M]'s claim against [S] and therefore in relation to his claim against the MIB'[47].

However, that was not the end of the matter, as M had a claim against the other negligent driver, B [48], who had played no part in M and S's joint criminal enterprise.

'Since [M] was jointly responsible for the dangerous driving, he is in the same position as [S], the actual rider of the bike, as regards a claim in negligence against [B]. The question in each case is whether the fact that the bike was being ridden dangerously provides a defence to the claim. The answer to that question is one with potentially wide ramifications, capable of affecting any driver involved in an accident with a negligent third party in circumstances where he or she is driving dangerously or is committing any other road traffic offence of sufficient seriousness to amount to turpitude for the purposes of the *ex turpi causa* defence.'[49]

The claim against B was unaffected by M's participation in the joint criminal enterprise, whether on grounds of duty of care or of causation:

'If the duty of care analysis formerly applied in the joint enterprise cases had any application here, it would tell decisively against the *ex turpi causa* defence succeeding. It is clear that the dangerous driving of the bike had no effect whatsoever on Mr Bell's duty of care or on the standard of care reasonably to be expected of him.'[50]

'... I do not think that the fact that the criminal conduct was one of the two causes is a sufficient basis for the *ex turpi causa* defence to succeed. Our attention has not been drawn to any remotely comparable case where it has in fact succeeded: for reasons I have explained, cases involving a claim by one party to a criminal joint enterprise against another party to that joint enterprise are materially different. In my judgment, the right approach is to give effect to both causes by allowing [M] to claim in negligence against [B] but, if negligence is established, by reducing any recoverable damages

---

45 In *Joyce v O'Brien*, the claimant fell out of the back of a van while he and the first defendant were making their getaway during their theft of some ladders. Elias LJ noted that the court was 'concerned in this case with its application in one particular context, namely where one criminal is injured by the negligence of another when they are both engaged in a criminal enterprise', a situation to which the *ex turpi* defence would often apply but where 'the jurisprudential basis for reaching that conclusion is a matter of some dispute' [5], quoted in *McCracken v Smith* at P319 [35].
46 *Joyce v O'Brien*, 80 [29].
47 *McCracken v Smith* (above) at P326 [48] (Richards LJ).
48 The appeal in *McCracken* was concerned solely with the claim against B: P326 [48].
49 P326 [49].
50 P326 [50].

in accordance with the principles of contributory negligence so as to reflect [M]'s own fault and responsibility for the accident.'[51]

The Court of Appeal found the minibus driver B to have driven negligently, on the basis that he had seen the two motorbikes before the material accident and that they had, again, been within his reasonable visibility for about 6 seconds before he manoeuvred the minibus towards them[52]. The Court of Appeal assessed the 'causal contribution of the dangerous riding of the bike for which [M] was responsible'[53] as contributory negligence of 65%, comprising an agreed 15% for failure to wear a helmet and 50% for 'his participation with [S] in a criminal joint enterprise to ride the bike dangerously'[54].

As to the extent of criminality necessary to satisfy the threshold test of 'turpitude' set by the Supreme Court in *Les Laboratoires Servier v Apotex Inc* (not a road traffic case), namely:

'The *ex turpi causa* principle is concerned with claims founded on acts which are contrary to the public law of the state and engage the public interest. The paradigm case is, as I have said, a criminal act. In addition, it is concerned with a limited category of acts which, while not necessarily criminal, can conveniently be described as 'quasi-criminal' because they engage the public interest in the same way ...'[55]

– the Court of Appeal in *McCracken v Smith* had 'no doubt' that 'participation ... in a joint enterprise to ride the bike dangerously... did amount to turpitude', referring to the offence of dangerous driving under RTA 1988, s 2, 'punishable on conviction on indictment by up to two years' imprisonment ... On no view is it a trivial offence'[56]. Christopher Clarke LJ added this discussion of the level of criminality or turpitude required to trigger *ex turpi* in a road traffic claim:

'Difficult questions may, however, arise in future as to the degree of blameworthiness needed for the doctrine to apply. In *Les Laboratoires Servier v Apotex Inc* the Supreme Court: (a) referred to the earlier rejection by the House of Lords of the "affront to the public conscience" test as unprincipled; (b) rejected a fact based discretionary approach; (c) said that "the paradigm case of an illegal act engaging the defence is a criminal offence"; and (d) treated the *ex turpi causa* principle as being founded on acts which are contrary to the public law of the state and engage the public interest; and (e) recognised that the doctrine might not apply to offences of strict liability where the claimant was not privy to the fact making the act unlawful.'

'The reach of modern criminal law into the field of road traffic is, however, extensive. Leaving aside dangerous driving, careless driving is, itself, an offence. Causing death thereby is punishable with imprisonment. There are

---

51 P326-327 [52].
52 P328 [58-59].
53 P327 [55].
54 P330 [67], though see criticism of this approach to calculation of contributory negligence by Yip J in *Clark v Farley* [2018] EWHC 1007 (QB); [2019] RTR 21 [77], discussed below.
55 *Les Laboratoires Servier v Apotex Inc* (above) 446 [25] (Lord Sumption).
56 *McCracken v Smith* (above) P324 [43], '*ex turpi causa*: the application of the principles to the facts of this case'.

a number of offences, punishable otherwise than by imprisonment under the Road Traffic Act 1988, including: motor racing on highways (s 12); riding a motorcycle without the required protective headgear (s 16); leaving a vehicle in a dangerous position (s 22); carrying a passenger on a motorcycle contrary to s 23 (s 23); failing to comply with traffic directions given by a constable or traffic officer (s 35) or the indications given by traffic signs (s 36); using a vehicle in a dangerous condition (s 40A); and contravention of a construction and use requirement as to brakes, steering gear or tyres, or use of a motor vehicle which does not comply with such a requirement, or causing or permitting a motor vehicle to be so used (s 41A). Speeding itself is a crime not punishable by imprisonment: Road Traffic Regulation Act 1984 s 89.'

'There will be circumstances in which the criminal act in question (e.g. of the driver) is: (a) causative of an accident in which a passenger has been injured; and (b) something for which the passenger himself is criminally responsible because he has aided or abetted, counselled or procured it. Is the passenger who encourages the driver to execute a manoeuvre, which it is careless to perform, to be deprived of compensation from the negligent driver when the resulting collision with another car causes him injury?'

'In *Joyce v O'Brien* Elias LJ said at [51] that the doctrine did not apply to "minor traffic offences", whilst recognising that in certain cases there may be a problem in determining whether the offence attracted the application of the doctrine or not. That begs the question as to what is meant by 'minor'. It may be that the dividing line should be between those offences which are, and those which are not, punishable by imprisonment. Or it may be that the criterion is simply whether the public interest requires the doctrine to apply to a crime of the category in question.'[57]

The judgment in *McCracken* has been criticised by some legal commentators[58]. It preceded the judgment of the Supreme Court in *Patel*. However, in *Clark v Farley*[59], a subsequent road traffic personal injury claim by a passenger, the law of *ex turpi* as set out in *McCracken* was applied with the benefit of the Supreme Court's judgment in *Patel*.[60] The facts required for the principle to operate were found unproven by the defendant[61]. The claimant was a passenger on an off-road motorbike. The claimant was not wearing a helmet. The motorbike upon which the claimant was a passenger collided head-on with another motorbike. The defendant was the rider of the other motorbike. The use of neither vehicle was insured. The MIB, joined as second defendant, 'claimed that the claimant's claim was barred on the ground that the claimant was involved in a joint illegal enterprise with the first and third defendants of dangerous driving'.

---

57   *McCracken v Smith* (above) at P335-336 [83-86].
58   See Merkin & Hemsworth, *The Law of Motor Insurance* (2nd edn, 2015) at 4-72.
59   *Clark v Farley* [2018] EWHC 1007 (QB, Yip J); [2019] RTR 21.
60   *Clark v Farley* [35]: 'there is 'no need to modify or place a gloss upon the approach in *McCracken v Smith* and *Joyce v O'Brien*' after the judgment of the Supreme Court in *Patel*.
61   See eg. *Clark v Farley* at [46-47]: 'The real issues relate to the defences of ex turpi causa and contributory negligence, in relation to which the defendants bear the burden of proof... As explained by Lord Carswell in *In re D* [2008] UKHL 33 at [28], the fact that a serious allegation is made does not: 'require a different standard of proof or a specially cogent standard of evidence, merely appropriately careful consideration by the tribunal before it is satisfied of the matter which has to be established.''

In relation to the evidence required to prove a joint criminal enterprise to drive dangerously, Yip J held that:

> 'The question of joint enterprise must now be considered in light of the Supreme Court decision in *R v Jogee* [2017] A.C. 387[62]. In relation to dangerous driving, [99] falls to be considered:
>
>> "Where the offence charged does not require *mens rea*, the only *mens rea* required of the secondary party is that he intended to encourage or assist the perpetrator to do the prohibited act, with knowledge of any facts and circumstances necessary for it to be a prohibited act."
>
> '*Jogee* was decided after *McCracken*. However, having regard to the conclusion at [24] that *McCracken's* 'presence on the bike must have been, and have been intended to be, an encouragement to [the rider] to ride as he did', the outcome was clearly entirely consistent with *Jogee*.'
>
> 'Having had the opportunity to consider *Jogee*, [counsel] modified their submissions somewhat from the position taken in the written closing submissions. It is agreed that for the defence of *ex turpi causa* to succeed, I must find that the claimant intended to encourage or assist the rider to ride dangerously. Mere foreseeability is not enough, although it may provide evidence from which the relevant intention can be inferred.'[63]

Applying the law to the facts of *Clark v Farley*, Yip J noted that 'the facts are similar (superficially at least)'[64] to those of *McCracken*, in which the *ex turpi* defence would have extinguished the claim against a rider also implicated in the joint enterprise. However, Yip J found on the facts of *Clark* that the claimant passenger was *not* implicated in a joint criminal enterprise to ride the motorbikes dangerously. Despite the description of the site of the accident as 'the Mad Mile':

> 'The police were not aware of a particular problem; there is no evidence of previous accidents; the adults from the community were aware of sometimes hearing bikes on the Mad Mile but did not appear to be particularly concerned about the activity there.'[65] and:

> 'I am satisfied that the claimant, like other youths in the area, would have known that people went to the Mad Mile to ride their off-road motorcycles. However, the evidence before me does not establish, on a balance of probabilities, that the claimant had been to the Mad Mile for that purpose before.'[66]

---

62 *R v Jogee* [2016] UKSC 8; *Ruddock v The Queen* [2016] UKPC 7, both reported at [2017] AC 387.
63 [40–42], and see [43–44] for counsel's agreed formulation of the issues on joint enterprise in that case.
64 [32].
65 [51].
66 [53].

'I accept that it is reasonable to infer that [the claimant] had some interest in motorbikes and probably in riding on one from the fact that he was invited and went to the Mad Mile.'[67]

'On the evidence available in this case, I have not found that [the claimant] must have known that the bike was likely to be ridden dangerously. On the available evidence, he was a newcomer to the Mad Mile and he had not been present very long before the accident occurred. He plainly intended to be carried on the motorcycle as it travelled along the path. However, there is simply no evidence from which I can infer that he intended the bike to be ridden dangerously.'[68]

'The evidence does not establish that [the claimant] in fact encouraged or that he intended to encourage [the rider who carried him as a passenger] to ride in a way that would not allow him to stop in the distance he could see to be clear. Referring to [99] of *Jogee*, I find that there is no evidence that he intended to encourage [the rider] to drive dangerously with knowledge of the facts and circumstances necessary for it to be dangerous.'[69]

'I have given careful consideration to the approach of the Court of Appeal in *McCracken*. However, by a fairly narrow margin, I find that this case is to be distinguished on its facts. The defendants have not established that [the claimant] was party to a criminal joint enterprise with [the rider] to drive dangerously.'[70]

Yip J found that each of the two riders was jointly and severally liable to the claimant and apportioned liability equally between them[71].

As to contributory negligence, Yip J did not follow the calculation of the Court of Appeal in *McCracken*, as:

'My understanding (I believe shared by both leading counsel) is that the correct approach is to look at relative blameworthiness and causative potency as a whole, rather than assessing elements of contributory negligence separately and adding the percentages together.'[72]

On that basis, taking into account both the claimant's failure to wear a helmet (as to which the parties had confidentially reached agreement as to a reduction) and his failure 'to have foreseen the inherent risk in riding pillion along the path', Yip J assessed the claimant's contributory negligence as a whole at 40%[73].

In a further RTA claim in which the defendant invoked *ex turpi*, *Wallett v Vickers*[74], the High Court, quoting the cases above including *Jogee*, emphasised that it was

---

67 [54].
68 [59].
69 [61].
70 [62].
71 [68-71].
72 [77].
73 [72-78].
74 *Wallett v Vickers* [2018] EWHC 3088 (QB, Males J); [2019] PIQR P6. Not a passenger case but a claim by the partner of a driver killed while racing another vehicle, defended by the surviving driver – unsuccessfully – as *ex turpi*.

insufficient for a defendant to assert a criminal joint enterprise in an *ex turpi* defence of a road traffic claim without proving all elements of such enterprise – including mental intention – in evidence before the trial judge. Further, addressing the issue of the level of criminal driving offence required for the *ex turpi* defence to operate (raised by Christopher Clarke LJ in *McCracken*, above), Males J noted that:

> 'Towards the other end of the spectrum [from manslaughter], careless driving is a criminal offence but nobody would suggest that careless driving by the claimant prevents the recovery of damages (reduced as appropriate on account of contributory negligence) in a road traffic case where both drivers are partly to blame. In such a case the recovery of damages does not offend public notions of the fair distribution of resources and poses no threat to the integrity of the law. On the contrary, the recovery of damages is in accordance with public policy. The claimant is not compensated for the consequence of his own criminal act. Rather, as a result of the reduction for contributory fault, he is compensated only for that part of the damage which the law regards as having been caused by the defendant's negligence.'[75]

In a non-passenger claim, *RO v Gray*[76], the claimant and defendant drivers became involved in an extended altercation after the claimant acted violently, aggressively and in an intimidating manner towards three taxi passengers. The defendant attempted to open the doors of the van driven by the claimant, who then drove the van into collision with the defendant's car. The defendant pursued the claimant's van in his car, forcing the claimant's van into collision with a wall, injuring the claimant. The defendant was convicted of causing serious injury by dangerous driving and of driving while disqualified and sentenced to 3 ½ years' imprisonment. The claimant was not prosecuted, although his barrister 'accepted that the claimant could have been prosecuted for careless driving in respect of the deliberate ramming … and criminal damage in respect of the damage caused' and the judge was 'satisfied that the claimant's conduct amounted to dangerous driving on two occasions' as well as to assault[77]. The claimant sued the defendant for assault and battery, to which the defendant (whose role was taken by the Motor Insurers' Bureau) raised the *ex turpi* defence. The claim being for a battery (an intentional tort to which no contributory negligence defence applied when the LR(CN)A 1945 was enacted) the defence of contributory negligence could not apply[78].

The High Court was referred to the cases discussed above in argument but it was agreed by the parties that the court 'was required to apply a policy-based test in accordance with the template provided by the Supreme Court in *Patel v Mirza* [2017] AC 467'[79]. In so doing, the judge pointed to the 'rationale for the decision in *Patel* and guidance on how to apply it, [which] is to be found between paras 99 and 110 of Lord Toulson JSC's judgment'[80].

Lord Toulson's judgment in *Patel* emphasises the importance of the statutory context in which the *ex turpi* defence is invoked. In particular, Lord Toulson singled

---

75 [38].
76 *RO v Gray* [2021] EWHC 2770; [2022] 1 WLR 1484 (QB, Judge Bird sitting as a High Court judge).
77 [55].
78 *Pritchard v Co-operative Group Ltd* [2011] EWCA Civ 329; [2012] QB 320.
79 *RO v Gray* (above) [12].
80 *RO v Gray* [138].

out the failure of the MIB's *ex turpi* argument in *Hardy v Motor Insurers' Bureau*[81] that its agreement with the Minister for Transport to satisfy any judgment against a motorist for a liability required to be covered under a motor insurance policy would not allow a contract to insure the driver against his own deliberate criminal conduct. Lord Toulson quoted Diplock LJ (as he then was) in *Hardy*:

'The rule of law on which the major premise is based – *ex turpi causa non oritur actio* – is concerned not specifically with the lawfulness of contracts but generally with the enforcement of rights by the courts, whether or not such rights arise under contract. All that the rule means is that the courts will not enforce a right which would otherwise be enforceable if the right arises out of an act committed by the person asserting the right (or by someone who is regarded in law as his successor) which is regarded by the court as sufficiently anti-social to justify the court's refusing to enforce that right.'[82]

Lord Toulson described Diplock LJ as observing "that the purpose of the relevant statutory provision[83] was the protection of persons who suffered injury on the road by the wrongful acts of motorists. This purpose would have been defeated if the common law doctrine of illegality had been applied so as to bar the plaintiff's claim"[84].

To return to *RO v Gray*, Judge Bird there addressed the issue of the level of wrongdoing of the claimant:

'In my judgment, the claimant's conduct on the evening in question was deplorable and disgraceful. It fell well below the standards that can be expected in a law-abiding and decent society and it could have been expected to warrant criminal sanctions. The threats made to the defendant from the safety of the van and the deliberate ramming of the Citroën are serious matters. The chasing after the taxi, forcing it to stop and kicking it are serious matters. The threats to the taxi passengers and the attack on the second passenger are also serious matters. However, the gravity of the claimant's wrongdoing (taken in its totality or considered only to the extent that it concerned the defendant) is not at the top of the range (compare acts of homicide in both *Gray [v Thames Trains Ltd]* [2009] AC 1339 and *Henderson*[85]). In my judgment, the claimant's conduct is closer to the bottom of the range than it is to the middle. As Edis J (as he then was) said in *Flint v Tittensor* [2015] 1 WLR 4370, para 42:

"This is the kind of relatively minor criminality which is not uncommon late at night in our cities. It is deplorable and alarming, and can sometimes escalate into more serious violence. In categorising it as I have, I am not condoning it. It is a fact of life which many people unfortunately have to deal with from time to time."'[86]

---

81 [1964] 2 QB 745 (CA).
82 *Hardy v MIB* (above) at 767.
83 The compulsory insurance requirement at the time of *Hardy* under RTA 1930 Part II then RTA 1960 Part VI and now RTA 1988 Part VI.
84 *Patel* (above) at 500 F [102].
85 *Henderson v Dorset Healthcare University NHS Foundation Trust* [2020] UKSC 43; [2021] AC 563.
86 *RO v Gray* (above) at 1517 [164].

In particular, the judge was not:

> 'however, satisfied in the present case that the claimant's illegality did not (in the sense required) cause his own loss. Whilst it is true to say that the loss would not have occurred but for the claimant's wrongdoing (there is no doubt that if he had not been involved in an altercation with the taxi passengers and then threatened the defendant, driven into his car and supported [the claimant's passenger]'s direct attack on him, no harm would have come to him) it is clear that the immediate cause of the loss was the defendant's dangerous driving. The claimant's wrongdoing merely providing the occasion for the defendant to do harm. Certainly, in the instant case, the claimant does not need to rely on his own wrongdoing to make good his claim.'[87]

As *RO v Gray* was an assault claim, contributory negligence could not apply, so judgment was entered for the claimant for damages to be assessed without reduction[88].

In 2020 the Supreme Court gave judgment in a mortgage fraud case *Grondona v Stoffel & Co*[89]. The *ex turpi* principle was not applied, as the law already accepted that an equitable interest in property passed to the respondent notwithstanding that the agreement for sale was tainted by illegality[90].

> 'As Lord Toulson JSC explained in *Patel* ..., the notion that persons should not be permitted to profit from their own wrongdoing is unsatisfactory as a rationale of the illegality defence... The true rationale of the illegality defence ... is that recovery should not be permitted where to do so would result in an incoherent contradiction damaging to the integrity of the legal system.'

> 'The appellants correctly identify deterrence as one underlying policy of the criminal law against fraud. I doubt, however, that permitting a civil remedy to persons in the position of the respondent would undermine that policy to any significant extent.'[91]

Although not a passenger case, the credit hire case of *Ali v HSF Logistics Polska SP Zoo*[92] is noteworthy as it suggests that *ex turpi* can operate in conjunction with another principle (causation) to bar a claim for a particular type of damage. The High Court on appeal from the County Court considered whether a claim for hire charges premised upon loss of use of the damaged vehicle after the accident was barred by the failure of the vehicle owner to have their car MOT tested, where it was not evidenced that the owner would have had the car so tested if the accident had not occurred. The trial judge below had refused to apply *ex turpi* on the basis of disproportionality (*Patel* point (c), above) but had dismissed the claim for lack of causation of the car being kept out of use by the accident. The appellant argued that this was to reintroduce the illegality argument, which the judge had rejected on the proportionality ground. Dismissing the appeal, Mr Justice Martin Spencer

---

87   [166].
88   See *Pritchard v Co-op* (above) and *RO v Gray* [178].
89   [2020] UKSC 42; [2021] AC 540.
90   *Grondona*, Lord Lloyd-Jones JSC [34].
91   *Grondona*, Lord Lloyd-Jones JSC [46, 29].
92   *Ali v HSF Logistics Polska SP Zoo* [2023] EWHC 2159 (Martin Spencer J).

held (relying upon 1998 dicta of Clarke LJ in *Hewison v Meridian Shipping*[93]) that 'there is a form of illegality relating not to the whole action but to the loss or damage claimed and which is not the result of an application of public policy'[94].

Adult carrier's standard of care in relation to children's safety equipment

11.11 The duty of an adult carrier of children includes not only maintenance of the vehicle[95] but also the use of safety equipment appropriate for children, according to its instructions.

In *Hughes v Williams & Williams*[96], the liable defendant driver sought contribution from the mother of the injured child claimant (the third party, also Williams but unrelated to the defendant), on the ground that the mother had contributed to the child claimant's injury by transporting her in a car on a booster seat which the mother knew from the instructions (which she had read) to be unsuitable due to the child's age and size. An alternative and safe child seat, with a five-point harness, had also been in the car at the time of the injury. The trial judge allowed the contribution claim and assessed the mother's contribution to the claimant's injuries at 25% (applying the same reduction as would have applied in relation to contributory negligence under *Froom v Butcher*[97]). The Court of Appeal noted that the case 'concerned a safety device which should not have been used at all rather than a safety device which was not being used properly'[98].

Similarly, use of the wrong safety equipment was the issue in *Jones v Wilkins (Wynn and another, part 20 defendants)*[99]. A child of two years and nine months was travelling on their mother's lap in the front passenger seat of a car driven by the child's aunt, restrained only by the lap portion of her mother's adult seatbelt. The expert evidence was that an approved child restraint would have avoided the claimant's injuries almost or virtually entirely. As in the later case of *Hughes* (above), the adults' use of the wrong safety equipment for the child was found to have contributed 25% to the child's injuries in the ensuing head-on collision with the defendant's vehicle.

As noted above, an occupier of a vehicle carrying children 'must be prepared for children to be less careful than adults' when considering the safety of the children in the vehicle[100].

As noted above, the AV Bill 2023-24 (HL Bill 1), cl 87(4) requires as a condition of the grant of an automated passenger permit the publication of reports by the permit holder 'in particular about the steps which it takes ... (b) to safeguard passengers...'.

---

93   [2002] EWCA Civ 1821; [2003] ICR 766.
94   *Ali v HSF* [20].
95   See 'duty of carrier in relation to defects in the vehicle', above.
96   [2013] EWCA Civ 455; PIQR P17, 248 (discussed in relation to the contribution claim and principles of apportionment in Chapter 9, 'RTA claims').
97   [1976] 1 QB 286 (CA). See Chapter 9, 'RTA claims'.
98   Black LJ, as she then was [61].
99   [2001] RTR 19, 283 (CA), cited in *Hughes v Williams & Williams* (above) at [31].
100 OLA 1957, s 2(3)(a).

Post-Brexit treatment of rights of passengers in bus and coach transport

11.12 CRA 2015, s 48 addresses the question 'what services contracts are covered?' by Part 1 Chapter 4 of the Act.

CRA 2015, s 48(3A) provides that:

'This Chapter does not apply to anything that is governed by Regulation (EU) No 181/2011 of the European Parliament and of the Council of 16 February 2011 concerning the rights of passengers in bus and coach transport and amending Regulation (EC) No 2006/2004.'

EU Regulation No 181/2011 provides increased rights for disabled passengers[101], as well as other matters including that:

'Passengers should, in addition to compensation in accordance with applicable national law in the event of death or personal injury or loss of or damage to luggage due to accidents arising out of the use of the bus or coach, be entitled to assistance with regard to their immediate practical needs following an accident. Such assistance should include, where necessary, first aid, accommodation, food, clothes and transport.'[102]

Art 7 of EU Regulation No 181/2011 as it applies in the law of England and Wales now reads as follows, pursuant to the Rights of Passengers in Bus and Coach Transport (Amendment etc) (EU Exit) Regulations 2019[103], Part 3 reg 4(5)(a):

'*Article 7 Death or personal injury to passengers and loss of or damage to luggage*

1. Passengers shall, in accordance with any applicable law (other than this Regulation), be entitled to compensation for death, including reasonable funeral expenses, or personal injury as well as to loss of or damage to luggage due to accidents arising out of the use of the bus or coach. In case of death of a passenger, this right shall as a minimum apply to persons whom the passenger had, or would have had, a legal duty to maintain.

2. The amount of compensation shall be calculated in accordance with any applicable law (other than this Regulation). Any maximum limit provided by any such applicable law to the compensation for death and personal injury or loss of or damage to luggage shall on each distinct occasion not be less than:

    (a) £190,000 per passenger;

    (b) £1,000 per item of luggage. In the event of damage to wheelchairs, other mobility equipment or assistive devices the amount of compensation shall always be equal to the cost of replacement or repair of the equipment lost or damaged.'

---

101 EU regulation No 181/2011, art 9-18.
102 Above, preamble [6] and art 7-8.
103 SI 2019/141.

Art 8 of EU Regulation No 181/2011, as applied by the Rights of Passengers in Bus and Coach Transport (Amendment etc) (EU Exit) Regulations 2019 reg 4(6), reads as follows:

> '*Article 8 Immediate practical needs of passengers*
>
> In the event of an accident arising out of the use of the bus or coach, the carrier shall provide reasonable and proportionate assistance with regard to the passengers' immediate practical needs following the accident. Such assistance shall include, where necessary, accommodation, food, clothes, transport and the facilitation of first aid. Any assistance provided shall not constitute recognition of liability.
>
> For each passenger, the carrier may limit the total cost of accommodation to £70 per night and for a maximum of 2 nights.'

EU Regulation No 181/2011 arts 9 to 17 ('*rights of disabled persons and persons with reduced mobility*') are retained with amendment in English and Welsh law by the Rights of Passengers in Bus and Coach Transport (Amendment etc) (EU Exit) Regulations 2019. The rights include the prohibition of provision of such transport on the grounds of disability or reduced mobility (art 9). Art 17 of the EU Regulation as applied by the 2019 Regulations provides for liability of carriers and terminal managing bodies to compensate for causing loss of or damage to wheelchairs, other mobility equipment or assistive devices. Art 18 of the EU Regulation ('exemptions') was omitted by the 2019 Regulations.

The Rights of Passengers in Bus and Coach Transport (Amendment etc) (EU Exit) Regulations 2019 were made under the Ministerial power to prevent, remedy or mitigate any failure of retained EU law to operate effectively or any other deficiency in retained EU law[104], pursuant to the European Union (Withdrawal) Act 2018 s 8(1) and in particular 8(2)(a) and (g)[105].

See also the AV Bill 2023-24 (HL Bill 1), cl 87, described above.

B Passenger claims involving Advanced Driver Assistance Systems (ADAS)

Standard of care of a driver using ADAS

11.13 As the law stands, the standard of care of a driver is unaltered by their use of an ADAS system.

It is possible that the courts might look for evidence of particular care when an accident occurs during use of an ADAS system which relinquishes part of the human driver's control in a novel way. However, there has been no alteration of

---

104 Explanatory Note to SI 2019/141.
105 '(2) Deficiencies in retained EU law are where the Minister considers that retained EU law (a) contains anything which has no practical application in relation to the United Kingdom or any part of it or is otherwise redundant or substantially redundant, … (g) contains EU references which are no longer appropriate.'

the standard of care in relation to cruise control[106], an established driver assistance system, so it is questionable whether the standard would alter in relation to other more recent ADAS systems (such as the 'hands off, eyes on' assisted driving system reported to have been approved for use on certain motorways in the UK[107]). The point has yet to be adjudicated or legislated.

The new regulatory background of the AV Bill 2023-24, which includes a power to amend type approval legislation for driver assistance systems (cl 91) will be relevant.

Passenger sharing control of an ADAS vehicle

11.14   The statutory definition of 'driver' allows for more than one person to be driving a vehicle. So a passenger who shares control of a vehicle with the person in the driving seat (for example, when misusing an ADAS system) can be held liable[108].

Duty of carrier to a passenger in a remotely driven vehicle

11.15   As discussed in Chapter 5, 'passenger services and public transport', the Law Commission of England and Wales' consultation on remote driving (June 2022 to February 2023) dealt with the immediate issue of testing prototype vehicles using remote driving, and particularly using a 'beyond line-of-sight' remote driver as a safety driver outside the vehicle. The Law Commission advised government that such testing should currently be permitted if within a Vehicle Special Order[109] or (in the longer term) a licensing system yet to be introduced by new primary legislation (now the AV Bill 2023-24 (HL Bill 1)).

In relation to the testing of public passenger vehicles, the Law Commission noted that current law allowed the Secretary of State for Transport to dispense with conditions for fitness for a public passenger vehicle adapted to carry more than eight passengers but lacking type approval 'where it is expedient to do so for the purpose of making tests or trials of a vehicle or its equipment' (PPVA 1981, s 11)[110]. However, like regulations 104 and 107 of the Road Vehicles (Construction and Use) Regulations 1986[111], that was not a law drafted with remote driving in mind[112], and is subject to the Law Commission's conclusions in its advice to government that 'in the short term ... those who use remote 'beyond line-of-sight' driving should be required to demonstrate that their system is safe and obtain a VSO' and in 'the longer term ... all organisations who conduct remote driving should obtain a

---

106 See Chapter 4, 'driving'.
107 Ford media centre website 'Ford brings hands-free driving technology to motorways in Great Britain' (13 April 2023).
108 See *Tyler v Whatmore* [1976] RTR 83, discussed in Chapter 4, 'driving'.
109 See Chapter 3, 'testing'.
110 Law Commission of England and Wales' Remote Driving: advice to government, February 2023 p 44, 4.30-31. And see p 42, 4.18, in relation to CUR 1986 reg 107 (prohibition against leaving a vehicle unattended) and the RTA 1988, s 42 offence in relation to a passenger vehicle.
111 SI 1986/1078.
112 Above, p 42, 4.20.

licence' under 'a licensing scheme to promote safety and shift responsibility to the organisation behind remote driving' which 'will require new primary legislation'[113].

The Law Commissions also noted a potential hazard of allowing commercial activity to take place during a trial, particularly in relation to the carriage of passengers, namely that 'it is possible that unscrupulous operators will try and avoid regulation by claiming they are trialling'[114] – a possibility which is illustrated by attempted evasion of the compulsory insurance requirement in the case of some electric vehicles[115]. The Law Commission took 'a cautious approach to trials which provide a commercial service carrying passengers'[116] but concluded that 'VSOs should permit the commercial carriage of goods and delivery of vehicles on a case-by-case basis'[117].

Since the publication of the Law Commission's advice to government on remote driving, it has been reported that a non-remotely driven car has been approved for use on roads while using a subscription-based 'hands off, eyes on' technology on motorways, allowing the driver to remove their hands from the steering wheel[118]. As at the time of writing, it is not yet clear on what basis that system has been approved by the Department for Transport, although a feature of the reported approval is its geographical restriction to certain (though extensive) stretches of motorway.

The AV Bill 2023-24 (HL Bill 1) proposes strict control of remote driving, including the new proposed RTA 1988, s 34B offence of using a vehicle without a driver or licensed oversight (cl 53).

C   Passenger claims involving Automated Vehicles

AEVA 2018

11.16   The direct claim under AEVA 2018, s 2 is available to 'an insured person'[119] (meaning 'any person whose use of the vehicle is covered by the policy … of insurance that satisfies the conditions in section 145 of the Road Traffic Act 1988'[120]) 'or any other person'[121] who suffers damage as a result of an accident caused by an insured [authorised[122]] automated vehicle when driving itself on a road or other public place in Great Britain[123]. It is also available to 'a person' who suffers damage as a result of such an accident, where an owner is permitted to use

---

113   Above, p 47, 4.48.
114   Above, p 54-55, 5.34.
115   See *Winter v DPP* [2002] EWHC 1524 (cosmetic pedals not reasonably capable of propelling electric tricycle, which was therefore a motor vehicle) discussed in Chapter 4, 'driving'.
116   Law Commission of England and Wales' Remote Driving: advice to government, February 2023, p 55, 5.38.
117   Above, p 55-56, 5.38 to 5.41 (conclusion 6).
118   Ford media centre website 'Ford brings hands-free driving technology to motorways in Great Britain' (13 April 2023).
119   AEVA 2018, s 2(1)(c).
120   AEVA 2018, s 8(1)(b) and (2).
121   AEVA 2018, s 2(1)(c).
122   Amendment proposed by AV Bill 2023-24 (HL Bill 1), cl 45, Sch 2, para 5(3)(a). See Chapter 2, 'specifications'.
123   AEVA 2018, s 2(1).

an [authorised] automated vehicle in such a place without insurance by virtue of RTA 1988, s 144(2) (prescribed exempted public bodies) or because the vehicle is in the public service of the Crown[124].

The AEVA 2018, s 2 claim is therefore available (subject to defences[125]) to any person who suffers damage as a result of such an accident – including not only a passenger in the vehicle but also its 'driver'. That traditional distinction between the two categories of vehicle occupant would seem not to affect the availability of an AEVA 2018, s 2 claim, as both are effectively passengers of the automated vehicle while it is driving itself. As discussed in Chapter 6, 'insurance', AEVA 2018 expands the boundaries of traditional, third party motor insurance by providing compulsory insurance for the benefit of the first party insured person, who is likely (in the traditional human relationship to the vehicle) to be the 'driver'. In practical terms, the 'driver' has become a 'passenger' for the purpose of an AV claim.

Civil liability for assault by a third party in an unattended automated vehicle

11.17   Please see Chapter 5, 'passenger services and public transport' and the discussion of a carrier's responsibility for rowdy co-passengers in the 'outline' section of this chapter, above.

D Passenger claims involving Electric Vehicles

Regulation of e-scooters in relation to passengers

11.18   An e-scooter is a motor vehicle[126], whose legal characteristics include that it is 'designed to carry no more than one person'[127].

As a motor vehicle not exempted[128] from the requirement for compulsory motor insurance, a person must not use an e-scooter 'on a road or other public place unless there is in force in relation to the use of the vehicle by that person such a policy of insurance as complies with the requirements of' Part VI of the Road Traffic Act 1988[129].

As discussed above, 'Section 148 [RTA 1988] invalidates certain exceptions in a compulsory insurance policy in so far as they relate to the liabilities which have to be insured' (including purported restrictions relating to 'the number of persons that the vehicle carries'[130]) and 'Section 149 invalidates any restriction of liability to or acceptance of the risk of negligence on the part of a passenger.'[131]

---

124 AEVA 2018, s 2(2).
125 See discussion of AEVA 2018 in Chapter 6, 'insurance', and in the various 'claims' chapters.
126 *DPP v King* [2008] EWHC 447 (Admin).
127 Road Vehicle (Registration and Licensing) Regulations 2002, SI 2002/2742 (as amended by the Electric Scooter Trials and Traffic Signs (Coronavirus) Regulations and General Directions 2020, reg 2(3)), reg 33(1)(d).
128 For exempted vehicles see RTA 1988, s 189.
129 RTA 1988, s 143(1).
130 RTA 1988, s 148(2)(c).
131 *R (Roadpeace Ltd) v Secretary of State for Transport* [2017] EWHC 2725, [2018] 1 WLR 1293 (Admin), 1300 E [12] (Ouseley J).

As discussed above, other defences including contributory negligence and *ex turpi causa non oritur actio* (no claim arises from a base cause) remain potentially arguable, depending upon the facts of the case.

As discussed in other chapters, the Transport Bill announced in May 2022 was intended to reclassify e-scooters for compulsory insurance purposes. As at the date of writing, the Bill has not been published (it did not appear in the King's Speech in November 2023) and the effects of such reclassification have not been specified.

Regulation of e-bikes (electrically assisted pedal cycles) in relation to child passengers

11.19 An electrically assisted pedal cycle (an EAPC) specified as such in the Electrically Assisted Pedal Cycles Regulations 1983[132] is not classified as a motor vehicle[133], so its use on a road or other public place in Great Britain does not carry the obligations required of the use of a motor vehicle, such as compulsory insurance[134].

As discussed in Chapter 6, 'insurance', an EAPC is defined as a pedal cycle with two or more wheels[135], fitted with pedals by means of which it is capable of being propelled and with 'no motor other than an electric motor which –

(i) has a maximum continuous rated power which does not exceed 250 watts;

(ii) cannot propel the vehicle when it is travelling at more than 15.5 miles per hour.'[136]

An EAPC 'shall not be driven on a road by a person under the age of fourteen'[137]. However, there is no prohibition upon children being carried as passengers on an EAPC, and some EAPCs have been designed especially to carry children as passengers.

Although the point has not been adjudicated, an EAPC would appear to be a 'vehicle' within the meaning of OLA 1957, s 1, so the rider of an EAPC carrying children 'must be prepared for children to be less careful than adults', pursuant to s 2(3)(a).

The *ex turpi causa* defence, as applied to e-scooter and EAPC passenger claims

11.20 The point has yet to be adjudicated, but the *ex turpi* judgments in relation to trail bikes (discussed in the 'outline' section, above) set out the principles.

---

132 SI 1983/1168.
133 RTA 1988, s 189(1)(c), Road Traffic Regulation Act 1984 s 140(1)(c).
134 Cf. RTA 1988, s 143.
135 Electrically Assisted Pedal Cycles Regulations 1983, SI 1983/1168, reg 3, as amended by the Electrically Assisted Pedal Cycles (Amendment) Regulations 2015, SI 2015/24, made under RTA 1988, s 189.
136 EAPCR 1983 reg 4.
137 RTA 1988, s 32(1).

Contributory negligence in relation to helmets, as applied to e-scooter and EAPC passenger claims

11.21 Just as was the case in relation to seatbelts when it was established that failure to wear a seatbelt could constitute contributory negligence (in *Froom v Butcher*, in 1976[138]), there is no requirement in law to wear a helmet when travelling on an EAPC. However, the lack of legal compulsion does not prevent the court reducing compensation for contributory fault in not wearing a helmet (see *Smith v Finch*[139], which applies *Froom* to failure to wear a cycle helmet).

The regulatory position in relation to e-scooters is different. The government classifies an e-scooter as a motorcycle (within the subclass of moped)[140], so the starting point is that a motorcycle helmet complying with British Standard 6658:1985 must be worn as a matter of law[141]. However, that legal requirement has been removed in relation to e-scooters being used in a trial[142], so a trial e-scooter can be ridden without wearing a helmet as a matter of law, even though use of a helmet is one of the several requirements still applying to public use of a privately-owned e-scooter.

Again, applying *Froom* and *Smith*, the absence of legal compulsion to wear a helmet does not release the injured rider or passenger from reduction of their compensation for causative contributory fault, should they fail to wear a helmet and suffer injury.

---

138 [1976] 1 QB 286 (CA). See Chapter 9, 'RTA claims'.
139 [2009] EWHC 53 (QB, Griffith Williams J). Also discussed in Chapter 9.
140 Answer by Trudy Harrison MP to parliamentary question by Jim Shannon MP, UN 21181, tabled on 20 June 2022, answered 23 June 2022.
141 Motor Cycle (Protective Helmets) Regulations 1998, SI 1998/1807, reg 4(1), 5(1).
142 MC(PH)R 1998, reg 4(2A), added by the Electric Scooter Trials and Traffic Signs (Coronavirus) Regulations and General Directions 2020, SI 2020/663, reg 3(2)(b).

Chapter 12

Employer's liability claims

'... in 1897, the first of the Workmen's Compensation Acts was passed, providing compensation for injury at work on a basis akin to social insurance. Liability did not depend on the negligence of the employer or of any of its employees. Compensation became payable whenever an employee was incapacitated by an accident 'arising out of and in the course of employment', one of the most litigated phrases in the English language.'

'There is no doubt that a variety of factors led to the introduction of the legislation [from 1802 to 2005] outlined above[1]... It is clear that a free market in labour untrammelled by regulation on health and safety grounds was not tolerable to many sections of society, and not just workers, once capitalist methods of production intensified by the advances of technology took hold.'

Munkman on Employer's Liability (2019)[2]

Chapter Contents

A Outline of the Laws of Employer's Liability Claims

12.01 Technology is often a culprit. The law of employer's liability[3] started with statutes to protect the safety of workers (who included, in increasing numbers,

---

1 The Health and Morals of Apprentices Act 1802 to the Regulatory Reform (Fire Safety) Order 2005, SI 2005/1541.
2 17th edn, chapter 1, 'the development of employer's liability law' by Daniel Bennett [1.26 'the Workmen's Compensation Acts' and 1.47 'motives and causes']
3 This is not a full account of the law of employer's liability and does not explore some concepts, for example 'the course of employment'. The reader should also consult specialist works such as *Munkman on Employer's Liability* (above) and *Charlesworth and Percy on Negligence* (15th edn, 2022), chapter 12.

children[4]) in the factories of the industrial revolution[5]. Judges for many years sought to restrict the liabilities of employers (chiefly by the doctrine of 'common employment', whereby 'if the cause of the injury was the negligence of a fellow employee, the employer was not to be held vicariously liable unless the employee could prove that the fellow worker was incompetent and that the employer had thereby been negligent in engaging him'[6]) before the courts accepted that employers owed to their employees a set of personal, non-delegable duties of care[7]. The health and safety legislation of the later twentieth century, including European Community directives, made some employer's compensation duties strict[8], before domestic legislation in 2013 greatly reduced the extent to which regulatory breaches could sound in damages[9].

Technology provides new facts for old laws. This is true of transport with, for example, the Supreme Court ruling that the claimant Uber drivers were 'workers' for the purpose of the Employment Rights Act 1996[10] and the Court of Appeal that taxi-hailing Apps may be analysed according to legal principles established in the 18th century[11]. But some central problems remain. The manufacture of battery-powered electric vehicles and the mining of materials for electronics raise environmental and labour concerns similar to those of the nineteenth century[12]. Law and technology are still in flux.

Employer's common law duties of care

12.02 Employer's liability concerns liability to employees. However it also extends to vicarious liability to members of the public who might be injured by an employee. This chapter is concerned with the former liability, but the second type of liability should also be borne in mind.

At common law, an employer's duty to take reasonable care for the safety of its employees arises primarily in the tort of negligence[13]. Where an action 'could be said to be equally poised in contract and in tort, I should have held that the plaintiff could rely upon that aspect which put him in the more favourable position'[14].

---

4 *Munkman* chapter 1, 1.9-11.
5 *Munkman* chapter 1, 1.9.
6 *Munkman* chapter 1, 1.13. The doctrine of common employment was limited (first by the judicial ruling that it was ineffective where the employer was in breach of statutory duty: *Groves v Lord Wimborne* [1898] 2 QB 402 (CA)) and eventually extinguished (by the Law Reform (Personal Injuries) Act 1948). See *Munkman* chapter 1, 1.24, 1.36.
7 *Wilsons and Clyde Coal v English* [1938] AC 57 (HL (Sc)), (see Lord Wright at 78).
8 See *Munkman* chapter 1, 'The European revolution', 1.60-1.88.
9 The Enterprise and Regulatory Reform Act 2013 (ERRA 2013), Part 5 ('reduction of legislative burdens') s 69, which from 25 April 2013 amended the Health and Safety at Work Act 1974 s 47 to provide that 'Breach of a duty imposed by a statutory instrument containing (whether alone or with other provision) health and safety regulations shall not be actionable except to the extent that regulations under this section so provide' (HSWA 1974 s 47(2)). See *Munkman* chapter 1, 'Deregulation', 1.89-92.
10 *Uber BV v Aslam* [2021] UKSC 5; [2021] RTR 29.
11 *R (United Trade Action Group Ltd) v Transport for London* [2022] EWCA Civ 1026; [2022] RTR 32. See chapter 5, 'passenger services and public transport'.
12 See House of Commons Library Research Briefing 'Electric Vehicles and Infrastructure', CBP-7480 (20 December 2021) p 70, fn 290.
13 *Davie v New Merton Board Mills Ltd* [1959] AC 604, 619 (Viscount Simonds).
14 *Chesworth v Farrar* [1967] 1 QB 407, 416 (Edmund Davies J). Cited in *Charlesworth and Percy*, chapter 12, 12-16, though not an employer's liability case.

However, 'confusion' (and the inflation of costs) should be avoided by the unnecessary duplication of tortious and implied contractual bases of employer's liability[15].

Whether or not a duty of care in negligence arises in relation to the pleaded injury and loss or expense is a matter of analysis on the facts of each case[16]. But duties of care often arise in certain kinds of relationship:

'In many kinds of relationships the existence and extent of a duty of care has been recognised by the law over a long period. Examples may be found in the duties of road users and of navigators at sea to avoid collisions … and of employers for the general safety of their workers.'[17]

The employer's duty to take care for the general safety of its workers has been broken down into a list of particular duties, to provide:

- a safe place of work;
- safe equipment;
- a safe system of work; and
- competent co-employees.

'Because they are aspects of the duty to take reasonable care, these categories are not exhaustive. Each duty must also be examined to ascertain its scope'[18]. For instance:

'Equipment is not just the machinery the employee operates, but necessarily includes the maintenance of that machinery so that it operates safely and for the provision to the employee of any safety or protective equipment necessitated by the risks inherent in the employment duty… Similarly, in respect of a safe system of work the employer does not fulfil its duty simply by providing it; it must also take reasonable steps to see that it is carried out.'[19]

The employer's common law duties of care are not absolute:

'… the courts should be vigilant to see that the common law duty owed by a master to his servants should not be gradually enlarged until it is barely distinguishable from his absolute statutory obligations.'[20]

'… the overall test is still the conduct of the reasonable and prudent employer, taking positive thought for the safety of his workers in the light of what he knows or ought to know; where there is a recognised and general practice which has been followed for a substantial period in similar circumstances without mishap, he is entitled to follow it, unless in the light of common

---

15 *Davie v New Merton Board Mills Ltd* (above), 619 (Viscount Simonds).
16 In relation to remoteness of damage and the scope of the duty of care in negligence, see *Manchester Building Society v Grant Thornton UK LLP* [2021] UKSC 20; [2021] 3 WLR 81 and *Meadows v Khan* [2021] UKSC 21; [2021] 3 WLR 147.
17 *Munkman*, chapter 2, 2.4.
18 *Munkman*, chapter 2, 2.49.
19 As above.
20 *Latimer v AEC Ltd* [1953] AC 643, 658 (Lord Reid).

sense or newer knowledge it is clearly bad; but, where there is developing knowledge, he must keep reasonably abreast of it and not be too slow to apply it; and where he has in fact greater than average knowledge of the risks, he may be thereby obliged to take more than the average or standard precautions. He must weigh up the risk in terms of the likelihood of injury occurring and the potential consequences if it does; and he must balance against this the probably [sic] effectiveness of the precautions that can be taken to meet it and the expense and inconvenience they involve. If he is found to have fallen below the standard to be properly expected of a reasonable and prudent employer in these respects, he is negligent.'[21]

Following 'a relevant code of practice or other official or regulatory instrument' will often provide evidence of safe practice, but the mere fact of such reliance does not provide an impenetrable shield to liability:

'There is no rule of law that a relevant code of practice or other official or regulatory instrument necessarily sets the standard of care for the purpose of the tort of negligence... Thus to follow a relevant code of practice or regulatory instrument will often afford a defence to a claim in negligence. But there are circumstances where it does not do so. For example, it may be shown that the code of practice or regulatory instrument is compromised because the standards that it requires have been lowered as a result of heavy lobbying by interested parties; or because it covers a field in which apathy and fatalism has prevailed amongst workers, trade unions, employers and legislators ...; or because the instrument has failed to keep abreast of the latest technology and scientific understanding.'[22]

Some jobs inherently involve a high risk of injury, as in *Hopps v Mott MacDonald Ltd and Ministry of Defence*[23], where the claimant was a civilian employee of the first defendant, injured in an explosion in Iraq in 2003, while a passenger in an unarmoured military vehicle. The judge found that, while the employer 'had delegated the responsibility for the security of its staff to the MOD', the 'delegation was not, however, total'[24]. The claimant alleged negligence against the first defendant employer in failing properly to assess the risks of injury to him[25] by reference to information available to it as to the security situation, thereby allowing him to be transported rather than kept within a base[26], and causing or increasing his injuries by allowing him to be carried in an unarmoured vehicle[27]. The judge described the employer's duty to provide a safe system of work in such a high-risk situation as follows:

'An employer's duty of care requires him to take reasonable care to devise and operate a safe system of work. What is reasonable depends on the circumstances. In the present case they were highly unusual. The claimant

---

21 *Stokes v Guest, Keen and Nettlefold (Bolts and Nuts) Ltd* [1968] 1 WLR 1776, 1783d-f (Swanwick J).
22 *Baker v Quantum Clothing Group Ltd* [2011] UKSC 17; [2011] 1 WLR 1003, 1052, [101] (Lord Dyson JSC).
23 [2009] EWHC 1881 (QB) (Christopher Clarke J).
24 Above [49].
25 Above [55].
26 Above [57].
27 Above [59].

had voluntarily agreed to go to a dangerous place in the aftermath of a war. He did so partly for his own benefit (the rewards being markedly greater than he would have received in a less dangerous role); but also as a brave personal contribution to the rebuilding of a shattered economy to the benefit, whether perceived or not, of the Iraqi people. He did so as a civilian, not as a soldier, who may on occasion have to bear risks of a different order of magnitude. He was entitled to have such protection as was, in all the circumstances, reasonable, having regard to what was or ought to have been known by the military about prevailing conditions. He ran the risk that, even with such protection, he might suffer grievous injury, even death. A determination of what in these circumstances was required is not straightforward because there are a number of relevant considerations to be taken into account and, to some extent, balanced.'[28]

The claim failed, both for reasons of causation (an armoured vehicle would not have provided greater protection) but also because of the scope and purpose of the claimant's job:

'I would not accept that the danger level was such that the MM [first defendant] team should have been kept in base or at least out of Basrah until 6 or more weeks had elapsed for the delivery of such a vehicle. The effect of doing that would have been to afford the claimant protection from IEDs [improvised explosive devices]. But it would also have precluded him and other MM employees from doing their job. That in turn would have had a serious effect on the implementation of the EIP [Emergency Infrastructure Plan, on which the claimant was working], which was intended to bring about as swift a repair as was possible, and would have increased or, at the least, done nothing to reduce, the risks (disillusionment, unrest, violent defiance) associated with the continuation of a crumbling infrastructure. It would also have contributed to a growing humanitarian crisis.'[29]

'For these reasons I propose to dismiss the claimant's claim. The fact that I have done so in no way reduces the great credit due to him for the contribution which, at much personal cost, he has made to improving the lot of the Iraqi people.'[30]

Employer's statutory liabilities

12.03 In addition to the common law duties of care, employers are subject to certain statutory duties, where breach (post-ERRA 2013) explicitly leads to civil liability.

Although these are statutory duties, to be applied according to their own provisions, they can be regarded as practical extensions of the common law duty (safe place of work, safe work equipment, etc). In effect, they bridge practical problems of litigation which would otherwise be impassable for most injured claimants.

---

28 Above [87 – 88].
29 Above [131].
30 Above [133].

The difficulty of establishing an employer's reasonable foresight of and liability in negligence for a defect in work equipment supplied by a third party is one such problem. The Employer's Liability (Defective Equipment) Act 1969, s 1(1), (2) provides that:

'Where after the commencement of this Act—

(a) an employee suffers personal injury in the course of his employment in consequence of a defect in equipment provided by his employer for the purposes of the employer's business; and

(b) the defect is attributable wholly or partly to the fault of a third party (whether identified or not),

the injury shall be deemed to be also attributable to negligence on the part of the employer (whether or not he is liable in respect of the injury apart from this subsection), but without prejudice to the law relating to contributory negligence and to any remedy by way of contribution or in contract or otherwise which is available to the employer in respect of the injury.

(2) In so far as any agreement purports to exclude or limit any liability of an employer arising under subsection (1) of this section, the agreement shall be void.'

'The broad approach' of EL(DE)A 1969 'is to protect an employee by providing a remedy which otherwise would not be available unless negligence was first established against the employer'[31]. As defined by the Act, 'equipment' includes 'any plant and machinery' and a 'vehicle'[32]. The Act binds the Crown[33]. 'Defect' is not defined by the Act but has been judicially defined as including 'anything which renders the plant, etc, unfit for the use for which it is intended, when used in a reasonable way and with reasonable care'[34] and as meaning 'a lack or absence of something essential to completeness' (referring to completeness in terms of protection: there in the sense of a plank normally fitted to a saw-bench 'to protect persons working near the saw-bench from the part of the saw which was under the bench')[35].

(Please note that in the context of product liability, 'defect' is defined differently by the Consumer Protection Act 1987, Part I, s 3, as being present 'if the safety of the product is not such as persons generally are entitled to expect', subject to the elaborations upon that definition in the remainder of that section. See Chapter 10, 'vehicle defect claims' for discussion of product liability.)

In relation to road vehicles, there is now also the direct liability of insurers and of certain public bodies and of the Crown (permitted uninsured owners) under AEVA 2018, s 2(1) and (2).

---

31 *Charlesworth and Percy*, chapter 12, 12-67.
32 EL(DE)A 1969 s 1(3).
33 EL(DE)A 1969 s 1(4).
34 *Yarmouth v France* (1887) 19 QBD 647, 658 (Lindley LJ), followed in *Knowles v Liverpool City Council* [1992] PIQR P425, P431 (Purchas LJ).
35 *Tate v Latham & Son* [1897] IQB 502 (CA), 506 (Bruce J).

AEVA 2018, s 2(2) is of likely greater relevance to an employer's liability claim (amendments proposed by the Automated Vehicles Bill 2023-24 (HL Bill 1), cl 45, Sch 2, para 5(3)(a) are shown underlined):

'(2) Where –

  (a) an accident is caused by an <u>authorised</u> automated vehicle when driving itself on a road or other public place in Great Britain,

  (b) the vehicle is not <u>being used by an insured person</u> at the time of the accident,

  (c) section 143 of the Road Traffic Act 1988 (users of motor vehicles to be insured or secured against third-party risks) does not apply to the vehicle at that time—

    (i)   because of section 144(2) of that Act (exemption for public bodies etc), or

    (ii) because the vehicle is in the public service of the Crown, and

  (d) a person suffers damage as a result of the accident,

  the owner of the vehicle is liable for that damage.'

As described in Chapter 6, 'insurance', AEVA 2018, s 2(2) provides for the direct liability of an owner, in the place of an insurer, where the owner is a public body or the Crown permitted to use the vehicle without insurance 'because of section 144(2)' RTA 1988 or 'because the vehicle is in the public service of the Crown'.

In this book, the AEVA 2018, s 2(2) owner is referred to as the 'permitted uninsured owner', though that is the writer's paraphrase of s 2(2)(c) rather than statutory language. RTA 1988, s 144(2) provides an extensive list of public bodies so exempted from the compulsory third party motor insurance requirement of s 143. The full list of public bodies in RTA 1988, s 144(2) (to which AEVA 2018, s 2(2)(c)(ii) adds the Crown where the vehicle is in its public service) is not repeated here for reasons of space but lists vehicles owned by various public bodies starting with 'the council of a county or county district in England and Wales'[36].

As noted above, EL(DE)A 1969 and AEVA 2018, s 2 extend existing duties owed by others (third party manufacturer of equipment, defendant user of an automated vehicle) to others closer to the claimant (employer; insurer or permitted uninsured owner of an automated vehicle) to relieve the injured claimant of an otherwise heavy burden in litigation. This is apparent from commentary on both Acts: on EL(DE)A 1969 ('to protect an employee by providing a remedy which otherwise would not be available unless negligence was first established against the employer'[37]) and on AEVA 2018, s 2 ('following a claims 'event' the process follows the insurance route – as now – rather than becoming a 'consumer-manufacturer' product liability action, which is inevitably longer and more costly'[38]).

The similarity is even more particular than that. Both Acts recognise the difficulties for an injured claimant to prove liability for an equipment fault, so simplify an

---

36 RTA 1988, s 144(2)(a)(i).
37 *Charlesworth and Percy*, above.
38 House of Commons Library Research Briefing 'Automated and Electric Vehicles Act 2018', CBP 8118 (15 August 2018)

otherwise complex and expensive legal action by making a more easily identified defendant (employer under EL(DE)A 1969; compulsory motor insurer or permitted uninsured owner of an automated vehicle under AEVA 2018) liable to the claimant on proof of a short prescribed list of facts (in essence, causation of injury by work equipment defect attributable to third party (EL(DE)A 1969); causation of accident by automated vehicle when driving itself – AEVA 2018). In both Acts, a defendant found statutorily liable is permitted then to claim against the liable third party[39], on the logic that the liable employer/insurer/permitted uninsured owner is better resourced to prove the complexities of a defective equipment claim than an individual claimant worker/road user.

It is possible that, in an individual automated vehicle accident claim, an owner of an automated vehicle might as a matter of fact and law be both the employer of the injured party and the permitted uninsured owner under AEVA 2018, s 2(2). If so, that defendant might face statutory liabilities under both EL(DE)A 1969 and AEVA 2018, s 2(2). However, an assessment of the merits of the two statutory bases of action will depend upon the facts of each case, and the differences should be noted. For example:

- AEVA 2018, s 2 requires no proof of 'defect' but focusses instead upon whether the self-driving of an automated vehicle was a cause (which includes a partial cause[40]) of an accident on a road or other public place in Great Britain;

- Unlike AEVA 2018, s 2, EL(DE)A 1969 does not require proof of the equipment's status within an insurance regime as an element of the statutory liability.

So, in summary, in an employer's liability context both EL(DE)A 1969 and AEVA 2018 can be regarded as practical statutory extensions of the employer's duty to provide safe work equipment.

Risk assessment as precursor to employer identifying, particularising and discharging duty of care

12.04 In *Kennedy v Cordia (Services) LLP*, the Supreme Court described the importance of a risk assessment:

> '... it has become generally recognised that a reasonably prudent employer will conduct a risk assessment in connection with its operations so that it can take suitable precautions to avoid injury to its employees... The requirement to carry out such an assessment, whether statutory or not, forms the context in which the employer has to take precautions in the exercise of reasonable care for the safety of its employees. That is because the whole point of a risk assessment is to identify whether the particular operation gives rise to any risk to safety and, if so, what is the extent of that risk, and what can and should be done to minimise or eradicate the risk. The duty to carry out such an assessment is therefore ... logically anterior to determining what precautions a reasonable employer would have taken in order to fulfil his common law duty of care.

---

39 EL(DE)A 1969 s 1(1); AEVA 2018, s 5.
40 AEVA 2018, s 8(3)(b).

'It follows that the employer's duty is no longer confined to taking such precautions as are commonly taken or, as Lord Dunedin put it, such other precautions as are so obviously wanted that it would be folly in anyone to neglect to provide them. A negligent omission can result from a failure to seek out knowledge of risks which are not in themselves obvious.'[41]

So a risk assessment is not merely a formal document but must be purposeful – 'a blueprint for action'[42] whose suitability and sufficiency will point to the adequacy of the precautions taken by an employer[43] (a view endorsed by the Supreme Court[44]).

The general principles of prevention are set out in the Management of Health and Safety at Work Regulations 1999[45], reg 4 and Sch 1:

'(a) avoiding risks;

(b) evaluating the risks which cannot be avoided;

(c) combating the risks at source;

(d) adapting the work to the individual, especially as regards the design of workplaces, the choice of work equipment and the choice of working and production methods, with a view, in particular, to alleviating monotonous work and work at a predetermined work-rate and to reducing their effect on health;

(e) adapting to technical progress;

(f) replacing the dangerous by the non-dangerous or the less dangerous;

(g) developing a coherent overall prevention policy which covers technology, organisation of work, working conditions, social relationships and the influence of factors relating to the working environment;

(h) giving collective protective measures priority over individual protective measures; and

(i) giving appropriate instructions to employees.'

Compulsory insurance for employer's liability

12.05 The Third Parties (Rights Against Insurers) Acts 1930 and 2010 preserve third party rights against insurers in the event of the insolvency of the assured.[46]

The Employer's Liability (Compulsory Insurance) Act 1969, s 1(1) provides that:

'Except as otherwise provided by this Act, every employer carrying on any business in Great Britain shall insure, and maintain insurance, under one or more approved policies with an authorised insurer or insurers against liability for bodily injury or disease sustained by his employees, and arising out of

---

41 [2016] UKSC 6; [2016] 1 WLR 597, 628 [110-111] (Lord Reed and Lord Hodge JJSC).
42 *Allison v London Underground* [2008] EWCA Civ 71 [58] (Smith LJ).
43 As above, [59].
44 *Kennedy v Cordia* (above), 622 [89].
45 SI 1999/3242.
46 See Chapter 6, 'insurance', 'List of the main developments in British motor insurance law'.

and in the course of their employment in Great Britain in that business, but except in so far as regulations otherwise provide not including injury or disease suffered or contracted outside Great Britain.'

'Employee' is defined as 'an individual who has entered into or works under a contract of service or apprenticeship with an employer whether by way of manual labour, clerical work or otherwise, whether such contract is expressed or implied, oral or in writing'[47].

There are exceptions to the compulsory EL insurance requirement by reference to certain familial relationships with the employer and employees not ordinarily resident in Great Britain[48], and certain types of employer including prescribed public bodies[49].

Because employment can include liabilities arising from road traffic, compulsory motor insurance under EL(CI)A 1969 and the Road Traffic Acts are interrelated. As described in Chapter 6, 'insurance':

- RTA 1988, s 145(4)(a) does not require a policy of insurance 'to cover liability in respect of the death, arising out of and in the course of his employment, of a person in the employment of a person insured by the policy or of bodily injury sustained by such a person arising out of and in the course of his employment'.

- RTA 1988, s 145(4)(a) was originally enacted in the Road Traffic Act 1930[50], to release motor insurers from the obligation to insure for matters already covered by optional employer's liability insurance (later made compulsory by EL(CI) A 1969).

- To comply with the requirement for insurance cover of all passengers other than the driver under the European Union's Third Motor Insurance Directive[51], this permitted statutory exclusion was subsequently limited in its application by RTA 1988, s 145(4A) introduced in 1992[52], which provided that, in the case of a person 'carried in or upon a vehicle, or entering or getting on to, or alighting from, a vehicle', the exclusion under s 145(4)(a) would not apply 'unless cover in respect of the liability referred to in that paragraph is in fact provided pursuant to a requirement of the Employers' Liability (Compulsory Insurance) Act 1969'.

- AEVA 2018 disallows the original permitted exemption for third party employee cover. 'Where the vehicle in question is an automated vehicle', AEVA 2018 disapplies[53] RTA 1988, s 145(4)(a). This appears to recognise both the possible commercial use of automated vehicles carrying employees as passengers, and the complexity which resulted from the original exemption of employers' liability cover from third party insurance under the Road Traffic Acts.

---

47 EL(CI)A 1969, s 2(1).
48 EL(CI)A 1969, s 2(2).
49 EL(CI)A 1969, s 3.
50 RTA 1930, s 36(1)(b)(i).
51 Council Directive 90/232/EC.
52 RTA 1988, s 145(4A) added from 31 December 1992 by Motor Vehicles (Compulsory Insurance) Regulations 1992, SI 1992/3036, reg 3(2). See commentary in *The Law of Compulsory Motor Vehicle Insurance* (Routledge, 2021) by Özlem Gürses, chapter 4 [4.17 to 4.30].
53 End of RTA 1988, s 145, added by AEVA 2018, s 20, Sch 1, para 19(3).

The benefit to the employee of compulsory indemnity insurance is a benefit that passes with a transfer of employment, pursuant to the Transfer of Undertakings (Protection of Employment) Regulations 2006, reg 4[54].

Contributory negligence of employee

12.06 Contributory negligence principles have been discussed in a previous chapter[55].

In relation to contributory negligence in an employer's liability claim based upon breach of statutory duty, the Court of Appeal held that 'a high standard of proof was required to shift the entire blame for a breach of statutory duty from an employer to an injured employee'[56]. That was in reliance upon a 1969 judgment of the House of Lords (*Boyle v Kodak Ltd*) which dealt with an 'absolute' regulatory health and safety duty:

> '… once the plaintiff has established that there was a breach of an enactment which made the employer absolutely liable, and that that breach caused the accident, he need do no more. But it is then open to the employer to set up a defence that in fact he was not in any way in fault but that the plaintiff employee was alone to blame.'[57]

ERRA 2013 has since reduced the regulatory duties leading to civil liability.

Employer's right to seek contribution from others

12.07 If an employer becomes liable as a concurrent tortfeasor[58] to compensate a claimant for injury caused by the negligent driving of his employee – but *only* on the basis of vicarious liability for the negligence of that single employee – then the employer has a right to full contribution, ie an indemnity, under the Civil Liability (Contribution) Act 1978 (CL(C)A 1978) (if its provisions are satisfied) against its employee based upon the employee's breach of their employment contract, particularly of the implied term to take reasonable care when driving.[59]

However, CL(C)A 1978 right cannot be to a full contribution (an indemnity) if the employer is concurrently liable otherwise than by vicarious liability for the single employee. If the employer is also liable vicariously liable for the wrong of another

---

54 TUPE 2006, SI 2006/246. *Martin v Lancashire County Council* [2000] 3 All ER 544 (CA), applied in *Baker v British Gas Services (Commercial) Ltd* [2018] EWHC 2302 (QB); [2018] PIQR P3, P36-37 [63-67] (Amanda Yip QC sitting as a Deputy High Court Judge, as she then was).
55 chapter 9, 'RTA claims'.
56 *Anderson v Newham College* [2003] EWCA Civ 505; [2003] ICR 212, 217 [12] (Sedley LJ).
57 *Boyle v Kodak Ltd* [1969] 1 WLR, 667c-d (Lord Reid). See the discussion in *Munkman* [6.29-31].
58 See Chapter 9, 'RTA claims', for discussion of concurrent wrongs and CL(C)A 1978.
59 *Lister v Romford Ice and Cold Storage Co Ltd* [1957] AC 555 (HL), where contribution was under the Law Reform (Married Women and Tortfeasors) Act 1935, the precursor to CL(C) A 1978. The majority of the House of Lords rejected the submission that the compulsory third party insurance regime of the Road Traffic Act 1930 should give the employee contractual immunity against such contribution to their employer.

employee and/or is itself personally liable, then CL(C)A 1978 claim against each wrongdoing employee cannot be for an indemnity but only for a contribution[60].

Recent and likely future AAEV regulations affecting employer's liability claims

12.08   As discussed in Chapter 4, 'driving', regulations governing the use of advanced and automated equipment while driving have either recently been brought into effect or are imminent, and the government has announced its intention to legalise the use of e-scooters on roads outside the current extent of legal use (rental scooters in mandated trial areas):

- The Road Vehicles (Construction and Use) Regulations 1986[61], reg 110, prohibits the use while driving of a mobile telephone or a hand-held device, other than a two-way radio, which is capable of transmitting and receiving data (with exceptions for using a mobile telephone in a 'genuine emergency', for remote controlled parking functions and for contactless payments).

- From 6 July 2022, all new vehicles that are placed onto the market or registered or entered into service in the European Union must be equipped with certain ADAS systems[62]. Those systems include Advanced Emergency Braking (AEB) and Intelligent Speed Assistance (ISA, which signal to the driver that the applicable speed limit is exceeded). It seems likely but has yet to be officially confirmed that the British government will adopt a similar rule – both to achieve parity for British drivers and manufacturers but also because such systems are common to many current new vehicles.

- In anticipation of listing or authorisation of the first 'automated' vehicles (under either AEVA 2018, s 1 or AVA 2024, Part 1, when enacted), and in accordance with the UK government's position that the driver of an automated vehicle may watch non-driving related material on an in-built screen while the vehicle is driving itself, the Road Vehicles (Construction and Use) Regulations 1986, reg 109(1) has been amended to permit a driver 'to see ... information ... of any sort...' displayed on a built-in screen in an automated vehicle driving itself within the meaning of AEVA 2018, s 8(1)(a) and providing that the vehicle is not requesting the driver to take back control[63]. A consequent revision to the Highway Code has been proposed.

- The government announced in May 2022 that it intended to legalise the use of e-scooters on roads and other public places. However, this measure was postponed in December 2022 and has not reappeared. It did not feature in the King's Speech in November 2023.

---

60 *Jones v Manchester Corporation* [1952] 2 QB 852 (CA). This decision preceded *Lister* (above), hence Denning LJ's doubts about extant authority for the implication of a contractual term allowing indemnity, though he considered it within the court's discretion to order contribution or indemnity under the 1935 Act (870-871). Another note is that the case preceded the Employer's Liability (Compulsory Insurance) Act 1969, hence Denning LJ's concluding comment [872].
61 SI 1986/1078.
62 EU Regulation 2019/2144 of the European Parliament and of the Council of 27 November 2019.
63 Road Vehicles (Construction and Use) (Automated Vehicles) Order 2022, SI 2022/470, art 3 (in force from 1 July 2022).

Hypothetical AAEV facts which might give rise to employer's liability claims

12.09 Predicting the future is of course impossible. However, future employer's liability issues in road traffic cases might feature these new trends:

- In freight, the use of 'platooning' heavy goods vehicles in convoy, in which the lead vehicle is driven and following vehicles are automated, or all vehicles are automated.

- Delivery by automated or remotely-driven vehicles. Delivery might be of goods, or of the vehicles themselves (in the case of rental vehicles).

- The increased use of micro-mobility vehicles (such as e-scooters) as work vehicles.

- The use of automated delivery vehicles as a moving office, in which humans work while the vehicle drives itself.

- Issues as to the adequacy of work equipment, for example protective equipment such as helmets for users of micro-mobility vehicles, and advanced and automated driving systems for reasons of safety (eg. automated emergency braking systems).

- The adequacy of training for workers using novel vehicle technologies.

- The use of charging cables and micromobility vehicles left in public spaces.

Employer's liability to employees taking part in testing of new vehicles or systems

12.10 The reader is referred to Chapter 3, 'testing'.

The duties to third parties relating to testing (including risk assessment and the provision of compulsory insurance) apply to employees taking part in the test as well.

The principles of employer's liability apply. In particular, the possibility of carelessness and of accident is implicit in an assessment of risk (see for example the MHSWR 1999 general principles of prevention, above).

Insurance for employees is, like third party motor insurance, compulsory, and RTA 1988 and EL(CI)A 1969 refer to each other.

Official guidance as to testing (including the CCAV code of practice in relation to trialling of advanced vehicle technologies) is detailed but not comprehensive. For example, the CCAV guidance makes clear that an organisation carrying out a test must ensure its legality. That is consistent with the fact-sensitive approach to codes of practice in the judgment of Lord Dyson JSC in *Baker v Quantum Clothing Group Ltd* (see above) and with the similar approach to mandatory standards relevant to product liability in the judgment of Mrs Justice Andrews in *Gee and others v DePuy International Ltd*[64].

---

64 [2018] EWHC 1208 (QB) [170 – 178]. See Chapter 10, 'vehicle defect claims'.

B Employer's Liability Claims involving Advanced Driver Assistance Systems (ADAS)

12.11 As discussed in Chapter 4 ('driving'), British case law on civil liability has not yet treated the use of any advanced driver assistance system as altering the driver's standard of care in law.

The Highway Code does not prohibit the use of ADAS systems: 'As the driver, you are still responsible for the vehicle if you use a driver assistance system (like motorway assist)'; 'You may use driver assistance systems while you are driving. Make sure you use any system according to the manufacturer's instructions' (rules 150 and 160).

Consistently with that official guidance, criminal cases (in sentencing) indicate the aggravating features of an offence resulting from the careless use of ADAS:

'It was not an offence to set the cruise control to the maximum possible speed, but to do so called for a corresponding degree of vigilance in the steering and braking of the vehicle... Reading documents while driving on cruise control is another matter. It is a deliberate, not simply a negligent, removal of one's attention from driving.'[65]

As discussed above, negligence on the part of an employee driver is likely to allow the vicariously liable employer the right of contribution under CL(C)A 1978, if the other requirements are met – to the point of indemnity if the entire negligence is with the employee driver.

However, the use of ADAS is likely also to raise the issue of adequate training on the part of the employer. ADAS systems are increasingly varied, and knowledge in their use cannot be assumed. The absence of a suitable and sufficient risk assessment in relation to the use of such systems by an employee driver would be likely to sound against the employer.

C Employer's Liability Claims involving Automated Vehicles

Contributory negligence of employee in an AEVA 2018 claim

12.12 In the context of automated vehicle claims under AEVA 2018, the Act prescribes defences which can extinguish the statutory liability under s 2:

'The insurer or owner of an [authorised[66]] automated vehicle is not liable under section 2 to the person in charge of the vehicle where the accident that it caused was wholly due to the person's negligence in allowing the vehicle to begin driving itself when it was not appropriate to do so.'

---

65 *R v Brian France* [2002] EWCA Crim 1419; [2003] 1 Cr. App. R. (S) 25 [18, 47], discussed in Chapter 4.
66 Proposed amendment under AV Bill 2023-24 (HL Bill 1), cl 45, Sch 2, para 5(3)(b).

(AEVA 2018, s 3(2), 'contributory negligence etc')

'An insurance policy in respect of an [authorised] automated vehicle may exclude … the insurer's liability under section 2(1) for damage suffered by an insured person arising from an accident occurring as a direct result of—

(a) software alterations made by the insured person[67], or with the insured person's knowledge, that are prohibited under the policy, or

(b) a failure to install safety-critical software updates that the insured person knows, or ought reasonably to know, are safety-critical.'

(AEVA 2018, s 4(1), 'accident resulting from unauthorised software alterations or failure to update software')

AEVA 2018, s 3(2) would be consistent with *Boyle v Kodak*[68], if deployed in an AV claim where the claimant was employed by the AEVA 2018, s 2(2) owner, because s 3(2) requires entire causation of the accident by the claimant's negligence.

However, the s 4(1) exclusion of the AEVA 2018, s 2(1) liability is specific to a liable *insurer*, so would not rest upon any employer's liability but upon the insurer's direct liability under s 2(1). AEVA 2018, s 4(1) allows an insurance policy exemption to have effect against the AEVA claimant (the third party having the benefit of the RTA insurance), so might be regarded by the courts purely as an insurance exemption.

Nevertheless, the software-updating exemption to AEVA 2018, s 2(1) liability highlights a safe system of work point to which employers should be alert: vehicles equipped to be automated vehicles and some other advanced vehicles require software updates, typically delivered over the air, ie by WiFi, by means of prompts to the user via an App. The responsibility and means for updating software in vehicles provided for employment are likely to be matters which courts will expect employers to specify. That is particularly because of the effect of the AEVA 2018, s 4 exemption, which motor insurers can be expected to include in motor insurance policies taken out by employers and others.

Employer's right to claim against others in an AEVA 2018 claim

12.13 As has been noted elsewhere[69], AEVA 2018 does not allow for contribution under CL(C)A 1978 and does not use the word 'contribution' in its own third party claim section (s 5). Instead, AEVA 2018, s 5 provides either defendant made liable by s 2 (insurer or – in the writer's phrase – permitted uninsured owner) with a

---

67 The current definition under AEVA 2018 is that "insured person", in relation to an insured vehicle, means any person whose use of the vehicle is covered by the policy in question': AEVA 2018, s 8(2). However, the AV Bill 2023-24 (HL Bill 1), cl 45, Sch 2 ,para 5(6)(b)(ii) and (iii) are set to delete s 8(2) and replace it with new wording for s 8(1)(b): 'a person is an "insured person", in relation to a vehicle, if there is in force in relation to that person's use of the vehicle on a road or other public place in Great Britain a policy of insurance that satisfies the conditions in section 145 of the Road Traffic Act 1988'.
68 '… it is then open to the employer to set up a defence that in fact he was not in any way in fault but that the plaintiff employee was alone to blame'. See above.
69 See Chapter 9, 'RTA claims'.

'right to claim against any other person liable to the injured party in respect of the accident'.

Whether this s 5 right is restricted, by implication, to the 'same damage' as that suffered by the victim (as would be the case for a contribution claim under CL(C) A 1978) is debatable, and examined in Chapter 9, 'RTA claims'.

Given the likelihood that a claim against an RTA 1988, s 144(2) public body under AEVA 2018, s 2(2) will sometimes be against a public body which is at the time of the accident the employer of the user of the vehicle, it seems that such a public body would be entitled to make a claim in relation to its AEVA 2018, s 2(2) liability against its employee in charge of an automated vehicle, if it was able to demonstrate a lack of reasonable care in that employee's use of the automated vehicle.

Precisely how that might be formulated would depend upon the facts of the case, but it might be put not only on the basis of breach of an implied term of reasonable care in driving (*Lister v Romford Ice and Cold Storage Ltd*, above) but also on the basis of AEVA 2018, s 3(2) ('accident ... wholly due to the person's negligence in allowing the vehicle to begin driving itself when it was not appropriate to do so'). It might be that the latter would even be a more likely approach to an AEVA 2018, s 5 claim than the entirely human driving situation upon which *Lister* – a judgment handed down in 1956 – was based. However, the *Lister* approach (implied term that employee will use reasonable care when driving the vehicle which they are employed to drive[70]) is factually wider than the situation required by AEVA 2018, s 3(2) ('allowing the vehicle to begin driving itself when it was not appropriate to do so') and s 3(2) is not (unlike the permitted contractual insurance exemption of AEVA 2018, s 4[71]) said to be the only available instance of contributory negligence.

A point to be determined by the courts will be the extent of contributory fault in automated vehicle liability claims, particularly in the subset of vehicle-related employer's liability claims to which *Lister* belongs. The point is likely to be highly fact-sensitive – especially in the new regulation of 'driving' that automated driving systems are likely to require[72].

A different situation allowing an AEVA 2018, s 5 claim by the s 2 liable insurer or permitted uninsured owner is where a defect in the hardware or software of the vehicle is identified, and the liable party wishes to pursue a claim against the manufacturer, software developer or other. This situation is discussed in Chapter 10, 'vehicle defect claims'.

D Employer's Liability Claims involving Electric Vehicles

12.14 Where there is an employment relationship, the duties owed to an employee include the provision of safe equipment.

---

70 *Lister* (above) 580 (Lord Morton).
71 AEVA 2018, s 2(6).
72 See Chapter 4, 'driving', especially the AV Bill 2023-24 (HL Bill 1) proposed codification of the user-in-charge's immunities in relation to transition from self-driving.

In relation to jobs involving the use of e-bikes and e-scooters, which travel at speeds often faster than bicycles and which (in the case of e-scooters) are less stable than bicycles, that raises the particular issue of the adequacy of safe protective equipment such as suitable helmets (not necessarily bicycle helmets in the case of an e-scooter) and potentially other equipment (such as gloves and high-visibility clothing).

In relation to electric cars, vans and lorries, duties in relation to driving are the same as for internal combustion engine (ICE) vehicles, with the addition of the possible further hazards of:

● tripping over unsafely arranged charging cables (see Chapter 6, 'insurance')

● failure to update software (see above)

● unfamiliarity with controls in an electric vehicle (which tend to be more screen-based than a traditional dashboard) and

● the faster acceleration from standing of electric vehicles as compared to ICE vehicles.

Additional risks such as these (and this is not an exhaustive list) should be considered as part of the employer's risk assessment in relation to any particular electric vehicle, and to be likely necessary topics for training.

Chapter 13

Highway claims

'Members of the public who drive cars on the highways of this country are entitled to expect that the highways will be kept properly in repair. They are entitled to complain if damage is caused by some obstruction or condition of the road or its surroundings that constitutes a public nuisance. And they are, of course, entitled to complain if they suffer damage by the negligence of some other user of the highway. But an overriding imperative is that those who drive on public highways do so in a manner and at a speed that is safe having regard to such matters as the nature of the road, the weather conditions and the traffic conditions. Drivers are first and foremost themselves responsible for their own safety.'

(Lord Scott, 2004)[1]

"*Caparo* [*Industries plc v Dickman*] [1990] 2 AC 605 did not impose a universal tripartite test for the existence of a duty of care, but recommended an incremental approach to novel situations, based on the use of established categories of liability as guides, by analogy, to the existence and scope of a duty of care in cases which fall outside them. The question whether the imposition of a duty of care would be fair, just and reasonable forms part of the assessment of whether such an incremental step ought to be taken."

(Lord Reed, 2019)[2]

Chapter Contents

---

1   *Gorringe v Calderdale Metropolitan Borough Council* [2004] UKHL 15; [2004] 1 WLR 1057 [77].
2   *N and another v Poole Borough Council (AIRE Centre and others intervening)* [2019] UKSC 25; [2020] AC 780, 835 [64].

A Outline of the Laws of Highway Claims

Nature of highway claims

13.01 Highway claims have been categorised according to their facts as claims arising from interference with access to the highway, obstruction of the highway and the condition of the highway[3].

In terms of legal categorisation, highway claims exist within a broad landscape which includes trespass, nuisance and negligence, to which Parliament has (by removing the maintaining authority's previous immunity from suit) added a particular statutory liability upon a highway authority to maintain the highway[4].

Highway claims in tort 'ought to represent a sensible balance or compromise between private and public interest'[5]. Highway claims have engaged legal debates as to the extent of the duties of public authorities, including the principle that there is usually no liability in negligence for pure omissions and the question of whether the content of public powers can be relied upon to establish, particularise or heighten a duty of care owed by a public authority in private law (as Lord Scott described it, to 'jack up' the public authority's common law duty of care[6]). Such arguments have coincided in leading highway claim cases, because a claim based upon breach of statutory duty under HA 1980, s 41 is construed narrowly so is often unavailable. Claimants have therefore sought other legal bases of claim and have submitted that particular common law duties are evidenced by the existence of public statutory powers[7].

Those points are discussed below. When considering the duties of care of public authorities in new or particular settings, the courts will hold to precedent, as Lord Reed made clear in 2018 (dealing with the duty of care owed by police to an innocent bystander while police officers carried out an arrest):

> 'In the ordinary run of cases, courts consider what has been decided previously and follow the precedents (unless it is necessary to consider whether the precedents should be departed from). In cases where the question whether a duty of care arises has not previously been decided, the courts will consider the closest analogies in the existing law, with a view to maintaining the coherence of the law and the avoidance of inappropriate distinctions. They

---

3   See *Winfield and Jolowicz on Tort* (20th edn, 2020) at 15-079 to 15-085 and *Clerk & Lindsell on Torts* (23rd edn, 2020) at 19-180 to 19-193. This chapter is not an exhaustive treatment of the law of highway claims, for which see also those and Stephen Sauvain KC, Ruth Stockley and Ned Westaway *Highway Law* (6th edn, Sweet and Maxwell, 2022).
4   Highways (Miscellaneous Provisions) Act 1961, s 1(1): 'The rule of law exempting the inhabitants at large and any other persons as their successors from liability for non-repair of highways is hereby abrogated.'; now HA 1980, s 41 (duty to maintain highways maintainable at public expense).
5   *Mills v Barnsley Metropolitan Borough Council* [1992] PIQR P291, 295, Steyn LJ (as he then was).
6   *Gorringe* [54].
7   See *Stovin v Wise, Norfolk County Council (Third Party)* [1996] AC 923 (HL) and *Gorringe* (above). The argument is not unique to negligence; in *Ali v Bradford Metropolitan District Council* [2010] EWCA Civ 1282; [2012] 1 WLR 161, discussed below, the claimant unsuccessfully argued that HA 1980, s 130 evidenced a claim in nuisance.

will also weigh up the reasons for and against imposing liability, in order to decide whether the existence of a duty of care would be just and reasonable.'[8]

Nuisance

13.02 *Clerk and Lindsell on Torts* defines nuisance as follows:

'Nuisance is an act or omission which is an interference with, disturbance of or annoyance to, a person in the exercise or enjoyment of: (a) a right belonging to him as a member of the public, when it is a public nuisance; or (b) his ownership or occupation of land or of some easement, profit, or other right used or enjoyed in connection with land, when it is a private nuisance.'[9]

Standard of duty in nuisance

13.03 In *Goldman v Hargrave*, Lord Wilberforce wrote that:

'... the tort of nuisance, uncertain in its boundary, may comprise a wide variety of situations, in some of which negligence plays no part, in others of which it is decisive.'[10]

Clerk and Lindsell on Torts observes that statements as to the standard of duty in nuisance (variously that it is strict, or based upon foreseeability):

'if taken out of context and applied generally to nuisance as a whole, naturally produce contradiction and perhaps confusion, and in the light of such disparate statements the standard of duty has been considered a vexed and difficult question. But if, as Lord Wilberforce says, there is no single standard applicable to all situations covered by the tort of nuisance, it is illusory to seek a single answer to the question. Instead, attention should be directed towards identifying different kinds of situations and the appropriate standard of duty in each.'[11]

For example, in *Dymond v Pearce*, the Court of Appeal held that leaving a lorry on the highway for a considerable period for the driver's convenience constituted a nuisance by obstruction of the highway which was actionable if that obstruction caused damage to a member of the public. However, on the facts of the case (including that the lorry was lit both by a streetlamp and its own lights) the sole cause of the accident was the negligence of the claimant motor cyclist who rode into the parked lorry and, accordingly, the nuisance was not a cause of the claimant's

---

8   *Robinson v Chief Constable of West Yorkshire Police* [2018] UKSC 4; [2018] AC 736, Lord Reed
     [29]. And see Lord Reed in *N v Poole BC*, quoted at the head of this chapter.
9   *Clerk & Lindsell on Torts*, 19-01.
10   *Goldman v Hargrave* [1967] 1 AC 645 (PC), Lord Wilberforce at 657 A. *Overseas Tankship
     (UK) Ltd v Miller Steamship Co Pty Ltd (The Wagon Mound No. 2)* [1967] AC 617 (PC), the
     source of Lord Wilberforce's observation, was a case in which foreseeability was essential
     to liability in nuisance: see in particular Lord Reid in *The Wagon Mound No. 2* at 639 B to
     640 B ('Comparing nuisance with negligence ...').
11   *Clerk & Lindsell on Torts*, 19-31.

injury, so the claim for damages was dismissed. Sachs LJ observed that the judge's finding that the nuisance by obstruction was not causative of the accident was:

'in effect a finding that the sole cause of the accident was the motor cyclist's negligence. On the facts, that was in my judgment a correct conclusion. It entails a parallel conclusion that the nuisance was not a cause of the plaintiff's injuries: that, indeed, in the vast majority of cases, is an inevitable conclusion once negligence on the part of the driver of a stationary vehicle is negatived, for only rarely will that which was found not to be a foreseeable cause of an accident also be found to have been in law the actual cause of it.'[12]

Police, Crime, Sentencing and Courts Act 2022, s 78

13.04 The Police, Crime, Sentencing and Courts Act 2022 (PCSCA 2022), s 78 (offence of intentionally or recklessly causing public nuisance) 'does not affect the civil liability of any person for the tort of public nuisance' (s 78(8)(b))[13].

Highway access claims

Access claims 'cease as soon as the highway is reached'

13.05 Access claims are limited to private access from the claimant's premises to the highway:

'A person who owns premises abutting on a highway enjoys as a private right the right of stepping from his own premises on to the highway, and if any obstruction be placed in his doorway, or gateway, or, if it be a river, at the edge of his wharf, so as to prevent him from obtaining access from his own premises to the highway, that obstruction would be an interference with a private right. But immediately that he has stepped on to the highway, and is using the highway, what he is using is not a private right, but a public right.'[14]

The judge in that case agreed 'that the local authority must not so use their power [to erect public lighting] as to commit a nuisance'[15]. *Clerk and Lindsell* notes that 'this private right' of access to the highway 'ceases as soon as the highway is reached and any subsequent interference, for example with the right to carry goods from the premises to a van standing in the roadway, is a public nuisance if it is a nuisance at all'[16].

---

12 *Dymond v Pearce* [1972] 1 QB 496, 503 C-D.
13 PCSCA 2022, s 78 in force from 28 June 2022: Police, Crime, Sentencing and Courts Act 2022 (Commencement No.1 and Transitional Provision) Regulations 2022, SI 2022/520, reg 5(j).
14 *Chaplin and Co Ltd v Westminster Corporation* [1901] 2 Ch 329, 334 (Buckley J, as he then was).
15 Above, 336.
16 *Clerk & Lindsell on Torts* (23rd edn, 2020), 19-180. The note in a previous edition was cited by Akenhead J in *Hiscox Synidcates Ltd v The Pinnacle Ltd* [2008] EWHC 1386 (QB, TCC) [14].

A difference between trespass and nuisance

13.06   As *Winfield and Jolowicz* puts it:

'Trespass to land is the name given to that form of trespass which is constituted by unjustifiable interference with the possession of land.'[17]

But, to constitute an interference with land amounting to trespass:

'the interference must be direct and immediate. If it is indirect or consequential, it may be a nuisance, but will not be a trespass. So if I plant a tree on your land, that is trespass; but if the roots or branches of a tree on my land project into or over your land, that is a nuisance.'[18]

Highway obstruction claims

13.07

'It is perfectly clear that anything which substantially prevents the public from having free access over the whole of the highway which is not purely temporary in nature is an unlawful obstruction.'[19]

Whether an obstruction is a nuisance depends upon:

'whether the obstruction was of a permanent or a temporary nature. If it is a permanent obstruction then, as indicated in the Court of Appeal decision in *Harper v GN Haden & Sons Ltd* [1933] 1 Ch 298[20], that no question of reasonableness arises, whereas if it is temporary the obstruction will only amount to a nuisance if it is unreasonable… where there is a non-*de minimis*[21] obstruction which is not ancillary to the passage and repassage on the highway, that is not likely to be reasonable. There is a difference between the position of a vehicle that has stopped, as in *Nagy v Weston*[22], and other physical objects placed in the road such as a skip or, as in this case, a bin.'[23]

An example of a *de minimis* obstruction would be 'a rack of newspapers outside a newsagent'[24]. A 1,100 litre bin was not a *de minimis* obstruction[25].

Uses ancillary to the passage and repassage on the highway include the following:

---

17   *Winfield and Jolowicz on Tort* (20th edn, 2020) at 14-001.
18   Above, 14-010, citing *Smith v Giddy* [1904] 2 KB 448 at 451 and *Davey v Harrow Corp* [1958] 1 QB 60.
19   *Seekings v Clark* (1961) QBD, 269, quoted in *East Hertfordshire District Council v Isabel Hospice Trading Ltd* [24].
20   Where temporary scaffolding was held to be reasonable and not a public nuisance.
21   *De minimis*: too trivial or minor to merit consideration.
22   [1965] 1 WLR 280. Van parked in street lay-by, by bus stop, for 15 minutes to sell hot dogs. Driver asked on several occasions by police constable to move. Held to be a nuisance.
23   *East Hertfordshire District Council v Isabel Hospice Trading Ltd*, Jack Beatson QC sitting as a Deputy High Court Judge (as he then was), 29 August 2000, QB [2001] JPL 597 [15, 28]. Wheeled 1,100 litre bin 'kept in the rear of the shop in the corner formed by the protruding wall of the adjacent premises' since the previous year held to be a nuisance.
24   Above [35], citing *Seekings*.
25   Above.

'... a tired pedestrian may sit down and rest himself. A motorist may attempt to repair a minor breakdown... Now, even then, such user must be reasonable in extent. The tired pedestrian or the motorist with the breakdown can only rest for a reasonable while.'[26]

In *Director of Public Prosecutions v Jones*[27], a case concerned with the lawfulness of protest, Lord Irvine LC did not accept 'that, to be lawful, activities on the highway must fall within a rubric 'incidental or ancillary to' the exercise of the right of passage' on the highway. Rather:

'... any 'reasonable and usual' mode of using the highway is lawful, provided it is not inconsistent with the general public's right of passage. I understand Collins LJ's acceptance in *Hickman v Maisey*[28], at pp 757-758, of Lord Esher MR's judgment in *Harrison v Duke of Rutland*[29] in that sense.'[30]

That an obstruction is widespread, or usually tolerated by neighbours, does not prevent it being found by the court to be a nuisance:

'... it is a widespread practice for shopkeepers such as greengrocers and hardware merchants to display their goods on the footpaths in front of the shops. If the law was strictly enforced in every case we do not see how it could be successfully contended that such practices do not constitute an obstruction of the footpaths, rendering the shopkeepers liable to proceedings under various statutory provisions... But it is notorious that these statutory provisions are not enforced with strictness, and that proceedings are but rarely brought either by the urban authorities or by private individuals... In the vast majority of cases the ordinary citizen would be apt to regard a strict enforcement of the statutory provisions as unneighbourly and unnecessary, and calculated to produce an amount of ill-feeling out of all proportion to any good which might be achieved. Nevertheless, when the matter is brought before the Court it is the duty of the Court to pronounce on the legal position.'[31]

In the year 2000, there was 'no difference in the approach used in the criminal cases and the civil cases to the question whether there was an obstruction, an unlawful obstruction'[32]. From 28 June 2022[33], PCSCA 2022, s 78 (the offence of intentionally or recklessly causing public nuisance) came into effect, abolishing the common law offence of public nuisance[34]. Section 78 'does not affect the civil liability of any person for the tort of public nuisance'[35]. So common law principles

---

26 *Hubbard v Pitt* [1976] 1 QB 142 (CA) at 149 G – 150 A (Forbes J).
27 [1999] 2 AC 240 (HL).
28 [1900] 1 QB 752, 757-758 (CA).
29 [1893] 1 QB 142 (CA), 146-147.
30 *DPP v Jones*, Lord Irvine at 255 E-F.
31 *Black v Mitchell* [1951] NI 145, quoted in *East Hertfordshire District Council v Isabel Hospice Trading Ltd* [18].
32 *East Hertfordshire District Council v Isabel Hospice Trading Ltd* [29], citing Glidewell LJ in *Hirst & Agu v Chief Constable of West Yorkshire* (1987) 85 Cr App R 143, 148, and Lord Denning in *Hubbard v Pitt* (above).
33 PCSCA 2022, s 78 in force from 28 June 2022: Police, Crime, Sentencing and Courts Act 2022 (Commencement No 1 and Transitional Provision) Regulations 2022, SI 2022/520, reg 5(j).
34 PCSCA 2022, s 78(6).
35 PCSCA 2022, s 78(8)(b).

as to civil liability for public nuisance continue; however, with the commencement of the offence under PCSCA 2022, s 78, the relationship between the criminal and civil definitions of public nuisance might not be as close after 28 June 2022 as it was before.

No liability upon a highway authority for continuing a nuisance which it had not created

13.08 In *Ali v Bradford Metropolitan District Council* the Court of Appeal held that it is not for the courts to impose liability on a highway authority for continuing a nuisance (in that case an accumulation of mud and debris) which it had not created, since that would usurp the proper role of Parliament and interfere with a carefully regulated statutory scheme which contained specific provisions regulating the powers and duty of a highway authority with respect to the removal of obstructions and established a method for enforcement of the duty. HA 1980, s 130 ('protection of public rights'[36]) was concerned with the protection of the legal rights of the public at large to use the public highway and with legal rights of access, not with the safety of the condition of the highway. That section placed no express obligation on a highway authority to remove obstructions and none was to be implied, since HA 1980, s 150 ('duty to remove snow, soil etc from the highway') made express provision for such a duty[37]. HA 1980, s 130 did not give rise to a private law action for damages for breach and any duty owed under the section was a public law duty enforceable only as such.[38]

Highway condition claims

The legal setting of highway condition claims

13.09 Claims in relation to the condition of highways have a special place in the legal landscape. In *Gorringe v Calderdale Metropolitan Borough Council*, the House of Lords described the history of

- the original *purely public duty* to keep a highway maintainable at public expense in repair (a duty placed originally upon the inhabitants of a parish, for which they appointed a surveyor funded by levying a rate),

- the consequent immunity of the public authority from *private law liability* for failure to repair such a highway, and

---

36 Including HA 1980, s 130(1) ('It is the duty of the highway authority to assert and protect the rights of the public to the use and enjoyment of any highway for which they are the highway authority, including any roadside waste which forms part of it'), s 130(3) ('it is the duty of a council who are a highway authority to prevent, as far as possible, the stopping up or obstruction of … the highways …') and 130 (5) ('a council may, in the performance of their functions under the foregoing provisions of this section, institute legal proceedings in their own name, defend any legal proceedings and generally take such steps as they deem expedient').

37 HA 1980, s 150(2): 'If a highway authority fail to remove an obstruction which it is their duty under this section to remove, a magistrates' court may, on a complaint made by any person, by order require the authority to remove the obstruction within such period (not being less than 24 hours) from the making of the order as the court thinks reasonable, having regard to all the circumstances of the case.'

38 *Ali v Bradford Metropolitan District Council* [2010] EWCA Civ 1282; [2012] 1 WLR 161. See Toulson LJ (as he then was) [39].

- Later – to fill the space of that immunity – the enactment of a particular *statutory duty* to keep the highway in repair[39], breach of which established a private law liability by the public authority to the claimant in damages, by the Highways (Miscellaneous Provisions) Act 1961 s 1, now by the Highways Act 1980 s 41[40].

That civil statutory liability to maintain the highway under HA 1980, s 41 is restricted in its application. The reason lies in its history:

'... the duty to take active steps to keep the highway in repair was special to the highway authority and was not a private law duty owed to any individual. Thus it was said that highway authorities were liable in tort for misfeasance but not for non-feasance... The true position was that no one had ever been liable in private law for non-repair of a highway. But all this was changed by section 1(1) of the Highways (Miscellaneous Provisions) Act 1961. The public duty to keep the highway in repair was converted into a statutory duty owed by the highway authority to all users of the highway, giving a remedy in damages for its breach. The new private law duty was however limited to the obligation which had previously rested upon the inhabitants at large, namely, to put and keep the highway in repair.'[41]

'The common law immunity enjoyed by highway authorities and abolished by section 1(1) of the 1961 Act related only to liability for failure to repair a highway. Liability for damage arising otherwise than from the non-repair of a highway was not affected.'[42]

The rationale for restricting the application of the s 41 statutory duty is that HA 1980 provides, irrespective of the civil liability under s 41, for:

'the absolute duty of the highway authority, which remains absolutely bound, as a matter of public law, to maintain the highway without any qualification, and thus whether or not any lack of reasonable care is involved... That absolute duty is enforceable by a variety of public law remedies, including judicial review and complaint to the Crown Court under s 56. If the court finds that the highway is 'out of repair', an order to put it in repair must follow: s 56(2). The consequences of the absolute nature of this liability are stressed in both *Haydon* [43](at 360C) and *Goodes* (at 378D) as one of the reasons why the limitation of the duty to maintain remains even in modern times.'[44]

---

39 HA 1980, s 329(1) ('further provision as to interpretation') provides that ''*maintenance*' includes repair, and '*maintain*' and '*maintainable*' are to be construed accordingly'.

40 *Gorringe*, Lord Hoffmann [11-14]; Lord Scott [48-52]; Lord Rodger [80-81]. See also Lord Hoffmann's judgment in *Goodes v East Sussex County Council* [2000] 1 WLR 1356; [2000] RTR 366.

41 *Gorringe*, Lord Hoffmann [13]-[14].

42 *Gorringe*, Lord Scott [50].

43 The dissent of Lord Denning MR, against the majority in *Haydon v Kent County Council* [1978] 1 QB 343 (Goff and Shaw LJJ), that clearance of snow and ice was not (then, before the 2003 addition of such a duty to HA 1980, s 41) within the highway authority's statutory duty to maintain the highway. In *Goodes v East Sussex County Council* (above) the House of Lords preferred Lord Denning's approach, which Lord Hoffmann described as 'completely convincing'.

44 *Valentine v Transport for London* [2010] EWCA Civ 1358; [2011] RTR 24, [11].

It follows that civil liability in damages for failure to maintain the highway is restricted to 'the fairly narrow scope'[45] of HA 1980, s 41 (the duty to maintain the highway, ie. to put and keep it in repair), but that other legal bases of claim remain available in cases concerned not with maintenance of the highway but with another duty of care acquired by the highway authority:

'In a case, therefore, where the damage complained of has been caused not by a failure to maintain the highway but by something done by the highway authority, or for which the highway authority have become responsible ..., liability continued after 1961 as before, to be determined by the common law principles of negligence or, as the case may be, public nuisance. It is only where the alleged liability arises out of a failure 'to maintain' the highway that the section 41(1) [HA 1980] duty and the section 58(1) defence come into play.'[46]

For example, in *Gorringe*, the House of Lords agreed with the Court of Appeal (both in that case and in *Lavis v Kent County Council*[47]) that the statutory duty under HA 1980, s 41 to keep the highway in repair does not include the provision of information by means of street furniture or painted signs[48], so did not require the restoration of a 'slow' sign once painted on the road surface at a sharp bend but since worn away (particularly where the danger of rounding the corner at speed ought to have been obvious to the injured claimant driver). The alternative basis of claim in negligence did not apply to include the provision of signs, as reasonable foreseeability of injury by an omission to act 'is insufficient to justify the imposition of liability upon someone who simply does nothing: who neither creates the risk nor undertakes to do anything to avert it... the imposition of such a liability upon a highway authority through the law of negligence would be inconsistent with the well-established rules which have always limited its liability at common law'[49]. Lord Scott noted that a case relied upon by the claimant in *Gorringe*, *Bird v Pearce*[50] (failure by local authority to provide temporary signs after its obliteration of road markings delineating minor and major roads at a junction during road resurfacing, contributing to road traffic collision) was a claim in negligence on the basis of the authority's creation of a new danger, and was not a claim supporting s 41 liability[51].

HA 1980, s 41 claim

13.10 HA 1980, s 41(1) and (1A) provide that:

'(1) The authority who are for the time being the highway authority for a highway maintainable at the public expense are under a duty, subject to subsections (2) and (4) below[52], to maintain the highway.

---

45 *Gorringe*, Lord Scott [52].
46 Above [51].
47 (1992) 90 LGR 416, 418 (Steyn LJ, as he then was).
48 *Gorringe*, Lord Hoffmann [15].
49 Lord Hoffmann [17].
50 [1979] RTR 369 (CA).
51 *Gorringe*, Lord Scott [65]-[66] and Lord Rodger [85].
52 HA 1980, s 41(2) and (4) relate to responsibility for maintenance of the highway where the Minister has made an order under s 10 directing that a highway proposed to be constructed by him or by a strategic highways company shall become a trunk road. For the context, see 'the Trunk Roads Act 1936' in 'Appendix: History'.

(1A)In particular, a highway authority are under a duty to ensure, so far as is reasonably practicable, that safe passage along a highway is not endangered by snow or ice.'

'The highway authority must provide not merely for model drivers, but for the normal run of drivers to be found on their highways, and that includes those who make the mistakes which experience and common sense teaches are likely to occur.'[53]

The statutory duty to maintain the highway is 'limited to the obligation which had previously rested upon the inhabitants at large, namely, to put and keep the highway in repair'[54]. So for example (as in *Gorringe*), a road marking does not form part of the physical or structural condition of the roadway, so does not engage HA 1980, s 41.[55]

Although removal of ice and snow would not previously have been within the s 41 duty, those additions to the duty were made by statutory amendment in 2003 (by the Railways and Transport Safety Act 2003, s 111, adding HA 1980, s 41(1A)[56]).

The s 41 duty to maintain the highway is 'not confined to the 'surface' of the road; the surface is simply treated as one important part of what is to be maintained, which is the 'structure and fabric of the roadway''[57]. The duty therefore includes maintenance of a highway drainage system, so extends beyond the surface of the highway used by traffic and pedestrians to highway drains beneath the surface[58]. Although 'not every flood is evidence of a failure to maintain':

'An effective drainage system is an intrinsic part of the design of a modern road, and like any other part of the road it needs to be properly maintained. As a matter of common sense, it is difficult to see why a statutory duty to maintain the road should exclude it.'[59]

Save for the removal of ice and snow, now subject to HA 1980, s 41(1A), the duty to maintain under s 41 relates 'to the fabric of the road including its substructure such as drains' and 'does not extend to a duty to remove surface-lying material, obstructions or spillages, whether or not they result in some danger.'[60]

---

53   *Rider v Rider* [1973] QB 505, 514 F-G (Sachs LJ) and see 517 C-D (Karminski LJ) and 518 A (Lawton LJ). And see *Mills v Barnsley MBC* (above).
54   *Gorringe*, Lord Hoffmann [14].
55   *Gorringe*, Lord Hoffmann [15], Lord Scott [67].
56   See *Gorringe* [14, 52], noting that the statutory revision was in response to the judgment of the House of Lords in *Goodes v East Sussex County Council* (above), which had decided that the HA 1980, s 41 duty did not then require the removal of ice and snow. *Sandhar v Department for Transport, Environment and the Regions* [2004] EWCA Civ 1440; [2005] 1 WLR 1632 was a claim decided after the amendment but arising from a pre-amendment (1996) event, to which the new part of the statutory duty did not apply retrospectively [11].
57   *Mitchell v Department for Transport, Mott MacDonald Ltd as Part 20 defendants* [2006] EWCA Civ 1089; [2006] 1 WLR 3356, Carnwath LJ [40], quoting *Dublin United Tramways Co Ltd v Fitzgerald* [1903] AC 99, Lord Robertson, 109-110.
58   *Burnside v Emerson* [1968] 1 WLR 1490 (CA); *Mitchell* (above).
59   *Mitchell*, Carnwath LJ [3].
60   *Valentine v Transport for London* (above), following *Goodes v East Sussex County Council* (above).

HA 1980, s 58 defence

13.11

'To mitigate the effect of allowing a private cause of action for breach of an absolute duty, the Act gave highway authorities a special statutory defence, which is now in section 58 of the Highways Act 1980.'[61]

HA 1980, s 58 provides as follows:

'(1) In an action against a highway authority in respect of damage resulting from their failure to maintain a highway maintainable at the public expense it is a defence (without prejudice to any other defence or the application of the law relating to contributory negligence) to prove that the authority had taken such care as in all the circumstances was reasonably required to secure that the part of the highway to which the action relates was not dangerous for traffic.

(2) For the purposes of a defence under subsection (1) above, the court shall in particular have regard to the following matters:

   (a) the character of the highway, and the traffic which was reasonably to be expected to use it;

   (b) the standard of maintenance appropriate for a highway of that character and used by such traffic;

   (c) the state of repair in which a reasonable person would have expected to find the highway;

   (d) whether the highway authority knew, or could reasonably have been expected to know, that the condition of the part of the highway to which the action relates was likely to cause danger to users of the highway;

   (e) where the highway authority could not reasonably have been expected to repair that part of the highway before the cause of action arose, what warning notices of its condition had been displayed;

   but for the purposes of such a defence it is not relevant to prove that the highway authority had arranged for a competent person to carry out or supervise the maintenance of the part of the highway to which the action relates unless it is also proved that the authority had given him proper instructions with regard to the maintenance of the highway and that he had carried out the instructions.

(3) This section binds the Crown.'

The list of matters to which the court 'shall have regard' under s 58(2) is not exhaustive, but those matters:

'are all objective matters going to the condition of the highway and what the authority may reasonably have been expected to know about it. There is a good reason for this. The obligation to maintain highways in a structural

---

61   *Goodes*, Lord Hoffmann at 1362 F (in the WLR), 374 C (in the RTR).

condition which makes them free from foreseeable danger to traffic using the road in the ordinary way is an unqualified obligation of highway authorities of long standing. If Parliament had wanted to weaken that fundamental obligation, now contained in section 41, it would have done so. Section 58 had a different purpose. Section 58 was designed simply to afford a defence to a claim for damages brought against a highway authority which was able to demonstrate that it had done all that was reasonably necessary to make the road safe for users, not an authority which decided that it was preferable to allocate its resources in other directions because other needs were more pressing than doing what was reasonably required to make the roads safe.'[62]

So the fact that other duties under HA 1980 invoke other matters, such as the availability of resources[63], is not relevant to s 58. It was wrong for a judge to take into account 'the financial considerations which led the highway authority to adopt the programme which it did' when deciding whether or not the s 58 defence was established[64].

Whether a common law duty of care can be based upon a statutory power

13.12   In *Gorringe*, the claimant submitted, as an alternative legal basis of claim to HA 1980, s 41, that the Defendant local authority owed her a duty of care which flowed from its power under RTA 1988, s 39(2) and (3) to carry out measures to promote road safety and provide her with information and advice relating to the use of roads (a similar argument was made in *Stovin v Wise*, in which the HA 1980, s 41 statutory duty had been unavailable, as the danger had not been part of the highway[65], so the power to serve a notice on the owner of land directing him to alter a fence or wall or bank under s 79 was there relied upon by the claimant as evidence of a common law duty[66]).

RTA 1988, s 39 provided that:

'(1) The Secretary of State may, with the approval of the Treasury, provide for promoting road safety by disseminating information or advice relating to the use of roads.'

'(2) Each local authority must prepare and carry out a programme of measures designed to promote road safety and may make contributions towards the cost of measures for promoting road safety taken by other authorities or bodies.'

'(3) Without prejudice to the generality of subsection (2) above, in pursuance of their duty under that subsection each local authority – (a) must carry out studies into accidents arising out of the use of vehicles on roads or parts of roads, other than trunk roads, within their area, (b) must, in the light of those studies, take such measures as appear to the authority to be appropriate to prevent such accidents, including the dissemination

---

62   *Wilkinson v City of York Council* [2011] EWCA Civ 207, Toulson LJ (as he then was) [35].
63   See HA 1980, s 150(3)(c) (in relation to the public duty to remove snow, soil etc from the highway).
64   *Wilkinson*, Toulson LJ [33].
65   *Stovin*, Lord Hoffmann, 942 G.
66   *Stovin*, Lord Nicholls, 929 A-B.

of information and advice relating to the use of roads, the giving of practical training to road users or any class or description of road users, the construction, improvement, maintenance or repair of roads for which they are the highway authority ... and other measures taken in the exercise of their powers for controlling, protecting or assisting the movement of traffic on roads, and (c) ...'[67]

The claimant:

'accepted, and rightly, that section 39 cannot possibly be construed so as to justify the conclusion that a private action in damages can be brought for breach of the statutory duty. Mrs Gorringe's contention is that section 39 can nonetheless be used to jack up the council's common law duty of care to a standard sufficient to enable the failure to provide suitable signage to constitute a breach of the duty.'[68]

The House of Lords disagreed, holding that a breach of the statutory duty to the public under RTA 1988, s 39 does not provide the basis for a claim in negligence.

The argument on RTA 1988, s 39 engaged what Lord Steyn (delivering a judgment individually on the subject, while agreeing with the unanimous judgment that s 39 did not provide such a basis of claim in *Gorringe*) described as the subject of:

'negligence and statutory duties and powers. This is a subject of great complexity and very much an evolving area of the law. No single decision is capable of providing a comprehensive analysis. It is a subject on which an intense focus on the particular facts and on the particular statutory background, seen in the context of the contours of our social welfare state, is necessary. On the one hand the courts must not contribute to the creation of a society bent on litigation, which is premised on the illusion that for every misfortune there is a remedy. On the other hand, there are cases where the courts must recognise on principled grounds the compelling demands of corrective justice or what has been called 'the rule of public policy which has first claim on the loyalty of the law: that wrongs should be remedied'... Sometimes cases may not obviously fall in one category or the other. Truly difficult cases arise.'[69]

A 'principled distinction ... not always in the forefront of discussions' was:

'in a case founded on breach of statutory duty the central question is whether from the provisions and structure of the statute an intention can be gathered to create a private law remedy? In contradistinction in a case framed in negligence, against the background of a statutory duty or power, a basic question is whether the statute excludes a private law remedy? An assimilation of the two inquiries will sometimes produce wrong results.'[70]

In *Stovin v Wise*, Lord Hoffmann had observed that 'the minimum preconditions for basing a duty of care upon the existence of a statutory power' are:

---

67 RTA 1988, s 39 as quoted by Lord Hoffmann in *Gorringe* [53].
68 *Gorringe*, Lord Scott [54].
69 *Gorringe*, Lord Steyn [2].
70 *Gorringe*, Lord Steyn [3].

'first, that it would in the circumstances have been irrational not to have exercised the power, so that there was in effect a public law duty to act, and secondly, that there are exceptional grounds for holding that the policy of the statute requires compensation to be paid to persons who suffer loss because the power was not exercised'[71]

That was the view of the majority in *Stovin* (Lord Goff, Lord Jauncey and Lord Hoffmann), which had found neither condition to be satisfied against the council in that case. However, Lord Slynn and Lord Nicholls had dissented, both favouring the imposition of a duty upon the public authority, so the outcome of *Stovin* was that the council's appeal succeeded by a majority.

By contrast, in *Gorringe* the court was unanimous as to the outcome. However, Lord Steyn viewed the law differently both to the majority in *Stovin v Wise* and, while concurring in the result, to other members of the court in *Gorringe*. Lord Steyn noted the later 'qualification' of Lord Hoffmann's observations in *Stovin v Wise* by Lord Hutton's observations, in *Barrett v Enfield London Borough Council*, that:

'where a plaintiff claims damages for personal injuries which he alleges have been caused by decisions negligently taken in the exercise of a statutory discretion, and provided that the decisions do not involve issues of policy which the courts are ill-equipped to adjudicate upon, it is preferable for the courts to decide the validity of the plaintiff's claim by applying directly the common law concept of negligence than by applying as a preliminary test the public law concept of *Wednesbury* unreasonableness (see *Associated Provincial Picture Houses Ltd v Wednesbury Corpn* [1948] 1 KB 223) to determine if the decision fell outside the ambit of the statutory discretion. I further consider that in each case the court's resolution of the question whether the decision or decisions taken by the defendant in exercise of the statutory discretion are unsuitable for judicial determination will require, as Lord Keith stated in *Rowling v Takaro Properties Ltd* [1988] AC 473, 501, a careful analysis and weighing of the relevant circumstances.' [72]

Lord Steyn quoted Professor Paul Craig's 'notably careful and balanced analysis' of the principles in caselaw in relation to the interplay of public authority decisions and private law claims:

'There are many instances where a public body exercises discretion, but where the choices thus made are suited to judicial resolution. The mere presence of some species of discretion does not entail the conclusion that the matter is thereby non-justiciable. In the United States, it was once argued that the very existence of discretion rendered the decision immune from negligence. As one court scathingly said of such an argument, there can be discretion even in the hammering of a nail. Discretionary judgments made by public bodies, which the courts feel able to assess, should not therefore preclude the existence of negligence liability. This does not mean that the presence of such discretion will be irrelevant to the determination of liability. It will be of relevance in deciding whether there has been a breach of the duty of care. It is for this reason that the decisions in *Barrett* [*v Enfield London*

---

71   *Stovin*, 953.
72   [2001] 2 AC 550, 586 D-F, quoted by Lord Steyn in *Gorringe* [4].

Borough Council] and *Phelps* [*v Hillingdon London Borough Council*[73]] are to be welcomed. Their Lordships recognised that justiciable discretionary choices would be taken into account in deciding whether the defendant had acted in breach of the duty of care. There may also be cases where some allegations of negligence are thought to be non-justiciable, while others may be felt suited to judicial resolution in accordance with the normal rules on breach.'[74]

The other members of the court in *Gorringe* agreed with the outcome of the case but not with Lord Steyn's judgment on the broader public and private duty issue. Lord Hoffmann maintained his view on the actionability in private law of the subject matter of a public law duty:

'Speaking for myself, I find it difficult to imagine a case in which a common law duty can be founded simply upon the failure (however irrational) to provide some benefit which a public authority has power (or a public law duty) to provide...'[75]

Although Lord Hoffmann also observed that:

'this appeal is concerned only with an attempt to impose upon a local authority a common law duty to act based solely on the existence of a broad public law duty. We are not concerned with cases in which public authorities have actually done acts or entered into relationships or undertaken responsibilities which give rise to a common law duty of care. In such cases the fact that the public authority acted pursuant to a statutory power or public duty does not necessarily negative the existence of a duty.'[76]

Lord Scott agreed with but was 'inclined to go further' than Lord Hoffmann in *Stovin v Wise*:

'In my opinion, if a statutory duty does not give rise to a private right to sue for breach, the duty cannot create a duty of care that would not have been owed at common law if the statute were not there.... In short, I do not accept that a common law duty of care can grow parasitically out of a statutory duty not intended to be owed to individuals.'[77]

And, as to the public authority's duty to provide road safety information under RTA 1988, s 39, Lord Scott considered that:

'The statutory duty is an entirely general one. It imposes a 'target' duty and no more than that. It cannot be read as intending to create specific duties owed to individuals. The subsection (3) duties are more specific but, still, are only target duties. The statutory policy was that highway authorities should devise and implement road safety measures. The policy was not that private individuals should be able to bring private actions for damages for their failure to do so.'[78]

---

73 [2001] 2 AC 619.
74 *Gorringe*, Lord Steyn [5]. See Lord Steyn's full judgment at [1-6].
75 *Gorringe*, Lord Hoffmann [32].
76 *Gorringe*, Lord Hoffmann [38].
77 *Gorringe*, Lord Scott [71].
78 *Gorringe*, Lord Scott [72].

Lord Brown was against the superimposition of a common law duty of care upon the public duty, unless a public authority had assumed such a duty of care by virtue of its relationship with the claimants. In contrast to the child welfare subject matter of other cases, he highlighted the context of road traffic claims, which in his Lordship's view (echoing Lord Hoffmann's conclusion in *Stovin v Wise*[79]) tended to allow other means of recovery than suing the highway authority:

> 'In the highway context, by contrast, the claimant (or some other road user involved in the accident) will almost inevitably himself have been at fault. In these circumstances it seems to me entirely reasonable that the policy of the law should be to leave the liability for the accident on the road user who negligently caused it rather than look to the highway authority to protect him against his own wrong.'[80]

The House of Lords' approach in *Gorringe* is now subject to the Supreme Court's reformulation of the law as to the circumstances in which a public authority owes a common law duty of care, in its 2019 judgment in *N and another v Poole Borough Council*[81], where both the Court of Appeal and the Supreme Court held that a council was not under a duty of care to protect its tenants from abusive neighbours. The Supreme Court summarised the new formulation as follows:

> '(1) that public authorities may owe a duty of care in circumstances where the principles applicable to private individuals would impose such a duty, unless such a duty would be inconsistent with, and is therefore excluded by, the legislation from which their powers or duties are derived; (2) that public authorities do not owe a duty of care at common law merely because they have statutory powers or duties, even if, by exercising their statutory functions, they could prevent a person from suffering harm; and (3) that public authorities can come under a common law duty to protect from harm in circumstances where the principles applicable to private individuals or bodies would impose such a duty, as for example where the authority has created the source of danger or has assumed a responsibility to protect the claimant from harm, unless the imposition of such a duty would be inconsistent with the relevant legislation.'[82]

Highway liabilities in negligence: acts and omissions

13.13 A further theme in highway claim cases framed in negligence as an alternative basis of claim to HA 1980, s 41 is the usual rule that, save for in special circumstances, there is no justification for 'the imposition of liability upon someone who simply does nothing: who neither creates the risk nor undertakes to do

---

79   *Stovin*, Lord Hoffmann at 958 B-E: '... Drivers of vehicles must take the highway network as they find it...'
80   *Gorringe*, Lord Brown [100].
81   [2019] UKSC 25; [2020] AC 780, 835 [64].
82   Above, at 835-836 [65].

anything to avert it'[83]. Lord Nicholls (dissenting from the majority view in *Stovin v Wise* that no duty arose against a highway authority with power to serve a notice upon a landowner to remove a bank which obscured visibility) described 'familiar instances' where such a duty does exceptionally arise at common law:

'parent and child, employer and employee, school and pupil ... Perhaps the established category nearest to the present case comprises occupiers of land and their neighbours. An occupier is under a common law duty to take positive action to remove or reduce hazards to his neighbours, even though the hazard is not one the occupier brought about. He must take reasonable steps to this end, for the benefit of his neighbours: see *Goldman v. Hargrave* [1967] 1 AC 645. If an occupier's tree is struck by lightning and catches fire, he must take reasonable steps to prevent the fire spreading. He must act as would a reasonable occupier in his position.'[84]

In *Stovin v Wise*, Lord Hoffmann disagreed with Lord Nicholls' view that there was sufficient proximity between the parties and that therefore 'the council was more than a bystander' to the claimant motorcyclist injured as a result of an accident at an obscured junction[85]. Speaking for the majority, Lord Hoffmann criticised the reasoning of the Court of Appeal (who had found the public authority liable in negligence for not more urgently effecting the work to remove the bank which obscured the claimant's view) and observed that:

'One must have regard to the purpose of the distinction as it is used in the law of negligence, which is to distinguish between regulating the way in which an activity may be conducted and imposing a duty to act upon a person who is not carrying on any relevant activity. To hold the defendant liable for an act, rather than an omission, it is therefore necessary to be able to say, according to common sense principles of causation, that the damage was caused by something which the defendant did. If I am driving at 50 miles an hour and fail to apply the brakes, the motorist with whom I collide can plausibly say that the damage was caused by my driving into him at 50 miles an hour. But Mr. Stovin's injuries were not caused by the negotiations between the council and British Rail *[as to the removal of the bank]* or anything else which the council did. So far as the council was held responsible *[at first instance and by the Court of Appeal]*, it was because it had done nothing to improve the visibility at the junction.'[86]

That passage is notable for its use of an exception to the 'no liability for omission principle' drawn from driving motor vehicles (omitting to brake is not an omission but part of the activity of driving). In his dissenting judgment in *Stovin*, Lord Nicholls made the following further observation as to why failing to apply a parking brake does not usually allow omission to be raised by way of defence to negligent driving:

---

83   *Gorringe*, Lord Hoffmann [17]: 'The law does recognise such duties in special circumstances: see, for example, *Goldman v Hargrave* [1967] 1 AC 645 on the positive duties of adjoining landowners to prevent fire or harmful matter from crossing the boundary. But the imposition of such a liability upon a highway authority through the law of negligence would be inconsistent with the well-established rules which have always limited its liability at common law.'

84   *Stovin*, Lord Nicholls, 930 G-H.

85   *Stovin*, Lord Nicholls, 931.

86   *Stovin*, 945 D-E.

'The distinction between liability for acts and liability for omissions is well known. It is not free from controversy. In some cases the distinction is not clear cut. The categorisation may depend upon how broadly one looks when deciding whether the omission is a 'pure' omission or is part of a larger course of activity set in motion by the defendant. Failure to apply the handbrake when parking a vehicle is the classic illustration of the latter. Then the omission is the element which makes the activity negligent.'[87]

Omissions in driving have therefore been treated as part of the activity of driving. For example, in *Valentine v Transport for London*, the Court of Appeal cited the further example of pleading a driver's failure to keep a proper lookout, 'which is in reality a complaint that he performed badly the positive act of driving'[88].

Liability of the police in relation to dangers on highways

13.14 In *Robinson v Chief Constable of West Yorkshire Police*[89], the Supreme Court disapproved the notion that the police have immunity from civil suit. The case was not a road traffic matter but concerned 'a quite delicate operational decision involving co-ordination between four officers, with a view to the arrest of suspected drug dealers, in a public place'[90]. In the course of the arrest there was a struggle as a result of which the claimant, an innocent bystander, was injured.

The Supreme Court elaborated upon the reasons for differentiating between act and omission in the law of negligence. Lord Reed explained that:

'The distinction between careless acts causing personal injury, for which the law generally imposes liability, and careless omissions to prevent acts (by other agencies) causing personal injury, for which the common law generally imposes no liability, is not a mere alternative to policy-based reasoning, but is inherent in the nature of the tort of negligence. For the same reason, although the distinction, like any other distinction, can be difficult to draw in borderline cases, it is of fundamental importance. The central point is that the law of negligence generally imposes duties not to cause harm to other people or their property: it does not generally impose duties to provide them with benefits (including the prevention of harm caused by other agencies). Duties to provide benefits are, in general, voluntarily undertaken rather than being imposed by the common law, and are typically within the domain of contract, promises and trusts rather than tort. It follows from that basic characteristic of the law of negligence that liability is generally imposed for causing harm rather than for failing to prevent harm caused by other people or by natural causes. It is also consistent with that characteristic that the exceptions to the general non-imposition of liability for omissions include situations where there has been a voluntary assumption of responsibility to prevent harm (situations which have sometimes been described as being close or akin to contract), situations where a person has assumed a status which carries with it a responsibility to prevent harm, such as being a parent

---

87 *Stovin*, Lord Nicholls at 930 A-B.
88 *Valentine v Transport for London* (above), Hughes LJ (as he then was) [32]. And see Chapter 18, 'personal security claims'.
89 [2018] UKSC 4; [2018] AC 736.
90 *Robinson*, Lord Mance [97].

or standing in loco parentis, and situations where the omission arises in the context of the defendant's having acted so as to create or increase a risk of harm.'[91]

As to an argument which had been accepted by the trial judge, Lord Mance wrote that the delicacy of the police operation might be suggested to raise 'special considerations, negativing any duty of care'. But, in his Lordship's view:

'we should not accept that suggestion. Rather we should now recognise the direct physical interface between the police and the public, in the course of an arrest placing an innocent passer-by or bystander at risk, as falling within a now established area of general police liability for positive negligent conduct which foreseeably and directly inflicts physical injury on the public.'[92]

Tindall v Chief Constable of Thames Valley Police[93] illustrated the distinction between acts (capable of carrying liability) and omissions (only exceptionally so capable) in the context of policing of the highway. Just after 5 am on 4 March 2014 the police had attended the site of a road traffic accident which they understood to be attributable to ice on the road, erected a 'Police Slow' sign by the carriageway while attending but removed the sign upon their departure about 23 minutes later. 'One officer made a call to his control centre requesting a gritter, though it is alleged that his request was insufficiently 'robust' and did not communicate the urgency of the situation'[94]. About 20 to 25 minutes after the officers' departure, the deceased drove his car towards the area which the police had attended and died in the ensuing collision with an oncoming vehicle which was out of control on the ice. His widow claimed against the police in negligence, for leaving the site in a dangerous state and without any warning to other drivers of the persisting danger of the ice. On the question of 'whether the police are to be taken as having assumed responsibility to an individual member of the public so as to give rise to a duty to exercise reasonable care to protect them from harm', the Court of Appeal derived nine 'principles … of high authority' from the caselaw, including the seventh principle that:

'in cases involving the police the courts have consistently drawn the distinction between merely acting ineffectually … and making matters worse'[95]

– and the ninth principle, that:

'In determining whether a public authority owes a private law duty to an individual, it is material to ask whether the relationship between the authority and the individual is any different from the relationship between the authority and other members of the same class as the individual: see *Gorringe*, per Lord Scott.'[96]

---

91   *Robinson*, Lord Reed [68(4)]. And see *N v Poole BC* (above).
92   *Robinson*, Lord Mance [97] and see Lord Reed [70]: the police 'generally owe a duty of care when such a duty arises under ordinary principles of the law of negligence, unless statute or the common law provides otherwise…'.
93   [2022] EWCA Civ 25; [2022] 4 WLR 104.
94   *Tindall*, Stuart-Smith LJ [6].
95   *Tindall*, Stuart-Smith LJ [23, 66], citing authority from *East Suffolk Rivers Catchment Board v Kent* [1941] AC 74 (HL) onwards.
96   *Tindall*, Stuart-Smith LJ [54].

Applying the nine principles to the claim and finding that the police had not made matters worse[97], the Court of Appeal agreed with the defendant that the claim should have been struck out for disclosing no reasonable cause of action against the police.

B Highway claims involving Advanced Driver Assistance Systems (ADAS)

Access to and obstruction of the highway

13.15 Although no such ADAS case has yet been adjudicated, access and obstruction cases are likely to be determined according to the principles set out above.

A potential, novel feature of such a case might be if an ADAS vehicle were suddenly to halt due to a system malfunction and a collision with following vehicles ensued, which claim might (if pleaded in nuisance against the driver of the ADAS vehicle) engage the hypothetical situation described by Sachs LJ in *Dymond v Pearce* (1972):

> 'What would be the position if, even though the lorry driver had not been negligent in leaving the lorry as it was in fact left, yet there had occurred some unexpected supervening happening such as an onset of heavy weather, sea mist or fog or, for instance, a sudden rear light failure (potent cause of fatalities) – which had so affected the situation that the lorry became the cause of an accident? Should the risk fall entirely on those using the highway properly? Or should some liability attach to the person at fault in creating a nuisance? ... If he was thus liable, this might be the only class of case in which an action in nuisance by obstruction of the highway could succeed where one in negligence would fail...'[98]

Edmund Davies LJ, agreeing with the result of *Dymond* but in the minority on the legal analysis, considered foreseeability of danger to be an essential element of a highway obstruction claim based upon nuisance:

> 'In *Maitland v Raisbeck & R T & J Hewitt Ltd* [1944] K.B. 689, 691-692 Lord Greene MR said:
>
> > "Every person ... has a right to use the highway, and, if something happens to him which, in fact, causes an obstruction to the highway, but is in no way referable to his fault, it is wrong to suppose that *ipso facto*[99] and immediately a nuisance is created. A nuisance will obviously be created if he allows the obstruction to continue for an unreasonable time or in unreasonable circumstances, but the mere fact that an obstruction has come into existence cannot turn it into a nuisance... . If that were not so, it would seem that every driver of a vehicle on the road would be turned into an insurer in respect of latent defects in his machine."

---

97 [66]-[68].
98 *Dymond* (above), Sachs LJ, in the majority on the legal analysis, at 503 E to G.
99 By that very fact or act.'

'… Claims in nuisance for personal injuries sustained by colliding with vehicles obstructing highways do not affect the general rule that negligence is not a necessary element in nuisance… But in my judgment a different approach is called for where damages are sought to be recovered in respect of personal injuries said to have been caused by nuisance arising from the inexcusable presence of vehicles on highways. If deliberately created and clearly giving rise to danger to road users, fault is implicit and liability incontestable, But if an obstruction be created, here too, in my judgment, fault is essential to liability in the sense that it must appear that a reasonable man would be bound to realise the likelihood of risk to highway users resulting from the presence of the obstructing vehicle on the road… [*citing the example in 1535 authority of a man digging a trench across a road*] The trench being dug "across" the highway, and the horseman "riding that way by night" are the typical ingredients of a situation where any reasonable person must have realised that a danger to highway users was being created. That, as I see it, remains to-day an essential ingredient in cases for personal injuries brought in circumstances such as those existing in the present case.'[100]

So an ADAS highway obstruction case might incline towards a negligence rather than a 'strict liability' standard in nuisance.

Condition of the highway

Failures in signage or road markings upon which an ADAS relies

13.16 Current law is that signage and road markings are not part of the fabric of the road so are not within the statutory duty of the highway authority to maintain under HA 1980, s 41. Other statutory duties which are not themselves actionable in private law cannot be relied upon to 'jack up' the highway authority's common law duties[101].

Unless a public authority has taken upon itself any other relevant duty actionable in private law, it is likely that failure to maintain or reinstate signs or road markings upon which an ADAS system in a vehicle might rely would not be actionable against the highway authority in the event of an accident causing damage or injury. The injured claimant's likely remedy would be against, if anyone, another road-user in negligence or, if the accident involved an automated vehicle while driving itself, under AEVA 2018, s 2, or possibly (if evidenced) against another party in relation to a vehicle defect[102].

Failures in connectivity equipment which forms part of the fabric of the road

13.17 If there were a maintenance fault in equipment intrinsic to the road which caused or contributed to an accident involving an ADAS vehicle (if, for example, an ADAS system in the vehicle connected to equipment integral to the road), a claimant might argue that the HA 1980, s 41 duty has been engaged, in

---

reliance upon *Mitchell v Department for Transport, Mott MacDonald Ltd as Part 20 defendants*[103] (drainage system part of the fabric and structure of the roadway). A claimant might be a compensator seeking contribution under the Civil Liability (Contribution) Act 1978[104]. Whether a court would favour this argument would depend upon the facts of the case, including whether the fault was in hardware or software (the latter being actionable only in limited circumstances[105]). The issue has yet to be adjudicated.

C Highway claims involving Automated Vehicles

Access to and obstruction of the highway

13.18 No automated vehicle highway claim has yet been adjudicated. In the case of a road traffic accident, the most likely legal basis of claim would be the AEVA 2018, s 2 claim against the insurer or permitted uninsured owner (according with the observations of the Law Lords in *Gorringe* and elsewhere that claims in RTA cases are likely to be against other motorists) [106].

If the AEVA 2018, s 2 claim were unavailable (for example, because a vehicle was uninsured in an unpermitted way), then the principles applicable to sub-automated vehicles (ie. ADAS and conventional cars, vans etc) would apply.

Condition of the highway

13.19 The same position as set out above would apply. If AEVA 2018, s 2 were unavailable to an injured claimant, then other potential legal bases of claim (from HA 1980, s 41 to common law duties) might assist.

As in the case of ADAS, if a maintenance fault in equipment intrinsic to the road caused or contributed to an accident involving an automated vehicle (if, for example, an automated driving system connected to equipment forming part of the fabric and structure of the road), a claimant might argue that the HA 1980, s 41 duty has been engaged, in reliance upon *Mitchell v Department for Transport, Mott MacDonald Ltd as Part 20 defendants*[107]. The point has yet to be adjudicated. The claimant might be a compensator seeking contribution under CL(C)A 1978.

D Highway claims involving Electric Vehicles

Access to and obstruction of the highway

13.20 No claim has yet been adjudicated, but dockless rental vehicles (such as e-bikes and e-scooters) raise the possibility of claims in relation to access to and obstruction of the highway. The principles are as set out in the 'outline' section above.

---

103 [2006] EWCA Civ 1089; [2006] 1 WLR 3356. See 'outline' section of this chapter.
104 See Chapter 9, 'RTA claims'.
105 See the discussion of the actionability of downloaded software in chapter 10, 'vehicle defect claims'.
106 See Chapter 6, 'insurance'.
107 See 'outline' section of this chapter.

Condition of the highway

13.21   There has been one highway condition claim against a public authority in relation to an e-scooter, from which the claimant alleged she fell when the scooter hit a pothole in the road. The judgment of the Barnet County Court has not been officially reported but press and legal professional reports[108] suggest that the claim was dismissed on the single evidential finding that the claimant had failed to prove that the pothole in question was the cause of her loss of control of the e-scooter. The defendant is said to have made a submission of *ex turpi causa non oritur actio*[109] on the basis of the alleged unlawful use of the scooter, but the judgment is not understood to have determined that issue.

---

108 *Drago v London Borough of Barnet* (March 2023, unreported). See The Sunday Times website article 'Illegal e-scooter rider loses £30,000 injury claim in first UK court case of its type' (10 March 2023) and Keoghs solicitors' website article 'First e-scooter claim for compensation fails' (17 April 2023).
109 'No claim arises from a base cause', discussed in Chapter 11, 'passenger claims'.

Delivery claims

'*Nota*[1] reader, it is good policy for him who takes any goods to keep, to take them in special manner, *scil.*[2] to keep them as he keeps his own goods, or to keep them the best he can at the peril of the party; or if they happen to be stolen or purloined, that he shall not answer for them; for he who accepteth them, ought to take them in such or the like manner, or otherwise he may be charged by his general acceptance. So if goods are delivered to one to be delivered over, it is good policy to provide for himself in such special manner, for doubt of being charged by his general acceptance, which implies that he takes upon him to do it.'

(Lord Coke, 1601)[3]

Chapter Contents

A Outline of the laws of delivery by road vehicle

14.01 This chapter describes the laws of delivery of goods, often referred to as carriage of goods.

In the context of road vehicles, the laws of delivery typically apply to two sets of facts:

- the delivery of goods by road vehicle, and

- the delivery of a road vehicle itself (for example, to its owner after purchase or repair, or to a person hiring the vehicle).

---

1 *Nota bene:* 'note well'.
2 *Scilicet*, from *scire licet* ('one is permitted to know'): 'that is to say; namely' (OED).
3 *Southcote's Case* Pasch. 43 Eliz.; 76 E.R 1061.

As in other topics (vehicle defects, highway claims etc), the laws of carriage arise from numerous sources:

> 'The English law in question is the common law of contract, tort, bailment and agency as it applies to contract for the carriage of goods by land, together with certain doctrines, which are peculiar to the law of carriage ... Also important are the standard contract terms governing road ... transport ... together with the international conventions relative to carriage by road (CMR) ... which apply to international carriage ...'[4]

Use of a delivery vehicle will also be subject to other legal requirements described elsewhere in this book, including compulsory insurance and obligations to employees, passengers etc.

The following is an outline of key principles potentially applicable to civil AAEV delivery claims. AAEV delivery technology is at an early stage, so points of AAEV delivery law have yet to be adjudicated. Given the variety of laws affecting carriage of goods the reader should in any event refer to specialist works[5].

Contract

14.02   The doctrine of 'common carrier' or carrier at common law (discussed below) imposed strict liability:

> 'at common law for loss of or damage to the cargo subject only to exceptions for acts of God and the Queen's enemies. The absence of negligence was irrelevant'[6].

This strict liability was the peril of the carrier being 'charged by his general acceptance' with ensuring the integrity of goods in his care, in Lord Coke's phrase from 1601[7].

So providers of delivery services avoided the strictness of the duties of common carrier by using special contractual terms – following Lord Coke's advice that they provide for themselves in 'special manner'[8]. In carriage by road, such special terms now appear in industry-standard conditions such as the Road Haulage Association conditions of carriage (as at the time of writing, RHA 2020) and the British International Freight Association standard trading conditions (likewise, BIFA 2021).

On the other hand, terms of exclusion and limitation of liability are now regulated, especially by the Unfair Contract Terms Act 1977 and by the Consumer Rights Act

---

4   *Palmer on Bailment* (3rd edn, 2009), 16-001.
5   For example, *Chitty on Contracts* (34th edn, 2021), chapter 38, 'carriage by land'; *Clerk & Lindsell on Torts* (23rd edn, 2020), chapter 16 'wrongful interference with goods'; *Palmer on Bailment* (above); *Contracts of Carriage by Land and Air*, Malcolm A. Clarke and David Yates (i-law, part of Lloyd's List Intelligence, 2nd edn, 2008). Given the dates of some of those works, the reader should take care to update (to take account, for example, of CRA 2015 and AEVA 2018).
6   *Volcafe Ltd v Cia Sud Americana de Vapores SA* [2018] UKSC 61; [2019] AC 358, Lord Sumption [8].
7   Comment at the end of *Southcote's Case*, quoted at the head of this chapter.
8   As above.

2015. While emphasising (in a pre-CRA 2015 case) the 'very important role' of the 1977 Act 'in protecting vulnerable consumers from the effects of draconian contract terms', the Court of Appeal was 'less enthusiastic about its intrusion into contracts between commercial parties of equal bargaining strength, who should generally be considered capable of being able to make contracts of their choosing and expect to be bound by their terms'[9].

There is a plethora of contractual issues. A selection of key points applicable to AAEV delivery cases follows.

The choice of delivery vehicle is a matter for the carrier. However, the carrier's choice might place it in breach of contract where (for example) the type of vehicle is fundamental to the contract of carriage, as it was in *Gunyon v South Eastern and Chatham Railway Companies' Managing Committee*[10], where 'the whole basis of the contract' was that the goods (cherries) were perishable so would be carried on a passenger train and not (as happened for part of the journey) on a goods train. The effect in that case was to deprive the carrier of the benefit of exception clauses in their contract, which the court held no longer applied[11].

In relation to consumer goods contracts, the consumer is not bound to accept a delivery of the wrong quantity of goods (CRA 2015, s 25) nor delivery of goods by instalments (CRA 2015, s 26)[12].

A consumer sales contract is to be treated as including a term that the trader must deliver the goods to the consumer, without undue delay and, in any event, not more than 30 days after the day on which the contract is entered into (CRA 2015, s 28, which also provides the consumer's rights in the event of breach).

In a consumer sales contract, the goods remain at the trader's risk until they come into the physical possession of the consumer or a person identified by the consumer to take possession of the goods, unless the carrier is commissioned by the consumer to deliver the goods and is not a carrier named by the trader as an option for the consumer (CRA 2015, s 29).

Tort

14.03   The sources of the tort law of interference with goods are voluminous and its mechanisms are complex. As *Clerk & Lindsell* notes:

'Much of its complexity … stems from history. English law never developed a single wrong of wrongful interference with goods: instead, it developed a congeries of different and often overlapping torts. Thus a defendant

---

9   *Granville Oil and Chemicals Ltd v Davies Tuner and Co Ltd* [2003] 1 All ER 819, Tuckey LJ at 829 [31].
10 [1915] 2 KB 370, Sankey J (as he then was) at 378.
11 'I do not think that where a railway company has promised to perform the conveyance in a certain manner, with an attendant right to take advantage of certain stipulations made in their favour, they can put upon the consignor a mode of conveyance which he has not contracted for and yet retain in their own favour the stipulations referable to the agreed mode of conveyance only.' (Sankey J, 378).
12 See both sections for the consumer's rights in those circumstances.

wrongfully interfering with a claimant's chattels may be liable for any of three torts: conversion, trespass to chattels, and a tort which will be referred to here as 'reversionary injury'. Before 1978 he could also be guilty of a fourth, detinue; but this was abolished by the Torts (Interference with Goods) Act 1977. In all these torts, moreover, liability may overlap...'[13]

Trespass to chattels 'lies for any direct and wrongful interference with possession'; Conversion 'lies in the unlawful appropriation of another's chattel'; reversionary injury is a tort for the benefit of an owner who is not in possession of the goods or who does not have an immediate right to possession of them – 'an owner out of possession' – who suffers 'damage to the reversion'[14]. Detinue was a tort relating to wrongful detention of a chattel which became absorbed into the tort of conversion, so it was abolished as a discrete tort and made conversion by TIGA 1977[15].

Tortious and contractual liabilities relating to delivery of goods overlap, and (subject to UCTA 1977 and CRA 2015) exemption clauses may apply in relation to tortious liability[16].

Bailment

14.04 *Halsbury's Laws* describes bailment as follows:

'Under modern law, a bailment arises whenever one person (the bailee) is voluntarily in possession of goods belonging to another person (the bailor). The legal relationship of bailor and bailee can exist independently of any contract, and is created by the voluntary taking into custody of goods which are the property of another, as in cases of sub-bailment or of bailment by finding. The element common to all types of bailment is the imposition of an obligation, because the taking of possession in the circumstances involves an assumption of responsibility for the safe keeping of the goods. A claim against a bailee can be regarded as a claim on its own, *sui generis*[17], arising out of the possession had by the bailee of the goods.'[18]

Like torts of interference with goods, the law of bailment is a jumble of notions, which have changed over time[19]. As *Chitty on Contracts* puts it

'The reality of the matter is that there is no one theory which seems to be capable of providing a comprehensive definition of bailment. It consists of an amalgam of different ideas.'[20]

Chitty identifies four key ideas of bailment:

'1. "the bailee must be in possession of the goods";

---

13 *Clerk & Lindsell on Torts*, 16-01.
14 Above, 16-02.
15 TIGA 1977, s 2.
16 See *Chitty* at 38-044.
17 'Of its own kind'.
18 *4 Halsbury's Laws of England* (5th edn, 2020) paras 101, 106.
19 See, for example, Oliver Wendell Holmes' account (from an American perspective) of the changes in bailment up to 1881, in *The Common Law*, lecture V, 'bailment'.
20 *Chitty* (34th edn, 2021), 35-006, 'no one unifying theory'.

2. "there must have been a "voluntary assumption" of possession; in other words, the consent of the bailee is necessary";

3. "the bailee must be aware of the existence of the bailor";

4. "it would appear that it is no longer necessary that the bailor consent to the bailee taking possession of the goods; a bailment can exist even when the bailor is unaware of the fact that the bailee has possession of his goods.""[21]

There are five types of bailment:

'(1) the gratuitous deposit of a chattel with the bailee, who is simply to keep it for the bailor;

(2) the delivery of a chattel to the bailee, who is to do something without reward for the bailee to or with the chattel;

(3) the gratuitous loan of a chattel by the bailor to the bailee for the bailee to use;

(4) the pawn or pledge of a chattel by the bailor to the bailee, who is to hold it as a security for a loan or debt or the fulfilment of an obligation; and

(5) the hire of a chattel or services by the bailor to the bailee for reward.'[22]

Claims by bailees in relation to cars

14.05 The Court of Appeal summarised the law of claims by bailees of cars in the credit hire case *Armstead v Royal Sun Alliance Co Ltd*:

'A person who possesses, but does not own, a chattel such as a motor car is a bailee of the motor car. The common law has long recognised the right of those in possession of the damaged chattel to bring a claim for the cost of repairing the damage and for consequential economic losses under the law of bailment. The history of the law of bailment was traced in the Attorney-General's argument in *The Winkfield* [1902] P. 42 by reference to the fifth lecture on the common law by Oliver Wendell Holmes, Jr. It was suggested that the law had developed from remedies made available to those affected by cattle stealing at a time in history described in the lectures as 'the primitive condition of England'. The person in possession of the cattle at the time of the theft had authority to pursue the wrongdoer and was entitled to exercise the authority of the owner to follow the cattle and to raise a claim for their return. This seems to have been on the basis that the person in possession of the cattle would have been liable to the owner for the loss of the cattle... Consistently with the approach to claims by a bailee set out in *The Winkfield* it is established that a driver in possession of a motor car but who is not the owner, may bring a claim for damages for loss of use of a car, see *O'Sullivan v Williams* [1992] R.T.R. 402 at 405B.'[23]

---

21 As above.
22 *Halsbury's Laws*, above.
23 [2022] EWCA Civ 497; [2022] RTR 23, Dingemans LJ [40]–[43]. At the time of writing the Supreme Court is due to give judgment on the appeal from the Court of Appeal, on the issue 'can the terms of a contract signed between the hirer of a motor car and the hire car company be relied upon to calculate the damages claimed by the hirer against the insurance company of a negligent driver who collided with the hire car?'.

So a deliverer of a vehicle which is damaged by (for example) the negligence of another during its delivery may claim as bailee both in relation to repairs and to the loss of use of the damaged vehicle.

Duty of bailee in relation to loss of goods

14.06 The 'bailee of the goods is responsible for their return to their owner. If he failed to return them it rested upon him to prove that he did take reasonable and proper care of the goods'[24].

Quantification of compensation in bailment

14.07 The internal contractual arrangements between the bailor and bailee cannot be a basis for recovering losses, as the law stands at the time of writing. There is:

> 'a loose analogy between the attempt to quantify damages by reference to clause 16 of the [*bailor*] Helphire['s] agreement [*with the bailee hirer of its car*] and a situation where one branch of a large company might invoice another branch of a large company (under the company's own internal arrangements) for losses caused by an incident for which a third party is liable. The invoiced sum might or might not accord with the losses which might be proved in an action by the company, but such an internal arrangement can hardly form the basis for proving the loss and bind the third party to pay the invoiced sum.'[25]

The Supreme Court is due to give judgment in the appeal in *Armstead* on this issue as at the time of writing.

Some points peculiar to the laws of carriage

Common carrier

14.08 The law of carriage distinguishes between a 'common carrier' and a 'private carrier'. *Chitty on Contracts* summarises the characteristics of 'common carrier' as follows:

> 'A common carrier is a person who publicly professes, orally or by conduct, to undertake for reward to all such persons, indiscriminately, who desire to employ him, the transportation of goods provided that he has room'[26] and who engages in that business habitually[27].

In 2018 the Supreme Court noted that:

---

24 *Joseph Travers & Sons Ltd v Cooper* [1915] 1 KB 73, 88 (CA, Buckley LJ); *Houghland v R R Low (Luxury Coaches) Ltd* [1962] 1 QB 694 (CA) (gratuitous bailment).
25 *Armstead v Royal Sun Alliance Co Ltd* (above), Dingemans LJ [52].
26 *Chitty*, 38-007.
27 *Chitty*, 38-011.

'The characteristic feature of a common carrier was that he held himself out as accepting for carriage the goods of all comers on a given route, subject to capacity limits. As such, he was strictly liable at common law for loss of or damage to the cargo subject only to exceptions for acts of God and the Queen's enemies. The absence of negligence was irrelevant.'[28]

A 'private carrier' will 'in virtually all cases' be any carrier who is not a common carrier[29]. A key difference between common and private carriers is the extent of their liabilities:

'A common carrier effectively undertakes, save in circumstances recognised by the common law as providing an exception, to indemnify the owner of the goods he carries for any loss or damage sustained by the goods; whereas a private carrier is liable, as a consequence of the bailment of the goods to him, only if his conduct amounts to negligence.'[30]

However, the concept of common carrier has diminished in importance, because (as Lord Coke advised) common law carrier's obligations may be modified by contract[31].

Importance of standard contractual terms of delivery

14.09   The standard contractual terms of the Road Haulage Association[32] stipulate that the carrier 'is not a common carrier and accepts goods for carriage only on that condition and on the conditions set out below'. As the Supreme Court has noted in relation to shipping (and has been quoted in relation to carriage of goods by land):

'although the position of common carriers is commonly referred to by way of background in the case law…, it is no longer a useful paradigm for the common law liability of a shipowner. Common carriers have for many years been an almost extinct category. For all practical legal purposes, the common law liability of a carrier, unless modified by contract, is the same as that of bailees for reward generally.'[33]

Such is the practical effect of the carrier's ability to modify terms of carriage by contract that (as Clarke and Yates put it)

'The movement of goods by road within the United Kingdom is governed by private conditions of carriage, notably those published for the use of its members by the Road Haulage Association Ltd. (RHA). Other conditions are in use. They have no statutory force.'[34]

---

28 *Volcafe*, above, Lord Sumption [8].
29 *Chitty*, 38-011.
30 *Chitty*, 38-012, 018 and 024.
31 *Southcote's Case*, quoted at the head of this chapter; *Chitty*, 38-013.
32 Road Haulage Association Limited Conditions of Carriage, as at the time of writing in their 2020 version (RHA CC 2020).
33 *Volcafe*, above, Lord Sumption [8], quoted by *Chitty* in its 'carriage by land' chapter at 38-010.
34 Clarke and Yates, 1.251, 'carriage of goods by road within the United Kingdom', 'introduction'.

Potentially shortened limitation periods for claims against carriers

14.10 A limitation period otherwise available under the Limitation Act 1980 might be shortened by a contractual term which, unless such term is unavailable (for example as an unfair term)[35], will stand. Parties to litigation should therefore be especially aware of time in a delivery claim.[36]

The Carriers Act 1830

14.11 The Carriers Act 1830 was passed to mitigate the strict liability of common carriers (such as stagecoach owners) for potentially very valuable items, by providing in particular for a declaration of value for certain items and the opportunity for the carrier to levy an increased charge.

The Act remains in force but is of limited application, as it applies to a 'mail contractor, stage coach proprietor, or other common carrier by land for hire'[37], which categories are now of limited application, via motor technology and the use of standard terms to avoid the strict duties of the common carrier.

International Carriage of Goods

14.12 As for vehicle specifications[38], the international carriage of goods is subject to the law of the United Nations. The Geneva Convention on the Contract for the International Carriage of Goods by Road of 1956 (abbreviated, by reference to its title in French, to CMR[39]) was implemented in the United Kingdom on 5 June 1967, by the Carriage of Goods by Road Act 1965[40]. The CMR applies:

> 'to every contract for the carriage of goods by road in vehicles for reward, when the place of taking over of the goods and the place designated for delivery, as specified in the contract, are situated in two different countries, of which at least one is a Contracting country, irrespective of the place of residence and the nationality of the parties.'[41]

Chitty notes that:

> 'As a result of the United Kingdom government's acceptance of treaties such as these and their successors, the particular treaty régimes have become binding on the United Kingdom and as such can be said to form part of the

---

35 See eg. the unfair terms provisions of UCTA 1977 and CRA 2015. Applicable rules will vary according to the facts of each case so the reader should research the applicable rules carefully (for example, remedies rules such as CRA 2015 s 22: time limit for consumer's short-term right to reject goods).
36 See *Chitty*, 38-048, 'time for making claims'.
37 CA 1830 s 1.
38 See Chapter 2.
39 Convention relative au Contrat de Transport International de Marchandises par Route.
40 CGRA 1965 s 1, Carriage of Goods by Road Act 1965 (Commencement) Order 1967 SI 1967/819, art 1.
41 CMR art 1(1) at CGRA 1965 Sched 1.

English law of carriage by land insofar as their terms have been incorporated in Acts of Parliament either directly or by reference.'[42]

Delivery claims law and AAEVs

14.13 The principles of delivery claims are set out above. The principles are likely to be altered by AAEV technologies. The alterations are impossible to predict, especially because of the antiquity and variety of the applicable laws and the novelty of the technologies (which include automated vehicles). Some initial points of relevance to AAEV delivery claims are described below.

B Delivery Claims involving Advanced Driver Assistance Systems (ADAS)

The limits of RTA 1988 compulsory insurance coverage in relation to property damage

14.14 ADAS-equipped motor vehicles are subject to RTA 1988 and to the boundaries of compulsory motor insurance. In relation to compulsory cover for property damage, RTA 1988, s 145 provides as follows:

'145. Requirements in respect of policies of insurance.

(1) In order to comply with the requirements of this Part of this Act, a policy of insurance must satisfy the following conditions.

(2) The policy must be issued by an authorised insurer.

(3) Subject to subsection (4) below, the policy—

   (a) must insure such person, persons or classes of persons as may be specified in the policy in respect of any liability which may be incurred by him or them in respect of the death of or bodily injury to any person or damage to property caused by, or arising out of, the use of the vehicle on a road or other public place in Great Britain …

   …

(4) The policy shall not, by virtue of subsection (3)(a) above, be required –

   …

   (b) to provide insurance of more than £1,200,000[43] in respect of all such liabilities as may be incurred in respect of damage to property caused by, or arising out of, any one accident involving the vehicle, or

   (c) to cover liability in respect of damage to the vehicle, or

---

42 *Chitty*, 38-003.
43 As at the time of writing the financial limit under RTA 1988 s 145(4)(b) is £1,200,000 (pursuant to the Motor Vehicles (Compulsory Insurance) Regulations 2016, SI 2016/1193, reg 2(2), from 31 December 2016).

(d) to cover liability in respect of damage to goods carried for hire or reward in or on the vehicle or in or on any trailer (whether or not coupled) drawn by the vehicle, or

(e) to cover any liability of a person in respect of damage to property in his custody or under his control, or

(f) to cover any contractual liability.'

Remotely driven vehicles already regulated

14.15 Four types of remotely operated vehicles are already regulated[44]. Among the types of remotely operated vehicles already regulated is a type intentionally not covered by the Law Commission of England and Wales' consultation[45] on the law applicable to remote driving, namely:

'Pedestrian-controlled road maintenance vehicles that are not constructed or used to carry a driver or passenger which are a recognised category of special vehicles.'[46]

Article 50 of the Road Vehicles (Special Types) (General) Order 2003 so permits the use of such a vehicle, as one of a number of special vehicles authorised for use on roads while not complying with construction and use etc regulations under RTA 1988, s 41, pursuant to the Secretary of State for Transport's power so to order under RTA 1988, s 44.

RV(AST)(G)O 2003, art 50 provides as follows in relation to the controls and definition of a pedestrian-controlled road maintenance vehicle:

'(4) The vehicle must be equipped with –

(a) an efficient braking system capable of bringing the vehicle to a standstill and of being set so as to hold the vehicle stationary; or

(b) if the vehicle does not have a braking system, sufficient other means capable of achieving the same results.

(5) 'Road maintenance vehicle' means a motor vehicle that is specially constructed or adapted for the purposes of carrying out one or more of the following operations-

(a) gritting roads;

(b) laying road markings;

(c) clearing frost, snow or ice from roads; or

(d) any other work of maintaining roads.'[47]

---

44 See Chapter 4, 'driving': 'remote driving'.
45 Law Commission RD issues paper (above), page 13, 2.33.
46 Road Vehicles (Authorisation of Special Types) (General) Order 2003, SI 2003/1998, part 5 ('miscellaneous special vehicles'), art 50(1), made under RTA 1988 s 44 ('authorisation of use on roads of special vehicles not complying with regulations under s 41').
47 RV(AST)(G)O 2003, art 50(4) and (5).

There are further types of pedestrian-controlled vehicle which are given special status by RTA 1988, though in a different way. RTA 1988, s 189 (and Road Traffic Regulation Act 1984 s 140) provides that the following vehicles are *not* to be treated as 'motor vehicles' for the purposes of the Road Traffic Acts, so releasing their use from requirements including compulsory third-party insurance:

'(1) For the purposes of the Road Traffic Acts—

(a) a mechanically propelled vehicle being an implement for cutting grass which is controlled by a pedestrian and is not capable of being used or adapted for any other purpose,

(b) any other mechanically propelled vehicle controlled by a pedestrian which may be specified by regulations made by the Secretary of State for the purposes of this section and section 140 of the Road Traffic Regulation Act 1984, and

(c) an electrically assisted pedal cycle of such a class as may be prescribed by regulations so made,

is to be treated as not being a motor vehicle.

(2) In subsection (1) above *'controlled by a pedestrian'* means that the vehicle either-

(a) is constructed or adapted for use only under such control, or

(b) is constructed or adapted for use either under such control or under the control of a person carried on it, but is not for the time being in use under, or proceeding under, the control of a person carried on it.'

The RTA 1988, s 189 definition is distinct from the power to order special types of vehicle under s 44. Although s 189 includes a power to regulate to exclude a mechanically propelled, pedestrian controlled vehicle from the 'motor vehicle' definition of RTA 1988, it does not appear to include a RV(AST)(G)O 2003, art 50 pedestrian-controlled road maintenance vehicle, which arises under RTA 1988, s 44 and which art 50(5) of the 2003 order defines as 'a motor vehicle'.

So the 'remotely-operated' vehicle is already known to the law. What is new is the technological capacity to remotely control a vehicle from a distance, and from beyond its operator's line of sight.

The Law Commission of England and Wales issues paper and advice on remote driving

14.16 In June 2022, the Law Commission of England and Wales published an issues paper on remote driving[48]. A consultation followed, after which the Law Commission published its advice to government on remote driving in February 2023[49].

---

48 Law Commission of England and Wales, 'Remote Driving Issues Paper' (24 June 2022).
49 Law Commission of England and Wales, 'Remote Driving: Advice to Government' (February 2023).

In relation to innovative delivery vehicles, the Law Commission took into account the existing operation of delivery vehicles ('last-mile delivery pods') which were subject to remote monitoring and remote driving assistance if required[50]. It also took into account plans for remote driving as a means of delivering rental vehicles[51].

The Law Commission summarised its advice to government on its website as including the following steps:

'**Short term measures to address gaps in the law:** current laws do not expressly prohibit the use of remote driving technology where the driver is beyond line of sight – clarity in the law is urgently required. A new prohibition measure could be brought in immediately.'

'**Safety requirements for remote driving:** under these short-term measures, companies wanting to use remote driving beyond line-of-sight on roads without an in-vehicle safety driver could submit a safety case to the Vehicle Certification Agency and apply for a vehicle special order.'

'**A new regulatory system to govern remote driving over the long term:** these short-term measures would provide some clarity, but penalties and enforcement powers are limited. A new comprehensive regulatory regime for remote driving would require an Act of Parliament.'

'**Licences for remote driving operations:** subject to satisfying a safety standard, organisations intending to use remote driving would be able to obtain a licence.'

'**Safety concerns justify a ban on remote driving from overseas:** given the lack of enforcement powers, remotely driving a vehicle from overseas should be prohibited.'

'**Criminal and civil liability:** while remote drivers should be prosecuted for the same crimes as in-vehicle drivers, they should not be liable for any problems beyond their control, such as those due to connectivity issues or faulty remote driving equipment. Remote driving companies should instead be subject to regulatory sanctions and in serious cases, prosecution. Victims of road incidents caused by remote driving should receive no-fault compensation.'[52]

The Automated Vehicles Bill 2023-24 (HL Bill 1)

14.17 The Automated Vehicles Bill 2023-24 (HL Bill 1) was published on 8 November 2023. It follows the Law Commissions' recommendations and advice. In particular, Part 1, Chapter 2 (cll 12-13) of the Bill propose a system of licensing of operators for vehicle use without a user-in-charge. The AV Bill 2023-24, cl 53 proposes a new criminal offence of using a vehicle without a driver or licensed oversight.

---

50 Law Commission RD issue paper (above), pages 4-5.
51 Law Commission RD issues paper (above), pages 3, 63.
52 Article on Law Commission website, 'Remote driving review: robust regulation needed before technology is on UK roads' (20 February 2023).

C Delivery Claims involving Automated Vehicles

14.18   As at the time of writing, no vehicle has been listed as 'automated' under AEVA 2018, s 1.

The limits of compulsory motor insurance in relation to property damage and the effect upon the tortious claim under AEVA 2018

14.19   The claim in tort[53] against an insurer or permitted uninsured owner for 'damage' suffered as a result of an accident caused by an automated vehicle when driving itself on a road or other public place in Great Britain under AEVA 2018, s 2 includes damage to property but excludes damage to:

'(a)   the [authorised[54]] automated vehicle,

(b)   goods carried for hire or reward in or on that vehicle or in or on any trailer (whether or not coupled) drawn by it, or

(c)   property in the custody, or under the control, of—

  (i)   the insured person (where subsection (1) [*liability of insurer*] applies), or

  (ii)   the person in charge of the [authorised[55]] automated vehicle at the time of the accident (where subsection (2) [*liability of permitted uninsured owner*] applies).'[56] And:

'In respect of damage to property caused by, or arising out of, any one accident involving an [authorised[57]] automated vehicle, the amount of the liability under this section of the insurer or owner of the vehicle is limited to the amount for the time being specified in section 145(4)(b) of the Road Traffic Act 1988[58] (limit on compulsory insurance for property damage).'[59]

D Delivery Claims involving Electric Vehicles

Electric vehicles are within the current system of vehicle specification

14.20   As described in other chapters[60], electric vehicles are within the current system of vehicle specification. Some vehicles are classified as motor vehicles, so their use carries requirements including compulsory liability insurance, while others (such as EAPCs) are exempted from those requirements[61].

---

53 AEVA 2018, s 6(4).
54 Amendment proposed by AV Bill 2023-24 (HL Bill 1), cl 45, Sch 2, para 5(3)(a).
55 Amendment proposed by AV Bill 2023-24 (HL Bill 1), cl 45, Sch 2, para 5(3)(a).
56 AEVA 2018, s 2(3).
57 Amendment proposed by AV Bill 2023-24 (HL Bill 1), cl 45, Sch 2, para 5(3)(a).
58 As at the time of writing the limit is £1,200,000 (see above).
59 AEVA 2018, s 2(4).
60 Not yet published (and absent from the King's Speech in November 2023). See Chapters 2 'specifications', 4 'driving' and 6 'insurance'.
61 See RTA 1988, s 189(1)(c) and the Electrically Assisted Pedal Cycles Regulations 1983, SI 1983/1168, as amended by the Electrically Assisted Pedal Cycles (Amendment) Regulations 2015, SI 2015/24, for the EAPC exemption. See chapter 4, 'driving'.

The limits of RTA 1988 compulsory insurance coverage in relation to property damage

14.21   Use of an electric vehicle which is within the RTA 1988 'motor vehicle' definition is, as the time of writing – and in the absence of mooted future rules giving special treatment to e-scooters[62] – subject to the same requirements for compulsory third party motor insurance as are described in relation to ADAS vehicles (above) and are set out in Chapter 6 of this book ('insurance').

Compulsory insurance in relation to property damage is limited by those provisions[63.]

---

62 The government's announcement of the Transport Bill in the last Queen's Speech in May 2022 included the intention to give special legal treatment to e-scooters and the House of Commons Transport Select Committee addressed the possibility of a reduced form of compulsory insurance for e-scooter use. However, the Transport Bill was subsequently removed from the government's parliamentary agenda for the 2022–23 session and (unlike the AV Bill 2023–24 (HL Bill 1)) did not appear in the King's Speech of 7 November 2023. See Chapter 6, 'insurance'.
63 See 'delivery claims involving ADAS vehicles', above.

Chapter 15

Electric vehicle charging claims

'The inherent difference between the electric vehicle and other types of self-propelled carriage is that it does not carry its energy in the form of fuel, and does not *generate* its own power in the same way that is the case with petrol cars and steam cars. Instead of that, it carries a storage battery (or electric accumulator) which is capable of supplying a certain amount of power in the form of electric current, and this battery has to be 'recharged' with electricity as often as the available energy has been expended.'

The editor of The Automotor Journal (London, 1906)[1]

'The UK Government is accelerating the transition to zero emission cars and vans. In November 2020, as part of the Government's 10 point plan for a green industrial revolution, the then Prime Minister announced that the sale of new petrol and diesel cars would be phased out by 2030 and that all new cars and vans would be zero emission by 2035.'

House of Commons Library Briefing Paper (2023)[2]

As this chapter relates to a single type of vehicle (the electric vehicle), it is not subdivided into 'advanced', 'automated' and 'electric' vehicle topics.

Outline: the regulation of electric vehicle charging facilities

15.01   The Alternative Fuels Infrastructure Regulations 2017 (AFIR 2017)[3] 'ensure the way that alternative fuels (electricity and hydrogen) are supplied to vehicles or ships is consistent across the UK'[4]. AFIR 2017 'must be enforced by the Secretary

---

1   *Motors and Motor Driving* (the Badminton library of sports and pastimes, ed. Alfred E. T. Watson, 4th edn, Longmans, Green and Co, 1906) at p 268 (chapter XIII, 'electric cars'). That and *The Automotor Journal* accessed online via Google Books.
2   House of Commons Library Briefing Paper 'Electric vehicles and infrastructure' by Dr Holly Edwards, Iona Stewart, Becky Mawhood and Paul Bolton (CBP-7480, 21 February 2023). *Please note* that this passage and this chapter were written before Prime Minister Sunak's alterations to this pledge in late September 2023.
3   AFIR 2017, SI 2017/897, and see UK government, Office for Product Safety and Standards 'Guidance on the Alternative Fuels Infrastructure Regulations 2017' (February 2021).
4   UK government, Office for Product Safety and Standards 'Guidance on the Alternative Fuels Infrastructure Regulations 2017' (February 2021) page 4, 1.1.

of State'[5] by means including compliance notices and civil penalties in the event of non-compliance[6].

AEVA 2018, Part 2 ('electric vehicles: charging'[7]) provides for 'the creation of regulations relating to the installation and operation of charging points and hydrogen refuelling points for electric vehicles'[8].

The regulation-making powers under AEVA 2018, ss 9, 10, 13–19 and 20(1) and the Schedule to the Act[9] came into force on 21 April 2021[10] and s 11 (power to regulate for provision of public charging or refuelling points by large fuel retailers and service area operators) on 27 May 2022[11]. As at the time of writing AEVA 2018, s 12 (Secretary of State's[12] duty to consider making regulations imposing requirements on large fuel retailers under s 11 if an elected mayor makes a request for such regulations to be made) is not yet in force, pending proposed amendments to the section.

Enforcement of regulations is provided for by AEVA 2018, s 16, which allows regulations to provide for enforcement in relation to a contravention of charging regulations made under AEVA Part 2, including setting the procedure to be followed in imposing a penalty[13] and 'for a determination for the purposes of the regulations to be made by the Secretary of State or a prescribed person'[14].

The Electric Vehicles (Smart Charge Points) Regulations 2021[15] were made under AEVA 2018, Part 2 and came into force on 30 June 2022[16]. They 'require electric vehicle charge points sold in Great Britain for domestic or workplace use to have

---

5 AFIR 2017, reg 7. The preamble to AFIR 2017 states that the 'Secretary of State is a Minister designated for the purpose of that section [European Communities Act 1972 s 2(2)] in relation to energy and energy sources'.

6 AFIR 2017, reg 11.

7 The subtitle is misleading as AEVA 2018, Part 2 applies to hydrogen as well as electric vehicle refuelling. This was pointed out in parliamentary debate and leads to the oddity of the Automated and Electric Vehicles Act 2018 not defining an 'electric vehicle', for the legislative definition of which see AFIR 2017, reg 2. See chapter 16, 'smaller electric vehicle claims'.

8 Explanatory note to AEVA 2018 para 1. AEVA 2018, s 18 (2): 'A power to make regulations under this Part is exercisable by the Secretary of State by statutory instrument'

9 AEVA 2018, s 9 ('definitions'), 10 ('public charging or refuelling points: access, standards and connection'), 13 ('information for users of public charging or refuelling points'), 14 ('transmission of data relating to charge points'), 15 ('smart charge points'), 16 ('enforcement'), 17 ('exceptions'), 18 ('regulations'), 19 ('report by Secretary of State on operation of this Part'), 20(1) ('minor and consequential amendments' bringing the Schedule to the Act into effect) and the Schedule ('minor and consequential amendments').

10 Automated and Electric Vehicles Act 2018 (Commencement No.1) Regulations 2021, SI 2021/396, reg 3(b).

11 Automated and Electric Vehicles Act 2018 (Commencement No.2) Regulations 2022, SI 2022/587, reg 3.

12 The Interpretation Act 1978 defines 'Secretary of State' as 'one of Her [*sic*] Majesty's Principal Secretaries of State' (IA 1978 Sch 1). In relation to most transport issues, 'Secretary of State' is taken to mean the Secretary of State for Transport, and that seems to be the case both in relation to AEVA 2018 and in relation to regulations relating to vehicle charging under AEVA 2018, Part 2. It was, for example, the Department for Transport which laid the 2023 draft Public Charge Point Regulations 2023 (see below) before Parliament. AFIR 2017 refers to a different Secretary of State (see above).

13 AEVA 2018, s 16(2)(c).

14 AEVA 2018, s 16(2)(g).

15 EV(SCP)R 2021, SI 2021/1467.

16 EV(SCP)R 2021, reg 1(1).

smart functionality, and a default off-peak setting to encourage EV owners to charge at times of lower demand (and cost)'[17]. EV(SCP)R 2021 do *not* apply to non-smart cables (meaning an electrical cable which is a charge point but which is not able to send and receive information[18]), to public charge points nor to rapid charge points[19]. EV(SCP)R 2021 must be enforced by the Secretary of State[20].

From 15 June 2022, but with transitional provision as to commencement[21], the Building Regulations 2010[22] were amended in England[23] to require 'the installation of electric vehicle charge points or cable routes for electric vehicle charge points when certain kinds of building work are undertaken'[24].

On 2 November 2023 the government made regulations under AEVA 2018, Part 2 – the Public Charge Point Regulations 2023[25]. PCPR 2023 will be in force from 24 November 2023 and will 'impose certain requirements on charge point operators that operate public charge points'[26], among which are requirements as to reliability, display prices and ensure pay-as-you-go contactless payments. PCPR 2023 must be enforced by the Secretary of State (reg 12).

Accessible charging facilities

15.02   The suitability of EV charging points for people with accessibility needs is the subject of a 2022 standard by the British Standards Institution[27], sponsored by the charity Motability. That standard includes guidance as to charge point design, placement, the surroundings of the charge point, digital platforms and information.

Duties of private providers of EV charging facilities

15.03   Whether and by what legal means the supply of electricity to charge an electric vehicle triggers statutory implied terms might depend upon the nature of the supply. Electricity is within the definition of 'goods' under CRA 2015, s 2, with water and gas, but 'if and only if they are put up for supply in a limited volume or

---

17 House of Commons Library Briefing Paper 'Electric vehicles and infrastructure' by Dr Holly Edwards, Iona Stewart, Becky Mawhood and Paul Bolton (CBP-7480, 21 February 2023), page 67.
18 EV(SCP)R 2021 reg 3(3)(b).
19 EV(SCP)R 2021 reg 3(1).
20 EV(SCP)R 2021 reg 15(1).
21 Building Regulations etc (Amendment) (England) (No.2) Regulations 2021, SI 2021/1392, reg 4.
22 SI 2010/2214.
23 By the Building Regulations etc (Amendment) (England) (No.2) Regulations 2021, above. In relation to Wales, see Welsh government website 'Electric vehicle charging strategy for Wales' (23 March 2021).
24 Explanatory note to SI 2021/1392.
25 SI 2023/1168.
26 Explanatory note to PCPR 2023.
27 *Electric vehicles -accessible charging – specification*, BSI PAS 1899:2022, at BSI website 'PAS 1899:2022 Electric vehicles – accessible charging – specification' (accessed 27 July 2023).

set quantity'[28]. Whether this would be true of a contract with a supplier of electricity to a home or the supplier of a public EV charging facility would be a matter of fact.

Irrespective of its status as 'goods', there is authority for the implication of terms as to quality of electricity supplied as a service, at common law, where the provision of electrical power is within the contract. In *Bentley Bros v Metcalfe and* Co, the claimant's employee was injured when excess electrical power caused a machine hired to the claimant by the defendant for use on the defendant's premises to overrun. Supply of electricity was included in the contract of hire. The Court of Appeal held that:

> 'the principle which governs the relation of the parties upon a purchase and sale, that the article bought should be fit and proper for the purpose for which it is to be used, is equally applicable to the supply of power.'[29]

Duties of public bodies in relation to EV charging facilities

15.04   Please see discussion of the actionability in private law of public authorities' duties, in Chapter 13, 'highway claims'.

If electricity is defined as 'goods' and its supply is pursuant to a particular statutory obligation embodying a public duty, then that supply might not amount to a sale of such goods[30]. The leading practitioner's work on sale of goods extends this argument to the supply of electricity, whether or not the supplier is a public body or a privately owned corporation[31]. Whether such an argument would apply to EV charging has not been adjudicated.

Duties of those using EV charging facilities

15.05   Those using charging facilities are under duties including a duty not to obstruct the highway[32]. This duty might be engaged by (for example) placing an EV charging cable on a road or pavement during charging. Whether and the extent to which charging cables constitute an unlawful obstruction or a negligent hazard has yet to be adjudicated. For the time being, users of charging cables should take care to reduce the potential factual and legal risks of such cables during charging by, for example, placing them away from the parts of the highway or pavement which other people are likely to cross.

---

28 CRA 2015 s 2(8).
29 [1906] 2 KB 548, 553 (Cozens-Hardy LJ, as he then was). See more recent statutory law as to mixed contracts and the inclusion of hire within goods contracts: see for example chapter 10, 'vehicle defect claims'.
30 See *Pfizer Corpn v Ministry of Health* [1965] AC 512 (HL) which concerns provision of medication for a fee paid by the patient but provided through the National Health Service, discussed in *Benjamin's Sale of Goods* (11th edn, 2021) at 1-071.
31 See *Benjamin's Sale of Goods*, above.
32 See Chapter 13, 'highway claims'.

Compulsory third party motor insurance and use of EV charging facilities

15.06   Please see Chapter 6, 'insurance', for discussion of whether the use of electric vehicle charging facilities might be within the 'use' of a motor vehicle on a road or other public place in Great Britain subject to the compulsory insurance requirements of RTA 1988, Part VI. This will also depend upon the classification of the vehicle as a 'motor vehicle' (or not) within RTA 1988[33].

---

33 See also Chapter 16, 'smaller electric vehicle claims'.

Smaller electric vehicle claims

'Though I doubt very much whether it was in the mind of the Legislature that a vehicle of this kind [*an electrically-propelled bathchair*] would come into existence, I am forced to the conclusion on the language of the Act that this is a motor car within the Act.'

(Lord Reading CJ, 1917[1])

'In order to tackle congestion, improve air quality and reduce damage to infrastructure, the limited road space available must be used efficiently. Encouraging the use of PLVs [*powered light vehicles*], by incorporating them into local and national policy, will achieve this.'

(The Motorcycle Industry Association, representing the PLV industry, 2019[2])

Chapter Contents

A   Outline of the law of smaller electric vehicles

Scope of this chapter

16.01   This chapter describes the laws applying to civil claims involving road vehicles which are smaller than most cars. That is a broad category, including electric four-wheeled vehicles and electric motorbikes, as well as some powered 'micro mobility' vehicles which the government has described collectively as 'powered transporters':

'The term "powered transporters" covers a variety of novel personal transport devices which are mechanically propelled (propelled by a motor) as well as or instead of being manually propelled. It includes e-scooters, Segways,

---

1   *Elieson v Parker* (1917) 81 JP 265.
2   MCIA paper 'The route to tomorrow's journeys: powered light vehicles, practical, efficient and safe transport for all' (2019), page 16.

hoverboards, go-peds (combustion engine-powered kick-scooters), powered unicycles, and u-wheels'[3]

This book deals with electric vehicles, although that is not the only potential means of low or zero-emission propulsion[4].

Powered transporters and light powered vehicles (LPVs[5]) are described together in this chapter as 'smaller electric vehicles'. That is the writer's shorthand for a group of vehicles within which a variety of rules apply. The group encompasses a range of vehicles, from the very small (the powered unicycle or u-wheel[6]) to four-wheeled vehicles nearly the size of cars but limited to lower speeds[7]. A chapter which set out the laws relating to all such vehicles would both overwhelm the book and soon be outpaced by innovation. So this chapter considers a selection of small electric vehicles. The vehicles which perhaps best illustrate the variety of rules within the smaller electric vehicles category are *powered unicycles, e-scooters* and *e-bikes*.

A Transport Bill reforming the law of smaller electric vehicles was announced in the Queen's Speech in May 2022 but was postponed in December 2022. The Transport Bill 2022-23 was never published. It did not appear in the King's Speech of 7 November 2023. The two bills relevant to advanced, automated and electric vehicle law in the King's Speech 2023 were the Automated Vehicles Bill 2023-24 (HL Bill 1), which is discussed in other chapters, and the Pedicabs (London) Bill 2023-24 (HL Bill 2), described below.

Some introductory points follow. The first topic is how the law classifies electric vehicles.

Electric vehicles are 'motor vehicles' within RTA 1988, unless exempted

16.02   The legal character of a 'motor vehicle' is determined strictly by reference to the language of the statutory definition. The legal character of a vehicle is not to be defined by broader terms outside the legal definition, such as its novelty[8] nor (as has been repeated in submissions in several cases, to no avail) on the basis that it is merely 'a toy'[9].

RTA 1988 defines "motor vehicle' and other expressions relating to vehicles' at s 185. In particular:

---

3   Gov.uk 'Guidance: Powered Transporters' (updated 13 July 2020)
4   Other zero-emission vehicles include hydrogen fuel celled vehicles and non-fuel celled vehicles such as the bicycle.
5   This chapter adopts LPV (rather than PLV) as that is the term adopted by the UK government: UK government, Department for Transport paper 'Decarbonising Transport: A Better, Greener Britain' (2021), page 96.
6   A single, powered wheel which the rider straddles (either standing on footrests or sitting on a saddle) and which (using gyroscopes) accelerates according to the angle of the vehicle.
7   UNECE categories L6 and L7, below.
8   *Elieson v Parker*, above.
9   *Elieson v Parker*, above; *DPP v Saddington* [2001] RTR 15 (QBD); *DPP v King* [2008] EWHC 447 (Admin). In *DPP v King*, Walker J held that distinguishing between a motor vehicle and a toy was a misdirection in law [13].

' *"motor vehicle"* means, subject to section 20 of the Chronically Sick and Disabled Persons Act 1970 (which makes special provision about invalid carriages, within the meaning of that Act), a mechanically propelled vehicle intended or adapted for use on roads[10]' And:

' *"motor car"* means a mechanically propelled vehicle, not being a motor cycle or an invalid carriage, which is constructed itself to carry a load or passengers and the weight of which unladen—

(a) if it is constructed solely for the carriage of passengers and their effects, is adapted to carry not more than seven passengers exclusive of the driver and is fitted with tyres of such type as may be specified in regulations made by the Secretary of State, does not exceed 3050 kilograms,

(b) if it is constructed or adapted for use for the conveyance of goods or burden of any description, does not exceed 3050 kilograms, or 3500 kilograms if the vehicle carries a container or containers for holding for the purposes of its propulsion any fuel which is wholly gaseous at 17.5 degrees Celsius under a pressure of 1.013 bar or plant and materials for producing such fuel,

(c) does not exceed 2540 kilograms in a case not falling within sub-paragraph (a) or (b) above,

…

"motor cycle" means a mechanically propelled vehicle, not being an invalid carriage, with less than four wheels and the weight of which unladen does not exceed 410 kilograms'[11].'

A vehicle is 'mechanically propelled' even if powered by electricity[12].

The statutory definition catches all motor vehicles unless they are exempted[13]. So, for example, an e-scooter is a motor vehicle[14].

Some electric vehicles which would otherwise fit the statutory definition are exempted – such as electrically assisted pedal cycles, ie e-bikes[15]. The statutory exemptions appear in RTA 1988, s 189 ('certain vehicles not to be treated as motor vehicles') which provides as follows:

---

10 RTA 1988, s 185(1). For the test of whether a vehicle is 'intended or adapted for use on roads', see *DPP v Saddington*, above, discussed in Chapter 6, 'insurance'.
11 RTA 1988, s 185(1).
12 *Elieson v Parker*, above.
13 See RTA 1988, s 189: 'Certain vehicles not to be treated as motor vehicles'.
14 *DPP v King*, above. In an answer to a parliamentary question on 23 June 2022, the Department for Transport particularised an e-scooter as a moped: 'As motor vehicles having fewer than 4 wheels and weighing less than 410 kg unladen, e-scooters are classed as motorcycles as defined in Section 185 of the Road Traffic Act 1988 and, because of their low speed, within the subclass of moped'.
15 RTA 1988, s 189(1)(c) and the Electrically Assisted Pedal Cycles Regulations 1983, SI 1983, SI 1168 ('EAPCR 1983'), as amended by the Electrically Assisted Pedal Cycles (Amendment) Regulations 2015, SI 2015/24.

'(1) For the purposes of the Road Traffic Acts –

    (a) a mechanically propelled vehicle being an implement for cutting grass which is controlled by a pedestrian and is not capable of being used or adapted for any other purpose,

    (b) any other mechanically propelled vehicle controlled by a pedestrian which may be specified by regulations[16] made by the Secretary of State for the purposes of this section and section 140 of the Road Traffic Regulation Act 1984, and

    (c) an electrically assisted pedal cycle of such a class as may be prescribed by regulations[17] so made,

is to be treated as not being a motor vehicle.

(2) In subsection (1) above *"controlled by a pedestrian"* means that the vehicle either—

    (a) is constructed or adapted for use only under such control, or

    (b) is constructed or adapted for use either under such control or under the control of a person carried on it, but is not for the time being in use under, or proceeding under, the control of a person carried on it.'

The nature of the 'illegality' of some smaller electric vehicles

16.03 There is a perception that some smaller electric vehicles (for example, e-scooters) are in themselves illegal. But, as the government puts it:

'There is no specially-designed legal regime for powered transporters. This means that they are covered by the same laws and regulations that apply to all motor vehicles.'[18]

The law attaches conditions to the use of 'motor vehicles' (as so defined by statute[19]) on roads and other public places. Those conditions relate to matters of public financing of roads and to road safety, so include conditions as to vehicle type approval, vehicle and driver licensing and compulsory third-party insurance. Breaches of those statutory conditions of use are criminal offences[20]. So the user of a vehicle which the law defines as a 'motor vehicle' must satisfy several conditions in order to use it lawfully on a road or other public place; if they do not do so,

---

16   See Chapter 14 ('delivery claims') for discussion of road maintenance vehicles controlled by a pedestrian as permitted by the Road Vehicles (Authorisation of Special Types) (General) Order 2003, SI 2003/1998, part 5 ('miscellaneous special vehicles'), art 50(1), made under RTA 1988, s 44 ('authorisation of use on roads of special vehicles not complying with regulations under s 41').

17   EAPCR 1983 (as amended), above.

18   Gov.uk 'Guidance: Powered Transporters' (updated 13 July 2020)

19   See RTA 1988, s 185.

20   See eg RTA 1988, s 63(1) (offence of using on a road a vehicle to which type approval requirements apply without certificates of conformity complying with ss 54 to 58), 87 (offence of driving or permitting a person to drive a vehicle without a driving licence for vehicle of that class) and 143(2) (offence of using motor vehicle on road or other public place without policy of insurance complying with RTA 1988, Part VI); Vehicle Excise and Registration Act 1994 s 29 (offence of using or keeping an unlicensed vehicle).

they will be behaving criminally. As the government says in its online guidance on powered transporters, the position is that:

'For motor vehicles to use public roads lawfully, they must meet a number of different requirements. These include insurance; conformity with technical standards and standards of use; payment of vehicle tax, licensing, and registration; driver testing and licensing; and the use of relevant safety equipment.'

'If the user of a powered transporter could meet these requirements, it might in principle be lawful for them to use public roads. However, it is likely that they will find it very difficult to comply with all of these requirements, meaning that it would be a criminal offence to use them on the road.'[21]

So a motor vehicle (such as an e-scooter) is not itself unlawful; but using a motor vehicle on a road or other public place without satisfying the statutory conditions of use (vehicle approval, driver and vehicle licensing, insurance etc) is unlawful. For the users of some small electric vehicles this presents practical difficulties which the law does not yet tackle. For example, even if a vehicle is approved and its use is insured etc, the registration plate size requirements of the Road Vehicles (Display of Registration Marks) Regulations 2001[22], non-compliance with which is a criminal offence[23], are likely to be difficult to satisfy in the case of a smaller motor vehicle such as an e-scooter (which probably explains the liberation of *trial* e-scooters from registration requirements[24]).

Riding on footpaths etc

16.04   The Highway Act 1835, s 72 ('penalty on persons committing nuisances by riding on footpaths, &c') remains law and provides that:

'If any person shall wilfully ride upon any footpath or causeway by the side of any road made or set apart for the use or accommodation of foot passengers; or shall wilfully lead or drive any horse, ass, sheep, mule, swine, or cattle or carriage of any description, or any truck or sledge, upon any such footpath or causeway; or shall tether any horse, ass, mule, swine, or cattle, on any highway, so as to suffer or permit the tethered animal to be thereon; every person so offending in any of the cases aforesaid shall for each and every such offence forfeit and pay any sum not exceeding level 2 on the standard scale, over and above the damages occasioned thereby.'

RTA 1988, s 34 ('prohibition of driving mechanically propelled vehicles elsewhere than on roads') covers mechanically propelled vehicles other than those exempted

---

21   Government guidance on powered transporters, above.
22   SI 2001/561, regs 14 ('size and spacing of characters') and 14A ('size and spacing of characters: special cases'), made under VERA 1994, s 23(3) and (4) ('registration marks').
23   VERA 1994, s 59.
24   Regulation 4(2A) of the Road Vehicle (Registration and Licensing) Regulations 2002, SI 2002/2742, as amended by regulation 2(3) of the Electric Scooter Trials and Traffic Signs (Coronavirus) Regulations and General Directions 2020, SI 2020/663; Gov.uk 'E-scooter trials: guidance for users' (13 July 2020, updated 17 July 2023).

by s 189(1)(a) to (c). Subject to the exemptions set out in the remainder of s 34, s 34(1) provides that

'Subject to the provisions of this section, if without lawful authority a person drives a mechanically propelled vehicle –

(a) on to or upon any common land, moorland or land of any other description, not being land forming part of a road, or

(b) on any road being a footpath, bridleway or restricted byway,

he is guilty of an offence.'

The effect of unlawful use upon smaller electric vehicle claims: the '*ex turpi causa*' defence

16.05 As discussed in Chapter 11, 'passenger claims' in relation to the application of the so-called[25] illegality defence (*ex turpi causa non oritur actio*[26]) to road traffic injury claims involving joint criminal enterprise, the Court of Appeal in *McCracken v Smith* addressed the level of criminality on the part of a claimant required for *ex turpi* to bar their road traffic accident claim. Christopher Clarke LJ noted that:

'Difficult questions may, however, arise in future as to the degree of blameworthiness needed for the doctrine to apply. In *Les Laboratoires Servier v Apotex Inc* the Supreme Court: (a) referred to the earlier rejection by the House of Lords of the "affront to the public conscience" test as unprincipled; (b) rejected a fact based discretionary approach; (c) said that "the paradigm case of an illegal act engaging the defence is a criminal offence"; and (d) treated the *ex turpi causa* principle as being founded on acts which are contrary to the public law of the state and engage the public interest; and (e) recognised that the doctrine might not apply to offences of strict liability where the claimant was not privy to the fact making the act unlawful.

'The reach of modern criminal law into the field of road traffic is, however, extensive. Leaving aside dangerous driving, careless driving is, itself, an offence. Causing death thereby is punishable with imprisonment. There are a number of offences, punishable otherwise than by imprisonment under the Road Traffic Act 1988, including: motor racing on highways (s 12); riding a motorcycle without the required protective headgear (s 16); leaving a vehicle in a dangerous position (s 22); carrying a passenger on a motorcycle contrary to s 23 (s 23); failing to comply with traffic directions given by a constable or traffic officer (s 35) or the indications given by traffic signs (s 36); using a vehicle in a dangerous condition (s 40A); and contravention of a construction and use requirement as to brakes, steering gear or tyres, or use of a motor vehicle which does not comply with such a requirement, or causing or permitting a motor vehicle to be so used (s 41A). Speeding itself is a crime not punishable by imprisonment: Road Traffic Regulation Act 1984 s 89...

---

25 'although described as a defence, it is in reality a rule of judicial abstention...': *Les Laboratoires Servier v Apotex Inc* [2014] UKSC 55; [2015] AC 430, 445 [23] (Lord Sumption).
26 'No claim arises from a base cause'.

'In *Joyce v O'Brien*[27] Elias LJ said at [51] that the doctrine did not apply to 'minor traffic offences', whilst recognising that in certain cases there may be a problem in determining whether the offence attracted the application of the doctrine or not. That begs the question as to what is meant by 'minor'. It may be that the dividing line should be between those offences which are, and those which are not, punishable by imprisonment. Or it may be that the criterion is simply whether the public interest requires the doctrine to apply to a crime of the category in question.'[28]

In a subsequent judgment of the High Court, Males J (as he then was) expressed a firmer view:

'Towards the other end of the spectrum [*from manslaughter*], careless driving is a criminal offence but nobody would suggest that careless driving by the claimant prevents the recovery of damages (reduced as appropriate on account of contributory negligence) in a road traffic case where both drivers are partly to blame. In such a case the recovery of damages does not offend public notions of the fair distribution of resources and poses no threat to the integrity of the law. On the contrary, the recovery of damages is in accordance with public policy. The claimant is not compensated for the consequence of his own criminal act. Rather, as a result of the reduction for contributory fault, he is compensated only for that part of the damage which the law regards as having been caused by the defendant's negligence.'[29]

As at the time of writing, *ex turpi* has yet to be considered in a judgment in a smaller electric vehicle claim[30]. The precise scope of the rule remains difficult to pin down, even in the road traffic context[31].

Incomplete regulation of smaller electric vehicles

16.06   As at the time of writing the use of smaller electric vehicles on public roads is not fully regulated. The incompleteness of regulation is especially clear in the case of micro mobility vehicles such as privately-owned e-scooters and powered unicycles, despite the increasingly common use of such vehicles on roads and other public places. As the government puts it:

'There is no specially-designed legal regime for powered transporters.'[32]

---

27   [2013] EWCA Civ 546; [2014] 1 WLR 70.
28   *McCracken v Smith* [2015] EWCA Civ 380; [2015] PIQR P19 [83-86].
29   *Wallett v Vickers* [2018] EWHC 3088; [2019] PIQR P6 [38].
30   A highway repair claim in the County Court involving an allegation of a fall from an e-scooter said to have been caused by a pothole was reportedly dismissed for lack of proof that the pothole in question caused the fall, without deciding any point on the regulation of e-scooters or *ex turpi*: Keoghs solicitors article 'First e-scooter claim for compensation fails' (17 April 2023).
31   See, for example, *Ali v HSF Logistics Polska SP Zoo* [2023] EWHC 2159, discussed in Chapter 11 (passenger claims).
32   Gov.uk 'Guidance: Powered Transporters' (updated 13 July 2020)

Trials intended to test the viability of a longer-term legal position for e-scooters are ongoing. Publication of a Transport Bill intended to include such regulation, announced in Parliament in May 2022, is still delayed[33].

As the law stands at the time of writing, an e-scooter is a 'motor vehicle' within the RTA 1988, s 185[34], although the government has relaxed some of the requirements for personal use of e-scooters in identified trial areas[35], including pushing the requirement for compulsory liability insurance to the commercial operators of trials[36] and disapplying in relation to trial e-scooters the requirement for use of a helmet[37].

E-bikes are exempted from the statutory definition of a 'motor vehicle' under RTA 1988[38].

International classification of light powered vehicles

16.07   Several types of small vehicle are within a particular category of international classification for the purpose of vehicle type approval[39]. These are 'light powered vehicles' (LPVs), which in their electric versions are sometimes referred to as zero emission LPVs (ZELPVs)[40]. The government describes LPVs as:

> 'two, three and four wheeled passenger or cargo vehicles. They are small and lighter than many other vehicle types and so can have a significant impact on urban transport systems, particularly when used in place of other forms of low occupancy vehicles. Their size also makes them complementary to increased public transport use and the growth of cycling and walking infrastructure.'[41]

LPVs are classified as the 'L' group of vehicles by the United Nations Economic Commission for Europe (UNECE) Consolidated Resolution on the Construction of Vehicles[42]. UNECE regulations are applied by national governments (including the UK government) to classify vehicles for the purpose of approving those vehicles for

---

33   Parliament Live TV, Transport Select Committee 7 December 2022 at 9:43, Sec of St for Transport the Rt Hon Mark Harper MP. Other than the Automated Vehicles Bill 2023-24 (HL Bill 1) and the Pedicabs (London) Bill (HL Bill 2), no broader Transport Bill featured in the King's Speech of 7 November 2023.
34   *DPP v King* [2008] EWHC 447 (Admin).
35   Electric Scooter Trials and Traffic Signs (Coronavirus) Regulations and General Directions 2020, SI 2020/663.
36   Gov.uk 'E-scooter trials: guidance for users' (13 July 2020, updated 17 July 2023).
37   Motor Cycle (Protective Helmets) Regulations 1998, reg 4(2A), added by the Electric Scooter Trials and Traffic Signs (Coronavirus) Regulations and General Directions 2020, SI 2020/663, reg 3(2)(b).
38   RTA 1988, s 189 'certain vehicles not to be treated as motor vehicles'; e-bikes are at s 189(1)(c).
39   See Chapter 2, 'specifications'.
40   UK government, Department for Transport paper 'Decarbonising Transport: A Better, Greener Britain' (2021), page 96.
41   As above.
42   UNECE Inland Transport Committee, World Forum for Harmonization of Vehicle Regulations, Revised consolidated version of the Resolution on the Construction of Vehicles (R.E.3), ECE/TRANS/WP.29/78/Rev.6 (11 July 2017).

sale and use within their country[43]. The L group vehicles as listed within the UNECE regulation are as follows:

' *"Category L"*: A two-wheeled vehicle with an engine cylinder capacity in the case of a thermic engine not exceeding 50 cm and whatever the means of propulsion a maximum design speed not exceeding 50 km/h [*just over 31 mph*].

"Category L2":A three-wheeled vehicle of any wheel arrangement with an engine cylinder capacity in the case of a thermic engine not exceeding 50 cm and whatever the means of propulsion a maximum design speed not exceeding 50 km/h [*just over 31 mph*].

"Category L3": A two-wheeled vehicle with an engine cylinder capacity in the case of a thermic engine exceeding 50 cm or whatever the means of propulsion a maximum design speed exceeding 50 km/h [*just over 31 mph*].

"Category L4": A vehicle with three wheels asymmetrically arranged in relation to the longitudinal median plane with an engine cylinder capacity in the case of a thermic engine exceeding 50 cm or whatever the means of propulsion a maximum design speed exceeding 50 km/h [*just over 31 mph*] (motor cycles with sidecars).

"Category L5": A vehicle with three wheels symmetrically arranged in relation to the longitudinal median plane with an engine cylinder capacity in the case of a thermic engine exceeding 50 cm or whatever the means of propulsion a maximum design speed exceeding 50 km/h [*just over 31 mph*].

"Category L6": A vehicle with four wheels whose unladen mass is not more than 350 kg, not including the mass of the batteries in case of electric vehicles, whose maximum design speed is not more than 45 km/h [*just under 28 mph*], and whose engine cylinder capacity does not exceed 50 cm for spark (positive) ignition engines, or whose maximum net power output does not exceed 4 kW in the case of other internal combustion engines, or whose maximum continuous rated power does not exceed 4 kW in the case of electric engines.

"Category L7": A vehicle with four wheels, other than that classified for the category L6, whose unladen mass is not more than 400 kg (550 kg for vehicles intended for carrying goods), not including the mass of batteries in the case of electric vehicles and whose maximum continuous rated power does not exceed 15 kW.'[44]

---

43   See Chapter 2, 'specifications' and UK government, Department for Transport, Vehicle Certification Agency (VCA) website 'What is Vehicle Type Approval?', 'Type Approval Category Definitions' (3 November 2022).

44   UNECE revised consolidated version of the Resolution on the Construction of Vehicles (R.E.3), art 2, 'classification of power-driven vehicles and trailers'. In the UNECE regulation, the digit for each sub-category (L1 etc) is written in small subtext, but for reasons of legibility I intentionally abandon that formatting in the quoted passage. In the UNECE regulation, category L is subtitled 'motor vehicles with less than four wheels'; however, sub-categories L6 and L7 both describe 'a vehicle with four wheels', so I do not repeat the subtitle here. The conversion of speeds from km/h to an approximate equivalent speed in mph is mine; for any practical purpose the reader should carry out their own more precise calculation.

Regulatory characteristics of a selection of smaller electric vehicles which are in common use

16.08   The following table shows the main regulatory characteristics of a selection of smaller electric vehicles which are in common use.

Example of small vehicle	Non-legal labels	Label in GB law	UNECE L Class	Whether 'motor vehicle' under RTA 1988	Main[45] exemptions from particular GB driving laws (if a 'motor vehicle')
Powered unicycle	Micro mobility vehicle; powered transporter[46]	Motor vehicle (likely a motor cycle)[47]	None	Yes	None (though query, for example, how such a small vehicle, if otherwise compliant, could comply with registration plate rules[48])
E-scooter[49]	Micro mobility vehicle; powered transporter[50]	Electric scooter[51]	L1	Yes: motorcycle[52]	Registration and helmet requirements removed for *trial* e-scooter use[53]

45   Eg. for reasons of space this table does not cover vehicle excise and registration laws (see the Vehicle and Registration Act 1994) nor driver licensing (RTA 1988, Part III).
46   Gov.uk 'Guidance: Powered Transporters' (updated 13 July 2020).
47   RTA 1988, s 185(1). *"Motor cycle"* means a mechanically propelled vehicle, not being an invalid carriage, with less than four wheels and the weight of which unladen does not exceed 410 kilograms'.
48   Road Vehicles (Display of Registration Marks) Regulations 2001, SI 2001/561, regs 14 ('size and spacing of characters') and 14A ('size and spacing of characters: special cases'), made under VERA 1994, s 23(3) and (4) ('registration marks').
49   NB. that the law as to e-scooters would alter if the Transport Bill (unpublished at the time of writing) became law on the basis of the government's announced intention (in the Queen's Speech of May 2022) to place e-scooters in a new legal category of vehicles. See other chapters, especially Chapters 4, 'driving', and 6, 'insurance'.
50   Gov.uk 'Guidance: Powered Transporters' (updated 13 July 2020)
51   Road Vehicle (Registration and Licensing) Regulations 2002, SI 2002/2742, reg 33(1A).
52   RTA 1988, s 185(1): *"motor cycle'* means a mechanically propelled vehicle, not being an invalid carriage, with less than four wheels and the weight of which unladen does not exceed 410 kilograms'.
53   Motor Cycle (Protective Helmets) Regulations 1998, reg 4(2A), added by the Electric Scooter Trials and Traffic Signs (Coronavirus) Regulations and General Directions 2020, SI 2020/663, reg 3(2)(b); Road Vehicle (Registration and Licensing) Regulations 2002, SI 2002/2742, reg 4(2A) as amended by regulation 2(3) of the EST etc 2020 Regulations and General Directions.

E-bike with two wheels	E-bike	Electrically Assisted Pedal Cycle (EAPC)[54]	L1	No: exempted, if within EAPCR 1983[55]	NA: not a 'motor vehicle' in GB law if within EAPCR 1983
E-bike with three wheels (eg three-wheeled child carrier e-bike)	Child carrier e-bike	Electrically Assisted Pedal Cycle (EAPC)[56]	L2	No: exempted, if within EAPCR 1983[57]	NA: not a 'motor vehicle' in GB law if within EAPCR 1983
Powered wheelchair or mobility scooter	Powered wheelchair; mobility scooter	'Invalid carriage'[58] and 'mechanically propelled vehicle'[59]	Depends upon specifications, eg number of wheels[60]	No: excluded from definition of 'motor vehicle'[61]	NA: not a motor vehicle.

Figure 1: the main regulatory characteristics of a selection of common smaller electric vehicles

B Smaller Advanced Driver Assistance Systems (ADAS) Electric Vehicle Claims

16.09   Small electric vehicle technology is an innovating field. It is possible that advanced driver assistance systems will be installed in smaller electric vehicles – particularly three and four-wheeled vehicles in the L5 to L7 groups.

Some smaller electric vehicles are used for deliveries. Some use partially automated technologies subject to remote assistance. Some operate as prototype vehicles in the context of tests or trials[62].

---

54   RTA 1989 s 189(1)(c).
55   RTA 1988, s 189(1)(c); EAPCR 1983 (as amended). See especially regs 4 and 5 and *DPP v Saddington* (above); *Winter v DPP* [2002] EWHC 2482; [2003] RTR 14 and *DPP v King* (above)
56   RTA 1988, s 189(1)(c); EAPCR 1983 (as amended).
57   RTA 1988, s 189(1)(c); EAPCR 1983 (as amended).
58   In the dated language of RTA 1988, s 185(1) (definitions of 'invalid carriage' and 'motor vehicle') and the Chronically Sick and Disabled Persons Act 1970, s 20 ('use of invalid carriages on highways').
59   RTA 1988, s 185(1).
60   And see official guidance as to matters including speeds of class 2 and 3 mobility scooters and powered wheelchairs at Gov.uk 'Mobility scooters and powered wheelchairs: the rules' (accessed 24 July 2023).
61   RTA 1988, s 185(1); CSDPA 1970, s 20.
62   Under the Road Vehicles (Authorisation of Special Types) (General) Order 2003, SI 2003/1998, as amended ('RV(AST)(G)O 2003'). See Chapter 3, 'testing'.

See also Chapters 2, 'specifications', 3, 'testing', 4, 'driving' and 14, 'delivery claims'.

C Smaller Automated Electric Vehicle Claims

16.10   As at the time of writing no vehicle has yet been listed as 'automated' under AEVA 2018 s 1. So no 'automated' vehicle yet exists as a matter of law.

If and when such vehicles come into legal existence, whether by means of AEVA 2018, s 1 listing or by its successor authorisation scheme under the Automated Vehicles Act 2024 (now the AV Bill 2023-24 (HL Bill 1)), the AEVA 2018 insurance and liability provisions will come into effect in relation to those vehicles.

See also Chapters 6, 'insurance' and 9, 'RTA claims'.

D Smaller Electric Vehicle Claims

Statutory definition of 'Electric Vehicle'

16.11   An oddity on the face of AEVA 2018 is that it does not define the phrase 'electric vehicle'. The definitions section of AEVA 2018, Part ('Electric Vehicles: Charging') only defines 'vehicle':

' *"vehicle"* means a vehicle that is intended or adapted for use on roads.'[63]

That was a deliberate legislative decision. Despite the title of the Act, AEVA 2018 Part 2 legislates beyond electric vehicles and includes hydrogen-fuelled propulsion. Parliamentary debate on what became AEVA 2018, s 9 included this passage:

'... this part of the Bill is focused on charging or refuelling infrastructure for vehicles. Such infrastructure is defined by reference to its capacity to recharge either battery or hydrogen-propelled vehicles. We think that the Bill includes the relevant definitions necessary in relation to refuelling points. In addition, there is a definition of "electric vehicle" in legislation already, as the definition contained in the Alternative Fuels Infrastructure Regulations made last year mirrors the definition proposed by the noble Baroness, Lady Worthington. Given that the definitions in the Bill already work as intended, we do not think there is a need to duplicate the definition of "electric vehicle" within the Bill.'[64]

The definition of 'electric vehicle' appears in those 2017 regulations:

' *"electric vehicle"* means a motor vehicle equipped with a powertrain containing at least one non-peripheral electric machine as energy convertor

---

63   AEVA 2018, s 9.
64   Baroness Sugg, House of Lords Hansard, volume 791, column 790, 17 May 2018

with an electric rechargeable energy storage system, which can be recharged externally;'[65]

As an electric vehicle is 'mechanically propelled'[66], such a vehicle already falls within the RTA 1988, s 185 definition of 'motor vehicle', though it is possible that the definitions in the 2017 and (for e-scooters) 2002 regulations[67] might also be relevant in future cases.

E-scooters

Statutory Definition of 'Electric Scooter'

16.12 An 'electric scooter' is defined (in relation to registration and licensing) by the Road Vehicle (Registration and Licensing) Regulations 2002[68], reg 33(1A) ('nil licences') as follows:

' *"electric scooter"* means a vehicle which-

(a) is fitted with an electric motor with a maximum continuous power rating not exceeding 500 watts;

(b) is not fitted with pedals that are capable of propelling the vehicle;

(c) has two wheels, one front and one rear, aligned along the direction of travel;

(d) is designed to carry no more than one person;

(e) has a maximum weight, excluding the driver, not exceeding 55 kgs;

(f) has a maximum design speed not exceeding 15.5 miles per hour;

(g) has a means of directional control through the use of handlebars which are mechanically linked to the steered wheel;

(h) has a means of controlling the speed through hand controls; and

(i) has a power control that defaults to the 'off' position;'

E-scooter regulation

16.13 As a 'motor vehicle'[69], an e-scooter is subject to the requirements and penalties provided by the RTA 1988 (including those requiring third party motor insurance and a driving licence[70]). As the government guidance on powered transporters puts it:

---

65   Alternative Fuels Infrastructure Regulations 2017, SI 2017/897, reg 2, 'interpretation'.
66   RTA 1988, s 185 and *Elieson v Parker*, above.
67   AFIR 2017 (above); Road Vehicle (Registration and Licensing) Regulations 2002, SI 2002/2742, below.
68   SI 2002/2742, reg 33(1A), as amended by the Electric Scooter Trials and Traffic Signs (Coronavirus) Regulations and General Directions 2020, reg 2(3).
69   *DPP v King*, above.
70   RTA 1988, s 87, 'drivers of motor vehicles to have driving licences'; Gov.uk 'E-scooter trials: guidance for users' (13 July 2020, updated 17 July 2023).

'It is illegal to use a powered transporter on a public road without complying with a number of legal requirements, which potential users will find very difficult'[71]

In 2020, the government regulated to allow trials of e-scooters on public roads in identified trial areas[72]. The purpose was to assess the suitability of e-scooters for eventual use on all roads[73]. Regulations liberated trial e-scooter use from some legal requirements including vehicle registration and wearing a helmet[74] and permitted trial e-scooters to use cycle lanes[75]. The attractions from the trial user's perspective included the provision of insurance by the trial operator[76]. E-scooter trials were due to end on 30 November 2022[77] but in July the Department for Transport stated its preference for an 18-month extension of the trials, if a local authority so wished, to the end of May 2024[78].

The government announced in the Queen's Speech in May 2022 that it intended to regulate the use of low-speed, zero-emission vehicles including e-scooters on roads and other public places. The government told Parliament the following day that:

'…it is our intention that the [*Transport*] Bill will create a low-speed, zero-emission vehicle category that is independent from the cycle and motor vehicle categories. New powers would allow the Government to decide the vehicles that fall into this new category in future and how they should be regulated to make sure that they are safe to use. We hope that e-scooters will be the first of these vehicles.'[79]

The Transport Bill was due to be debated in parliament during the 2022 to 2023 session but in December 2022 the Secretary of State for Transport told the House of Commons Transport Select Committee that the entire Bill had been postponed[80]. The Transport Bill was not published. It did not appear in the King's Speech in November 2023.

E-scooter helmets

16.14 An e-scooter is a motor cycle[81] so a rider of an e-scooter is required to wear protective headgear, by regulation 4(1) of the Motor Cycles (Protective Helmets)

---

71 Gov.uk 'Guidance: Powered Transporters' (updated 13 July 2020).
72 Electric Scooter Trials and Traffic Signs (Coronavirus) Regulations and General Directions 2020, SI 2020/663.
73 Explanatory note to Electric Scooter Trials and Traffic Signs (Coronavirus) Regulations and General Directions 2020, SI 2020/663.
74 Electric Scooter Trials and Traffic Signs (Coronavirus) Regulations and General Directions 2020, SI 2020/663, regs 2 and 3.
75 Electric Scooter Trials and Traffic Signs (Coronavirus) Regulations and General Directions 2020, SI 2020/663, reg 5.
76 Gov.uk 'E-scooter trials: guidance for users' (13 July 2020, updated 17 July 2023).
77 Gov.uk 'E-scooter trials: Guidance for local areas and rental operators' (updated 22 February 2022).
78 DfT answer 6 July 2022 to parliamentary question by Gill Furniss MP 1 July 2022, UIN 28907.
79 Baroness Vere, House of Lords Hansard Volume 822, columns 30 to 31, 11 May 2022.
80 Parliament Live TV, Transport Select Committee 7 December 2022 at 9:43, Sec of St for Transport the Rt Hon Mark Harper MP.
81 Provided that it meets the definition in RTA 1988, s 185(1): 'a mechanically propelled vehicle, not being an invalid carriage, with less than four wheels and the weight of which unladen does not exceed 410 kilograms'. And see the government's characterisation of an e-scooter as 'a motorcycle as defined in section 185 … within the subclass of moped' in Answer by Trudy Harrison MP to parliamentary question by Jim Shannon MP, UN 21181, tabled on 20 June 2022, answered 23 June 2022.

Regulations 1998[82]. By amendment from 4 July 2020, that regulation does not apply to 'to any person driving an electric scooter being used in a trial'[83].

Even for trial e-scooters, the government's guidance is to recommend use of a helmet for e-scooter journeys (which accords with the law that failure to use a helmet need not be a criminal offence to amount to contributory negligence in a civil claim[84]) and it advises that

> 'local authorities [*conducting e-scooter trials*] may wish to include the provision of helmets or availability at the point of hire in their agreement(s) with operators.'[85]

E-scooter liability insurance

16.15   Unlike e-bikes and what the law still calls 'invalid carriages', e-scooters are not exempt from the compulsory motor insurance requirements of RTA 1988, Part VI[86]. So, as at the time of writing the current system of compulsory third-party insurance for the use of a motor vehicle on a road or other public place in Great Britain applies in full force to e-scooters.

An e-scooter is defined in law as 'a vehicle which is designed to carry no more than one person'[87]. In practice, that does not prevent the occasional use of e-scooters to carry more than one person. RTA 1988, s 148 provides as follows:

'148. Avoidance of certain exceptions to policies

(1) Where a policy is issued for the purposes of this Part of this Act, so much of the policy as purports to restrict the insurance of the persons insured by the policy, by reference to any of the matters mentioned in subsection (2) below shall, as respects such liabilities as are required to be covered by a policy under section 145 of this Act, be of no effect.

(2) Those matters are—

  …

  (c) the number of persons that the vehicle carries'

The future form of insurance law for e-scooters is unknown. A possibility is that the duty to insure e-scooter use under RTA 1988, s 143 will be retained by the individual user upon liberalisation of private use beyond the trials. An alternative (perhaps indicated by the intended creation of a new category of vehicles 'independent from the cycle and motor vehicle categories', as the government told Parliament in May 2022) is that s 143 will be substantially amended in relation to e-scooters.

---

82 SI 1998/1807.
83 MC(PH)R 1998, reg 4(2A), added by the Electric Scooter Trials and Traffic Signs (Coronavirus) Regulations and General Directions 2020, SI 2020/663, reg 3(2)(b).
84 *Smith v Finch* [2009] EWHC 53 (QB) [44] (Griffith Williams J), discussed in Chapter 9, 'RTA claims'.
85 Gov.uk 'E-scooter trials: Guidance for local areas and rental operators' (updated 22 February 2022).
86 See RTA 1988, ss 185 and 189.
87 Road Vehicle (Registration and Licensing) Regulations 2002 (above), reg 33(1A).

The Motor Insurers' Bureau has supported motor insurance reform to provide a 'lighter touch' insurance approach, in which the compulsory motor insurance requirement still applies to the use of e-scooters on roads but is subject to financial limits to compensation[88]. And some respondents to the government's *Future of Transport Regulatory Review* in 2020:

> 'suggested that different types of insurance could be available, rather than motor insurance which applies to mopeds. This included options such as add-ons to home insurance, a standalone personal liability product, or some form of taxation. It was also suggested insurance should also be required for [e-bikes], or that requirements could be linked to the speed, weight or power of the vehicle.'[89]

The form of a liability insurance scheme to secure payment of compensation to e-scooter accident victims, if the conditions for e-scooter use were reduced in a future Transport Bill, is not yet clear. Asked in January 2023 about the effect of e-scooters upon insurance requirements, the government stated that it will consult before regulating further for private and rental e-scooters[90]. No Transport Bill dealing with e-scooters appeared in the King's Speech in November 2023.

'Powered Transporter/micro mobility' vehicles other than e-scooters, eg. the powered unicycle

Statutory definition of 'micro mobility' vehicles or 'powered transporters'

16.16   There is no statutory definition of 'micro mobility' vehicles or 'powered transporters'. As the government's guidance on powered transporters says:

> 'There is no specially-designed legal regime for powered transporters. This means that they are covered by the same laws and regulations that apply to all motor vehicles.'[91]

Regulation of 'micro mobility' vehicles or 'powered transporters'

16.17   As described above, a vehicle which satisfies the statutory definition of 'motor vehicle' without exemption will be subject to the several requirements of use on roads and other public places set out in RTA 1988 and elsewhere, including (for example) type approval, the provision of compulsory liability insurance and the display of registration details on plates of the prescribed size[92]. That such

---

88   'The Motor Insurers' Bureau supported insurance for e-scooters, saying that they will 'inevitably give rise to additional accidents'. It said this should be a lighter-touch approach than car insurance requirements and that the amount of cover, and the cost, should reflect the lower risk presented by e-scooters': House of Commons Transport Select Committee 'E-scooters: pavement nuisance or transport innovation' (2 October 2020), para.54. And see Bolt Burdon Kemp solicitors 'The Future of E-scooter Regulation: a Stakeholder Discussion' (6 July 2022).
89   Department for Transport 'Future of Transport Regulatory Review: Summary of Responses' (October 2020), p 26, 27.
90   See DfT answer to question by Gill Furniss MP, asked 31 January 2023, answered 3 February 2023, UIN 136675.
91   Gov.uk 'Guidance: Powered Transporters' (updated 13 July 2020).
92   See 'outline' section of this chapter.

requirements (eg. registration plates of the prescribed size) might be impracticable in the case of a very small vehicle such as a powered unicycle or e-scooter does not provide exemption.

The Construction and Use regulations do not address micro mobility vehicles such as a powered unicycle directly. However, two regulations are potentially of relevance.

RV(CU)R 1986, reg 100, 'maintenance and use of vehicle so as not to be a danger, etc', provides that

'(1) A motor vehicle, every trailer drawn thereby and all parts and accessories of such vehicle and trailer shall at all times be in such condition, and the number of passengers carried by such vehicle or trailer, the manner in which any passengers are carried in or on such vehicle or trailer, and the weight, distribution, packing and adjustment of the load of such vehicle or trailer shall at all times be such, that no danger is caused or is likely[93] to be caused to any person in or on the vehicle or trailer or on a road.

Provided that the provisions of this regulation with regard to the number of passengers carried shall not apply to a vehicle to which the Public Service Vehicles (Carrying Capacity) Regulations 1984[94] apply.

(2) The load carried by a motor vehicle or trailer shall at all times be so secured, if necessary by physical restraint other than its own weight, and be in such a position, that neither danger nor nuisance is likely to be caused to any person or property by reason of the load or any part thereof falling or being blown from the vehicle or by reason of any other movement of the load or any part thereof in relation to the vehicle.

(3) No motor vehicle or trailer shall be used for any purpose for which it is so unsuitable as to cause or be likely to cause danger or nuisance to any person in or on the vehicle or trailer or on a road.'

The regulation relating to 'driver's control' (RV(CU)R 1986, reg 104) provides that

'No person shall drive or cause or permit any other person to drive, a motor vehicle on a road if he is in such a position that he cannot have proper control of the vehicle or have a full view of the road and traffic ahead.'

Breaches of RV(CU)R 1986 are criminal offences under RTA 1988, Part II, ss 40A–42.

In particular, RTA 1988, s 40A makes it an offence to use a vehicle in a dangerous condition:

'A person is guilty of an offence if he uses, or causes or permits another to use, a motor vehicle or trailer on a road when –

(a) the condition of the motor vehicle or trailer, or of its accessories or equipment, or

---

93 'Likely' means something more than a bare possibility, but less than a probability: *Bennington v Peter* [1984] RTR 383 (QB, Woolf J, as he then was).
94 SI 1984/1406.

(b) the purpose for which it is used, or

(c) the number of passengers carried by it, or the manner in which they are carried, or

(d) the weight, position or distribution of its load, or the manner in which it is secured,

is such that the use of the motor vehicle or trailer involves a danger of injury to any person.'

In a criminal case, *Rex v Tudor Manolache*[95], the Court of Appeal dismissed an appeal against a sentence of 14 months' imprisonment on pleas of guilty to causing death by careless driving of an electrically propelled unicycle, a 'Gotway', and for causing death by driving a vehicle without insurance, where no separate penalty was imposed for the second offence (the pleas were not to construction and use offences). The appellant was riding on a footpath and collided with an elderly pedestrian, Mr Leonard Bailey. The Court of Appeal noted that the unicycle:

'should never have been on a public road. It was capable of speeds of up to 26 mph in testing, although the advertised speed was up to 40 mph when loaded. It was illegal (except on private land) because it was not registered, it was not taxed and it was not insured. There was some evidence that the applicant had been warned about legal restrictions on use when he bought the vehicle.'[96]

The Court of Appeal rejected a submission that '[a]lthough it is accepted that the offence was aggravated by his presence on a path which he had no right to be on, and the lack of insurance or licence, it is said that these factors all flowed from the current classification of his Gotway':

'We disagree. The speed was indeed excessive, but that was not all. It was combined with what the applicant knew to be his dangerous inability to bring the unicycle to a rapid stop, on a path shared with pedestrians, because of the way it was constructed and operated. The applicant was not entitled to assume that pedestrians would be able to jump out of his way. Mr Bailey did in fact try to do that. However, the movement of the Gotway was too rapid and unpredictable for him, and that was to be expected. The illegality of the unicycle was an aggravating factor. To say that this flowed from its classification does not in any way diminish that. This was no merely technical infraction. The applicant's vehicle was completely unfit for driving on a public road or path, as this fatal accident demonstrated only too clearly.'[97]

How a court might determine civil liability against that background in a micro mobility vehicle road traffic accident claim – and whether or not the *ex turpi* principle might apply – are issues so far unadjudicated[98]. See Chapter 11, 'passenger claims'.

---

95 [2023] EWCA Crim 1116.
96 Above, at [5].
97 Above, at [14]–[15].
98 See discussion of criminal liability under RTA 1988, s 40A and RV(CU)R 1986 reg 100 for vehicles or loads in a dangerous condition in *Wilkinson's Road Traffic Offences* (30th edn, 2021), 8-40 to 8-53.

Liability insurance of 'micro mobility' vehicles or 'powered transporters'

16.18   Among the requirements of use of a 'motor vehicle' on a road or other public place is the provision of compulsory liability insurance. Criminal non-compliance with a legal pre-requirement of use of a motor vehicle on a road or other public place, such as type approval[99], will make such use uninsurable. The coincidence of innovation in small vehicle technology with the persistence of the established 'motor vehicle' definition has widened the exposure of compulsory motor insurers and the liabilities of the MIB in relation to uninsured drivers. The MIB now seeks a 'lighter touch' insurance approach in relation to compulsory insurance of e-scooters. The Transport Bill announced in May 2022 to introduce such an approach (among other matters) was postponed in December 2022 and did not appear in the King's Speech in November 2023.

Electrically assisted pedal cycles (EAPCs or e-bikes)

Statutory definition of an e-bike

16.19   RTA 1988, s 189(1)(c) provides that:

> 'For the purposes of the Road Traffic Acts … an electrically assisted pedal cycle of such a class as may be prescribed by regulations so made, is to be treated as not being a motor vehicle.'[100]

Regulation of e-bikes

16.20   The regulations are the Electrically Assisted Pedal Cycles Regulations 1983 (the EAPC Regulations)[101], reg 3 of which provides that:

> 'The class of electrically assisted pedal cycles prescribed for the purposes of … section 189 of the Road Traffic Act 1988 consists of pedal cycles with two or more wheels which comply with the requirements specified in Regulation 4 below.'

The EAPC Regulations, reg 4 specifies those requirements as

> 'that the vehicle shall: – …
>
> (b) be fitted with pedals by means of which it is capable of being propelled; and
>
> (c) be fitted with no motor other than an electric motor which –
>
>   (i) has a maximum continuous rated power which does not exceed 250 watts;
>
>   (ii) cannot propel the vehicle when it is travelling at more than 15.5 miles per hour.'

---

99   RTA 1988, s 63(1). See Chapter 2, 'specifications'.
100 RTA 1988, s 189(1)(c).
101 'The EAPC Regulations', SI 1983/1168, as amended by the Electrically Assisted Pedal Cycles (Amendment) Regulations 2015, SI 2015/24.

Liability insurance position in relation to the use of e-bikes on roads and other public places

16.21 EAPCs are exempt from the insurance requirement of RTA 1988, Part VI, by virtue of their exemption from the 'motor vehicle' definition[102].

The exemption cannot be obtained by cosmetic means by (for example) adding pedals to a vehicle which would otherwise be a 'motor vehicle'. The requirement of pedals 'by means of which [*the EAPC*] is capable of being propelled' is (as in the case of intention or adaptation for use on roads[103]) tested by an objective standard. In *Winter v DPP*[104], exemption from the insurance requirement had been attempted by the installation of largely ineffective pedals to an electric tricycle. Michael Supperstone QC, sitting as a Deputy High Court Judge[105], interpreted:

'the words 'fitted with pedals by means of which it is capable of being propelled' as meaning that the vehicle is 'reasonably capable of being propelled' by the pedals'

Because:

'the policy behind s.143 of the Road Traffic Act 1988, namely to safeguard road users and pedestrians from uninsured injury from a mechanically powered vehicle, by providing for compulsory insurance'

requires that:

'a purposive construction should be adopted to reg.4(b) to give effect to the intention of Parliament, which must be to require the pedals on an electrically assisted pedal cycle to be capable of propelling the vehicle in a safe manner in its normal day-to-day use.'

So the installation of pedals not 'reasonably' capable of propelling the vehicle 'in a safe manner in its normal day-to-day use' failed to avoid (via the EAPC exemption) the 'motor vehicle' classification and the consequent requirement for third party insurance.

So, an electrically assisted pedal cycle within RTA 1988, s 189(1)(c) and the EAPC regulations on that objective test will not require insurance.

Parked dockless e-bikes, e-scooters and nuisance

16.22 Please see Chapter 13, 'highway claims', for discussion of potential liability for dockless e-bikes and e-scooters parked so as obstruct the highway or access to it.

---

102 RTA 1988, s 189(1)(c).
103 *DPP v Saddington*, above.
104 *Winter v DPP* [2002] EWHC 1524 (Admin).
105 Later Mr Justice Supperstone.

Pedicabs in London

16.23 The Pedicabs (London) Bill 2023-24 (HL Bill 2) would, if enacted, empower Transport for London to regulate previously unregulated pedicabs by means of licensing, enforcement powers and criminal offences. The definition of pedicab includes a power-assisted pedal cycle (cll 1(2) and 7(1)).

The legal background is set out in the explanatory notes to the Bill (paras 5 to 7):

'There is no extant legislation which would allow the regulation of pedicabs in London. This is because the legislation which enables TfL to regulate taxis within London does not apply to pedicabs. Conflicting judicial decisions mean that pedicabs can only be regulated outside London, where different legislation applies.

Outside London, in England and Wales, pedicabs are treated as taxis for the purposes of the Town Police Clauses Act 1847 and Part II of the Local Government (Miscellaneous Provisions) Act 1976. Accordingly, pedicabs may be regulated as taxis under the provisions of the 1847 and 1976 Acts.

By contrast, within London, pedicabs are not treated as taxis for the purpose of the Metropolitan Public Carriage Act 1869, which is the equivalent legislation in London. Pedicabs are instead considered stage carriages in London pursuant to section 4 of the Metropolitan Public Carriage Act. The legislation governing stage carriages is no longer in force; there are therefore no licensing provisions, so pedicabs are unregulated in London.'

Chapter 17

Data and privacy claims

'There was another thought which a scanning of those tiny electronic headlines often invoked. The more wonderful the means of communication, the more trivial, tawdry or depressing its contents seemed to be.'

Arthur C Clarke (1968)[1]

'We find the references by the [*Divisional*] court to the possibility of future reconsideration of this issue [*whether there is a sufficient legal framework for the use of the Automated Facial Recognition technology*] a little curious. This is because either an interference is in accordance with the law or it is not. The issue of whether there is relevant law for this purpose is a binary question: see *In re Gallagher* [2020] AC 185, para 14 (Lord Sumption). The fact that this case involved the trial of a new technology does not alter the need for any interference with [*ECHR*] article 8 rights to be in accordance with the law.'

The Court of Appeal (2020)[2]

This chapter is of general application so does not differentiate between the categories of advanced, automated and electric vehicles. No data or privacy claim cases involving AAEVs have yet been reported.

Please see Chapter 26, 'data protection and privacy laws' for an outline of data protection and privacy law as it affects AAEVs.

Outline of legal bases of claim

17.01   Although 'English law does not recognise any direct action for the invasion of privacy … privacy is a value recognised by the law and protected in several ways': *Winfield and Jolowicz* classifies these as 'indirect protection afforded by torts such as trespass and nuisance', 'protection provided by various statutory provisions' including HRA 1998 and DPA 2018 and 'substantial development of the old law of breach of confidence, resulting in an offshoot that is sometimes called the tort of misuse of private information'[3].

---

1   Arthur C. Clarke, '2001: A Space Odyssey' (Hutchinson, 1968), chapter 9, 'Moon Shuttle'.
2   *Regina (Bridges) v Chief Constable of South Wales Police (Information Commissioner and others intervening)* [2020] EWCA Civ 1058; [2020] 1 WLR 5037 [58].
3   *Winfield and Jolowicz on Tort* (20th edn, 2020), ed James Goudkamp and Donal Nolan, 13-136.

Torts protecting data and privacy

17.02 Please see Chapter 13, 'highway claims', for an account of the torts of trespass and nuisance. In 2020, the editors of *Winfield and Jolowicz* were sceptical of their application to a surveillance claim, in part on the ground that 'neither tort is apt to deal with modern means of electronic and optical surveillance, which may be carried on from a great distance' [4].

While other legal bases of claim succeeded, a claim in nuisance failed in a claim against a defendant householder who used surveillance cameras pointing towards his neighbours' properties in alleged response to an attempted theft of his car but whose conduct towards his neighbour, the claimant, the court found to be actionable as statutory harassment and breaches of DPA 2018. In *Fairhurst v Goddard*, Her Honour Judge Melissa Clarke held (applying the Court of Appeal's judgment in *Fearn v Board of Trustees of the Tate Gallery*[5]) that mere overlooking from one property to another is incapable of founding an action in private nuisance and that the nuisance caused by a light activated by one of the cameras was not an undue interference with the claimant's enjoyment of her urban property, 'where night-time lights are a feature'[6].

However, since the judgment in *Fairhurst* the Supreme Court has (by a majority) reversed the Court of Appeal's judgment in *Fearn*, holding that anything – including visual intrusion[7] – which materially interferes with the ordinary use and enjoyment of neighbouring land by a person with a legal interest in that land is capable of being a nuisance and that, to amount to a nuisance, the interference has to be substantial, judged not by what the claimant found annoying or inconvenient but by the standards of an ordinary person in the claimant's position. In *Fearn*, the nuisance was viewing and photography of the claimants' homes by visitors to the defendant's gallery from the gallery's public viewing platform.

So, in principle nuisance is again relevant to a claim in relation to viewing and photography of a property by modern electronic means. Whether an interference is sufficient to constitute a nuisance will still depend (as in *Fairhurst*) upon an assessment of the evidence in each case, according to the standards of an ordinary person in the claimant's position.

Statutory bases of claim in relation to data and privacy

17.03 Potential statutory claims include:

- Protection from Harassment Act 1997 (PHA 1997), s 3 of which allows, in addition to injunctive relief, the civil remedy of damages 'for (among other things) any anxiety caused by the harassment and any financial loss resulting from the harassment'[8].

---

4   Above, 13.137.
5   [2020] EWCA Civ 104
6   *Fairhurst v Goddard* 12 October 2021, county court at Oxford, unreported [129-130].
7   [2023] UKSC 4; [2023] 2 WLR 339. See eg. Lord Leggatt JSC at [94].
8   PHA 1997 s 3(2). See *Fairhurst v Goddard* (above) as an example of a successful claim.

- Human Rights Act 1998 (HRA 1998), s 8 of which ('judicial remedies') provides (at s 8(1)) that

> 'In relation to any act (or proposed act) of a public authority which the court finds is (or would be) unlawful, it may grant such relief or remedy, or make such order, within its powers as it considers just and appropriate.'

HRA 1998, s 8 provides in detail for the circumstances in which damages may be awarded in relation to an unlawful act. In particular, under s 8(3):

> 'No award of damages is to be made unless, taking account of all the circumstances of the case, including—
>
> (a) any other relief or remedy granted, or order made, in relation to the act in question (by that or any other court), and
>
> (b) the consequences of any decision (of that or any other court) in respect of that act,
>
> the court is satisfied that the award is necessary to afford just satisfaction to the person in whose favour it is made.'

Although damages were claimed in *Bridges* (the AFR case), the Court of Appeal ruled 'that declaratory relief to reflect the reasons why this appeal has succeeded will suffice'[9].

- The GDPR and Data Protection Act 2018 (DPA 2018), art 82, ss 168 and 169 of which provide for compensation, including for distress.

The usual rules as to vicarious liability apply[10].

While the *Fairhurst* judgment in Oxford County Court (above) has been partly overtaken by the change of the law in relation to nuisance (in the *Fearn* claims), it is noteworthy that the judge in *Fairhurst* did not consider the use of an outward-looking doorbell security camera to be objectionable in itself on data protection grounds; it was the processing of audio data and the scope of the surveillance from other cameras which the court did not consider necessary for a legitimate data-processing purpose[11].

'Breach of confidence' and 'misuse of private information'

17.04 *Clerk and Lindsell* notes that 'two different frameworks of liability have emerged: one for breach of confidence and one for misuse of private information/privacy'[12].

> 'Where the obligation of confidence arises (either expressly or impliedly) in a contractual relationship, the breach of confidence may be categorised as

---

9 *Bridges* [210].
10 *Various Claimants v Wm Morrison Supermarkets plc* [2020] UKSC 12; [2020] AC 989.
11 *Fairhurst*, above [133]-[138].
12 *Clerk & Lindsell on Torts* (23rd edn, 2020), 26-02.

a breach of contract. However, the obligation can arise in a non-contractual setting'[13].

There are three elements to an action for *breach of confidence*:

'First, the information in respect of which relief is sought must have the 'necessary quality of confidence about it'. Secondly, the information must have been imparted in circumstances importing an obligation of confidence. The use of the word 'imparted', however, is now clearly too limited for the modern action, it now being established that there is no need for an initial confidential relationship. Thirdly, there must be an unauthorised use or disclosure of that information.'[14]

A chance discovery of an obviously confidential document can activate the duty. In *Attorney General v Guardian Newspapers (No 2)*, Lord Goff:

'expressed the circumstances in which the duty arises in broad terms, not merely to embrace those cases where a third party receives information from a person who is under a duty of confidence in respect of it, knowing that it has been disclosed by that person to him in breach of his duty of confidence, but also to include certain situations, beloved of law teachers – where an obviously confidential document is wafted by an electric fan out of a window into a crowded street, or where an obviously confidential document, such as a private diary, is dropped in a public place, and is then picked up by a passer-by.'[15]

Breach of confidence is remediable by measures including injunction, an order for delivery up or destruction of material and damages[16].

The action for *misuse of private information* is 'mediated by the analogy of the right to privacy conferred by Article 8 of the European Convention on Human Rights and has required a balancing of that right against the right to freedom of expression conferred by Article 10' and the correct approach is to balance those rights[17]. Everyone has a reasonable expectation of privacy. The cause of action 'focuses upon the protection of human autonomy and dignity – the right to control the dissemination of information about one's private life and the right to the esteem and respect of other people'[18].

In *Reid v Price*, Warby J assessed compensation for the tortious disclosure of personal information established 'on four different causes of action', namely breach of confidence, misuse of private information, breach of contract and breaches of DPA 2018 (the contract claim did not, in his Lordship's view, add anything to the claim). The court did not see 'any material difference between the approach to be taken to the claims in confidentiality, misuse of private information, and breach

---

13 Above, 26-04.
14 Above, 26-06.
15 [1990] 1 AC 109 [281E-F].
16 See *Clerk & Lindsell* 26-33 to 36.
17 *OBG v Allan* [2007] UKHL 21; [2008] 1 AC 1, Lord Hoffmann, 47-48 [118]; *Clerk & Lindsell* 26-40.
18 *Campbell v Mirror Group Newspapers* [2004] UKHL 22; [2004] 2 AC 457, 473 [51] (Lord Hoffmann).

of statutory duty. The essential task is to compensate the claimant …'. The court described the principles as follows:

> 'Compensation for the tortious disclosure of personal information should aim to restore the claimant to the position he would have occupied but for the tort. There is now a considerable body of academic writing on how this should be achieved … The authorities are not very numerous. But principles identified in *Mosley v News Group Newspapers Ltd* [2008] EWHC 1777 (QB) [2008] EMLR 20 include the following: damages may include compensation for distress, hurt feelings and loss of dignity; it may also be appropriate to take into account any aggravating conduct by the defendant which increases the hurt to the claimant's feelings; damages should be proportionate, they should not be open to criticism for arbitrariness; but they must be adequate to mark the wrong and provide a measure of solatium; it will be legitimate to pay some attention to the current level of personal injury awards; and the court should have in mind the tariff applied so far as defamation awards are concerned (though the analogy with defamation can only be pressed so far)… if damages are to be an effective remedy, they must not be subject to too severe a limitation; although vindicatory damages are not recoverable in this context, in misuse of private information and data protection claims, damages may be awarded for loss of autonomy or loss of control; the nature of the information disclosed and the degree of loss of control should bear on this aspect of the court's assessment of damages – the more intimate the information and the more extensive the disclosure, the greater the award.'[19]

---

19 *Reid v Price* [2020] EWHC 594 (QB) 1 [49]–[51].

Chapter 18

Personal security claims

'... it is not to be forgotten that, in ordinary households in this country, there are nowadays many things which might be described as possible sources of fire if interfered with by third parties, ranging from matches and firelighters to electric irons and gas cookers and even oil-fired central heating systems. These are commonplaces of modern life; and it would be quite wrong if householders were to be held liable in negligence for acting in a socially acceptable manner. No doubt the question whether liability should be imposed on defenders in a case where a source of danger on his land has been sparked off by the deliberate wrongdoing of a third party is a question to be decided on the facts of each case, and it would, I think, be wrong for your Lordships' House to anticipate the manner in which the law may develop: but I cannot help thinking that cases where liability will be so imposed are likely to be very rare.'

Lord Goff (1987)[1]

'The law of negligence is not an area where fixed absolutes of universal application are appropriate.'

Lord Nicholls (2004)[2]

Chapter Contents

A Outline of personal security claims involving vehicles 18.01
B Personal security claims involving Advanced Driver Assistance Systems (ADAS) 18.06
C Personal security claims involving Automated Vehicles 18.08
D Personal security claims involving Electric Vehicles 18.10

A Outline of personal security claims involving vehicles

18.01 This chapter considers civil liabilities affecting personal security against the physical[3] acts of third parties which might arise from the deployment of new road vehicle technologies. Such acts might also be criminal.

---

1 *Smith v Littlewoods Ltd* [1987] 1 AC 241 (HL), 274 B-D.
2 *Attorney-General of the British Virgin Islands v Hartwell* [2004] UKPC 12; [2004] 1 WLR 1273, 1280 [25].
3 Data security and privacy claims are discussed in chapter 17.

New technology can be put to deadly use. The Court of Appeal has repeatedly pointed to this extreme when describing the risks of driving:

'The court 'has consistently imposed upon the drivers of cars a high burden to reflect the fact that the car is potentially a dangerous weapon''[4]

As Lord Goff observed in 1987[5], the law is aware both of advances in commonplace technology and of its attendant risks when fixing the boundaries of a defendant's liability for its misuse by others. The broader context includes the observation that the safety risks of a car are numerous and the process of balancing risks when designing cars is complex. As Professor Jane Stapleton wrote in 1994:

'In designing, say, a car, the designer has to take into consideration a large range of issues relating to safety and risk: the strength of front, side and rear panels; brake and steering efficiency; rear-vision field; passenger restraints; dash-board configuration, etc. Each of these features relevant to safety must then be traded off against other factors which can also relate to safety. For example, automatic car door locks reduce the risk of child passengers opening the door but increase the risk of entrapment in the event of a crash.'[6]

That was to consider purely accidental risks, and was written in a pre-worldwide web era. The inclusion of connected vehicles in the 'internet of things' magnifies the potential for misuse. Automated vehicle technologies are at an early stage of deployment. This is not a list of all potential personal security claims which might arise from AAEVs. Some potential categories of claim can be imagined at this early stage, for example:

- liabilities to victims of crimes by third parties such as assault or robbery in automated passenger vehicles which are not physically attended by a human driver or conductor; and

- liabilities to victims of a crime by a third party which results in a vehicle collision, for example when a vehicle is used as a weapon.

The first of those situations is also discussed in Chapter 5, 'the laws of passenger services and public transport'[7]. The second situation is discussed in more detail in this chapter. As at the time of writing neither point has yet been adjudicated in an AAEV claim.

Liability for acts of a third party

18.02 A 'problem arises when the pursuer is seeking to hold the defender responsible for having failed to prevent a third party from causing damage to the pursuer or his property by the third party's own deliberate wrongdoing. In such a case, it is not possible to invoke a general duty of care; for it is well recognised that

---

4 *Lunt v Khelifa* [2002] EWCA Civ 801 (20), as quoted by Hale LJ in *Eagle v Chambers* [2003] EWCA Civ 1107; [2004] RTR 9, [16].
5 *Smith v Littlewoods Ltd*, quoted at the head of this chapter.
6 Jane Stapleton, *Product Liability* (Butterworths, 1994), page 259.
7 See chapter 5, 'the laws of passenger services and public transport', discussion of 'civil liability for assault by a third party in an unattended automated vehicle'. In relation to duties of highway authorities, see Chapter 13, 'highway claims'.

there is no *general* duty of care to prevent third parties from causing such damage…
The fundamental reason is that the common law does not impose liability for what
are called pure omissions.'[8]

'[T]here are special circumstances in which a defender may be held responsible
in law for injuries suffered by the pursuer through a third party's deliberate
wrongdoing'[9]. Lord Goff gave the following examples:

'In "special cases"[10], "a duty of care may arise from a relationship between
the parties", for example contractually, by licence, by employment of the
third party leading to vicarious liability, by a duty to control the third party or
by occupation of land[11];

"But there is a more general circumstance in which a defender may be held
liable in negligence to the pursuer, although the immediate cause of the
damage suffered by the pursuer is the deliberate wrongdoing of another.
This may occur where the defender negligently causes or permits to be
created a source of danger, and it is reasonably foreseeable that third parties
may interfere with it and, sparking off the danger, thereby cause damage
to persons in the position of the pursuer". The "classic example" was the
defendant's employee leaving a horse-cart unattended in the street where
a boy threw a stone at the horses, causing them to injure a police officer
who went to stop them. The Defendant's employee ought to have foreseen
that or a similar event occurring before he left the horses unattended.[12]
Smith v Littlewoods was a different case, in which the third party was not on
public land but was trespassing; Lord Goff wrote that "liability should only
be imposed under this principle in cases where the defender has negligently
caused or permitted the creation of a source of danger on his land, and
where it is foreseeable that third parties may trespass on his land and spark it
off, thereby damaging the pursuer or his property"[13].

'There is another basis upon which a defender may be held liable for damage
to neighbouring property caused by a fire started on his (the defender's)
property by the deliberate wrongdoing of a third party. This arises where
he has knowledge or means of knowledge that a third party has created
or is creating a risk of fire, or indeed has started a fire, on his premises, and
then fails to take such steps as are reasonably open to him (in the limited
sense explained by Lord Wilberforce in *Goldman v Hargrave* [1967] 1 A.C.
645, 663-664[14]) to prevent any such fire from damaging neighbouring
property. If, for example, an occupier of property has knowledge, or means
of knowledge, that intruders are in the habit of trespassing upon his property

---

8   *Smith v Littlewoods* (above), 270G-H and 271C, Lord Goff.
9   *Smith v Littlewoods*, 272.
10 Above, 272H.
11 Above 272D-H.
12 Above 272H-273C, citing *Haynes v Harwood* [1935] 1 KB 146.
13 Above 274B.
14 Tree in Australia struck by lightning; defendant surrounds fire with combustible material
    and lets it burn out; weather alters and re-ignites fire; defendant takes no further steps. The
    appeal came before the Privy Council. Lord Wilberforce noted that this was not a case in
    which the fire could simply have been extinguished once ('… other cases are not so simple.
    In such situations the standard ought to be to require of the occupier what it is reasonable
    to expect of him in his individual circumstances': 663E).

and starting fires there, thereby creating a risk that fire may spread to and damage neighbouring property, a duty to take reasonable steps to prevent such damage may be held to fall upon him... What is reasonably required would, of course, depend on the particular facts of the case. I observe that, in *Goldman v Hargrave*, such liability was held to sound in nuisance; but it is difficult to believe that, in this respect, there can be any material distinction between liability in nuisance and liability in negligence.'[15]

Lord Goff was not prepared to extend such a duty to require a householder to protect adjacent properties from theft by ensuring that their own property was always kept locked:

'The practical effect is that everybody has to take such steps as he thinks fit to protect his own property, whether house or flat or shop, against thieves. He is able to take his own precautions; and, in deciding what precautions to take, he can and should take into account the fact that, in the ordinary course of life, adjacent property is likely to be from time to time unoccupied (often obviously so, and sometimes for a considerable period of time) and is also likely from time to time not to be lockfast.'[16]

A similar result applied to theft of an unlocked minibus, which was later driven negligently by the thief, causing the death of the claimant's wife[17]. In *Smith v Littlewoods*, Lord Goff observed that:

'It is very tempting to try to solve all problems of negligence by reference to an all-embracing criterion of foreseeability, thereby effectively reducing all decisions in this field to questions of fact. But this comfortable solution is, alas, not open to us. The law has to accommodate all the untidy complexity of life; and there are circumstances where considerations of practical justice impel us to reject a general imposition of liability for foreseeable damage.'[18]

In *Mitchell v Glasgow City Council* (a claim in which the defendant was said tortiously to have omitted to have warned the deceased of the fact of a council meeting with the deceased's abusive neighbour, which was said to have led to the neighbour's lethal attack upon the deceased, who was unaware of the meeting so unable to avoid the neighbour) Lord Hope made three points on the law relating to claims based upon omission to prevent the criminal acts of third parties:

'The first is that foreseeability of harm is not of itself enough for the imposition of a duty of care: ... Otherwise, to adopt Lord Keith of Kinkel's dramatic illustration in *Yuen Kun Yeu v Attorney General of Hong Kong* [1988] AC 175, 192, there would be liability in negligence on the part of one who sees another about to walk over a cliff with his head in the air, and forebears to shout a warning. The second, which flows from the first, is that the law does not normally impose a positive duty on a person to protect others. As Lord Goff of Chieveley explained in *Smith v Littlewoods Organisation Ltd* [1987] AC 241, 270-271, the common law does not impose liability for

---

15 *Smith v Littlewoods*, above, 274D-G, and see to 275G for discussion of previous caselaw on such fires.
16 278D.
17 *Topp v London Country Bus (South West) Ltd* [1993] 1 WLR 976 (CA).
18 *Smith v Littlewoods*, 280B-C.

what, without more, may be called pure omissions. The third, which is a development of the second, is that the law does not impose a duty to prevent a person from being harmed by the criminal act of a third party based simply upon foreseeability: *Smith v Littlewoods Organisation Ltd*, at pp 272-279, per Lord Goff.'[19]

Lord Scott elaborated:

'A legal duty to take positive steps to prevent harm or injury to another requires the presence of some feature, additional to reasonable forseeability that a failure to do so is likely to result in the person in question suffering harm or injury… The requisite additional feature that transforms what would otherwise be a mere omission, a breach at most of a moral obligation, into a breach of a legal duty to take reasonable steps to safeguard, or to try to safeguard, the person in question from harm or injury may take a wide variety of forms. Sometimes the additional feature may be found in the manner in which the victim came to be at risk of harm or injury. If a defendant has played some causative part in the train of events that have led to the risk of injury, a duty to take reasonable steps to avert or lessen the risk may arise. Sometimes the additional feature may be found in the relationship between the victim and the defendant: (eg. employee/employer or child/parent) or in the relationship between the defendant and the place where the risk arises (eg. a fire on the defendant's land as in *Goldman v Hargrave* [1967] 1 AC 645). Sometimes the additional feature may be found in the assumption by the defendant of responsibility for the person at risk of injury (see *Smith v Littlewoods Organisation Ltd* [1987] AC 241, 272, per Lord Goff of Chieveley). In each case where particular circumstances are relied on as constituting the requisite additional feature alleged to be sufficient to cast upon the defendant the duty to take steps that, if taken, would or might have avoided or lessened the injury to the victim, the question for the court will be whether the circumstances were indeed sufficient for that purpose or whether the case remains one of mere omission.'[20]

Baroness Hale wrote that

'In essence, there must be some particular reason why X should be held to have assumed the responsibility for protecting Y from harm caused by the criminal acts of Z.'[21]

Claims against a public authority are now subject to the Supreme Court's reformulation of the law as to the circumstances in which a public authority owes a common law duty of care, in its 2019 judgment in *N and another v Poole Borough Council*[22], where both the Court of Appeal and the Supreme Court held that a council was not under a duty of care to protect its tenants from abusive neighbours. The Supreme Court summarised the new formulation as follows:

(1) that public authorities may owe a duty of care in circumstances where the principles applicable to private individuals would impose such a duty,

---

19 *Mitchell v Glasgow City Council* [2009] 1 AC 874, 884 [15].
20 *Mitchell*, 893 [39, 40].
21 *Mitchell*, 904 [76].
22 [2019] UKSC 25; [2020] AC 780, 835 [64].

unless such a duty would be inconsistent with, and is therefore excluded by, the legislation from which their powers or duties are derived; (2) that public authorities do not owe a duty of care at common law merely because they have statutory powers or duties, even if, by exercising their statutory functions, they could prevent a person from suffering harm; and (3) that public authorities can come under a common law duty to protect from harm in circumstances where the principles applicable to private individuals or bodies would impose such a duty, as for example where the authority has created the source of danger or has assumed a responsibility to protect the claimant from harm, unless the imposition of such a duty would be inconsistent with the relevant legislation.'[23]

Overall 'activity of driving' analysis prevails over 'omissions' approach to driving negligence

18.03 As discussed in other chapters[24], a potential extension of the 'pure omissions' exclusion to driving negligence (by pointing to an omission to brake, to keep a proper lookout, etc), in an attempt to avoid negligence liability by means of the exclusion, has been emphatically rejected by the courts. As Lord Hope said in *Mitchell*, distinguishing those three points from other 'commonplace' omissions:

'The context is therefore quite different from the case where a person is injured in the course of his employment or in a road traffic accident. In cases of that kind it can be taken for granted that the employer owes a duty of care to the person who is in his employment or that a duty is owed to other road users by the driver of a vehicle which causes an accident. If commonplace situations of that kind had to be analysed, the conclusion would be that the duty is owed not simply because loss, injury or damage is reasonably foreseeable. It is because there is a relationship of proximity between the employer and his employees and the driver and other road users. This is sufficient in law to give rise to a duty of care. The duty is created by the relationship, and the scope of the duty is determined by what in the context of that relationship is reasonably foreseeable. In such cases this is so obvious that there is no need to ask whether it is fair, or whether it is just and reasonable, that the pursuer should recover damages.'[25]

Baroness Hale wrote that

'A driver who takes to the roads and thus is an actor in the drama is liable for the things which he fails to do as well as for the things which he does.'[26]

'Source of danger': liability for third party's misuse of an obviously hazardous device provided by defendant

18.04 A defendant's liability for the acts of a third party can arise where a risk of serious harm emanates from the obviously hazardous nature of a particular device

---

23 Above, at 835-836 [65].
24 See Chapters 11, 'passenger claims', and 15, 'highway claims'.
25 *Mitchell*, 884 [16].
26 *Mitchell*, 904 [76].

provided to the third party by the defendant and the defendant knows (or ought reasonably to know) that the third party cannot be trusted safely to operate it. In *Attorney-General of the British Virgin Islands v Hartwell*[27]:

'the police authorities had entrusted a gun to an officer who was still on probation and had shown signs of instability and unreliability. As Lord Nicholls explained, in para 32, loaded hand guns are dangerous weapons and the serious risks if a gun is handled carelessly are obvious. On the other hand the precautionary steps required of a careful person are unlikely to be particularly burdensome. Where such an article is handed over, the class of persons to whom the duty of care is owed is wide and the standard of care required is high.'[28]

In *BVI v Hartwell*, Lord Nicholls exemplified the concept of duty of care by that owed by 'drivers of cars' who owe 'among other duties, a duty to other road users to take reasonable care to avoid inflicting personal injury on the latter'[29]. Lord Nicholls continued:

'Speaking generally, one of the necessary prerequisites for the existence of a duty of care is foresight that carelessness on the part of the defendant may cause damage of a particular kind to the plaintiff. Was it reasonably foreseeable that, failing the exercise of reasonable care, harm of the relevant description might be suffered by the plaintiff or members of a class including the plaintiff? 'Might be suffered' embraces a wide range of degrees of possibility, from the highly probable to the possible but highly improbable. Bearing in mind that the underlying concept is fairness and reasonableness, the degree of likelihood needed to satisfy this prerequisite depends upon the circumstances of the case. Reasonable foreseeability does not denote a fixed point on the scale of probability: see Lord Hoffmann in *Jolley v Sutton London Borough Council* [2000] 1 WLR 1082, 1091. There must be reasonable foreseeability of a risk which a reasonable person would not ignore. The risk must be 'real' in the sense that a reasonable person 'would not brush [it] aside as far-fetched': see Lord Reid in *Overseas Tankship (UK) Ltd v Miller Steamship Co Pty (The Wagon Mound (No 2))* [1967] 1 AC 617, 643. As the possible adverse consequences of carelessness increase in seriousness, so will a lesser degree of likelihood of occurrence suffice to satisfy the test of reasonable foreseeability.'[30]

BVI v Hartwell was not an omissions case: 'the police authorities were in possession of a gun and ammunition. They took the positive step of providing PC Laurent with access to that gun'[31]. However, discussing the *Dorset Yacht* case (in which damage caused to the claimant's property by borstal boys was attributable to omissions by the defendant's employees supervising them), Lord Nicholls noted that:

'Liability for omissions is less extensive than for positive acts. But that is not a satisfactory ground for putting the *Dorset Yacht* case on one side and distinguishing it from the present case. The better approach is to recognise

---

27 [2004] UKPC 12; [2004] 1 WLR 1273.
28 Lord Hope, summarising *BVI v Hartwell* in *Mitchell* at 885 [18].
29 *BVI v Hartwell*, 1279 [20].
30 *BVI v Hartwell*, 1279 [21].
31 *BVI v Hartwell*, 1281 [31].

that, as with the likelihood that loss will occur, so with the likelihood of wrongful third party intervention causing loss, the degree of likelihood needed to give rise to a duty of care depends on the circumstances... The law of negligence is not an area where fixed absolutes of universal application are appropriate. In each case the governing consideration is the underlying principle. The underlying principle is that reasonable foreseeability, as an ingredient of a duty of care, is a broad and flexible objective standard which is responsive to the infinitely variable circumstances of different cases. The nature and gravity of the damage foreseeable, the likelihood of its occurrence, and the ease or difficulty of eliminating the risk are all matters to be taken into account in the round when deciding whether as a matter of legal policy a duty of care was owed by the defendant to the plaintiff in respect of the damage suffered by him.'[32]

Echoing Cardozo J in *MacPherson v Buick Motor Company*[33], Lord Nicholls wrote that:

'The law has long recognised the special dangers associated with certain types of articles such as loaded firearms, explosives and poisons. In past days when the distinction mattered, articles such as these were classified as 'inherently dangerous'. Those who sent forth inherently dangerous articles were subject to a common law duty to take precautions... When the majority decision of the House of Lords in *Donoghue v Stevenson* [1932] AC 562 set the law of negligence on a new path, this special rule regarding inherently dangerous goods was subsumed into the wider, more general principles of negligence. This did not mean that thenceforth the scope of the duty of care and the required standard of diligence became the same in respect of all types of articles. Lord Atkin was at pains to point out that the nature of an article 'may very well call for different degrees of care'. He continued, at p 596:

"the person dealing with [an inherently dangerous article] may well contemplate persons as being within the sphere of his duty to take care who would not be sufficiently proximate with less dangerous goods; so that not only the degree of care but the range of persons to whom a duty is owed may be extended."

... Thus, where an article as dangerous as a loaded gun is handed over the class of persons to whom the duty of care is owed is wide and the standard of care required is high.'[34]

Or, as Lord Hope thereby concluded:

'As the possible adverse consequences of carelessness increase in seriousness, so will a lesser degree of likelihood of occurrence suffice to satisfy the test of reasonable foreseeability.'[35]

---

32 *BVI v Hartwell*, 1280 [25].

33 217 NY 382, 111 NE 1050 (1916), cited by the majority in *Donoghue v Stevenson* [1932] AC 562 (HL). See chapter 10, 'vehicle defect claims'.

34 *BVI v Hartwell*, 1282 [34, 36].

35 *Mitchell* at 885 [18].

In *Kalma and others v African Minerals Ltd and others*, the provision by the Defendant mining companies of motor vehicles[36] and other resources to the Sierra Leonean police for the purpose of preventing disruption at their mine was not a breach of its duty of care owed to protestors subsequently injured by police using excessive force on their own account. 'Such assistance was, as the judge found, common in Sierra Leone'[37]. It was not akin to the provision of the gun in *BVI v Hartwell*, as it did not create the danger and, on the judge's findings at trial, not providing those resources might have made the situation worse:

> 'As Lord Nicholls said in that case, loaded handguns are dangerous weapons and the serious risks if a gun is handled carefully are obvious. The same cannot be said of the provision of money, vehicles and accommodation to the police during a lengthy bout of civil unrest.'[38]

Liability of carriers to passengers for injurious acts of other passengers

18.05 A carrier is not responsible for the action of a passenger causing injury to another passenger unless it could reasonably have foreseen the danger.

In *East Indian Railway v Mukerjee* the explosion of fireworks in a railway carriage where passengers were smoking was not foreseeable by the railway company:

> 'The question then is reduced to this: whether there is any proof that the parcels carried by the two passengers exhibited such signs of their real nature as ought to have called the attention of the railway servants to them, and thus prevented such dangerous goods being carried. Their Lordships can find none.'[39]

In *Pounder v North Eastern Railway Company*, a passenger whose job it was to evict pitmen from their homes was recognised and assaulted by pitmen who were also travelling on the defendant's train. The defendant was not liable:

> 'The railway company are bound to take reasonable care for the safety of their passengers. The controversy was as to how that reasonable care was to be measured, and I am clearly of opinion that it can only be ascertained by reference to the ordinary incidents of a railway journey, and by reference to what must be taken to have been in the contemplation of the parties when the contract of carriage was entered into.'[40]

By contrast, in a 1959 American case described by Lord Scott in his judgment in the *Mitchell* case, *Bullock v Tamiami Trail Tours Inc*, false imprisonment, assaults and racial abuse by passengers on a racially-segregated bus, with the participation of the bus driver, resulted in the carrier being held liable, on the basis that 'a carrier, which could reasonably foresee injury to its passenger caused by a fellow

---

36 Conventional motor vehicles, not AAEVs.
37 *Kalma*, 124.
38 *Kalma*, 133.
39 [1901] AC 396 (PC), 400-401.
40 [1892] 1 QB 385 (QBD), Mathew J, 390.

passenger, in time to prevent its occurrence, was subjected to the highest degree of care to its passenger either to protect him from, or to warn him of, the danger'[41].

The scope of passenger protection through civil liability law has (as at the time of writing) not been adjudicated in an advanced, automated or electric vehicle passenger case in England and Wales, so the evidential effect of technologies likely to feature in AAEVs (such as in-vehicle footage and remote monitoring) and the legal effect of (for example) the Consumer Rights Act 2015 upon such claims has not been tested in court.

B Personal security claims involving Advanced Driver Assistance Systems (ADAS)

Incomplete regulatory framework for passenger security

18.06   A hands-free driving system has been approved for use on extensive areas of British motorway[42]. The current version of the Highway Code (the statutory guidance to motorists under the Road Traffic Act 1988[43]) does not deal with hands-free driving systems and requires the user of a vehicle to:

'drive or ride with both hands on the wheel or handlebars where possible. This will help you to remain in full control of the vehicle at all times. You may use driver assistance systems while you are driving. Make sure you use any system according to the manufacturer's instructions.'[44]

A motor vehicle is not a risk-free device; risks typical of a motor vehicle do not by themselves establish liability[45]. However, providing an especially risky device to a person insufficiently qualified to use it might generate liability even for the act of that third party[46].

In general terms, a lack of a regulatory framework is capable of generating liabilities[47]. The boundaries of the duty of care in relation to the use of ADAS have yet to be fixed. The regulatory framework for automated vehicles (which also affects driver assistance systems[48]) proposed by the Automated Vehicles Bill 2023-24 (HL Bill 1) has yet to be enacted and completed by (in relation to ADAS and

---

41 (1959) 266 F 2d 326, as described by Lord Scott in *Mitchell* (above) at 899-900 [59].
42 Ford motor company website article 'Ford brings hands-free driving technology to motorways in Great Britain' (13 April 2023); Rt Hon Jesse Norman MP, Minister of State, Department for Transport, in oral evidence to Transport Committee of House of Commons (oral evidence: self-driving vehicles, HC 519, 17 May 2023) at Q271.
43 RTA 1988 s 38. See discussion of the Highway Code in chapter 4, 'driving'.
44 Highway Code rule 160.
45 See for example *Wing v London General Omnibus Company* [1909] 2 KB 652, 662 (Vaughan Williams LJ): ' ... I do not think that an accident resulting from the tendency of motor omnibuses, however well constructed and designed, to skid is any evidence of negligence or of nuisance'. And see Fletcher Moulton LJ at 666-667.
46 *BVI v Hartwell*, above.
47 See *Regina (Bridges) v Chief Constable of South Wales Police (Information Commissioner and others intervening)* [2020] EWCA Civ 1058; [2020] 1 WLR 5037, discussed in Chapter 17, 'data and privacy claims'.
48 See the references to equipment to facilitate the driving or control of a vehicle, at AV Bill 2023-24 (HL Bill 1), cll 55, 91(1)(b)(i) and 93(4)(b).

automated vehicles) updated type approval requirements under the power in cl 91(1) and (in relation to automated vehicles) publication of the statement of safety principles for vehicle authorisation (cl 2) and by regulations relating to matters including safeguarding on automated passenger services (cl 87(4)(b)).

Liability for third party criminal use of an ADAS vehicle

18.07   There is no general presumption of a duty of care to a victim of a crime where a person makes a vehicle available to another, and that vehicle is subsequently used in a crime causing injury to a claimant[49]. The dangers inherent in the use of motor vehicles have not caused the law to treat them as inherently dangerous devices, comparable with devices such as firearms; the law has subsumed all such devices within the law of negligence[50].

Actual foresight of criminal behaviour might be the basis of a duty of care encompassing the conduct of a third party (as in a case where a third party known to be aggressive was employed by a defendant in order to intimidate others[51]).

Lord Atkin and Lord Nicholls pointed out that 'the nature of an article 'may very well call for different degrees of care''[52]. A vehicle with ADAS (which might include a hands-free driving system) and an automated vehicle are of different natures to the conventional, entirely human-driven motor vehicle. How the law might fix duties of care to victims of misuse of such vehicles is unclear.[53]

C Personal security claims involving Automated Vehicles

18.08   Please also see the discussion of ADAS, above.

AEVA 2018, s 2

18.09   AEVA 2018, s 2 provides for direct liability of the insurer or permitted uninsured owner of an AV 'where an accident is caused by an [authorised[54]] automated vehicle when driving itself on a road or other public place in Great Britain'[55] and the insured or any other person thereby suffers damage.

As discussed in Chapter 5, questions might arise as to whether the operator of a highly automated passenger service had assumed a duty of care to a passenger so as to embrace responsibility for the acts of a third party, by exception to the usual rule that the common law does not impose liability for pure omissions. It is

---

49 *Kalma*, above.
50 See *Wing v London General Omnibus* and Lord Nicholls in *BVI v Hartwell*, 1282 [34, 36], both above.
51 *Mattis v Pollock (trading as Flamingos Nightclub)* [2003] EWCA Civ 887; [2003] 1 WLR 2158, 2169 [33-34].
52 Lord Atkin in *Donoghue*, quoted by Lord Nicholls in *Smith v Littlewoods*, above.
53 See the discussion of the standard of care in Chapter 4, 'driving'.
54 Proposed amendment by AV Bill 2023-24 (HL Bill 1), cl 45, Sch 2, para 5(3)(a).
55 AEVA 2018, s 2(1)(a), 2(2)(a).

established that, for the purpose of criminal liability, the word 'accident' in the Road Traffic Acts can include both intentional and fortuitous acts (for example, driving a car deliberately at a locked gate)[56]. AEVA 2018, s 2 requires the '[authorised] automated vehicle when driving itself on a road or other public place in Great Britain' to be the cause of the accident.

Whether and how the direct action against the insurer or permitted uninsured owner under AEVA 2018, s 2 might apply to liability for third party criminal acts using or within an AV has yet to be adjudicated. The passenger safeguarding provision of the AV Bill 2023-24 (HL Bill 1) (cl 87(4)(b)) would, if enacted, be a relevant part of the regulatory background.

D Personal security claims involving Electric Vehicles

Smaller electric vehicles used in crime

18.10   The use of small motor vehicles as a tool of crime is well-known, given their usefulness in evading pursuit. Even in the case of powered scooters, their use by criminal gangs was reported in the early 20th century when the earlier version of the e-scooter, the 'Autoped', was popular[57].

The principles discussed in the 'outline' section above would apply to a claim in which a smaller electric vehicle was used in a crime and the claimant sought to attribute fault to the provider of the vehicle. Each case would depend upon its facts. It is possible that the nature of the vehicle, if obviously hazardous, would affect the scope of the defendant's duty of care, as in *BVI v Hartwell*.

Duties to and for children using smaller electric vehicles

18.11   The laws relating to e-bikes and e-scooters are different. The broad difference is that e-bikes are not classified as 'motor vehicles' and that e-scooters are so classified. As at the time of writing, there is no long-term regulatory framework for the use of e-scooters on roads and other public places; there is merely the interim framework for the use of 'trial' e-scooters[58].

The persistent lack of a regulatory framework, in the absence of a broader Transport Bill dealing with smaller electric vehicles, is problematic. In particular, the lack of a regulatory body has been identified by a coroner[59] as a factor contributing to the death of a 12 year-old child who fell into the path of a bus while riding a trial

---

56 *Chief Constable of Staffordshire v Lees* [1981] RTR 506 (DC). See discussion of 'accident' at *Blackstone's Criminal Practice 2023*, C1.1.
57 Jackie Mansky, 'The motorised scooter boom that hit a century before dockless scooters', The Smithsonian Magazine (18 April 2019)
58 See Chapter 16, 'smaller electric vehicle claims'.
59 Courts and Tribunals Judiciary website 'Mustafa Nadeem: prevention of future deaths report' (18 July 2023).

rental e-scooter which he was not licensed to ride (a requirement of use of a trial e-scooter, not loosened by the e-scooter trial regulations[60]).

Again, each case would turn upon its facts. Many cases exceptionally imposing a duty upon parents for the actions of children have – like *BVI v Hartwell* – been concerned with guns (airguns and firearms)[61]. Whether and how such cases might be relevant to duties of care owed to and for children using smaller electric vehicles has yet to be adjudicated.

---

60 RTA 1988, s 87, 'drivers of motor vehicles to have driving licences'; Gov.uk 'E-scooter trials: guidance for users' (13 July 2020, updated 17 July 2023).
61 See *Charlesworth and Percy on Negligence* (15th edn, 2022), 3-73, 'liability of parent for act of the child'. See also *Harris v Perry* [2008] EWCA Civ 907; [2009] 1 WLR 19 (injury on bouncy castle; issue of sufficiency of parental supervision) where the terms of the written agreement of hire of the equipment were among the facts relevant to the scope of the parental duty, and where the Court of Appeal accepted that constant parental supervision was practically impossible and should not be required by law.

Chapter 19

Procedure for additional claims

'The first draft [*of the Law Revision Committee's 1934 report on abolition of the rule against contribution between tortfeasors*] contained much material that would survive to the final version. Thus, it described the no contribution rule as being 'of obscure and uncertain origin' … and as having limited scope. It recommended that 'the common law rule should be altered as speedily as possible', and it also recommended that alteration should apply not only to joint tortfeasors in the strict sense, but also to situations where two tortfeasors had independently contributed to the same damage. 'This is the position', the report pointed out, 'which frequently arises where the plaintiff sustains a single damage from the combined negligence of two motor car drivers, and recovers judgment against both'. In short, the damages should be apportioned between the tortfeasors in all such cases.'

Professor Paul Mitchell, describing the work of the Law Revision Committee (the precursor of the Law Commission) on reform of the law of contribution[1]

Chapter Contents

A Outline of the procedural rules for additional claims

19.01 For discussion of the principles of apportionment (by reduction of damages for contributory negligence, contribution between concurrent tortfeasors and the apportionment of liability between several tortfeasors) and of their application to advanced, automated and electric vehicle claims, please see Chapter 9, 'RTA claims'. Please also see Chapter 6, 'insurance', for discussion of the AEVA 2018, s 5 claim against another responsible person.

---

1 Mitchell, *A History of Tort Law 1900-1950* (Cambridge, 2015), chapter 11, p 278.

This chapter discusses the procedural rules applying to additional claims, as they might apply in advanced, automated and electric vehicle cases. No 'other person' AAEV claims have yet been adjudicated, so the ways in which the courts will approach the practicalities of such claims are uncertain and the discussion in this book is therefore preliminary. Evidential and costs practicalities of RTA claims have been discussed in the same preliminary way in Chapter 9.

Underlying the procedural rules is the central distinction between the legal bases of the liable defendant's claim against the other person, which will be a matter of fact in each case. In the AAEV context, the central legal distinction is between:

- automated vehicle cases where the primary liability is under AEVA 2018, s 2 and the liable defendant insurer's (or permitted uninsured owner's) claim against another will arise under AEVA 2018, s 5; and

- cases where the primary liability does *not* arise under AEVA 2018, s 2 (for example, where the vehicle was *not* driving itself so as to cause the accident wholly or in part[2], either because it was an automated vehicle not driving itself or because it was an advanced, electric or other motor vehicle lacking an automated driving system), where a contribution claim will be under the Civil Liability (Contribution) Act 1978, if it meets the criteria of that Act[3].

There is the further feature of AEVA 2018, s 2 cases that an insurer etc might seek to raise both an AEVA 2018, s 5 claim in relation to its settlement of liabilities covered by AEVA 2018, s 2 and (if it has made further, extra-AEVA 2018 payments, for example for the value of the automated vehicle itself[4]) a CL(C)A 1978 claim for those further payments. As discussed in Chapter 9, 'RTA claims', it is not clear whether AEVA 2018, s 6(5) deprives the insurer etc of all rights to a CL(C)A 1978 claim, nor how (if possible) a 1978 Act claim could still be raised in tandem with an AEVA 2018, s 5 claim. These points have yet to be adjudicated.

CPR Part 20: counterclaims and other additional claims

19.02   The reader is referred to the full text of Part 20 of the Civil Procedure Rules 1998 and to its Practice Direction (respectively CPR Part 20 and 20 PD), and to caselaw on those rules[5]. Each case will turn on its facts and the reader should consult the full text.

CPR 20.1 provides in its entirety that: 'The purpose of this Part is to enable counterclaims and other additional claims to be managed in the most convenient and effective manner'.

CPR 20.2 sets the scope of the rule and defines its terms:

'(1) This Part applies to –

(a) a counterclaim by a defendant against the claimant or against the claimant and some other person;

---

2   AEVA 2018, s 2(1)(a), 2(2)(a), 8(3)(b).
3   See Chapter 9, 'RTA claims'.
4   AEVA 2018, s 2(3)(a).
5   See, for example, the commentary in the current edition of the annual *Civil Procedure* (Sweet & Maxwell), aka the *White Book*.

(b) an additional claim by a defendant against any person (whether or not already a party) for contribution or indemnity or some other remedy; and

(c) where an additional claim has been made against a person who is not already a party, any additional claim made by that person against any other person (whether or not already a party).

(2) In these Rules –

(a) 'additional claim' means any claim other than the claim by the claimant against the defendant; and

(b) unless the context requires otherwise, references to a claimant or defendant include a party bringing or defending an additional claim.'

CPR 20.3(1) provides that an 'additional claim shall be treated as if it were a claim for the purposes of these Rules, except as provided by this Part'. CPR 20.3(2) to (4) then provide for the different application of certain rules (eg. that CPR 12 (default judgment) 'applies to a counterclaim but not to other additional claim': CPR 20.3(3)).

CPR 20.4 provides for a defendant's counterclaim against a claimant, providing among other matters that this may be made by filing particulars of the counterclaim and '(a) without the court's permission if the defendant files the counterclaim with the defence; or (b) at any other time with the court's permission' (CPR 20.4(2)).

CPR 20.5 provides for a 'counterclaim against a person other than the claimant', providing that this requires the court's permission, unless the court orders otherwise by application on notice, and that the court will if it makes such an order give directions as to the management of the case.

CPR 20.6 provides for a defendant's additional claim for contribution or indemnity from another party, providing that this may be done 'by filing and serving on that party a notice containing a statement of the nature and grounds of the additional claim' and that:

'(2) A defendant may file and serve a notice under this rule –

(a) without the court's permission, if the defendant files and serves it –

(i) with the defence; or

(ii) if their additional claim for contribution or indemnity is against a party added to the claim later, within 28 days after that party files their defence; or

(b) at any other time with the court's permission.'

CPR 20.7 provides the procedure for making any other additional claim 'except (a) a counterclaim only against an existing party; and (b) a claim for contribution or indemnity made in accordance with rule 20.6' (CPR 20.7(1))[6]. An additional claim under CPR 20.7 'is made when the court issues the appropriate claim form' (CPR 20.7(2)), which must contain or be accompanied when served by particulars

---

6 The *White Book 2023* opines that CPR 20.7 'provides an alternative route' to 20.5, at volume 1, page 597, 20.5.3.

of the additional claim ((CPR 20.7(4)). 'A defendant may make an additional claim (a) without the court's permission if the additional claim is issued before or at the same time as they file their defence; (b) at any other time with the court's permission' (CPR 20.7(3)).

CPR 20.9 applies where 'the court is considering whether to (a) permit an additional claim to be made; (b) dismiss an additional claim; or (c) require an additional claim to be dealt with separately from the claim by the claimant against the defendant.' (CPR 20.9(1)). 'The matters which the court may consider include:

(a) the connection between the additional claim and the claim made by the claimant against the defendant;

(b) whether the additional claimant is seeking substantially the same remedy which some other party is claiming from them; and

(c) whether the additional claimant wants the court to decide any question connected with the subject matter of the proceedings –

   (i)   not only between existing parties but also between existing parties and a person not already a party; or

   (ii) against an existing party not only in a capacity in which they are already a party but also in some further capacity' (CPR 20.9(2)).

CPR 20.13 provides that:

'(1) Where a defence is filed to an additional claim the court must consider the future conduct of the proceedings and give appropriate directions.

(2) In giving directions under paragraph (1) the court must ensure that, so far as practicable, the original claim and all additional claims are managed together.'

B Procedure for additional claims in an Advanced Driver Assistance Systems (ADAS) case

19.03 As discussed in the 'outline' section above, ADAS cases do not fall within AEVA 2018 and – absent any change in the law relating to the safety or safe use of ADAS systems – will be adjudicated on their facts according to the legal principles described in this book (see, for example, Chapters 9, 'RTA claims', and 10, 'vehicle defects').

C Procedure for additional claims in an Automated Vehicle case

Does CPR Part 20 accommodate an AEVA 2018, s 5 claim?

19.04 CPR Part 20 appears broad enough to include an AEVA 2018, s 5 claim. In particular, CPR 20.2(1)(b) describes 'an additional claim by a defendant against any person (whether or not already a party) for contribution or indemnity *or some other remedy*' (italics added).

Can/should an AEVA 2018, s 5 claim be heard at the same time as a s 2 claim?

19.05 Under the preceding Act to CL(C)A 1978, the court had jurisdiction to determine a contribution claim between concurrently liable drivers of two motor vehicles who are already joined as defendants to an existing road traffic accident claim, without the need for separate contribution proceedings[7]. That was on the basis that the statute contained the phrase 'in any proceedings for contribution under this section the amount of the contribution recoverable from any person shall be such as may be found by the court to be just and equitable having regard to the extent of that person's responsibility for the damage'[8], wording essentially the same to that now in CL(C)A 1978, s 2(1).

Whether or not Parliament intended the same mechanism for AEVA 2018, s 5 is unclear. The second criterion of s 5 is that 'the amount of the insurer's or vehicle owner's liability to the injured party in respect of the accident … is settled'[9], and 'the time of that settlement' is the time at which the s 5 right of action accrues[10] and from which time starts to run for limitation purposes[11]. AEVA 2018, s 5 does not repeat the '…found by the court …' language of the contribution acts and CL(C) A 1978 is expressly excluded[12]. The active discouragement of multiple actions in CL(C)A 1978 (exemplified by the disentitlement of the claimant to costs of repeat actions in s 4) does not appear in AEVA 2018. It is arguable that AEVA 2018 seeks to separate the s 2 direct action (which simplifies the victim's means to recourse, by the bypassing of expensive product liability litigation) and the s 5 insurer etc's action (which passes the more difficult task to the more resourced insurer or public body), with the aim of avoiding, for the claimant, the cost and difficulty of product liability litigation.

The issue of the joining of AEVA 2018, ss 2 and 5 proceedings is, however, likely to be contentious – especially as early case management points (including the potential commonality of some evidence) are explored.

D Procedure for additional claims in an Electric Vehicle case

Addition of party not permitted to establish funds of potential defendant

19.06 As the law stands, some users of smaller electric vehicles are likely to be uninsured. For example, an owner of an e-bike is not required to have compulsory insurance cover for its use as it is exempted from the 'motor vehicle' definition by RTA 1988, s 189. The question might then arise as to the extent of the defendant's assets or the existence of other insurance.

---

7 *Croston v Vaughan* [1938] 1 KB 540 (CA).
8 *Croston*, Slesser LJ at 553-554.
9 AEVA 2018, s 5(1)(b).
10 AEVA 2018, s 5(5).
11 Limitation Act 1980, s 10A, inserted by AEVA 2018, s 20(1), Sch, para 9.
12 AEVA 2018, s 6(5).

The courts have resisted applications to join a party to establish the extent of funds available to satisfy a judgment. In group litigation relating to breast implants, *XYZ v Various (including Transform Medical Group (CS) Ltd and Spire Healthcare Ltd*, the High Court considered an application by an insurer to join another insurer who could have been made defendant to an additional claim without permission at the same time as entering the defence under CPR 20.7 but was not. The court found no compelling case for bringing the additional insurer into the claim.

> 'However attractively packaged this application may be it is an attempt … to establish in advance the depths of another insurer's pockets. If [*the applicant's*] submissions are correct, CPR 19.2 (2)(b) would entitle a claimant in a personal injury case to join into proceedings a defendant's insurers, seeking a declaration as to the scope of the insurance available to meet the claim. This would cut across years of jurisprudence to the effect that a claimant must take the defendant as he finds him.' [13]

The court noted that, 'had the claim been brought under [CPR] 20.7 and [*the respondent insurer*] had sought to sever the claim … [i]n accordance with CPR 20.9 …', the applicant would have faced the same difficulty as under CPR 19.2:

> 'There is no connection between their claim for a declaration and the claims currently being made… The question raised on the declaration is not connected with the subject matter of the proceedings'[14.]

---

13 [2014] EWHC 4056 (QB), Thirlwall J (as she then was) [27].
14 Above, at [30].

Chapter 20

Damages

'It is desirable that there should be a measure of damage which can be easily and definitely found.'

Greer LJ (1935)[1]

Note: this chapter raises points which are generic to advanced, automated and electric vehicle claims, for which categories there are at present no distinct damages cases. So this chapter is not separated into the sections generally used throughout this book.

Introduction

20.01   Damages sought will depend upon the legal base or bases of claim which arise upon the facts of each case. AAEV damages claims may arise in several factual and legal contexts[2]. As at the time of writing automated and many ADAS technologies have yet to be deployed and AAEV damages claims have yet to be litigated, so the course of arguments is unpredictable[3].

Some relevant trends in damages can be identified. An example in the AAEV field is the irrecoverability of damage to the automated vehicle itself[4] in a direct claim under AEVA 2018, s 2 – a feature of compulsory third party motor insurance under the Road Traffic Acts[5] which has passed into the direct claim against the insurer etc under AEVA 2018, s 2.[6]

Despite Greer LJ's hope (above, quoted recently in a test case on damage to highway furniture described below), the tendency has been towards extensive litigation of

---

1   *The London Corporation* [1935] P. 70, 78 (CA).
2   See other chapters in the civil liability part of this book.
3   For the whole topic the reader is referred to specialist works (eg. *McGregor on Damages*) and particularly to the judgments of the Supreme Court relating to remoteness of damage in *Manchester Building Society v Grant Thornton UK LLP* [2021] UKSC 20; [2022] AC 783 and *Khan v Meadows* [2021] UKSC 21; [2022] AC 852.
4   AEVA 2018, s 2(3)(a).
5   The exclusion of damage to the insured vehicle under RTA 1988, s 145(4)(c).
6   How this might affect the AEVA 2018, s 5 insurer etc's claim and a CL(C)A 1978 claim for contribution is discussed in Chapters 9, 'RTA claims', and 19, 'procedure for additional claims'.

damages points in cases arising from road traffic accidents[7]. The broader context is a system of RTA injury and damage compensation with compulsory motor insurance at its core, in which there is both a commercial and a motor vehicle users' interest in limiting expenditure[8].

Higher costs of collision repairs to vehicles

20.02 Motor vehicles have included microchips and computers since the late 1960s[9]. AAEVs carry more electronic equipment than previous vehicles, including sensors and connections within the outer structure of the vehicle which are vulnerable to damage in road traffic collisions. The higher cost of vehicle repairs for even minor collisions reflects this.

The insurance system for vehicles includes vehicle repair, with the qualification that first party vehicle damage is not within compulsory part of the motor insurance system[10]. Given the increasing value of vehicle components and vehicle repairs, that is a significant exclusion.

Highway furniture repair claims

20.03 Designated civil judges in the county court have heard cases in which the quantification of compensation due to national highway authorities for the repair of highway furniture in road traffic collisions has been disputed.

In *National Highways Ltd v Hubble, EUI Ltd and Parekh*[11], His Honour Judge Hassall heard three test cases. Much of the judgment relates to contentious pleading points (which might itself indicate that this area of litigation is not at an end). The essential dispute was whether (as the defendants submitted) 'a claim for diminution in value cannot exceed the pre-accident capital value of the thing damaged. [The defendants say] that the incidence of the cap is, in all three cases, identical to the new materials cost of the items of highway furniture replaced'[12] or whether (as the claimant submitted) diminution in value of the highway should also be compensated.

Among other points the defendants sought to argue that costs such as installation of replacement equipment in land should be disregarded:

---

7   As in the credit hire litigation which started with *Giles v Thompson* [1994] 1 AC 142 (HL) and continues.
8   See the quotation from *Winfield and Jolowicz on Tort* (20th edn, 2020, 1-028) at the head of Chapter 6 of this book, 'insurance': '… the tort system, at least in the personal injury context, is overwhelmingly financed by the public'.
9   See Appendix, 'History'.
10 RTA 1988 s 145(4)(c); AEVA 2018, s 2(3)(a). The further qualification that compulsorily insured third party property damage is capped (as at the time of writing at £1,200,000) by RTA 1988, s 145(4)(b) and AEVA 2018, s 2(4) is unlikely to affect most consumer motor vehicles.
11 *National Highways Ltd v Hubble*, County Court at Manchester, 13 January 2023, [2023] 1 WLUK 457.
12 Above, at [32].

'Even though, via concrete, wiring and nuts and bolts, the chattel has been joined to the highway, the body of the chattel itself is unchanged. Hence the measure of loss, it is argued, should also be unchanged: the same as if the tortfeasor had destroyed the column before it left the warehouse.'[13]

Judge Hassall held that:

'Once the exercise of construction is complete, whether hours or years later, the capital value of the finished article may bear little relation to the purchase price of its components. Hence the question in the instant cases is whether the claimant's pre-accident installation of the highway furniture in question altered the approach that the court would take to diminution in value if those items were damaged. If such a transition can occur, it is reasonable for the lawyer to ask: 'when does it?'[.] In my judgment, it is when the chattel is fixed to the highway, becoming in law a fixture and in practice a component part of a wider, physical whole. As Lord Lloyd said in *Elitestone Ltd v Morris and Another* [1997] UKHL 15:

"Thus blocks of stone placed one on the top of another without any mortar or cement for the purpose of forming a dry stone wall would become part of the land, though the same stones, if deposited in a builder's yard and for convenience sake stacked on the top of each other in the form of a wall, would remain chattels."

'This is the same for other items of highway furniture that may also be damaged in accidents, such as signs or overhead gantries.'[14]

The judge allowed that this would not be the case where items were never intended to be installed but were temporary (eg. mobile lighting columns) or had not been installed at the time of the tort (eg. posts lying by the roadside)[15].

Judge Hassall accordingly allowed the claim for diminution in loss of the highway, which 'should be measured as the notional reasonable cost of repairing the highway' and 'should be determined immediately after each accident occurred'[16]. A defendant bears the burden of proving otherwise:

'In my judgment, it matters not by what method a tortfeasor attempts to displace or limit the award that the court would otherwise make for diminution in value as measured by the reasonable cost of repairs: once the attempt is made, the onus lies upon the tortfeasor to establish the reasons for the displacement sought. If the reason is an argument about valuation so as to apply 'the cap,' then it is for the tortfeasor to establish each element of the argument, including the evidential basis for it.'[17]

---

13 *National Highways Ltd v Hubble* [147].
14 Above, at [148]-[151].
15 Above, at [152]-[153].
16 Above, at [259].
17 Above, at [206].

Damages in data breach claims

20.04 The General Data Protection Regulation, art 82 and Data Protection Act 2018, ss 168 and 169 provide for compensation for data protection breaches, including compensation for distress[18].

This is subject to the *de minimis* principle. The courts have applied a 'threshold of seriousness' approach so as to exclude damage which is 'no more than trivial'[19]. Viable claims are allocated proportionately to complexity and value and value will often be modest. See for example:

- *Ashley v Amplifon Ltd*[20]: accidental, one-off data breach of employment documents relating to an employment dispute, quickly remedied. Judge held that there were unanswered questions which might favour both sides, which should be put at trial. Transferred to county court. 'Access to justice includes the right to litigate modest claims for amounts that may seem trivial to lawyers but are not to the party seeking not just the money but to vindicate their rights. Whether the claim is worth the candle must be seen in that light'[21].

- *Johnson v Eastlight*[22]: inadvertent disclosure by email of rental statements to a single person for less than three hours, admitted and self-referred to ICO who confirmed no action would be taken. No personal injury claim made. Claim not struck out but transferred to county court, with 'all the hallmarks of a Small Claim Track claim'[23].

In *Lloyd v Google LLC*, the Supreme Court – dealing with DPA 1998 – held that recovery of damages for distress on a 'uniform per capita basis' so as to allow a representative action to proceed for all claimants would be contrary to the findings of the trial judge in the case that users had been affected differently by the breach:

'some affected individuals were 'super users' – heavy internet users. They will have been 'victims' of multiple breaches, with considerable amounts of [browser generated information] taken and used throughout the Relevant Period. Others will have engaged in very little internet activity. Different individuals will have had different kinds of information taken and used …'[24]:

'If liability is established, the ordinary application of the compensatory principle would therefore result in different awards of compensation to different individuals. Furthermore, the amount of any compensation recoverable by any member of the class would depend on a variety of circumstances particular to that individual. Individualised assessment of damages would therefore be required.'[25]

---

18 DPA 2018 s 168(1) and 169(5). See Chapter 17, 'data and privacy claims'.
19 *Lloyd v Google LLC* [2021] UKSC 50; [2022] AC 1217, 1268 [153].
20 [2021] EWHC 2921 (QB, Kerr J).
21 Above, at [80].
22 [2021] EWHC 3069 (QB, Master Thornett).
23 Above, at [24.5].
24 From the judgment of Warby J (as he then was) [2019] 1 WLR 1265 [91], quoted by the Supreme Court at 1250 [87].
25 *Lloyd v Google* (UKSC, above) at 1250 [87].

Part III

Criminal law

Chapter 21

'Moving' offences

'Existing law reflects a division between rules governing vehicle design on the one hand and the behaviour of drivers on the other… To accommodate [*automated vehicles*], we need a new vocabulary, new legal actors and new regulatory schemes.'

The Law Commission of England and Wales and the Scottish Law Commission (2022)[1]

Chapter Contents

A Outline of 'moving' offences applicable to AAEVs 21.01
B 'Moving' offences and Advanced Driver Assistance Systems (ADAS) 21.05
C 'Moving' offences and Automated Vehicles 21.06
D 'Moving' offences and Electric Vehicles 21.07

A Outline of 'moving' offences applicable to AAEVs

Categorisation of criminal offences for AAEVs in Part III of this book

21.01 This Part of the book categorises criminal offences applicable to AAEVs as follows:

1. 'Moving' vehicle offences, relating to AAEVs in motion and including offences relating to driving and to the automated and remote operation of vehicles (Chapter 21);

2. 'Keeping' offences, relating to criminal sanctions for failure to meet the pre-conditions of keeping and using a vehicle on the roads such as the provision of compulsory liability insurance (Chapter 22);

3. 'Construction' offences, relating to the vehicle features of AAEVs (Chapter 23);

4. 'Obstruction' offences, relating to the obstruction of roads by AAEVs (Chapter 24);

---

1 Law Commissions' final report on automated vehicles, *Automated Vehicles: Joint Report*, Law Com No 404, Scot Law Com No 258 (January 2022), p 11, 2.2-2.3.

5. 'Tampering' offences, relating to criminal interference with AAEVs and their systems both inside and outside the vehicle, as well as offences relating to information (Chapter 25).

Offences not yet enacted but likely to appear in the Automated Vehicles Act 2024 when enacted are cited as they appear in the current version of the Automated Vehicles Bill 2023-24 (HL Bill 1).

Scope of this book

21.02 This book does not list all criminal offences potentially applicable to AAEVs. The criminal offences applicable to road vehicles and to their use are voluminous and each case will depend upon its facts. For a study of the whole field of criminal law as it applies to road traffic the reader is referred to specialist works[2]. This book focusses upon existing offences of likely application to AAEVs. It also includes the offences which appear in the AV Bill 2023-24 (HL Bill 1).

This chapter discusses category 1, above: **'moving'** offences.

The Automated Vehicles Bill 2023-24 (HL Bill 1)

21.03 In their review of the laws of automated vehicles (November 2018 to January 2022), the Law Commission of England and Wales and the Scottish Law Commission made recommendations to government for legal reforms to accommodate automated vehicles[3]. The overarching recommendations were the establishment of a new safety regulator, a licensing system for automated passenger services and the continuous monitoring of the safety of automated vehicles in use. Criminal law reforms were recommended – including delineating the responsibility of the driver of an automated vehicle by the provision of immunity from driving offences during automated driving and providing for corporate liability including a new offence of misdescribing a lesser driving system as automated. Data protection and privacy were 'predominantly outside the scope of [the Law Commissions' AV law] project. However, some issues concerning data integral to the proposals made' were in the Law Commissions' third paper, on access to incident data[4].

The government announced in the Queen's Speech in May 2022 that it would publish a Transport Bill legislating for railway and road transport, to 'pave the way for the travel choices of tomorrow'[5]. In relation to automated vehicles the government's announcement reflected the AV law recommendations of the Law Commissions, whose project on AV law had concluded in January 2022, by describing the Bill as:

---

2 See for example *Wilkinson's Road Traffic Offences* (30th edn, 2021), *Blackstone's Criminal Practice* and Susan Cavender and Alistair Haggerty *A Practical Approach to Road Traffic Law* (Bloomsbury, 2023).
3 www.lawcom.gov.uk/project/automated-vehicles.
4 The Law Commissions, 'Automated Vehicles: Consultation Paper 3 – A regulatory framework for automated vehicles, a joint consultation paper', Law Commission Consultation Paper 252, Scottish Law Commission Discussion Paper 171 (18 December 2020), chapter 17, 'Access to Data', p 287, 17.2.
5 Baroness Vere, House of Lords Hansard Volume 822, columns 30 to 31, 11 May 2022.

'comprehensive legislation, which will enable the Government to set new safety standards and assign legal responsibilities to protect users of self-driving vehicles, as well as those on the streets around them. We will establish new legal entities to take responsibility for vehicles that drive themselves. In the event of any issues, this will prevent the occupants of the vehicles being unfairly held to account. The legislation will also ensure that the vehicles remain safe throughout their lives, and that they serve all parts of society when used in public transport networks.'[6]

In relation to electric vehicles the government stated that the Transport Bill 2022–2023 would regulate the use of low-speed, zero-emission vehicles including e-scooters on roads and other public places:

'…it is our intention that the [*Transport*] Bill will create a low-speed, zero-emission vehicle category that is independent from the cycle and motor vehicle categories. New powers would allow the Government to decide the vehicles that fall into this new category in future and how they should be regulated to make sure that they are safe to use. We hope that e-scooters will be the first of these vehicles.'[7]

The government largely accepted the detail of the Law Commissions' AV law recommendations in its policy paper 'Connected and Automated Mobility 2025' (CAM 2025), published in August 2022[8].

The Transport Bill was due to be debated in Parliament during the 2022–2023 session but in December 2022 the Secretary of State for Transport told the House of Commons Transport Select Committee that the entire Bill had been postponed[9]. That larger Transport Bill was not among the Bills announced for the 2023-24 Parliamentary session in the King's Speech on 7 November 2023. It remains unpublished. As at the time of writing, the regulatory framework for smaller electric vehicles such as e-scooters has not progressed to publication of a Bill.

The Automated Vehicles Bill 2023-24 (HL Bill 1) was announced in the King's Speech on 7 November 2023 and was published the following day, after its first reading in the House of Lords. The AV Bill 2023-24 mainly regulates automated vehicles (particularly in relation to initial authorisation, ongoing safety monitoring and the licensing of automated passenger services) although its provisions also affect ADAS systems in more limited respects, including type approval. It includes powers to change or clarify existing traffic legislation in relation to its application to a user-in-charge of an automated vehicle (cl 50) and to adapt assimilated type approval legislation to ADAS and AV systems (cl 91).

See Chapter 2, 'specifications', for an outline of the AV Bill 2023-24.

---

6 As above.
7 As above.
8 UK government policy paper 'Connected and automated mobility 2025: realising the benefits of self-driving vehicles' ('CAM 2025'), 19 August 2022.
9 Parliament Live TV, Transport Select Committee 7 December 2022 at 9:43, Sec of St for Transport the Rt Hon Mark Harper MP.

Table summarising main statutory 'moving' vehicle offences applicable to AAEVs and proposed offences under the AV Bill 2023-24 (HL Bill 1)

21.04

Act/Regs	Provision	Description
Highway Act 1835	s 72	Penalty on persons committing nuisances by riding on footpaths etc
Offences Against the Person Act 1861	s 35	Drivers of carriages injuring persons by furious driving
Road Traffic Regulation Act 1984	s 89	Speeding offences generally
RTA 1988	s 2	Dangerous driving[10]
	s 3	Careless, and inconsiderate, driving[11]
	s 4	Driving or being in charge of mechanically propelled vehicle when unfit to drive through drink or drugs
	s 23	No person in addition to driver of motor bicycle may be carried otherwise than sitting astride the motor cycle and on a proper seat securely fixed to the motor cycle behind the driver's seat.
	s 28	Dangerous cycling
	s 29	Careless and inconsiderate cycling
RTA 1988; Motor Cycle (Protective Helmets) Regulations 1998[12]	s 16; reg 4	Wearing of protective headgear (disapplied in relation to *trial* e-scooters[13])
RTA 1988	s 32	Riding an Electrically Assisted Pedal Cycle while under 14 or knowingly or suspecting that they are under 14 causing or permitting a person under 14 to do so
	s 33	Control of use of footpaths, bridleways and restricted byways for motor vehicle trials
	s 34	Prohibition of driving mechanically propelled vehicles elsewhere than on roads
RTA 1988; Road Vehicles (Construction and Use) Regulations 1986[14]	s 41D; regs 104, 110.	Breach of requirements as to control of vehicle, mobile telephones etc

---

10 And see RTA 1988, s 1 (causing death by dangerous driving), s 1A (causing serious injury by dangerous driving) and s 2A (meaning of dangerous driving).

11 And see RTA 1988, ss 2B and 2C (causing serious injury by careless, or inconsiderate, driving) and the offences at ss 3ZA to 3A.

12 SI 1998/1807.

13 MC(PH)R 1998, reg 4(2A), added by the Electric Scooter Trials and Traffic Signs (Coronavirus) Regulations and General Directions 2020, SI 2020/663, reg 3(2)(b).

14 SI 1986/1078, 'CUR 1986'.

Act/Regs	Provision	Description
RTA 1988; CUR 1986	s 42; other CUR	Breach of other CUR requirements, including reg 102 (carrying passenger on motorcycle without suitable supports or rests for the feet of passenger)
RTA 1988	s 87	Driver of motor vehicles to have driving licences
	s 96	Driving with uncorrected defective eyesight
	s 163	Driver on a road failing to stop a mechanically propelled vehicle when required to do so by a constable in uniform or a traffic officer
	s 168	Failure to give, or giving false, name and address in case of reckless or careless or inconsiderate driving or cycling
	s 170	Duty of driver to stop, report accident and give information or documents
Equality Act 2010	Part 12	Accessibility offences for taxis etc and public service vehicles[15]
Automated Vehicles Act 2024 (**not yet enacted**; sections quoted as clause numbers in AV Bill 2023-24, HL Bill 1)	Cl 48 (1) and (2)	Loss of immunity from criminal liability of user-in-charge of automated vehicle after authorised transition demand has ended
	Cl 48(4)	Loss of immunity from criminal liability of user-in-charge of automated vehicle for use without payment of road toll or charge
	Cl 48(5)-(6)	Loss of immunity from criminal liability of user-in-charge of automated vehicle for UIC feature used outside its authorisation as result of deliberate interference with equipment by or with knowledge of UIC
	Cl 53	Use of vehicle without driver or licensed oversight (proposed new offence at RTA 1988, s 34B)[16]
	Cl 53	Causing death or serious injury by using vehicle without driver or licensed oversight (proposed new RTA 1988, s 34C)
	Cl 53	Use of automated vehicle in a dangerous state (proposed new RTA 1988, s 3C)
	Cl 53	Causing death, or serious injury, by use of automated vehicle in dangerous state (proposed new RTA 1988, s 3D)

---

15 See Chapter 27, 'equality'.
16 See Chapter 3 for discussion of this proposed offence in relation to testing.

Act/Regs	Provision	Description
	Cl 53	Causing danger to road users resulting in automated vehicle killing or seriously injuring (proposed new RTA 1988, s 22b)
	Cl 54	Proposed new RTA 1988, s 3B, 'Disapplication to user-in-charge of automated vehicle': 'For the purposes of section 47 of the Automated Vehicles Act 2024 (user-in-charge of authorised automated vehicle not liable for manner of driving), any offence under the preceding sections is to be taken to be an offence arising from the way in which a vehicle is driven.'
	Cl 54	Proposed new RTA 198,8 s 3C: 'Use of automated vehicle in dangerous state'
	Cl 54	Proposed new RTA 1988, s 3D: 'Causing death, or serious injury, by use of automated vehicle in dangerous state'

B 'Moving' offences and Advanced Driver Assistance Systems (ADAS)

ADAS still to be regulated by secondary legislation

21.05 To date, ADAS systems have been regulated mainly by secondary legislation. The Construction and Use Regulations 1986[17] have been amended on several occasions to accommodate new technologies (such as remote parking using a mobile telephone[18]).

April 2023 saw the approval by government of a hands-free driving system for use on extensive areas of British motorways[19], without alteration of RTA 1988, CUR 1986, nor even (as at the date of writing) the applicable rule of the Highway Code[20].

The AV Bill 2023-24 does not set out a regulatory scheme for ADAS as it does (more stringently) for automated vehicles. But it lays foundations for ADAS-focused regulation in future – in particular by the power by regulations to adapt

---

17 Road Vehicles (Construction and Use) Regulations 1986, SI 1986/1078 (as amended).
18 CUR 1986, reg 110(5A), added from 11 June 2018 by the Road Vehicles (Construction and Use) (Amendment) Regulations 2018, SI 2018/592, reg 1 and 2(2).
19 Ford motor company website article 'Ford brings hands-free driving technology to motorways in Great Britain' (13 April 2023); Rt Hon Jesse Norman MP, Minister of State, Department for Transport, in oral evidence to Transport Committee of House of Commons (oral evidence: self-driving vehicles, HC 519, 17 May 2023) at Q271. And see Chapter 3, 'testing' for the permissions applicable to prototype vehicles.
20 HC rule 160: 'Once moving you should ... drive or ride with both hands on the wheel or handlebars where possible. This will help you to remain in full control of the vehicle at all times. You may use driver assistance systems while you are driving. Make sure you use any system according to the manufacturer's instructions.'

existing type approval legislation not only for vehicles that are designed to travel autonomously but also for:

'(b) any other type of vehicle that—

(i) includes equipment designed to allow its motion to be controlled other than by an individual in it, or to facilitate its being so controlled, or

(ii) is designed to incorporate or interact with software.' (cl 91(1)(b))

C 'Moving' offences and Automated Vehicles

Law Commissions' recommendations leading to the automated vehicle 'moving' offences in the AV Bill 2023-24 (HL Bill 1)

21.06   As to moving offences, at the conclusion of their review of automated vehicle law the Law Commissions proposed that:

'While a relevant [*Automated Driving System*] feature is engaged, the user-in-charge should not be liable for any criminal offence or civil penalty which arises from dynamic driving.

The immunity should not apply if the user-in-charge has taken steps to override or alter the system so as to engage the ADS when it is not designed to function.

The immunity should cease if the user-in-charge deliberately interferes with the functioning of the ADS.'[21]

'The new Act should create a defence to any driving offence committed in the period immediately following a handover. The defence should be that the defendant's driving did not fall below the standard reasonably expected of a competent and careful driver in the circumstances.'[22]

'The new Act should provide that a user-in-charge who fails to respond to a transition demand will acquire the legal responsibilities of a driver at the end of the transition period.'[23]

A user-in-charge's criminal liability would be of a different nature to that of a driver. Accordingly, the Law Commissions recommended that:

'A user-in-charge should not be liable for any of the driving offences set out in sections 1 to 3A[24] of the Road Traffic Act 1988.

Instead, a user in charge should be liable for a new offence of using a vehicle in an obviously dangerous state. The offence would be committed where:

(1) the user-in-charge used the vehicle in a dangerous state; and

---

21 Law Commissions' final report on automated vehicles (above), recommendation 44.
22 Recommendation 47.
23 Recommendation 48.
24 The principal 'driving' offences.

(2) it would be obvious to a competent and careful user-in-charge engaging the ADS that using the vehicle in its current state would be dangerous.

In deciding whether the vehicle is in a dangerous state, regard should be had to anything attached to or carried on or in it and to the manner in which it is attached or carried.

An aggravated form of the offence should apply where the use caused death or serious injury.'[25]

As to aggravated driving offences such as causing death by dangerous driving, the Law Commissions noted that:

'These offences will not be committed when a vehicle is driving itself. We do not think it is right to prosecute an ASDE Authorised Self-Driving Entity: the organisation that will be held responsible for a vehicle when driving itself for the behaviour of the vehicle simply because a human driver would be prosecuted in similar circumstances. However, if wrongdoing by the ASDE or NUIC operator leads to a death or serious injury, there is a moral case for liability, and the public will want to see this reflected in both the charge and the sentence.'[26]

D 'Moving' offences and Electric Vehicles

Application of some offences not just to 'motor vehicles'

21.07 Some offences apply not only to 'motor vehicles' – a definition from which some electric vehicles such as e-bikes are excluded[27] – but to 'mechanically propelled vehicles', a definition which includes electric vehicles[28]. For example, RTA 1988, s 34 prohibits 'driving mechanically propelled vehicles elsewhere than on roads'.

The Highway Act 1835, s 72, remains in force and requires no mechanical propulsion:

'If any person shall wilfully ride upon any footpath or causeway by the side of any road made or set apart for the use or accommodation of foot passengers; or shall wilfully lead or drive any horse, ass, sheep, mule, swine, or cattle or carriage of any description, or any truck or sledge, upon any such footpath or causeway; or shall tether any horse, ass, mule, swine, or cattle, on any highway, so as to suffer or permit the tethered animal to be thereon; ...; every person so offending in any of the cases aforesaid shall for each and every such offence forfeit and pay any sum not exceeding [level 2 on the standard scale], over and above the damages occasioned thereby.'

---

25 Law Commissions' Final AV report, recommendation 46.
26 Above, p 220, 11.61.
27 RTA 1988, s 189(1)(c); Electrically Assisted Pedal Cycles Regulations 1983, SI 1983/1168, reg 3.
28 *Elieson v Parker* (1917) 81 JP 265.

Death caused by careless driving of an electrically propelled unicycle

21.08   In *Rex v Tudor Manolache*[29], the Court of Appeal dismissed an appeal against a sentence of 14 months' imprisonment on pleas of guilty to causing death by careless driving of an electrically propelled unicycle, a 'Gotway', and for causing death by driving a vehicle without insurance, where no separate penalty was imposed for the second offence. The appellant was riding on a footpath and collided with an elderly pedestrian, Mr Leonard Bailey. The Court of Appeal noted that the unicycle:

> 'should never have been on a public road. It was capable of speeds of up to 26 mph in testing, although the advertised speed was up to 40 mph when loaded. It was illegal (except on private land) because it was not registered, it was not taxed and it was not insured. There was some evidence that the applicant had been warned about legal restrictions on use when he bought the vehicle.'[30]

The Court of Appeal rejected a submission that '[a]lthough it is accepted that the offence was aggravated by his presence on a path which he had no right to be on, and the lack of insurance or licence, it is said that these factors all flowed from the current classification of his Gotway':

> 'We disagree. The speed was indeed excessive, but that was not all. It was combined with what the applicant knew to be his dangerous inability to bring the unicycle to a rapid stop, on a path shared with pedestrians, because of the way it was constructed and operated. The applicant was not entitled to assume that pedestrians would be able to jump out of his way. Mr Bailey did in fact try to do that. However, the movement of the Gotway was too rapid and unpredictable for him, and that was to be expected. The illegality of the unicycle was an aggravating factor. To say that this flowed from its classification does not in any way diminish that. This was no merely technical infraction. The applicant's vehicle was completely unfit for driving on a public road or path, as this fatal accident demonstrated only too clearly.' 31

---

29 [2023] EWCA Crim 1116.
30 Above, at [5].
31 Above, at [14]–[15].

Chapter 22

'Keeping' offences

'In law, drivers have many responsibilities. Some relate to dynamic driving (such as following road signs or driving with due care and attention)... However, the law also imposes responsibilities on drivers which do not relate to dynamic driving.'

The Law Commission of England and Wales and the Scottish Law Commission (2020)[1]

Chapter Contents

A   Outline of 'keeping' offences applicable to AAEVs 22.01
B   'Keeping' offences and Advanced Driver Assistance Systems (ADAS) 22.04
C   'Keeping' offences and Automated Vehicles 22.05
D   'Keeping' offences and Electric Vehicles 22.07

A   Outline of 'keeping' offences applicable to AAEVs

Categorisation of criminal offences for AAEVs in Part III of this book

22.01   As at the time of writing, the criminal law does not yet cater expressly for advanced, automated and electric vehicles (save in relation to the requirement for automated vehicles to be insured within the RTA 1988, Part VI, per AEVA 2018).

The law for ADAS systems and automated vehicles will be progressed when the Automated Vehicles Bill 2023-24 (HL Bill 1) is enacted (subject to amendments) as the Automated Vehicles Act 2024 and regulations are made under that Act.

The Transport Bill announced in the Queen's Speech in May 2022 to reform the law in relation to smaller electric vehicles including e-scooters has not been published and did not appear in the King's Speech in November 2023. The criminal law in relation to smaller electric vehicles has therefore not been clarified and they remain regulated as motor vehicles (or not, if exempted) under RTA 1988 and its regulations.

---

1   The Law Commissions, 'Automated Vehicles: Consultation Paper 3 – A regulatory framework for automated vehicles, a joint consultation paper', Law Commission Consultation Paper 252, Scottish Law Commission Discussion Paper 171 (18 December 2020), p 14, 2.9.

This book categorises criminal offences applicable to AAEVs as follows:

1. 'Moving' vehicle offences, relating to AAEVs in motion and including offences relating to driving and to the automated and remote operation of vehicles (Chapter 21);

2. 'Keeping' offences, relating to criminal sanctions for failure to meet the pre-conditions of keeping and using a vehicle on the roads such as the provision of compulsory liability insurance (Chapter 22);

3. 'Construction' offences, relating to the vehicle features of AAEVs (Chapter 23);

4. 'Obstruction' offences, relating to the obstruction of roads by AAEVs (Chapter 24);

5. 'Tampering' offences, relating to criminal interference with AAEVs and their systems both inside and outside the vehicle, as well as offences relating to information (Chapter 25).

Scope of this book

22.02   This book does not list all criminal offences applicable to AAEVs. AAEVs are 'vehicles', the criminal offences applicable to them and to their use are voluminous and each case will depend upon its facts. For a study of the whole field of criminal law as it applies to road traffic the reader is referred to specialist works[2]. This book focusses upon existing offences of likely application to AAEVs.

This chapter discusses category 2, above: **'keeping'** offences.

Please see Chapter 21, 'moving' offences, for an outline of the Law Commissions' work in the consultations on automated driving (2018 to 2022) and remote driving (2022 to 2023) leading to the AV Bill 2023-24 (HL Bill 1).

Table summarising main statutory *'keeping'* vehicle offences (pre-Transport Bill) potentially applicable to AAEVs

22.03

Act/Regs	Provision	Description
RTA 1988	s 143	Users of motor vehicles to be insured[3]
	s 144A	Offence of keeping vehicle which does not meet insurance requirements
	s 154	Offence of wilfully not giving information as to insurance where claim made, or wilfully making false statement in reply to such demand

---

2   See for example *Wilkinson's Road Traffic Offences* (30th edn, 2021), *Blackstone's Criminal Practice* and Susan Cavender and Alistair Haggerty *A Practical Approach to Road Traffic Law* (Bloomsbury, 2023).

3   And see the offence under RTA 1988, s 3ZB (Causing death by driving: unlicensed and uninsured drivers) and *Rex v Tudor Manolache* [2023] EWCA Crim 1116 discussed in section D below.

Act/Regs	Provision	Description
	s 171	Duty of owner of vehicle to give information for verifying compliance with requirement of compulsory insurance
RTA 1988; RTRA 1984	RTA 1988, s 172; RTRA 1984, s 112	Duty to give information as to identity of driver etc in certain circumstances
Automated Vehicles Act 2024 (***not yet enacted***; *sections quoted as clause numbers in AV Bill 2023-24, HL Bill 1)*	Cl 49	'The user-in-charge of a vehicle is to be taken for the purposes of any enactment to be the driver of, and driving, the vehicle' (cl 49(1)). 'This clause clarifies that for the purposes of any enactment[4] … the user in charge is to be considered the driver of and driving the vehicle, although benefiting from the immunity provided in clause 47' (explanatory note to the AV Bill 2023-24, HL Bill 1-EN, para 228)
	Cl 45, Sch 2, para 4(2)	Amendment of RTA 1988, s 145 (requirements about insurance policies) to insert 'authorised' before 'automated vehicle'.

B 'Keeping' offences and Advanced Driver Assistance Systems (ADAS)

Insurance of mixed capability ADAS and AV vehicles

22.04 ADAS vehicles remain subject to the requirement for compulsory motor liability insurance in RTA 1988, Part VI. The question has arisen as to whether a vehicle with both ADAS and automated driving capabilities must be insured as an automated vehicle, including the cover required by RTA 1988, Part VI as amended by AEVA 2018 for an automated vehicle[5], even if there is no actual use of the automated system. Although there is at present no explicit law on the point, the government's view in April 2021 was that a vehicle which is listed as 'automated' must be insured as an automated vehicle, irrespective of whether automated driving is ever actually used:

'… respondents [*to the government's call for evidence*] expressed concerns about a situation where a vehicle is registered as an Automated Vehicle but the registered keeper has decided not to use the self-driving function or has had it disabled.'

---

4 AV Bill 2023-24 (HL Bill 1), cl 95 (not cl 44(1), as cited in the Explanatory Note at para 228) defines enactment as including 'an enactment comprised in—(a) an Act of the Scottish Parliament, (b) an Act or Measure of Senedd Cymru, (c) subordinate legislation within the meaning of the Interpretation Act 1978 (see section 21(1) of that Act), or (d) any instrument corresponding to such legislation made under an Act of the Scottish Parliament or an Act or Measure of Senedd Cymru;'

5 Eg. AEVA 2018 section 20(1) and paragraph 19(2) of the Schedule, adding RTA 1988, s 145(3A), which extends compulsory cover in relation to automated driving to the insured person (the first person in the insurance context). See Chapter 6, 'insurance'.

'If a vehicle is listed as an 'Automated Vehicle' then it must be insured as an Automated Vehicle, even if the registered keeper has no intention to use it as one.'

'The registered keeper is responsible for ensuring they have a valid insurance policy whether the vehicle is automated or not.'[6]

C 'Keeping' offences and Automated Vehicles

Law Commissions' recommendations of a new authorisation scheme for automated driving systems, leading to the AV Bill 2023-24 (HL Bill 1)

22.05 In their final paper on AV law, the Law Commissions recommended a new scheme of pre- and post-deployment safety assurance for automated vehicles, both before and during their use. In particular, the Law Commissions recommended that the new Act:

'should establish an authorisation scheme for vehicles equipped with ADS features to be used in Great Britain. The scheme should be administered by an authorisation authority'[7]

'should establish an in-use safety assurance scheme which gives an in-use regulator responsibilities to monitor the safety of authorised AVs and investigate infractions involving AVs, and powers to enforce its decisions'[8]

The new Act should empower the in-use regulator

'to impose the following regulatory sanctions:

(1) informal and formal warnings;

(2) civil penalties;

(3) redress orders;

(4) compliance orders;

(5) suspension of authorisation;

(6) recommendation of withdrawal of authorisation; and

(7) recommendation of attendance at a restorative conference.'[9]

Among other matters the regulator should also

---

6 Department for Transport, 'Safe use of automated lane keeping system (ALKS): summary of responses and next steps – moving Britain ahead' (April 2021) chapter 4 ('The Listing Methodology for Automated Vehicles') pages 42 and 43.

7 Law Commissions' final report on automated vehicles, *Automated Vehicles: Joint Report*, Law Com No 404, Scot Law Com No 258 (January 2022), recommendation 9.

8 Law Commissions' final report (above), recommendation 18.

9 Recommendation 24.

'have responsibility for developing and encouraging best practice with regards to ongoing AV cybersecurity. Where a lack of security gives rise to a safety concern, the regulator's powers to deal with safety concerns should apply'[10]

The Law Commissions defined 'user-in-charge' as 'an individual who is in a vehicle and in position to operate the driving controls while a relevant ADS [*automated driving system*] feature is engaged'[11]. In addition to moving offences[12],

'The user-in-charge should continue to be responsible for the following matters which do not arise from dynamic driving:

(1) Duties to carry insurance;

(2) Duties to maintain the vehicle in a roadworthy condition;

(3) Any parking offence which continues after the ADS feature is disengaged;

(4) Duties following accidents to provide information and report accidents;

(5) Duties to ensure that child passengers wear seatbelts;

(6) Duties relating to loading; and

(7) Strategic route planning, including duties to pay tolls and charges.

The new Act should include a regulation-making power to adapt the lists of dynamic and non-dynamic offences in the light of experience, including a power to allocate some or all roadworthiness responsibilities to the ASDE.'[13]

In relation to the operation of unattended passenger vehicles (No User In Charge vehicles, NUICs), the Law Commission made recommendations including the criteria for applying for a NUIC operator licence and safety management systems[14].

In response to the Law Commissions' recommendations, the government agreed that

'an in-use regulatory scheme must be established to ensure self-driving vehicles remain safe and legal throughout their lives and to collect evidence for the overall safety of self-driving compared to conventional driving.'[15]

'An ASDE [*Authorised Self-Driving Entity*] is the organisation that will be held responsible for a vehicle when it is driving itself. An ASDE will need to be registered, considering whether they are suitable to take on responsibility for a vehicle, such as having sufficient financial standing and good repute.'[16]

'We intend to set the following, broad duties on the ASDE:

---

10 Recommendation 33.
11 Recommendation 39.
12 See for example recommendations 40 to 44.
13 Recommendation 45.
14 See recommendations 50 to 64.
15 CAM 2025 (above), p 122.
16 CAM 2025, p 37.

- Ensuring that vehicles drive safely and legally throughout their life (which includes remaining compliant with their authorisation),

- Ensuring cybersecurity,

- Updating the safety case and any assessment of fairness,

- Providing data to the regulator,

- Communicating information to users, owners, and registered keepers,

- Continuing to meet ASDE requirements (such as financial standing and good repute),

- Processing data in compliance with data protection law,

- Collecting, storing, and sharing data to process insurance claims,

- Co-operation with government and other necessary parties.'[17]

Automated vehicle insurance compulsory, even if automated driving is disabled?

22.06   There is no settled law on the point, but the government's view is that an insurance policy fully compliant with RTA 1988, Part VI, including the amendments to that regime made by AEVA 2018 is required at law for use of a vehicle listed (or under AVA 2024 'authorised') as 'automated' under AEVA 2018, whether or not the user of the automated vehicle ever uses automated driving (see above and Chapter 6, 'insurance').

D 'Keeping' offences and Electric Vehicles

Regulatory regime for smaller electric vehicles incomplete

22.07   The requirements of the law in relation to the compulsory insurance of smaller electric vehicles is in a state of flux. Regulation has been delayed by the postponement of the Transport Bill[18]. The lack of a legal regime for e-scooters exemplifies the uncertainty.

There have been reports of prosecutors being uncertain as to the obligations of keepers and riders of smaller electric vehicles.

The lack of a regulatory body has been identified by a coroner[19] as a factor contributing to the death of a 12-year-old child who fell into the path of a bus while riding a trial rental e-scooter which he was not licensed to ride (a requirement of use of a trial e-scooter, not loosened by the e-scooter trial regulations[20]).

---

17 CAM 2025, p 121, described as a 'non-exhaustive list', with a final list to be provided in the Transport Bill.
18 See Chapters 6, 'insurance', and 16, 'smaller electric vehicle claims'.
19 Courts and Tribunals Judiciary website 'Mustafa Nadeem: prevention of future deaths report' (18 July 2023).
20 RTA 1988, s 87, 'drivers of motor vehicles to have driving licences'; Gov.uk 'E-scooter trials: guidance for users' (13 July 2020, updated 17 July 2023). See Chapter 18, 'personal security claims'.

Illegality of use of an electrically powered unicycle 'no merely technical infraction' but an aggravating factor in sentencing

22.08   In *Rex v Tudor Manolache*[21], the Court of Appeal dismissed an appeal against a sentence of 14 months imprisonment on pleas of guilty to causing death by careless driving of an electrically propelled unicycle, a 'Gotway', and for causing death by driving a vehicle without insurance, where no separate penalty was imposed for the second offence. The applicant was riding on a footpath and collided with an elderly pedestrian, Mr Leonard Bailey. The Court of Appeal noted that the unicycle:

'should never have been on a public road. It was capable of speeds of up to 26 mph in testing, although the advertised speed was up to 40 mph when loaded. It was illegal (except on private land) because it was not registered, it was not taxed and it was not insured. There was some evidence that the applicant had been warned about legal restrictions on use when he bought the vehicle.'[22]

The Court of Appeal rejected a submission that '[a]lthough it is accepted that the offence was aggravated by his presence on a path which he had no right to be on, and the lack of insurance or licence, it is said that these factors all flowed from the current classification of his Gotway':

'We disagree. The speed was indeed excessive, but that was not all. It was combined with what the applicant knew to be his dangerous inability to bring the unicycle to a rapid stop, on a path shared with pedestrians, because of the way it was constructed and operated. The applicant was not entitled to assume that pedestrians would be able to jump out of his way. Mr Bailey did in fact try to do that. However, the movement of the Gotway was too rapid and unpredictable for him, and that was to be expected. The illegality of the unicycle was an aggravating factor. To say that this flowed from its classification does not in any way diminish that. This was no merely technical infraction. The applicant's vehicle was completely unfit for driving on a public road or path, as this fatal accident demonstrated only too clearly.'[23]

---

21 [2023] EWCA Crim 1116.
22 Above, at [5].
23 Above, at [14]–[15].

Chapter 23

'Construction' offences

'If the nature of a thing is such that it is reasonably certain to place life and limb in peril when negligently made, it is then a thing of danger. Its nature gives warning of the consequences to be expected.'

Cardozo J (1916)[1]

Chapter Contents

A Outline of 'construction' offences applicable to AAEVs 23.01
B 'Construction' offences and Advanced Driver Assistance Systems (ADAS) 23.04
C 'Construction' offences and Automated Vehicles 23.05
D 'Construction' offences and Electric Vehicles 23.07

A Outline of 'construction' offences applicable to AAEVs

Categorisation of criminal offences for AAEVs in Part III of this book

23.01 As at the time of writing, the criminal law does not yet cater expressly for advanced, automated and electric vehicles (save in relation to the requirement for automated vehicles to be insured within the RTA 1988, Part VI, per AEVA 2018).

The law for ADAS systems and automated vehicles will be progressed when the Automated Vehicles Bill 2023-24 (HL Bill 1) becomes the Automated Vehicles Act 2024 and regulations are made under that Act. See Chapters 2, 'vehicle specifications' and 6, 'insurance'.

The Transport Bill announced in the Queen's Speech in May 2022 to reform the law in relation to smaller electric vehicles including e-scooters has not been published and did not appear in the King's Speech in November 2023. The criminal law in relation to smaller electric vehicles has therefore not been clarified and they remain regulated as motor vehicles (or not, if exempted) under RTA 1988 and its regulations.

---

1 *MacPherson v Buick Motor Company* 217 NY 382, 111 NE 1050 (1916).

This book categorises criminal offences applicable to AAEVs as follows:

1 'Moving' vehicle offences, relating to AAEVs in motion and including offences relating to driving and to the automated and remote operation of vehicles (Chapter 21);

2 'Keeping' offences, relating to criminal sanctions for failure to meet the preconditions of keeping and using a vehicle on the roads such as the provision of compulsory liability insurance (Chapter 22);

3 'Construction' offences, relating to the vehicle features of AAEVs (Chapter 23);

4 'Obstruction' offences, relating to the obstruction of roads by AAEVs (Chapter 24);

5 'Tampering' offences, relating to criminal interference with AAEVs and their systems both inside and outside the vehicle, as well as offences relating to information (Chapter 25).

Prospective offences under the AV Bill 2023-24 (HL Bill 1) are included in these chapters and in the table below.

Scope of this book

23.02   This book does not list all criminal offences applicable to AAEVs. AAEVs are 'vehicles', the criminal offences applicable to them and to their use are voluminous and each case will depend upon its facts. For a study of the whole field of criminal law as it applies to road traffic the reader is referred to specialist works[2]. This book focuses upon existing offences of likely application to AAEVs. It also outlines the reforms proposed by the Law Commissions to such offences.

This chapter discusses category 3, above: **'construction'** offences.

Table summarising main statutory 'construction' vehicle offences and proposed offences under the AV Bill 2023-24 (HL Bill 1)

23.03

Act/Regs	Provision	Description
Health and Safety at Work Act 1974	s 33	Offences under HSWA 1974, s 33, including both HSWA 1974 duties to employees and others[3] and duties under health and safety regulations, eg. (if a system fits definition of 'guided transport'[4]) duties under the Railways and other Guided Transport Systems (Safety) Regulations 2006.

---

2 See for example *Wilkinson's Road Traffic Offences* (30th edn, 2021), *Blackstone's Criminal Practice* and *A Practical Approach to Road Traffic Law*, Susan Cavender and Alistair Haggerty (Bloomsbury, 2023).
3 HSWA 1974, s 2, 3. See s 33 for offences under the Act.
4 RoGTS(S)R 2006, SI 2006/599 (as amended), reg 2: 'a system of transport, used wholly or mainly for the carriage of passengers, employing vehicles which for some or all of the time when they are in operation are guided by means of (a) rails, beams, slots, guides or other apparatus, structures or devices which are fixed and not part of the vehicle; or (b) a guidance system which is automatic'.

Act/Regs	Provision	Description
RTA 1988	s 23	No person in addition to driver of motor bicycle may be carried otherwise than sitting astride the motor cycle and on a proper seat securely fixed to the motor cycle behind the driver's seat.
RTA 1988; CUR 1986[5]	CUR 1986, reg 41 or 42	Construction regulations under CUR 1986, eg. maintenance and use of vehicle so as not to be a danger[6]; carrying passenger on motorcycle without suitable supports or rests for the feet of passenger[7]; prohibition of cathode ray tube television visible by driver showing unpermitted matters[8].
	s 63	Using or causing or permitting a vehicle or vehicle part to be used on a road without required type approval certificates
	s 65	Supplying a vehicle or vehicle part without required type approval certificates
	s 75	Vehicles not to be sold in unroadworthy condition or altered so as to be unroadworthy
	s 76	Fitting and supply of defective or unsuitable vehicle parts
Vehicle Excise and Registration Act 1994	s 42	Not fixing registration mark on vehicle
	s 43	Obscured registration mark
	s 59	Failure to fit registration mark complying with regulations as to size, shape and character of registration marks per regulations made under VERA 1994, s 23(4)(a)[9]
Automated Vehicles Act 2024 (**not yet enacted**; *sections quoted as clause numbers in AV Bill 2023-24, HL Bill 1*)	Cl 56	Amendment of RTA 1988, s 76 (above) to include software and installation of software.

---

5   Road Vehicles (Construction and Use) Regulations 1986, SI 1986/1078 (as amended).
6   CUR 1986, reg 100.
7   CUR 1986, reg 102. And see the definition of an electric scooter as 'a vehicle which … is designed to carry no more than one person': Road Vehicle (Registration and Licensing) Regulations 2002, SI 2002/2742, reg 33(1A)(d), as amended by the Electric Scooter Trials and Traffic Signs (Coronavirus) Regulations and General Directions 2020, regulation 2(3). See Chapter 16, 'smaller electric vehicle claims'.
8   CUR 1986, reg 109, as amended by Road Vehicles (Construction and Use) (Automated Vehicles) Order 2022, SI 2022/470, in force from 1 July 2022 (art 1(1)): see Chapter 2, 'specifications'.
9   Road Vehicles (Display of Registration Marks) Regulations 2001, SI 2001/561, regs 14 ('size and spacing of characters') and 14A ('size and spacing of characters: special cases'). See Chapter 16, 'smaller electric vehicle claims'.

Act/Regs	Provision	Description
	Cl 78	Offence of using terms restricted to an authorised automated vehicle which are not appropriate
	Cl 79	Offence in relation to communications likely to confuse as to autonomous capability
	Cl 80	Liability of corporate officers etc for offences under cll 78 and 79
	Cl 91	Provision for updating of type approval legislation for driver assistance and automated vehicles

B 'Construction' offences and Advanced Driver Assistance Systems (ADAS)

Construction regulations amended incrementally for ADAS

23.04 Devices to perform advanced functions in vehicles have been regulated incrementally by amendment of the Road Vehicles (Construction and Use) Regulations 1986 (CUR 1986)[10]. In particular, CUR 1986, reg 110 has been amended to permit the use of a hand-held mobile telephone for remote parking and contactless payments.

The Administrative Court has held that the use of a hand-held mobile telephone within a car to operate the car's music system via Bluetooth is 'interactive communication' between devices amounting to an offence under CUR 1986, reg 110[11].

The AV Bill 2023-24 (HL Bill 1), while still allowing for secondary legislation to govern type approval of ADAS systems, nevertheless focuses upon ADAS regulation by the power to update assimilated type approval legislation for both automated and driver assistance systems under cl 91(1).

C 'Construction' offences and Automated Vehicles

CUR 1986 amended in preparation for automated vehicles

23.05 CUR 1986, reg 109(1) has been amended in preparation for listing or authorisation[12] of the first automated vehicles to permit a driver 'to see ... information ... of any sort...' displayed on a built-in screen in an automated vehicle driving itself within the meaning of the AEVA 2018, s 8(1)(a) providing that the vehicle is not requesting the driver to take back control[13]. The amendment came

---

10 SI 1986/1078.
11 *Bendt v Crown Prosecution Service* [2022] EWHC 502 (Admin); [2022] RTR 17.
12 Under AEVA 2018, s 1 or, when enacted, the authorisation process in AVA 2024.
13 Road Vehicles (Construction and Use) (Automated Vehicles) Order 2022, SI 2022/470, art 3 (in force from 1 July 2022), per the Law Commissions' final report on automated vehicles, *Automated Vehicles: Joint Report*, Law Com No 404, Scot Law Com No 258 (January 2022), p 51-52, in particular 3.76-77 and recommendation 4.

into force on 1 July 2022[14], so will come into immediate practical effect upon listing or classification of the first automated vehicle.

The AV Bill 2023-24, once enacted as AVA 2024, will allow other regulation-making powers, eg. to update assimilated type approval legislation under cl 91.

Law Commission proposals for automated vehicle construction offences leading to the AV Bill 2023-24 (HL Bill 1)

23.06   In their final report, the Law Commissions recommended that:

'The Secretary of State for Transport should establish a domestic AV technical approval scheme to approve vehicles with ADS features which do not have UNECE[15] approvals and which are intended for use on GB roads.'[16]

'The new Act should establish an authorisation scheme for vehicles equipped with ADS features to be used in Great Britain. The scheme should be administered by an authorisation authority.'[17]

'The authorisation authority should assess each ADS feature in relation to the vehicle with which it is presented. If authorisation is granted, it should state whether each ADS feature is authorised for use with or without a user-in-charge.'[18]

'The authorisation authority should provide guidelines on the information to be included in the [*Authorised Self-Driving Entity's*][19] safety case and equality impact assessments, and assess both documents as part of authorisation.'[20]

'The in-use regulator should be given powers to collect relevant data from ASDEs and NUIC [*No User in Charge vehicle*[21]] operators so as to allow the regulator to compare the safety of automated and conventional vehicles.'[22]

'It should be a criminal offence to engage in a commercial practice in connection with driving automation technology designed for use on roads or in public places if the commercial practice uses:

(1) the terms 'self-drive', 'self-driving', 'drive itself', 'driverless' and 'automated vehicle';

---

14 Road Vehicles (Construction and Use) (Automated Vehicles) Order 2022, SI 2022/470, art 1.
15 United Nations Economic Commission for Europe. See Chapters 2, 'specifications' and Appendix, 'History', 1947.
16 Law Commissions' final AV law report (January 2022, above), recommendation 8.
17 Above, recommendation 9.
18 Recommendation 11.
19 ASDE: 'the entity that puts an AV forward for authorisation as having self-driving features. It may be the vehicle manufacturer, or a software designer, or a joint venture between the two': Law Commissions' final AV law report (January 2022, above) at p xvii and Chapter 5.
20 Above, recommendation 15.
21 NUIC vehicle: 'a vehicle equipped with one or more ADS [*automated driving system*] features designed to perform the entire dynamic driving task without a user-in-charge': above, p xix.
22 Recommendation 20.

(2) any other terms prescribed by the Secretary of State for Transport by regulations; or

(3) any symbol or kitemark approved by the authorisation authority to identify authorised ADS features;

unless the driving automation technology is specified as a self-driving feature by the authorisation authority under the authorisation scheme recommended in this report.

The offence should not be committed if the only use of the driving automation technology is by a person who, as part of their employment, test drives vehicles equipped with driving automation technologies (a 'safety driver').'[23]

'It should be a criminal offence to:

(1) engage in a commercial practice;

(2) which creates a likelihood of confusion among the public (or a part of the public) licensed to drive;

(3) over whether a driving automation technology needs to be monitored when used on a road or public place;

(4) when that driving automation technology has not been specified as a self-driving feature by the authorisation authority.'[24]

'A due diligence defence should be available in respect of both offences (recommendations 34 and 35) if:

(1) the commercial practice giving rise to the offence was engaged in from outside Great Britain; and

(2) the person engaging in the commercial practice took all reasonable precautions and exercised due diligence to prevent drivers in Great Britain from being misled.'[25]

'The new Act should give the enforcement agency powers to accept voluntary undertakings and to apply to a court for civil enforcement orders in respect of both offences (recommendations 34 and 35).'[26]

'The new Act should require the Secretary of State for Transport to nominate an enforcement agency responsible for pursuing civil enforcement and preventing the offending conduct.'[27]

(Recommendation 65 set out the 'duty of candour' criminal offences described in Chapter 25, 'tampering offences'.)

---

23 Recommendation 34.
24 Recommendation 35.
25 Recommendation 36.
26 Recommendation 37.
27 Recommendation 38.

The government agreed with the recommendations for pre and post-deployment safety regulation of AVs, particularly 'that an in-use regulatory scheme must be established to ensure self-driving vehicles remain safe and legal throughout their lives and to collect evidence for the overall safety of self-driving compared to conventional driving'[28].

The government stated that it would 'consult further' on the 'implications … of a broad power' to collect data[29]. As to recommendation 37:

'More details … on enforcement agency powers will be available as the Bill goes to Parliament and thinking is on-going as to how to meet Recommendation 38 on nominating an enforcement agency.'[30]

As to organisational liability, the government proposed:

'to set the following, broad duties on the ASDE:

- Ensuring that vehicles drive safely and legally throughout their life (which includes remaining compliant with their authorisation),

- Ensuring cybersecurity,

- Updating the safety case and any assessment of fairness,

- Providing data to the regulator,

- Communicating information to users, owners, and registered keepers,

- Continuing to meet ASDE requirements (such as financial standing and good repute),

- Processing data in compliance with data protection law,

- Collecting, storing, and sharing data to process insurance claims,

- Co-operation with government and other necessary parties.'[31]

The government supported criminal liability for misdescription of AV capabilities, though with the protection restricted to consumers:

'[the government] would not wish these new offences to apply to interactions between businesses. A business that will not use the vehicle, but may be intending to seek authorisation in the future, is not at risk of using a vehicle unsafely'[32].

That is reflected in the AV Bill 2023-24 cl 81(1) definition of 'end-user'.

---

28 UK government policy paper 'Connected and automated mobility 2025: realising the benefits of self-driving vehicles' ('CAM 2025'), 19 August 2022, p 122.
29 CAM 2025 p 122, re recommendation 20 (above).
30 CAM 2025 p 124.
31 CAM 2025, p 121, described as a 'non-exhaustive list', with a final list to be provided in the Transport Bill.
32 CAM 2025, p 123.

D 'Construction' offences and Electric Vehicles

Widespread use of smaller electric vehicles and lack of current regulatory regime

23.07 No broader Transport Bill having been published since its announcement in the Queen's Speech in May 2022, there is still no permanent regulatory regime for smaller electric vehicles. Current law sets requirements which cannot practically be met by many smaller electric vehicles in common use, even if they were to obtain type approval (for example, requirements as to the size of registration marks[33]).

While many privately-owned smaller electric vehicles may lack type approval, making their use an offence[34], the reality is that numerous such vehicles are in public use. Powers to stem their sale and supply are already in existence[35]. Conditions for the use of e-scooters on a trial basis in certain areas exist[36], but in the absence of a Transport Bill the regulatory approach to such vehicles in the longer term is unknown.

There have been reports of uncertainty as to the law of smaller electric vehicles among prosecutors. A coroner has sought clarification from the Secretary of State for Transport and others in relation to the lack of a regulatory body for e-scooters, after the death of a 12-year-old boy who was able to access a trial e-scooter despite his age and lack of the requisite driving licence[37.]

---

33 Road Vehicles (Display of Registration Marks) Regulations 2001, SI 2001/561, regs 14 ('size and spacing of characters') and 14A ('size and spacing of characters: special cases'). See Chapter 16, 'smaller electric vehicle claims'.
34 RTA 1988, s 63.
35 RTA 1988, s 75, 76.
36 See Chapters 3, 'testing' and 16, 'smaller electric vehicle claims'.
37 Courts and Tribunals Judiciary website 'Mustafa Nadeem: prevention of future deaths report' (18 July 2023).

'Obstruction' offences

'The offences [of unlawfully obstructing railways, in the Offences against the Person Act 1861] were created at a time when the railway was the only form of fast transport. There are now other forms of fast transport.'

The Criminal Law Revision Committee (1980)[1]

Chapter Contents

A Outline of 'obstruction' offences applicable to AAEVs

Categorisation of criminal offences for AAEVs in Part III of this book

24.01   As at the time of writing, the criminal law does not yet cater expressly for advanced, automated and electric vehicles (save in relation to the requirement for automated vehicles to be insured within the RTA 1988, Part VI, per AEVA 2018).

The law for ADAS systems and automated vehicles will be progressed when the Automated Vehicles Bill 2023-24 (HL Bill 1) is enacted (subject to amendments) as the Automated Vehicles Act 2024 and regulations are made under that Act. See Chapters 2, 'vehicle specifications' and 6, 'insurance'.

The Transport Bill announced in the Queen's Speech in May 2022 to reform the law in relation to smaller electric vehicles including e-scooters has not been published and did not appear in the King's Speech in November 2023. The criminal law in relation to smaller electric vehicles has therefore not been clarified and they

---

1   *Criminal Law Revision Committee's 14th Report, Offences against the Person* (1980, Cmnd 7844) at para 195, quoted in *R v Meeking* [2012] EWCA Crim 641; [2012] 1 WLR 3349, 3352 (by Toulson LJ, as he then was).

remain regulated as motor vehicles (or not, if exempted) under RTA 1988 and its regulations.

This book categorises criminal offences applicable to AAEVs as follows:

1. 'Moving' vehicle offences, relating to AAEVs in motion and including offences relating to driving and to the automated and remote operation of vehicles (Chapter 21);

2. 'Keeping' offences, relating to criminal sanctions for failure to meet the pre-conditions of keeping and using a vehicle on the roads such as the provision of compulsory liability insurance (Chapter 22);

3. 'Construction' offences, relating to the vehicle features of AAEVs (Chapter 23);

4. 'Obstruction' offences, relating to the obstruction of roads by AAEVs (Chapter 24);

5. 'Tampering' offences, relating to criminal interference with AAEVs and their systems both inside and outside the vehicle, as well as offences relating to information (Chapter 25).

Scope of this book

24.02   This book does not list all criminal offences applicable to AAEVs. AAEVs are 'vehicles', the criminal offences applicable to them and to their use are voluminous and each case will depend upon its facts. For a study of the whole field of criminal law as it applies to road traffic the reader is referred to specialist works[2]. This book focuses upon existing offences of likely application to AAEVs.

This chapter discusses category 4, above: **'obstruction'** offences.

Please see Chapter 21, 'moving' offences, for an outline of the Law Commissions' work in the consultations on automated driving (2018 to 2022) and remote driving (2022 to 2023) leading to the AV Bill 2023-24 (HL Bill 1).

Table summarising main statutory 'obstruction' vehicle offences and proposed offences under the AV Bill 2023-24 (HL Bill 1)

24.03

Act/Regs	Provision	Description
RTA 1988	s 22	Leaving vehicle in dangerous position
	s 22A	Causing danger to road users
	s 35	Refusing to comply with the instructions of a constable

---

2   See for example *Wilkinson's Road Traffic Offences* (30th edn, 2021), *Blackstone's Criminal Practice* and Susan Cavender and Alistair Haggerty *A Practical Approach to Road Traffic Law* (Bloomsbury, 2023).

Act/Regs	Provision	Description
RTA 1988; Road Vehicles (Construction and Use) Regulations 1986[3]	s 42; reg 103	Causing or permitting a motor vehicle or trailer to stand on a road so as to cause any unnecessary obstruction of the road
Police, Crime, Sentencing and Courts Act 2022	s 78	Intentionally or recklessly causing public nuisance
Automated Vehicles Act 2024 (**not yet enacted**; *sections quoted as clause numbers in AV Bill 2023-24, HL Bill 1*)	Cl 48(3)	Loss of immunity from criminal liability of user-in-charge of automated vehicle for parking offence if UIC voluntarily departs vehicle
	Cl 54(2)	Addition of new RTA 1988, s 22B (see s 22A above) to include '…the conduct constituting that offence causes an authorised automated vehicle to commit a traffic infraction'

B   'Obstruction' offences and Advanced Driver Assistance Systems (ADAS)

Law Commission's recommendations for remote driving offences

24.04   The Law Commission highlighted the obstruction risks of loss of connectivity between a vehicle and its remote operator, including the risk of obstruction to emergency vehicles[4]. The Law Commission recommended that an ERDO[5] be required as a condition of its licence (among other duties):

'(1) to ensure that the driver is able to drive safely by:

    (a)   taking reasonable care that connectivity is suitable;

    (b)   ensuring that in the absence of connectivity or driver input, the vehicle comes to a safe stop;

    …

(6)   not to impede traffic flow (for example by ensuring that vehicles are not left in inappropriate places)'[6]

---

3   SI 1986/1078, 'CUR 1986'.

4   The Law Commission of England and Wales, 'Remote Driving: Advice to government' (February 2023), p 62, 7.8(2), at www.lawcom.gov.uk/project/remote-driving.

5   'Entity for Remote Driving Operation': a new term coined by the Law Commission 'to describe a licensed organisation that employs remote drivers and is subject to a range of statutory duties' (February 2023 advice to government on remote driving, p vii).

6   The Law Commission of England and Wales, 'Remote Driving: Advice to government' (February 2023, above), p 72, 8.45.

The Law Commission (altering its earlier view in the remote driving issues paper) concluded that such duties should be regulatory and the subject of regulatory sanctions[7] (and should not themselves be the basis of a civil claim for breach of statutory duty[8]). As the law stands, criminal liability might also result from an obstruction (see table above).

As an interim measure for the regulation of remotely driven vehicles, the Law Commission proposed:

> 'a new construction and use regulation to prohibit beyond line-of-sight remote driving without an in-vehicle safety driver. The regulation would apply unless the organisation obtains a Vehicle Special Order.'[9]

C 'Obstruction' offences and Automated Vehicles

Law Commission proposals for automated vehicle offences leading to the AV Bill 2023–24 (HL Bill 1)

24.05 The Law Commissions made similar recommendations in relation to obstruction risks of automated vehicles[10] as the Law Commission of England and Wales later made in relation to remotely driven vehicles (above). They also jointly recommended, as a condition of their licensing, sharing of relevant data by ASDEs[11] and NUICOs[12]:

> 'with local transport authorities, police and emergency services, where necessary for the purposes of improving traffic flow or responding to emergency situations or dealing with road rule infractions.'[13]

In response to the Law Commissions' recommendations, the government agreed that

> 'an in-use regulatory scheme must be established to ensure self-driving vehicles remain safe and legal throughout their lives and to collect evidence for the overall safety of self-driving compared to conventional driving.'[14]

---

7   Above, p 73, 8.50.

8   The Law Commission's view was that this might fall within AEVA 2018 s 2.

9   The Law Commission of England and Wales, 'Remote Driving: Advice to government' (February 2023, above), p 49, 5.3. See Chapter 3, 'testing' and the proposed offence under AV Bill 2023-24 (HL Bill 1), cl 53 (RTA 1988, s 34B).

10 Law Commissions' final report on automated vehicles, *Automated Vehicles: Joint Report*, Law Com No 404, Scot Law Com No 258 (January 2022), p 185, 9.111(5), p 190, 9.139 and p 202, 10.52 in relation to trials.

11 ASDE: Authorised Self-Driving Entity: 'the vehicle manufacturer or software developer who puts an [*automated vehicle*] forward for authorisation as having self-driving features': Law Commissions' Final report on automated vehicles (January 2022, above), p 20, 2.41.

12 NUICO: 'No user in charge [vehicle] operator' (Law Commission Remote Driving Advice at p 4, 1.15(7)), ie. operator of fully automated vehicles.

13 Law Commissions' final report on automated vehicles (January 2022, above), p 86, 5.96(4) and recommendations 54 and 55. See Chapters 25, 'tampering offences' and 26, 'public laws of data and privacy' which deal with the information provisions of the AV Bill 2023-24 (HL Bill 1).

14 UK government policy paper 'Connected and automated mobility 2025: realising the benefits of self-driving vehicles' ('CAM 2025'), 19 August 2022, p 122.

The government intended 'to set ... broad duties on the ASDE', including 'Ensuring that vehicles drive safely and legally throughout their life (which includes remaining compliant with their authorisation)' and 'Co-operation with government and other necessary parties.'[15]

D 'Obstruction' offences and Electric Vehicles

Police, Crime, Sentencing and Courts Act 2022, s 78: 'intentionally or recklessly causing public nuisance'

24.06 The offence is subject to a defence of 'reasonable excuse for the act or omission': PCSCA 2022, s 78(3). Given the breadth of the new offence, there is a query as to whether it would apply to an accidental but allegedly 'reckless' halt of a vehicle on a motorway (eg. by loss of power), thereby causing a risk of or actual 'serious harm' or 'obstruction' under s 78(1)(b).

Smaller electric rental vehicles

24.07 Smaller electric rental vehicles (such as e-scooters and e-bikes) are capable of causing an obstruction, particularly 'dockless' rental vehicles left for the next hirer in a public space. Local authorities publish their own guidance to operators[16] and some authorities are introducing parking bays for dockless rental bikes[17]. Government guidance to operators of e-scooter trials[18] recommends that:

> 'Local authorities and operators should review current safety measures and consider improvements including:
>
> ...
>
> • parking incentives and penalties
>
> • improved geofencing (including reducing the complexity of geofencing for users)'

---

15 CAM 2025, p 121, described as a 'non-exhaustive list', with a final list to be provided in the Transport Bill.

16 See, for example, Dockless bike share code of practice for operators in London (Mayor of London and Transport for London, September 2018), section 8, 'Parking'.

17 See for example Lewisham Council website article 'Lewisham agrees new dockless bike partnership with Lime' (18 September 2023).

18 UK government 'Guidance: E-scooter trials: guidance for local authorities and rental operators' (updated 22 February 2022)

Chapter 25

'Tampering' offences

'The potential for interference with automated vehicles (AVs) is a matter of great public concern. Interferences with AVs could range from computer hacking, to standing in front of an AV to obstruct its movement, to spray-painting the vehicle's sensors.'

The Law Commission of England and Wales
and the Scottish Law Commission (2022)[1]

A Outline of 'tampering' offences applicable to AAEVs

Categorisation of criminal offences for AAEVs in Part III of this book

25.01   As at the time of writing, the criminal law does not yet cater expressly for advanced, automated and electric vehicles (save in relation to the requirement for automated vehicles to be insured within the RTA 1988, Part VI, per AEVA 2018).

The law for ADAS systems and automated vehicles will be progressed when the Automated Vehicles Bill 2023-24 (HL Bill 1) is enacted (subject to amendments) as the Automated Vehicles Act 2024 and regulations are made under that Act. See Chapters 2, 'vehicle specifications' and 6, 'insurance'.

The Transport Bill announced in the Queen's Speech in May 2022 to reform the law in relation to smaller electric vehicles including e-scooters has not been published and did not appear in the King's Speech in November 2023. The criminal law in relation to smaller electric vehicles has therefore not been clarified and they

---

1   Law Commissions' final report on automated vehicles, *Automated Vehicles: Joint Report*, Law Com No 404, Scot Law Com No 258 (January 2022), p 227, 12.1.

remain regulated as motor vehicles (or not, if exempted) under RTA 1988 and its regulations.

This book categorises criminal offences applicable to AAEVs as follows:

1. 'Moving' vehicle offences, relating to AAEVs in motion and including offences relating to driving and to the automated and remote operation of vehicles (Chapter 21);

2. 'Keeping' offences, relating to criminal sanctions for failure to meet the pre-conditions of keeping and using a vehicle on the roads such as the provision of compulsory liability insurance (Chapter 22);

3. 'Construction' offences, relating to the vehicle features of AAEVs (Chapter 23);

4. 'Obstruction' offences, relating to the obstruction of roads by AAEVs (Chapter 24);

5. 'Tampering' offences, relating to criminal interference with AAEVs and their systems both inside and outside the vehicle, as well as offences relating to information (Chapter 25).

Scope of this book

25.02   This book does not list all criminal offences applicable to AAEVs. AAEVs are 'vehicles', the criminal offences applicable to them and to their use are voluminous and each case will depend upon its facts. For a study of the whole field of criminal law as it applies to road traffic the reader is referred to specialist works[2]. This book focuses upon existing offences of likely application to AAEVs.

This chapter discusses category 5, above: **'tampering'** offences.

Please see Chapter 21, 'moving' offences, for an outline of the Law Commissions' work in the consultations on automated driving (2018 to 2022) and remote driving (2022 to 2023) leading to the AV Bill 2023-24 (HL Bill 1).

Provisional categorisation of AAEV 'tampering' offences

25.03   In the AAEV context, 'tampering' offences might be categorised provisionally as follows:

1   Tampering with the vehicle (which can be by means internal or external to the vehicle[3]);

2   Tampering with related equipment (which includes traffic equipment[4], computers[5] and an electronic system[6]);

---

2 See for example *Wilkinson's Road Traffic Offences* (30th edn, 2021), *Blackstone's Criminal Practice* and Susan Cavender and Alistair Haggerty *A Practical Approach to Road Traffic Law* (Bloomsbury, 2023).
3 *R v Meeking* [2012] EWCA Crim 641; [2012] 1 WLR 3349.
4 RTA 1988, s 22A(1)(c).
5 Computer Misuse Act 1990.
6 Terrorism Act 2000, s 1(2)(e).

3 Tampering with data (which could mean interference with data[7] or restricting access to data[8]).

Table summarising main statutory 'tampering' vehicle offences and proposed offences under the AV Bill 2023–24 (HL Bill 1)

25.04

Act/Regs	Provision	Description
Theft Act 1968	s 12	Taking motor vehicle or other conveyance without authority
RTA 1988	s 22A	Causing danger to road users (by interfering with a motor vehicle, trailer or cycle or with traffic equipment)
	s 25	Tampering with motor vehicle 'while a motor vehicle is on a road or on a parking place provided by a local authority'
Computer Misuse Act 1990	s 1	Unauthorised access to computer material
	s 2	Unauthorised access with intent to commit or facilitate commission of further offences
	s 3	Unauthorised acts with intent to impair, or with recklessness as to impairing, operation of computer, etc
	s 3ZA	Unauthorised acts causing, or creating risk of, serious damage
	s 3A	Making, supplying or obtaining articles for use in offence under s 1, 3 or 3ZA
Terrorism Act 2000	s 1	Definition of terrorism includes use or threat of action 'designed seriously to interfere with or seriously to disrupt an electronic system'[9]
Data Protection Act 2018	s 119	Offences of obstructing or without reasonable excuse refusing assistance to Commissioner inspecting data where necessary to discharge an international obligation of the UK
	s 132	Offences by Commissioner or member of Commissioner's staff relating to confidentiality
	s 144	False statements made in response to Commissioner's information notices[10]

---

7 DPA 2018, s 170, 171, 173.
8 DPA 2018, s 119, 144, 148, 184.
9 TA 2000, s 1(1)(e).
10 See DPA 2018, s 142, 'information notices'.

Act/Regs	Provision	Description
	s 148	Destroying or falsifying information after a person has been given an information notice or assessment notice[11]
	s 170	Unlawful obtaining of personal data
	s 171	Re-identification of de-identified personal data
	s 173	Alteration etc of personal data to prevent disclosure to data subject
	s 184	Offences of requiring certain 'relevant records'[12] in connection with certain employment matters or a contract for the provision of services or the provision of goods to that person
Automated Vehicles Act 2024 (**not yet enacted**; *sections quoted as clause numbers in AV Bill 2023-24, HL Bill 1*)	Cl 20	Offences of non-compliance with notices for information or interview by a body regulated within the automated vehicles regulatory scheme[13]
	Cll 24-25	Offences relating to information about safety[14]
	Cl 42(4)	Offence of disclosure of information in certain provisions of AVA 2024, Part 1 to unpermitted person or for unpermitted purpose[15]
	Cl 45, Sch 2, para 1	Amendment of Theft Act 1968, s 12 (above) to extend 'conveyance' to include authorised automated vehicle
	Cl 48(5)-(6)	Loss of immunity from criminal liability of user-in-charge of automated vehicle for UIC feature used outside its authorisation as result of deliberate interference with equipment by or with knowledge of UIC
	Cl 54(2)	Addition of new RTA 1988, s 22B (see s 22A above) to include '...the conduct constituting that offence causes an authorised automated vehicle to commit a traffic infraction'
	Cl 55	Amendment of RTA 1988, s 25 (above) to include in definition of mechanism of vehicle any automated or driver-assistance equipment, software and electronic information.

---

11 See DPA 2018, s 146, 'assessment notices'.
12 See DPA 2018, Sch 18, 'relevant records', which include certain health records (see Sch 18 para 1 and 2).
13 See Chapter 26, 'public law of data and privacy'.
14 As above.
15 As above.

Act/Regs	Provision	Description
	Cl 73(5)	Offence by inspector and others against protection of information[16]
	Cl 88(6)	Offence by recipient of information in relation to information-sharing condition of automated passenger service permit[17]

B 'Tampering' offences and Advanced Driver Assistance Systems (ADAS)

Extent of 'tampering' offence revisions of AV Bill 2023-24 (HL Bill 1) to RTA 1988, ss 22A and 25

25.05 The Law Commissions' proposals for reform of tampering laws in relation to automated vehicles were, it indicated, also applicable to ADAS vehicles. In relation to the suggested reform of the aggravated offence under RTA 1988, s 22A to bring it into accordance with Scots law, the Law Commissions acknowledged the force of the argument that such reform should apply to all vehicles:

'Although conventional vehicles are outside our terms of reference we see merit in extending the aggravated offence under section 22A to conventional vehicles and would urge the Government to consider this option.'[18]

The government response was against that proposal: other than agreeing to legislate to extend the application of RTA 1988, s 25 to 'to anything that is physically part of an automated vehicle, including sensors, and any software installed within it' (Law Commissions' recommendation 66, below), the government stated that 'no other offence will be extended beyond self-driving vehicles'[19].

This is reflected in the AV Bill 2023-24 (HL Bill 1), cl 55 (above), which applies to RTA 1988, s 25 but not s 22A.

C 'Tampering' offences and Automated Vehicles

Law Commissions' recommendations leading to AV Bill 2023-24 (HL Bill 1)

25.06 In their final report the Law Commissions made four recommendations in relation to wrongful interference:

'Legislative amendment should clarify that the tampering offence in section 25 of the Road Traffic Act 1988 applies to anything that is physically part of

---

16 As above.
17 As above.
18 Law Commissions' final AV report (above), p 237, 12.53.
19 UK government policy paper 'Connected and automated mobility 2025: realising the benefits of self-driving vehicles' ('CAM 2025'), 19 August 2022, p 125.

an automated vehicle, including sensors, and any software installed within it.'[20]

'The offence of taking a conveyance without authority under section 12 of the Theft Act 1968 should cover all motor vehicles'[21], '(not just those constructed for the carriage of people and with a driving seat.)'[22], so as to cover remotely-driven and automated delivery vehicles[23].

In accordance with Scots law[24], 'in England and Wales it should be an aggravated offence to wrongfully interfere with an AV, the road, or traffic equipment contrary to section 22A of the Road Traffic Act 1988, where the interference results in an AV causing death or serious injury.'[25]

'The mental element for the aggravated offence under section 22A should be intention to interfere with a vehicle, the road or traffic equipment.'[26], so as to remove the problem of the 'uncertain boundaries' of unlawful act manslaughter and gross negligence manslaughter pointed out by the Court of Appeal in *R v Meeking*[27].

As to tampering with infrastructure, the Law Commissions' view was that was adequately covered by existing offences[28].

The government's response to the Law Commissions' recommendations was as follows:

'We support the Commissions' recommendations relating to wrongful interference. We intend for recommendation 66 [*the tampering offence in section 25 of the Road Traffic Act 1988 applies to anything that is physically part of an automated vehicle, including sensors, and any software installed within it*] to be addressed as part of the forthcoming Transport Bill but will apply more broadly than just self-driving vehicles. More details will be available as the Bill enters Parliament.

'Further details of the other amendments to existing tampering and interference offences will also be available as the Bill enters Parliament, though no other offence will be extended beyond self-driving vehicles.'[29]

As to the information offences, the government agreed:

'with the Commissions' sixty fifth recommendation on the new duty of candour offences. It is important that, with the asymmetry of information inherent to this nascent technology, government has a final resort to penalise

---

20 Law Commissions' final AV report (above), recommendation 66.
21 Recommendation 67.
22 Law Commissions' Final AV Report (above), p 228, 12.5.
23 Above, p 231, 12.24.
24 Above, p 228, 12.5.
25 Recommendation 68.
26 Recommendation 69.
27 Law Commissions' Final AV Report (above), p 236, 12.48.
28 Above, p 231, 12.20-12.21.
29 CAM 2025 (above), p125.

ASDEs[30] and NUiC operators who fail to disclose, or mislead in the disclosure of, safety-relevant or operational information. We expect prosecutions to be very rare as the industry has expressed a strong desire to cooperate with government on the safety of self-driving vehicles.'[31]

The proposed additions of the AV Bill 2023-24 (HL Bill 1) are set out in the table above.

D 'Tampering' offences and Electric Vehicles

Rental smaller electric vehicles

25.07 A coroner has highlighted the use of rental e-scooters by people unlicensed to use them, in the context of the death in a road traffic collision of a 12-year-old boy riding a trial rental e-scooter, including evidence that payment could be made on the rental system using a child's bank account and that 'despite education and the facts of this death being known, children from the same school and other schools continued to use hire e-scooters illegally.'[32]

---

30 Authorised Self-Driving Entity: 'the vehicle manufacturer or software developer who puts an [*automated vehicle*] forward for authorisation as having self-driving features': Law Commissions' Final AV report (above), p 20, 2.41.
31 CAM 2025 (above), p 125.
32 Courts and Tribunals Judiciary website 'Mustafa Nadeem: prevention of future deaths report' (18 July 2023).

Part IV

Public law

Chapter 26

Data and privacy law

'In a world where global trade was coming to depend on the use of computers, and where the movement and manipulation of information was necessary for the healthy expansion of the global economy, threats [*from the 1970s onwards*] to restrict data exchange on the grounds of concern for personal privacy were taken extremely seriously. International organisations moved to deal with these problems and develop instruments designed to reconcile the twin aims of respect for personal privacy and the need to ensure free trade between nations.'

Rosemary Jay (2020)[1]

'It is vital that people have confidence in the relevant technology doing what it is supposed to, and that means the whole ecosystem of surveillance cameras and biometrics, not simply novel offshoots of it. More practically, it also means having equal confidence that the operators of those systems are doing what they are supposed to do; it means understanding the purposes for which the technology is being used, who authorised it and how they arrived at their decision that it was lawful and proportionate to do so in each case. And finally it means having clearly defined, published, accessible and intelligible policies publicly setting out the parameters, policies that will be regularly reviewed in light of experience.'

Professor Fraser Sampson (2022)[2]

'Data is changing the world and has become a new kind of infrastructure.'

Department for Transport (2023)[3]

Chapter Contents

---

1   Rosemary Jay, *Data Protection Law and Practice* (Sweet & Maxwell, 5th edn, 2020), 1-008.
2   Letter from the Biometrics and Surveillance Camera Commissioner to the ICO25 consultation team, 26 September 2022
3   Department for Transport policy paper 'Transport Data Strategy: Innovation through data' (28 March 2023), page 6.

A Outline of data protection and privacy laws affecting AAEVs

Significance of data protection and privacy laws to AAEVs

26.01 Data is an essential tool for transport and road planning. There are practical challenges to its use to modernise transport networks. For example:

> 'It is difficult for innovators to find out what data is available and under what conditions it can be accessed and used, as transport data can be fragmented – Traffic Regulation Orders data, for example, is held by over 150 [*local authorities*] in different formats and not all data is stored digitally.'[4]

Data is just as essential to the regulatory infrastructure, and to those providing and receiving services while using vehicles. It is essential to:

- the system of vehicle authorisation, safety monitoring and automated passenger service licensing set out in the Automated Vehicles Bill 2023-24 (HL Bill 1), hence the information requirements, protections and offences in that Bill[5];

- the effective provision and operation of a compulsory motor insurance scheme[6], especially by its usefulness to insurers and to courts to resolve liability issues[7]. The accessibility of relevant data to parties to litigation is likely to become an increasingly common feature of road traffic accident claims, as data systems available to vehicle users, to vehicle manufacturers and to public authorities become more widespread[8];

- the safe operation of advanced and automated systems dependent upon accurate navigation, hence the proposed power of the Secretary of State to require a traffic regulation authority to provide information about traffic regulation measures (AV Bill 2023-24 (HL Bill 1), cl 93).

In addition to the overriding concern for the physical safety of an automated system, the use of data by providers of transport and related services will also engage data protection and privacy laws unrelated to road traffic collisions[9]. As Marco Müller-ter Jung has written:

> 'The interconnecting and autonomation of vehicles means that vehicles collect enormous amounts of data, and exchange these with each other and with components of the transport infrastructure. Therefore, data protection law is of particular importance in the context of connected and autonomous mobility. This is because the breadth of data that is captured automatically is very

---

4 Department for Transport policy paper 'Transport Data Strategy: Innovation through data' (28 March 2023), page 12.
5 See 'automated vehicles' section below.
6 RTA 1988 Part VI.
7 See Chapter 9, 'RTA claims'.
8 The growth in accident-relevant data generation by vehicles is well known. The form of evidence gathered by police is also likely to alter, through systems such as the mobile device and desk-based Collision Recording and Sharing (CRaSH) application – see Department for Transport policy paper 'Transport Data Strategy: Innovation through data' (28 March 2023), page 36.
9 See in particular Chapters 9, 'RTA claims' and 17, 'data protection and privacy claims'.

large… At an early stage in the development of their products and business models, providers of connected and autonomous vehicles and systems will therefore have to analyze which data protection requirements have to be met in order to act in compliance with the law and to create trust in these new forms of mobility from the point of view of data protection law.'[10]

The use of data in connected vehicles raises particular security and privacy concerns. As the European Data Protection Board (the EU body created to ensure 'a correct and consistent application' of the General Data Protection Regulation[11]) wrote in its 'Guidelines on processing personal data in the context of connected vehicles and mobility related applications':

'The issues relating to data security and control already stressed regarding IoT [*the Internet of Things*] are even more sensitive in the context of connected vehicles, since it entails road safety concerns – and can impact the physical integrity of the driver – in an environment traditionally perceived as isolated and protected from external interferences.'

'Also, connected vehicles raises significant data protection and privacy concerns regarding the processing of location data as its increasingly intrusive nature can put a strain on the current possibilities to remain anonymous. The EDPB wants to place particular emphasis and raise stakeholders' awareness to the fact that the use of location technologies requires the implementation of specific safeguards in order to prevent surveillance of individuals and misuse of the data.'[12]

British data protection law is currently in a state of flux, with a post-Brexit data protection bill (the Data Protection and Digital Information Bill 2023-24[13]) yet to be enacted at the time of writing.

This chapter provides an overview of data protection and privacy law as it now affects advanced, automated and electric vehicles in England and Wales. Given the protean state of the law and the numerosity of potential points generated by innovation the reader should in any event also refer to specialist works and take care to check current law and standards[14].

---

10 Marco Müller-ter Jung 'Data protection for connected and autonomous vehicles' (article for Dot magazine, May 2019).
11 EU GDPR 2016 Chapter VII section 3; Statement of the Council's reasons, Position (EU) No 6/2016 of the Council at first reading with a view to adoption of GDPR 2016, at 8.1, in *European Data Protection Law* ed. Andreas Linder (2016) page 123.
12 European Data Protection Board, 'Guidelines 01/2020 on processing personal data in the context of connected vehicles and mobility related applications, Version 2.0, Adopted on 9 March 2021', para 44-45, available on EDPB website.
13 Bill 001 2023-24. The first version of the Bill, DPDI Bill 2022-23, was withdrawn by the Truss administration: House of Commons Library Research Briefing 'The Data Protection and Digital Information (No.2) Bill 2022-23' by John Woodhouse and others (28 March 2023), pages 15, 17. The second version (the Data Protection and Digital Information Bill (No 2) Bill 2022-23 (HC Bill 314)) was not enacted in that session and in the King's Speech of November 2023 was carried over to the 2023-24 Parliamentary Session as the Data Protection and Digital Information Bill 001 2023-24. In this book it is referred to as the Data Protection and Digital Information Bill 2023-24.
14 Specialist works on data protection include Jay, *Data Protection Law and Practice* (above). See also *Cyber Litigation: the Legal Principles* by Dean Armstrong KC, Fergus McCombie and Ceri Davis (Bloomsbury, 2021), chapter 4, 'causes of action in data protection law'.

The laws of data protection and privacy relevant to AAEVs

Human Rights Act 1998

26.02 The Human Rights Act 1998 gives effect in British law to certain rights in the European Convention on Human Rights (ECHR). The rights are listed in HRA 1998, Sch 1, and include:

- The right to life (ECHR Article 2)

- The right to liberty and security (ECHR Article 5)

- The right to a fair trial (ECHR Article 6)

- The right to respect for 'private and family life, … home and correspondence' (ECHR Article 8). 'There shall be no interference by a public authority with the exercise of this right except such as is in accordance with the law and is necessary in a democratic society in the interests of national security, public safety or the economic well-being of the country, for the prevention of disorder or crime, for the protection of health or morals, or for the protection of the rights and freedoms of others' (ECHR Article 8(2)).

- The right to freedom of expression, including 'freedom to hold opinions and to receive and impart information and ideas without interference by public authority and regardless of frontiers' (ECHR Article 10).

- 'The enjoyment of the rights and freedoms set forth in this Convention shall be secured without discrimination on any ground such as sex, race, colour, language, religion, political or other opinion, national or social origin, association with a national minority, property, birth or other status' (ECHR Article 14, the prohibition of discrimination).

- Some ECHR rights are absolute (eg. the prohibition on torture under Article 3, which hopefully will not arise in the AAEV context) while some (eg. the right to respect for private and family life under Article 8) are qualified, so might be interfered with by the State (see Article 8(2) above). However, 'The restrictions permitted under this Convention to the said rights and freedoms shall not be applied for any purpose other than those for which they have been prescribed' (Article 18, limitation on use of restrictions on rights).

(That is not a complete list of the ECHR rights, but a selection of those rights which seem potentially applicable to AAEVs in relation to data and privacy laws.)

'It is unlawful for a public authority to act in a way which is incompatible with a Convention right' (HRA 1998, s 6(1)). A 'public authority' includes '(a) a court or tribunal, and (b) any person certain of whose functions are functions of a public nature …' (s 6(3)), although 'In relation to a particular act, a person is not a public authority by virtue only of subsection (3)(b) if the nature of the act is private' (s 6(5)).

'So far as it is possible to do so, primary legislation and subordinate legislation must be read and given effect in a way which is compatible with the Convention rights' (HRA 1998, s 3(1) 'interpretation of legislation').

An award of damages may be made for breach of those rights if, having regard to other remedies, 'the court is satisfied that the award is necessary to afford just satisfaction to the person in whose favour it is made' (s 8(3) 'judicial remedies').

EU General Data Protection Regulation 2016 and Data Protection Act 2018

26.03 The Data Protection Act 2018 (DPA 2018) enacted the European Union's General Data Protection Regulation 2016 (the GDPR). Before the 2016 referendum on membership of the EU the British government committed to implementing the GDPR irrespective of the result of the referendum and the GDPR was given force in British law by DPA 2018[15].

Following Brexit, DPA 2018 was amended by the Data Protection, Privacy and Electronic Communications (Amendments etc) (EU Exit) Regulations 2019 (known as DPPEC)[16] to bring into effect a 'UK GDPR', which DPPEC define as the EU GDPR 2016 'as it forms part of the law of England and Wales, Scotland and Northern Ireland by virtue of section 3 of the European Union (Withdrawal) Act 2018'[17]. A Bill is currently before Parliament (the Data Protection and Digital Information Bill 2023-24) to enact a further version of a post-EU data protection regime in the UK, which the government has described as a simplified and more pro-growth approach[18].

The relevant parts of DPA 2018 are as follows. This is not a comprehensive account of the workings of the Act, but a focus upon those areas of the DPA 2018 which seem most likely to affect AAEVs.

DPA 2018, s 1 ('overview') provides that:

'(1) This Act makes provision about the processing of personal data.

(2) Most processing of personal data is subject to the GDPR...'

Both the GDPR and DPA 2018 are of broad application, and the latter (by invoking the former) sets strict rules for how personal information is dealt with. The following parts of DPA 2018, s 3 ('terms relating to the processing of personal data') define terms and show the breadth of the Act:

'3 *Terms relating to the processing of personal data*

(1) This section defines some terms used in this Act.

(2) 'Personal data' means any information relating to an identified or identifiable living individual …

(3) 'Identifiable living individual' means a living individual who can be identified, directly or indirectly, in particular by reference to—

(a) an identifier such as a name, an identification number, location data or an online identifier, or

---

15 See for example UK Government, Department for Exiting the European Union 'Policy Paper: The exchange and protection of personal data – a future partnership paper' (24 August 2017), paras 2-3: "At the point of our exit from the EU, the UK's domestic data protection rules will be aligned with the EU data protection framework. After leaving the EU, the UK will continue to play a leading global role in the development and promotion of appropriate data protection standards and cross-border data flows."
16 DPPEC 2019, SI 2019/419.
17 DPPEC 2019, reg 2.
18 Explanatory notes to DPDI Bill 2023-24, paras 1-2.

    (b) one or more factors specific to the physical, physiological, genetic, mental, economic, cultural or social identity of the individual.

(4) 'Processing', in relation to information, means an operation or set of operations which is performed on information, or on sets of information, such as—

    (a) collection, recording, organisation, structuring or storage,

    (b) adaptation or alteration,

    (c) retrieval, consultation or use,

    (d) disclosure by transmission, dissemination or otherwise making available,

    (e) alignment or combination, or

    (f) restriction, erasure or destruction,

    …

(5) 'Data subject' means the identified or identifiable living individual to whom personal data relates.

    …

(7) 'Filing system' means any structured set of personal data which is accessible according to specific criteria, whether held by automated means or manually and whether centralised, decentralised or dispersed on a functional or geographical basis.

    …'

DPA 2018 defines some terms in a complicated way, not by a single definition but by reference to the parts of the Act in which they are treated. It defers to a large extent to the terms of the GDPR itself, where the definition of terms is often clearer. For example, data controller and data processor are defined in GDPR 2016, art 4 as follows:

'(7) 'controller' means the natural or legal person, public authority, agency or other body which, alone or jointly with others, determines the purposes and means of the processing of personal data; …

(8) 'processor' means a natural or legal person, public authority, agency or other body which processes personal data on behalf of the controller;'

GDPR 2016 and DPA 2018 require that personal data be processed in accordance with the following **six data protection principles**. GDPR 2016, art 5(1), and DPA 2018, ss 34–40, in chapter 2 ('law enforcement processing'), set out the six data protection principles. DPA 2018, s 34(3) provides that: 'The controller in relation to personal data is responsible for, and must be able to demonstrate, compliance with this Chapter'.

The six data protection principles are:

1 **Lawfulness, fairness and transparency** (in relation to the data subject)

2 **Purpose Limitation** (limitation to the purposes of processing the data, which purposes must be specified, explicit and legitimate)

3 **Data Minimisation** (of processed data, to achieve the purpose)

4 **Accuracy** (of data, including the erasure of outdated information)

5 **Storage Limitation** (limitation of storage period to the time necessary for the purpose)

6 **'Integrity and Confidentiality'** (ie. secure storage)

The lawful purposes for the processing of personal data are set out in GDPR, art 6(1):

'(a) the data subject has given consent to the processing of his or her personal data for one or more specific purposes;

(b) processing is necessary for the performance of a contract to which the data subject is party or in order to take steps at the request of the data subject prior to entering into a contract;

(c) processing is necessary for compliance with a legal obligation to which the controller is subject;

(d) processing is necessary in order to protect the vital interests of the data subject or of another natural person;

(e) processing is necessary for the performance of a task carried out in the public interest or in the exercise of official authority vested in the controller;

(f) processing is necessary for the purposes of the legitimate interests pursued by the controller or by a third party, except where such interests are overridden by the interests or fundamental rights and freedoms of the data subject which require protection of personal data, in particular where the data subject is a child.

Point (f) of the first subparagraph shall not apply to processing carried out by public authorities in the performance of their tasks.'

Furthermore, special rules apply to sensitive ('special') personal data. GDPR 2016, art 9 defines **'special categories of personal data'**, processing of which is prohibited unless a prescribed situation applies.

The special categories of personal data of which processing is prohibited under GDPR 2016, art 9, unless specifically permitted, are:

'personal data revealing racial or ethnic origin, political opinions, religious or philosophical beliefs, or trade union membership, and the processing of genetic data, biometric data for the purpose of uniquely identifying a natural person, data concerning health or data concerning a natural person's sex life or sexual orientation' (art 9(1))

The exceptional circumstances in which processing of those sensitive personal data is permitted by GDPR 2016, art 9(2) are as follows:

'(a) the data subject has given explicit consent to the processing of those personal data for one or more specified purposes, except where Union or Member State law provide that the prohibition referred to in paragraph 1 may not be lifted by the data subject;

(b) processing is necessary for the purposes of carrying out the obligations and exercising specific rights of the controller or of the data subject in the field of employment and social security and social protection law in so far as it is authorised by Union or Member State law or a collective agreement pursuant to Member State law providing for appropriate safeguards for the fundamental rights and the interests of the data subject;

(c) processing is necessary to protect the vital interests of the data subject or of another natural person where the data subject is physically or legally incapable of giving consent;

(d) processing is carried out in the course of its legitimate activities with appropriate safeguards by a foundation, association or any other not-for-profit body with a political, philosophical, religious or trade union aim and on condition that the processing relates solely to the members or to former members of the body or to persons who have regular contact with it in connection with its purposes and that the personal data are not disclosed outside that body without the consent of the data subjects;

(e) processing relates to personal data which are manifestly made public by the data subject;

(f) processing is necessary for the establishment, exercise or defence of legal claims or whenever courts are acting in their judicial capacity;

(g) processing is necessary for reasons of substantial public interest, on the basis of Union or Member State law which shall be proportionate to the aim pursued, respect the essence of the right to data protection and provide for suitable and specific measures to safeguard the fundamental rights and the interests of the data subject;

(h) processing is necessary for the purposes of preventive or occupational medicine, for the assessment of the working capacity of the employee, medical diagnosis, the provision of health or social care or treatment or the management of health or social care systems and services on the basis of Union or Member State law or pursuant to contract with a health professional and subject to the conditions and safeguards referred to in paragraph 3;

(i) processing is necessary for reasons of public interest in the area of public health, such as protecting against serious cross-border threats to health or ensuring high standards of quality and safety of health care and of medicinal products or medical devices, on the basis of Union or Member State law which provides for suitable and specific measures to safeguard the rights and freedoms of the data subject, in particular professional secrecy;

(j) processing is necessary for archiving purposes in the public interest, scientific or historical research purposes or statistical purposes in accordance with Article 89(1) based on Union or Member State law which shall be proportionate to the aim pursued, respect the essence of the right to data protection and provide for suitable and specific measures to safeguard the fundamental rights and the interests of the data subject.'

GDPR 2016, art 9(3) adds that:

'Personal data referred to in paragraph 1 may be processed for the purposes referred to in point (h) of paragraph 2 when those data are processed by or under the responsibility of a professional subject to the obligation of professional secrecy under Union or Member State law or rules established by national competent bodies or by another person also subject to an obligation of secrecy under Union or Member State law or rules established by national competent bodies.'

GDPR 2016 further provides that:

- The GDPR does not apply in all circumstances. In particular, it does not apply to the processing of personal data '(c) by a natural person in the course of a purely personal or household activity' or '(d) by competent authorities for the purposes of the prevention, investigation, detection or prosecution of criminal offences or the execution of criminal penalties, including the safeguarding against and the prevention of threats to public security' (GDPR 2016, art 2(2)).

- Data controllers and processors must show how they comply with all of the data protection principles. This is the overarching 'accountability' requirement (GDPR 2016, art 5(2).

- 'The data subject shall have the right not to be subject to a decision based solely on automated processing, including profiling, which produces legal effects concerning him or her or similarly significantly affects him or her' (GDPR 2016, art 22). That shall not apply 'if the decision: (a) is necessary for entering into, or performance of, a contract between the data subject and a data controller; (b) is authorised by Union or Member State law to which the controller is subject and which also lays down suitable measures to safeguard the data subject's rights and freedoms and legitimate interests; or (c) is based on the data subject's explicit consent' (art 22(2)). 'In the cases referred to in points (a) and (c) of paragraph 2, the data controller shall implement suitable measures to safeguard the data subject's rights and freedoms and legitimate interests, at least the right to obtain human intervention on the part of the controller, to express his or her point of view and to contest the decision' (art 22(3)). Absent explicit consent by the data subject or processing for reasons of substantial public interest on the basis of law which shall be proportionate to the aim pursued, decisions under art 22(2) shall not be based upon special categories of personal data (art 22(4)).

- Data protection must be achieved by design (including by technical and organisational measures) and by default (GDPR 2016, art 25).

- The territorial reach of the regulation is wider than the previous law. It applies to data controllers and processors 'offering goods and services to data subjects who are within the Union', even where the controller or processor is established outside the EU (GDPR 2016, recital 23 and art 3).

- The meaning of 'personal data' is wider than previously understood. For example, information identifying online activity, such as an IP address, can be personal data, as can data that has been 'pseudonyomised' (GDPR 2016, recitals 26, 30 and art 32.

- Consent to data processing must be 'given by a clear affirmative act' and 'unambiguous'. Silence or not altering a pre-ticked box will not suffice. Consent must be capable of withdrawal at any time (GDPR 2016, recital 32 and art 7)

- Information to data subjects should be 'easily accessible and easy to understand' (GDPR recital 58, 'the principle of transparency', and art 12)

- The data subject has a right to have data provided in intelligible form to him or her and to transmit it to another controller, or where technically feasible to ask a data controller to transmit that data ('data portability' – GDPR 2016, recital 68 and art 20)

- Controllers and processors owe enhanced duties to ensure data security, by several measures including (for example) 'pseudonymising' personal data as soon as possible (GDPR 2016, recital 78)

- Where there is a 'high risk' in data processing 'to the rights and freedoms of natural persons', the controller shall carry out 'an assessment of the impact of the envisaged processing operations on the protection of personal data'. That is especially so 'where a type of processing' uses 'new technologies' (GDPR 2016, art 35)

- Member states may 'provide for more specific rules to ensure the protection of the rights and freedoms of in respect of the processing of employees' personal data' (GDPR 2016, art 88).

- The GDPR states its commitment to a balance between the data subject's security and the demands of increasingly sophisticated technologies and international data transfers. But it gives greater weight to the data security of the individual subject (GDPR 2016, recitals 6 and 7). That is its object.

Protection of Freedoms Act 2012

26.04 The Protection of Freedoms Act 2012 (PFA 2012), Part 2, Chapter 1, ss 29–36) currently regulates surveillance and provides for a code of practice in relation to camera surveillance and the appointment of a surveillance camera commissioner. However, DPDI Bill 2023-24, cl 112 before Parliament as at the time of writing proposes the 'removal of provision for regulation of CCTV etc' and the repeal of PFA 2012, Part 2, Chapter 1. The government's rationale for the abolition of the surveillance camera commissioner's powers is that:

> 'The Information Commissioner already has oversight of the use of personal data under the Data Protection Act 2018, including data captured via surveillance camera systems, by all controllers, including the police and local authorities... [T]he Information Commissioner will continue to provide independent oversight and regulation of this area, without duplication by the Surveillance Camera Code and Commissioner, making it easier for the police, local authorities and the public to understand and comply with any requirements.'[19]

PFA 2012 and the surveillance code of practice were considered by the Court of Appeal, in the context of local use of Automated Facial Recognition (AFR) technology for law enforcement purposes, in the *Bridges* case[20]. PFA 2012 is relevant in the road vehicles context both because it applies to Automatic Number Plate Recognition (ANPR) technology (PFA 2012, s 29(6)(a)) and because some vehicles available on the open market now include cameras not only to enable ADAS functions while the vehicle is in motion but also to record footage which can be archived – footage of

---

19 Explanatory note to the DPDI Bill 2023-24, para 720.
20 *Regina (Bridges) v Chief Constable of South Wales Police (Information Commissioner and others intervening)* [2020] EWCA Civ 1058; [2020] 1 WLR 5037.

the vehicle's surroundings both when the vehicle is in motion and when it is parked, by use of 'sentry' modes[21]. ANPR is used as a tool not only of law enforcement but also of traffic management. So PFA 2012, Part 2, Chapter 1 (should it survive, or should its duties in effect be absorbed by the Information Commissioner) is relevant to AAEVs.

B Public laws of data and privacy involving Advanced Driver Assistance Systems (ADAS)

Need for a sufficient legal framework regulating data and privacy issues for new vehicle technologies

26.05 In the *Bridges* case, the Court of Appeal found the legal framework for use of Automated Facial Recognition by South Wales Police to be insufficient, noting in particular that:

'We find the references by the [*Divisional*] court to the possibility of future reconsideration of this issue [*whether there is a sufficient legal framework for the use of the Automated Facial Recognition technology*] a little curious. This is because either an interference is in accordance with the law or it is not. The issue of whether there is relevant law for this purpose is a binary question: see *In re Gallagher* [2020] AC 185, para 14 (Lord Sumption). The fact that this case involved the trial of a new technology does not alter the need for any interference with [*ECHR*] article 8 rights to be in accordance with the law.'[22]

The use of cameras (for example) is already commonplace among ADAS-equipped vehicles. As described above, data protection and privacy law generally is in a state of flux. Regulatory reform is directed broadly to artificial intelligence; it is debatable whether it is yet sufficiently directed to particular sectors (such as AAEVs).

Algorithmic bias

26.06 In *Bridges*, the Court of Appeal found the South Wales Police to have been in breach of the public sector equality duty (PSED) under the Equality Act 2010, s 149 by having 'never sought to satisfy themselves, either directly or by way of independent verification, that the software program in this case does not have an unacceptable bias on grounds of race or sex' despite witness evidence in the case 'that that programs for AFR can sometimes have such a bias'[23]. In particular,

'it would appear that SWP were not aware of the dataset used to train the AFR system in this case. For that reason, [*the witness*] states, it would be difficult for SWP to confirm whether the technology is in fact biased. As a minimum for confirming whether an AFR system is biased, the database statistics, such as the number of males to females, and different races considered, would need to be known.'[24]

---

21 See PFA 2012, s 29(6)(b).
22 *Bridges*, above, at [58].
23 *Bridges*, above, [199].
24 *Bridges*, [193].

Biometric data

26.07   The first 'hands off, eyes on' driving system was approved for use on extensive parts of the British motorway system in April 2023, using driver-facing cameras aimed at the eyes to detect whether or not the driver was maintaining their view of the road ahead while not holding the steering wheel[25].

'Biometric data for the purpose of uniquely identifying a natural person' is a special category of personal data under GDPR 2016, art 9(1). GDPR 2016, art 4(14) defines 'biometric data' as:

> 'personal data resulting from specific technical processing relating to the physical, physiological or behavioural characteristics of a natural person, which allow or confirm the unique identification of that natural person, such as facial images or dactyloscopic [*fingerprint comparison*] data'.

Would the GDPR 2016, art 22 concept of 'automated processing' be engaged by an advanced or automated vehicle feature?

26.08   The DPDI Bill 2023-24, cl 12 seeks to amend UK GDPR 2016, art 22 – the data subject's right not to be subject to a decision based solely on automated processing, including profiling, which produces legal effects concerning him or her or similarly significantly affects him or her (see above).

Whether cl 12 is intended to relate to decisions made by an advanced or automated vehicle based upon processing of (for example) 'biometric data for the purpose of uniquely identifying a natural person'[26], such as a system based upon monitoring of the driver's behavioural or other identifying characteristics, is not made clear within the proposed clause.

The government's response to a consultation 'Data: a new direction' in June 2022 did not treat advanced and automated vehicles, but expressed a broad approach to data regulation so as not to restrict commercial uses of artificial intelligence:

> 'The government is considering how to amend [GDPR] Article 22 to clarify the circumstances in which the Article must apply. The government wants to align proposals in this area with the broader approach to governing AI-powered automated decision-making that will be set out as part of the upcoming white paper on AI governance. Reforms will cast Article 22 as a right to specific safeguards, rather than as a general prohibition on solely automated decision-making. Reforms will enable the deployment of AI-

---

25 Ford motor company website article 'Ford brings hands-free driving technology to motorways in Great Britain' (13 April 2023).
26 GDPR 2016, art 9, a special category of personal data. GDPR 2016, art 4(14) defines 'biometric data' as 'personal data resulting from specific technical processing relating to the physical, physiological or behavioural characteristics of a natural person, which allow or confirm the unique identification of that natural person, such as facial images or dactyloscopic [fingerprint comparison] data'.

powered automated decision-making, providing scope for innovation with appropriate safeguards in place.'[27]

The subsequent government AI White Paper of March 2023 did address self-driving vehicles and the need to close 'regulatory gaps'[28]. It might be that this was a reference to the authorisation and passenger services licensing schemes since proposed by the Automated Vehicles Bill 2023-24 (HL Bill 1) (see Chapters 2, 'specifications', 3, 4 'driving' and 5 'passenger services and public transport'), or it might have related to regulation more broadly.

The explanatory notes to the DPDI Bill 2023-24 describe the proposed power under an amended UK GDPR art 22D(3) to amend art 22(A) (definitions of automated processing and significant decisions) directly by regulations:

'These provisions will ensure that additional legal clarity on the circumstances in which safeguards must apply can be introduced if and when necessary and appropriate. For example, this might be necessary in light of the rapid advancement and adoption of technologies related to automated decision-making that may inform when meaningful involvement can be said to have taken place, as well as changing societal expectations of what constitutes a significant decision in a privacy context.'[29]

Whether 'automated processing' is intended to apply to advanced and automated vehicles is unclear. The AV Bill 2023-24 (HL Bill 1), cl 95 (below) seems to apply data protection legislation. Whether the data protection safeguards in relation to 'automated processing' apply, or might in future apply, in relation to ADAS and automated vehicle features ought to be addressed by guidance or regulations in relation to both Bills.

C Public laws of data and privacy involving Automated Vehicles

Information provisions of the AV Bill 2023-24 (HL Bill 1)

26.09   The regulatory framework of the AV Bill 2023-24 (HL Bill 1) illustrates the status of data as 'a new kind of infrastructure' of road transport, crucial to public safety as well as to commercial success[30]. It provides an extensive and detailed scheme of disclosure within both the authorisation and monitoring of automated vehicle safety process and the licensing of automated passenger services, with a range of policing powers reinforced by criminal offences. There are protections, but the emphasis is upon full disclosure.

---

27 UK government (Department for Digital, Culture, Media and Sport) paper 'Data – a new direction – government response to consultation' (23 June 2022), para 1.5, 'AI and machine learning'.

28 UK government (Department for Science, Innovation and Technology, Office for Artificial Intelligence) policy paper 'A pro-innovation approach to AI regulation' (29 March 2023), eg. at page 40, 3.2.5.

29 Explanatory notes to DPDI Bill 2023-24, para 186.

30 See the quotations at the head of this chapter.

The AV Bill 2023-24 provides a steely framework, to which much regulatory detail is yet to be added.

Data protection in general under the AV Bill 2023-24

26.10   The AV Bill 2023-24 (HL Bill 1), cl 95 provides:

'95 Disclosure of information: interaction with external constraints

(1) This section applies in relation to any provision for the disclosure, obtaining or use of information made by or under this Act.

(2) The provision does not require or authorise any disclosure, obtaining or use of information that—

   (a) contravenes the data protection legislation, or

   (b) is prohibited by any of Parts 1 to 7 or Chapter 1 of Part 9 of the Investigatory Powers Act 2016.

(3) But the provision is to be taken into account in determining whether the disclosure, obtaining or use of information would contravene the data protection legislation.

(4) The disclosure of information in accordance with the provision (as read subject to subsection (2)) does not breach—

   (a) any obligation of confidence owed by the person making the disclosure, or

   (b) any other restriction on the disclosure of information (however imposed).

(5) The provision does not require or authorise the disclosure or obtaining of information in respect of which a claim to legal professional privilege could be maintained in legal proceedings without the agreement of the person entitled to maintain that claim.

(6) In the application of subsection (5) in Scotland, the reference to legal professional privilege is to be read as a reference to confidentiality of communications.

(7) In this section "the data protection legislation" has the same meaning as in the Data Protection Act 2018 (see section 3 of that Act).'

Provision of information by regulated bodies

26.11   The AV Bill 2023-24 (HL Bill 1), Part 1, Chapter 3 deals with the 'provision of information by regulated bodies', within the 'regulatory scheme for automated vehicles'.

Clause 14 provides for the 'collection and sharing of information':

'(1) Authorisation requirements may include requirements as to the collection and sharing of information by an authorised self-driving entity.

(2) Operator licensing regulations may impose requirements as to the collection and sharing of information by a licensed no-user-in-charge operator.

(3) Those references to sharing include—

    (a) sharing with the Secretary of State or other public authorities, and

    (b) sharing with private businesses (such as vehicle manufacturers or insurers).

(4) Authorisation requirements or operator licensing regulations that require an authorised self-driving entity or licensed no-user-in-charge operator to share information must specify the purpose for which the information is to be shared.'

The AV Bill 2023-24 (HL Bill 1), cl 15 allows for authorisation requirements or operator licensing requirements to require a person who is, or is seeking to become, an authorised self-driving entity or a licensed no-user-in-charge operator 'to nominate an individual to be responsible for information that is, or has to be, provided by the person to the Secretary to the State for the purposes of this Part' (cl 15(1) and (2)).

Clause 17 allows the Secretary of State to 'issue an information notice to a regulated body if the Secretary of State considers it appropriate to do so for any of the investigative purposes' (cl 17(1)). Those are 'the domestic purposes and the international purpose' for which a notice is given, as set out in cl 16 and defined in cl 16(2) and (3):

'(2) The domestic purposes are the purposes of—

    (a) assessing whether a regulatory requirement is being, or has been, met—

        (i) by the regulated body, or

        (ii) in relation to authorised automated vehicles for which the regulated body is or has been responsible,

    (b) investigating whether, how or why an authorised automated vehicle has committed a traffic infraction while the regulated body was responsible for it,

    (c) assessing whether an authorised automated vehicle for which the regulated body is or has been responsible continues to satisfy the self-driving test by reference to the authorised locations and circumstances, and

    (d) investigating—

        (i) a suspected offence under section 24 by the regulated body, or another regulated body that is or has been responsible for a vehicle for which the regulated body is or has been responsible, or

        (ii) a suspected offence under section 25, or a suspected offence arising by virtue of section 26 or 27, that is predicated on an offence within sub-paragraph (i).[31]

---

31 See below for the offences under cll 24-27.

(3) The international purpose is the purpose of sharing information with an authority in a country or territory outside Great Britain (an "overseas authority"), where—

    (a) the overseas authority has requested the information,

    (b) the overseas authority has functions under the law of that country or territory that are similar to those referred to in subsection (2), and

    (c) the information is likely to assist the overseas authority in performing those functions in respect of the regulated body.'

The AV Bill 2023-24 (HL Bill 1), cll 17 and 18 allow the Secretary of State to issue respectively an information notice and an interview notice to a regulated body. Clause 19 allows either of those notices to require attendance by an individual.

'An information notice is a notice requiring the regulated body to provide information to the Secretary of State' (cl 17(2)).

Failure or likely failure to respond to an information notice is a prescribed reason for a justice of the peace to grant a warrant for entry, search and seizure under cl 28.

Clause 20 creates offences of non-compliance:

'(1) A regulated body commits an offence if it—

    (a) fails to provide information as required by an information notice,

    (b) provides, in purported compliance with an information notice, information that is false or misleading in a material respect, or

    (c) fails to comply with an information notice or interview notice as described in section 19(5)[32].

(2) It is a defence for the regulated body to prove that it took all reasonable precautions and exercised all due diligence to avoid the commission of the offence.

(3) A person commits an offence if—

    (a) the person is an individual identified in an information notice as described in section 19(2)(a)[33],

    (b) the person has been made aware of the contents of the notice, and

    (c) the person—

        (i) fails, without reasonable excuse, to attend at the place and time specified in the notice or provide information as required by the notice, or

---

32 AV Bill 2023-24 (HL Bill 1), cl 19(5): 'The regulated body complies with the notice if it takes all steps that it could reasonably be expected to take in order to (a) procure the attendance of the identified individual, or an individual within the described class, at the place and time specified in the notice, and (b) enable that individual to provide the information specified, or answer questions on the subject-matter indicated, in the notice.'

33 AV Bill 2023-24 (HL Bill 1), cl 19 (2)(a): 'The notice may identify a particular individual'.

(ii)   provides, in purported compliance with the notice, information that is false or misleading in a material respect, knowing it to be so or being reckless as to whether it is.

(4) A person commits an offence if—

(a) the person is an individual identified in an interview notice as described in section 19(2)(a),

(b) the person has been made aware of the notice, and

(c) the person—

(i)   fails, without reasonable excuse, to attend at the place and time specified in the notice,

(ii)   on being interviewed further to the notice, fails, without reasonable excuse, to answer a question, or

(iii)   on being interviewed further to the notice, answers a question in a way that is false or misleading in a material particular, knowing it to be so or being reckless as to whether it is.

(5) A person commits an offence if—

(a) the person destroys, suppresses or alters, or causes or permits the destruction, suppression or alteration of, any information, and

(b) the person does so with the intention of preventing the provision of accurate information in response to an information notice, or at an interview undertaken further to an interview notice.

(6) In subsection (5)—

(a) the reference to information required to be provided by an information notice includes anything in or on which that information is recorded;

(b) the references to suppressing information include destroying the means of reproducing information recorded otherwise than in a legible form.

(7) A person who commits an offence under this section is liable—

(a) on summary conviction in England or Wales, to imprisonment for a term not exceeding the general limit in a magistrates' court or a fine (or both);

(b) on summary conviction in Scotland, to imprisonment for a term not exceeding 12 months or a fine not exceeding the statutory maximum (or both);

(c) on conviction on indictment, to imprisonment for a term not exceeding 2 years or a fine (or both).'

Clauses 24 and 25 create 'offences relating to information about safety':

'24 False or withheld information relevant to vehicle safety

(1) A person commits an offence if—

(a) the person is, or is seeking to become, a regulated body,

(b) the person provides to the Secretary of State—

> (i) information about a vehicle for which the person is, has been, or is seeking to become responsible, or
>
> (ii) other information in connection with the person's role (or proposed role) as a regulated body, and
>
> (c) the information is false or misleading in a respect in which it is relevant to the safety of the person's automated vehicle operations...'

Clause 25 creates an 'aggravated offence where death or serious injury occurs'.

An offence under cl 20 or 24 is committed by the nominated individual for the information to which the offence relates (cl 26) and by any senior manager who consents to or connives in the commission of the offence (cl 27).

In the AV Bill 2023-24 (HL Bill 1), Part 1, Chapter 7 ('supplementary provision'), cl 41(1) requires that the Secretary of State imposes

> 'authorisation requirements designed to secure that the Secretary of State has available at all times—
>
> (a) a postal address, and
>
> (b) an electronic address,
>
> which can be used to issue notices under this Part to an authorised self-driving entity.'

And a similar requirement applies in relation to a no-user-in-charge operator if the Secretary of State makes operator licensing regulations (cl 41(2)).

Information connected with investigation by statutory inspectors

26.12 Part 3 Chapter 2 of the AV Bill 2023-24 (HL Bill 1) provides powers to statutory inspectors to investigate, seek and deal with information as to incidents involving authorised automated vehicles, including:

> 'If an inspector considers it necessary for the purposes of an investigation, the inspector may require a person—
>
> (a) to provide to the inspector, or allow the inspector access to, information, items or material in any manner the inspector considers appropriate;
>
> (b) not to access, disturb, move or alter anything specified by the inspector.' (cl 63(1));

Various powers 'in respect of any premises' under cl 64, including to:

> 'record (in whatever form) any document, equipment or other item or material on the premises, or any information contained in or accessible by means of any such document, equipment, item or material' (cl 64(2)(e));

> 'require any person on the premises to provide information or assistance for the purpose of—

(i)   enabling or facilitating the exercise of the preceding powers, or

(ii) allowing anything inspected, seized or recorded in the exercise of those powers to be better understood.' (cl 64(2)(f))'; and to

Use reasonable force if necessary when using the powers under cl 64(2) (except to enforce a requirement under cl 64(2)(f)), but only if accompanied by a constable.

Such further powers as to the manner in which information should be provided (other than a response to a request under cl 63) to the statutory inspector as the Secretary of State might make under cl 70;

The power by further regulations to require AV incident reports from police (cl 71);

The power to 'produce and publish information about the safety of authorised automated vehicles or about investigations' (cl 72(1)(a)). However, the AV Bill 2023-24 also provides for protection of information 'obtained by an inspector in connection with the inspector's functions' at cl 73, including providing that

'It is an offence for the person to—

(a)   disclose the information to any other person, or

(b)   use the information for a purpose other than the purpose for which it was obtained, except as authorised by or under this Part or any other enactment…'

Information relating to automated passenger services

26.13   The AV Bill 2023-24 (HL Bill 1) ('permits for automated passenger services'), Part 5, cl 88 provides that:

'(1) Permit conditions may, in particular, include conditions as to the collection and sharing of information.

(2)   That reference to sharing includes—

(a)   sharing with the appropriate national authority or other public authorities, and

(b)   sharing with private businesses (such as vehicle manufacturers or insurers).

…

(5)   The Secretary of State may make regulations authorising the recipient to—

(a)   disclose the information to another person for a purpose specified in the regulations, or

(b)   use the information for a purpose other than the purpose for which it was obtained.

(6)   It is an offence for the recipient to—

(a)   disclose the information to another person, or

   (b) use the information for a purpose other than the purpose for which it was obtained, except as authorised by regulations under subsection (5) or any other enactment…

   …

(9) Regulations under subsection (5) are not to be taken to authorise disclosure or use that would be liable to harm the commercial interests of any person, except to the extent that—

   (a) the regulations otherwise provide, or

   (b) the person disclosing or using the information reasonably considers such disclosure or use necessary in view of the purpose of the regulations.'

Information about traffic regulation measures

26.14   The AV Bill 2023-24 (HL Bill 1), Part 6 ('adaptation of existing regimes') allows the Secretary of State 'by regulations [to] make provision requiring a traffic regulation authority to provide prescribed information about a relevant traffic regulation measure' (cl 93). This is to serve both assistive and automated vehicle systems (cl 93(4)).

Regulations 'may, in particular, provide that information is to be provided in accordance with a specified model, standard or set of specifications as it exists from time to time' (cl 96(7)) and 'may apply in respect of traffic regulation measures made before the regulations come into force (including those made before this Act is passed)' (cl 96(8)).

Protection of information obtained

26.15   The AV Bill 2023-24 (HL Bill1) provides offences where the recipient of information discloses or uses information other than for the purpose for which it was obtained.

Clause 42 (within Part 1 of the AV Bill 2023-24, 'regulatory scheme for automated vehicles') provides that:

'(1) This section applies in relation to information that a person obtains—

   (a) further to authorisation requirements or operator licensing regulations of the sort described in section 14(1) and (2),

   (b) as a result of the exercise of a power in section 17, 18 or 29, or

   (c) further to regulations under section 40.

(2) In this section, "the recipient" means—

   (a) the person who obtains the information as described in subsection (1), or

   (b) any other person to whom the information is subsequently disclosed.

(3) The Secretary of State may make regulations authorising the recipient to—

   (a) disclose the information to another person for a purpose specified in the regulations, or

(b) use the information for a purpose other than the purpose for which it was obtained.

(4) It is an offence for the recipient to—

(a) disclose the information to another person, or

(b) use the information for a purpose other than the purpose for which it was obtained, except as authorised by regulations under subsection (3) or any other enactment.

(5) But it is a defence to prove that—

(a) the person from whom the information was obtained as described in subsection (1) consented to the disclosure or use, or

(b) the recipient reasonably believed that the disclosure or use was lawful, or

(c) in the case of a disclosure, that the information had already lawfully been disclosed to the other person.

(6) A person who commits an offence under subsection (4) is liable on summary conviction or conviction on indictment to a fine.

(7) A provision made by or under this Part that authorises the disclosure or use of the information is not to be taken to authorise disclosure or use that would be liable to harm the commercial interests of any person, except to the extent that—

(a) the provision otherwise provides, or

(b) the person disclosing or using the information reasonably considers such disclosure or use necessary in view of the purpose of the provision.'

The explanatory note to cl 42(7) states that it

'protects commercially sensitive information by providing a presumption that it should be excluded from any disclosures authorised in this Part.'

Notably, cl 42(7) relates to the AV Bill 2023-24 (HL Bill 1), Part 1, 'regulatory scheme for automated vehicles'. It does not relate to Part 3 (above), 'policing and investigation' in which (for example) the statutory inspector's power to 'produce and publish information about the safety of authorised automated vehicles or about investigations' (cl 72(1)(a)) appears, subject to the protection of the offence under cl 73 (see above).

There is a similar provision at cl 88(9), in relation to the collection, sharing and protection of information required as a condition of an automated passenger service permit (the AV Bill 2023-24, Part 5, see above).

D Public laws of data and privacy involving Electric Vehicles

26.16   Electric vehicles are unlikely to generate any data protection issues which depend solely upon their mode of propulsion. However, it is possible that the use of a particular type of service using electric vehicles might give rise to data protection and privacy issues: for example, the Public Charge Point Regulations 2023[34] reg 9(7) requires that a charge point operator's quarterly report to the Secretary of State must not contain any personal data of the caller and reg 10 'requires charge point operators to hold certain specified data and ensure that the data is accurate, regularly updated and provided to the Secretary of State, Distribution Network Operators, Transmission Owners and Electricity Systems Operators'[35]. Each case will depend upon its facts[36].

Purely domestic car-sharing

26.17 In the case of a purely domestic car share, it might be argued that the data protection laws have no application (see GDPR 2016, art 2(2)(c), above), although that would require a 'purely personal or household activity'.

---

34 SI 2023/1168.
35 Explanatory note to PCPR 2023.
36 See, for example, the point made on the public law challenge to the use of the AFR in *Bridges* [61] that 'what is in issue in this appeal is the local deployment of AFR within the area of [South Wales Police]. This appeal is not concerned with possible use of AFR in the future on a national basis. As Mr Sharland submits, it is well-established in the case law of the European Court of Human Rights that local policies can be relevant to satisfy the requirement of 'in accordance with the law'. Such policies do not necessarily have to be at a national level.'

Chapter 27

Equality law

'...an overall safety benefit [*of automated vehicles*] should not be at the expense of increasing risks for vulnerable groups.'

The Law Commission of England and Wales
and the Scottish Law Commission (2022)[1]

A   Outline of equality laws for AAEVs

Dangers of bias with AAEVs

27.01   The Law Commissions provided the following, non-exhaustive list of potential sources of bias in the design of vehicles. The dangers may arise in hardware and (of particular importance for AAEVs) in software. Bias could result in a collision, causing serious injury or death.

'... we cited several examples where bias has crept into the design of vehicles, or into the design of other automated systems. Air bags save many lives, but the first generation of air bags posed risks to smaller passengers, such as women of small stature, the elderly, and children, because they were developed with adult males in mind. Current facial recognition software may also exhibit a bias towards white, male faces. For non-white and non-male faces, the accuracy of facial recognition systems may decline significantly.'

'In the future, there are ways in which AVs [*automated vehicles*] might adversely affect protected groups, even if they reduce the risk for other groups. Systems may not have been trained to deal with the full variety of wheelchairs and mobility scooters; or they may struggle to recognise certain road user groups.

---

1   Law Commissions' final report on automated vehicles, *Automated Vehicles: Joint Report*, Law Com No 404, Scot Law Com No 258 (January 2022), p 82, 5.74.

These issues may be exacerbated if designers are drawn predominantly from one demographic group (such as young non-disabled men).'[2]

Conventional vehicles require human control, including 'a full view of the road and traffic ahead', and failure to comply is a criminal offence[3]. The law imposes requirements as to the physical fitness of drivers[4], including providing for the revocation of a driving licence 'because of disability or prospective disability'[5]. A hope for AAEV technologies and automated vehicles is that they might improve accessibility to transport as well as road safety, but the Law Commissions point out the need for vigilance on equality: 'an overall safety benefit should not be at the expense of increasing risks for vulnerable groups'[6].

Equality Act 2010

27.02   What follows is not a comprehensive guide to the Equality Act 2010 (EA 2010), and the reader should refer to its full text and relevant commentary for its application to a particular case. In the developing AAEV context, the terms of EA 2010 can be summarised as follows.

EA 2010 provides, in general terms:

- In its first section, a public sector duty regarding socio-economic inequalities[7].

- Protection against discrimination for nine characteristics, listed in EA 2010, s 4: age, disability, gender reassignment, marriage and civil partnership, pregnancy and maternity, race, religion or belief, sex, sexual orientation.

- Discrimination is categorised into three broad types: direct (less favourable treatment, because of a protected characteristic, than would have been given to others: s 13), combined (less favourable treatment because of a combination of two protected characteristics than would have been given to another lacking either characteristic: s 14[8]) and indirect discrimination (the application of a provision, criterion or practice which is generally applied but discriminatory in relation to a protected characteristic in that it puts people with that characteristic, and the particular claimant, at a disadvantage which is disproportionate to the legitimate aim of the provision: s 19).

- There are particular prohibitions of discrimination arising from the protected characteristics of disability (s 15), gender reassignment: absences from work (s 16) and for non-work and work cases for pregnancy and maternity (ss 17 and 18).

- EA 2010, ss 20–22 describe the duty to make reasonable adjustments for disabled persons.

---

2   Law Commissions' Final AV report (January 2022, above), p 27-28, 2.80-2.81.
3   RTA 1988 s 41D and Road Vehicles (Construction and Use) Regulations 1986, SI 1986/1078, reg 104, 'driver's control'.
4   RTA 1988 s 92-96.
5   RTA 1988 s 93.
6   Law Commissions' Final AV report (January 2022, above), p 82, 5.74.
7   EA 2010, s 1, below.
8   Not in force at the time of writing.

EA 2010 prescribes, in its first section, a public sector duty regarding socio-economic inequalities. It also provides specifically for equality in transport, in certain situations. Those sections are as follows.

EA 2010, s 1(1) sets out the public sector duty regarding socio-economic inequalities:

> 'An authority to which this section applies must, when making decisions of a strategic nature about how to exercise its functions, have due regard to the desirability of exercising them in a way that is designed to reduce the inequalities of outcome which result from socio-economic disadvantage.'

EA 2010, s 20 provides for the duty to make adjustments for disabled persons. The three requirements of the duty are described at s 20(3)–(5):

> '(3) The first requirement is a requirement, where a provision, criterion or practice of A's puts a disabled person at a substantial disadvantage in relation to a relevant matter in comparison with persons who are not disabled, to take such steps as it is reasonable to have to take to avoid the disadvantage.
>
> (4) The second requirement is a requirement, where a physical feature puts a disabled person at a substantial disadvantage in relation to a relevant matter in comparison with persons who are not disabled, to take such steps as it is reasonable to have to take to avoid the disadvantage.
>
> (5) The third requirement is a requirement, where a disabled person would, but for the provision of an auxiliary aid, be put at a substantial disadvantage in relation to a relevant matter in comparison with persons who are not disabled, to take such steps as it is reasonable to have to take to provide the auxiliary aid.'

In EA 2010, Part 3 ('Services and public functions', which does not apply to protected characteristics of age under 18 nor marriage and civil partnership: s 28(1)), s 29 sets out the prohibitions against discrimination in provision of services etc. EA 2010, s 29(3)–(6) specifically prohibit discrimination, harassment or victimisation. EA 2010, s 29(1) and (2) provide as follows:

> '(1) A person (a 'service-provider') concerned with the provision of a service to the public or a section of the public (for payment or not) must not discriminate against a person requiring the service by not providing the person with the service.
>
> (2) A service-provider (A) must not, in providing the service, discriminate against a person (B) –
>
> (a) as to the terms on which A provides the service to B;
>
> (b) by terminating the provision of the service to B;
>
> (c) by subjecting B to any other detriment.'

And, at s 29(7):

> 'A duty to make reasonable adjustments applies to—
>
> (a) a service-provider ...;
>
> (b) a person who exercises a public function that is not the provision of a service to the public or a section of the public.'

EA 2010, s 149 (the 'public sector equality duty') provides as follows:

'(1) A public authority must, in the exercise of its functions, have due regard to the need to –

    (a) eliminate discrimination, harassment, victimisation and any other conduct that is prohibited by or under this Act;

    (b) advance equality of opportunity between persons who share a relevant protected characteristic and persons who do not share it;

    (c) foster good relations between persons who share a relevant protected characteristic and persons who do not share it.

(2) A person who is not a public authority but who exercises public functions must, in the exercise of those functions, have due regard to the matters mentioned in subsection (1).

(3) Having due regard to the need to advance equality of opportunity between persons who share a relevant protected characteristic and persons who do not share it involves having due regard, in particular, to the need to –

    (a) remove or minimise disadvantages suffered by persons who share a relevant protected characteristic that are connected to that characteristic;

    (b) take steps to meet the needs of persons who share a relevant protected characteristic that are different from the needs of persons who do not share it;

    (c) encourage persons who share a relevant protected characteristic to participate in public life or in any other activity in which participation by such persons is disproportionately low.

(4) The steps involved in meeting the needs of disabled persons that are different from the needs of persons who are not disabled include, in particular, steps to take account of disabled persons' disabilities.

(5) Having due regard to the need to foster good relations between persons who share a relevant protected characteristic and persons who do not share it involves having due regard, in particular, to the need to—

    (a) tackle prejudice, and

    (b) promote understanding.

(6) Compliance with the duties in this section may involve treating some persons more favourably than others; but that is not to be taken as permitting conduct that would otherwise be prohibited by or under this Act.

(7) The relevant protected characteristics are— age;

    disability;

    gender reassignment;

    pregnancy and maternity; race;

    religion or belief; sex;

    sexual orientation.

(8) A reference to conduct that is prohibited by or under this Act includes a reference to—

(a) a breach of an equality clause or rule;

(b) a breach of a non-discrimination rule.

(9) Schedule 18 (exceptions) has effect.'

EA 2010, Sch 18, para 3 exempts from s 149:

'(1) ... the exercise of –

(a) a judicial function;

(b) a function exercised on behalf of, or on the instructions of, a person exercising a judicial function.

(2) The references to a judicial function include a reference to a judicial function conferred on a person other than a court or tribunal.'

EA 2010, Sch 18, para 4 exempts the House of Commons, the House of Lords, the Scottish Parliament and the National Assembly for Wales.

(Otherwise, EA 2010, Sch 18 excepts various other bodies and activities[9] which, at present, seem unlikely to affect the equality duty insofar as it might relate to AAEVs).

EA 2010, s 158 ('positive action') provides (insofar as might be relevant to AAEVs) as follows:

'(1) This section applies if a person (P) reasonably thinks that –

(a) persons who share a protected characteristic suffer a disadvantage connected to the characteristic,

(b) persons who share a protected characteristic have needs that are different from the needs of persons who do not share it, or

(c) participation in an activity by persons who share a protected characteristic is disproportionately low.

(2) This Act does not prohibit P from taking any action which is a proportionate means of achieving the aim of –

(a) enabling or encouraging persons who share the protected characteristic to overcome or minimise that disadvantage,

(b) meeting those needs, or

(c) enabling or encouraging persons who share the protected characteristic to participate in that activity.

(3) Regulations may specify action, or descriptions of action, to which subsection (2) does not apply.

...

---

9   EA 2010, Sch 18 otherwise exempts functions relating to pupils in schools and accommodation for children in community homes, immigration and nationality functions, the General Synod of the Church of England, the security and intelligence services and parts of the armed forces assisting GCHQ. A Minister of the Crown may amend the Schedule per Sch 18, para 5.

(6)   This section does not enable P to do anything that is prohibited by or under an enactment other than this Act.'

EA 2010 in relation to road transport

27.03   The subject of EA 2010, Part 12 is 'Disabled Persons: Transport'. EA 2010, Part 12, Chapter 1 (ss 160–173) deals with 'Taxis etc' and Chapter 2, including 2A, (ss 174–181D) deals with 'public service vehicles'.

Of those sections, the following are the most relevant:

In EA 2010, Part 12, Chapter 1 ('Taxis etc'):

- As at the time of writing, ss 160–164 are not yet entirely in force. These provide for taxi accessibility regulations[10]; exception to the control of the numbers of licensed taxis[11]; regulations for the provision of designated transport facilities[12]; making a taxi licence conditional upon compliance with taxi accessibility regulations[13] and exemption from such regulations[14].

- EA 2010, ss 164A–167 are in force. These prescribe the duties of the driver of a taxi which has been hired by or for a disabled person or by another person who wishes to be accompanied by a disabled person[15]; the assistive duties or driver of a designated, wheelchair-accessible taxi hired by a disabled person in a wheelchair, or by their companion[16]; the duties of a driver of a private hire vehicle or pre-booked taxi to take reasonable steps to assist the passenger to identify and find the vehicle that has been hired[17]; provision for medical exemption from those requirements[18] and the listing of designated vehicles[19]. Breaches of the duties are criminal offences.

- EA 2010, ss 168–173 are in force. These provide equivalent duties in the case of a disabled person who is accompanied by their assistance dog. Breaches of the duties are criminal offences. A private hire driver might seek medical exemption[20].

In EA 2010, Part 12, Chapters 2 and 2A ('Public service vehicles', all sections of which (ss 174–181D) are in force):

- EA 2010, ss 174–180 provide that the Secretary of State may make regulations for securing disabled persons' ability to get on and off regulated public service vehicles 'without unreasonable difficulty' and to travel in such vehicles 'in safety and reasonable comfort', particularly when using wheelchairs. Compliance must be certified, by inspection of the vehicle (s 176). It is an offence (s 175) to contravene those regulations.

---

10 EA 2010, s 160.
11 EA 2010, s 161.
12 EA 2010, s 162.
13 EA 2010, s 163.
14 EA 2010, s 164.
15 EA 2010, s 164A.
16 EA 2010, s 165.
17 EA 2010, s 165A.
18 EA 2010, s 166.
19 EA 2010, s 167.
20 EA 2010, s 171.

- EA 2010, ss 181A–181D empower the Secretary of State to make regulations requiring operators of bus services to make available to disabled passengers information relating to their service. The Secretary of State must issue guidance about the duties imposed on operators by regulations under s 181A (s 181C).

EA 2010, Sch 2, para 3, makes 'special provision about transport' in relation to reasonable adjustments for services and public functions. It is a detailed provision as to the adjustments which a service provider is and is not required to make in the context of private and public transport, which is not repeated here.

Accessibility of public transport

27.04 In *Paulley v FirstGroup plc*[21] the Supreme Court considered 'the lawfulness of a bus company's policy in relation to the use of the space provided for wheelchair users on its buses'.

On 24 February 2012, Mr Paulley, a wheelchair user:

'… arrived at Wetherby bus station, expecting to catch the 9.40 bus ('the Bus') to Leeds. On arrival at Leeds he intended to catch the train to Stalybridge to meet his parents for lunch. The Bus was operated by a subsidiary of FirstGroup PLC ('FirstGroup'), which is the parent company of a group of companies which operates a total of about 6,300 buses. The Bus was equipped with a lowering platform and a wheelchair ramp. The Bus also had a space (a 'space') for wheelchairs, which included a sign that read 'Please give up this space if needed for a wheelchair user.'

'When Mr Paulley started to board the Bus, the driver, Mr Britcliffe, asked him to wait because the space was occupied by a woman with a sleeping child in a pushchair. The space had a sign with the familiar designation of a wheelchair sign, and in addition it had a notice ('the Notice') saying 'Please give up this space for a wheelchair user'. Mr Britcliffe asked the woman to fold down her pushchair and move out of the space so that Mr Paulley could occupy it in his wheelchair. She replied that her pushchair did not fold down, and refused to move. Mr Paulley then asked whether he could fold down his wheelchair and use an ordinary passenger seat. Mr Britcliffe refused that request, because there was no safe way of securing the wheelchair and the Bus had to take a rather winding route.'

'As a result, Mr Paulley had to wait for the next bus, which left around 20 minutes later. The consequence of this was that Mr Paulley missed his train at Leeds, and had to take a later train which arrived at Stalybridge an hour later than he had planned.'[22]

The bus company's policy, at the time of the incident, was quoted in para 7 of the judgment:

---

21 [2017] UKSC 4; [2017] 1 WLR 423.
22 *Paulley*, [2 to 4].

'As part of our commitment to providing accessible travel for wheelchair users virtually all our buses have a dedicated area for wheelchair users; other passengers are asked to give up the space for wheelchairs. ... If the bus is full or if there is already a wheelchair user on board unfortunately we will not be able to carry another wheelchair user. ... Wheelchairs do not have priority over buggies, but to ensure that all our customers are treated fairly and with consideration, other customers are asked to move to another part of the bus to allow you to board. Unfortunately, if a fellow passenger refuses to move you will need to wait for the next bus.'

As the Supreme Court noted, that policy had 'changed somewhat' by the time the case came to trial, to the following:

'As part of our commitment to providing accessible travel for wheelchair users virtually all our buses have a dedicated wheelchair area for wheelchair users; other passengers are asked to give up the space for wheelchairs. ...

Wheelchair users have priority use of the wheelchair space. If this is occupied with a buggy, standing passengers or otherwise full, and there is space elsewhere on the vehicle, the driver will ask that it is made free for a wheelchair user. Please note that the driver has no power to compel passengers to move in this way and is reliant on the goodwill of the passengers concerned. Unfortunately, if a fellow passenger refuses to move you will need to wait for the next bus.'[23]

Mr Paulley sought damages for breach of EA 2010, s 29(2), on the ground that FirstGroup had failed to make 'reasonable adjustments' to its policy.

The Recorder allowed Mr Paulley's claim. The Court of Appeal reversed that decision and found against him. Mr Paulley appealed to the Supreme Court, who restored the Recorder's decision that the bus company had acted unlawfully[24], though (by a bare majority of four to three Justices) disallowing the Recorder's award of damages to Mr Paulley.

The majority's disallowance of damages was on the ground that the Recorder had not considered whether the reasonable adjustment (which, it was agreed, did not require the bus company to go so far as physically ejecting the uncooperative passenger) would have resulted in any different outcome. The minority concluded that there was at least a real prospect that the suggested adjustment (a firm request by the driver of the passenger refusing to move, followed if necessary by firmer action such as stopping the bus) would have resulted in a different outcome, so as to merit damages.

---

23 [8].
24 See Lord Neuberger PSC at 442 [66-67]: 'it was not enough for FirstGroup to instruct its drivers simply to request non-wheelchair users to vacate the space, and do nothing further if the request was rejected... I cannot see why a driver should not be expected to rephrase any polite request as a requirement, and, if that does not work and especially if the bus is ahead of schedule, why the driver should not be expected to consider whether there was any reason why the bus should not stop for a few minutes with a view to pressurising or shaming the recalcitrant non-wheelchair user to move.'. See also Lord Toulson JSC at 446 [83]: 'the concept of 'reasonable adjustments' under [EA 2010, s 29(7)] is intensely practical'.

The judgments of the Supreme Court in *Paulley* demonstrate a variety of perceptions as to the practicalities of transport for disabled persons. There was disagreement between the justices as to the meaning of the judgment below.

There was also a difference in judicial perception as to whether bad manners should be justiciable by the courts (Lord Sumption finding not, in the absence of an alternatively drafted regulation, though not considering this to be a case appropriate for a dissent[25]; Baroness Hale considering the question of 'how a priority policy might be enforced against recalcitrant passengers' to be 'something of a red herring', based both upon her experience of transport and the clarity of the law in question[26]).

Bias of an automated system and the public sector equality duty under EA 2010

27.05   In *R (Bridges) v Chief Constable of South Wales Police*[27] (the automated facial recognition case, discussed in Chapter 17, 'data and privacy claims'), the Court of Appeal held that the defendant police force's failure to satisfy itself that the AFR system did not have an unacceptable bias on grounds of race or sex was a breach of the public sector equality duty under EA 2010, s 149, even though there was no evidence that the system had any such bias. The lack of consideration of the dataset used to train the system was sufficient to show the breach[28].

> 'The reason why the PSED is so important is that it requires a public authority to give thought to the potential impact of a new policy which may appear to it to be neutral but which may turn out in fact to have a disproportionate impact on certain sections of the population... The whole purpose of the positive duty (as opposed to the negative duties in the Equality Act 2010) is to ensure that a public authority does not inadvertently overlook information which it should take into account.'[29]

B   Equality laws for Advanced Driver Assistance Systems (ADAS)

Algorithmic bias

27.06   The dangers of bias of a system such as AFR (see *Bridges*, above) also apply to an ADAS system which does not fit the definition of 'automated vehicle'. A computer system which operates with inadequate assessment of its potential bias might be in breach of the EA 2010.

---

25 [88]–[92].
26 [106]–[109].
27 [2020] EWCA Civ 1058; [2020] 1 WLR 5037.
28 *Bridges*, 5078D-E [193], 5079E-F [199].
29 *Bridges*, 5076 [179-182].

C Equality laws for Automated Vehicles

Law Commissions' recommendations on equality laws for Automated Vehicles

27.07   At the end of their survey of automated vehicle law the Law Commissions observed that equality affects all stages of a vehicle's life, from design onwards. The authorisation authority approving a vehicle is subject to the EA 2010, s 149 duty, so (for example), transition demands in vehicles seeking authorisation as automated 'need to be designed for those with hearing loss... an overall safety benefit should not be at the expense of increasing risks for vulnerable groups'[30]. The Law Commissions recommended that:

> 'the ASDE[31] should submit an equality impact assessment. This should show how it has taken account of the needs of vehicle users and others using the road, to ensure that people are not treated unequally on the basis of protected characteristics.'[32]

The Law Commissions made the following recommendations in relation to the equality issues of automated vehicles:

> 'The authorisation authority [*for vehicles equipped with ADS features to be used in Great Britain*] should provide guidelines on the information to be included in the safety case and equality impact assessments, and assess both documents as part of authorisation.'[33]

> 'The in-use regulator should have power to require ASDEs to provide suitable, clearly worded and easily comprehensible information to owners, users-in-charge and registered keepers throughout the life of a vehicle.'[34]

> 'The in-use regulator should be under a duty to engage with those with an interest in the safety of automated vehicles, including local traffic authorities, the emergency services, road user groups and experts in the field.'[35]

> 'The UK Government should establish a forum for collaboration on how road rules, traffic laws and guidance such as the Highway Code should apply to automated driving.'[36]

> 'The new Act should empower the Secretary of State for Transport and the Scottish and Welsh Ministers to issue interim permits for passenger services designed to use NUIC vehicles. The holder of an interim passenger permit would not be subject to taxi, private hire or PSV legislation.

---

30 Law Commissions' Final AV report (January 2022, above), p 82, 5.74.
31 ASDE: Authorised Self-Driving Entity: 'the vehicle manufacturer or software developer who puts an [*automated vehicle*] forward for authorisation as having self-driving features': Law Commissions' Final report on automated vehicles (January 2022, above), p 20, 2.41.
32 Law Commissions' Final AV report (January 2022, above), p 82, 5.74.
33 Above, recommendation 15.
34 Recommendation 23.
35 Recommendation 30.
36 Recommendation 31.

(1) A permit should only be granted if:

    (a) in the opinion of the accessibility advisory panel (recommendation 63), the service is likely to add to knowledge of how to provide automated services for older and disabled passengers by involving them in the service's design;...'[37]

'The new Act should establish an accessibility advisory panel to advise on granting interim passenger permits and assist in the development of national minimum accessibility standards for NUIC[38] passenger services.

The accessibility advisory panel should include:

(1) the Equality and Human Rights Commission;

(2) representatives for disabled and older persons; and

(3) representatives from industry.'[39]

'In the longer term, the Secretary of State for Transport should set national accessibility standards to apply to all self-driving passenger services using NUIC vehicles.'[40]

In its response to the Law Commissions' recommendations (the CAM 2025 report of August 2022), the government stated that it:

'intend[ed] to require any organisation seeking authorisation of their vehicle as self-driving to submit an assessment of fair outcomes, including considerations of data bias, which must include how they avoid their vehicles unfairly discriminating against certain people as well as vulnerable road users, and their considerations of the importance of accessibility for people with different disabilities. ... [W]e are considering whether those organisations responsible for the behaviour of self-driving vehicles, known as Authorised Self-Driving Entities (ASDEs), should be under a duty to report data relating to discriminatory behaviour by their vehicle(s) to the in-use regulatory scheme, which will also take evidence from third parties. The scheme could then consider whether the effect on specified groups is unacceptable and take action to resolve issues.'[41]

'We support the idea behind Recommendation 23; that a user of a self-driving vehicle must understand how the vehicle operates in order to use it safely,...'[42]

'In Recommendations 30 and 31, the Law Commissions highlight the need for dedicated consultative mechanisms for self-driving vehicle regulation,

---

37 Recommendation 61(1)(a).
38 NUIC: 'No user-in-charge vehicle', 'a vehicle equipped with one or more ADS features designed to perform the entire dynamic driving task without a user-in-charge': Law Commissions' final AV report (January 2022, above), p xix.
39 Recommendation 63.
40 Recommendation 64.
41 UK government policy paper 'Connected and automated mobility 2025: realising the benefits of self-driving vehicles' ('CAM 2025'), 19 August 2022, p 36.
42 CAM 2025, p 122.

especially on road rules. In their responsible innovation report, the Centre for Data Ethics and Innovation (CDEI) have proposed how to operationalise these recommendations with the creation of a new science advisory committee – the Committee on Automated Vehicle Ethics and Safety (CAVES) – a sub-group of which will look at road rules.'[43]

The AV Bill 2023–24 (HL Bill 1) equality provisions for passengers of automated services

27.08 AV Bill 2023-24 (HL Bill 1), Part 5, 'permits for automated passenger services', cl 87(3) requires the appropriate national authority, in deciding whether to grant a permit, to 'have regard to whether, and to what extent, the granting of the permit is likely to lead to an improvement in the understanding of how automated passenger services should best be designed for, and provided to, older or disabled passengers'.

Clause 87(4) provides that

'Where the appropriate national authority grants a permit, it must include a permit condition (of the sort described in section 82(5)(b)) requiring the permit holder to publish reports about the automated passenger services which it provides, and in particular about the steps which it takes—

(a) to meet the needs of older or disabled passengers, and

(b) to safeguard passengers more generally.'

D Equality laws for Electric Vehicles

Accessible charging facilities

27.09 The suitability of EV charging points for people with accessibility needs is the subject of a 2022 standard by the British Standards Institution[44], sponsored by the charity Motability. That standard includes guidance as to chargepoint design, placement, the surroundings of the chargepoint, digital platforms and information.

See also Chapter 15, 'EV charging claims'.

---

43 CAM 2025, p 123.
44 *Electric vehicles -accessible charging – specification,* BSI PAS 1899:2022, at BSI website 'PAS 1899:2022 Electric vehicles – accessible charging – specification' (accessed 27 July 2023).

Chapter 28

Highway law

'Automated technology enables a much more flexible approach to road pricing. One problem with a daily charge is that once the vehicle has paid the charge for the day, it can continue to circulate within the zone without further disincentive. However, if the vehicle can generate reliable data to show where it has travelled and at what time, it will be possible to introduce more sophisticated pricing schemes... With a digitised system, there is also the possibility of dynamic pricing, where charges vary depending on the level of congestion in the city at that particular time.'

The Law Commission of England and Wales
and the Scottish Law Commission (2019)[1]

Chapter Contents

A   Outline of the public laws of highways

Regulation of road space

28.01   The Highways Act 1980 (HA 1980), the Road Traffic Regulation Act 1984 (RTRA 1984) and the Traffic Management Act 2004 (TMA 2004) are the main public laws governing road space[2].

---

1   Law Commission of England and Wales and Scottish Law Commission 'Automated Vehicles: Consultation Paper 2 on Passenger Services and Public Transport' (CP 245, DP 169, October 2019), p149, 7.79.
2   This is not a comprehensive account of highway laws but an overview relevant to AAEVs. For a fuller account see specialist works such as *Highway Law* by Stephen Sauvain KC, Ruth Stockley and Ned Westaway (Sweet and Maxwell, 6th edn, 2022).

Changes in vehicle types and technologies, and in work and movement patterns were evident even before the coronavirus pandemic. The pandemic accelerated those changes[3].

TMA 2004 requires a local traffic authority, among other matters, to secure 'the expeditious movement of traffic' and 'the avoidance, elimination or reduction of road congestion or other disruption to the movement of traffic' (s 16, 'the network management duty'). 'Traffic' is not limited to vehicles and includes pedestrians (s 31). So far as reasonably practicable, an authority must 'identify things (including future occurrences) which are causing, or which have the potential to cause, road congestion or other disruption to the movement of traffic on their road network' and 'consider any possible action' in response (s 17). The local authority shall have regard to statutory guidance published by the national authority, relating to performance of the duties imposed by ss 16 and 17 (s 18).

The Secretary of State for Transport publishes statutory guidance on traffic network management under TMA 2004, s 18. The menu of legal provisions allowing changes in road layout includes, for example, powers to improve highways – cycle tracks, guardrails etc – under HA 1980 Part V, and the powers to make traffic regulation orders outside Greater London (RTRA 1984, s 1), experimental traffic orders (RTRA 1984, s 9) or to order temporary prohibitions or restrictions on roads (RTRA 1984, s 14)[4].

The statutory guidance relating to traffic network management was revised during the 2020 to 2021 pandemic, to encourage changes in use of road space to support active travel. Initial guidance in May 2020 was updated in April 2022:

> 'Emergency legislation made in May 2020 to temporarily introduce an emergency procedure for the making of temporary traffic orders expired on 30 April 2021. Any TROs made using the emergency procedures under the Traffic Orders Procedure (Coronavirus) (Amendment) (England) Regulations 2020[5] can continue to be in place for up to 18 months. Traffic authorities will, however, need to consider the reason for the measures included in each TTRO or ETRO and whether the case for them remains valid … Any TROs made since 1 May 2021 need to follow the existing procedures set out in the Local Authorities' Traffic Orders (Procedure) (England and Wales) Regulations 1996[6].' [7]

In the foreword to the network management guidance updated in April 2022, the then Secretary of State for Transport wrote that:

---

3 With (for example) alterations to the statutory guidance on traffic network management, particularly in relation to experimental traffic orders, 'on 9 May 2020 and updated on 23 May 2020, 13 November 2020 and 30 July 2021': Department for Transport 'Statutory guidance. Traffic Management Act 2004: network management to support active travel' (1 April 2022).

4 And see 'an overview of the powers' in the Law Commissions' second AV law paper (October 2019, above), p 132-133.

5 SI 2020/536.

6 SI 1996/2489.

7 Department for Transport 'Statutory Guidance. Traffic Management Act 2004: network management to support active travel' (updated 1 April 2022; withdrawn on 2 October 2023).

'Local authorities should continue to make significant changes to their road layouts to give more space to cyclists and pedestrians and to maintain the changes they have already made. Of course, not every scheme is perfect, and a minority will not stand the test of time. But we are clear that schemes must be given that time. They must be allowed to bed in, must be tested against more normal traffic conditions and must be in place long enough for their benefits and disbenefits to be properly evaluated and understood.'[8]

On 2 October 2023 the TMA 2004 statutory guidance of 1 April 2022 was withdrawn by the government 'with immediate effect' and the government webpage upon which it appeared referred the reader to the government's plan for drivers' document of October 2023.

In *R (on the application of Better streets for Kensington and Chelsea) v Kensington and Chelsea RLBC*[9], in the context of traffic network management powers used on the rapid basis mandated during the pandemic without prior consultation, it was held that there was no duty on the local authority to consult before removing a cycle lane installed under those powers. No obligation to consult was found to have arisen. The court noted that

'the controversial nature of the proposal in question – which the removal of the cycle lanes undoubtedly was – is not a touchstone for deciding whether conspicuous unfairness has arisen as a result of a failure to consult. Indeed, the more controversial the proposal, the more likely it is that the subject matter lies in the political realm, where the courts are rightly cautious to intervene.'[10]

Other relevant road management laws include the New Roads and Street Works Act 1991 (NRSWA 1991) which, with TMA 2004 and 'supported by relevant regulations and codes of practice, provide a legislative framework for street works by undertakers (including utility companies) and the road works carried out by highway authorities – to the extent that these must be co-ordinated by street authorities'[11].

Traffic network management measures are subject to the Equality Act 2010:

'Accessibility requirements and the Public Sector Equality Duty apply to all measures, both temporary and permanent. In making any changes to their road networks, authorities must ensure that elements of a scheme do not discriminate, directly or indirectly and must consider their duty to make reasonable adjustments anticipating the needs of those with protected characteristics, for example, by carrying out equality impact assessments on proposed schemes. Engagement with groups representing disabled people and others with protected characteristics should be carried out at an early stage of scheme development.'[12]

---

8   As above.
9   [2023] EWHC 536 (Admin); [2023] RTR 24.
10 Lane J, [53].
11 Department for Transport 'Code of Practice for the co-ordination of street and road works' (5th edn, 31 March 2023), p 6.
12 As above, and see chapter 27, 'equality'.

The public duty to maintain highways under HA 1980, s 41 is actionable in private law but other public law highway duties would only exceptionally be actionable, in accordance with the principles in *Gorringe v Calderdale Metropolitan Borough Council*[13].

National Highways Digital, Data and Technology Strategy

28.02 The National Highways' digital, data and technology strategy (2021) includes 'the need to innovate, modernise and realise the benefits of emerging technologies, which have the potential to revolutionise travel on our roads'.[14]

National Transport Delivery Plan for Wales

28.03 In 2023 the Welsh Government published its National Transport Delivery Plan for Wales, with an emphasis upon the use of technology to better integrate freight transport and passenger journeys on public transport to support decarbonisation[15].

Road pricing

28.04 Road pricing powers are in the Transport Act 2000 (Part III, Chapter I, ss 163–177A) and for London in the Greater London Authority Act 1999 (s 295, 'road user charging'), which allows the Mayor to exercise the Authority's functions as to road user charging (Sch 23, para 2).

Under TA 2000, s 109A:

> 'A local transport authority whose area is in Wales must submit their local transport plan to the National Assembly for Wales [Senedd Cymru or the Welsh Parliament[16]] for its approval ... The [Senedd] may approve a local transport plan under this section if (but only if) it considers –
>
> (a) that the plan is consistent with the Wales Transport Strategy, and
>
> (b) that the policies contained in the plan are adequate for the implementation in the authority's area of the Strategy.'[17]

In their second AV law report, in October 2019, the Law Commissions considered road pricing, the 'most significant example' of which was then the London congestion charge, extended in April 2019 'to address problems of air quality' by the Ultra-Low Emission Zone (ULEZ) scheme[18]. The ULEZ area was further extended taking effect in August 2023.

---

13 2004] UKHL 15; [2004] 1 WLR 1057; see also *N and another v Poole Borough Council (AIRE Centre and others intervening)* [2019] UKSC 25; [2020] AC 780. See Chapter 13, 'highway claims'.
14 National Highways website 'Digital, data and technology strategy' (May 2021).
15 Welsh Government website 'Policy and Strategy. National transport delivery plan 2022 to 2027 (14 February 2023, updated 3 August 2023).
16 Senedd and Elections (Wales) Act 2020, s 2.
17 TA 2000, s 109A(1) and (4). And see s 170 ('charging schemes: consultation and inquiries').
18 Law Commissions' second AV law paper (October 2019, above), p 145, 7.80.

A challenge to the 2023 ULEZ expansion on three issues (whether confirmation of the order extending the area was within the statutory power; whether the Mayor provided sufficient information in his consultation before expansion; whether a grant of funds to Transport for London for a vehicle scrappage scheme was unlawful due to geographical restrictions on grants, insufficient consultation information and an inadequate consultation exercise) was dismissed by the High Court on all three grounds[19]. In particular, the standard applicable to material published for the purpose of a consultation ('whether reasons sufficient to permit the opportunity properly to respond had been provided') is:

'not a standard of perfection or anything close to it; it is one resting on a practical notion of what is sufficient to permit an informed response'

even where it could:

'fairly be said that some parts of the material published for the purposes of the consultation require careful reading'[20].

In relation to the scrappage scheme grant:

'The Mayor was not subject to any free-standing obligation to approve any grant payment to support a scrappage scheme. Whether he did, and if so in what amount, were political choices within his discretion, subject only to the usual public law constraints. Nor was the Mayor subject to any legal obligation that prescribed the terms of any scrappage scheme he might choose to fund. On this matter too, so far as concerned any legal obligation, the Mayor had something of a free hand. Any decision he took could be the subject of legal scrutiny based on ordinary *Wednesbury*[21] principles, but in this context any application of those principles would permit him significant latitude to decide as he considered appropriate.'[22]

In their second AV law paper (October 2019), the Law Commissions noted the potential for road pricing when combined with AV technology:

'Automated technology enables a much more flexible approach to road pricing. One problem with a daily charge is that once the vehicle has paid the charge for the day, it can continue to circulate within the zone without further disincentive. However, if the vehicle can generate reliable data to show where it has travelled and at what time, it will be possible to introduce more sophisticated pricing schemes. We envisage that HARPS[23] vehicles might pay a price per mile travelled, with the possibility of different mileage rates depending on the roads, occupancy and time of day. With a digitised

---

19 *London Boroughs of Hillingdon, Bexley, Bromley and Harrow and Surrey County Council v The Mayor of London and Transport for London* [2023] EWHC 1972 (Admin).
20 *LB Hillingdon and others* (above), Swift J [29].
21 *Associated Provincial Picture Houses Limited v Wednesbury Corporation* [1948] 1 KB 223 (CA), 229 (Lord Greene MR).
22 *LB Hillingdon and others* (above), Swift J [41].
23 'HARPS: Highly automated road passenger services. The term refers to a service which uses highly automated vehicles to supply road journeys to passengers without a human driver or user-in-charge. Some services may resemble taxi, private hire or bus services; others may look and operate differently': Law Commissions' second AV law paper (October 2019, above), p xi.

system, there is also the possibility of dynamic pricing, where charges vary depending on the level of congestion in the city at that particular time.'[24]

However, the Law Commissions concluded (in January 2022) that:

'... many consultees thought that road pricing raises issues which extend far beyond HARPS, including how to approach road taxation in the post-fossil fuel world. We do not feel able to make any recommendations on this issue at this time, in the absence of a more general Government strategy on the replacement for fuel duty.'[25]

B Public laws of highways for Advanced Driver Assistance Systems (ADAS)

Maintenance of road features upon which ADAS systems might depend

28.05 An untested question is whether there is a public law duty on a highway or similar authority to equip a road so as to allow ADAS systems on a vehicle to function.

The duty to keep in good repair a highway that is maintainable at the public expense (HA 1980, s 41) does not include the duty to maintain signs or markings painted on the surface of the road (*Gorringe v Calderdale Metropolitan Borough Council*[26]). A public law matter upon which camera-based ADAS systems might depend in darkness – the lighting of highways (HA 1980, s 97) – arises from a statutory discretion, rather than a requirement ('A highway authority may provide lighting...')[27].

C Public laws of highways for Automated Vehicles

The Law Commissions on traffic network management laws for automated vehicles

28.06 In chapter 7 of their second AV law report, the Law Commissions considered traffic management, as well as parking and use of kerbside space. In relation to traffic management, they noted the existence of:

'regulatory tools to manage the use of Highly Automated Road Passenger Services (HARPS) on UK roads. Initially, automated driving systems are likely to operate only in limited numbers in narrowly defined locations and

---

24 Law Commissions' second AV law paper (October 2019, above), p 149, 7.79.
25 Law Commissions' final report on automated vehicles, *Automated Vehicles: Joint Report*, Law Com No 404, Scot Law Com No 258 (January 2022), p, p197, 10.23.
26 Above.
27 *Sheppard v Mayor, Aldermen and Burgesses of the Borough of Glossop* [1921] 3 KB 132 (CA), followed in *Fisher v Ruislip-Northwood Urban District Council and Middlesex County Council* [1945] 1 KB 584 (CA), 600 (Lord Greene MR: "... they merely had the power to light at their discretion ...").

conditions. However, once the technological challenges have been met, the deployment of automated vehicle technology may be rapid.'[28]

The Law Commissions noted (presciently, as their paper preceded the expansion of TROs during the pandemic of 2020 to 2021) that 'TROs could be used in new and experimental ways', including:

'to restrict automated vehicles on a given road. Alternatively, TROs could be used to prohibit all vehicles other than automated vehicles, providing segregated lanes. We envisage that, as automation takes off, traffic authorities will use these powers to make many decisions about how HARPS vehicles are used in their areas. At the most basic level, TROs will be used to decide where HARPS vehicles can stop, wait and park and whether they can use bus lanes. There is also the possibility of HARPS only roads or roads where HARPS vehicles are prohibited.'[29]

The AV Bill 2023–24 (HL Bill 1) and public laws of highways

28.07   The AV Bill 2023-24 (HL Bill 1) includes the following provisions:

- Clause 57(1)-(4) provide how police may make an automated stop of an AV.

  'This clause clarifies that where a person would have power to direct a vehicle to stop that person will be able to use an appropriate communication protocol to direct an authorised automated vehicle to stop. If the vehicle does not stop in response to the communication protocol it will commit a traffic infraction in the same way as a human who fails to observe a signal.'[30]

- Clause 58 provides for the power to seized and detain vehicles, and for regulations to be made which will provide for appropriate storage of vehicles and for owners to be told what has happened to their vehicle and how to recover it.

- Clause 71(1) provides that:

  'The Secretary of State may, by regulations, require a chief officer of police to report to an inspector incidents which –

  (a)   occur in the area of the chief officer's police force, and

  (b)   are of a description set out in the regulations.'

- Clause 92 proposes amendments to RTA 1988 s 67-69 in relation to the provisions for roadside testing of vehicles.

  'This clause extends the existing powers of vehicle examiners to cover authorised automated vehicles for the purposes of determining whether these vehicles meet authorisation or operator licensing requirements.'[31]

---

28 Law Commissions' second AV law paper (October 2019, above), p 131, 7.1.
29 Law Commissions' second AV law paper (October 2019), p 131-132, 7.5-7.6.
30 Explanatory notes to AV Bill 2023-24 (HL Bill 1 – EN), para 246.
31 As above, para 360.

- Clause 93 empowers the Secretary of State by regulations to require a traffic regulation authority to provide prescribed information about a relevant traffic regulation.

  'Traffic regulation orders (TROs) are the legal orders made by traffic regulation authorities that set the rules around a road's use or its design. They contain information about, for example, the location and times of use of bus lanes or parking bays, speed limits, height and width restrictions, and temporary road closures for street and road works. The data contained in TROs is a valuable data set and will be needed for autonomous vehicles. The data will, for example, mean that information on the legal parameters of the road can be built into the vehicle and will be available to support the safe operation of vehicles.'[32]

- Clause 93(4) makes clear that the power in relation to TROs is exercisable both for advanced and automated vehicle technologies:

  'Regulations under this section may be made only if the Secretary of State considers that the provision of information in accordance with the regulations will help to enable information about the effects of traffic regulation measures to be communicated to or acted upon by –

  (a) authorised automated vehicles, or

  (b) electronic equipment designed to undertake or facilitate the driving of other vehicles on roads.'

D Public laws of highways for Electric Vehicles

Provision of EV charging points by a London Authority

28.08 Powers for the provision by a London local authority or by Transport for London of charging points for electric vehicles appear in the London Local Authorities and Transport for London Act 2013, Part 5, ss 16 to 18, which also features the offence of using prohibited charging apparatus at a charging point (s 19). LLATLA 2013, s 1(1) provides that:

'A London authority may provide and operate charging apparatus for electrically powered motor vehicles –

(a) in any public off-street car park under the management and control of the authority;

(b) on any highway for which they are responsible as highway authority.'

Provision of EV charging points outside London

28.09 Outside London, the provision of EV charging points is as provided by the Automated and Electric Vehicles Act 2018, Part 2, and regulations made under AEVA 2018, Part 2, which are described in chapter 15, 'EV charging claims' (to

---

32 As above, para 363.

date, the Public Charge Point Regulations 2023[33]). Those rules make requirements of providers of charging facilities.

As also described in chapter 15, the Alternative Fuels Infrastructure Regulations 2017 (AFIR 2017)[34] 'ensure the way that alternative fuels (electricity and hydrogen) are supplied to vehicles or ships is consistent across the UK'[35]. The AFIR 'must be enforced by the Secretary of State'[36] by means including compliance notices and civil penalties in the event of non-compliance[37].

The network management duty under TMA 2004, s 16, to secure 'the expeditious movement of traffic' and 'the avoidance, elimination or reduction of road congestion or other disruption to the movement of traffic' might – in at least some locations – imply the provision of sufficient public EV charging points.

---

33 SI 2023/1168.
34 AFIR 2017, SI 2017/897, and see UK government, Office for Product Safety and Standards 'Guidance on the Alternative Fuels Infrastructure Regulations 2017' (February 2021).
35 UK government, Office for Product Safety and Standards 'Guidance on the Alternative Fuels Infrastructure Regulations 2017' (February 2021) page 4, 1.1.
36 AFIR 2017, reg 7. The preamble to AFIR 2017 states that the 'Secretary of State is a Minister designated for the purpose of that section [European Communities Act 1972, s 2(2)] in relation to energy and energy sources'.
37 AFIR 2017, reg 11.

Chapter 29

Human rights law

'… either an interference is in accordance with the law or it is not. The issue of whether there is relevant 'law' for this purpose is a binary question… The fact that this case involved the trial of a new technology does not alter the need for any interference with article 8 rights to be in accordance with the law.'

The Court of Appeal (2020)[1]

Chapter Contents

A   Outline of human rights laws and AAEVs

29.01   This chapter describes human rights laws as they might be activated in their public law context by advanced, automated and electric vehicles.

Chapter 17, 'data and privacy claims' outlined civil claims for breaches of the Human Rights Act 1998, in the context of data protection and privacy, and Chapter 26 describes the public laws of data protection and privacy. HRA 1998 claims might arise in other contexts. Civil liability of public authorities has also been discussed in Chapters 13 and 18 (highway claims and personal security claims).

Public law liabilities might also arise under statutes other than HRA 1998 (for example, under the Equality Act 2010, discussed in Chapter 27). Environmental public law is discussed in Chapter 30.

The rights and freedoms protected by HRA 1998

29.02   HRA 1998 protects the following rights and fundamental freedoms set out in the Convention for the Protection of Human Rights and Fundamental Freedoms,

---

1   *Regina (Bridges) v Chief Constable of South Wales Police (Information Commissioner and others intervening)* [2020] EWCA Civ 1058; [2020] 1 WLR 5037, 5055 [58].

agreed by the Council of Europe at Rome on 4th November 1950 as it has effect for the time being in relation to the United Kingdom (the Convention[2]):

'(a) Articles 2 to 12 and 14 of the Convention,

(b) Articles 1 to 3 of the First Protocol, and

(c) Article 1 of the Thirteenth Protocol,

as read with Articles 16 to 18 of the Convention.'[3]

HRA 1998, s 2(1) requires that a 'court or tribunal determining a question which has arisen in connection with a Convention right must take into account any … judgment, decision, declaration or advisory opinion of the European Court of Human Rights' and certain opinions and decisions of the European Commission of Human Rights and Committee of Ministers of the Council of Europe 'whenever made or given, so far as, in the opinion of the court or tribunal, it is relevant to the proceedings in which that question has arisen'.

HRA 1998, ss 4 and 5 provide for declarations of incompatibility in primary and subordinate legislation.

HRA 1998, s 6 provides as follows:

'It is unlawful for a public authority to act in a way which is incompatible with a Convention right.

(2) Subsection (1) does not apply to an act if –

(a) as the result of one or more provisions of primary legislation, the authority could not have acted differently; or

(b) in the case of one or more provisions of, or made under, primary legislation which cannot be read or given effect in a way which is compatible with the Convention rights, the authority was acting so as to give effect to or enforce those provisions.

(3) In this section 'public authority' includes –

(a) a court or tribunal, and

(b) any person certain of whose functions are functions of a public nature,

but does not include either House of Parliament or a person exercising functions in connection with proceedings in Parliament.

…

(5) In relation to a particular act, a person is not a public authority by virtue only of subsection (3)(b) if the nature of the act is private.

(6) 'An act' includes a failure to act but does not include a failure to –

(a) introduce in, or lay before, Parliament a proposal for legislation; or

(b) make any primary legislation or remedial order.'

---

2 HRA 1998, s 21(1).
3 HRA 1998, s 1(1).

The protected rights and fundamental freedoms under HRA 1998, s 1(1) are set out in Sch 1 to the Act. In summary, they are as follows:

ECHR Articles 2 to 12 and 14 (including Arts 16 to 18, with which all of the protected rights are read):

Art 2: right to life

Art 3: prohibition of torture

Art 4: prohibition of slavery and forced labour

Art 5: right to liberty and security

Art 6: right to a fair trial

Art 7: no punishment without law

Art 8: right to respect for private and family life

Art 9: freedom of thought, conscience and religion

Art 10: freedom of expression

Art 11: freedom of assembly and association

Art 12: right to marry

Art 14: prohibition of discrimination

Art 16: restrictions on political activity of aliens

Art 17: prohibition of abuse of rights

Art 18: Limitation on use of restrictions on rights

Arts 1 to 3 of the First Protocol:

Art 1: protection of property

Art 2: right to education

Art 3: right to fair elections

Art 1 of the Thirteenth Protocol:

Abolition of the death penalty

Automated and surveillance systems and ECHR Art 8

29.03 AAEV technology involves both automated systems and surveillance, both of which have engaged Art 8 (the right to respect for private and family life) in *Bridges*[4], the Automated Facial Recognition (AFR) case and in *Fairhurst*, the doorbell camera case[5].

---

4 *Regina (Bridges) v Chief Constable of South Wales Police (Information Commissioner and others intervening)* [2020] EWCA Civ 1058; [2020] 1 WLR 5037. See Chapters 17 and 26.
5 *Fairhurst v Goddard* 12 October 2021, county court at Oxford, unreported. See Chapter 17.

B Human rights laws and Advanced Driver Assistance Systems (ADAS)

Future ADAS technologies and challenges uncertain

29.04 Future ADAS technologies are uncertain, so the scope of potential interferences with rights such as privacy, as well as other rights, is unknown.

As in the cases described above, it seems likely that future cases will involve a combination of rights protected by a combination of several laws (not limited to HRA 1998, EA 2010, DPA 2018 and nuisance).

The Supreme Court's expansion of nuisance to include visual intrusion[6] is also likely to be relevant to AAEVs, given their camera technologies.

State's general or systemic duty to protect the right to life

29.05 In *Savage v South Essex Partnership NHS Foundation Trust (MIND and others intervening)*, the House of Lords observed that:

'Fundamentally, article 2 [*ECHR*] requires a state to have in place a structure of laws which will help to protect life. In *Osman v United Kingdom* 29 EHRR 245, 305, para 115, the European court identified the 'primary duty' of a state under the article as being:

"to secure the right to life by putting in place effective criminal law provisions to deter the commission of offences against the person backed up by law-enforcement machinery for the prevention, suppression and sanctioning of breaches of such provisions."[7]'

In the road traffic context (which was not the context of *Savage*), the extensive criminal law provisions of the Road Traffic and other Acts and the national law enforcement machinery for road traffic surely complies with that duty. It is perhaps an open question, however, as to how long a regulatory system still centred upon 'driver control'[8] can continue to do so, without reform to accommodate increasingly innovative and unfamiliar ADAS systems, of which 'hands free' driving systems are an example[9]. The Automated Vehicles Bill 2023-24 describes a rigorous and detailed scheme of regulation for automated vehicles and empowers further regulation of ADAS systems. On its first reading the government stated that the AV Bill 2023-24 (HL Bill 1) was compatible with the Convention rights, pursuant to HRA 1998, s 19(1)(a)[10].

---

6 *Fearn v Board of Trustees of the Tate Gallery* [2023] UKSC 4; [2023] 2 WLR 339. See Chapter 17, 'data and privacy'.
7 [2009] 1 AC 681, 694 [19].
8 RTA 1988, s 41D and Road Vehicles (Construction and Use) Regulations 1986, SI 1986/1078, reg 104.
9 See Chapters 4, 'driving', and 21, 'moving offences'.
10 First page of the Bill.

The undeveloped state of regulation in the face of a new technology is irrelevant to the breach of an HRA 1998 right. In *Bridges*, the Court of Appeal found 'references by the [Divisional] court to the possibility of future reconsideration of this issue a little curious' and confirmed that:

> '… either an interference is in accordance with the law or it is not. The issue of whether there is relevant 'law' for this purpose is a binary question: see *In re Gallagher* [2020] AC 185, para 14 (Lord Sumption). The fact that this case involved the trial of a new technology does not alter the need for any interference with article 8 rights to be in accordance with the law.'[11]

C Human rights laws and Automated Vehicles

Challenge to AEVA 2018, s 1 listing or AVA 2024 authorisation of an 'automated' vehicle on human rights grounds

29.06   The regulatory system for classifying a vehicle as 'automated' is unfinished, as the government agrees with the Law Commissions that the present system of 'listing' a vehicle as automated under AEVA 2018, s 1 is not adequate and should be replaced[12]. The AV Bill 2023-24 (HL Bill 1) is the legislative proposal for its replacement.

As discussed above, a regulatory scheme will be tested by the courts on its terms as they exist[13]. If the first automated vehicle is 'listed' under AEVA 2018, s 1, then that will be before the AV Bill 2023-24 (HL Bill 1) is enacted, as that Bill replaces 'listing' with a fuller regulatory scheme. If the first automated vehicle is 'authorised' under the Automated Vehicles Act 2024, supported by (as yet unpublished) statement of safety principles and regulations made under AVA 2024, then that will be under a fuller scheme.

D Human rights laws and Electric Vehicles

Road infrastructure

29.07   Road infrastructure for AAEVs will be subject to a number of duties, depending upon the facts of the case, likely including the public sector equality duty under EA 2010, s 149[14]. See Chapter 27, 'equality'.

The suitability of EV charging points for people with accessibility needs is the subject of a 2022 standard by the British Standards Institution[15], sponsored by the charity Motability. That standard includes guidance as to charge point design, placement, the surroundings of the charge point, digital platforms and information.

---

11 *Bridges* (above), 5055 [58].
12 UK government policy paper 'Connected and automated mobility 2025: realising the benefits of self-driving vehicles' ('CAM 2025'), 19 August 2022, p 126.
13 *Bridges* (above), 5055 [58].
14 See Chapters 13, 'highway claims', 15, 'EV charging claims', 27, 'equality' and 28, 'public highway laws'.
15 *Electric vehicles -accessible charging – specification,* BSI PAS 1899:2022, at BSI website 'PAS 1899:2022 Electric vehicles – accessible charging – specification' (accessed 27 July 2023).

Chapter 30

Environmental law

'Although electric vehicles offer 'clear benefits' for local air quality due to zero exhaust emissions at street level, they still emit particulate matter from road, tyre and brake wear. This means EVs cannot entirely eliminate issues of air pollution in cities... The number of EVs currently approaching the end of their life is relatively small, however the EV market is growing which in turn will lead to more batteries reaching the end of their on-vehicle life.'

(House of Commons Library Briefing Paper (2023)[1]

'... choices can be made about the direction and nature of both environmental law and technology. Those choices are not simply choices about regulatory strategy and technological innovation, but choices about how we choose to imagine the world and how we choose to live in it.'

Professor Elizabeth Fisher (2017)[2]

Chapter Contents

A   Outline of environmental laws of AAEVs

A wide, pluralistic concept

30.01   As Professors Fisher, Lange and Scotford note, environmental law 'is a legally, scientifically, and socio-politically complex subject'[3], 'a pluralistic subject in scholarly terms'[4], rooted in national culture and drawing upon laws as various as

---

1   House of Commons Library Briefing Paper 'Electric vehicles and infrastructure' by Dr Holly Edwards, Iona Stewart, Becky Mawhood and Paul Bolton (CBP-7480, 21 February 2023), p 10, 73.
2   'Imagining Technology and Environmental Law', chapter 15 of *The Oxford Handbook of Law, Regulation and Technology* (ed. Roger Brownsword, Eloise Scotford and Karen Yeung, Oxford University Press, 2017) at p 376.
3   Elizabeth Fisher, Bettina Lange and Eloise Scotford *Environmental Law: Text, Cases and Materials* (Oxford University Press, 2nd edn, 2019), p 2.
4   Above, Chapter 10, 'Environmental law in the legal culture of the United Kingdom', p 293.

521

pre-Industrial Revolution common laws such as nuisance[5] to twenty first century international directives on the disposal of vehicles and electronic waste[6].

Some recent environmental cases relevant to AAEVs

30.02 A selection of recent cases relevant to AAEVs, discussed in other chapters of this book, demonstrates the range of environmental law as a topic:

- *Fearn*[7] (nuisance includes visual intrusion)

- *Bridges*[8] (automated surveillance in a public space engages the Human Rights Act 1998, Equality Act 2010, Protection of Freedoms Act 2012 and Data Protection Act 2018)

- *London Borough of Hillingdon and others*[9] (expansion of Ultra Low Emission Zone and grant to vehicle scrappage scheme within Mayor of London's legal powers).

Environment Act 2021 (EA 2021)

30.03 EA 2021, s 1 regulates by targets. EA 2021, s 1(1) to (4) provide as follows:

'(1) The Secretary of State may by regulations set long-term targets in respect of any matter which relates to –

    (a) the natural environment, or

    (b) people's enjoyment of the natural environment.

(2) The Secretary of State must exercise the power in subsection (1) so as to set a long-term target in respect of at least one matter within each priority area.

(3) The priority areas are –

    (a) air quality;

    (b) water;

    (c) biodiversity;

    (d) resource efficiency and waste reduction.

(4) A target set under this section must specify –

    (a) a standard to be achieved, which must be capable of being objectively measured, and

    (b) a date by which it is to be achieved.'

---

5 Above, p 297.
6 Above, Chapter 16, 'Waste regulation', p 550.
7 *Fearn v Board of Trustees of the Tate Gallery* [2023] UKSC 4; [2023] 2 WLR 339.
8 *Regina (Bridges) v Chief Constable of South Wales Police (Information Commissioner and others intervening)* [2020] EWCA Civ 1058; [2020] 1 WLR 5037.
9 *London Boroughs of Hillingdon, Bexley, Bromley and Harrow and Surrey County Council v The Mayor of London and Transport for London* [2023] EWHC 1972 (Admin).

Environmental Acts of Senedd Cymru

30.04   The Senedd has passed environmental legislation including the Well-being of Future Generations (Wales) Act 2015 and the Environment Act (Wales) 2016. The 2015 Act imposes a duty to carry out sustainable development on each public body (s 3), where:

'…*'sustainable development'* means the process of improving the economic, social, environmental and cultural well-being of Wales by taking action, in accordance with the sustainable development principle (see section 5), aimed at achieving the well-being goals (see section 4).' (WBFGWA 2015, s 2)

'… any reference to a public body doing something *'in accordance with the sustainable development principle'* means that the body must act in a manner which seeks to ensure that the needs of the present are met without compromising the ability of future generations to meet their own needs.' (WBFGWA 2015, s 5(1)).

The well-being goals are explicitly environmental (WFGWA 2015, s 4, table 1):

Goal	Description of the goal
A prosperous Wales.	An innovative, productive and low carbon society which recognises the limits of the global environment and therefore uses resources efficiently and proportionately (including acting on climate change); and which develops a skilled and well-educated population in an economy which generates wealth and provides employment opportunities, allowing people to take advantage of the wealth generated through securing decent work.
A resilient Wales.	A nation which maintains and enhances a biodiverse natural environment with healthy functioning ecosystems that support social, economic and ecological resilience and the capacity to adapt to change (for example climate change).
A healthier Wales.	A society in which people's physical and mental well-being is maximised and in which choices and behaviours that benefit future health are understood.
A more equal Wales.	A society that enables people to fulfil their potential no matter what their background or circumstances (including their socio economic background and circumstances).
A Wales of cohesive communities.	Attractive, viable, safe and well-connected communities.
A Wales of vibrant culture and thriving Welsh language.	A society that promotes and protects culture, heritage and the Welsh language, and which encourages people to participate in the arts, and sports and recreation.
A globally responsible Wales.	A nation which, when doing anything to improve the economic, social, environmental and cultural well-being of Wales, takes account of whether doing such a thing may make a positive contribution to global well-being.

In 2023 the Welsh Government published its National Transport Delivery Plan for Wales, citing WFGWA 2015[10].

Scope of this chapter

30.05   This chapter focuses upon two environmental law issues of likely application to AAEVs:

- regulation of tyre and brake particulate matter emissions;
- regulation of electronic waste recycling;

Those issues affect ADAS, AVs and EVs, so this chapter considers each of those issues in turn and is not subdivided into 'ADAS', 'automated vehicle' and 'electric vehicle' sections.

Please see other chapters in relation to other public and private laws with an environmental aspect – for example, Chapters 13, 'highway claims', and 28, 'public highway laws'.

B   AAEVs and particulate matter emissions

EA 2021, ss 2 and 74–77

30.06   EA 2021, s 2 applies to England and Wales[11] and sets environmental targets for particulate matter:

'(1) The Secretary of State must by regulations set a target ('the $PM_{2.5}$ air quality target') in respect of the annual mean level of $PM_{2.5}$ in ambient air.

(2) The $PM_{2.5}$ air quality target may, but need not, be a long-term target.

(3) In this section '$PM_{2.5}$' means particulate matter with an aerodynamic diameter not exceeding 2.5 micrometres.

(4) Regulations setting the $PM_{2.5}$ air quality target may make provision defining '*ambient air*'.

(5) The duty in subsection (1) is in addition to (and does not discharge) the duty in section 1(2) to set a long-term target in relation to air quality.

(6) Section 1(4) to (9) applies to the $PM_{2.5}$ air quality target and to regulations under this section as it applies to targets set under section 1 and to regulations under that section.

(7) In this Part '*the $PM_{2.5}$ air quality target*' means the target set under subsection (1).'

Powers under EA 2021, ss 74–77 to recall motor vehicles for environmental reasons have yet to be brought into force.

---

10 Welsh Government website 'Policy and Strategy. National transport delivery plan 2022 to 2027 (14 February 2023, updated 3 August 2023), p 9.
11 EA 2021, s 146(1).

Environmental Targets (Fine Particulate Matter) (England) Regulations 2023

30.07 The regulations under EA 2021, s 2(1) are the Environmental Targets (Fine Particulate Matter) (England) Regulations 2023[12]. The regulations 'extend to England and Wales but apply in relation to England only' (reg 1(4)).

Reg 2 defines 'ambient air' as 'outdoor air, excluding the air in workplaces where members of the public do not have regular access'.

Reg 4 'sets the target to ensure that the annual mean concentration of $PM_{2.5}$ in ambient air is equal to or less than 10 micrograms per cubic metre by 31st December 2040.'[13]

Reg 7 sets the population exposure reduction target 'to ensure that there is at least a 35% reduction in population exposure to $PM_{2.5}$ by 31st December 2040, as compared with a baseline period of 1st January 2016 to 31st December 2018.'[14]

C AAEVs and electronic waste recycling

End-of-Life Vehicles (Producer Responsibility) Regulations 2005

30.08 The End-of-Life Vehicles (Producer Responsibility) Regulations 2005[15] (as EU-derived domestic legislation continuing to have effect under EU(W)A 2018, s 2) 'require a producer to submit to the Secretary of State an application for approval of the system he has established to collect vehicles for which he is responsible (reg 10). A producer's system for collection must contain sufficient capacity to treat those end-of-life vehicles for which he is responsible (reg 12). The system for collection must also be reasonably accessible to any person who wants to deliver an end-of-life vehicle to it (reg 11)'[16].

Waste Batteries and Accumulators Regulations 2009

30.09 The Waste Batteries and Accumulators Regulations 2009[17] apply to vehicle batteries, although the battery providing the power to drive an electric vehicle is classified not as an 'automotive' battery (which is 'a battery used for automotive starter, lighting or ignition power'[18]) but as an 'industrial' battery, 'used as a source of power for propulsion in an electric vehicle'[19]. A 'hybrid' vehicle is likely to have both types of battery[20].

---

12 SI 2023/96.
13 Explanatory note to SI 2023/96.
14 As above.
15 SI 2005/263.
16 Explanatory note to SI 2005/263.
17 SI 2009/890.
18 WBAR 2009, reg 2(1).
19 As above.
20 Environment Agency 'Guidance. Waste Batteries and accumulators: technical guidance' (31 August 2021).

WBAR 2009, Part 5 (regs 35 to 46, 'producer obligations: industrial and automotive batteries') requires producers to take back waste batteries free of charge from end-users on request. In particular:

- Reg 36 imposes obligations on producers of automotive batteries to collect waste automotive batteries free of charge from final holders of such batteries on request (reg 2 defines a final holder of automotive batteries in summary as (a) a trade remover of automotive batteries (b) a scrap metal dealer (c) an authorised treatment facility as defined by EoLV(PR) 2005 (above) (d) a waste disposal authority);

- Reg 38 requires producers to ensure that all waste batteries they take back or collect are delivered for treatment and recycling to an approved battery treatment operator or an approved exporter;

- Regs 39 to 41 require producers to report on and keep records of the amount of batteries placed by them on the market for the first time in the UK and the amount of waste batteries collected by them and delivered for treatment and recycling.

- Regs 42 to 46 require producers to be registered with the Secretary of State.

WBAR 2009, Part 7 applies to all types of battery and sets requirements for the disposal, treatment and recycling of batteries, including the prohibition on disposing of waste automotive and industrial batteries in a landfill or by incineration (reg 56) and the requirement for approval of battery treatment operators and exporters (reg 57).

Waste Electrical and Electronic Equipment Regulations 2013

30.10   The Waste Electrical and Electronic Equipment Regulations 2013[21] do not apply to electrical and electronic equipment (EEE):

> 'which is ...
>
> (b) specifically designed and installed as part of another type of equipment that is excluded from or does not fall within the scope of these Regulations, which can fulfil its function only if it is part of that equipment' (WEEER 2013, reg 7(b)).

WEEER 2013, Schs 1 and 2 respectively categorise and give examples of EEE to which the regulations apply; vehicles do not explicitly feature (although category 7 is 'toys, leisure and sports equipment').

Government guidance on WEEER 2013 gives as examples of such excluded equipment:

> 'a built-in satellite navigation system installed into cars...'

> 'transport for persons or goods, excluding electric 2 wheeled vehicles which are not type-approved'

---

21 SI 2013/3113.

'off-road mobile machinery for professional use only' and

'equipment designed only for research and development use and only available via business to business (B2B)'[22].

EA 2021, s 50 and Sch 4

30.11   EA 2021, s 50 and Sch 4 extend to England and Wales, Scotland and Northern Ireland[23] and provide that the 'the relevant national authority may by regulations make provision for imposing producer responsibility obligations on specified persons in respect of specified products or materials'[24]. To date, the section has been used to amend packaging waste regulations[25].

---

22 Government (Office for Product Safety and Standards; DEFRA) 'Guidance. Regulations: Waste Electrical and Electronic Equipment (WEEE)' (1 January 2021); Environment Agency 'Guidance. Electrical and electronic equipment (EEE) covered by the WEEE regulations' (2 August 2023).
23 EA 2021, s 146(3)(a)(i).
24 EA 2021, Sch 4, para 1(1).
25 Producer Responsibility Obligations (Packaging Waste) (Amendment) (England and Wales) Regulations 2022, SI 2022/1222.

Chapter 31

The new public laws of advanced and automated vehicle safety

To accommodate [automated vehicles], we need a new vocabulary, new legal actors and new regulatory schemes."

The Law Commission of England and Wales
and the Scottish Law Commission (2022)[1]

Outline

31.01   The Automated Vehicles Bill 2023-24 (HL Bill 1) sets out the detailed regulatory scheme for automated vehicle safety designed by the Law Commissions over four years (2018 to 2022) and since refined by the UK government's Centre for Connected and Autonomous Vehicles (CCAV) and Department for Transport. The various parts of the scheme are described in earlier chapters. The 'general monitoring duty ... for monitoring and assessing the general performance of authorised automated vehicles on roads and other public places in Great Britain' (cl 38) is emblematic of the new approach.

Among the distinctive features of the scheme are the quantity of safety-related powers which it gives to government (the Secretary of State) and the safety powers which are also exercisable by traffic commissioners and by statutory inspectors. Many of those powers – of interview, seizure of evidence and search of premises – are essentially police powers. The strength with which the State intends to police advanced and automated technologies is clear from the AV Bill 2023-24. That should not come as a surprise: it was apparent from the Law Commissions' final recommendations in January 2022 that a proactive safety scheme – atypical of previous motor vehicle regulation – was intended for automated vehicles.

31.02   This chapter is not split into the sub-topics of advanced, automated and electric vehicles used in earlier chapters, as the powers described in the Bill are broad (some apply both to advanced and automated vehicles – see cll 78, 79 and 91, for example) and many vehicles to which it will apply are likely to be electrically propelled.

This chapter deals with the sanctions of the new regulatory scheme of the AV Bill 2023-24 (HL Bill 1) and appeals against those sanctions. It is not an exhaustive list

---

1   Law Commissions' final report on automated vehicles, *Automated Vehicles: Joint Report*, Law Com No 404, Scot Law Com No 258 (January 2022), p 11, 2.2-2.3.

of all powers and procedures under the AV Bill (the reader is referred to the text of the Bill, as it moves through Parliament) but a selection of notable points.

The scheme of the AV Bill is a work in progress – the regulations which can be made under its numerous powers have yet to be published, like the statement of safety principles (cl 2) which will inform those regulations and those who will work under them. The Bill itself, though expected to become the Automated Vehicles Act 2024 in similar terms, is yet to have its second reading in the House of Lords (where it was introduced) as at the time of writing of this book.

The types of operation which the AV Bill 2023-24 (HL Bill 1) seeks to regulate are:

- An authorised self-driving entity (ASDE), the body with 'general responsibility for ensuring that an authorised automated vehicle continues to satisfy the self-driving test by virtue of its authorised automation features' (cl 6(4)(a), under the Part 1 'regulatory scheme for automated vehicles');

- A 'licensed no user-in-charge operator' (NUICO), meaning 'a person for the time being licensed under operator licensing regulations' (cl 44(1)) in relation to a 'no user-in-charge journey' ('a journey by a vehicle with an authorised no-user-in-charge feature during which (at any point) (a) that feature is engaged, or (b) there is no individual in the vehicle who is exercising control of it': cl 12(2)) under the power to establish an operator licensing scheme by regulations (cll 12-13, also under the Part 1 'regulatory scheme for automated vehicles'); and

- An 'automated passenger service', meaning 'a service that consists of the carrying of passengers in a road vehicle that: (a) is designed or adapted to travel autonomously;, or (b) is being used for a trial with the aim of developing vehicles that are so designed or adapted' (cl 82(2)), permitted under cl 82 (within Part 5, 'permits for automated passenger services').

Powers of the Secretary of State

31.03 The powers of the Secretary of State under the AV Bill 2023-24 (HL Bill 1) include the power to vary, suspend or withdraw an automated vehicle authorisation (cll 8-9). Clause 8 of the Bill provides:

'(1) The Secretary of State may vary, suspend or withdraw an automated vehicle authorisation with the agreement of the authorised self-driving entity for the authorised automated vehicle concerned.

(2) The Secretary of State may vary, suspend or withdraw an automated vehicle authorisation without that agreement if the Secretary of State is satisfied that a unilateral ground has arisen in respect of the authorisation.

(3) The Secretary of State may suspend or temporarily vary an automated vehicle authorisation without that agreement if the Secretary of State—

    (a) suspects that a unilateral ground has arisen in respect of the authorisation, and

    (b) proposes to enquire into whether it has.

(4) For the purposes of this section, a unilateral ground arises in respect of an authorisation if—

(a) an authorisation requirement is not or has not been met in respect of the authorised vehicle,

(b) the authorised vehicle has committed a traffic infraction, or

(c) the authorised vehicle no longer satisfies the self-driving test by reference to all authorised locations and circumstances.

(5) A suspension or variation under subsection (3) may not be kept in force after the process of enquiry has concluded, except for so long as may be necessary to allow action to be taken under subsection (2).

(6) An authorisation may be suspended or varied under subsection (2) even if it is already suspended, or varied in the same way, under subsection (3) (in which case the new suspension or variation supersedes the existing one).

(7) Part 1 of Schedule 1—

(a) makes provision about the procedure applicable in connection with variation, suspension or withdrawal under subsection (2) or (3) (including rights of appeal), and

(b) provides for a further case in which an authorisation may be varied, suspended or withdrawn without agreement.'

The Secretary of State also has the ability to prescribe descriptive language for advanced and automated vehicles and their components:

Cl 78(1) of the Bill provides:

'The Secretary of State may, by regulations, specify words, expressions, symbols or marks as appropriate for use in connection with road vehicles only if used in connection with authorised automated vehicles (whether generally or of a description given in the regulations).' (cl 78(1))

The Secretary of State is also the enforcer of criminal offences in relation to the misuse of descriptive terms:

'It is the duty of the Secretary of State to enforce sections 78 and 79.' (cl 81(4), Sch 5 para 1(1))[2]

Powers of Statutory Inspectors

31.04   Under the AV Bill 2023-24 (HL Bill 1), cll 60-77 (within Part 3 of the Bill, 'policing and investigation', Chapter 2, 'investigation of incidents by statutory inspectors'), statutory inspectors have wide powers 'of identifying, improving understanding of, and reducing the risks of harm arising from the use of authorised automated vehicles on roads in Great Britain' (cl 61(1)), to investigate AV incidents or potential incidents, whether or not on a road (cl 62) and a duty to report any findings of their investigations to the Secretary of State (cl 68).

---

2   And AV Bill 2023-24 (HL Bill 1), cl 81(4), Sch 5, para 2 adds this paragraph to the list of enforcer's legislation under the Consumer Rights Act 2015, s 77, Sch 5, para 9(1)(a), by amendment to para 10 of that Schedule.

Regulations may allow for 'whether and how interested persons are to be given the opportunity to comment on a draft report' (cl 68(4)(d)).

The powers include, at cl 63(1), a statutory inspector's power to require:

> 'a person to take positive action to provide them with or allow them access to information, items, or material. For example, this could include access to an automated vehicle and the associated data that has been collected during the period around an incident of interest. Paragraph (b) provides that this may include an inspector requiring a person to refrain from doing something, such as disturbing, altering or moving anything specified by the inspector.' (Explanatory notes to the AV Bill 2023-24, HL Bill 1 – EN, para 261).

– and powers to enter and search premises (cl 64).

Under cl 67 investigation powers can be directed at police officers. Under cl 65 a statutory inspector can stop traffic and pedestrians.

Under cl 72 an inspector may 'produce and publish information about the safety of authorised automated vehicles or about investigations'. The Explanatory notes refer (at para 300) to the Marine Accident Investigation Branch's Safety Digests, which describe incidents in plain language and 'draw out the lessons to be learned'[3].

The regulatory scheme under the AV Bill supports multidisciplinary operations. Under cll 72(1)(b) and (3) a statutory inspector may support the functions of investigators in other transport fields: including merchant shipping, civil aviation, railways and space transport.

Civil sanctions against regulated bodies under the AV Bill 2023-24 (HL Bill 1), Part 1, 'regulatory scheme for automated vehicles'

31.05   Under the AV Bill 2023-24 (HL Bill 1), cll 34-37, the Secretary of State may order a range of civil sanctions against regulated bodies. These are compliance notices, redress notices and monetary penalties.

A compliance notice is defined in cl 34, (4)-(7) of which provide that:

> '(4) A compliance notice is a notice requiring the person to whom it is issued to take such actions within subsection (5) as are specified in the notice.
>
> (5) The actions that may be specified are—
>
> (a) in the case of a notice under subsection (1), actions that the Secretary of State considers appropriate in order to secure, or make it more likely, that the regulated body complies with the regulatory requirement in the future;

---

3   'Safety Digest: Lessons from Marine Accident Reports' (Marine Accident Investigation Branch (MAIB), February 2023)

(b) in the case of a notice under subsection (2), actions that the Secretary of State considers appropriate in order to avoid, or make less likely, the future commission of similar traffic infractions by authorised automated vehicles for which the authorised self-driving entity is responsible.

(6) The actions may be specified by referring (with or without further particulars) to the actions necessary to achieve a result described in the notice.

(7) A compliance notice must—

(a) explain the Secretary of State's reasons for issuing the notice, and

(b) specify the time by which, or period during which, the specified actions must be taken.

(8) The reference in subsection (4) to taking action includes refraining from taking action; and "actions" in this section is to be read accordingly.'

A redress notice is defined in cl 35, (4)-(9) of which provide that:

'(4) A redress notice is a notice requiring the person to whom it is issued to take such actions within subsection (5) as are specified in the notice.

(5) The actions that may be specified are actions that the Secretary of State considers appropriate in order to rectify, mitigate, or compensate for (whether directly or indirectly) the loss, damage, inconvenience or annoyance that has been suffered.

(6) A redress notice must—

(a) explain the Secretary of State's reasons for issuing the notice, and

(b) specify the time by which, or period during which, the specified actions must be taken.

(7) If a redress notice requires a regulated body to pay a sum of money to another person, the sum may be recovered by that person as a civil debt.

(8) The reference in subsection (4) to taking action includes refraining from taking action; and "actions" in this section is to be read accordingly.

(9) In this section, "users of roads" includes persons exercising statutory functions in relation to roads.'

Monetary penalties are provided for in cl 36, which provides as follows:

'(1) The Secretary of State may issue a monetary penalty notice to a regulated body if satisfied that—

(a) a regulatory requirement is not, or has not been, met by the body, or

(b) the body has failed to comply with—

(i) an information notice,

(ii) an interview notice,

(iii) a compliance notice, or

(iv) a redress notice.

(2) The Secretary of State may issue a monetary penalty notice to an authorised self-driving entity if satisfied that an authorised automated vehicle has committed a traffic infraction while the entity was responsible for it.

(3) Subsection (2) does not apply if it appears to the Secretary of State that the commission of the traffic infraction was wholly caused by a failure of a licensed no-user-in-charge operator to comply with a requirement under operator licensing regulations.

(4) A monetary penalty notice is a notice requiring the regulated body to pay a monetary penalty, of a sum specified in the notice, to the Secretary of State.

(5) Subsection (6) applies in relation to a monetary penalty notice issued under subsection (1) if it appears to the Secretary of State that the failure to which the notice relates is or may be a continuing one.

(6) The monetary penalty notice may provide for a sum specified in the notice to be added to the penalty for each day in the period—

    (a) beginning with the day after the day on which the notice is issued, and

    (b) ending with—

        (i) the day on which the failure is brought to an end, or

        (ii) such earlier day as is specified in the notice.

(7) A monetary penalty notice must—

    (a) explain the Secretary of State's reasons for issuing the notice, and

    (b) specify the time by which, and manner in which, the penalty must be paid.

(8) If a monetary penalty is not paid in time—

    (a) the penalty (or the unpaid part of it) carries interest at the rate for the time being specified in section 17 of the Judgments Act 1838;

    (b) the Secretary of State may recover the penalty (or the unpaid part of it), with the interest, as a civil debt.

(9) The Secretary of State must, by regulations, provide for the determination of—

    (a) a maximum sum that may be specified under subsection (4), and

    (b) a maximum sum that may be specified under subsection (6).

(10) Those regulations may determine the sum by reference to the turnover of the regulated body or other entities or undertakings that are connected with the regulated body in a manner specified in the regulations; and if they do so they may also make provision about—

    (a) what counts as "turnover";

    (b) how turnover is to be calculated or assessed.

(11) A regulated body is not, in respect of the same conduct or omission, liable both to conviction of an offence under section 24 or 25[4] and to a monetary penalty under this section (so the occurrence of one, unless overturned or cancelled, means that the other can no longer take place).'

---

4   258 (January 2022), p 11, 2.2-2.3.
And AV Bill 2023-24 (HL Bill 1), cl 24, 'false or withheld information relevant to vehicle safety'; cl 25 'aggravated offence where death or serious injury occurs'. See Chapter 25, 'tampering offences'.

Cl 37 makes supplementary provisions including that the procedure applicable in connection with such notices (including the recovery of costs and right of appeal) is set out in Sch 1. Ceasing to be a regulated body does not protect against defaults under cll 33-37 while a regulated body (cl 37(4)).

Appeals against decisions on authorisations and civil sanctions under the AV Bill 2023-24 (HL Bill 1), Part 1, 'regulatory scheme for automated vehicles'

31.06   AV Bill 2023-24 (HL Bill 1), Sch 1, Part 1 sets out the procedure in relation to enforcement action under Part 1 of the Bill, including the ordinary procedure and the procedure for urgent suspension or temporary variation.

The AV Bill 2023-24 (HL Bill 1), Sch 1, para 3 provides for appeals against variation, suspension or withdrawal of an automated vehicle authorisation under cl 8(2) or (3) (above). The potential grounds of appeal are:

'(a) in a case where the Secretary of State acted under section 8(2) in reliance on section 8(4)(a), that the failure to meet authorisation requirements did not occur;

(b) in a case where the Secretary of State acted under section 8(2) in reliance on section 8(4)(b), that the commission of a traffic infraction did not occur;

(c) in a case where the Secretary of State acted under section 8(2) in reliance on section 8(4)(c), that the Secretary of State's conclusion was based on a mistaken finding of fact;

(d) that the decision to vary, suspend or withdraw the authorisation was unreasonable;

(e) that the Secretary of State failed to comply with paragraph 1 or 2, or made some other procedural error, in respect of the variation, suspension or withdrawal.'

The explanatory notes to the AV Bill 2023-24 (para 383) state that:

'This paragraph provides a right of appeal against unilateral authorisation measures. It is intended to allow the tribunal to intervene where the Secretary of State makes incorrect factual findings, fails to follow proper procedure, or acts unreasonably – in a public law sense – but not to allow the tribunal to substitute its own judgement on matters of evaluation, such as whether the self-driving test is satisfied. The relevant tribunal will be the First-tier Tribunal unless procedure rules allocate matters to the Upper Tribunal.'

Under Sch 1, para 3(3) and (4):

'(3) If satisfied that any of those grounds is made out, the Tribunal must allow the appeal and—

(a) direct that the variation, suspension or withdrawal be undone, or

(b) remit the matter to the Secretary of State with a direction that the Secretary of State consider, in accordance with the findings of the

> Tribunal and by such time as the Tribunal specifies, whether to undo the variation, suspension or withdrawal.
>
> (4) Otherwise, the Tribunal must dismiss the appeal.'

The AV Bill 2023-24 (HL Bill 1), Sch 1, para 7 treats appeals against a compliance notice, redress notice, monetary penalty notice or costs notice. Schedule 1, para 7(1)-(4) provide as follows:

> '(1) A person to whom a compliance notice, redress notice, monetary penalty notice or costs notice is issued may appeal to the Tribunal.
>
> (2) The grounds on which an appeal may be brought are—
>
> > (a) in the case of a compliance notice or redress notice—
> >
> > > (i) that the failure to meet requirements, or commission of a traffic infraction, on the grounds of which the notice was issued did not occur, or
> > >
> > > (ii) that the actions specified in the notice, or the time or period specified for taking them, are unreasonable;
> >
> > (b) in the case of a monetary penalty notice—
> >
> > > (i) that the failure to meet requirements, or commission of a traffic infraction, on the grounds of which the notice was issued did not occur, or
> > >
> > > (ii) that the sum or amount specified in the notice, or the time or manner specified for paying it, is unreasonable;
> >
> > (c) in the case of a compliance notice, redress notice or monetary penalty notice issued under section 34(2), 35(2) or 36(2), that the commission of a traffic infraction on the grounds of which the notice was issued was caused as described in section 34(3), 35(3) or 36(3);
> >
> > (d) in the case of a costs notice—
> >
> > > (i) that costs relied on in arriving at the sum specified in the notice were not reasonably incurred as described in paragraph 6(3), or
> > >
> > > (ii) that the time or manner specified for payment is unreasonable; that the Secretary of State failed to comply with a requirement of paragraph 5, or made some other procedural error, in respect of the notice.
>
> (3) If satisfied that any of those grounds is made out, the Tribunal must allow the appeal and do whichever of the following it considers appropriate—
>
> > (a) cancel the notice,
> >
> > (b) remit the matter to the Secretary of State with a direction that the Secretary of State consider, in accordance with the findings of the Tribunal and by such time as the Tribunal specifies, whether to cancel or vary the notice under section 37(2), or
> >
> > (c) if the appeal is allowed on a ground in sub-paragraph (2)(b)(ii) or
> >
> > (d), vary the notice.
>
> (4) Otherwise, the Tribunal must dismiss the appeal.'

As in relation to an appeal against an authorisation decision:

'... "the Tribunal' means the First-tier Tribunal. This is qualified in sub section (10), which allows the Tribunal Procedure Rules to provide for an appeal to the Upper Tribunal instead of the First Tier Tribunal. This gives the flexibility for the Tribunal Rules to make adjustments to the appeals process in the future, for example, so that more important cases may directly go to the Upper Tribunal.' (Explanatory note at para 401).

Civil sanctions for infringements of automated passenger permit scheme under the AV Bill 2023–24 (HL Bill 1), Part 5

31.07   The AV Bill 2023-24 (HL Bill 1), cl 84 and Sch 6 provide civil sanctions for infringements of an automated passenger service permit (including "the permit holder says or does anything that would lead a reasonable passenger (or potential passenger) of the service to think that the service was provided under a [automated passenger] permit" where "the service is not such as could be provided under the permit" (cl 84(2)). The civil sanctions under Sch 6 are compliance notices and monetary penalties as well as costs notices.

Appeals against civil sanctions for infringements of automated passenger permit scheme under the AV Bill 2023–24 (HL Bill 1), Part 5

31.08   There is a right of appeal to the Tribunal on similar terms to the appeal in Sch 1, grounds for which are in Sch, 6 para 6:

'(a) in the case of a compliance notice—

    (i)   that the infringement of the permit scheme on the grounds of which the notice was issued did not occur, or

    (ii) that the actions specified in the notice, or the time or period specified for taking them, are unreasonable;

(b) in the case of a monetary penalty notice—

    (i)   that the infringement of the permit scheme, or failure of compliance, on the grounds of which the notice was issued did not occur, or

    (ii) that the sum specified in the notice, or the time or manner specified for paying it, is unreasonable;

(c) in the case of a costs notice—

    (i)   that costs relied on in arriving at the sum specified in the notice were not reasonably incurred as described in paragraph 4(3), or

    (ii) that the time or manner specified for payment is unreasonable;

(d) that the appropriate national authority failed to comply with paragraph 3 [serve a notice of intent and consider any representations in response by the permit holder], or made some other procedural error, in respect of the notice.' (Sch 6 para 6(2)).

History

'The rational study of law is still to a large extent the study of history. History must be a part of the study, because without it we cannot know the precise scope of rules which it is our business to know. It is a part of the rational study, because it is the first step toward an enlightened scepticism, that is, towards a deliberate reconsideration of the worth of those rules.'

Oliver Wendell Holmes Jr, 'The Path of the Law' (1897)[1]

Summary

Question: What is the history of advanced, automated and electric vehicles?

Answer: It is the history of three technologies:

(1) **Motors** (the history of the two dominant types of motor which power road vehicles – the electric motor and the internal combustion engine – and of the development of motorised road vehicles)

(2) **Electronics** (which allows the miniaturisation of components within motors and computers) and

(3) **Computers** (including robots[2], the internet[3] and artificial intelligence[4]).

---

1 10 Harvard Law Review (1897), at http://moglen.law.columbia.edu/LCS/palaw.pdf
2 Robot: 'A machine capable of carrying out a complex series of actions automatically, especially one programmable by a computer' (Oxford English Dictionary, 2010).
3 The internet: 'A global computer network providing a variety of information and communication facilities, consisting of interconnected networks using standardised communication protocols' (OED). Or, as Dr Paul Lambert puts it: 'a global network of computers all speaking the same language' (Dr Paul Lambert, *Gringras: The Laws of the Internet* (5th edn, Bloomsbury Professional, 2018), at 1.1).
4 Artificial Intelligence, or 'AI': the OED defines Artificial Intelligence as 'the theory and development of computer systems able to perform tasks normally requiring human intelligence, such as visual perception, speech recognition, decision-making, and translation between languages'. It is important to emphasise that definition, which Professor Michael Wooldridge, head of computer science at the University of Oxford, reflects when he writes that 'the mainstream of AI research today is focused around getting machines to do specific tasks which currently require human brains (and also, potentially, human bodies), and for which conventional computing techniques provide no solution'. By contrast, 'the grand dream' version of AI – 'to build machines that are self-aware, conscious and autonomous in the same way that people like you and me are' is, to quote Professor Wooldridge, 'difficult to approach directly, and although it makes for great books, movies and video games, it isn't in the mainstream of AI research' (See 'What AI is and isn't', in the Introduction to *The Road to Conscious Machines: the Story of AI* by Michael Wooldridge, Pelican, 2020).

Those three technologies developed individually (though closely in the case of electronics and computers) before combining, relatively recently, in the subject of this book: advanced, automated and electric vehicles.

The law has developed in response to those technologies. This appendix describes the main laws of road transport, as they first arose. The chapters describe in detail the current versions of those laws.

The history[5]

'**Motor.** A machine, especially one powered by electricity or internal combustion, that supplies motive power for a vehicle or for another device with moving parts.'

'**Electronics.** The branch of physics and technology concerned with the design of circuits using transistors and microchips, and with the behaviour and movement of electrons in a semiconductor, conductor, vacuum or gas.'

'**Computer.** An electronic device which is capable of receiving information (data) in a particular form and of performing a sequence of operations in accordance with a predetermined but variable set of procedural instructions (program) to produce a result in the form of information or signals.'[6]

Part One: 1769 to 1865:
Engines, the battery and a red flag

Motors, 1769 to 1865

1769, France. Nicholas Cugnot's steam road locomotive, 'a three-wheeled steam-powered vehicle with a boiler and engine perched on the front'. Initially 'authorised by the Minister of War for the carriage of cannon', funding is withdrawn after the vehicle hits a wall inside the Paris arsenal in 1771.[7]

---

5   For reasons of space this is not a comprehensive history of each of these three technologies and all of their legal consequences. This history focuses upon the points material to advanced, automated and electric vehicle law in the UK. The aim is to give the context to current laws, and to examine the similarities and differences between current practical needs and the needs of the past, from which the laws of road vehicles have developed. I have adopted a chronological approach. Please note that, in so doing, I have generally included only the first example of a particular innovation or change. That is true both of the facts (eg. the first appearance of a particular technology) and the law (eg. the first enactment of compulsory third party motor insurance in the UK). I have not included subsequent factual or legal refinements in this chapter, unless the refinement significantly illuminates the context (in my view). Material legal refinements (eg. the further development of compulsory motor insurance in British law, after its introduction in the Road Traffic Act 1930 and during British membership of the European Union) are described in the relevant chapter. Speed limits have fluctuated, and (again for reasons of space and relevance) I have not included every detail of speed limits. The divisions into eras are mine, based upon notable developments in one or more of the three technologies. These are lofty aims, of which I am likely to fall short, so readers should feel free to suggest additional points for future editions!
6   All three definitions from the 2010 edition of the Oxford English Dictionary (OED).
7   Merkin and Hemsworth, *The Law of Motor Insurance* (second edition, 2015), 1-02

1781, Britain. William Murdoch makes a working model of the first British steam carriage.[8]

1788. Scottish engineer James Watt invents the flyball governor, a sensor device using the centrifugal force of spinning balls to release pressure and thereby control the speed of a steam engine (a precursor of Ralph Teetor's 1950 cruise control for cars, and of electronic driver assistance devices).[9]

1825. The British steam road locomotive industry grows, but 'companies formed to exploit this new form of travel nevertheless did not thrive, presumably the victims of speculation and the absence of limited liability for investors'.[10]

1838. The first British steam-powered car, built by Walter Hancock 'Hancock's car was a steam phaeton [an open carriage] which carried four people including the driver, but had the severe disadvantage of disrupting the rest of the traffic system, not in the least because it frightened horses'.[11]

1844 and 1846, USA. Two versions of a petrol-fuelled internal combustion engine (ICE) are patented by Stuart Perry, a New York inventor.[12]

1860, France. Jean Joseph Étienne Lenoir, a Belgian engineer, patents his two-cycle internal combustion engine (his version is generally credited as the first ICE because it was the more commercially successful)[13]. Lenoir's version uses an electric spark plug to ignite a fuel mixture of air and illuminating gas.

Electronics, 1769 to 1865

1800, Italy. Alessandro Volta, a professor of chemistry, makes the 'Voltaic Pile': 'a stack of thin, alternating zinc and silver discs sandwiched between layers of brine-soaked cardboard or felt'. 'When the top, zinc disc was connected to the bottom silver one by a copper ribbon, a steady stream of electric current began to flow along the copper strand'.[14] As Benjamin Franklin would later rename it, the first battery.

1800. British chemist Humphrey Davy discovers that electricity can transmit through air.[15]

1820. French mathematician André-Marie Ampère shows that electric current generates a magnetic field (by showing that two wires through which current runs in the same direction are repelled from each other, while running currents in opposite directions causes the wires to be attracted to each other).[16]

---

8   Merkin and Hemsworth 1-02
9   Wooldridge page 13.
10   Merkin and Hemsworth 1-04
11   Merkin and Hemsworth 1-04
12   James J Flink, *The Automobile Age* (MIT press, 1990, 2001 edition), page 11
13   Flink page 11
14   Derek Cheung and Eric Brach, *Conquering the Electron* (Lyons Press, 2020), page 13
15   Cheung and Brach page 102
16   Cheung and Brach page 17

1821, Britain. Michael Faraday builds the first model of an electric motor: a metal rod is suspended in a beaker containing electrically-conductive liquid (mercury) and a magnet. When current flows through the metal rod, the rod rotates around the magnet. When the direction of the current is switched, the rod rotates in the other direction. The magnetic force of the electric current interacts with the magnetic force of the magnet to produce motive energy.[17]

1839, Britain. The first commercial telegraph system (a system for transmitting messages along a wire) is used on a London railway line.[18]

1844, USA. Samuel Morse demonstrates America's first telegraph system, at the US Supreme Court building.[19]

Computers, 1769 to 1865

1838, Britain. Charles Babbage resigns his post as Lucasian Chair of Mathematics at Cambridge University, to concentrate upon building his calculating machines, including the never-built 'Analytical Engine'.[20]

1843, Britain. Ada Lovelace publishes her notes on Babbage's proposed analytical engine, proposing that it could be 'programmed' (by the use of holes punched into cards) to answer any question, not merely to calculate.[21]

Road Transport Law, 1769 to 1865

1835. The **Highway Act 1835**[22] provides for upkeep of highways, offences on and by the highway and (at section LXXVI) that the name of its owner shall be painted on the side of every wagon.

1861. The **Locomotive Act 1861**, 'Whereas the use of locomotives is likely to become common on turnpike and other roads …'[23] permits the use of steam locomotives on roads, but is short-lived.[24]

1865. Parliament passes the **Locomotives Act 1865**, 'the legislative nail in the coffin' of steam vehicles. Its restrictions 'effectively made the use of steam boilers impractical'.[25] 'Under the influence of horse-drawn transportation interests, the turnpike trusts that administered the highways levied discriminatory tolls against mechanical road vehicles... This so-called **Red Flag Act** limited the speed of 'road locomotives' to 2 mph [miles per hour] in towns and 4 mph on the open highway and required that an attendant walk sixty yards ahead carrying a red flag by day and a red lantern by night. Until its repeal at the request of wealthy automotive

---

17 Cheung and Brach pages 20, 21
18 Cheung and Brach page 35
19 Cheung and Brach page 36
20 Sydney Padua, *The Thrilling Adventures of Lovelace and Babbage* (Particular Books, 2015), page 35
21 Padua page 22
22 Unless stated otherwise, all the statutes mentioned are British.
23 Preamble to the Locomotive Act 1861
24 Merkin and Hemsworth 1-05
25 Merkin and Hemsworth 1-05

pioneers in 1896, the act militated against development of the automotive idea, for by 1890 light steam vehicles were capable of being driven 15 mph for long distances over British roads'.[26] Among its many prohibitions: 'the whistle of such locomotive shall not be sounded for any purpose whatever'[27].

Part Two: 1866 to 1900:
The first age of electric cars, the battle of the engines, the bicycle and the birth of worldwide communication

Motors, 1866 to 1900

1876, Germany. Nicolaus Otto's engine compresses the fuel-air mixture in the working cylinder and operates a four-cycle principle (intake, compression, power, exhaust).

1885, Germany. Gottlieb Daimler (one of Otto's engineers) and his assistant, Wilhelm Maybach, build 'the prototype of the modern motor-car's power plant' [28], the vertical 'high speed' engine.

1885, Germany. Karl Benz builds the first motor car, a three-wheeled petrol-driven vehicle with an internal combustion engine.[29]

1885, Britain. James Kemp Starley designs the 'Safety Bicycle' – the modern form of the bicycle, with equal-sized wheels and a chain drive.[30]

1887, USA. First electric streetcar (or trolley) system installed by Frank Sprague in Richmond, Virginia.[31]

1888, Britain. John Boyd Dunlop makes the first practical pneumatic (air-filled) tyre.[32]

1890. London underground system completely electrified.[33]

1891, France. The Panhard et Levassor car: the prototype of the modern gasoline automobile, with engine placed vertically in front of the chassis (instead of under the seats or in the back).[34]

---

26 Flink page 2
27 Section 3 of the Locomotives Act 1865, the long section in which the Red Flag provision also appeared.
28 Flink page 11
29 Flink page 12, Merkin and Hemsworth 1-06
30 Flink pages 3, 4, *Pedal your way through the bicycle's bumpy history* (article by Evan Andrews on history.com, https://www.history.com/news/pedal-your-way-through-the-bicycles-bumpy-history)
31 Flink pages 3, 137, 138
32 Encyclopedia Britannica
33 Cheung and Brach page 20
34 Flink page 17

1893, Germany. Maybach invents the modern carburettor, which sprays a fine jet of gasoline into the air stream being sucked into the engine. This leads to 'dramatic improvement of the four-cycle, Otto type engine'.[35]

1893, Germany. Rudolf Diesel patents the isothermal-combustion/adiabatic expansion engine, which is more efficient and can run on lower grade fuels, because the fuel-air mixture is ignited by pressure (fuel is introduced into a cylinder in which air had already been compressed to a very high pressure).[36]

1893, Germany. Benz produces his four-wheel car with 3 horsepower and electric (rather than open-flame) ignition.[37]

1893, USA. Margaret A Wilcox invents the car heater (by moving warm air flow from the engine).[38]

1895, Britain. First successful British petrol-powered car: a two horsepower tricycle built by Herbert Austin, employed at Wolseley (builder of sheep-shearing tools and, also from 1895, bicycle parts).[39]

1895, France, June. The Paris-Bordeaux race. Includes Panhard and Levassor's car with two-cylinder, 4 horsepower Daimler-Phoenix engine travelling at 15 mph and a longest servicing stop of only 15 minutes.[40]

1895, USA, December. Ogden Bolton patents an electrical bicycle[41]. Not the first such innovation (batteries had been attached to tricycles in the 1880's) but among the first to electrically power a bicycle.

1897, Germany. Rudolf Diesel produces an engine which can run on heavy oil.[42]

1897, USA. Until 1907, the Pope Manufacturing Company of Hartford, Conneticut, formerly the USA's leading bicycle manufacturer, produces electric cars.[43]

1898, USA. Andrew L Riker organises the Riker Motor Vehicle Company in Elizabeth, New Jersey, to make electric cars.[44]

1899, USA. The Lead Cab Trust starts its project to place fleets of electric cabs in American cities.[45] First year in which 'United States census of manufactures' publishes figures for the automobile industry. The census shows that ten New

---

35 Flink pages 11, 12
36 Flink page 12
37 Flink pages 12, 13
38 Post on Facebook by Museum of American Speed, 27 December 2017: https://www.facebook.com/MuseumofAmericanSpeed/posts/for-todays-women-in-automotive-history-wednesday-wed-like-to-honor-margaret-a-wi/1618560924868484/
39 Flink page 20
40 Flink page 17
41 Electricbike.com, *Electric bike history, patents from the 1800's*, 9 November 2013: https://www.electricbike.com/e-bike-patents-from-the-1800s/
42 Flink page 12
43 Flink pages 8, 9
44 Flink page 8
45 Flink page 9

England manufacturers, making electric and/or steam vehicles, were responsible for the most significant part of the industry's output.[46]

1900, USA. Review in June 1900 'American Monthly Review of Reviews' opines that the gasoline automobile had 'developed more all-round qualities than any other carriage. In spite of its clumsy and complicated mechanism, it does not easily get out of order. It will climb all ordinary hills; it will run through sand, mud or snow; it makes good speed over long distances – say, an average of fifteen miles an hour … It carries gasoline enough for a 70 mile journey, and nearly any country store can replenish the supply.'[47]

1900, Britain. By 1900, 59 British companies have entered automobile manufacturing.[48]

Electronics, 1866 to 1900

1873, USA. A single company (Western Union) controls 90% of the US telegraph system.[49]

1874, France. Belgian inventor Zenobe Gramme's alternating current (AC) generator illuminates the Paris Opéra.[50]

1876, USA. Alexander Graham Bell demonstrates transmission of a voice signal through wire: the telephone.[51]

1879, USA. Thomas Edison demonstrates his electric lighting system at Menlo Park, New Jersey. It is a direct current (DC) system.[52]

1888, Germany. Heinrich Hertz discovers electromagnetic waves invisible to the human eye, including radio waves.[53]

1893, USA. George Westinghouse wins the battle of the currents, winning the competition to illuminate the Chicago World's Fair with his alternating current (AC) system, defeating Edison's bid for his direct current (DC) system.[54]

1897, Britain. Professor J J Thompson demonstrates, through research into particles in cathode rays, that there are smaller particles than the atom.[55]

1899. Italian electrical engineer Guglielmo Marconi establishes a wireless radio link across the English Channel to France (and a trans-Atlantic link two years later).[56]

---

46 Flink page 24
47 Flink page 10
48 Flink page 20
49 Cheung and Brach page 46
50 Cheung and Brach pages 83, 85
51 Cheung and Brach pages 54, 55
52 Cheung and Brach pages 80, 81
53 Cheung and Brach pages 28, 66 to 68
54 Cheung and Brach page 89
55 Cheung and Brach page 107
56 Cheung and Brach page 71

Computers, 1866 to 1900

1887, USA. Herman Hollerith builds an electric tabulating machine, using punch-cards to process the results of the 1890 census.[57]

Road Transport Law, 1866 to 1900

1896, Britain. Parliament passes the **Locomotives on Highways Act 1896**, abolishing the provisions of the Red Flag Act and establishing a 14 miles per hour speed limit on the open highway. In further contrast to the 1865 Act, it requires every locomotive to 'carry a bell or other instrument capable of giving audible and sufficient warning of the approach or position of the carriages'[58]. *Horseless Age* (an automotive journal in the USA) says of the British Act:

> 'The sum and substance of these provisions may be reduced roughly to the general axiom that the vehicle must be at all times under the control of its operator, and that the speed at which it may be allowed to travel depends upon its weight and the conditions of the road.'[59]

Part Three: 1901 to 1938:
Internal combustion wins the battle of the engines. Safety features, compulsory insurance and negligence liability appear. A thinking machine is conceived.

Motors, 1901 to 1938

1901, USA, January 10. Oil struck at the gusher 'Spindletop' at Beaumont, Texas. Oil previously used in the US in small quantities, for lighting. With the Spindletop strike, gasoline becomes a cheap, mass commodity in the USA.[60]

1901, Britain. British Standards Institution (BSI) founded (with the original title of the Engineering Standards Committee) by Sir John Wolfe-Barry, designer of Tower Bridge, believing that agreed technical standards for the manufacture of goods and services would speed up production and reduce costs. Receives royal charter in 1929 and changes title to BSI in 1931. BSI 'kitemark' registered in 1903.[61]

1903, USA. Ford motor company incorporated.[62]

1903, USA. Mary Anderson patents the windscreen wiper.[63]

---

57   United States Census Bureau: https://www.census.gov/history/www/census_then_now/ notable_alumni/herman_hollerith.html
58   Section 3 of the Locomotives on Highways Act 1896, entitled 'Locomotives to carry a bell'.
59   *Horseless Age*, Vol II, No.1, New York, November 1896
60   Flink page 10
61   BSI website: https://www.bsigroup.com/en-GB/about-bsi/our-history/#chapter5 Institute of Chartered Engineers (ICE) website: https://www.ice.org.uk/what-is-civil-engineering/ what-do-civil-engineers-do/british-standards-institution
62   Flink page 27
63   National Public Radio website: https://www.npr.org/2017/07/25/536835744/alabama-woman-stuck-in-nyc-traffic-in-1902-invented-the-windshield-wiper?t=1600859619797

1905, USA. Society of Automotive Engineers (SAE) founded: 'a small but influential group of American automobile trade journalists and engineers who organised in 1905 to improve the state of automotive technology through the publication of articles'.[64]

1905, Britain. Rolls-Royce produces first automobile with a V-8 engine (8 for total number of cylinders, V for the angled shape made by the 2 banks of cylinders).[65]

1906, France. Banque Automobile becomes first of several French institutions to finance purchase of cars on credit.[66]

1907, USA. By 1906 to 1907, manufacture of automobiles in the USA has shifted from New England to the Midwest. Rural markets replace urban markets for automobiles. 'The early, overwhelming choice of the internal combustion engine by midwestern manufacturers was influenced by the region's poor roads, which were nearly impossible for electrics to negotiate, and by the universal availability of gasoline [petrol] for fuel in sparsely settled rural areas lacking electricity'.[67]

1907, USA. Pope Manufacturing company goes into receivership. The Lead Cab Trust declines and collapses, after underperformance of its electric cabs and financial scandal.[68]

1908. USA. Model T Ford released.[69]

1908, USA. Cadillac demonstrates interchangeability of parts (an essential part of mass manufacture) in the Cadillac Model B, winning the Dewar Trophy of the Royal Automobile Club (RAC) in the UK by reassembling three Cadillac cars from their mixed parts and driving them 500 miles, with perfect scores.[70]

1909, France. Use of a catalyst to reduce pollutants in exhaust (a catalytic converter) first proposed, by French chemist Michel Frenkel (but not put into effect until the mid-1970's, with regulation in the USA in 1975).[71]

1909, Britain. Dorothée Levitt, the first female British racing driver, instigates the use of a (handheld) rear-view mirror when driving.[72]

1910, USA. The SAE produces the first common standard for automobile parts, adopting 224 standards by 1921. SAE President Howard E Coffin says that the lack of intercompany standardisation was 'responsible for nine tenths of the production troubles and most of the needless expense in the manufacture of motorcars'.[73]

---

64   Flink page 8. SAE website: https://www.sae.org/about/history
65   Flink page 214
66   Flink page 190
67   Flink page 24
68   Flink page 9
69   Flink pages 28, 37
70   Flink page 36
71   Royal Society of Chemistry website: https://edu.rsc.org/feature/the-evolution-of-catalytic-converters/2020252.article
72   Brighton Museums website: https://brightonmuseums.org.uk/discover/2020/07/06/the-fastest-girl-on-earth-trailblazing-dorothy-levitt/
73   Flink page 71

1912, USA. Cadillac introduces the self-starter (replacing the use of a hand crank to start the internal combustion engine). Electric cars had been distinct from ICE cars by needing no engine starter, so the new self-starter in motor cars 'sealed the doom of the electric car' (James J Flink).[74]

1914, USA. Florence Lawrence invents the direction indicator (originally an extending arm, rather than a light) in 1914 and subsequently a brake signal (Florence Lawrence was, incidentally, also a silent film star, the daughter of Charlotte Bridgwood[75] and later the President of her mother's company).[76]

1914 to 1918. Automobiles supersede other means of military transport during the First World War. Wartime production needs expand work of automobile manufacturers. (eg. Austin in UK, where the Longbridge plant produces military trucks, ambulances and armoured cars and diversifies to make shells, guns, planes, plane engines, generating sets and pumping equipment). Factories modernise. The automobile industry expands in wartime.[77]

1915, USA. First company formed in USA purely to finance automobile sales.[78]

1915, USA and UK. The first mass-produced motorised scooter: the Autoped. 'Essentially an enlarged child's scooter with an engine mounted over the front wheel'[79]. The precursor of the electric scooter (the e-scooter), the Autoped of 1915 is advertised as:

> 'an ideal short distance conveyance for business or professional men or women to and from their places of business; for women to go shopping or calling; for physicians to make their regular daily calls or to answer hurry calls; for the older children to go about quickly for outing or school; for servants when they are sent on errands; for grocers, druggists and other merchants for quick delivery purposes; for commercial salesman to call on the trade; for employees to ride to and from work; for collectors; repairmen; messengers, and for anybody else who wants to save money, time and energy in going about. All will enjoy the comfort and pleasure of AUTOPEDING.'[80]

1916, USA. 21 December: *Automobile* magazine opines that 'the parking problem every day in big cities … grows more acute … We are facing something which was never foreseen in the planning of our towns, a thing which has come upon us so swiftly that there has been no time to grasp the immensity of the problem till we are almost overcome by it'.[81]

---

74 Flink page 212
75 Inventor of the electric windscreen wiper, in 1917. See below.
76 Automobile Association website: https://www.theaa.com/breakdown-cover/advice/evolution-of-car-safety-features Womenshistory.org: https://www.womenshistory.org/education-resources/biographies/florence-lawrence
77 Flink page 75
78 Flink page 191
79 Jackie Mansky, *The motorised scooter boom that hit a century before dockless scooters,* the Smithsonian Magazine, 18 April 2019: https://www.smithsonianmag.com/history/motorized-scooter-boom-hit-century-dockless-scooters-180971989/
80 Quoted in the Smithsonian Magazine article (footnote above)
81 *Automobile* 35 (Dec 21, 1916), Flink page 151 and note 37 at page 417

1917, USA. June McCarroll invents the highway central lane-separation line, after her car is run off the road by an oncoming truck.[82]

1917, USA. Charlotte Bridgwood, president of the Bridgwood Manufacturing Company, patents the first electric windscreen wiper.[83]

1919, Britain. Ministry of Transport created.[84]

1920s, Britain. Large numbers of new roads built and adapted in Britain, under the new Ministry of Transport.[85]

1921, Britain. Dorothée Pullinger, designs the Galloway car (1921-1928) with better controls (eg. gear and handbrake levers within the car, distance to pedals shortened). Galloway adopts the colours of the suffragettes and apprentices women engineers.[86]

1921, USA. Benjamin Katz patents the automobile headrest. Hydraulic brakes introduced, in the Model A Duessenberg car.[87]

1922, Britain. Austin Seven introduced. Until the Morris Minor (1929), it is the most competitive British car to the Ford Model T, well-priced and more suitable to British conditions: 'British roads were slow and congested … British cars tended to emphasise manoeuvrability, light steering and good engine torque and to de-emphasise high-speed cruising ability'.[88]

1925, USA. End of the automobile boom in the USA, with the saturation of new cars after 1925. Most cars in USA are financed by credit. New car sales decline. Manufacturers respond by adding new features.[89]

1927. Laminated safety glass introduced to windscreens, to prevent shattering upon impact.[90]

1929, USA, 24 September. First fully 'blind' flight of a piloted aircraft using autopilot (developed by the Sperry gyroscope company).[91]

1929, USA, October. The stock market crash, precipitating the Great Depression (1929-1939). Clarence E Eldridge, sales manager of the REO Motor Car Company, tells the Minnesota Automobile Dealers Association, as the stock market crashes, that

---

82 https://www.atlasobscura.com/places/doctor-june-mccarroll-monument
83 https://www.denso-am.eu/media/corporate-news/2019/deneur19_13_female-pioneers-mary-anderson-and-charlotte-bridgwood/
84 Merkin and Hemsworth 1-09
85 Historic England website
86 https://www.bbc.co.uk/news/uk-scotland-35414177
87 Both at AA website: https://www.theaa.com/breakdown-cover/advice/evolution-of-car-safety-features
88 Flink page 255 (quoting Peter S Dunnett)
89 Flink pages 189, 191, 192
90 AA website: https://www.theaa.com/breakdown-cover/advice/evolution-of-car-safety-features
91 Lockheed Martin website: https://www.lockheedmartin.com/en-us/news/features/history/sperry.html National Aviation Hall of Fame website: https://www.nationalaviation.org/our-enshrinees/sperry-elmer-ambrose-sr/

'there has been built up by this greatest of all industries a capacity for building, and a capacity for selling, approximately twice as many automobiles as the market, either present or potential, can absorb ... the basic problem is not one of how to sell used cars or to handle the used car problem, but how more intelligently to adjust production to the absorptive capacity of the market'.[92]

1931, Germany. Mercedes-Benz produces the first modern independent front suspension.[93]

1932, USA. Ford introduces the Ford V-8 engine. Ford casts the engine block as a single unit, greatly reducing manufacturing costs and making an 8-cylinder engine practical for low-priced cars.[94]

1933, USA. Struggling banks in Michigan, financed largely by automobile companies, are closed by a state banking holiday ordered by the state governor, precipitating the national collapse of the US banking structure.[95]

1933, Japan. Tobuta casting company and Nippon industries (later combining as Nissan, in 1934) manufacture the Datsun car.[96]

1934, USA. General Motors perform the first crash test.[97]

1935, Britain. Ford plant at Dagenham (started 1929) completed. Planned as Ford's European manufacturing centre and the largest automobile factory outside the USA.[98]

1937, USA. Automatic transmission first used, in General Motors' buses. Appears in passenger cars in 1940 and is a standard feature in 90% of American-made, full-size cars by 1974.[99]

1938, USA. Katharine Blodgett invents non-reflecting glass, a particular safety attribute for car windscreens.[100]

Electronics, 1901 to 1938

1901. Marconi establishes wireless radio link across the Atlantic ocean.[101]

---

92   Flink pages 193, 212 and 421, quoting Clarence E Eldridge, 'One million too many cars', *Motor* 52 (November 1929): 30-33
93   Flink page 215
94   Flink pages 205, 215, 230
95   Flink pages 222 to 224
96   Flink page 271
97   AA   website: https://www.theaa.com/breakdown-cover/advice/evolution-of-car-safety-features
98   Flink page 256; *Buildings and infrastructure for the motor car* (Historic England, 2013) at: https://historicengland.org.uk/images-books/publications/iha-buildings-infrastructure-motor-car/heag138-buildings-and-infrastructure-for-motor-car-iha/
99   Flink page 207
100 MIT website: https://lemelson.mit.edu/resources/katherine-blodgett
101 Cheung and Brach page 73

1909, USA. Robert Millikan measures the subatomic particles demonstrated by Thompson in 1897 and calls them 'electrons': particles which, in some substances, will break free from their atoms in the presence of an electric field.[102]

1930. First car radio produced by Motorola (first factory-fitted into a British car – by Crossley – in 1933).[103]

1931, Britain. Alan H Wilson's paper showing how electrons pass in bands across semiconductors. 'Solid State' electronics is born, allowing for more compact electronic devices.[104]

Computers, 1901 to 1938

1936, Britain. Alan Turing publishes the paper *On computable numbers, with an application to the Entscheidungsproblem'*, to address the problem that 'had been posed by the mathematician David Hilbert in 1928. The *Entscheidungsproblem* ['decision problem'] asks whether there are mathematical questions [ie. questions requiring a 'yes/no answer'] which can be answered simply by following a recipe' (an algorithm) 'or whether there are problems for which there is no recipe for finding an answer'[105].

To address the decision problem, Turing innovates by considering the question in physical, mechanical terms, as a machine: 'It is possible to invent a single machine which can be used to compute any computable sequence'[106]. 'To settle Hilbert's problem, all you had to do was show that there was some decision problem that could not be answered by any Turing machine'[107]. Turing's machine reads symbols on a paper tape which is fed into it and can obliterate those symbols or add its own[108]:

> 'Let us imagine the operations performed by the computer to be split up into 'simple operations' which are so elementary that it is not easy to imagine them further divided. Every such operation consists of some change of the physical system consisting of the computer and his tape. We know the state of the system if we know the sequence of symbols on the tape, which of these are observed by the computer (possibly with a special order), and the state of mind of the computer'.[109]

The computer is born – and the seed of artificial intelligence is sown, as each Turing machine can answer questions about computations carried out by other Turing

---

102 Cheung and Brach page 107
103 Sunday Times Driving website: https://www.driving.co.uk/news/test-your-knowledge-when-was-first-car-radio-introduced/
104 Cheung and Brach page 179
105 Wooldridge page 17
106 Section 6 of Turing's 1936 paper, at the Turing Scrapbook website: https://www.turing.org.uk/scrapbook/machine.html
107 Wooldridge page 18
108 Roger Penrose, *The Emperor's New Mind* (Oxford, 1989, 2016 edition), page 48
109 Part 9 of Turing's paper, at the Turing Scrapbook website: https://www.turing.org.uk/scrapbook/machine.html

machines. So each machine is a 'universal computing machine', as Turing describes it.[110]

Road Transport Law, 1901 to 1938

1903. The **Motor Car Act 1903** comes into force on 1 January, making reckless driving an offence, requiring drivers to be 17 years of age and licensed, introducing minimum braking requirements and requiring registration of the car and raising speed limit to 20mph. The Motor Cars (Use and Construction) Order 1904 follows.

Circa 1909. English courts resist the argument that placing a motor vehicle on a road constitutes the strict tort (civil wrong) of nuisance, preferring instead to decide road traffic accident cases on the basis of reasonable care, within the tort of negligence (as, for example, in *Wing v London General Omnibus Company* [1909] KB 652 (CA)).

1909, Paris. **Convention with respect to the International Circulation of Motor Vehicles**, 'with a view of facilitating, as far as possible, the international circulation of motor vehicles'. The convention (which is not comprehensive by later standards) covers both vehicle specifications and driver behaviour. For example, Article 1 sets out conditions for examination, by a competent authority or authorised association, of the suitability for use on the highway of 'every motor car', alternatively that the car 'must belong to a type approved in the same manner'. Article 2 provides that 'The driver of a motor-car must possess qualifications which provide a sufficient guarantee of public safety'. Article 3 provides for the 'issue and recognition of international travelling passes'. Great Britain is among the signatories[111].

1926, Paris. The **International Convention relative to Motor Traffic** modifies and expands the 1909 convention, setting more detailed requirements for vehicles in international use including (for example) the requirement for front and rear registration plates, and for uniform road signs[112]. As in 1909, the Convention deals both with vehicle specifications and with driver behaviour (for example, the requirement under Article 8 to comply with the laws of the country in which they are travelling).

1930, Britain. The **Road Traffic Act 1930** introduces compulsory third party motor insurance (Part II) and the Highway Code ('such directions as appear to [the Minister for Transport] to be proper for the guidance of persons using roads ... from time to time revise[d]': s.45) as well as codifying other areas, including the licensing of public service vehicles. Speed limits are set (by section 10 and schedule 1) by reference to the type of vehicle and the type of tyres (eg. 20 mph for a heavy car with pneumatic tyres but 16 mph with soft or elastic tyres). In the same year, the **Third Parties' (Rights Against Insurers) Act 1930** is enacted

---

110 Part 6 of Turing's paper
111 Signed at Paris, 11 October 1909. A copy of the Convention, published in the American Journal of International Law in October 1910, is available on JSTOR, at https://archive.org/details/jstor-2212082.
112 Paris, 24 April 1926, and ratified by Great Britain in 1929. Copy in the Foreign, Commonwealth and Development Office treaty archive, at https://treaties.fco.gov.uk/awweb/pdfopener?md=1&did=64295

to protect the rights of third parties against a bankrupt person insured against third party liabilities, by transferring to and vesting in the third party the bankrupt etc person's contractual rights against their insurer. Together, those two Acts of 1930 (in the words of Lord Justice Goddard, writing in 1942) –

> 'would naturally have led the public, at least those who were neither lawyers nor connected with the business of insurance, to believe that if thereafter they were, through no fault of their own, injured or killed by a motor car they or their dependants would be certain of recovering damages, even though the wrong-doer was an impecunious person. How wrong they were quickly appeared. Insurance was left in the hands of companies and underwriters who had imposed what terms and conditions they chose.'[113]

1931, Britain. The first edition of the **Highway Code**.

1931, Switzerland. The signing of two further conventions on international road traffic at the **League of Nations**: the **Convention on Taxation of Foreign Motor Vehicles** (releasing foreign vehicles used temporarily in the signatory states from local taxation)[114] and (expanding upon the 1926 Paris Convention) the **Convention concerning the unification of road signals**[115] ('Desiring to increase the safety of road traffic and to facilitate international road traffic by a uniform system of road signalling' ie. uniform road signs).

1934, Britain. The **Road Traffic Act 1934** imposes a general speed limit of 30 mph in built-up areas, introduces a mandatory driving test and introduces 'a series of further provisions in relation to policies or securities which were aimed at strengthening the position of the third party victim, by giving the victim a direct right to enforce judgments against insurers' under section 10, the originator of the current section 151 of the Road Traffic Act 1988, 'and by controlling the terms upon which liability cover could be written'[116]. As to control of terms, in 1942 Lord Justice Goddard (in the same judgment quoted above) explains the abuse of insurance terms that the 1934 Act was designed to correct, and its insurance provisions as follows:

> 'Insurance was left in the hands of companies and underwriters who could impose what terms and conditions they chose. Nor was there any standard form of policy, and any company who could fulfill the not very onerous financial requirements that were necessary for acceptance as an approved insurer could hedge round the policies with so many warranties and conditions that no one advising an injured person could say with certainty whether, if damages were recovered against the driver of the car, there was a prospect of recovering against the insurers. I myself once tried a case, *Richards v. Port of Manchester Insurance Co., Ld.*[117], where the insurers were enabled to escape liability if at

---

113 *Zurich General Accident and Liability Insurance Co Ltd v Morrison* [1942] KB 53, 61-62
114 No.3185. League of Nations Treaty Series Volume CXXXVIII 1933 page 149, at the United Nations' online archive of League of Nations treaties, at https://treaties.un.org/doc/Publication/UNTS/LON/Volume%20138/v138.pdf
115 No.3459. League of Nations Treaty Series Volume CL 1934 page 247, at the United Nations' online archive of League of Nations treaties, at https://treaties.un.org/doc/Publication/UNTS/LON/Volume%20150/v150.pdf
116 Merkin and Hemsworth, *The Law of Motor Insurance* (2nd edition, 2015) at 1-17.
117 (1934) 50 Ll. L. Rep. 88

the time of the accident the car was being driven by a Jew, a bookmaker, or an actor. It was indeed a state of affairs of which the words of Lord Moulton, in *Joel v. Law Union & Crown Insurance Co.*[118], were forcibly applicable. 'I wish,' he said in dealing there with a life policy, 'I could adequately warn the public against such practices on the part of insurance offices. I am satisfied that few of those who insure have any idea how completely they leave themselves in the hands of the insurers should the latter wish to dispute the policy when it falls in.' But in the case of motor car insurance it was the third parties who needed the warning, and unfortunately they had no voice as to the warranties or conditions that were inserted in policies, though it was only because they held a policy that careless drivers were enabled to drive and put other persons in peril. It is not surprising therefore, that by 1934 Parliament interfered, and by section 10 of the Act of that year they took steps towards remedying a position which to a great extent nullified the protection that compulsory insurance was intended to afford. Generally speaking, section 10 was designed to prevent conditions in policies from defeating the rights of third parties, but insurers were still allowed to repudiate policies obtained by misrepresentation or non-disclosure of material facts. This right, however, was made subject to certain conditions and restrictions contained in subsection (3) of section 10. It seems to me that what the legislature had in mind was that, if an insurer was intending to repudiate a policy, it was only fair that the injured third party should know the grounds on which repudiation was sought before he went to the expense of endeavouring to establish his claim against the assured, who, if not entitled to indemnity, might be unable to satisfy a judgment. It was to prevent an injured party incurring further useless expense. Hence the necessity of the notice prescribed by the proviso to the subsection[119]. The protection afforded is little enough.'[120]

As Lord Sumption, Justice of the Supreme Court, writes in 2019, 'The statutory regime [for compulsory motor insurance] has become more elaborate and more comprehensive since 1934, but the basic framework has not changed'[121].

---

118 [1908] 2 KB 863, 885

119 'By sub-s. 3 the right of the insurer to avoid the policy is preserved, provided that, in an action commenced before or within three months after the commencement of the action in which the third party obtains judgment, he obtains a declaration that the policy was obtained by the non-disclosure of a material fact or by a representation of fact which was false in some material particular. If this sub-section had stopped there, the benefit conferred by sub-s. 1 on third parties would have been seriously curtailed, but a proviso is added for their protection by which the benefit of the declaration is not to avail the insurer as against a third party who obtains his judgment in proceedings commenced before the commencement of the insurer's action, unless the insurer has, before or within seven days after the commencement of his own action, given notice to the third party 'specifying the non-disclosure or false representation 'on which he proposes to rely,' and the third party can then apply to be added as a party to the insurer's action. The object of this proviso clearly is to enable the third party to decide whether, in view of the allegations contained in the notice, it is worth his while to incur the expense of proceeding with his action and to allow him, as a person interested in disputing the insurer's claim, to be heard in opposition to it.' *Zurich General Accident and Liability Insurance Co Ltd v Morrison*, Lord Greene M.R. at 56

120 *Zurich General Accident and Liability Insurance Co Ltd v Morrison* at 61-62, continuing the passage cited in this chapter in relation to the 1930 Acts.

121 *Cameron v Liverpool Victoria Insurance Company Limited (Motor Insurers' Bureau intervening)* [2019] UKSC 6 [2019] 1 WLR 1471, 1474, para.2

1935. Britain. The **Law Reform (Married Women and Tortfeasors) Act 1935** overrules the common law rule (established since the 18th century) that there could be no contribution between tortfeasors. The 1935 Act allows judicial apportionment of liability. As the Law Revision Committee (precursor of the Law Commission) pointed out when recommending the reform, this position 'frequently arises where the plaintiff sustains a single damage from the combined negligence of two motor car drivers, and recovers judgment against both'.[122]

1936, Britain. The **Trunk Roads Act 1936** regulates 'a national strategic road network, and would later come to include the new Motorways, which began to open in the late 1950s'[123]. 'Trunk road' was the term adopted for nationally strategic highways, as they began to be organised by number from the 1920s (with the Great North Road becoming the A1). The reason for the use of the word 'trunk' is unexplained by the 1936 Act and is open to speculation. The Oxford English Dictionary defines 'trunk road' as 'an important main road used for long distance travel'.

Part Four: 1939 to 1972:
War needs research and manufacturing, post-war regulation organises international trade and new vehicle features proliferate

Motors, 1939 to 1972

1940, USA. The Jeep (elision of GPV – General Purpose Vehicle) produced for use by US armed forces. 'After the war, surplus military jeeps inaugurated a market for off-road recreational vehicles that persists into the present'.[124]

1940, USA. 1940 Packard the first car to offer factory-installed air conditioning.[125]

1946, France. Michelin introduces steel-belted radial tyres, improving durability and traction on wet surfaces (not generally adopted in USA until late 1970's).[126]

1946, Britain. Birth of the International Organisation for Standardisation (abbreviated worldwide to ISO), with meeting of delegates from 25 countries at the Institute of Civil Engineers in London to discuss the future of international standardisation[127].

1947, USA. Tucker Sedan is first car with padded dashboards, to reduce injury in impact.[128]

1949, USA. Chrysler introduces disc brakes.[129]

---

122 Professor Paul Mitchell, *A history of tort law 1900-1950* (Cambridge, 2015), chapter 11
123 National Highways website, 'History of modern A roads', https://nationalhighways.co.uk/our-roads/history-of-modern-a-roads/.
124 Flink pages 211, 276
125 Automobile magazine, 24 June 2010: https://www.automobilemag.com/news/automotive-air-conditoning-history/
126 Flink page 292
127 ISO website: https://www.iso.org/about-us.html
128 AA website: https://www.theaa.com/breakdown-cover/advice/evolution-of-car-safety-features
129 Flink page 247

1950, USA. The invention of cruise control. Engineer (and former SAE president) Ralph Teetor, who is blind, patents 'speedostat', a device to automate speed and to inform the driver (by resistance to the accelerator pedal) who can then either maintain the automated speed or override it.[130] Speedostat was described in 1954 by *Popular Mechanics* magazine as 'a kind of power-operated accelerator, or governor with extras. It definitely takes us several miles farther down the road to automatic pilots for cars.'

1951, USA. Chrysler introduces power steering.[131]

1951, Germany. Walter Linderer conceives idea of an airbag, to cushion car occupants in impacts. Airbag idea continues in development by others, until its deployment (including crash-sensing technology) in the late 1960s.[132]

1951, Germany. Mercedes Benz engineer Béla Barényi registers patent for the crumple zone, to absorb force of impact in areas away from car occupants.[133]

1954, USA. Ford introduces the 'safety package' consisting of safety door latches, a collapsible steering column, a padded dashboard and optional seat belts, before those measures were required by law – 'only to discover that safety did not sell to style-conscious consumers'.[134]

1954, Germany. Mercedes introduces fuel injection (on the 300SL sports car), reducing exhaust emissions and increasing fuel efficiency.[135]

1958, Britain. The Preston bypass (now part of the M6) opens, the first motorway in Britain[136] (the M1 opens the following year[137]).

1959, Sweden. Volvo introduce the three-point seatbelt developed by Nils Bohlin.[138]

1960 to 1963, USA. First generation of the Chevrolet Corvair, whose rear axle design was said to have contributed to oversteer and to many accidents, including accidents injuring family members of several automobile company executives.

---

130 David Sears, *the sightless visionary who invented cruise control*, the Smithsonian magazine, 8 March 2018: https://www.smithsonianmag.com/innovation/sightless-visionary-who-invented-cruise-control-180968418/
131 Flink page 247
132 AA website: https://www.theaa.com/breakdown-cover/advice/evolution-of-car-safety-features
133 Mercedes website: https://www.mercedes-benz.com/en/classic/bela-barenyi-the-lifesaver/
134 Flink page 290
135 Daimler website: https://media.daimler.com/marsMediaSite/en/instance/ko/A-short-history-of-injection-engines-Mercedes-Benz-is-a-pioneer-in-direct-petrol-injection.xhtml?oid=9361801
136 UK government website: https://www.gov.uk/government/news/englands-first-motorway-turns-60-with-major-technology-upgrade
137 UK government website: https://www.gov.uk/government/publications/history-of-road-safety-and-the-driving-test/history-of-road-safety-the-highway-code-and-the-driving-test#contents
138 Volvo website: https://www.media.volvocars.com/global/en-gb/media/pressreleases/250014/volvo-cars-celebrates-60-years-of-sharing-safety-knowledge-with-open-for-all-digital-library

1961, USA. Publication of *The Death and Life of Great American Cities*[139] by Jane Jacobs, campaigner for the accommodation of road traffic within urban neighbourhoods, against the mass relocation of urban housing to allow city-centre space for large highways.

1965, USA. Consumer campaigner Ralph Nader focusses upon the Chevrolet Corvair and Ford Pinto in his book *Unsafe at any speed: the designed-in dangers of the American automobile*, public response to which influences the National Traffic and Motor Vehicle Safety Act 1966 in the USA.[140]

1965, Britain. Installation of seatbelts in vehicles in UK made compulsory.[141]

1966, USA. First Fuel cell electric vehicle (FCEV), the GMC Electrovan, produced by General Motors. 'The fuel used was pure liquid hydrogen and liquid oxygen. The Electrovan achieved a top speed of 70 MPH and had a range of 120 miles. However, the whole fuel cell system turned the 6-seat van into a 2-seater due to the large hydrogen and oxygen tanks along with the piping ... After test driving in the GM facility and being shown off to journalists, the project was discontinued due to the prohibitive cost and lack of hydrogen infrastructure at that time.'[142]

Electronics, 1939 to 1972

1939 to 1942, Britain. Robert Dippy develops radio triangulation to fix the location of targets for bomber aircraft.[143]

1940, Britain. Professor John Randall and Henry Boot make a compact, portable radar device for use by submarine-hunter aircraft, using solid-state, semiconductor technology.[144]

1943, Britain. Austrian scientist Paul Eisler invents printed circuit board technology, (PCB), making entire circuit boards both compact and less fragile, by the removal of dangling wires.[145]

1948, USA. Bell laboratories publicly announces the solid state transistor (the precursor to the microchip), as an alternative to the larger and more fragile vacuum tube.[146]

1950 to 1956. Semiconductor technology continues to advance. Gordon Teal of Bell laboratories having pioneered the production of structurally perfect

---

139 Jane Jacobs, *The Death and Life of Great American Cities* (1961, Random House)
140 Ralph Nader, *Unsafe at any speed: the designed-in dangers of the American automobile* (1965, Grossman publishers); Flink page 288
141 UK government website: https://www.gov.uk/government/news/thirty-years-of-seatbelt-safety
142 Dr. Nan Qin, Dr. Ali Raissi and Dr. Paul Brooker *Analysis of Fuel Cell Vehicle Developments,* Florida Solar Energy Center, September 2014, FSEC Report Number: FSEC-CR-1987-14, sponsored by U.S. Department of Transportation's University Transportation Centers Program, page 3: http://fsec.ucf.edu/en/publications/pdf/fsec-cr-1987-14.pdf
143 Cheung and Brach page 156
144 Cheung and Brach pages 151, 152
145 Cheung and Brach page 232
146 Cheung and Brach Chapter 13

germanium and silicon crystals, the same laboratory produces the first large scale photovoltaic cells (solar panels) in 1956. Siemens synthesise the gallium arsenide (GaA) conductor in 1953, which will later allow Light Emitting Diodes (LEDs).[147]

1958, USA. Jean Hoerni invents the planar process, whereby transistors are manufactured within a single, flat surface.[148]

1958, USA. In response to the Soviet Union's orbit of the Earth by Sputnik, the USA establishes two governmental agencies: the National Aeronautics and Space Administration (NASA) and the Defense Advanced Research Projects Agency (DARPA).[149]

1960, USA. The LASER (light amplification by stimulated emission of radiation) invented by Theodore Maiman of Hughes research laboratory.[150]

1961, USA. First monolithic integrated circuit, or 'chip', designed by Robert Noyce and built by Jay Last of Fairchild semiconductors. 'This was a historic achievement, and it marked the beginning of the modern electronic era. With the chip, mankind could now precisely control the complex flow of electrons in a functional circuit built on a tiny piece of silicon'.[151]

1962, USA. Nick Holonyak Jr makes the first light emitting diode (LED).[152]

1965, USA. In an article, chemist, chip pioneer and founder of Intel, Gordon Moore, coins 'Moore's Law' about future computing capability. Moore predicts that the number of transistors on a chip would double every 12 months (he later amends this to every 18 months).[153]

1968. First use of a computer in a consumer vehicle: a transistorised, electronically-controlled fuel injection (EFI) system manufactured by Bosch, installed in type 3 Volkswagen models.[154]

1970. First fibre-optic cable (the technology pioneered by Charles Kao, which would later allow broadband connectivity).[155]

1971, USA. The first microprocessor (a computer on a single chip, or System on a Chip (SOC)): the 4004 by Intel, measuring 0.32 by 0.42cm and containing about 2,300 transistors.[156]

---

147 Cheung and Brach pages 201, 289-290
148 Cheung and Brach page 238
149 Cheung and Brach page 231
150 Cheung and Brach page 294
151 Cheung and Brach page 239
152 Cheung and Brach page 290
153 Cheung and Brach page 249
154 Article *Computer Chips inside the car*, accessed 21 May 2021: https://www.chipsetc.com/computer-chips-inside-the-car.html#
155 Cheung and Brach page 300
156 Cheung and Brach page 258

Computers, 1939 to 1972

1943, USA. Warren McCulloch and Walter Pitts propose a mathematical model for the working of neurons in the human brain: the precursor of the 1958 perceptron model, to create neural nets. 'They realized that neurons could be modelled as electrical circuits – more specifically, simple logical circuits'.[157]

1949, Britain. William Grey Walter, member of the Ratio Club, a group for practitioners of cybernetics (which 'blended ideas from engineering, mathematics and brain sciences to try and find general, unifying ways of understanding how behaviour is generated and information processed in brains … [cybernetics was] a forerunner of artificial intelligence and cognitive science'[158]) builds 'tortoise' robots, which move according to signals received by two sensors: a light sensor and a touch sensor. The forerunner of vehicles responding in an automated way to signals from sensors.

1950, Britain. Alan Turing publishes his paper *Computing machinery and intelligence*, in which he reframes the question 'can machines think?'

> 'in terms of a game which we call the 'imitation game'. It is played with three people, a man (A), a woman (B), and an interrogator (C) who may be of either sex. The interrogator stays in a room apart from the other two. The object of the game for the interrogator is to determine which of the other two is the man and which is the woman.'
>
> …
>
> 'What will happen when a machine takes the part of A in this game? Will the interrogator decide wrongly as often when the game is played like this as he does when the game is played between a man and a woman?'
>
> …
>
> 'It will simplify matters for the reader if I explain first my own beliefs in the matter. Consider first the more accurate form of the question. I believe that in about fifty years time it will be possible to programme computers with a storage capacity of about 10^9 to make them play the imitation game so well that an average interrogator will not have more than 70 per cent chance of making the right identification after five minutes of questioning. The original question, 'Can machines think?' I believe to be too meaningless to deserve discussion. Nevertheless I believe that at the end of the century the use of words and general educated opinion will have altered so much that one will be able to speak of machines thinking without expecting to be contradicted. I believe further that no useful purpose is served by concealing these beliefs. The popular view that scientists proceed inexorably from well-established fact to well-established fact, never being influenced by any unproved conjecture, is quite mistaken. Provided it is made clear which are proved facts and which

---

157 Wooldridge page 174
158 Owen Holland and Phil Husbands, *Pioneers of cybernetics: Grey Walters' robot tortoises and the Ratio Club*, Chapter 5 of *Robots: the 500-year quest to make machines human* (the Science Museum, 2017). British Pathé news footage of Grey Walter's robot, Toby (1951), at https://www.youtube.com/watch?v=wQE82derooc

are conjectures, no harm can result. Conjectures are of great importance since they suggest useful lines of research.'

...

'It is not possible to produce a set of rules purporting to describe what a man should do in every conceivable set of circumstances. One might for instance have a rule that one is to stop when one sees a red traffic light, and to go if one sees a green one, but what if by some fault both appear together? One may perhaps decide that it is safest to stop. But some further difficulty may well arise from this decision later. To attempt to provide rules of conduct to cover every eventuality, even those arising from traffic lights, appears to be impossible. With all this I agree.' [159]

1952, USA. Computer scientist Grace Murray Hopper of the US Navy (later Rear Admiral Hopper) completes the first 'compiler', translating mathematical code into machine code understood by computers – the precursor of word-based computer languages usable by non-mathematicians, which she later also helped to develop (Grace Hopper also wrote the first computer manual and is said to have coined the terms 'bug' and 'debugging' in relation to computer faults, after finding a moth lodged in a Mark II computer at Harvard in 1945).[160]

1958, USA. Frank Rosenblatt's 'perceptron' computer, for the US Office of Naval Research, (the first machine learning, neural net to be implemented).[161]

'An IBM 704 – a 5-ton computer the size of a room – was fed a series of punch cards. After 50 trials, the computer taught itself to distinguish cards marked on the left from cards marked on the right.'[162]

Each artificial 'neuron' is fed several inputs, and the neuron activates when the total weight of inputs reaches a pre-set value (so, eg., a neuron with 3 inputs, two of which are worth 1 and one is worth 2, can be set to fire when it receives a total weight of 2, which could happen either by inputs one and two firing, or input three alone firing). A network of many such neurons – the neural network – can be built, and then the network can be taught how to act, by the programmer setting the appropriate numeric weights for each of the many neurons within the system. So the neural network is capable of machine learning.

The practical application of the neural network was limited, by the technology, to single-layer neural networks which could not achieve learning close to human abilities. The limits of the hardware eventually led to the stagnation of AI research: an 'AI Winter' from the 1970's. But later technology allowed multi-layer neural networks, which expanded the capacity of machine learning.

1972, USA. DARPA demonstrates its ARPANET: the Advanced Research Projects Network.

---

159 Turing scrapbook https://www.turing.org.uk/scrapbook/test.html
160 Yale university website: https://news.yale.edu/2017/02/10/grace-murray-hopper-1906-1992-legacy-innovation-and-service
161 Wooldridge page 175
162 Cornell university website: https://news.cornell.edu/stories/2019/09/professors-perceptron-paved-way-ai-60-years-too-soon

'This military network was intended to connect computers across the American continent, with one special feature. If one part of this great network was destroyed, the communications system would remain operative. The information passing through the system was required to detour around the damaged part and arrive at its destination by another route'[163]

This is achieved in part by sending data in packets, rather than in a continuous stream; if any packets are lost or blocked, they can be re-sent. The internet – 'the largest network of computers in the world'[164] is born.

Road Transport Law, 1939 to 1972

1945, Britain, June. The **Law Reform (Contributory Negligence) Act 1945** comes into force. A further reform recommended by the Law Revision Committee, before the Second World War, to allow apportionment of fault between a defendant and a claimant where the latter was also at fault, applying the Admiralty Court practice of apportionment, rather than the previous principle of contributory negligence as a complete defence. As in the case of joint tortfeasors, this reform is of particular significance in road traffic accident cases.[165]

1945, October. The **United Nations Charter**[166] (signed in San Francisco in June) comes into force. At its signing, US President Truman described the UN Charter as

'a solid structure upon which we can build a better world. History will honor you for it. Between the victory in Europe and the final victory, in this most destructive of all wars, you have won a victory against war itself.'

The purposes of the Charter include (Article 1(2))

'To achieve international co-operation in solving international problems of an economic, social, cultural, or humanitarian character'

Its six principal organs (starting with the security council) include (Article 7 and see Chapter X, below) 'an Economic and Social Council' and

'Such subsidiary organs as may be found necessary may be established in accordance with the present charter'

Regional arrangements are permitted, provided the Security Council is kept informed (Articles 52 to 54)

Chapter IX provides for 'International Economic and Social Co-operation' and particularly that (Article 57(1)):

---

163 Gringras 1.3
164 Gringras 1.3
165 Mitchell Chapter 13
166 Speech of President Harry S Truman at the closing session of the United Nations Conference (26 June 1945), website of the American Presidency Project, University of California, Santa Barbara

The various specialized agencies, established by intergovernmental agreement and having wide international responsibilities, as defined in their basic instruments, in economic, social, cultural, educational, health, and related fields, shall be brought into relationship with the United Nations in accordance with the provisions of Article 63.

Chapter X (Articles 61 to 72) makes detailed provision for the **Economic and Social Council (ECOSOC)**. Among its powers and functions (Article 62(1) and (3)):

'The Economic and Social Council may make or initiate studies and reports with respect to international economic, social, cultural, educational, health, and related matters and may make recommendations with respect to any such matters to the General Assembly to the Members of the United Nations, and to the specialized agencies concerned.'

Article 68 provides that:

'The Economic and Social Council shall set up commissions in economic and social fields and for the promotion of human rights, and such other commissions as may be required for the performance of its functions.'

And Article 71 provides that:

'The Economic and Social Council may make suitable arrangements for consultation with non-governmental organizations which are concerned with matters within its competence. Such arrangements may be made with international organizations and, where appropriate, with national organizations after consultation with the Member of the United Nations concerned.'

1946, Britain. The **Motor Insurers' Bureau (MIB)** is created to cover claims against uninsured drivers. 'The UK motor insurance industry, anxious to avoid legislation requiring them to participate in [the 1937 Cassel Committee's] proposed guarantee fund, decided to accept a non-statutory scheme for the compensation of uninsured drivers and the newly-formed [MIB] established by motor insurers entered into an agreement with the government which achieved just that result'.[167]

1947. The **United Nations Economic Commission for Europe (UNECE)** established by ECOSOC, as one of the five regional commissions of the UN.[168]

1947. The Final Act of the **General Agreement on Tariffs and Trade (GATT)** is signed by six of its 23 contracting parties (Belgium, Canada, Luxembourg, the Netherlands, the United Kingdom and the United States)[169]. The GATT (the precursor to the **World Trade Organisation**, WTO, formed in 1995) aims to remove national tariffs on imports, which it sees as restraining international trade.

---

167 Merkin and Hemsworth 1-18, 1-20
168 UNECE website https://www.unece.org/mission.html
169 World Trade Organisation (WTO) website: https://www.wto.org/english/tratop_e/gatt_e/ task_of_signing_e.htm; Andrea Barrios Villareal, *International Standardisation and the Agreement on Technical Barriers to Trade* (Cambridge, 2018)

A tool of that liberalisation of international trade is the development of common international standards for goods and services.

1949, Switzerland. **The UN Convention on Road Traffic 1949 (the Geneva Convention)**. Replaces the 1926 International Convention relative to Motor Traffic (above). Later superseded by the UN Convention on Road Traffic 1968 (the Vienna Convention), below.

1958, **UNECE Agreement to harmonise vehicle standards (the 1958 Agreement)**. 'Building a better world', in President Truman's description of the purpose of the UN Charter, includes the motor industry. The aim of the 1958 agreement is to reduce technical barriers to international trade in vehicles and vehicle parts. The UK becomes a party in 1963. The World Forum for Harmonisation of Vehicle Regulations – also known as Working party 29 of UNECE – sets regulations for vehicle standards.[170]

1965, UK. The **Motor Vehicles (Construction and Use) Regulations 1966**[171] require all cars first registered after 1 January 1965 to be fitted with seat belts in the front seats. However, despite repeated efforts by some members of parliament[172], successive British governments resist making the wearing of seatbelts compulsory until 1983.[173]

1968, Austria. **UN Convention on Road Traffic 1968 (the Vienna Convention)** to promote road safety and 'facilitate international road traffic', building upon the **1949 Geneva Convention**. The UK does not ratify the Vienna Convention until decades later, on 28 March 2018, and it comes into force in UK law on 28 March 2019, 'as part of the government's preparations for leaving the EU'[174]). The Global Forum on Road Traffic Safety – also known as UNECE Working Party 1 – administers the Vienna Convention. [175]

---

170 See the Law Commission of England and Wales and the Scottish Law Commission, *Automated Vehicles, a joint preliminary consultation paper*, CP 240, DP 166 (November 2018) at page 23, 2.50. Cited in this book as the Law Commission, *Automated Vehicles* CP 240 (November 2018).

171 SI 1996/1288

172 Royal Society for the Prevention of Accidents (RoSPA), *Road Safety Factsheet: seatbelts: history*, on RoSPA website at https://www.rospa.com/rospaweb/docs/advice-services/road-safety/vehicles/seatbelt-history.pdf

173 House of Commons library, *Motor vehicles: seat belts and child restraints*, Standard Note SN/BT/43, last updated 1 December 2010

174 Specifically, as foreseen in March 2018, to ensure the ability of British drivers to use British licences to drive in certain states in the absence of agreements with the EU or states: 'Being party to this Convention ensures that in the event that the UK leaves the EU, without either an EU wide deal, or a comprehensive set of bilateral agreements on driver licensing, holders of UK driving licences can ensure recognition if they hold the relevant International Driving Permit … The government decided that ratifying the 1968 Convention was necessary because, while the UK has long been a party to the 1949 Convention, not all Member States are party to that Convention, which meant that there was a gap which needed to be addressed. If the UK had not ratified the 1968 Convention, there would be no Convention that covered motorists who wished to drive in 5 EU Member States, specifically Croatia, Estonia, Germany, Latvia and Lithuania.' *Explanatory memorandum to the Motor Vehicles (International Circulation) (Amendment) (EU Exit) Order 2019, 2019 No.563*, UK Department of Transport, paragraphs 7.1 and 7.2, on UK government website at https://www.legislation.gov.uk/uksi/2019/563/pdfs/uksiem_20190563_en.pdf

175 See the Law Commission, *Automated Vehicles* CP 240 at page 23, 2.50

1972, Britain. The **Road Traffic Act 1972** consolidates road traffic and insurance law.

1973, Britain. On 1 January 1973, the UK becomes a member of the European Economic Community, the **European Communities Act 1972** comes into force, and EEC law becomes supreme to British law. The supremacy of EEC (later European Union, or EU) law will directly shape British law in many everyday areas – including the regulation of motor vehicles and driving – for nearly fifty years, before the withdrawal of Britain from the EU in January 2020.

Part Five: 1973 to 1988:
Oil runs short, emissions run high, computers appear in homes and in cars

Motors, 1973 to 1988

1973. Oil price rises and fuel shortages after Organisation of Arab Petroleum Exporting Countries (OAPEC) embargo sales of oil to USA, UK and other countries supportive of Israel in the 1973 Arab-Israeli war.[176] Ralph Teetor's cruise control becomes an essential tool in the USA, as speed limits are reduced from 70 to 55 miles per hour in response to the fuel shortages.[177]

1975, USA. California regulates to require catalytic converters on 1975 cars sold in the state[178] (not introduced until 1993 in the UK[179]).

1976, USA. Introduction of electronic engine controls to decrease fuel emissions (in response to government regulation) while increasing performance. Development starts of Electronic Control Units (ECU). For example, General Motors announce partnership with Motorola semiconductor to develop a custom microcomputer for use in GM vehicles, to monitor fuel emissions.[180]

1978, Germany. Mercedes demonstrates its anti-lock braking system (ABS), describing it as follows:

> 'The anti-lock braking system uses a computer to monitor the change in rotational speed of each wheel during braking. If the speed slows too quickly (such as when braking on a slippery surface) and the wheel risks locking, the computer automatically reduces the brake pressure. The wheel accelerates

176 Flink page 389
177 Clay McShane, *The automobile: a chronology of its antecedents, development and impact* (Routledge library editions, 1997, revised 2017); David Sears, *The sightless visionary who invented cruise control*, the Smithsonian magazine, 8 March 2018: https://www.smithsonianmag.com/innovation/sightless-visionary-who-invented-cruise-control-180968418/
178 Flink page 388
179 Royal Automobile Club (RAC) website: https://www.rac.co.uk/drive/advice/car-maintenance/catalytic-converters/
180 Flink page 392. Chipsetc.com: https://www.chipsetc.com/computer-chips-inside-the-car.html#

again and the brake pressure is increased again, thereby braking the wheel. This process is repeated several times in a matter of seconds.'[181]

1979. Further oil price rises after the Iranian revolution.[182]

1979, USA. The Stanford Cart, a long-term project by Stanford University (conceived in 1960 as a prototype moon vehicle, in its 1977 version with a TV camera relaying images to a computer), navigates across a room, avoiding an obstacle (a chair).[183]

1981. World automotive manufacturers introduce the Vehicle Identification Number (VIN) to show the manufacturer, year of production, place of production and vehicle characteristics of each individual vehicle.[184]

1982. Voice reminders introduced in some cars (eg. 1982 Datsun Maxima). 'Knight Rider' television drama series starts, featuring a crime-fighting talking car.[185]

1982, USA. Study by the National Research Council, concludes that, in the post-Second World War period to the early 1980s, competition in the US automobile industry 'occurred largely on the basis of the economies of scale, styling, and sales and service networks ... innovation became increasingly incremental in nature and, in marketing terms, invisible'.[186]

1984, UK. Work begins on the first Japanese car factory located in UK: Nissan Sunderland.[187]

Mid 1980s. Oil prices stabilise, with new reserves in Mexico and the North Atlantic.[188]

1985, USA, June. General Motors acquires Hughes Aircraft company. Chairman Roger B Smith says that the acquisition allows GM to 'redefine' the automobile 'from a mechanical product with a few electrical subsystems to one with major electromechanical and electronic elements'. The Wall Street Journal reports that GM expects the Hughes acquisition to result in

> 'a marketing edge over competitors. It sees lasers one day helping guide vehicles under poor visibility conditions; microelectronics and sensors under the hood improving engine performance; cockpit-like computerised dashboards, and space age materials in a range of uses. And on the factory

---

181 Daimler website: https://media.daimler.com/marsMediaSite/en/instance/ko/Brake-Assist--a-safety-asset-from-Mercedes-Benz.xhtml?oid=9913939
182 Flink page 390
183 Fabian Kröger, *Automated driving in its social, historical and cultural contexts*, Chapter 3 of *Autonomous driving: technical, legal and social aspects* (edited by Markus Maurer, J. Christian Gerdes, Barbara Lenz and Hermann Winner, Springer Open, 2016) p58; Computer History Museum (California) website: https://www.computerhistory.org/timeline/ai-robotics/
184 BSI webite: https://www.bsigroup.com/en-GB/industries-and-sectors/automotive/uk-world-manufacturer-identifier-wmi/
185 McShane page 152. Autotrader website: https://www.autotrader.com/car-news/miracle-1980s-talking-car-265020
186 Flink pages 278, 424
187 Nissan website: https://www.nissan.co.uk/experience-nissan/news/ten-millionth-vehicle-built-at-nissan-sunderland-plant.html
188 Flink page 390

floor, Hughes's advanced computer science – especially artificial intelligence capabilities – could offer far more efficient ways to assemble a car.'[189]

1985, USA, July. Etak produces the first car navigational computer, the precursor to modern satellite car navigation (SatNav). It uses both maritime navigation and computer gaming technology.[190]

1985, Germany. Mercedes introduces acceleration skid control (ASR), automatic locking differential (ASD) and automatically engaged four-wheel drive (4MATIC). Mercedes says that:

> 'What all these systems have in common is the recording and limiting of wheel slip by means of advanced micro-electronics and hydraulics with the aim of improving the so-called longitudinal dynamics of a motor vehicle.'[191]

1986, USA. Mimi Vandermolen, designer at Ford, introduces ergonomic design to US cars by positioning all controls within the driver's reach in the Ford Taurus.[192]

Electronics, 1973 to 1988

1975, USA. Steven Sasson, an engineer at Eastman Kodak, invents digital photography and makes the first digital camera. Eastman Kodak initially rejects it, on Sasson's account, in part because 'no one would ever want to look at their pictures on a television set'[193].

1980, USA. Professor Carver Mead of the California Institute of Technology (CalTech) develops computer-aided chip design, allowing design of chips without specialism in semiconductors, and subsequently allowing Gate Array and Field-Programmable Gate Arrays (FPGAs):

> 'Rather than requiring the physical connection of their components, these FPGAs were already fully finished and connected. However, the routing or wiring of the components could be reconfigured by the user via software inputs'.[194]

1984, USA. Motorola launches the DynaTAC mobile telephone, also known as 'the brick' (as used by the character Gordon Gecko in the 1987 film 'Wall Street').[195]

---

189 Flink page 397
190 McShane p156; Fastcompany.com, at https://www.fastcompany.com/3047828/who-needs-gps-the-forgotten-story-of-etaks-amazing-1985-car-navigation-system
191 Daimler website: https://media.daimler.com/marsMediaSite/en/instance/ko/Brake-Assist--a-safety-asset-from-Mercedes-Benz.xhtml?oid=9913939
192 Core77.com: https://www.core77.com/posts/39532/Mimi-Vandermolen-the-Ergonomics-Genius-Behind-Fords-'Rounded-Edge-Revolution
193 Steven Sasson quoted in article, *Kodak's first digital moment* by James Estrin, New York Times, 12 August 2015: https://lens.blogs.nytimes.com/2015/08/12/kodaks-first-digital-moment/
194 Cheung and Brach page 274
195 Science Museum website: https://www.sciencemuseum.org.uk/objects-and-stories/invention-mobile-phones

1985, Britain. On New Year's Day, Vodafone launches the first British mobile telephone network (an analogue system).[196]

1985, Britain. Sophie Wilson and Steve Furber of Acorn Computers invent the ARM1 microprocessor chip, which 'allows for very fast data processing by reducing the amount of instructions a computer can perform to the minimum'. This microchip allows the later invention of smartphones.[197]

1987. European leaders sign the Bonn GSM (Groupe Spécial Mobile, subsequently changed to Global System for Mobile Communications) agreement to establish common terms of service for mobile telephones. GSM systems were now second generation, digital systems (in which the signals are converted into binary code), known as '2G'.[198]

1988. First trans-Atlantic fibre-optic cable.[199] First LCD flatscreen TV.[200]

Computers, 1973 to 1988

1975, USA. First microcomputer (the forerunner of the home computer): the Altair 8800, using the Intel 8080 chip as its central processing unit.[201]

1984, USA. Apple launches the Mac home computer, with a graphical user interface (GUI), showing documents as pictures, to which the user could navigate with a 'mouse'.[202]

1986, USA. The second age of machine learning neural nets: David E Rumelhart and others propose a new method, 'Parallel Distributed Processing' (PDP), including a new algorithm, 'Backpropagation' (Backprop), which 'works by looking at cases where a neural net has made an error in its classification' and 'propagates the error backwards through the network through each preceding layer' to 'find the steepest way to descend in the map, in stages, all the way from the current error down to the lowest error of all'. Backprop 'made possible a whole slew of applications for neural nets, which went far beyond the simple demonstrations of perceptron models of 20 years earlier'.[203] But, again, machine learning stagnated, because 'computers of the time were just not powerful enough to handle the new techniques'.[204]

196 Science Museum website: https://www.sciencemuseum.org.uk/objects-and-stories/invention-mobile-phones
197 Science Museum website: https://www.sciencemuseum.org.uk/objects-and-stories/computer-your-pocket-rise-smartphones Royal Society website: https://royalsociety.org/topics-policy/industry-innovation/case-studies/wilson/
198 Science Museum website: https://www.sciencemuseum.org.uk/objects-and-stories/invention-mobile-phones
199 Cheung and Brach page 301
200 Cheung and Brach page 311
201 Cheung and Brach page 260
202 Wooldridge page 144
203 Wooldridge page 183
204 Wooldridge page 184

Road Transport Law, 1973 to 1988

1983. The **Motor Vehicles (Wearing of Seat Belts) Regulations 1982**[205] make the wearing of seatbelts compulsory in the front of cars in Britain, from 31 January 1983 (18 years after front seatbelts were required as a vehicle specification by British law)[206]. The wearing of rear seatbelts becomes compulsory in the UK even later: for children on 1 September 1989[207] and for adults on 1 July 1991[208].

1984. The **Data Protection Act 1984** receives royal assent: 'An Act to regulate the use of automatically processed information relating to individuals and the provision of services in respect of such information' (the 1984 Act is later superseded by DPA 1998 and then DPA 2018). Eric Howe becomes the first Data Protection Registrar in September 1984.[209]

1987. The **Consumer Protection Act 1987** is enacted, as a result of EU directive of 1985 concerning liability for defective products. It replaces fault (which can be difficult to prove) with defectiveness of a product, defined as 'if the safety of the product is not such as persons generally are entitled to expect' and makes producers, those who hold themselves out as producers, importers and suppliers liable.[210]

1988. The **Road Traffic Act 1988** consolidates road traffic and insurance law.

Part Six: 1989 to 2004:
The worldwide web and Wi-Fi connect people and devices, manufacturers explore self-driving cars

Motors, 1989 to 2004

1990, USA. James J Flink, in *The Automobile Age*, concludes that:

> 'The current renaissance in automotive technology is a renaissance almost entirely engendered by electronic and aerospace technology; the major technological forces for change in American life at present are the computer, the robot, the laser beam and telecommunications.'[211]

205 SI 1982/1203
206 From 1 January 1965: see above, the Motor Vehicles (Construction and Use) Regulations 1966 (SI 1966/1288). House of Commons library, *Motor vehicles: seat belts and child restraints*, Standard Note SN/BT/43, last updated 1 December 2010; Royal Society for the Prevention of Accidents (RoSPA), *Road Safety Factsheet: seatbelts: history*, on RoSPA website at https://www.rospa.com/rospaweb/docs/advice-services/road-safety/vehicles/seatbelt-history.pdf
207 The Motor Vehicles (Wearing of Seat Belts by Children in Rear Seats) Regulations 1989 (SI 1989/1219)
208 The Motor Vehicles (Wearing of Seat Belts in Rear Seats by Adults) Regulations 1991 (SI 1991/1255)
209 Information Commissioner's Office (ICO) website: https://ico.org.uk/about-the-ico/our-information/history-of-the-ico/our-history/
210 *Clerk & Lindsell on Torts*, 23rd edition (Sweet and Maxwell, 2020) at 10-01, 10-55, 10-75
211 Flink page 408

1994, Sweden. Volvo introduces side impact airbags, as part of its side impact protection system, designed to spread the force of an impact across the side of the car.[212]

1995, Germany. Mercedes introduces electronic stability (electronic stability program, or ESP) to improve vehicular stability.[213]

1995, Japan. Mitsubishi launches first adaptive cruise control system, able to alter automated speed according to distance to vehicle ahead, but unable to automate braking (the driver is prompted to brake by audible and visual signals).[214]

1995, Europe. End of the PROMETHEUS project – 'a research programme headed by car manufacturers from six European countries' and 'the largest R&D [research and development] project ever in the field of driverless cars'. 'The project defined the state of the art for autonomous vehicles', including particular technologies such as Lane Keeping Support, Collision Avoidance and Autonomous Intelligent Cruise Control.[215]

1996, Germany. Mercedes introduces the brake assist system (BAS):

> 'Brake Assist (BAS) shortens the stopping distance in an emergency – when the driver applies the brakes too hesitantly or too gently in a critical situation. In such a case, the system automatically generates the maximum available brake boosting effect in split seconds, thereby shortening the car's stopping distance significantly.'[216]

1996. The European New Car Assessment Programme (**Euro NCAP**) launched. A five-star rating of the safety features of new cars.[217]

1997, Japan. Toyota Prius, the 'world's first mass-produced petrol hybrid electric vehicle' (PHEV) launched.[218]

1998, Germany. Mercedes launches a more sophisticated adaptive cruise control system, including automated braking.[219]

---

212 Volvo website: https://www.media.volvocars.com/global/en-gb/media/pressreleases/250014/volvo-cars-celebrates-60-years-of-sharing-safety-knowledge-with-open-for-all-digital-library

213 Mercedes website: https://emercedesbenz.com/autos/mercedes-benz/s-class/mercedes-benz-history-esp-makes-its-debut-in-the-mercedes-benz-s-600-coupe/

214 Autonomous Vehicle International website: the history of adaptive cruise control: https://www.autonomousvehicleinternational.com/features/adas-3.html

215 Wooldridge pages 224, 225. University of Portsmouth website: https://researchportal.port.ac.uk/portal/en/projects/ european-eureka-project--programme-for-a-european-traffic-of-highest-efficiency-and-unprecedented-safety-prometheus(7258e5d4-51ec-4114-84b1-f107e2dd9cb5).html

216 Daimler website: https://media.daimler.com/marsMediaSite/en/instance/ko/Brake-Assist--a-safety-asset-from-Mercedes-Benz.xhtml?oid=9913939

217 Euro NCAP website: https://www.euroncap.com/en/about-euro-ncap/timeline/euro-ncap-launched/

218 Official blog of Toyota UK: https://blog.toyota.co.uk/history-toyota-prius

219 Autonomous Vehicle International website: the history of adaptive cruise control: https://www.autonomousvehicleinternational.com/features/adas-3.html; Daimler website: https://media.daimler.com/ marsMediaSite/en/instance/ko/DISTRONIC-The-car-learns-to-see.xhtml?oid=41510718

2000. Toyota Prius released in the UK.[220]

2004, Sweden. Volvo introduces the blind spot information system, a camera-based system which illuminates the wing mirror when a vehicle enters the blind spot zone.[221]

Electronics, 1989 to 2004

1999, USA. One of the several groups using unlicensed radio frequencies as an alternative to wired internet connections coins the term **'WiFi'**, a compaction of 'Wireless Fidelity'. In 2003, Wi-Fi pioneer and electrical engineering Professor Teresa Meng tells Wired Magazine that 'Five or ten years from now, we won't worry about communications with wires. You'll just open your laptop or PDA [Personal Digital Assistant – precursor of the smartphone] and the data will be there'.[222]

1999. The first **'Bluetooth'** device released. 'Bluetooth' is a short-range Wi-Fi system, designed to connect devices situated close to each other. The first Bluetooth device is a wireless headset. 'Bluetooth' is named after King Harald 'Bluetooth' Gormsson, who united Denmark and Norway in 958 (he had a distinctive, dead tooth). 'Bluetooth' is a collaboration between many manufacturers, led by Intel, Ericsson and Nokia.[223]

2003. Third generation of mobile telephones (3G) launched in the UK, allowing transmission of video and video calls.[224]

Computers, 1989 to 2004

1989. British scientist Tim Berners-Lee invents the **worldwide web**, while working at CERN (Conseil Européen pour la Recherche Nucléaire)[225]. The worldwide web is 'a common language that allows one computer to understand another when they communicate across telecommunications lines'[226].

1993. Tim Berners-Lee and CERN release the worldwide web ('www') software into the public domain, enabling worldwide communication between computers, via the internet.[227]

1997, USA. Ramnath Chellappa coins the term **'cloud computing'**[228] (the use of a network of remote servers hosted on the internet to store, manage and process

---

220 Official blog of Toyota UK: https://blog.toyota.co.uk/history-toyota-prius
221 Volvo website: https://www.media.volvocars.com/global/en-gb/media/pressreleases/4923
222 Wired magazine article 'The Wi-Fi Revolution', 1 May 2003 https://www.wired.com/2003/05/wifirevolution/
223 Bluetooth website: https://www.bluetooth.com/about-us/bluetooth-origin/
224 BBC website http://news.bbc.co.uk/1/hi/technology/2808761.stm
225 CERN website: https://home.cern/science/computing/birth-web
226 Gringras 1.15
227 CERN website: https://home.cern/science/computing/birth-web
228 'the practice of using a network of remote servers hosted on the internet to store, manage and process data, rather than a local server or personal computer' (OED).

data, rather than a local server or personal computer[229]) in his paper *Intermediaries in cloud computing: a new computing paradigm.*[230]

1999, USA. Nvidia (founded 1993) releases its GeForce 256, which it describes as the first **Graphics Processing Unit (GPU)**. GPUs are capable of such high levels of data processing (to render three-dimensional images for computer gaming) that they find other uses, including the further development of machine learning neural nets.[231]

Road Transport Law, 1989 to 2004

1990. The **Computer Misuse Act 1990** enacted and comes into force: 'An Act to make provision for securing computer material against unauthorised access or modification; and for connected purposes'.

2000, 2 October. The **Human Rights Act 1998** comes into force, bringing into British law express rights to life and to respect for private and family life, among others.

2003, 19 January. The **European Communities (Rights against Insurers) Regulations 2002**[232] come into force, giving a party who 'has a cause of action against an insured person in tort or (as the case may be) delict', arising out of an accident, 'without prejudice to his right to issue proceedings against the insured person, [the right to] issue proceedings against the insurer which issued the policy of insurance relating to the insured vehicle, and that insurer shall be directly liable to the entitled party to the extent that he is liable to the insured person'.[233]

Part Seven: 2005 to 2019:
The disruption of the automotive industry (machine learning enters its third age, self-driving cars are born, electric cars are reborn, mobile Apps change passenger travel, the Automated and Electric Vehicles Act 2018 is enacted, 5G arrives)

Motors, 2005 to 2019

2005, USA. In the second DARPA (Defense Advanced Research Projects Agency) grand challenge (to produce an autonomous car that can drive itself 150 miles across the desert), a converted Volkswagen Touareg, STANLEY, designed by a team at Stanford University led by Sebastian Thrun, completes the course first, in just

---

229 OED
230 Emory university profile of Professor Ramnath Chellappa: https://goizueta.emory.edu/faculty/profiles/ramnath-k-chellappa
231 Wooldridge page 187; Nvidia website: https://www.nvidia.com/en-gb/about-nvidia/corporate-timeline/
232 SI 2002/3061
233 Regulation 3(2)

under 7 hours (in the first challenge in 2004, no vehicle had completed more than 8 miles).[234]

2006, USA. **Automated Emergency Braking (AEB)** introduced on some cars in USA, to detect obstacle in front of car and to brake if driver fails to do so.[235]

Circa 2007, USA. **'Ridesharing'** appears (a taxi service which uses an algorithm to assign a vehicle at short notice, allowing passengers without a common destination to share a taxi).[236]

2007, USA. The DARPA Urban Challenge (for an autonomous car to traverse an urban area, constructed on a disused airfield, while obeying local traffic laws, interacting with manned traffic and 'performing complex manoeuvres such as merging, passing, parking, and negotiating intersections'). Won by a team from Carnegie Mellon university, which completed the course at an average speed of 14 mph.[237]

2008, USA. Electric car manufacturer **Tesla releases its first car**, the luxury Roadster, described (on its 2020 website) as 'an all-electric supercar'.[238]

2009, USA. In wake of the 2008 financial crisis, US government provides financial support (the 'bailout') to two of the 'big three' auto manufacturers (GM and Chrysler) to prevent collapse of US automotive industry.[239]

2009, USA. Google starts its self-driving car project (subsequently renamed **Waymo**).[240]

2010, USA. **Uber** provides its first ride, to a passenger in San Francisco who has hailed the driver using Uber's mobile app.[241]

2011. The fully-electric **Nissan Leaf** car launches in Europe (having launched in December 2010 in Japan and the USA), described as 'the world's first 100-percent electric, zero-emission car designed for the mass market'.[242]

2012, USA, June. Tesla launches the Model S, 'the world's first premium electric sedan'.[243]

---

234 Wooldridge pages 225, 226; Stanford website: https://news.stanford.edu/news/2005/october12/stanleyfinish-100905.html
235 National Highway Traffic Safety Administration (NHTSA) website: https://www.safercar.gov/Vehicle+Shoppers/Safety+Technology/aeb-1/
236 McShane
237 Wooldridge page 226; DARPA website: https://www.darpa.mil/about-us/timeline/darpa-urban-challenge
238 Tesla website: https://www.tesla.com/about https://www.tesla.com/en_GB/roadster
239 *The Auto bailout 10 years later: was it the right call?* Wharton School, University of Pennsylvania website: https://knowledge.wharton.upenn.edu/article/auto-bailout-ten-years-later-right-call/
240 Waymo website: https://waymo.com
241 Uber website: https://www.uber.com/en-GB/newsroom/history/
242 Nissan website: https://www.nissan-global.com/EN/NISSAN/LEAF/
243 Tesla website: https://www.tesla.com/en_GB/blog/tesla-motors-begin-customer-deliveries-model-s-june-22nd?redirect=no; Wooldridge page 228

2012, Britain, June. The first Uber journey in London.[244]

2014, USA, January. The Society of Automotive Engineers (SAE) publishes Taxonomy and Definitions for Terms Related to On-Road Motor Vehicle Automated Driving Systems (J3016_201401) – the **SAE Levels of autonomous driving**.[245]

2014. British autonomous driving software company **Oxbotica (now Oxa)** founded by Professors Paul Newman and Ingmar Posner.[246]

2014, USA. Tesla is reported to have introduced hardware ready for its 'Autopilot' system.[247]

2015, USA, August. The first reported 'hack' of a conventional car. Dr Charlie Miller and Chris Valasek report that they were able to attack the driver assistance, Wi-Fi and radio systems of a Jeep Cherokee remotely and to take remote control of its steering and braking and of the volume of the radio.[248]

2015, USA, September. US Environmental Protection Agency (EPA) issues 'a Notice of Violation of the Clean Air Act to Volkswagen AG, Audi AG, and Volkswagen Group of America, Inc (collectively, 'Volkswagen'). The notice alleges that Volkswagen installed software in its model year 2009-2015 2.0 litre diesel cars that circumvents EPA emissions standards'. A week after the Notice, EPA announces 'that **defeat device** screening protocols would be included in compliance oversight programs going forward'.[249]

2015, USA, October. Tesla releases its **Autopilot** system, by software update. The Tesla British blog describes Autopilot as follows:

> 'Autopilot allows Model S to steer within a lane, change lanes with the simple tap of a turn signal, and manage speed by using active, traffic-aware cruise control. Digital control of motors, brakes, and steering helps avoid collisions from the front and sides, as well as preventing the car from wandering off the road. Your car can also scan for a parking space, alert you when one is available, and parallel park on command.'

> 'Tesla Autopilot relieves drivers of the most tedious and potentially dangerous aspects of road travel. We're building Autopilot to give you more confidence behind the wheel, increase your safety on the road, and make highway driving more enjoyable. While truly driverless cars are still a few years away, Tesla Autopilot functions like the systems that airplane pilots use when conditions are clear. The driver is still responsible for, and ultimately in control

---

244 https://www.uber.com/en-GB/newsroom/5-years-moving-london/, accessed 12 October 2022.
245 SAE website: https://www.sae.org/standards/content/j3016_201401/ (original and subsequent versions of SAE J3016)
246 Oxbotica website: https://www.oxbotica.com/about-us/
247 Electrek website: https://electrek.co/guides/tesla-autopilot/
248 Dr Charlie Miller & Chris Valasek, *Remote Exploitation of an Unaltered Passenger Vehicle*, 10 August 2015, at http://illmatics.com/Remote%20Car%20Hacking.pdf
249 EPA website: https://www.epa.gov/vw/learn-about-volkswagen-violations; Date in §3 of judgment of Mr Justice Waksman in *Crossley and others v Volkswagen, Audi, Skoda, Seat and others* [2019] EWHC 783 (QB) (*the VW NOx emissions group litigation*)

of, the car. What's more, you always have intuitive access to the information your car is using to inform its actions.'[250]

2015, UK, November. **UK Autodrive** starts on-road trials of autonomous vehicles, including **Aurrigo**'s self-driving pods, (project ends October 2018).[251]

2016, USA (Florida), May. First fatal accident involving a Tesla autopilot system, when a Tesla S collides with a truck.[252]

2017, UK (Cambridge), February. Self-driving start-up, **Wayve**, established.[253]

2017, Europe, July. Audi launches '**traffic jam pilot**' in its A8 model, describing it as

'the world's first system that enables SAE level 3 conditional automation. Audi presents the innovation in the new A8, which handles the task of driving in traffic jam or slow-moving highway traffic up to 60 km/h (37.3 mph)'[254]

(But regulators do not allow level 3 cars to operate, so in May 2020 Audi is reported to have announced that it is withdrawing the system[255]. The start of the UK government's consultation on whether such systems should be allowed in the UK follows 3 months later, in August 2020.[256])

2017, China, December. Beijing becomes first Chinese city to introduce regulations to allow tests of autonomous vehicles.[257]

2018, USA (Arizona), March. First pedestrian fatal accident involving an AV. Uber self-driving vehicle under testing with a safety driver collides with pedestrian pushing her bicycle across a road.[258]

2019, Britain, April. Foundation of the **Connected Places Catapult**:

'a new organisation which combines the Transport Systems and Future Cities Catapults, ... The new Connected Places Catapult will accelerate smarter living and travelling, in and between the places of tomorrow. The new Catapult will grow businesses with innovations in mobility services and the built environment, that enable new levels of physical, digital and social connectedness ...'

---

250 Tesla GB blog, *your autopilot has arrived*, 14 October 2015: https://www.tesla.com/en_GB/blog/your-autopilot-has-arrived

251 UK Autodrive website: http://www.ukautodrive.com/the-uk-autodrive-project/

252 Tesla GB blog: https://www.tesla.com/en_GB/blog/tragic-loss

253 https://wayve.ai

254 Audi website: https://www.audi-mediacenter.com/en/audimediatv/video/footage-audi-a8-audi-ai-traffic-jam-pilot-3785

255 Autovista article, *Audi A8 will not feature level 3 autonomy*, 11 May 2020, at https://autovistagroup.com/news-and-insights/audi-a8-will-not-feature-level-3-autonomy

256 UK government website: https://www.gov.uk/government/consultations/safe-use-of-automated-lane-keeping-system-on-gb-motorways-call-for-evidence

257 South China Morning Post website: https://www.scmp.com/tech/enterprises/article/3096495/these-chinese-autonomous-vehicle-start-ups-are-keeping-their-eye

258 National Transportation Safety Board (NTSB), Preliminary report into Uber pedestrian fatal accident March 2018, Arizona, at https://www.ntsb.gov/investigations/AccidentReports/Reports/HWY18MH010-prelim.pdf

'The Connected Places Catapult will focus on working across boundaries, bureaucracies, public and private sectors, on a whole system approach to achieve this goal. Like the legacy organisations before it, the new Catapult will engage academic networks, diverse SME ecosystems, business and government departments as it seeks to foster new markets, boost demand for innovation and increase the supply of proven products and services across transport, cities, towns and villages.'[259]

2019, Britain, July. **BSI** launches its connected and autonomous vehicles (CAV) standards programme.[260]

2019, UK (London), October. Five (now **Five AI**) leads government-backed 'Streetwise project' testing autonomous driving on public roads.[261]

Electronics, 2005 to 2019

2007, USA. First **iPhone**, using System on a Chip (SOC) technology for each of its various functions (camera, music player etc) and an LCD screen with touch sensors.[262]

2012, Britain, October. Fourth generation mobile telephone service (4G) launched in 11 cities, increasing speed and size of data transfers.[263]

2019, UK, May: EE launches first fifth generation (5G) mobile telephone networks in UK, in limited parts of six cities. 5G 'offers faster internet speeds and the ability to connect thousands of different devices in a small area'.[264]

Computers, 2005 to 2019

2006, USA. **Amazon web services** (AWS) launches its cloud computing infrastructure service to businesses.[265]

2010, Britain. The third age of machine learning: deep learning. Demis Hassabis, Mustafa Suleyman and Shane Legg found **DeepMind**, 'to solve intelligence', by advancing the link between neuroscience and logic established by earlier machine learning pioneers. In particular, DeepMind draws upon Hassabis' and Legg's studies in computer science and neuroscience, and Hassabis' experience as a chess prodigy, and asks how to translate animal learning traits such as attention, episodic

---

259 Connected Places Catapult website: https://ts.catapult.org.uk/news-events-gallery/news/connected-places-catapult-set-to-accelerate-smarter-living-and-travelling/

260 BSI website: https://www.bsigroup.com/en-GB/about-bsi/media-centre/press-releases/2019/july/bsi-launches-standards-programme-to-accelerate-british-leadership-in-automated-vehicles/

261 https://www.autonomousvehicleinternational.com/opinion/what-the-uks-most-advanced-av-trials-teach-us-about-building-public-trust.html

262 Cheung and Brach page 312

263 BBC News website: https://www.bbc.co.uk/news/technology-20121025

264 BBC News website: https://www.bbc.co.uk/news/technology-48458280 UK government guide to 5G: https://www.gov.uk/ government/publications/5g-mobile-technology-a-guide

265 Amazon website: https://aws.amazon.com/about-aws/

and working memory and continual learning into a machine learning system. In an early success, a DeepMind system wins an Atari video game with a strategy it was not taught but devised itself.[266]

2016, South Korea, March. DeepMind's **AlphaGo** (a 'deep-learning' neural net artificially intelligent system) beats Lee Sedol, a world champion, in a tournament of the board strategy game, Go, by four games to one.[267]

Road Transport Law, 2005 to 2019

2015. British government creates its **Centre for Connected and Autonomous Vehicles (CCAV)**, a joint unit of the Department for Business, Energy & Industrial Strategy (BEIS) and Department for Transport (DfT). CCAV is charged with 'developing regulation, investing in innovation and skills and engaging the public to realise the benefits of new transport technologies and to create a thriving connected and self-driving vehicle sector in the UK'.[268]

2015, 1 October. The **Consumer Rights Act 2015** comes into force. It applies to consumer contracts, including to digital content.

2018, March. **UK ratifies the UN Vienna Convention on road traffic 1968**, as part of its preparations for leaving the EU. It comes into force in the UK on 28 March 2019.[269]

2018, 25 May. **EU General Data Protection Regulation (the GDPR)** and the **Data Protection Act 2018** come into force. Described by Professor Lillian Edwards of Newcastle University as 'the most significant data privacy reform process in history'.[270]

2018, June. First appearance in **Highway Code** of guidance on remote parking and driver assistance systems. The initial revision (3 June 2018) is withdrawn weeks later (27 June) with the explanation that those rules had not completed the statutory process. They are reissued later in the year, after the Automated and Electric Vehicles Act 2018 (below) is given royal assent.[271]

2018, July. The **Automated and Electric Vehicles Act 2018** enacted (but provisions relating to automated vehicles are not then brought into force). The Act does not refer to the SAE levels but provides its own definition of 'automated vehicle'.

---

266 Demis Hassabis, Dharshan Kumaran, Christopher Summerfield and Matthew Botvinick, *Neuroscience-Inspired Artificial Intelligence*, Neuron, Volume 95, Issue 2, P245-248, 29 July 2017; Wooldridge p184

267 Wooldridge p197; the film 'AlphaGo' (on YouTube at https://www.youtube.com/watch?v=WXuK6gekU1Y)

268 CCAV website: https://www.gov.uk/government/organisations/centre-for-connected-and-autonomous-vehicles/about

269 UK Department of Transport's explanatory memorandum to the Motor Vehicles (International Circulation) (Amendment) (EU Exit) Order 2019, 2019 No.563, at https://www.legislation.gov.uk/uksi/2019/563/pdfs/uksiem_20190563_en.pdf

270 Edwards and others, *Law, Policy and the Internet* (Hart, 2019) page 77

271 Highway Code on gov.uk: https://www.gov.uk/guidance/the-highway-code/updates

2018, November. **Revisions take effect to the Highway Code** to provide guidance on use of remote parking and driver assistance systems. The guidance reiterates the need for human concentration and control, eg. at rule 150: 'As the driver, you are still responsible for the vehicle … You MUST have full control over these systems at all times'. Rule 239 requires constant control of remote parking. Rule 160 requires the driver to understand the manufacturer's instructions for vehicle systems: 'Make sure you use any system according to the manufacturer's instructions'.

2018, UK, November. The **Law Commissions of England and Wales and of Scotland** start their consultation 'to examine options for regulating automated road vehicles' with the publication of their first paper, *Automated Vehicles: a joint preliminary consultation paper*.[272]

2019, UK, March. **UN Vienna Convention 1968 on road traffic comes into force in UK**. The Vienna Convention requires, centrally, that a driver must 'at all times be able to control his vehicle' (Art 8.5). But UNECE accommodates automated vehicle development, by (a) allowing assisted driving where the system complies with international standards and can be overridden or switched off by the driver (clarification, 2016) (b) resolving to adopt a flexible framework for automated technologies (Working Party 1, September 2018) and (c) proposing a new UN regulation to approve vehicles with Automated Lane Keeping System (ALKS) feature (June 2020).

Part Eight: 2020 to 2023: Brexit, pandemic and a new Automated Vehicles Bill

Motors, 2020 to 2023

2020, Europe, May. Audi is reported to have announced that it is withdrawing the SAE level 3 driving system which was to be activated in the Audi A8, already produced in 2018, because of the lack of regulation allowing it.[273]

2020, Britain, August. **Aurrigo autonomous shuttle bus** transports players and caddies at the Wales open golf tournament.[274]

2022, Britain, May. Oxbotica (now **Oxa**) carries out **first European test of a zero-occupancy autonomous vehicle on a publicly accessible road**.[275]

272 Law Commission Consultation Paper 240, Scottish Law Commission Discussion Paper 166, 8 November 2018, at https://www.lawcom.gov.uk/project/automated-vehicles/
273 Autovista article, *Audi A8 will not feature level 3 autonomy*, 11 May 2020, at https://autovistagroup.com/news-and-insights/audi-a8-will-not-feature-level-3-autonomy
274 Aurrigo website: https://aurrigo.com/news/
275 Oxa website article, *Europe-first zero-occupancy autonomous vehicle journey on-road completed by Oxbotica*, 20 May 2022, at https://oxa.tech/news-and-insights/europe-first-zero-occupancy-autonomous-vehicle-journey-on-road-completed-by-oxbotica/

2023, Britain, April. Ford reports that it has introduced a **'hands free' SAE level 2 driving system** to Great Britain.[276]

Electronics, 2020 to 2023

2020, USA, September. Tesla announces intention to cut cost of its electric vehicles, and increase their range, by manufacturing their own spiral 'tabless' batteries, without cobalt.[277]

Computers, 2020 to 2023

2022, USA, November. OpenAI launches **ChatGPT**.[278]

Road Transport Law, 2020 to 2023

2020, 31 January, 11pm. UK leaves the European Union and enters a transition period that is due to run until the end of the year. The **European Union (Withdrawal) Act 2018** repeals the European Communities Act 1972. EU Law ceases to have primacy over British law, though section 2 contains a saving that 'EU-derived domestic legislation' as defined by the 2018 Act, 'as it has effect in domestic law immediately before exit day, continues to have effect in domestic law on and after exit day'.

2020, 11 March. World Health Organisation (WHO) declares coronavirus a pandemic. 25 March, the **Coronavirus Act 2020** is enacted.

2020, April. The High Court rules that the software function used by Volkswagen and its subsidiaries in **the VW NOx emissions case ('Dieselgate')** was a 'defeat device' prohibited by European Union regulation.[279]

2020, Switzerland, June. UNECE proposes a new regulation to approve vehicles with the Automated Lane Keeping System (ALKS) feature: **UN Regulation No. 157 – Automated Lane Keeping Systems (ALKS)**[280].

2020, Britain, August. UK Government's Centre for Connected and Autonomous Vehicles (CCAV) launches its call for evidence in relation to Advanced Lane Keeping

---

276 Ford media center website article, *Ford brings hands-free driving technology to motorways in Great Britain*, 13 April 2023, at https://media.ford.com/content/fordmedia/feu/gb/en/news/2023/04/13/ford-brings-hands-free-driving-technology-to-motorways-in-great-.html

277 Carly Page, *Tesla's Model S Plaid wasn't the biggest Battery Day announcement*, article in Wired, 23 September 2020: https://www.wired.co.uk/article/tesla-model-s-plaid-battery-day

278 Will Douglas Heaven, *The Inside Story of how ChatGPT was built from the people who made it*, article in MIT Technology Review, 3 March 2023, at https://www.technologyreview.com/2023/03/03/1069311/inside-story-oral-history-how-chatgpt-built-openai/

279 Judgment of Mr Justice Waksman in *Crossley and others v Volkswagen, Audi, Skoda, Seat and others* [2019] EWHC 783 (QB) (*the VW NOx emissions group litigation*)

280 UN Regulation No. 157 – Automated Lane Keeping Systems (ALKS), on UN website at https://unece.org/transport/documents/2021/03/standards/un-regulation-no-157-automated-lane-keeping-systems-alks

Systems (ALKS) and, among other questions, whether ALKS (and other 'traffic jam chauffeur' types of systems) should cause a vehicle to be treated as 'automated' under the Automated and Electric Vehicles Act 2018, so as to require the Secretary of State for Transport to bring the 2018 Act into force.[281]

2021, September. UN proposes amendment to the **1968 UN Convention on Road Traffic (the Vienna Convention), to accommodate automated driving**. The proposed amendment reads:

'ARTICLE 34 bis

Automated driving

'The requirement that every moving vehicle or combination of vehicles shall have a driver is deemed to be satisfied while the vehicle is using an automated driving system which complies with:

(a) domestic technical regulations, and any applicable international legal instrument, concerning wheeled vehicles, equipment and parts which can be fitted and/or be used on wheeled vehicles, and

(b) domestic legislation governing operation.

The effect of this Article is limited to the territory of the Contracting Party where the relevant domestic technical regulations and legislation governing operation apply.'

And the proposed revision to Article 1 defines 'automated driving system' as follows:

'ARTICLE 1

Definitions

(ab) 'Automated driving system' refers to a vehicle system that uses both hardware and software to exercise dynamic control of a vehicle on a sustained basis.

(ac) 'Dynamic control' refers to carrying out all the real-time operational and tactical functions required to move the vehicle. This includes controlling the vehicle's lateral and longitudinal motion, monitoring the road, responding to events in the road traffic, and planning and signalling for manoeuvres.'

2020, 24 December. UK and EU agree terms for their post-Brexit relationship[282].

2021, February. In ***Uber BV and others v Aslam and others***[283] the UK Supreme Court rules against Uber on the question of whether the respondent drivers in

---

281 UK government website: https://www.gov.uk/government/consultations/safe-use-of-automated-lane-keeping-system-on-gb-motorways-call-for-evidence
282 Press release from UK Prime Minister's Office (webpage describing itself as withdrawn), at https://www.gov.uk/government/publications/agreements-reached-between-the-united-kingdom-of-great-britain-and-northern-ireland-and-the-european-union; European Commission press release, at https://ec.europa.eu/commission/presscorner/detail/en/ip_20_2531
283 [2021] UKSC 5, [2021] I.C.R. 657

London were 'workers' within the meaning of section 230(3)(b) of the Employment Rights Act 1996, section 54(3)(b) of the National Minimum Wage Act 1998 and regulation 2(1) of the Working Time Regulations 1998. The Supreme Court holds that, on the facts found by the employment tribunal, which showed that the service performed by the drivers was very tightly defined and controlled by the company and that the drivers had little or no ability to improve their economic position through professional or entrepreneurial skill, the tribunal had been entitled to find that the claimants were 'workers' for the purposes of those provisions. The Supreme Court's judgment opens: 'New ways of working organised through digital platforms pose pressing questions about the employment status of the people who do the work involved' (Lord Leggatt JSC).

2021, April. On 21 April 2021, Part 1 of the AEV Act 2018 is brought into force, by the **Automated and Electric Vehicles Act 2018 (Commencement No. 1) Regulations**[284]. However, no list of automated vehicles under section 1 of the Act is then published by the Secretary of State for Transport.

The explanation for the bringing-into force of the Act, without the list of automated vehicles to which it would apply, comes the following week (28 April 2021), in the government's statement of its proposed way ahead on regulation of the Automated Lane Keeping System (after the UK government's ALKS consultation in the wake of the UN ALKS regulation, above). The UK government's conclusion is that it:

'expects that vehicles fitted with ALKS for use on GB roads will be automated vehicles under the Automated & Electric Vehicles Act 2018 …. However, rather than list all vehicles fitted with ALKS by default, individual models will be listed after they have received whole vehicle type approval (WVTA). This will enable the Secretary of State to review evidence that may have come to light before the formal decision as to whether to list the vehicle model is made.' and:

'Since no automated vehicle will yet have been listed upon commencement of AEVA, we will not be publishing the list.'[285]

2021, October. UK government **lays before Parliament the UN's proposed amendment to the 1968 UN Convention on Road Traffic (the Vienna Convention) to accommodate automated driving**[286]. UK government states in an **Explanatory Memorandum** on the proposed amendment that:

'For the UK the amendment to the 1968 Convention is merely clarificatory, setting out a route whereby countries can regulate automated driving to

---

284 SI 2021/396

285 Pages 41 and 43 of CCAV document *Safe use of Automated Lane Keeping System (ALKS). Summary of responses and next steps. Moving Britain ahead*, 28 April 2021, at https://assets.publishing.service.gov.uk/government/uploads/system/ uploads/attachment_data/file/980742/safe-use-of-automated-lane-keeping-system-alks-summary-of-responses-and-next-steps.pdf

286 Proposal of Amendment to Article 1 and new Article 34 BIS of the 1968 Convention on Road Traffic, UK government (Secretary of State for Foreign, Commonwealth and Development Affairs) Miscellaneous Series No.5 (2021), on UK government website at https://www.gov.uk/government/publications/proposal-of-amendment-to-article-1-and-new-article-34-bis-of-the-1968-convention-on-road-traffic-ms-no52021

continue to adhere to the requirement, (common to both Conventions[287]), that every vehicle shall have a driver in a way which suits their own domestic law and traffic rules. As the UK is already regulating automated driving in accordance with the principles set out in the amendment to the 1968 Convention, its wording is no more than a restatement for the UK of what we are doing already.'

and, in relation to implementation of the proposed amendment in the UK:

'No new domestic legislation is required. The Government is preparing a minor amendment to the Highway Code to provide information on driver responsibilities in automated vehicles, and plans a longer term programme of regulatory reform to provide a legal framework for automated vehicles which will be done in compliance with international conventions as amended.'[288]

2022, January. Law Commission of England and Wales and Scottish Law Commission conclude their review of automated vehicle law with final joint paper making recommendations.[289]

2022, May. UK Government announces Transport Bill 2022-23 in the Queen's Speech.[290]

2022, July. UK Government announces **extension of e-scooter trials to May 2024**.[291]

2022, August. UK Government responds to Law Commissions' AV law recommendations, in 'CAM 2025' paper.[292]

December 2022. UK Government confirms **postponement of entire Transport Bill** from the 2022-23 Parliamentary Session.[293]

---

287 The 1968 Vienna Convention and its precursor, the 1949 Geneva Convention on Road Traffic.

288 *Explanatory Memorandum on the Proposal of Amendment to Article 1 and new Article 34 BIS of the 1968 Convention on Road Traffic*, Command Paper No: CP 540, at paragraphs 3.1 and 5.1, on UK government website at https://www.gov.uk/government/publications/proposal-of-amendment-to-article-1-and-new-article-34-bis-of-the-1968-convention-on-road-traffic-ms-no52021

289 At www.lawcom.gov.uk/project/automated-vehicles.

290 Baroness Vere, House of Lords Hansard vol 822, 11 May 2022, columns 30 to 31, at https://hansard.parliament.uk/lords/2022-05-11/debates/7185EB58-3987-46EA-97A2-8884332BF759/QueenSSpeech

291 DfT answer 6 July 2022 to parliamentary question by Gill Furniss MP 1 July 2022, UIN 28907.

292 UK Government, *Connected & Automated Mobility 2025: Realising the benefits of self-driving vehicles in the UK* (CP 719, August 2022) at https://assets.publishing.service.gov.uk/government/uploads/system/uploads/attachment_data/file/   1099173/cam-2025-realising-benefits-self-driving-vehicles.pdf

293 Parliament Live TV, Transport Select Committee 7 December 2022 at 9:43, Sec of St for Transport the Rt Hon Mark Harper MP.

2023, January, USA (Nevada). The Mercedes 'Drive Pilot', an SAE level 3 ALKS system, is legalised in Nevada.[294]

2023, February. **Law Commission of England and Wales publishes its advice to government on the law of remote driving.**[295]

2023, April. Report by its manufacturer of approval of a **hands-free driving system** on certain UK motorways.[296] Approval confirmed by Department for Transport[297.]

2023, November. **Automated Vehicles Bill 2023–24** has its first reading in Parliament (as HL Bill 1), intended to become the **Automated Vehicles Act 2024.**

---

294 Mercedes Benz website 'Certification for SAE Level 3 System for U.S. Market' (26 January 2023).
295 At https://www.lawcom.gov.uk/project/remote-driving/
296 Ford media center website article, *Ford brings hands-free driving technology to motorways in Great Britain*, 13 April 2023, at https://media.ford.com/content/fordmedia/feu/gb/en/news/2023/04/13/ford-brings-hands-free-driving-technology-to-motorways-in-great-.html
297 Rt Hon Jesse Norman MP, Minister of State, Department for Transport, in oral evidence to Transport Committee of House of Commons (oral evidence: self-driving vehicles, HC 519, 17 May 2023) at Q271, Government emphasising that this was not a self-driving system.

Index